EXPLORING THE DIGITAL DOMAIN

An Introduction to Computing with Multimedia and Networking

EXPLORING THE DIGITAL DOMAIN

An Introduction to Computing with Multimedia and Networking

Ken Abernethy & Tom Allen   Furman University

Vasily Kandinsky, *Arc and Point*, February 1923. Solomon R. Guggenheim Museum

Brooks/Cole Publishing Company
I(T)P®An International Thomson Publishing Company

Pacific Grove • Albany • Belmont • Boston • Cincinnati • Johannesburg • London • Madrid • Melbourne • Mexico City • New York • Scottsdale • Singapore • Tokyo • Toronto

Sponsoring Editor: Kallie Swanson
Production Service: Graphic World Publishing Services
Production Coordinator: Marjorie Z. Sanders, Marlene Thom
Marketing Manager: Nathan Wilbur
Manuscript Editor: Nancy Kruse-Hannigan
Interior Design: Julia Gecha

Interior Illustration: Graphic World Illustration Studio
Photo Editor: Linda Rill
Cover Design: Roger Knox
Cover Art: Judith Larzelere
Typesetting: Graphic World, Inc.
Cover Printing: Phoenix Color Corp.
Printing and Binding: World Color Corp./Versailles

For more information, contact PWS Publishing at Brooks/Cole Publishing Company:

BROOKS/COLE PUBLISHING COMPANY
511 Forest Lodge Road
Pacific Grove, CA 93950
USA

International Thomson Publishing Europe
Berkshire House 168-173
High Holborn
London WC1V 7AA
England

Thomas Nelson Australia
102 Dodds Street
South Melbourne, 3205
Victoria, Australia

Nelson Canada
1120 Birchmount Road
Scarborough, Ontario
Canada M1K 5G4

International Thomson Editores
Seneca 53
Col. Polanco
11560 México, D F., México

International Thomson Publishing GmbH
Königswinterer Strasse 418
53227 Bonn
Germany

International Thomson Publishing Asia
60 Albert Street
#15-01 Albert Complex
Singapore 189969

International Thomson Publishing Japan
Hirakawacho Kyowa Building, 3F
2-2-1 Hirakawacho
Chiyoda-ku, Tokyo 102
Japan

Printed in the United States of America

10 9 8 7 6 5 4 3 2 1

Library of Congress Cataloging-in-Publication Data

Abernethy, Ken.
   Exploring the digital domain : an introduction to computing with multimedia and networking / Ken Abernethy, Tom Allen.
     p. cm.
   Includes bibliographical references and index.
   ISBN 0-534-95516-9
   1. Multimedia systems. 2. Computer networks. I. Allen, J. Thomas, 1948- . II. Title.
   QA76.575.A34 1999
   004.6—dc21
                                      98-49444
                                      CIP

Credits continue on p. 774.

*To my father, Hugh Daniel Abernethy, on his 90th birthday,
and in loving memory of my mother, Susie Campbell Abernethy.*

—KCA

*To my wife and the principal co-author of our remarkable
children, Kathleen.*

—JTA

BRIEF CONTENTS

CONTENTS

PART 3   Text and Numbers   245

PART 4   Sights and Sounds   353

PREFACE

In a few short years, most of us have changed our opinions dramatically about computers and computing. Almost overnight, the machines that once were "curiosities," "interesting," or even "intimidating" have become "necessities" and "must-haves" for our homes and offices. This remarkable change in attitudes is due to the equally remarkable adaptability of computer systems to perform myriad tasks quickly and easily. Even the most vocal antitechnologues have become addicted to the conveniences of electronic document preparation and electronic mail. Surprisingly, though, few computer users are able to exploit many of the newer capabilities that these machines offer. Most users are familiar with word processing, but only a few have the know-how to publish their documents on the World Wide Web. The worlds of image processing, digital sound, multimedia presentations, know-bots, MUDs, and MOOs are as yet undiscovered territory for many. Although most computer users would swear to the utility of their system, the bottom line is that only a fraction of its riches have been mined by many of them. To be able to exploit these new and interesting capabilities, computer users must achieve a new standard of computer literacy. This book is our attempt to push the old boundaries of computer literacy into new ground.

Computer literacy is a slippery notion. The term functions much like the terms *democracy, freedom,* and *common sense.* Just about everyone knows precisely what they mean, but no one seems to be able to agree on that meaning. And like democracy and freedom, we all agree that computer literacy is a good thing, even if we don't mean quite the same thing by it. If you are not convinced of these claims, examine the proliferation and variety of computer literacy courses on our college and university campuses. Today, most of these courses have evolved to include a wide assortment of topics and skills. They include a few apparent fundamentals: studying practical software such as word processing, spreadsheets, and (recently) Internet applications; some basic concepts about computer technology; and a consideration of social and ethical issues related to computing and information management. Many courses address a few other topics such as the history of computing, software development, the disciplines of computer science, and, perhaps, some type of elementary programming experience. But the variety in which these topics are packaged and delivered is dizzying.

To complicate matters more, computer literacy today is a swiftly moving target. What skills should we choose to develop? In the area of applications, for example, software vendors are continually upgrading, revising, and replacing their products with new features and looks. You can be sure that as soon as you gain some level of comfort and familiarity with one product, it will be entirely replaced by some new version. Even the choice of applications seldom sits still. The word processors and spreadsheets that were "gee-whiz" only five years ago are strictly "ho-hum" to a generation that was first introduced to computers in primary or secondary school. To maintain interest and relevance, the ante must be raised accordingly.

If students acquire training on specific applications, these skills will depreciate as rapidly as the software versions on which they are based.

Instead of training, students would profit more from a conceptual understanding of what these applications are about. Armed with this knowledge, they might better adapt to the changing environment.

Hardware platforms are changing rapidly as well. Nearly all desktop computer systems today have increased storage and performance capacities. These newer systems make it possible to perform meaningful work in such areas as sound, image, and video processing—work that would have been unthinkable only a few years ago.

Several years ago it would also have been impractical to discuss computing applications without recognizing the great differences in their look, feel, and functionality on different hardware/software platforms. But today, due in some measure to market forces and to the influences of networking for desktop systems, there is a slow but evident convergence among software applications. The incredibly rapid growth of the Internet is another significant factor. In a few short years, Internet access has evolved from a curiosity to almost a mainstay. The popularity of the World Wide Web is the chief reason for this explosive growth. The remarkable ease and utility of publishing on the Web has had a significant impact on the way that we organize and deliver information locally and abroad. (In fact, these changes are so rapid that they outpace any attempt to describe their status and significance with traditional printed media.) The impact on computing literacy is obvious. Three years ago, most people would have considered knowledge and familiarity with Internet tools to be interesting but strictly a frill or optional. Today, students demand this knowledge as part of the basic package.

We think that there are a number of important lessons to be learned from considering these issues. First, and obviously, the current state of computer literacy must take into account the changes in the computing environments of the workplace and home. It should incorporate more about multimedia and networking. Moreover, whatever computer literacy means, it probably should not be bound to particular systems, software versions, and so on. These are static goals, and our target is a moving one. For similar reasons, it is much more practical to study the applications by what they do rather than the idiosyncrasies of how they appear on a particular machine. All these point to a standard that is both more conceptual and more dynamic than past ones. We have wrestled with many of these issues on our own campus. This text is derived from our experiences offering a computer literacy course to a clientele that is capable, somewhat experienced, and inquisitive about the why's and wherefore's as much as the how's and how-to's. We do not presume to have resolved the issue of what is computer literacy once and for all. However, we believe that our approach has benefits and can be applied to other, similar situations.

This approach is both thematic and conceptual. The organizing theme for our book is that the computer system is not merely a tool but rather itself a medium for representing, storing, manipulating, and communicating different forms of information: text, numbers, graphics, images, sounds, and video. The common denominator for these differing forms of information is the fact that they must be digitized to be stored on and handled by our computers. Data within this digital domain can be studied, combined, transformed, and transmitted with an apparent ease that belies the true complexities of these tasks. But not all is golden—information converted to digital form must bear some costs: approximations, alterations, and limits. The *digerati* (a person literate in digital media) understands the nature of digital media—both their uses and limitations. Thus, this book focuses on digital media rather than the customary survey of applications software designed to process these media.

We have tried to adopt a conceptual approach to treating these topics as well. Our assumption is that if you explain why something behaves the way it does, a quick study can apply this knowledge to related instances. We believe that it is more useful, for example, to understand the basic functions of an operating system than to learn a specific set of commands to invoke these functions. In the same vein, what you learn about *Word Whiz 7.32* will be yesterday's news; but what you learn about document preparation in general and such specific issues as character coding and file formats will survive. Of course, concepts without instances are vague. So, we have offered a number of concrete examples for these general ideas. This, of course, includes specific operating systems and software products. However, these are illustrations, and we make no pretense to be treating any of these software systems completely.

TEXT ORGANIZATION AND FEATURES

The textbook contains six units and two appendices. Each unit has several chapters organized by a unifying theme. The first unit introduces the student to the digital domain via the World Wide Web. The Web is a natural choice since it demonstrates at once the powerful integrative capabilities of the computer system as well as the convenience and utility of networking. The student is also introduced to the concept of digital media. A separate chapter on the World Wide Web provides an early introduction to publishing on the Web. The second unit supplies a foundation for understanding how computers can accomplish these amazing feats. The conventional topics of hardware and software are treated, but the perspective is dominated by the types of desktop systems that the student is likely to encounter in the lab, at work, and at home. There are separate chapters on programming and how operating systems manage our computers. The third unit features the traditional media of text and numbers as well as databases. Digital imaging, graphics, sound, music, video, and the related issues of data compression are the focus of the fourth unit. The fifth unit contains chapters on data communications and networks—large and small. The final unit culminates with some larger issues that are best considered after some maturity with computing: integrating multimedia and artificial intelligence.

Each of the chapters concludes with a summary of central ideas, suggested projects for further study, a list of the key terms, and some questions for reviewing important concepts. Most of the chapters incorporate Focus sidebars. These are boxes that contain examples, details, or related facts that augment the discussion of topics addressed in the chapter. These are intended for the curious student who wants to know more about the topics. Building on the model for this book that we developed in the (former) Beta Edition, two new features have been added to this first edition. Many of the chapters include short exercises that students may perform at their computers. These At Your Computer sections are intended to illustrate ideas introduced in that chapter and provide hands-on experience that apply these concepts. In the previous edition, social and moral issues were treated in a separate chapter. For this edition, we have integrated these topics within the chapters. Social Themes sections introduce the student to the moral, social, and political implications of computer use and information systems. We have greatly expanded the range of topics covered as well. This includes current issues such as intellectual property and copyrights, risks of software, secrecy and encryption, the impact of computers on photojournalism, and others.

Also new in this first edition are two appendices: an extensive glossary of key terms introduced in the text and a brief synopsis of HTML tags for creating basic Web pages.

A significant feature separate from the text is its accompanying World Wide Web site. The *Exploring the Digital Domain* Web site is an integral part of the overall product. Throughout the book, we highlight subjects that are referenced on related Web pages. These pages contain expanded material, updated information, and links to other documents. As mentioned, some of the topics that the book incorporates are so dynamic that only the Web can be a suitable medium for their delivery. An even broader and cross-referenced glossary of key terms can be found there as well. Tutorials and some of the laboratory activities that we employ are also referenced there. Many of these can be examined as Web pages or downloaded as PDF files for printing. (We would be very happy to incorporate references to additional lab materials from instructors interested in sharing them with colleagues.) Chapter outlines offered as multimedia presentations are there, too. Students may find them useful as study guides. Instructors may wish to use them for creating overheads or electronic presentations. Most of these are PowerPoint files; all may be downloaded for editing and use. A printed text is static; but a Web site is a dynamic, evolving entity. We hope to augment the book and enhance its currency and relevance with an assemblage of resources within these Web pages.

An instructor's manual is available to text adopters in both print and Web formats. It offers PowerPoint outlines for each chapter; answers to the chapter exercises; answers or suggestions for implementing projects; and, of course, sample questions for composing tests on the material. There are also suggestions for organizing lectures with readings based on our experiences with using these materials for the past four years.

COORDINATING COURSEWORK WITH THIS TEXT

A significant challenge for producing any textbook is to present sufficient coverage of topics to suit a variety of tastes and needs. The result is usually overkill: the breadth of coverage is often too great for most college courses. We have been quite conscious of this dilemma in the preparation of this text. Most of the chapters and many of the units have been written with few dependencies on earlier materials. This affords an instructor considerable flexibility in organizing and coordinating this text with his or her approach and course.

We offer several suggested treatments employing this text. These are based on different approaches as well as different schedules. At our university, for example, we have used the text in introductory computing for both general and specialized audiences. General audiences are served by a course that features computing applications with an emphasis on multimedia and networking. We also offer a course primarily for students in arts and communications on the use of computers for graphic design and publishing. On the other hand, we believe that the text would be useful for approaches that emphasize computing technology, traditional computing applications, and information systems. Many introductions to the discipline of computer science emphasize programming. We believe that the book would also be appropriate for providing an alternative approach for general audiences as a prelude to programming courses. (In fact, the book is currently being used as a general introductory text for training programmers in the Caribbean Institute of Technology in Jamaica.) The table below offers chapter coverage for these possible treatments—assuming different schedules.

CT = emphasis on computing and computing technology
CA = emphasis on computing and computing applications
IS = emphasis on computing and information systems
MN = emphasis on computing with multimedia and networking
GAP = emphasis on computing and graphic arts and publishing
CS-0 = an alternative introduction to computer science for general education

Treatments	CT		CA		IS		MN		GAP		CS-0	
Chapter	10-12 weeks	14-15 weeks	10-12 weeks	14-15 weeks	10-12 weeks	14-15 weeks	10-12 weeks	14-15 weeks	10-12 weeks	14-15 weeks	10-12 weeks	14-15 weeks
1	X	X	X	X	X	X	X	X	X	X	X	X
2	X	X	X	X	X	X	X	X	X	X	X	X
3		X	X	X			X	X	X	X	X	X
4	X	X	X	X	X	X	X	X	X	X	X	X
5	X	X	X	X	X	X	X	X	X	X	X	X
6	X	X			X	X					X	X
7	X	X	X	X	X	X	0	0			X	X
8	X	X	X	X	X	X		X				X
9	X	X	X	X	X	X		X	X	X		
10	X	X	X	X	X	X	0					X
11			X	X		X	X	X	X	X		X
12			X	X			X	X	X	X		
13			X	X			X	X	X	X		X
14								0	X	X		
15		X							0	X	X	X
16	X	X		X	X	X	X	X	0	X	X	X
17	X	X			X	X	X	X		X	X	X
18	X	X		X	X	X	X	X	X	X	X	X
19					X	X	X	X	X	X	X	X
20					0	X					X	X

O = optional

ACKNOWLEDGMENTS

We have class-tested this material for several years and would like to thank our students who helped us to improve the text by their questions, comments, and reactions. Several of our colleagues also participated in class-testing versions of this text. We would like to thank Margaret Batchelor, Bryan Catron, Paula Gabbert, Ray Nanney, and Kevin Treu. Our thanks go to the following reviewers for their comments and general support of the project.

Elizabeth Adams   *Richard Stockton College*
William Allen   *University of Central Florida*
Julia Benson   *DeKalb College*
Gary G. Bitter   *Arizona State University*
David Alan Bozak   *State University of New York at Oswego*
Kim Bridges   *University of Hawaii*
Bryan Catron   *Furman University*
Ronald Curtis   *William Paterson College*
Daniel Everett   *University of Georgia*
Edward Fox   *Virginia Polytechnic Institute*
Kathleen M. Goelz   *Rutgers University*
Elaine Haight   *Foothill College*
R. Wayne Headrick   *New Mexico State University*
Trevor Jones   *Duquesne University*
Ed Kaplan   *Bentley College*
David Kay   *University of California-Irvine*
Peter L. Liu   *Malone College*
Daniel D. Ludwig   *Virginia Polytechnic Institute*
Barbara J. Maccarone   *North Shore Community College*
Vicki McCullough   *Palomar College*
Bamshad Mobasher   *University of Minnesota*
Rob Perkins   *Central Washington University*
Robert Probasco   *University of Idaho*
Jane Ritter   *University of Oregon*
Paul W. Ross   *Millersville University*
Krystal Scott   *Oklahoma Baptist University*
Raoul N. Smith   *Northeastern University*
Roberta Stokes   *Miami-Dade Community College–Kendall*
Thomas D. L. Walker   *Virginia Polytechnic Institute*
Peter Wegner   *Brown University*
Jerry Wei   *University of Notre Dame*

We would also like to express our gratitude to a number of individuals at PWS Publishing and Brooks/Cole who worked on this project. Special thanks to Michael J. Sugarman, who first encouraged us to pursue it. We also would like to thank David Dietz and Ann Lengel for managing the publication of the Beta Edition. Kallie Swanson, the computer science editor, and Suzanne Jeans, product development editor at Brooks/Cole, managed the completion of this first edition. Nancy Kruse-Hannigan served as copy editor for this first edition. Our thanks to them as well. We owe a special expression of gratitude to our tireless development editor, Kitty Pinard, who coordinated the beta testing of the text. She managed the numerous reviewers, instructors' and students' diaries from the class-testing of these materials, and surveys sampling computer literacy courses nationwide. Kitty also offered many useful ideas for reorganizing and improving the text and provided continued enthusiasm for the project. Veteran readers of textbook prefaces are familiar with the expressions of appreciation to the authors' families for the many hours that they did without them. This is no exaggeration. Our sincere thanks (and apologies) go to our families.

To my wife, Sherry, thanks for all your support and encouragement, and for covering all the many bases I let slip while working on this project.—KCA

To my wife, Kathleen, and my children, John and Kara, thanks for your patience. I hope to be able to help more with chores and projects, and go to more of your games and events than during these past four years.—JTA

A FINAL NOTE

We encourage your reactions and comments on any portion of the text. Please feel free to contact us or our publisher. You may use the automated electronic mail links or the electronic forms for both students and instructors located on our Web site. If you have suggestions for links or additions to the Web pages that support this text, we would greatly appreciate them. If you have materials that you would like to link to our pages, please contact us. See you in the Digital Domain.

Ken Abernethy
Tom Allen
Department of Computer Science
Furman University

EXPLORING THE DIGITAL DOMAIN

An Introduction to Computing with Multimedia and Networking

INTRODUCTION

Vasily Kandinsky, *Arc and Point*, February 1923. Solomon R. Guggenheim Museum

The world of information is going digital. A computer system is not merely a tool but rather itself a medium for representing, storing, manipulating, and communicating different forms of information: text, numbers, graphics, images, sounds, and video. The common denominator for these differing forms of information is that they all can be digitized for use by our computers. This data can be studied, combined, transformed, and transmitted with an apparent ease that belies the true complexities of these tasks. Digitized data and the systems that handle it constitute the **digital domain.** In this chapter, you will get an overview of the digital domain.

OBJECTIVES

- *The evolution of information within the digital domain*

- *The electronic computer as a media machine*

- *The role of multimedia computing in the digital domain*

- *The importance of networking for the digital domain*

- *The World Wide Web and how it enhances the digital domain*

CHAPTER 1

INFORMATION IN THE DIGITAL DOMAIN

Vasily Kandinsky, *Arc and Point*, February 1923. Solomon R. Guggenheim Museum

THE DIGITAL EVOLUTION

The evolution to digital forms of information has influenced the workplace, the marketplace, our schools, and our homes. In some instances, the changes have been dramatic; in others they have been subtle—almost imperceptible. Considered together, these changes have been highly significant, helping to redefine the ways in which we think about and use information to communicate with each other. Our primary goal in this book is to guide your exploration of this digital domain. Let's begin with a few examples of how the digital domain influences our use of and access to information.

Digital Documents

Typewriters have become relics of an age forgotten in favor of electronic digital word processing. You can now create, edit, and format documents with a flexibility and speed unthought of before documents were prepared on computers. The typesetting of books like this one now depend more on digital methods than traditional, conventional techniques. In the past, publishing was the province of the professional; today even school children can produce a typeset book. In short, digital documents are easier to create, store, transmit, and manipulate. One consequence of digital document preparation is that we now create a lot more documents—notes, letters, reports, and books—than ever before.

Digital Numeric Processing

Since their first appearance more than fifty years ago, computers have assisted us in many tasks that involve numerical computation. The earliest computers supported national defense and other government functions. They calculated ballistic tables for artillery, performed computations for developing the first atomic bomb, processed census information, and even predicted presidential elections. Unfortunately, these early computers were expensive and required considerable skill and expertise to operate. Today, the accessibility of computers for numeric processing is widespread. Spreadsheets and statistical and mathematical software offer powerful tools for numerical computation and are easy to use. Most of these tools also have graphing and visualization features that convert large data sets and models to more convenient and accessible forms. Today anyone can command both processing power and productivity for "number crunching" from a desktop computer that far outstrips that of the early giant computers. See Figure 1.1 for a comparison of appearances.

Digital Music

Most of the music that you listen to is recorded, stored, and played back using digital methods. Compared to phonograph and audio tape, compact disc digital audio offers much higher fidelity sound. Phonographs and tapes have inherent noise noticeable in playback; their media usually suffer from the wear and tear of constant replay as well. Not so for

FIGURE 1.1

Let's compare a 1960 vintage mainframe computer and a modern desktop computer. Surprisingly, the desktop computer has many times more computing power than the giant mainframe had!

FIGURE 1.2

A recently introduced digital camera from Casio costs less than $300 and can store as many as 96 digital photographs. The built-in LCD viewing panel (similar to those on many camcorders) allows the photographer to view a picture, then decide whether to delete it or store it in the camera's electronic memory.

compact discs. CDs are less noisy and wear out much more slowly, making digital recording a much better archive for important performances. Today we can only imagine how brilliant were the talents of performers such as Enrico Caruso, Toscaninni, and George Gershwin. Their surviving recordings are dim and fading replicas. On the other hand, today's artists can be preserved for all posterity. When you tell your grandchildren how they just don't make music like they used to, you'll be able to prove it by inflicting on them recordings of your favorites that sound just as new as they did the day you bought them.

Digital Photography

When the family is forcibly collected at the photography studio for a portrait, the photographer most likely uses digital methods to capture and process your likenesses. After the shooting, the photographer can use a computer system to display instantly the proofs that used to take weeks to process. Thus, you can be photographed and choose which shots you want almost instantly. At the same time, the photographer can show you samples of how these photos may be retouched or processed to make you look even better than you naturally do. Professional photography has made the move to digital methods. Journalistic photography today is often processed digitally; fewer "wet" darkrooms are left in the offices of newspaper and magazine publishers. Recently, consumer versions of digital cameras have become more affordable. See Figure 1-2. Armed with these and image processing software, you too can produce results that match those of many professionals.

Digital Graphic Arts

Computer graphics is the artificial generation of images. The field has evolved from computing curiosity to the mainstream. Today, commercial artists employ computer graphics extensively to produce images for newspapers, magazines, and television. Computer-generated animation is used to create or enhance commercials, television shows, and full-length feature films. For example, the science fiction series *Babylon 5* employs computer-generated graphics for nearly all its action sequences; many of its filmed scenes are created with actors superimposed on graphic image backgrounds rather than shot against conventionally made scenery. *Beauty and the Beast* and *Jurassic Park* are examples of films that employed computer animation extensively and with dramatic effect. The feature film *Toy Story* was produced entirely using computer animation techniques.

Digital Television

Television is migrating to the digital domain as well. Today you can purchase a small, 18-inch diameter satellite dish and receiver for a few hundred dollars. In spite of its size, it can receive hundreds of television channels beamed directly from satellites in fixed orbit around the earth. The picture that you receive is crisp, detailed video, and the audio is CD-quality stereo sound. All of this is possible because the transmission and processing are digital. Compared to conventional cable TV service, digital satellite television offers higher fidelity, greater choice, and fewer interruptions of service. It is usually more economical, too. The future of television will no doubt be digital. The proposed U.S. standard for high-definition TV (HDTV) is a digital one. HDTV offers tremendous gains in resolution that mean unparalleled realism in picture quality.

Virtual Reality

FIGURE 1.3

Items like computerized headsets and gloves allow a user to be immersed in a computer-generated reality. Such devices are dropping in price and improving in performance as virtual reality moves into the mainstream.

Virtual reality (VR) is a new technology that immerses the user into the illusion of a three-dimensional world built from 3-D graphic models and sophisticated animation techniques. In contrast to a viewer merely watching conventional graphics that are projected onto a video display, the viewer dons special video goggles, headsets, and even gloves for manipulating objects in a specially designed model world. See Figure 1.3. The objective is to create an artificial experience of new phenomena, with the conjured experience having a natural look and feel. Early versions of VR have created artificial rooms and buildings, projected users on journeys across the surface of Mars, and produced trips to virtual art galleries—complete with an extensive collection of art objects. These applications of VR technology have been largely experimental or exploratory. In the near future, as the technology develops, more serious commercial applications will appear. For instance, VR promises to be an invaluable training medium. In medical applications, it can be used to train surgeons. Using ultrasound imaging, VR can also augment the surgeon during live operations as well as by providing additional "visual" cues about the displacement and location of a patient's organs and tissues.

Digital Communications

Person-to-person telephone service is a fact that we all take for granted. Compared to realizing radio and television broadcasting, achieving such service is incredibly complex. A radio transmission can be broadcast across the airwaves. Listeners can receive it merely by purchasing a receiver and tuning in the signal. On the other hand, for telephony, each user must be capable of reaching any other user at any time. The communication must be exclusive and two-way; broadcast methods will not do. Consider that there are billions of users worldwide and that sizable distances separate them. Under these circumstances, telephone service is amazing. Digital methods have helped to extend service to all points of the globe and have improved performance at the same time. Digitizing voice and data have made transmission faster. Digital techniques are used to combine and transmit thousands of conversations simultaneously on a single carrier. Digital switching systems process and route hundreds of thousands of calls per hour. As commercial communication carriers have converted to digital media and techniques, consumer services have expanded, but the costs have not. In the future, all-digital networks promise to add processing power and intelligence to our telephone service.

The Internet

The explosive growth of long-distance networks and the creation of the global Internet are direct consequences of the digitization of commercial communication. Computer networks that were once restricted to a local area can now connect to thousands of other networks around the world. Dedicated network lines called **backbones** carry millions of individual packets of digital data. These packets hop from one network to another until they reach their intended destination. In this manner, you can send and receive electronic mail, transfer files of data and software, or browse through information on a computer system located thousands of miles away. All of this is possible almost instantly and from the convenience of your own desktop.

The World Wide Web

The use of the Internet has literally exploded over the past several years. A major force in this growth has been the World Wide Web (or Web for short) and the availability of user-friendly programs, called Web **browsers** (Netscape Communicator and Microsoft Internet Explorer are two of the most popular), for accessing its wealth of multimedia information. The **World Wide Web** is a confederation of computer systems that adhere to a common set of guidelines for storing and presenting information to users. These guidelines make it completely straightforward for computer users all over the world to publish multimedia information they have created or collected to all other Web users. Web browser programs like Netscape Communicator and Internet Explorer exploit the Web's commonality to make all information on the Web accessible in an extremely easy-to-use graphical user interface. This ease of use has made the Web a universal success and phenomenon.

Collections of organized information stored and made available to Web users in a single location are often referred to as **Web sites.** Indeed, you will shortly learn about the Web site that accompanies this text. The individual computer files that comprise a Web site are called **Web pages.** You can always scroll to view all the information on a Web page (although it may extend over many screens). You use the mouse to click over connecting links that access one Web page from another. We'll give the details of how this is done later in the chapter. Most Web sites contain several (perhaps many) Web pages connected to each other for easy access.

As just one example of the Web's use, a group in California recently organized a Web site called *24 Hours in Cyberspace.* This site organized a collection of digital video, photos, text, and live audio from Web users from around the globe in an attempt to chronicle and capture one 24-hour period in the life of our planet. All this information could be thought of as Web version of a "coffee table" book. But this "book" had a difference—it became available to everyone with Web access almost the instant it was created! Of course, the *24 Hours in Cyberspace* effort was largely a publicity stunt, but nonetheless it demonstrated the extraordinary power and worldwide visibility of the Web. Bringing together reports, opinions, and observations—complete with pictures, video, and sounds—from around the world within minutes of their creation, and making the collected work available to each of the millions of Web users worldwide, is a dramatic demonstration of the astounding power and potential of networked computers as communication facilitators.

These examples illustrate the ways in which digital information has improved or supplanted other conventional forms and how such information can be made available worldwide almost instantly. Of course, none of these capabilities would be possible without the technology of the electronic digital computer. How will this technology ultimately change our world and our lives? Will these changes be for the better or the worse? No one knows the complete answers to such questions. What is clear is that life in the 21st century will be inextricably intertwined with a changing communications paradigm, and the new paradigm will exhibit an increasing dependence on and exploitation of computers and computer networks. Preparation for life in this new era will require, even demand, an understanding of the technologies underlying these fundamental changes. This book is intended as a guide to help you achieve this understanding.

MULTIMEDIA

We usually think of computers as tools. We use computers to do this and that. One of the goals of this book is to convince you that a computer system is a medium, not just a helper or instrument. A **medium** is a vehicle or agent for something. For example, air is the medium for sound; writing is a medium for words and thoughts. The computer is a medium for ideas and information. Computers can be used not only to express but communicate these ideas as well. They can store knowledge and facts. But more importantly, computer systems can store and manipulate information in many different forms.

What Is Multimedia?

Informational media include text, illustrations, photographs, animation, video, sounds, voice, and music. The modern computer is an all-purpose medium for informational media. Regardless of the media, the computer system represents, stores, and transmits all in its native digital form. That a computer converts text and graphics, for example, to a digital format means that it can process them in similar fashion and at the same time. **Multimedia** refers to the integration of various forms of information such as text, graphics, sound, and images.

The modern computer system is a multimedia machine; that is, it is capable of integrating two or more conventional forms of informational media in a single electronic document. Because we can express and combine various forms of information using a computer, we can interact, explore, and learn even more from that information. In this way, the computer becomes a vehicle for knowledge rather than just a tool that stores, distributes, and displays information.

Why Multimedia?

Why should you be interested in multimedia computing? Our answer is simple: It is both natural and inevitable. Multimedia computing offers a more natural way to express and convey ideas. If you don't buy that proposition, there is another reason. Multimedia computing—and therefore, large and small corporations, governments, and organizations around the world—is where computing is going. If you want to keep in touch with computing, you will need to understand and master it.

Natural forms of communication are seldom one-dimensional activities. Though we often take it for granted, communicating involves a rich context. Consider the following sentence:

He didn't say that you were wrong.

Its meaning seems plain and simple. Now say it out loud: first stress the word "say"; then a second time, stress the word "you." The same sentence takes on two very different meanings. Suppose that we can see the speaker. In one instance, she has a calm, matter-of-fact look; in another case, she is mugging and exaggerating her gestures. Again, the same words express very different ideas. Clearly, the eye and the ear convey additional meaning beyond a simple transcript of the words. Similarly, we can capture and convey ideas more effectively if we can express them in a richer context. A picture can amplify words; sounds can evoke experiences; the spoken word is often more persuasive than the written one. These are just a few instances that persuade us of the importance of providing a fuller, richer context when communicating. Figure 1.4 illustrates.

Expressing ideas, thoughts, and facts in a single form or medium is unnatural. It can conceal, obscure, or otherwise lose important informational content rather than convey it. Of course, we often employ a singular medium to express our ideas because it offers some practical advantages. Expressing ideas in text, for example, fixes them in time and offers efficient storage that can exist apart from or survive our thoughts. But, if we have technology available that allows us to express ideas in a richer, more natural form—and just as easily—ignoring it would be foolish. We can see from the example above that providing a fuller, richer

FIGURE 1.4

Multimedia reference materials, illustrated by this screen from the multimedia CD "Passage to Vietnam," provide enhanced learning opportunities appealing to a variety of our senses. Shown here is a virtual gallery of the photojournalist Nicole Bengireno, who explains her photos as you view them.

context when communicating enables people to better understand our meaning.

The technology behind multimedia computing is a recent development, but communicating in this manner is not. That children are comfortable with these richer forms of communication attests to their simplicity and directness. Technology is now catching up so that technology-enhanced communications can become more natural for us all.

NETWORKING

This book describes how the computer can be used to create, express, and communicate ideas in various forms. Some of the ideas discussed in this book are new and evolving; others are as old as the advent of electronic digital computers more than fifty years ago. After all, modern computer systems are electronic digital machines; they have always had this capability for combining and transmitting informational media. However, desktop or personal computers have only recently had the power to exploit these capabilities for both multimedia and data communications over networks.

The remarkable advances in the price/performance ratio of computer hardware over the past few years, together with a new generation of computer software, are driving dramatic developments in this innovative computer use. In the early days of computing, it was recognized that the speed of computers was especially useful for processing large amounts of numeric and text information. Today, developments in software and hardware are creating opportunities to exploit the computer's capabilities for representing and processing different, richer forms of information that enhance our intellectual abilities. Thus, the traditional model of employing computation for numbers and text is being replaced by a new paradigm. At the heart of these developments is the emergence of two primary technologies: the ability of modern desktop computer systems to collect, store, retrieve, display, and generally manage information in a variety of media and the possibilities for cooperative work using fully interconnected computers and computer networks.

What Is Networking?

The computer system serves as a common denominator by converting all media to the digital domain. Programs that run on the computer exploit this digital denominator more explicitly by combining and processing various media in new and interesting ways. In short, multimedia computing means that a number of informational technologies are converging. Their combination and interplay create new possibilities.

Computer networks are also playing a dominant role in integrating technology into our lives. **Networks** connect computers in our offices and labs; they also can link us to other computers across the nation and around the world. Using networks, computer systems can share resources and information. That many forms of information can be exchanged instantaneously over long distances has changed the way we work and play. For example, employees in many corporations and other organizations rely more on electronic mail than conventional mail for communication with coworkers.

Indeed, networks have created a new habitat, commonly called **cyberspace.** These new opportunities have a profound effect on ways we work and interact with one another. Not only is information more readily available, it is also richer and strikingly more dynamic. In cyberspace, you are immersed in and engaged by information rather than merely possessing it.

Why Networking?

Communication technologies have existed for a long time. So, what is special about data communications over computer networks? First, the technology driving data communications offers far greater capacity and speed than any other previous form. For example, we now have the capability to store and send whole libraries of information much more quickly than sending a simple message by ordinary postal service. Because this data is represented digitally, we can combine and communicate various forms of information simultaneously, for example, text, audio, and images.

Connectivity means more than simply people communicating with other people. Computer networks also make it possible for individuals to communicate with other computers over long distances. For instance, from your home computer, you can easily borrow both software and processing power from a computer system far away. You can also ask the distant computer system to supply you with the latest stock market quotes, college basketball scores, or international news. Figure 1.5 illustrates. When traveling, you can telephone your computer system at home or office to check for electronic mail or messages.

In the past, computers were isolated and largely incompatible. Today, networks support communication from computer to computer as well. Computer systems can request and receive services from other computers automatically and invisibly to the user. This offers a number of advantages. Borrowing processing from a remote system extends the capabilities of your own computer. It also means that computers of different scale and performance can exchange the results of processing almost seamlessly. Distributing the work of processing among cooperating computer

FIGURE 1.5

The latest news, sports, weather, entertainment, and more are all easily accessible from today's networked desktop computers.

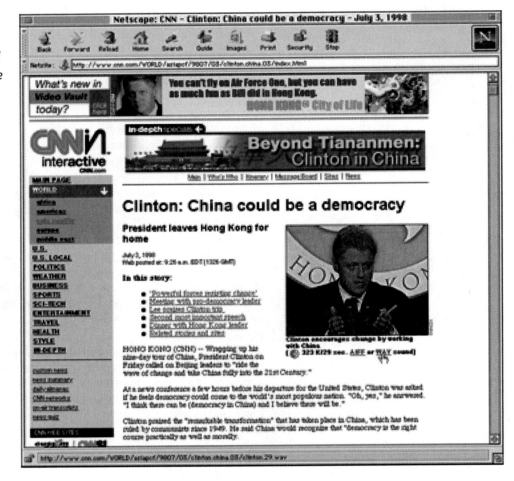

systems is still in its infancy. We can expect that it will have a profound effect on computing in the future. Indeed, the idea of individual or autonomously functioning computer systems will very likely become archaic. Perhaps William Gibson's vision in *Neuromancer* of the worldwide network of cooperating computer systems called the *Matrix* holds more fact than fancy. (It was Gibson who coined the term "cyberspace" to denote this new dimension.)

Admittedly, terms such as "multimedia" and "connectivity" are buzzwords today; talk about them is sometimes more hype than substance. Consider the following parable. We take for granted the interactive capabilities of computing equipment today, but this wasn't always the case. It was not until the mid-1950s that computer systems commonly employed display monitors based on the cathode ray tube (CRT) technology. The first genuinely interactive program to exploit this medium was a drawing program called Sketchpad. The program was designed by Ivan Sutherland at M.I.T. as part of his doctoral dissertation, completed in 1963. Sketchpad allowed the user to create and edit drawings on the screen by manipulating buttons and a light pen. The fact that changes to the drawing could be seen immediately was revolutionary. In the years following, terms such as "online" and "interactive computing" became buzzwords that conjured up the exotic in computing. Today, however, if a hardware vendor touted its machine as supporting interactive software, the natural reaction would be underwhelming. Of course, the software will be interactive; no one would bother with it otherwise.

By the same token, multimedia computing and almost universal network connectivity may be thought of as somewhat exotic today. The idea of integrating media in an application may be considered interesting, but not essential. Distributed processing between computers across networks seems just as avant-garde. The fact remains: What is revolutionary today in computing is evolutionary tomorrow, and matter-of-fact the day after tomorrow. Five years from now, the term "multimedia" will simply be redundant. Integrating informational media over connected systems will be the way that communicating is done, plain and simple. Interestingly, computer technology has a knack for driving itself. Whether or not you get on board, the digital train is leaving the station.

WHO BENEFITS FROM MULTIMEDIA COMPUTING AND NETWORKING?

Our own enthusiasm for networking and multimedia computing is based more on their advantages than on prophecies of manifest destiny. What are some of these concrete, practical benefits for the ways in which we work and live? Computing with multimedia and networking is important for at least three segments of society: information consumers, information providers, and informational workers. These three groups represent most of society; they touch nearly all walks of life and most forms of endeavor.

● An **information consumer** is anyone who either needs or stands to benefit from relevant information services. Consumers may employ that information for a variety of tasks associated with both work and leisure.

● **Information providers** are the vendors and distributors of information services. These include the enterprises of publishing, entertainment, education, and all others whose mission, at least in part, involves imparting information to consumers.

● An **informational worker** is someone whose profession depends on the analysis, assessment, and manipulation of specific forms or classes of information. Informational workers include a wide variety of professions: scientists, physicians, tax lawyers, journalists, professors, managers, graphic artists, and many others.

For example, suppose that you are planning a vacation to Scotland. As a potential tourist, you become an information consumer. Where should you go? When is the best time to go? How should you get there? Where should you stay? A travel agent is a relevant information provider for this undertaking. The agent can provide useful information on flights, accommodations, and itineraries. The pilot of your flight depends on informational workers like the meteorologist who forecasts the atmospheric conditions over the Atlantic. How can multimedia computing improve or enhance these activities? The travel agent could consult a multimedia database that provides descriptions and photographs of hotels from which to choose. Possible itineraries could be plotted and maps automatically generated that show the travel routes. You, the information consumer, could examine these documents in the comfort of your own home after downloading the information from a commercial network that offered these and many other services. A meteorologist might use multimedia computing to help forecast for your flight. Complex three-dimensional models representing atmospheric dynamics can be depicted graphically to model current conditions. Some of this information may even be supplied to the pilot by means of computerized displays and audio format. In these and many other ways, multimedia computing can affect the manner in which we do our work and even choose our leisure time activities.

Digitization and the Information Consumer

The information consumer can benefit from digitization of information in a variety of ways. Here is a brief catalog of the kinds of services that are or will soon be available. In each instance, consider the advantages that these digital services have over comparable ones delivered using more conventional methods.

● **Research and Reference Materials.** Converting reference information to electronic form has immediate dividends. It can be stored more efficiently and accessed or transferred much more quickly than conventional forms. Add the multimedia factor to this, and the dividends are even greater. Information that combines text, graphics, images, video, and sound is richer, more engaging, and easier to absorb than traditional printed reference materials. Also, that it is electronic means that it can be distributed far and wide. To take advantage of a printed encyclopedia, for example, you must own it or have access to it. Electronic research and reference materials do not have to be physically present. You can access them remotely over networks. As an added benefit, information providers don't have to worry about damage to or loss of electronic information in the same way that libraries, for instance, must for their printed collections.

● **Education.** The purpose of institutional education is to prepare an individual to meet the challenges of living. In short, educators prepare students to spend a life educating themselves. Computing technology will play an important role in this education for several reasons. First, technology itself will be significant in both workplace and the home. Students must understand and master it to succeed in the future. Just as important for the educator, computing technology will become a new partner in the process of general education. As a resource and a tool, computing technology has myriad applications in the classroom, lab, and library. Computers can bridge long distances, they can conjure up worlds and experiences, they can assist and monitor learners, and they can be repositories for a wealth of information in many forms.

● **Games and Entertainment.** Fantasy adventure computer games such as *Myst, Riven* (see Figure 1.6), and *7th Guest* have created intoxicating diversions that are enhanced by realistic three-dimensional graphics, engrossing sound effects, and music. With their simple, natural interfaces for interacting with them, these games effectively integrate several informational media to create a more engaging, realistic experience.

The digital dividend will be extended to other entertainment forms in the future. Interactive television promises to immerse the viewer in the performance or event being broadcast. For example, imagine controlling the camera shots at a World Series game directly from your remote control. You choose from a number of camera positions; at the same time, you can control the mix and sound levels of the players and

FIGURE 1.6
Fantasy games such as Riven create an incredibly rich and entertaining environment for exploration.

the fans. Choose your own replays and slow-motion, stop-action sequences. (This must be couch potato heaven!)

● **Telemarketing.** A lot of people scoffed when networks such as QVC launched 24-hour shopping channels. The success of such home shopping networks speaks to a simple fact about human nature: When a service is delivered in a form that is easily accessible, we embrace it. Electronic marketing via networks and home computers is another version of this simple idea, offering individuals the opportunity to choose from a wide variety of products. It can provide the consumer with demos, advertisements, and electronic catalogs. Using catalogs, individuals can order products even more quickly and easily than through shopping channels.

Using computer networks as a market medium has a distinct advantage over television marketing. Television is a broadcast medium. Even cable transmissions depend on the economics of scale: Masses must receive these mass communications to justify the expense. Computer networks, however, communicate more like telephones; they support point-to-point communications. This means that information can afford to be highly specialized and tailored for each individual consumer. Computer telemarketing can thus create micromarkets. In the future, we might expect to find more specialized retailers that exploit the digital advantage and fewer mass retailers on the scale of the venerable Sears & Roebuck model.

Digitization and the Information Provider

The information service industry will also benefit from the digital boon. Here is a sample of the ways in which information services have been and will be improved.

● **Consumer and Retail Kiosks.** **Kiosks** are public facilities designed to make information available to many people. Kiosks are typically placed in locations having high visibility and heavy consumer traffic. Computer kiosks replace traditional informational booths found on street corners and in malls, hospitals, office buildings, and the like.

The advantages of a multimedia kiosk are its attractiveness, flexibility, and convenience for its consumers. Interactive displays permit consumers to search for relevant information in a self-directed manner and at a self-paced rate. These computer-based kiosks can also collect information about their own use, too. Such feedback may be very useful, even vital, for the information provider.

● **Network Information Delivery.** The growth of data communication networks is staggering. Business and commerce could hardly be conducted today without electronic mail, file transfers, and remote log-ins. These applications permit us to share resources with other persons and systems—sometimes distantly. At the same time, individuals have benefited from the growth of commercial network access providers such as CompuServe and America Online. These services offer connectivity to users who wish to gather information or share ideas with others. The future promises even greater growth and opportunity. Increased load capacities (often called bandwidth) for existing networks will allow richer sources of information, such as video and audio, to be transmitted in real time. Wireless networking will extend connectivity beyond office and home to remote spots. In the not too distant future, computers, telephones, and televisions will merge into a seamless appliance for communication.

● **Sales and Commercial Presentations.** An effective presentation is one that gains our attention and enables us to retain the information presented. How many sales talks or commercial presentations have you endured in which the speaker simply talked at the audience? Presentations that make effective uses of graphics or video for illustration are not only more interesting, they are usually more memorable. It is a fact that we can absorb and retain visual data at a rate over twice that of verbal or textual data. Multimedia presentations make the development and delivery of such multifaceted communication much easier.

● **Simulations and Training.** Most companies and institutions need to train employees in a variety of subjects. Training is an expensive and difficult endeavor for a number of reasons. It is difficult to manage because its success depends on fitting a range of topics to a variety of individuals with different aptitudes and learning styles. Training also requires constant updating to be relevant. Computer-based training can help diminish some of these obstacles and their associated expense. Flight simulators are a good example of computer training modules that simulate activities for the trainee in a concrete, hands-on, and individualized manner. These training modules can be updated easily to reflect new conditions or objectives. In addition, because the computer is the vehicle for training, it can gather important information about the trainee's performance. Some training modules even have built-in intelligence to evaluate that performance and make decisions on how to enhance it with other activities. All of this is done automatically and economically.

● **Electronic Publishing.** Electronic books offer several advantages that conventional printed texts do not. First, information can be enriched with appropriate multimedia content; speech, images, and video can enhance the message. Second, electronic information can be organized in different and innovative ways. A printed text is a linear document—you read one page after another from beginning to end.

An electronic book, however, might be designed to be read in many different orders. As in a do-it-yourself tour, you are free to choose those paths that are most interesting. Finally, electronic documents can be edited and updated easily. New editions can be prepared and disseminated much more quickly and cheaply than those of conventional printed books.

Even print publishing can benefit from the conversion to the digital domain. Readers can pick and choose segments of texts for personalized editions—called on-demand or just-in-time publishing. For example, some companies today offer individually tailored versions of textbooks that contain only those units or chapters that fit the course's content or the instructor's teaching style. The review, selection, and preparation of these on-demand texts can be handled almost entirely electronically.

Digitization and the Informational Worker

Informational or knowledge workers can also expect the digitization of the workplace to produce palpable gains. Here are some of the most common areas of productivity.

● **Multimedia Databases.** Databases are collections of data stored on a computer and organized for convenient and easy retrievals. In addition to the conventional text and numeric data, multimedia databases collect digital graphics, video, and audio samples that increase the value of the database immensely.

● **Data Visualization.** Large amounts of data often overwhelm the individuals who attempt to analyze or assess it. Visual representations ranging from graphs and plots to complex dynamic models aid these endeavors. Multimedia computing enhances analysis by automating the visualization process.

● **Groupware or Cooperative Computing.** Most informational enterprises engage in tasks requiring the cooperative effort of workers. Groupware extends the idea of a team by supporting the team with various computing services. For example, suppose a team is working on a budget proposal. Perhaps the basic budget document originates with one team member but is passed electronically to others for their suggestions, corrections, and additions. After various team members have made their contributions, the entire team can review and approve the final proposal without the necessity of a face-to-face meeting. Networked multimedia computing enhances the productivity of teams by improving communication while automating records and document archives.

● **Personal Communications.** In addition to the existing technologies of voice telephony, electronic mail, and text-based network services, the digital dividend contributes enhanced forms of communication. Video-conferencing can link multiple sites rather than just point to point. Participants can see the other groups and themselves in separate windows on a computer screen. At the same time, the group can manipulate a common document in another window. Multimedia e-mail involves transmitting both voice and images along with or in place of conventional text files. In fact, speech recognition and synthesis can automate many normal mail and phone messaging tasks.

A TOUR OF THE WORLD WIDE WEB

This book is about exploring the digital domain. The interactive use of multimedia information and the tapping of the tremendous potential inherent in modern computer networks energize this domain. We have tried to convey some of the excitement that we have for the usefulness and the impact of the digital domain. It is impossible to give an accurate and complete description of multimedia information using text and static pictures alone. Nor does text alone adequately convey the incredible enabling power of easily accessible international computer networks. The impact of the digital domain is best appreciated when it is experienced, and we have provided a way for you to engage actively in this exploration. We hope that this activity will be a valuable and motivating context on which the remainder of our exposition can build.

We mentioned earlier the ease with which Web browsers allow access to an assortment of materials. Netscape Communicator and Microsoft Internet Explorer are two of the most popular browsers. In this activity, we will guide you through a quick tour of the World Wide Web employing Netscape Communicator or Internet Explorer and resources we have prepared on the Web site that serves as a companion resource for this text. (Don't be concerned if you have a different Web browser; you should be able to translate the instructions for getting to the *Exploring the Digital Domain* Web site easily enough.)

We have just a few pretour instructions. Whenever you see text on a Web page in color or underlined, this means that text is connected or linked to additional Web resources. The underlined text is called a **hyperlink,** or **link** for short.

When you move the mouse pointer over a link, it will change into an icon shaped like a small hand with a pointing finger. Clicking a link will automatically connect you to the linked Web page. The new page may be on the same computer you're currently accessing, or it may be on a computer on the other side of the world. It won't matter to you because the transfer is done automatically at the click of your mouse. Outlined icons, graphics, and images on Web pages are also frequently linked to other Web sites as well. Again, a simple mouse click over the icon or image will do the trick.

Finally, there are several very useful buttons on the browser toolbars. These are shown for both the Netscape Communicator and Internet Explorer browsers in Figure 1.7. Keep in mind that it may take your computer a few minutes to link to some Web sites—just how long will depend on how fast your computer is, how busy the Internet is, and how much information the new Web page contains. Web pages with lots of images take longer to load than those with fewer images. If you become impatient with a Web site loading process, you can stop the process by clicking the Stop button on your browser's toolbar. A very handy navigational tool is the Back button. Clicking it will reverse your journey and take you back to the previous Web page you visited. Using this button, you can easily return to pick up your tour after a side trip. Now, let's get started!

1 Find the icon representing the Netscape Communicator or Internet Explorer browser, which must have been previously installed on your computer. (If you cannot locate such an icon, consult your instructor for further instructions.)

FIGURE 1.7

The toolbars for the (a) Netscape Communicator 4.0 and (b) Internet Explorer 4.0 browsers contain buttons that can be clicked to initiate many frequently used browser commands.

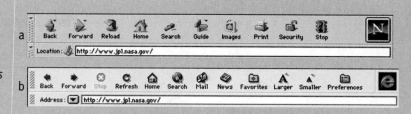

2 Double-click this icon to establish an Internet connection and open the browser's graphical user interface. If you are using Netscape Communicator, you should see a screen similar to the one shown in Figure 1.8; Internet Explorer users should see a screen organized similar to the one shown in Figure 1.9. Your actual screen may be different if another default page loads when you launch the browser on your machine.

3 Click **File** at the left top of the window to open the **File** pull-down menu. (If you're using a Macintosh, you'll need to keep the mouse button depressed to display the menu.) From the **File** menu select the command *Open Location*.

A dialog box for communicating information to the browser program will appear.

4 Type the following address in the dialog box:

http://s9000.furman.edu/DD

When you are sure that the address is correctly entered, click the Open button in the dialog box to instruct the browser to transfer to the Web page at this address.

5 In a short period of time (depending on the speed of your computer and the type of its connection to the Internet), you should see the *Exploring the Digital Domain* home page. A **home**

FIGURE 1.8

The Netscape Communicator 4.0 browser user interface contains a menu bar from which commands may be accessed via pull-down menus. The toolbar represents commands that may be activated by clicking the appropriate button. Shown here is the entry page for the Jet Propulsion Laboratory.

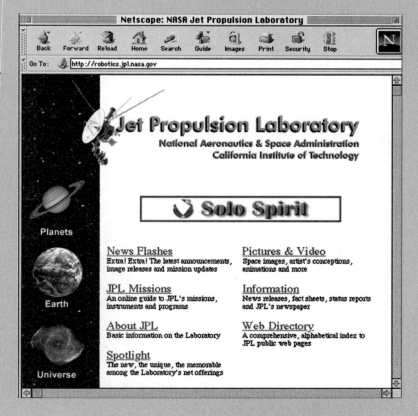

FIGURE 1.9
The Internet Explorer 4.0 browser user interface contains a menu bar from which commands may be accessed via pull-down menus. The toolbar represents commands that may be activated by clicking the appropriate button.

page is the entry point or anchor page for an electronic document stored and delivered via the Web. You will access this page frequently throughout your readings to seek more information about ideas discussed in the text and to explore additional topics.

6 To save this location for future reference, add the address to your browser's bookmark list. A **bookmark list** is a collection of locations that can be easily referenced without your having to remember and type in their Web addresses. To do this in Netscape Communicator, choose the *Add Bookmark* command from the **Bookmarks** pull-down menu. In Internet Explorer, choose the *Add Page to Favorites* command from the **Favorites** pull-down menu. The name of the current page will be stored in the bookmark list. To return to that location, you need only select the name of the page from the list (accessing either the **Bookmarks** or **Favorites** menu, depending on which browser you're using). The browser will do the rest; it looks up the proper address and connects to the site.

7 For now, we're interested in accessing the interactive World Wide Web tour stored on the *Exploring the Digital Domain* Web site. To do this, click on the *World Wide Web Tour* link; you will next see the *Exploring the Digital Domain World Wide Web Tour* page. You're now ready to complete the tour on your own—exploring interactively those topics that particularly interest you.

8 The tour bus is about to pull onto the information superhighway. You're the tour guide! Go where you like, explore the sights and sounds, and return on your own schedule. We would issue one warning, though: Allow plenty of time for your tour—surfing the Web can be addictive!

ABOUT THE *EXPLORING THE DIGITAL DOMAIN* WEB SITE

FIGURE 1.10
The World Wide Web *icon signifies an electronic reference to related materials that augment or update items discussed in the text.*

Within this text, we have tried to describe the excitement and effectiveness of the powerful new information and communication paradigms that are evolving. But the flavor and impact of multimedia information and the ease with which modern networking makes an incredible array of such information available must be experienced for a full appreciation. You've just completed your first tour of the World Wide Web, so you have an idea of the variety and richness of information available there. We encourage you to treat the companion Web site as an integral part of this text. All text chapters have associated essays, demonstrations, software tutorials, and sometimes just interesting distractions accessed through the accompanying Web site. To help guide your access to these additional resources, we will use a Web icon, shown in Figure 1.10, in the text margin whenever we wish to point you to something of interest on the Web site. You may consult these resources as you wish, picking and choosing as you work through the text proper. We encourage you to explore them all.

SUMMARY

Today's computer systems are far more than computational and text processing tools. They provide a new communication paradigm for representing and communicating information in a wide variety of media: text, numbers, graphics, images, sounds, and video. All these differing forms of information can be digitized, combined, transformed, and transmitted with relative ease employing worldwide computer networks.

Digitized multimedia data and the systems that handle it constitute the digital domain. The digital domain has had a pervasive and transforming influence on the workplace, the marketplace, our schools, and our homes, redefining the ways in which we think about and use information to communicate with each other. That many forms of information can be exchanged instantaneously over long distances will continue to change the way we work and play. Electronic mail has already become the norm for communication with coworkers in many organizations; the World Wide Web is the information resource of first choice for many people; and a school or workplace without networked computers is becoming hard to imagine.

The powerful combination of the modern computer as an all-purpose platform for informational media and ubiquitous computer networks is enabling the integration of technology into our lives at an unprecedented rate. And rapid developments in software, hardware, and networking technologies continue to create new opportunities to realize the computer's potential for enhancing our intellectual abilities and activities. At the heart of these developments is the emergence of two primary technologies: the ability of modern desktop computer systems to collect, store, retrieve, display, and generally manage information in a variety of media, and the possibilities for cooperative work using fully interconnected computers and computer networks. These two technologies are the principal subjects of this text.

PROJECTS

1 Describe the availability of networking on your campus. How pervasive is it? Is electronic mail available to all students? Assuming it is available, is it convenient for you to get access to electronic mail?

2 Using newspapers and news magazines that were on the newsstand *in the past two weeks,* can you find two articles that you would classify as being about the digital domain? Assuming so, summarize each of those articles in a paragraph or two.

3 Write a short essay on how the digital domain can fundamentally change an industry. Use the publishing industry as one illustrative example. Add some other examples of your own choosing.

4 Check some newspaper or magazine ads to find out what an entry-level multimedia computing system might cost. Include a multimedia computer with a CD-ROM, a color printer, a color scanner, and a digital camera in your system. Summarize your findings in a table, giving a range of products and prices (low, medium, and high, perhaps).

5 Do some research to find out how the national newspaper *USA Today* is published. Summarize your findings in a brief report.

6 Do some research on how the movie *Toy Story* was produced. Summarize your findings in a brief report.

Key Terms

bookmark list	information provider	multimedia database
browsers	informational worker	network
cyberspace	Internet	virtual reality
digital domain	link (Web page)	Web page
home page	medium	Web site
information consumer	multimedia	World Wide Web

QUESTIONS FOR REVIEW

1 Describe the digital domain in your own words.

2 Give your own definition of the term *cyberspace*.

3 How is computing technology changing the ways in which we communicate with each other? Are these changes for the better or worse in your opinion?

4 How does the use of multimedia information affect the communication process? Give some specific examples to support your answer.

5 Describe how networking is supporting the integration of technology into our lives. Try to project the future impact of networking technology.

6 Can you think of ways, in addition to those catalogued in the text, in which information consumers will benefit from multimedia computing and networking in the future?

7 Can you think of ways, in addition to those catalogued in the text, in which information providers will likely exploit multimedia computing and networking in the future?

8 What is an informational worker?

9 Can you think of ways, in addition to those catalogued in the text, in which informational workers will come to depend on multimedia computing and networking in the future?

10 What is a Web site? A Web page?

11 What is a Web browser?

12 Describe some of the ways the evolution to digital forms of information has influenced the workplace.

13 Name some ways multimedia computing can enhance the educational process.

14 Identify three of your favorite stops on the World Wide Web Tour that you accessed from the *Exploring the Digital Domain* Web site. What about these particular sites appealed to you?

As mentioned in the last chapter, computers are the spearhead for the revolution in information technology today. The revolution is marked by the convergence or assimilation of many different technologies into one, seamless platform. Ten years ago, computers, telephones, televisions, books, postal service, audio, and most other informational technologies were distinctive, alternative forms for representing, storing, and delivering thoughts, ideas, and expressions of feelings. Today the boundaries between these technologies are melting. In the future, distinguishing them may be impractical. What has fueled this revolution? As we alluded previously, the conversion of information technology to the digital domain is the single most important factor. But what is the digital domain? Why is it so important? What advantages does it offer over conventional technologies? These and other related issues are the subject of this chapter.

OBJECTIVES

- *The nature of the digital domain*

- *Distinguishing analog versus digital data*

- *The advantages of electronic digital media*

- *The universal language of computers: binary encoding of data*

- *The basics of how information is converted to digital (binary) form*

CHAPTER 2

THE DIGITAL DOMAIN

Vasily Kandinsky, *Red Oval (Rotes Oval)*, 1920. Solomon R. Guggenheim Museum

WHAT IS THE DIGITAL DOMAIN?

All forms of information, or **data,** in the modern electromagnetic computer are encoded by way of a discrete symbol system. **Discrete** means definite or distinct, so a discrete system is a set of interpretations, each of which is distinct, unambiguous, and precise. This means that any legitimate symbol sequence has a definite meaning that cannot be confused with that of any other symbol sequence.

For example, the letters of the alphabet compose a discrete symbol system. Each letter is distinct; no two letters can be confused. The same is true for combinations of such symbols. For instance, the words "torn" and "worn" are clearly different. Regardless of what these words might mean in a given language (English), the written words are quite distinct. The precision and clarity afforded by discrete symbols systems, of course, are very useful for most practical matters. To illustrate the point, consider these instructions: "Bring some chairs into the room" and "Bring three chairs into the room." Which instruction is easier to interpret? Obviously, the second one is precise and unambiguous. It is consistently repeatable as well; any two persons who carried it out would fetch the same number of chairs.

Just as words denote and express our thoughts and feelings, the computer represents and stores information in the symbols of a formal language. The formal language of a computer is based on a digital symbol system. **Digital** means a discrete system whose symbols are numbers. Using numbers for symbols has some advantages over other discrete symbol systems.

Digital symbol systems are easier to implement. Modern technologies can generate symbols based on numbering more reliably and economically than other types of symbols. Whether the medium is electronic or otherwise, creating, transmitting, and storing symbols that are numeric, that is, based on counting, is easier. (Remember that Paul Revere employed a digital messaging system for convenience, too: 1 = "by land," 2 = "by sea.")

Numbers have a natural ordering, too. We can exploit this ordering when devising coding systems to make our work easier. For example, suppose that we arranged each person in a group by height and assigned them a number in ascending order from shortest to tallest. It would be a simple matter to decide whether one person is taller or shorter than another by comparing their designated numbers. Person 3 is shorter than person 5, but taller than person 1. Such decisions could be made without any further measurements. The facts are embedded in our coding system.

That all data is represented in computers as numbers means that a common underlying symbol system serves as the basis for all forms of expression. This is another significant feature. Think of how advantageous it would be if everyone used precisely the same alphabet the world over. Even if this alphabet were used to represent different languages, it would still mean that publishing (storing information) and communications (transmitting information) would be a great deal easier than it is now.

All computing is based on the fact that numbers are used to denote the things that interest us. Whether these numbers represent words, pictures, sounds, music, measurements, qualities, or whatever else we choose, they are all collections of numbers in the end. The collective set of numeric coding schemes used to represent the data that computers process constitutes what we call the digital domain. As you shall see, all computerized information is captured, stored, processed, and transmitted in the digital domain. And this is the chief source of the great power and flexibility of modern computing. Understanding the scope and range of the digital domain reveals the true potential of the computer as a communications and multimedia machine.

ANALOG VERSUS DIGITAL INFORMATION

Even though modern information technologies are based on digital representations of data, many natural forms of representing information are analog. Strictly speaking, the terms "analog" and "digital" fit more comfortably in the discourse of signal processing—the realm of communications technologies. Considering these concepts in the context of how information may be represented in general, however, is useful. **Analog** representations are continuous over some dimension, such as time. Sound provides a good example for how information may be represented in analog form. Sounds are rapid vibrations that are transmitted as variations in air pressure. If you were to measure the intensity of a pure tone, for instance, it would be plotted as a continuously undulating line or **wave,** like the one depicted in Figure 2.1. Its amplitude or intensity would vary smoothly and continuously over time.

Continuity is an essential feature of analog information. At every instant, we can measure the amplitude of a sound, for example. Hence, the curve in Figure 2.1 plots an infinite amount of information because a continuous curve has an infinite number of points. Just about everything in nature is susceptible to an analog representation. Besides sound, light, water, electricity, wind, and so on are all measurable using analog methods.

In contrast, digital information is, of course, discrete. A digital representation of sound, for example, would be a series of instantaneous pulses. The intensity of the pulse is measured at distinct intervals of time. Between these intervals no measurements are made. Figure 2.2 shows the same sound illustrated in Figure 2.1, but represented digitally. In contrast to analog forms, a digital representation contains a finite

FIGURE 2.1

Sound can be plotted as a wave whose amplitude varies continuously over time. Here is a simple wave pattern.

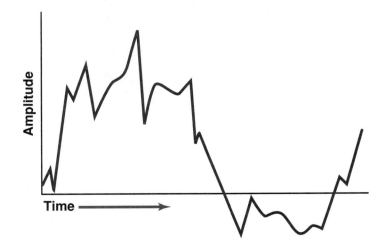

FIGURE 2.2

A sampled version of the sound wave in Figure 2.1 is shown here. The bars represent sampled amplitudes measured at regular intervals. These values can be used to reconstruct a facsimile of the original analog signal.

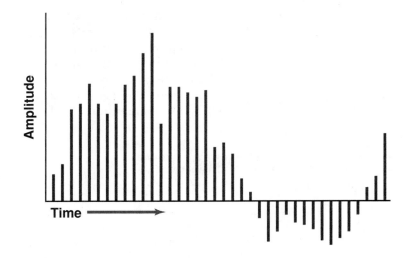

amount of information. Digital information sacrifices exactness for a precise, compact representation.

Even so, if the number of intervals over time is sufficient, a digital representation is a good facsimile of its analog counterpart. In fact, under the right conditions, digital and analog representations can be exchanged for one another with acceptable accuracy. Thus, analog information such as sound, images, and the like can be **digitized** or converted to a digital representation. Conversely, the digital information stored and processed on a computer system can be converted to analog form for other uses. Compact discs, for instance, store music in digital form, but a CD player converts it back to analog form to drive your speakers.

ADVANTAGES OF THE DIGITAL DOMAIN

So far we have emphasized the digital or discrete character of computing. Keep in mind that computers are electronic machines, too. This is a significant factor: The operation of a computer system is based on the flow, processing, and interchange of electronic signals. Electronic devices are very fast; the operating speeds of a modern computer system are measured in billionths of a second. Even its slowest devices, those hampered by mechanical components, operate at speeds that are blindingly fast to us. Digital electronic signals offer great flexibility, too. They may be amplified, combined, sorted out, filtered, and manipulated in various ways.

Because the digital domain is predominantly an electronic one, this marriage of electronic technology with digital data representation results in a number of distinct advantages over conventional technologies based on analog forms. To appreciate the power and flexibility of digital forms of information, let's consider each of these factors briefly.

⬤ **Precision.**   As mentioned, the underlying language of digital media is numeric. Numbers are distinct and unambiguous; this means that digital representations can be manipulated precisely. For example, a conventional black-and-white photograph likely contains hundreds of shades of gray. See Figure 2.3. A digitized photograph, however, assigns a distinct value for each separate shade of gray. We could match two shades of gray in separate areas of a digitized image simply by comparing their numbers. If the numbers are the same, the shades are identical. Matching shades of gray in a conventional photograph would be subjective, more difficult, and therefore less reliable.

● **Ordinality.** Numbers express ordering, too; for example, 1 comes before 2, 2 before 3, and so on. This concept of ordering is called **ordinality.** The encoding of digital data can take advantage of this built-in ordinality. For example, we can arrange the shades of gray discernible in a black-and-white image from darkest black to the lightest white. We could then assign increasing values so that low numbers mean dark shades and high values light ones, as in Figure 2.4. This makes comparing two shades in a digital image a simple matter—the darker shade has a lower number. Ordering values has a variety of important uses for nearly all forms of data.

FIGURE 2.3

The blocks in the top half of the diagram show a close-up view of a digitized image composed of uniformly sized areas called pixels (for picture elements). The pixels denote shades of gray in a monotone (black-and-white) photo. Can you identify the pixels that have the same shades of gray by visual inspection? Note, for example, the two boxed pixels in the image. Are they the same shade of gray? Contrasts with the surrounding blocks often play tricks on the eye and make it difficult to determine. When the shades of gray are represented by numbers (as in the bottom half of the diagram), it is easy to decide. Both the numbers are the same. This is how a computer compares digital data.

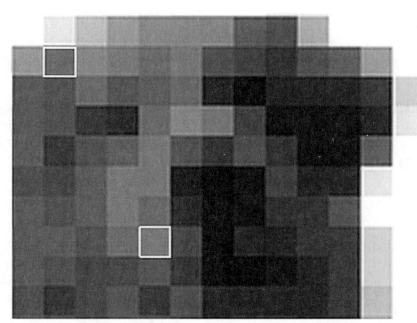

15	14	12	10	8	9	8	6	5	10	14	15	15
10	7	9	7	7	7	4	3	2	4	6	10	15
6	4	6	4	5	7	2	0	1	2	2	2	12
6	4	3	1	7	8	7	3	1	0	1	1	14
6	3	5	5	7	5	3	4	2	0	1	5	15
5	3	6	7	7	1	0	0	3	1	2	13	15
5	5	6	8	7	2	0	0	2	3	4	14	15
6	5	4	7	7	3	0	1	1	3	3	12	15
6	4	4	3	4	2	0	0	1	2	3	13	15
4	3	4	5	2	4	2	2	2	1	2	12	15

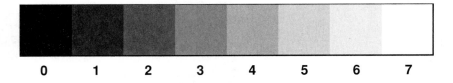

FIGURE 2.4

Eight shades of gray from darkest to lightest can be arranged in order and numbered from 0 to 7, respectively. Deciding whether a particular portion of an image is lighter or darker than another can be decided by comparing their number values. If a given value is lower than some other, it is darker. If it is higher, then it is lighter.

Efficient Storage. Digital media are physically represented and stored using electronic, electromagnetic, or optical technologies. All of these offer the basic advantage of compact storage. In other words, the amount of information stored per unit of measure is much greater than with any conventional media. For example, the single letter "e" on this page takes up as much width as roughly 300 copies of "e" when they are stored on a compact disc.

If we assume that a typical page has 70 symbols per line (counting punctuation and spaces) and has 50 lines, then the average page stores about 3500 symbols. If a typical printed book numbered 300 pages, it would store more than 1 million symbols. Yet these totals are puny compared to the capacities of different forms of computer storage, as shown in Table 2.1. A single floppy disk could store the equivalent of almost one and one-third books. A typical CD-ROM could store more than 500 books. By contrast, if the hard drive of your system could store up to 1 billion symbols, it would take a printed book with more than 285,000 pages to match this capacity.

TABLE 2.1

Using a printed book as a standard measure, the capacities of different forms of computer storage are compared.

COMPARING MEDIA		
Page	=	70 symbols × 50 lines
Book	=	300 pages
Floppy Disk	=	1.33 books (1.4 million symbols)
CD-ROM	=	571.4 books (600 million symbols)
Hard Drive	=	952.4 books (1 billion symbols)

Fast Transfer. The technologies supporting digital media can transport or transfer digital data rapidly compared to other forms. For example, an average typist can transcribe 40 to 60 words per minute. On the other hand, the slowest connector on a desktop computer can transfer data at a rate almost 1800 times as fast. Other types of connections are even faster.

Absolute Replication. If you photocopy a document or image, the resulting copy is not a perfect duplicate. Xerography, like photography, is an analog process; each time a duplicate is itself duplicated, a small but noticeable degradation of the image occurs. If we continued to photocopy each new copy, eventually the imperfections and noise inherent in the process would become clearly visible. On the other hand, when you duplicate a digital picture or document, the copy replicates the original. Not only is there no degrading of the signal, the copy is indistinguishable from the original. (After all, both are just lists of numbers.) This constitutes **absolute replication.** This is why a musical performance recorded to digital compact disc sounds the same time after time. The same is not true for analog phonograph records and tape; wear and tear ultimately

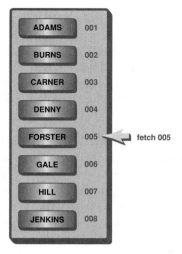

FIGURE 2.5

Digital data can be organized in standard units. These units can be numbered or addressed for convenient access. The names are stored in numbered bins. If we know the number of a particular item, we can fetch it directly, which is called random access. Random access is a fast and efficient means of locating digital data.

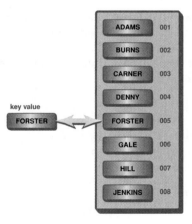

FIGURE 2.6

Digital data can also be searched based on content as well. For example, using the key we can try to find a match with a list of names stored in the bins. This is called selective access. We do, of course, have to examine a number of items before finding a match, but selective access is useful when we are trying to find items that share similar characteristics.

corrupt the recording. The capability for unlimited, absolute replication is an important characteristic of digital media.

● **Resolution Independence or Scalability.** Roughly speaking, **resolution** defines the capacity for detail contained in a message or signal. For example, a television picture has a resolution that is based on and limited by the number of scan lines that constitute the screen. Audio signals also have limited capacities for representing the highs and lows of the original sound. Signals with greater resolution usually have higher fidelity. In an analog system, the sender and receiver of a signal must be perfectly matched. Specifically, the receiver must be capable of handling the resolution of the signal created by the sender.

Digital systems are not so limited. In fact, for digital systems, the quality of the received signal can be easily scaled to the characteristics of the receiver rather than those of the original source. Practically speaking, this means that computers with very different performance characteristics can transfer and portray the same data. For example, high-resolution images and high-fidelity sound can be processed and portrayed acceptably by systems that are not equipped to handle such resolution. The resolution of the digital data is independent of the machines processing it. This ability of machines to transmit, receive, and process data with a greater resolution than the machine is capable of producing is called **scalability.** As you will learn later, scalability is one of the chief factors that enable different computers to communicate information with one another even though they have very different capabilities for displaying and processing that information.

● **Random and Selective Access.** Digital data can be organized to permit two distinct forms of access. Because discrete data consists of physically distinct chunks of symbols, we can organize it so. In other words, we can stuff digital data into bins or convenient pockets for later access. If we know exactly where each of these bins is located, then we can access that data directly. This is called **random access.** See Figure 2.5. By contrast, in analog systems, access is always sequential. Consider, for example, an audio cassette tape. To play a song stored in the middle of the tape, you must physically move past all the songs that precede it.

Digital data can be searched out selectively, too. **Selective access** means that the item is found based on analyzing its content for desired properties. For example, the locations of all the occurrences of a given word in a document can be found by searching through the text for sequences of letters that match it. See Figure 2.6.

● **Compression.** Information is interesting to us because it is neither totally redundant nor completely random. An unmodulated droning sound contains little or no information for us. In fact, if it is not too loud, after a while we become inured to it and fail to notice it at all. On the other hand, when you view your television screen between channels, you see a snowy picture filled with random noise. Nothing is discernible about it either. Information lies somewhere in between randomness (TV snow) and total redundancy (droning sound). Information has some redundancy or patterns, but it also has some novelty or disruption of redundancy.

When information is represented digitally—that is, numerically—we can exploit this propensity for patterns. In short, we can describe the extent to which information contains redundancy and novelty numerically.

This is the heart and soul of **data compression** techniques. In other words, we may replace numeric sequences by other, more concise numeric sequences, yet reproduce the originals when needed. Compressed data requires less space for storage and is transmitted more quickly. As you shall see, data compression is a convenience for some and a necessity for other, richer forms of information. (You will find out more about data compression in Chapter 15.)

● **Content Analysis and Synthesis.** Digital data is subject to processes that analyze and combine it in useful ways. This, of course, is the intent of computing. For example, a large collection of photographs stored conventionally (in albums, perhaps) can be unwieldy. The same collection stored as digitized images can be processed using selective techniques that look for specific structures or content. Thus, the images can be classified and sorted for quick access. At the same time, digital images can be abstracted and combined in new ways, offering even greater practical uses.

DIGITAL BASICS: BINARY BITS AND BYTES

As mentioned earlier, digital representations of information involve numerically encoding it as data. The numeric coding scheme for all forms of digital data, however, is a binary one rather than the decimal one we are accustomed to. The **binary numbering system** is a base-2 positional numbering system. Let us elaborate in more detail.

A **positional notation** is one in which the order or position of each symbol conveys a special meaning. In a nonpositional notation, each occurrence of a given symbol has the same meaning as any other occurrence. For example, if we counted sheep using simple tick marks, four sheep might be represented in this manner.

$$| | | |$$

Each tick means one sheep; the order of the ticks adds no special significance to the number. Decimal notation, on the other hand, is a positional scheme. The decimal numbers

$$346$$

$$463$$

both contain the same symbols, but they denote different numbers. In the first decimal number, the 3 denotes three hundreds (3×10^2), the 4 denotes four tens (4×10^1), and the 6 signifies six units (6×10^0). In a positional notation, both the numerals and their respective positions are significant for denoting the number.

As you can see, each digit position in the decimal notation represents some product of a power of 10. We can rewrite any number in the base-10 system as the sum of the products of its powers of 10:

$$(3 \times 10^2) + (4 \times 10^1) + (6 \times 10^0)$$
$$300 \quad + \quad 40 \quad + \quad 6 \quad = 346$$
$$[\text{hundreds} + \text{tens} + \text{units}]$$

In base 10, there are exactly ten different numerals available as symbols $\{0, 1, 2, \ldots, 9\}$.

We are so accustomed to using decimal notation that it seems both natural, and intuitive. In spite of this fact, other base positional notations are available to represent numbers. Octal is base 8. Each symbol denotes a power of eight, and numerals are limited to the set $\{0, 1, 2, \ldots, 7\}$. The numerals 346 in an octal representation are as follows:

$$(3 \times 8^2) + (4 \times 8^1) + (6 \times 8^0)$$
$$192 \quad + \quad 32 \quad + \quad 6 \quad = 230 \text{ (decimal)}$$

Binary is a base-2 notation. This means that each symbol represents a power of 2, and there are two available numerals for representing numbers, that is, $\{0, 1\}$. Suppose that 110011 expresses a binary value. Its interpretation would be as follows:

$$(1 \times 2^5) + (1 \times 2^4) + (0 \times 2^3) + (0 \times 2^2) + (1 \times 2^1) + (1 \times 2^0)$$
$$32 \quad + \quad 16 \quad + \quad 0 \quad + \quad 0 \quad + \quad 2 \quad + \quad 1 \quad = 51 \text{ (decimal)}$$

Because binary is a positional notation, the order of symbols is still significant for determining the number denoted. But because binary is base 2, there are only two possible symbols, and each position is a power of 2. This means that quantities expressed in binary notation will likely require more symbols than decimal notation. For example, the decimal number 111 would be expressed in binary as 1101111.

$$(1 \times 2^6) + (1 \times 2^5) + (0 \times 2^4) + (1 \times 2^3) + (1 \times 2^2) + (1 \times 2^1) + (1 \times 2^0)$$
$$64 \quad + \quad 32 \quad + \quad 0 \quad + \quad 8 \quad + \quad 4 \quad + \quad 2 \quad + \quad 1 \quad = 111$$

Binary notation is very simple because only one of two values is needed to express any binary digit. This is the main reason why binary numbering is preferred for encoding data in a computer system. Binary numbers are simply easier to store, transmit, and process electronically than is our conventional decimal notation. Consequently, all forms of digital data are represented fundamentally using some binary coding scheme. Whether the data denotes text, numbers, pictures, sounds, or whatever, it is encoded on a computer system as some sequence of binary digits.

Each *binary digit* is called a **bit.** A single bit, though, is not very expressive. At most, it can denote one of two values. Instead, bits are usually combined to form larger sequences or strings. A very common unit is a string of eight bits called a **byte.** A byte can denote $2 \times 2 \times 2 \times 2 \times 2 \times 2 \times 2 \times 2 = 2^8$ or 256 possible values, that is, from 0 (00000000) to 255 (11111111). One byte could be used to encode a single item of information potentially having as many as 256 interpretations, depending on its value. For example, one byte is sufficient to denote both uppercase and lowercase alphabets, as well as other printed character symbols used to compose text. Suppose that we assigned uppercase A the value of 00000000 (0), B the value 00000001 (1), C the value 00000010 (2), and so on. The lowercase letter a could be encoded starting at 00011011 (27), b the value 00011100 (28), through z with the value 00011000 (48). This would still leave plenty of assignments for punctuation, numerals, special symbols, and the like. We could denote 256 shades of gray or colors for some piece of a picture and store that picture element in a single byte, too. And, of course, we could use a single byte to denote a simple, unsigned integer value from 0 to 255, as well.

These are just some of the ways in which binary numbering can be used to encode data of various forms. It may be necessary to combine bits into larger strings or sequences, but the principle remains the same. All meaningful forms of information are represented by some collection and configuration of binary numbers.

In every computer system, each item of data is usually constrained to some maximum number of bits called its **precision.** For example, a text symbol may have a precision of 8 bits or a byte; integers may have a precision of 32 bits or 4 bytes. Whether it is a byte or larger, the precision is always finite. This, of course, implies that any digital symbol system used for computer storage is finite as well. Only so many meanings can be denoted when there is a finite limit on the number of different values used to represent them. This principle is called **finite precision.** As you will see in subsequent treatments, whether you are representing numbers, text, pictures, sounds, or whatever, finite precision will often have significant consequences for that coding scheme.

More information

CONVERTING INFORMATION TO DIGITAL FORM

Any piece of information that is stored, transmitted, or otherwise processed by computers must be represented in binary digital form. The process of converting information into a binary representation is called **digitization.** The nature of this process, however, depends on whether the original information is analog or discrete.

Digitizing Discrete Forms of Information

You will recall that discrete forms of information are those whose interpretations are distinct and unambiguous. Text and numbers represent information in a discrete form. To digitize a discrete form of information, all that is necessary is to agree on a mapping of the original symbol system to a binary numbering. Consider the following example.

Suppose we want to represent any decimal number using a binary scheme that encodes each digit of that number. This means that the original number is divided into individual digits and each digit is encoded distinctly. As a result, the string of binary codes denotes the original decimal number. A natural way of mapping each digit to a binary number is simply to represent it by its pure binary equivalent. Consequently, we could use the following table as a mapping of our symbol systems.

Base 10		Base 2
0	=	0000
1	=	0001
2	=	0010
3	=	0011
4	=	0100
5	=	0101
6	=	0110
7	=	0111
8	=	1000
9	=	1001

Digits 8 and 9 require a minimum of four bits to encode them, so we will adopt a uniform precision of four bits for each digit code. This makes it more convenient to both store and convert values back and forth. How then would we convert 346 to this digital form? By substituting each decimal numeral with the corresponding four-bit pattern, we get the sequence

$$0011 \quad 0100 \quad 0110$$
$$3 \qquad\quad 4 \qquad\quad 6$$

In fact, a method very similar to this one, called **binary coded decimal** (or **BCD**), is used by many computer systems to represent some forms of numeric information.

Even though this technique of representing numbers is acceptable, there are some trade-offs. First, digitized numbers using this scheme are variable-length codes. Specifically, the length of the code sequences depends on how many decimal digits were present in the original number. When converting back to decimal form, we have to account for how many four-bit sequences are needed to interpret the original number accurately. If a series of numbers was stored in this manner consecutively in a series of bytes, for example, we have to keep track of where one number ends and another starts. A second problem is performing arithmetic with numbers digitized in this manner. Multiplying 346 by 3 would require converting the numbers to some other form to complete the operation—and then converting it back using our binary-based code. (Can you see why this is necessary?) For these reasons, although it is perfectly suitable for some applications, BCD and our simplified version of it are not the favored methods used to digitize numeric information.

The moral of this story, though, is a simple one. Any coding scheme that you adopt will have some benefits and some trade-offs. In later chapters, we will examine in greater detail how various forms of information are normally digitized. In these treatments, we will consider both the strengths and weaknesses of these techniques. An appreciation of these factors is essential for managing digital information effectively.

Digitizing Analog Forms of Information

Most natural forms of information are analog. For instance, consider a shade of red. How red is it? There is no precise way to determine this. It is not difficult to compare it with other shades. We might even be able to order them or even match identical or resembling shades. Even so, we do not normally deal with colors using a discrete representation or measure.

On the other hand, a discrete representation is precisely what is required to digitize analog forms of information such as pictures, recorded sounds, and so on. For analog data, the process of digitization requires two steps: sampling the information and quantizing the sample. **Sampling**—as the name suggests—means choosing some discrete sample of the information as representative of the whole. Once this is done, the sample can be measured, or **quantized,** using a discrete scale that can be mapped to a binary encoding.

Admittedly, this all sounds pretty complicated, but the principle is not. In fact, you have probably employed this method when using an ordinary bathroom scale to weigh yourself. Such scales use a spring-loaded mechanism to measure weight as a function of the pressure exerted on that mechanism. The more you weigh, the more compression the springs register. Older models use an analog dial that reacts to the spring compression measured continuously as pounds over time.

Suppose that you step onto such a scale. How much do you weigh? Normally, when you first step on such a scale, the dial fluctuates greatly as the spring mechanism attempts to stabilize under the force of your body weight. If the mechanism is sensitive, it will react to even the slightest changes in pressure. The result is that the dial fluctuates continuously—even if only by small amounts. If you fidget or shift your weight, the scale will fluctuate appreciably. At some point, though, you will decide that the dial registers a representative measure of your current weight. When you decide to read the scale, you are sampling the information. In other words, even though the measure may fluctuate continuously over time, this instant's reading is an acceptable sample of its overall content.

But what does the dial read? The dial is usually marked conveniently with a sequence of hash marks and numbers that serve as a discrete scale for expressing your weight. Thus, the measuring scale has been quantified, so each reading can be assigned a discrete value that is both distinct and unambiguous. Suppose that the arrow sits between two hash marks on the scale. The normal thing to do is to round off the value to one of these numbers. Even though the scales measure your weight *exactly,* you often have to compromise such analog measures to express them *precisely.* The process of quantizing an analog measure to a discrete scale almost always involves some estimation or rounding for the sake of precision.

Precision is a very useful attribute, usually worth some loss of accuracy. Besides being concise, precise measurements are unequivocal or repeatable. For example, if you tell someone that you weigh 150 pounds, he or she can understand that by repeating what it means. (Imagine filling a bag with sand until it weighs 150 pounds and then trying to lift and carry it. You would get an accurate idea of what 150 pounds means.) Accordingly, we are often willing to sacrifice some tolerance for exactness to achieve precision.

The process of sampling and quantization in the digital domain is similar, but it varies depending on the original form of information being digitized. Consider the case of converting a black-and-white photograph of a dog to digital form. See Figure 2.7a. The goal, of course, is to convert the photo to some sequence of binary numbers so that its important properties are captured with both acceptable accuracy and precision.

In this instance, because the original is a photo, the sampling would be done spatially rather than over time. It would involve breaking up the structure of the picture into smaller elements that faithfully represent its pictorial content. A convenient way to do this is to place a grid over the photo that divides it into separate, but equally sized areas. The areas should be small enough to capture meaningful detail. Each of the squares in the grid, like the one in Figure 2.7b, is called a **picture element** or **pixel.** Each pixel is a sample from the original picture taken from the spatial domain. In Figure 2.7b, the sample rate is 28 × 44 for a total of 1232 pixels. If you examine the grids in the figure, you may note that some of them contain more than one shade. For example, at the boundaries, part of a grid may contain both dog and the white background. Digital information, however, must be unambiguous. Consequently, the process of sampling usually incorporates some technique whereby ambiguous information is rendered uniform. In Figure 2.7c, the pixels are averaged to produce uniform shades of gray within.

FIGURE 2.7

Digitizing the photo of man's best friend involves two stages, sampling and quantizing. The process of sampling is shown here in two steps. First, the original image (a) is subdivided into regular units called pixels, as shown in (b). The area enclosed by the pixel boundaries is averaged to produce a uniform shade of gray. This averaging is shown in (c). Some of the detail in the original image may be lost if the sampling resolution is too coarse. Quantizing converts the shade of each pixel to a discrete value or number on a uniform scale, as shown in (d). Shades are matched as closely as possible to those values permitted by the scale. These numbers are then stored in a format that can be converted back to an image for display. The scale should have enough range to capture the differences in shades from the sampled image. If the range is too small, fidelity will be lost.

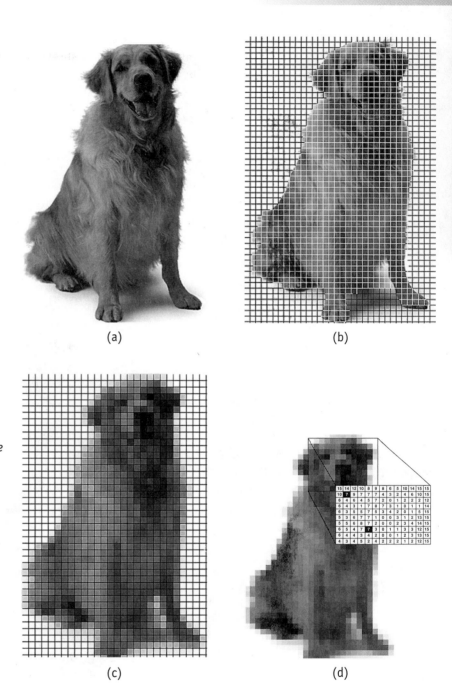

(a)   (b)

(c)   (d)

Quantizing this sampled photo means converting the shade of intensity within a given pixel to some precise quantity. Assume that we decide to adopt a scale of 16 different discernible shades from black to white. To quantize each pixel, we have to decide which shade value most accurately represents the pixel content. We could assign the values 0 through 15 to denote ascending intensities from darkest black to brightest white, as shown in Figure 2.7d.

Converting these 16 values to a binary representation is easy enough. We could use a straight binary encoding of the original values requiring a precision of 4 bits per pixel. Our sample image (1232 pixels) could be stored as a series of 616 bytes (2 pixels per byte).

This is basically how images are digitized for processing using computers. As the example attests, two very different sources of error are inherent to the process. First, the sampling rate may introduce some error. In Figure 2.7b, some of the pixels contain more than one shade of gray or intensity. These differences must be discounted in favor of a single interpretation. When the digitized image is converted back to a visible form, as in Figure 2.7c, some sampling error is evident. If the sampling rate is poorly matched to the content of the image, the details of the original may be irretrievably lost, as shown in Figure 2.8b. A second kind of error may be introduced during quantization. The measuring scale

FIGURE 2.8

Errors in the digitizing process can arise from several sources. Compare the original image (a) with these less-than-perfect instances. Poor sampling resolution, that is, using too few pixels, can result in an image that is so blocky (b) that it is almost unrecognizable. Likewise, a low dynamic range for pixel values can create an image that has false contours. In (c), the resolution is high, but the pixels are quantized at only four shades of gray. Finally, (d) shows how a noisy imaging system can introduce a speckled effect in the digitized image.

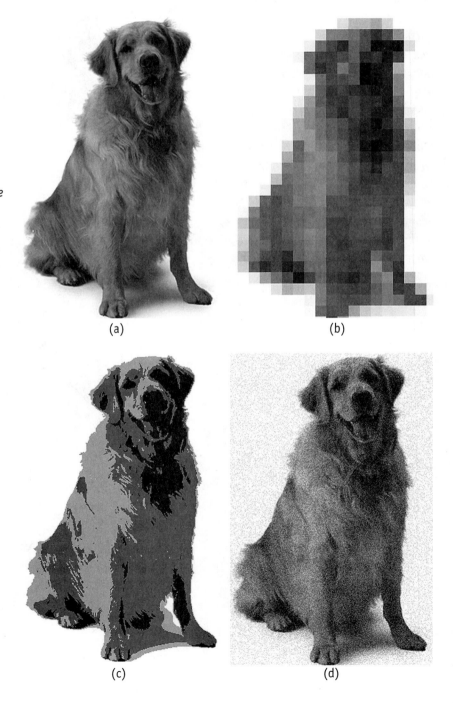

(a) (b)

(c) (d)

may be too coarse; specifically, it may not have a sufficient range of values to differentiate details appropriately. For example, in Figure 2.8c, using only four shades of gray results in false contours on the surface of the dog. This means differentiating areas sharply in the digital image that vary more smoothly in the original.

How then do you choose an appropriate sampling rate and a sufficient range of values for digitizing analog information? Fortunately, it is not entirely a hit-or-miss proposition. As you will learn in later chapters, given the type of signal that we are digitizing, we can predict sampling rates and dynamic ranges that will minimize the effects of these types of errors.

On the other hand, another potential source of error in the digitization process resists any theoretically derived controls: noise. **Noise** refers to unpredictable errors that are introduced into the digitization process, usually by the medium itself. For example, digitizing an image may result in errors that are artifacts of the imaging system itself (the lens, for instance). Noise is random misinformation. And most digitizing methods must account for some sources of noise if the results of the process are both accurate and robust. Figure 2.8d illustrates how a noisy imaging system may produce a digitized image with unwanted artifacts.

DIGITIZING DATA

You have learned that the process of converting continuous or analog forms of information to digital form is a two-stage process. The first step is to transform continuous data to a discrete form. This is done by sampling. Choosing a sampling rate that approximates the original data with acceptable accuracy is crucial. For pictures and graphics, the sampling rate is defined by the resolution of the image, that is, the number of pixels used to represent it. The second stage is quantizing—converting the discrete samples to a numeric representation. The scale—the range of numbers—used for quantizing is also an important factor in how faithfully the digital version approximates the original. For images, scale is referred to as the dynamic range.

To find out more about these concepts and how computers convert images to digital form, consult the "At Your Computer" section in Chapter 2 on the *Exploring the Digital Domain* Web site. There you will find a series of examples that illustrate how resolution and dynamic range can affect the outcome of digitizing analog images.

At Your Computer

Social Themes

Copyright Laws in the Digital Domain

Copyrights and Intellectual Property

The growth of digital technologies has posed new challenges for our traditional interpretations of individual rights and protections. The World Wide Web, for example, brings a wealth of information and material directly to your home, office, or lab. At the press of a mouse button or a keystroke, you can instantly transport text, pictures, graphics, sounds, music, or video. All of this stuff constitutes what is glibly called "content" in the industry. But this content is provided by somebody and is likewise created by somebody. And, protecting the rights of creators and producers is a hallmark of our society.

Traditionally authors, the creators of intellectual property, are protected by a broad assortment of laws that safeguard trademarks, patents, trade secrets, and copyrights. **Trademarks** protect words, names, symbols, and logos normally used in commerce. **Patents** protect the rights of individuals who make discoveries or inventions. **Trade secrets** cover information, designs, and devices that companies wish to keep secret to retain commercial advantages from their creations. **Copyrights** protect authors of original works from damages caused by others who might improperly reproduce or use materials without the author's permission. Copyrighted materials include literary works; musical pieces; dramatic works; dance and pantomime works; pictorial, graphic, or sculptured pieces; motion pictures and video; sound recordings; and architectural designs. These laws are not extended to intellectual ideas or discoveries, to concepts and principles, nor to a process or procedure. In short, copyrights protect the *expression* of an idea, not the idea itself.

Copyrights carry both positive and negative rights. As an author, you may use and distribute an original work. You are permitted to create derivative works based on that original. For example, an author may adapt a copyrighted book as a screenplay. These are positive rights. As an author, you have the right to prevent others from copying, distributing, and deriving works from your original work. These are negative rights in the sense that you can seek redress from those who violate these prohibitions. As in other property cases, the owner must lay claim to these rights by seeking the prosecution of offenders. To prove copyright infringement, the author or holder of the copyright must (1) establish ownership, (2) prove that copying took place, and (3) show that the positive rights of the owner were impeded by this act.

Copyright infringement can be exonerated in one of two ways: by seeking the express consent of the author to use the materials or by appealing to the principle of **fair use,** a defense based on the notion that limited use leads to a greater good: the increase in the amount of intellectual property available to society. Thus, educational, scientific, and some journalistic uses are permissible because they advance the cause of knowledge, which benefits everyone in society. The courts have wrestled considerably with the concept of fair use, and a number of factors mitigate its application. Copying limited amounts of nonartistic materials for noncommercial purposes is generally permissible.

Copying and Downloading Items from the Web

The emergence of the World Wide Web as a medium has posed a number of issues that challenge our traditional interpretations of copyrights. The digital technology of the World Wide Web makes copying original materials extremely simple and convenient for all users. Whenever you inspect a page your browser downloads the files that make up that page. **Downloading** constitutes copying materials because digital replicas of the text, images, and other components must be transmitted over a network to your computer to be viewed. These copies, however, are transient—the legal term is "ephemeral." They exist only temporarily. Even so, it is very easy to save these items in a more permanent state for other uses.

Here are several cases of employing materials downloaded from the Web. Which of these are cases of copyright infringement? Which could be argued with a fair use defense?

1 A person incorporates verbatim a substantial portion of text downloaded from a Web site into a report. The report is printed and distributed publicly without attributing the source of the downloaded material.

2 A person incorporates a large portion of a text document downloaded from a Web site into a report. The report does correctly attribute the authorship of the downloaded material incorporated. The report is printed and distributed publicly.

3 A person downloads a graphic or picture from a Web site and posts it on his or her own home page without noting the source or origin of the image.

4 A person downloads a graphic or picture from a Web site and posts it on his or her own home page. On the page, the source of the image is noted.

5 A person downloads a graphic or picture from a Web site but reduces it size and scale and replicates it over and over to create a pattern or design. This repeated pattern is then used as a background for the Web page.

6 A person uses his or her browser to download a copy of the formatting code for an especially attractive or interesting page designed by another. The individual then modifies that code by replacing some of the text and graphics and posts it as a page on his or her own Web site.

Did you say "all"? It is very likely that each of these cases qualifies as copyright infringement. Case 1 is both a violation of copyright and plagiarism. The culprit in this instance not only copies someone else's work but also tries to take credit for it as well. By contrast, the individual in case 2 probably doesn't seem so culpable. Posting copied material without the consent of the author, however, makes him or her a copyright pirate nonetheless. Giving credit by itself does not constitute fair use. Cases 3 and 4 are very similar to those of 1 and 2, respectively. That we are dealing with images rather than writings is not significant. In case 5, the person infringes on the author's sole rights to produce derivatives of an original. Even if the resulting product is very different from the original, this act may still constitute copyright infringement. The last case, case 6, is similar to case 5, though not quite as clear cut. It would be defensible to use the design of another page as a means of learning how to create similar effects. However, producing a substantially similar design—with little modification or enhancement—would likely fail as fair use.

Linking Pages from the Web

As you have probably noticed, a number of Web pages contain external links to other pages. These links provide access to pages not stored on the referring page's local server. These linked pages are usually created by different authors. Is this legal? Do we have to gain the permission of the author to use external links on our own Web pages? Such uses are generally permissible due to the principle of implied public access. The fact that an author posts his or her pages on a publicly accessible server means that anyone is free to view those pages. Consequently, in most cases, we can legally create links to publicly accessible pages because a link does nothing more than notify readers of the pages' whereabouts.

Authors may limit access to their own pages using various means. Pages may be protected so that only authorized users have access. Extreme measures like these, however, do not have to be taken. An author can either expressly prohibit links to his or her pages or object to those who have created such links. In these instances, posting such external links on your own Web pages would probably constitute improper use. For this reason, the safest policy is to notify or seek consent from authors when you create external links to their pages.

Unfortunately, law and legal precedent are not clear on all these matters. The current laws have evolved from older technologies, and they could hardly be expected to anticipate the realities of future ones. The digital technology of the World Wide Web severely challenges the rules of the game because it has radically altered the playing field. Simply put, the means and opportunity for copyright infringement are abundant in this new medium. Thus, a new method of distribution for intellectual property has upset the established balance between producers and consumers. Whether the remedies are legal, technological, or both, these issues will not be resolved until this balance is restored.

Social Themes

S U M M A R Y

There are two fundamental categories for representing data. Analog representations measure some property continuously over such dimensions as time and space. Digital data is based on discrete symbolic representations that incorporate numbering. Even though digital and analog representations of information are exchangeable, there are decided advantages to representing and storing digital data on an electronic computer system. The precision and natural ordinality of digital data make it easier to process and evaluate. Digital data created on an electronic computer system is stored and transmitted more economically than is possible using other technologies. Digital data may be accessed in a variety of ways; digital data can be replicated over and over again without loss of information. Digital systems are scalable; their processing capabilities assist in analyzing and combining data in useful ways.

In succeeding chapters, you will learn more about the digitization of both discrete and analog forms of information. Whether the original information is discrete or analog, it is converted to a sequence or stream of binary numbers that are stored in, processed by, and transmitted between computer systems. If the original information is already in discrete form, digitizing means assigning a binary coding for its meaningful values or symbols. Converting analog data to a digital form is a two-step process. The data is rendered discrete by sampling, and the samples are quantized to produce a binary encoding. This common denominator of the digital domain is what makes multimedia forms of information possible.

PROJECTS

1 Make a list of at least ten different forms of information. For each, decide whether its representation is discrete or analog. For example, numbers and text are discrete forms, but natural sound and radio signals are analog.

2 One of the advantages of digitizing information is that it may be represented and stored much more efficiently than in conventional forms. To gain a better grasp of this fact, solve the following problem. Find out how many volumes of books are held in your college or university library collection. Assuming that a single CD-ROM could hold approximately 500 books, how many discs would it take to store the entire library collection?

3 One of the advantages of digitizing information is that data can be *compressed* into forms that are much smaller than the original digital representations. The method of data compression involves transforming the original data stored in a file to a smaller encoded version. The encoded file must be decoded to restore it to its original content for normal use. Images, for example, are often compressed for storage and transmission over networks. The file, though, must be decompressed for viewing. Thus, the compression of images saves storage space and transmission time.

As you know, most Web pages contain graphic images that must be copied to your computer in order to be viewed using your browser program.

These images are typically compressed so that they will be transmitted more rapidly. Consult some of the links from the World Wide Web Tour introduced in Chapter 1. Download or copy several images from different pages to your computer system. [Using Netscape Communicator, for example, point to the image and click the right mouse button to reveal a pop-up menu. (Macintosh users must hold down the mouse button until the menu appears.) Choose the *Save Picture As . . .* command. You will be asked where to save the image. Jot down its name and location for later reference.]

Using one of the tools listed on the *Projects Page* for this chapter, find out to what extent each of these images has been compressed. (Follow the directions on the *Projects Page* for downloading and using the appropriate tool for your system.)

4 Representing base ten numbers on a computer system requires encoding each value using a binary number. In general, the largest quantity that can be expressed by N-bits is $2^N - 1$. For example, the largest number expressible in four bits is $2^4 - 1 = 15$. What is the minimum number of bits needed to express the following base ten integer magnitudes?

- **a** 1,000
- **b** 1,000,000
- **c** 1,000,000,000

5 The status of copyrights is not always clear to readers who consult materials on the World Web Web. Investigate how materials are posted by sampling some sites.

Specifically, consult some of the links from the World Wide Web Tour introduced in Chapter 1. How many of these sites offer copyright information about the origin and use of materials that they include? Classify these sites into one of four groupings: (a) those that have no copyright posted; (b) those that provide only a dated copyright notice, for example "© 1998"; (c) those that have a copyright notice *and* offer specific instructions for use with permission; and (d) those that permit use without written permission. Based on a sample of at least 20–30 sites, what is the breakdown for these categories?

Projects

Key Terms

absolute replication	digitization, digitized	precision
analog	discrete	quantizing
binary (numbering system)	downloading	random access
binary coded decimal	fair use	resolution
bit (binary digit)	finite precision	sampling
byte	noise	scalability
compression, data	ordinality	selective access
copyrights	patents	trade secrets
data	pixel (picture element)	trademarks
digital	positional notation	wave

QUESTIONS FOR REVIEW

1 Identify several distinguishing characteristics of modern information technologies (e.g., telephone, radio, and television). Which of these characteristics are most important, in your opinion?

2 Contrast analog and digital forms of information.

3 What is a digital symbol system? Give an example.

4 What are some advantages of digital as opposed to analog representation of information?

5 Contrast positional and nonpositional number systems.

6 How are the decimal and binary number systems alike? How do they differ?

7 Define a bit and a byte.

8 Describe the process called "digitization." Give some examples to illustrate your definition.

9 Assume the binary coded decimal digital coding scheme for decimal numbers described in the chapter. Exactly why is it necessary to convert such numbers to decimal or, perhaps, binary before performing arithmetic operations? Consider the example, multiplying 346 (represented as 001101000110) by 3 (represented as 0011).

10 Identify the two steps involved in digitizing analog forms of information.

11 Describe how a sound wave is translated to digital form.

12 What is a pixel? What are pixels used for?

13 What does the term *noise* mean within the context of the digitization process?

14 Describe several ways that errors can be introduced into the digitization process.

15 Why is sampling required when analog information is digitized?

16 Identify and describe several advantages that electronic digital media have over conventional forms of information storage.

17 Compare the storage capacities of typical floppy disks, hard disks, and CD-ROMs.

18 Give two reasons why data compression is important in the digital domain.

19 What is meant by the term *finite precision* in digital data storage?

20 What is meant when we say that electronic digital media provide a *precision* that conventional media forms do not? Discuss the trade-offs inherent in gaining this precision.

21 What is meant when we say that electronic digital media provide scalability?

22 How do electronic digital media and conventional forms of media storage compare in providing the capability of replication?

23 How do electronic digital media and conventional forms of media storage compare in providing selective access to information?

24 How do electronic digital media and conventional forms of media storage compare in providing the capabilities for information content analysis?

25 What advantages do electronic digital media provide over conventional media forms in the transfer of information?

26 This book is titled *Exploring the Digital Domain*. In your own words, define and explain the "digital domain."

In Chapter 2 you learned how the computer can be used to store information in a variety of media. Indeed, a hallmark of the digital domain is that wide varieties of information can be reduced to a digital common denominator bits and bytes. Of course, storing information is just part of the picture. We do not realize the real power of the digital domain until we utilize these bits and bytes for a good purpose. This utilization often depends on transporting digital information. The combined abilities to digitize information from various media and to move it across town, across the country, or across the world in a matter of seconds are what truly energize the digital domain. In this chapter, we continue our study of the major entity connecting the digital domain—the World Wide Web.

In Chapter 1, you took a quick tour of the World Wide Web (or the Web, for short). Even if this was your first experience on the Web, you no doubt already appreciate what an incredibly rich source of information the Web can be. And the Web is really still in its infancy. The Web was invented as an aid for scientific researchers in 1989, but it has since emerged as the basis for a whole new communications paradigm. Today, there are many thousands of Web sites and millions of users worldwide, and these numbers grow daily.

There are many questions about the Web that your tour did not resolve. Just what exactly is the World Wide Web? How does it operate? What makes it so appealing and useful? How can you make your own information available on the Web? What does the future hold for its development and use? In this chapter, we will explore these and other questions, as you learn more about the technology that promises to make computing an integral part of our everyday lives.

OBJECTIVES

- How the World Wide Web is organized

- How the client/server computing model enables the capabilities of the Web

- How Web browser software, like Internet Explorer and Netscape Communicator, makes the Web's information almost universally accessible

- The fundamentals of designing basic Web documents employing HTML (Hypertext Markup Language)

CHAPTER 3

CONNECTING THE DIGITAL DOMAIN: THE WORLD WIDE WEB

Vasily Kandinsky, *Several Circles (Einige Kreise)*, 1926. Solomon R. Guggenheim Museum

THE WEB IS A GLOBAL HYPERMEDIA REPOSITORY

In 1989, Tim Berners-Lee and a group of researchers at the European Particle Physics Laboratory (known as CERN) proposed a project for the electronic dissemination of research and related information. These researchers had been using the existing Internet (which you'll learn more about in Chapter 18) for information exchange, but they found its facilities for sharing information lacking. They envisioned instead a hypertext system that would allow members of the scientific community to communicate, edit, and view information easily—this system became known as the World Wide Web.

Hypermedia

Electronic documents with built-in links to additional information are called **hypertext.** Such documents are linked electronically by means of **hyperlinks.** Hyperlinks can be represented and accessed in many different ways, but most hypertext systems make integral use of a mouse to select links. For example, words or phrases on Web pages linked to additional information are typically shown in a different color and underlined. A single click of the mouse over a hyperlink transports you to the linked page or resource. These links allow you to use hypertext documents in a nonlinear way. Instead of reading such documents from start to finish, the way you might read most ordinary documents, you can use the hyperlinks to create your own path through the connected group of documents. In fact, this ability to create your own paths through hypertext documents is their central distinguishing feature.

And as your experience with the Web has demonstrated, this cross-referenced material can involve a variety of media—images, sounds, and movie clips as well as text. Indeed, images can themselves be links to other information. A hypertext document composed of different media is called a **hypermedia document.** This term extends to include *all* the connected information as well as any document that links to that information. In this sense, you can see how the World Wide Web can be viewed as a huge hypermedia "document" or repository.

The hyperlinks in the Web hypermedia repository have another remarkable characteristic: They connect information stored on computers at distant sites. The user of such links traverses physical distances automatically and transparently. From its modest beginnings, the Web has grown to truly global proportions. Today, it encompasses far more than scientific research. Information on the Web comes in almost infinite variety. Here are just a few examples:

- Astronomical data from the Observatory at Pisa
- Film reviews and movie minutiae from Wales
- Top ten lists from David Letterman's talk show
- The latest research on computer vision and image understanding
- Weather predictions and latest satellite imagery
- Campus information from thousands of colleges and universities worldwide
- Online help and information from many computer vendors, both hardware and software

- An electronic edition of the magazine *Wired* with features, discussion groups, and advertisements

Recall from Chapter 1 that information on the Web is organized as a collection of **Web pages.** These pages contain text, graphics, sound, even video, and, of course, links to other related documents. The user clicks a link to transfer from the current document to a new one. Linked pages create a structure for the information that the user may employ in various ways. Many documents are organized by levels in a hierarchical structure. The first document, called the **home page,** often acts like a central hub with a main menu. It explains the purpose or contents of the document. Home pages also contain various links to other pages that are part of the overall document. Figure 3.1 illustrates.

Because the Web is conceived as a distributed information system, these other pages may be stored on the same computer or may be found on remote systems across the world. In this way, the reader not only traverses information according to inclination but also travels from site to site in the Web. All of this, of course, is easy and effortless. In fact, if it were not for the time lapses due to fetching items from distant sites, the user could be easily deceived into thinking that all the information was stored neatly on his or her local system.

Clients, Servers, and Protocols

One of the distinctive features of the Web is that it is based on an open, distributed system. This means that computer systems that differ in scale and performance capabilities can communicate with one another freely. How is all of this managed with such ease and transparency? The secret is that the Web is built on client/server computing.

FIGURE 3.1

In a typical Web site organization, the site home page usually acts as a kind of index to the other pages at the site. Links on the home page connect to other pages, whose links, in turn, connect to other pages, and so on.

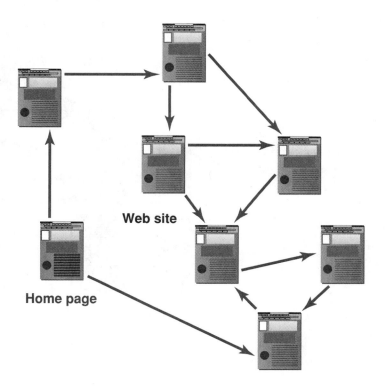

Web site

Home page

The World Wide Web is a confederation of computer systems that adhere to a set of guidelines for the storage and communication of electronic information. **Web servers** are computer systems that store and make available Web pages and other resources (like images and sounds). Other computers, acting as **Web clients,** request Web pages or resources from Web servers.

Any type or scale of machine can function as either a Web server or a Web client. It is not uncommon for Windows-based PCs and Macintoshes, for example, to play the roles of both clients and servers. Using your desktop computer as a client will likely put you in touch with a variety of different computers acting as servers—all during the same session.

All of this is managed in a way that hides the complexity from the user by means of agreed-upon guidelines called protocols. **Protocols** are sets of rules that govern how some activity will take place. The World Wide Web protocol, now being maintained by a standards group known as the **World Wide Web Consortium (W3C),** governs how information is exchanged on the Web and is, in fact, what defines and makes the Web possible. Three components constitute the Web protocol, known widely by their acronyms: URL, HTTP, and HTML. Figure 3.2 illustrates.

A **URL** (for *Uniform Resource Locator*) is the agreed-upon protocol for giving the address of a page or resource available on a Web server. Suppose that a user is reading text from a Web page currently displayed on his or her system. When the user clicks a hyperlink to another page or resource, the client transmits a request for the appropriate information to the server addressed in the URL stored as part of the hyperlink. (You'll see exactly how this is done a little later.)

Let's look a little more closely at the structure of a URL. Consider the URL for the Web site accompanying this text, namely:

```
http://s9000.furman.edu/DD/index.html
```

FIGURE 3.2

Web servers store Web pages and make them accessible to client machines. For a user at the client to view a page, the client must issue a request to the server for the page to be transferred. The server then transmits the page, with instructions for its display. Once the client receives the page, it displays it in a way appropriate for the client machine.

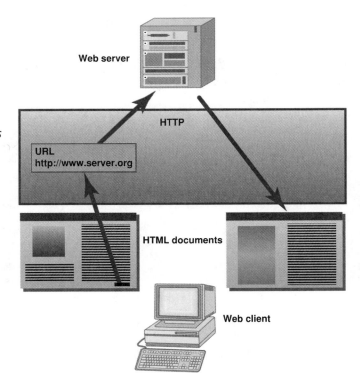

Web server

HTTP

URL
http://www.server.org

HTML documents

Web client

We can break this URL down into pieces that indicate standard information about the address it represents. Most URLs have a similar structure.

http://	Means that the page or resource being requested is located on a remote Web server.
s9000.furman.edu	Designates the registered name of the Web server holding the page or resource being requested
DD/index.html	Is information about where on the Web server's hard disk the page or resource is located

The set of rules that govern the exchange of information between Web clients and Web servers is **HTTP** (for *Hypertext Transfer Protocol*). Consider again the example of selecting a hyperlink to another Web page or resource. The page or resource may reside on the same server that contains the original page, or it may be found on a remote system. It doesn't matter. The web client makes these requests automatically, and they are delivered to the appropriate server, located by its URL. Once the server receives the request, it interprets the request and transmits the appropriate information. Notice how the workload is distributed. The client does not have to worry about the details of how the information is stored. It needs only the URL of the page or resource it is requesting. Retrieving the information and sending it back to the client is the work of the server.

Once the client receives the requested information, it takes over the task once again and decides how to display what was received. This process is governed by the **HTML** (for *Hypertext Markup Language*) protocol. HTML offers specific directions on how the Web client is to format and display text and images, play sounds, and so on. As its name suggests, HTML is, in fact, a language whose purpose is to allow its users to write documents for display on the World Wide Web. We'll have a lot more to say about HTML later in this chapter where you will learn to construct your own HTML documents.

SURFING THE WEB

Viewing Web pages and clicking (and hence following) their built-in hyperlinks is colloquially referred to as **Web surfing.** Web surfing is easy and engaging. We hope that you have already experienced this—when you took the World Wide Web tour in Chapter 1. In this section, we'll explore some of the additional skills you need to be an effective Web surfer.

Browsers

When a Web page is transmitted to the client, a special program on the client system, called a **Web browser,** handles the task of interpreting and displaying the page—a task sometime referred to as **loading** a Web page. Browsers, with their graphical interfaces, make Web surfing an easily mastered activity. As you know, there are a number of popular Web browsers. Although the browsers may differ in some details, they are essentially similar and operate on the same basic concepts. We will describe some of these concepts and illustrate their implementation within the two most popular browsers, Netscape Communicator and Internet Explorer.

HTML documents are, in fact, instructions on how to format a document. The Web browser simply implements the instructions in a manner appropriate for the client machine. When images, sounds, or video are transmitted, the browser converts these—often with the help of a utility program—into a form that your machine can play or display.

Browsers come in a variety of forms. The earliest browsers offered by CERN had text-based interfaces. The user entered numbers and letters to select hypertext links. Other text-based browsers were developed and used in the early days of the Web. The genuine watershed event for the Web was the introduction of the first graphical-based browser called **Mosaic.** The original Mosaic program was conceived by Marc Andreesen, an undergraduate student at the University of Illinois at Urbana-Champaign who worked part time for the National Center for Supercomputing Applications (NCSA). Andreesen developed the program with the assistance of several others at NCSA. Versions were released (free of charge) in 1993 for a variety of different computers, including the Macintosh and Windows-based computers.

Mosaic handles multimedia documents and has an interface that is graphical and easy to use. It proved to be an overwhelming success. In fact, its popularity spawned tremendous growth in the amount and variety of information available on the Web as well as the numbers of users who sought this information. Today, Mosaic has been replaced by newer and more powerful Web browsers like **Netscape Navigator** and **Communicator** (produced by the company founded by Marc Andreesen), Microsoft's **Internet Explorer,** and the browsers provided by America Online and others.

Some Basic Browser Features

In this section we will quickly survey some typical browser features. Note that all the screen shots shown are from either Internet Explorer 4.0 or Netscape Communicator 4.0, the current versions (at the time of writing) of the two most popular browsers. However, new versions of these two browsers come out rather frequently, as each tries to keep "one up" on the other, its main competition. It's quite possible that you're using a newer (or even an older) version of one of these. The concepts we present will be valid no matter which browser and version you're using, but you may find certain features placed in slightly different positions within your browser interface.

When we start a browser program, we say that we are conducting a **session** with the browser. In a given session, we may visit many pages. Each page of a Web document is presented in a browser window similar to that shown in Figure 3.3. Let's take a quick tour of this window, which is displayed using the Netscape Communicator browser.

- The title bar displays the name of the Web page currently displayed.

- The tool bar contains buttons for some standard surfing functions—moving back to the previous page viewed in this browser session, for-

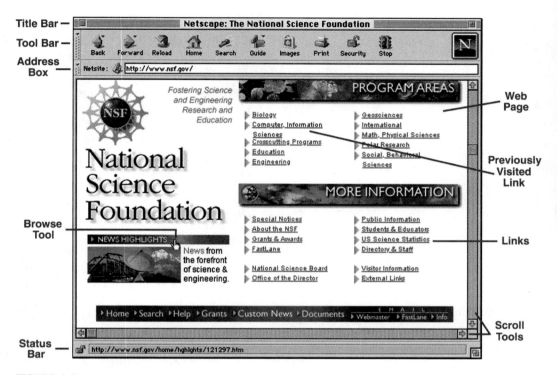

FIGURE 3.3

A Web document is displayed using Netscape Communicator 4.0. A typical Web document window contains a number of components, both gadgets and information. The HTML document itself is displayed in the window surrounded by Netscape tools and status indicators.

ward (assuming you've already moved back) in the chain of pages being viewed in this session, returning to your home page—as well as other actions. We'll explore these in more detail shortly.

- Hyperlinks within text are typically underlined and displayed in a different color. A link that you have already visited (in this session or another recent one) is shown in yet another color.

- Graphic objects and images can also be hyperlinks. You can discover these links by observing the shape of the mouse pointer as you move it over the object (see the description of the browse tool next) or by noticing that the objects are often outlined in the same color in which the text hyperlinks are displayed.

- When you move the mouse pointer over a hyperlink, the pointer takes the shape of a hand (with a finger pointing), called the **browse tool.** As you know, you follow a link by moving the browse tool over the link and clicking the mouse button.

- Scroll tools (box and arrows) along the window's right and bottom edges may be used to advance or retrace the view in the window.

- The status bar offers a brief message about what event will occur if the mouse is clicked in the current pointer location. For example, in Figure 3.3, the message gives the URL of the hyperlink under the current position of the browse tool.

● In the address or location box, the Web address for the page currently being viewed is given. You may enter a URL directly into this box and press the Return or Enter key to move to the corresponding Web page.

The page displayed using the Netscape Communicator browser in Figure 3.3 is shown displayed in Internet Explorer in Figure 3.4. Notice the similarities in the two windows. There are, of course, some differences, but the similarities are numerous and striking. Each browser also has a menu bar providing access to a number of pull-down menus enabling many common browser activities.

Changing Your Browser's Properties

Both the Netscape Communicator and Internet Explorer browsers provide options to change the appearance of the browser window. For example, you can turn the display of the URL address bar, the tool bar, and the status bar off or on as you prefer. You might turn one or more of these off when you want to expand the actual Web page viewing area within your browser window.

Figures 3-5 and 3-6 illustrate one of several options dialog boxes you can access to change various settings for Netscape Communicator and Internet Explorer, respectively. In Internet Explorer, you can access these option dialog boxes by clicking the Preferences button in the tool bar or by selecting *Preferences* under the **Edit** pull-down menu. In Netscape Communicator, you select *Preferences* under the **Edit** pull-down menu.

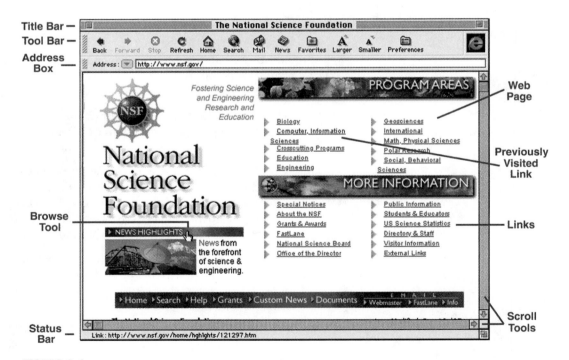

FIGURE 3.4

The same document viewed by Netscape Communicator 4.0 in Figure 3.3 is viewed here by Internet Explorer 4.0. Notice the similarities between the two browser windows.

FIGURE 3.5

This dialog box sets some of the characteristics of the Netscape Communicator 4.0 browser.

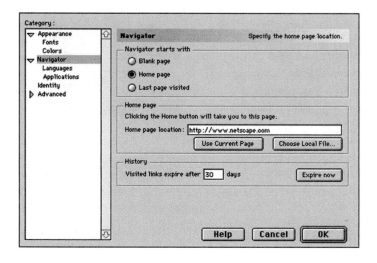

FIGURE 3.6

This dialog box sets some of the characteristics of the Internet Explorer 4.0 browser. Although similar options can be set in Netscape Communicator and Internet Explorer, the dialog boxes are organized into slightly different categories.

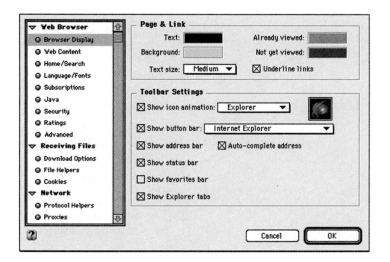

If you're doing a search of the Web seeking information on a specific topic, you can speed the process considerably by selecting an option in your browser to suppress the loading of images on the Web pages you search. Indeed, a significant hindrance to speedy Web cruising is the time spent loading images that enhance the basic text of a Web page. When the image suppression option is selected, the Web page images won't be transferred; instead they will be replaced by a small icon representation. This is accomplished in the *Advanced* options dialog box in Netscape Communicator and in the *Web Content* dialog box in Internet Explorer. When automatic image loading is turned off, you can load images for any page by clicking the Images button in the tool bar in Netscape Communicator or by selecting *Load Images* in the **View** pull-down menu in Internet Explorer.

Using the Browser Tool Bar

You were briefly introduced to the Netscape Communicator and Internet Explorer tool bars in Chapter 1. The tool bars put some of the most

FIGURE 3.7

This figure compares (a) The Netscape Navigator 4.0 and (b) Internet Explorer 4.0 toolbars. Note that the two toolbars contain many common buttons. Clicking a button initiates the indicated task.

(a)

(b)

commonly used browser commands within a mouse click. Let's summarize some of the commands common to both Internet Explorer and Netscape Communicator tool bars. Refer to Figure 3.7 to see the location and form of the various button icons on the two tool bars.

- The Back button displays the previous Web page viewed in the current browser session.

- The Forward button displays the next Web page in the sequence of viewed pages—the one you would have just left had you clicked the Back button.

- The Reload, or Refresh, button will correct a scrambled Web page. Sometimes when a page is loading, network line noise interferes with one or more page components. When this occurs, click the Reload button to restart the page transfer process.

- The Home button displays the currently configured home page for the browser. This is the page that is displayed when you first open the browser. It is initially preset to a page chosen by the browser company, but you have the option of changing this to any page you like.

- The Stop button allows you to interrupt the transfer of Web pages. As you already know, some Web pages can take quite a while to load. This may occur because they contain lots of images or because the Web server and/or the transmission line is very busy. At any rate, being able to interrupt a Web page transfer is convenient at times.

- The Search button transfers you to the browser's search page interface. On this page you can enter keywords to initiate Web searches in one of any number of third-party search tools. We'll discuss Web searches in the next section.

- The animated icon (at the far right in each tool bar) is not a button but is there for information. When the icon is animated, it indicates that the browser is working to load a page.

Each browser has other buttons on its tool bar. For example, the Print button in the Netscape Communicator tool bar opens the *Print* dialog box to allow you to print the Web document currently being viewed. To print in Internet Explorer, you access the *Print* command under the **File** menu. A Web "page" may be many printer pages long, so you should exercise some caution (scroll to see how long the document is and whether you really need to print all of it) before you initiate printing of entire Web documents. You will learn the functions of some of the other buttons later in the chapter.

WEB SEARCH TOOLS

If you know the URL for a Web site, accessing that site is easy. Accessing known sites is certainly important, but more often than not, you may actually be *searching* for information when you surf the Web. You may be interested in finding information about polar bears, for instance. The Web has tools to help you conduct such searches that enhance the Web as a powerful information source.

There are two very popular methods for finding information on the Web: index sites and search engines. There are a number of **index sites** to Web information—you saw a simple example of a Web site index when you used the World Wide Web tour pages within the Web site for this text in Chapter 1. On those pages, we have collected a relatively small number of links to Web sites organized by general topic. You will find much more extensive, better organized, and more complete indices to Web information. These indices are typically hierarchically organized to allow you to repeatedly refine a search for Web sites about a particular topic.

The Netscape Communicator Guide button on the tool bar presents a Web page containing links to a number of Web site indices, illustrated in Figure 3.8. For example, the *What's New* link provides a listing (complete with hyperlinks, of course) of Web sites recently placed on the Web. The *What's Cool* link provides a service similar to the *What's New*

FIGURE 3.8

This page is displayed when the user clicks the Guide button on the Netscape Communicator 4.0 toolbar. This page gives the user access to a number of different searchable web directories.

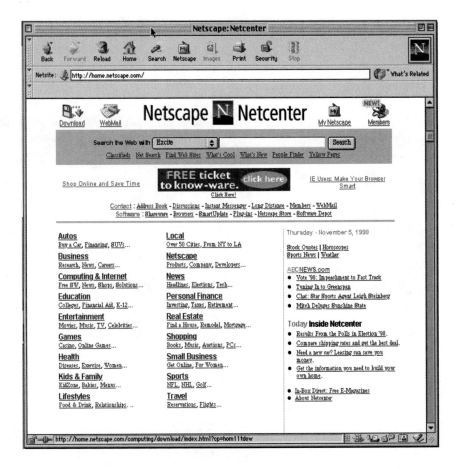

link. The list provided, however, is not restricted to new sites (although it is frequently updated), but rather concentrates on sites the Netscape staff have found particularly interesting or noteworthy. The Search button on the Internet Explorer tool bar takes you to a page that contains a number of links to Web indices as well.

Another way to search for information on the Web is to use special software products designed explicitly for this purpose. Such programs, commonly called **search engines,** give users the ability to perform keyword searches for specific topics. Every browser includes easy access to one or more search engines and Web indices. The Search button on each browser's tool bar opens a page containing a dialog box for a Web search engine. You may select the particular search engine you prefer to use from among the choices presented (Yahoo!, Magellan, InfoSeek, Excite, and AltaVista are likely to be among these choices). The search engine interface page for Internet Explorer is shown in Figure 3.9.

Figure 3.10 portrays the web page from Yahoo!—one of the most popular Web search tools. Although it is probably more accurate to call Yahoo! a searchable directory, it is often referred to as a search engine. Yahoo! actually links to the search engine AltaVista for keyword searches beyond its own searchable directory. Notice in Figure 3.9 that the two keywords "Polar" and "Bears" have been entered by the user as the key for the search. Yahoo!, and other search engines like AltaVista, Excite, InfoSeek, Lycos, and Magellan, respond to the user's request for information about some topic by producing lists (indices), complete with built-in hyperlinks, of Web sites around the world that contain information about the desired topic. Figure 3.10 shows the beginning of the list returned by Yahoo! for the two keywords "Polar" and "Bears."

Clicking the link over which the browser tool is positioned in Figure 3.10 loads the Web page shown in Figure 3.11. The various Web search engines have similar but slightly different capabilities and approaches to

FIGURE 3.9

This search engine access page is presented when the user clicks the Search button on the Internet Explorer 4.0 toolbar. This page allows the user to enter one or more keywords and/or key phrases and select one of several search engines to conduct a Web search.

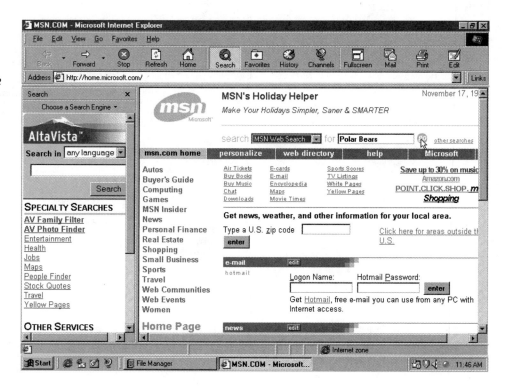

FIGURE 3.10

This screen shows just a few of the sites in the list of sites containing information about polar bears returned by Yahoo! (Text and artwork copyright © 1998 by Yahoo! Inc. All rights reserved. YAHOO! and the YAHOO! logo are trademarks of YAHOO! Inc.)

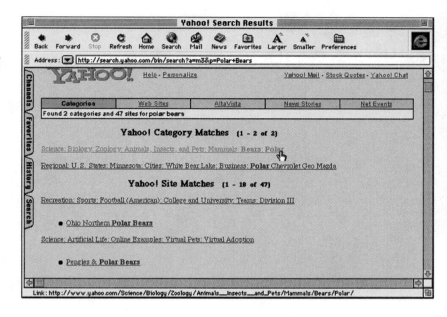

FIGURE 3.11

Clicking the hyperlink indicated in Figure 3.10 produces this page of additional links. Each link can be followed to Web sites containing information about polar bears. Clicking the Back button returns the user to the annotated index to try another link if desired. Using a search engine in conjunction with the Back button can usually produce the kind of information you seek in a reasonable amount of time. (Text and artwork copyright © 1998 by Yahoo! Inc. All rights reserved. YAHOO! and the YAHOO! logo are trademarks of YAHOO! Inc.)

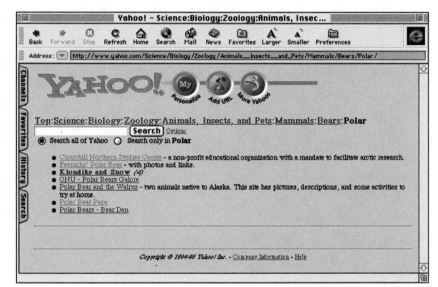

searching for Web information. You should explore several of them to decide which you prefer and which are most suitable for particular kinds of searches. Most have built-in help facilities to guide you.

Search engines are tools designed to find information about a specific topic. If you wish to browse for information in a general category, however, these are likely to return far more Web sites than you will have the time or inclination to explore. Keep in mind that the search engines are designed to retrieve a list of *all* sites on the Web that contain information about a particular topic. An alternative way to browse by general topic is to use the Web indices. These indices have been selected and culled by someone. They will generally provide a more efficient way to browse for information about a general topic than the longer, unedited indices returned by search engines. Of course, some overlap does occur between these two types of search tools; experimenting with a variety of them from both categories is a good idea.

focus

EFFECTIVE WEB SEARCHES USING ALTAVISTA

AltaVista, produced by the research unit of Compaq Computer Corporation, is one of the most popular Web search engines. As you learned already, Yahoo! uses it to facilitate searches outside its own searchable directory. AltaVista can also be used as a stand-alone keyword search tool. By way of example, we will examine some of AltaVista's searching capabilities; you will find similar capabilities in other Web search engines as well. Most of these products have built-in help information to instruct you about their use, and we encourage you to experiment with several of them.

When a user specifies one or more keywords or phrases to AltaVista, it searches for these terms in every Web page in its extensive Web index. This index is produced and updated by special programs that constantly search the Web for new and updated pages. Authors of Web pages can also submit their own pages (or other pages, for that matter) for inclusion in the index. Any page that has been on the Web for a

few days or more is quite likely to be included in the index.

When you enter a list of keywords in the AltaVista keyword input box, as illustrated in Figure 3.12, AltaVista searches for documents with one or more of those words present. The more occurrences of keywords it finds in a document, the higher priority it places on that document. Documents are reported to you in decreasing priority order.

AltaVista has a number of convenient features that make Web searches easy and more likely to produce the desired information. Among its features are the following.

Natural Language Queries

You can submit a list of keywords or a question to AltaVista in ordinary language. No special syntax is required. If you enter a keyword list, the search engine searches for occurrences of the words you enter but does not insist that all those words appear in every document retrieved. The

FIGURE 3.12

You can search by keywords in the search engine AltaVista. AltaVista is one of the most popular Web search engines and provides features for refining Web keyword and key phrase searches. Notice that 62,044 documents (with some duplication) containing the keywords "polar bears" were found! (AltaVista and the AltaVista logo are trademarks or source marks of Compaq Computer Corporation. Used with permission.)

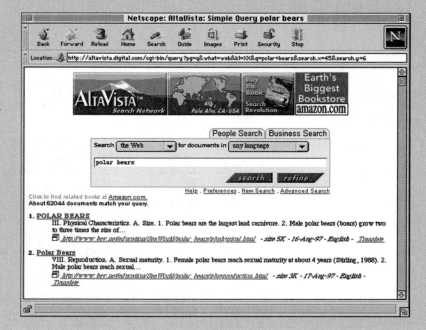

important thing is to include enough words to specify your topic, but no more. The more keywords you specify, the longer the search may take because AltaVista looks for documents containing *any* of the keywords.

For example, if you want to find information about the project to reintroduce wolves into Yellowstone National Park, you might type this simple keyword list:

```
wolves Yellowstone
```

AltaVista will return sites of documents containing either of these words, but the highest priority sites (that is, the ones returned at the top of the list) will contain both words—assuming there are such documents.

If you prefer, instead of entering the list of keywords, you could enter your query as a question. For example, you might type

```
what is the status of the wolf
project in Yellowstone?
```

AltaVista will examine the question and extract its own list of keywords (ignoring the words like *what, is,* and *the* used to construct the question).

Requiring and/or Excluding Words from Searches

If you wish to insist that a certain word or words appear in all the documents retrieved, you can indicate this by preceding the word with a plus (+) sign. To exclude any document containing a certain word, you precede that word by a minus (−) sign. For example, suppose we wish to find information about wolf reintroduction in places other than Yellowstone National Park. We might enter the following keywords:

```
wolf wolves +reintroduction
-Yellowstone
```

This sequence will find documents that do include the word *reintroduction* but do not include the word *Yellowstone*. Documents retrieved would not have to include either of the words *wolves* or *wolf,* although those sites that do include one or both of these words would be retrieved first.

Searching for Exact Phrases

If you wish to insist that certain words occur together (such a sequence is called a *key phrase*) in documents retrieved, you can specify this by placing the phrase inside quotes. For example, you might enter

```
"Yellowstone wolf project"
```

This approach can greatly narrow a search. The search will not return documents that contain any of the words listed unless they occur in exactly the phrase you've specified. If you have missed the phrase by a word or two, you may not receive the document(s) you're after. For example, if the phrase "Yellowstone Park wolf project" appears in a document, but the phrase "Yellowstone wolf project" (without the word "Park") does not, such a document will not be retrieved via the above key phrase.

It's wise to use key phrases carefully, making sure the phrase occurs just as you have it listed in the documents of interest. Nonetheless, there are certainly times when searching for a phrase makes good sense. For example, if you're interested in finding information about Yellowstone National Park, it would be better to enter the phrase

```
"Yellowstone National Park"
```

rather than the list

```
Yellowstone National Park
```

The list would return lots of pages of no interest (all pages containing the word "National" or the word "Park"), but a search for the phrase would return only those pages containing the three words in sequence.

Using a Wildcard Character in Searches

Sometimes you may wish to search for an item that could appear in several different forms. Alta-Vista allows you to use a wildcard character (*) for this purpose. For example, you might enter

```
+Yellowstone +wol*
```

to account for the occurrence of either "wolf," "wolves," or "wolfpack." The * indicates that the ending of the word is of no consequence and should be ignored by the search engine. Hence, this will return documents containing both the word "Yellowstone" and a word beginning with the letters "wol."

Case-Sensitive or Case-Insensitive Searching

If you use only lowercase letters in a keyword, then AltaVista will search for the word without regard to the case of its characters. For example, if you enter

```
wolf
```

the search engine will return documents containing "wolf," "Wolf," or "WOLF." On the other hand, if you enter

```
Wolf
```

the uppercase letter signals to AltaVista that you wish to return only those documents containing "Wolf." Documents containing "wolf" or "WOLF" (but not "Wolf") will be ignored.

Nontext Searches

AltaVista can also search for items on a Web page other than text. For example

```
image:wolf*
```

returns pages that display or refer to image files whose names begin with the letters "wolf." Similarly,

```
title:wolf
```

returns pages whose titles contain the word "wolf." AltaVista allows a dozen or so of these kinds of searches (consult the AltaVista help information available from the AltaVista Web page for details).

As you can see from these examples, search engines can be very powerful tools for finding information on the Web. On many occasions, though, your searches will turn up a large number of Web documents that are not relevant. The list of documents returned is annotated (with brief descriptions or excerpts from the page) and hyperlinked to the actual documents themselves. You can eliminate many of the documents returned based on the annotations. For those that look promising, or those for which the annotation doesn't give enough information to make a decision, you may use the built-in hyperlinks to examine a document to see if it does, in fact, contain useful information. Of course, you wouldn't want to have to check out 10,000 documents in this manner, so a careful application of the search engine's capabilities usually pays off.

Constructing well-planned queries and doing a bit of "leg work" in consulting sites will usually mean success in finding information on the Web. A final word of caution is in order. Remember that the Web is an open, uncontrolled repository. Anyone with the know-how and the means can post Web pages. Although much of the information on the Web is useful and accurate, you will find some of it frivolous, misleading, or just plain incorrect. Often, knowing the reputation of the author of the page (or the company or organization sponsoring the site) provides a degree of confidence in the information. You can also seek additional Web sources for the same or similar information. The Web can be a great source of quick information, but it pays to double check that information before placing too much confidence in it. By all means, learn to use this terrific resource, but always use it with a degree of caution.

Keeping Track of Web Sites Using Bookmark Lists

Lab Activity

Often you will wish to record specific Web sites for later use. Fortunately, browsers make this easy by automating the process of remembering your favorite Web sites. You may create a **bookmark list,** a personalized index of Web sites that allows you to return to a site with ease.

For example, Netscape Communicator provides a **Bookmarks** (indicated by the icon shaped like a bookmark) pull-down menu to which you can easily add links to sites that you have visited. To do this, you just choose the *Add Bookmark* command in the **Bookmarks** menu while you are viewing the desired Web page. The title of the Web page (always displayed in the browser title bar) will then be added to the **Bookmarks** menu along with a built-in link to its URL. You can even create a hierarchical structure by designating sublists within your bookmarks list. Later, you can access any of these stored sites by simply selecting it from the **Bookmarks** menu.

In Internet Explorer, bookmarks are added and stored in the **Favorites** pull-down menu. You can access the sites by selecting them from the **Favorites** menu, or you can open a *Favorites* folder by clicking the Favorites tool bar button. Once the folder is open, you can double-click on any site you wish to load.

AT YOUR COMPUTER

SEARCHING THE WEB

In this activity, you will use AltaVista to engage in some Web-based research on Ayers Rock. You may already know where and what Ayers Rock is, but if you don't, you will soon. And even if you already know these basic facts, chances are very good that you'll learn some new things about this fascinating natural phenomenon.

1 Before you begin, read the Focus box, "Effective Web Searches Using AltaVista." Then begin this activity by accessing the AltaVista Web search engine. Instructions for doing this in both Netscape Communicator and Internet Explorer follow.

Netscape Communicator Users: Click the Search button on the tool bar (or select *Search Inter-*

net under the **Edit** menu). On the ensuing screen, find the AltaVista link (in a list labeled *Search Engines*) and click on it.

Internet Explorer Users: Click the Search button on the tool bar. On the ensuing screen, select AltaVista as the search engine. Proceed to step 2 and enter your first keywords on this screen; you will be transferred to the AltaVista dialog screen for later entries.

2 Enter the following keywords in the AltaVista search input box:

Ayers Rock

Click the Search button on the page. Record the number of entries that AltaVista locates.

3 Let's try once more. Use the Back button to return to the AltaVista dialog page, as shown in Figure 3.13. This time, enter the same keywords, but use a plus sign as follows:

+Ayers Rock

Click the Search button on the page. Once again, record the number of entries that Alta-Vista locates. How does this number compare with the number of entries you found in step 2? Explain the difference.

4 Let's try one more approach. Return to the Alta-Vista dialog page. This time, enter the key phrase (with quotes):

"Ayers Rock"

Click the *Search* button on the page. Once again, record the number of entries that Alta-Vista locates. How does this number compare with the number of entries you found in steps 2 and 3? How do you account for the difference?

5 Visit several of the sites near the top of the most recently returned list. Record some facts about Ayers Rock that you learn from these sites. Bookmark any particularly noteworthy sites that you find for a later project. Did you find, for example, where Ayers Rock is, what it is, and how large it is? Did you find a map showing the location of Ayers Rock? Did you find any photographs of Ayers Rock?

6 Let's suppose for a moment that we really do want a map showing the location of Ayers Rock. Assuming you didn't find one in the few sites you visited above, let's do another search. Return to the AltaVista dialog page. Try the following (or substitute a question or keyword list of your own design).

Where is Ayers Rock?

Any luck? How many foreign language sites did your search return? Let's try again. Return to the AltaVista dialog page, and use the following keywords. This time, select only English language sites in the pull-down menu on the AltaVista page.

+"Ayers Rock" +map

You're on your own. Keep looking until you find a map of Australia showing where Ayers

---

FIGURE 3.13

This screen shows a search for information about Ayers Rock in AltaVista. When a search does not produce a satisfactory list, return to the search engine and alter the search words or phrase. (AltaVista and the AltaVista logo are trademarks or source marks of Compaq Computer Corporation. Used with permission.)

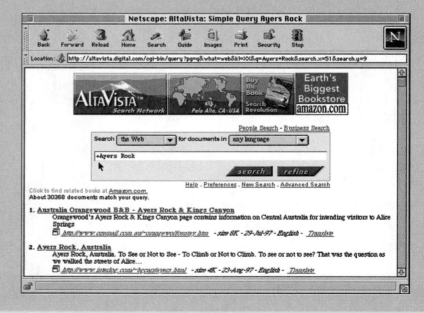

Rock is located. Bookmark this page when you find it.

7 Let's now focus our search on finding some images of Ayers Rock. You no doubt found a few images in some of the sites you've already visited, but as you know, we can do a more specific search. Return to the AltaVista dialog page, and type in the following search criterion:

```
image:"Ayers Rock"
```

Any luck? What happened? Remember, this syntax causes the search engine to look for file names containing the keyword or phrase we enter. Not too surprising that we didn't find a lot of such file names. File names are usually short and contain no spaces. Let's try again with

```
image:ayers
```

Much better! Bookmark a few of your favorite sites from this group for a later project.

Social Themes

Censorship on the Web

The World Wide Web has rapidly gained acceptance in homes and offices around the world—in short, it has become a mass medium. It should come as no surprise that, just as with other forms of mass media, censorship has become an issue. What drives efforts to limit the information available on the Web and other mass media? The following list contains some of the major concerns:

- Parents fears that their children will gain access to explicit information about sex, drugs, and other topics the parents deem inappropriate.
- Most citizens deplore the potential for the wide dissemination of material advocating hate crimes, bigotry, and other antisocial behaviors.
- Totalitarian governments fear that information about free elections and democratic processes could undermine their control over their populations.
- Some groups object to the open dissemination and discussion of "inside information" (including potential misinformation) on medical, legal, economic, religious, and other matters.

These are neither unusual nor unheard-of concerns. In fact, the traditional mass media are subject to societal controls—some self-imposed, others legally binding—in all these areas. But there is an important difference between these media and the Web. Traditional mass media are dominated by a relatively few individuals and corporations. The dissemination of information by these media can be controlled largely at the source. For example, newspapers and magazines can be shut down or have their products pulled from distribution; television and radio stations can have their broadcast privileges revoked; strong public opinion (including boycotts) can send compelling signals to the movie and entertainment industry. When laws are broken, prosecution can focus on relatively few individuals or companies, and successful prosecution efforts have a reasonable chance of affecting that industry.

On the other hand, the Web is a huge, distributed, largely uncontrolled medium. It is operated by thousands of individuals in thousands of locations, in many different countries, and within many different social and cultural environments. Controlling the source in this situation becomes next to impossible. Legal sanctions would have to span and be accepted by many jurisdictions. Even finding persons to hold responsible for originating offending information may be difficult, and preventing others from "filling the gap" once offending information has been removed may not be practical.

In February 1996, President Clinton signed into law the Communications Decency Act (CDA). This act attempted to establish limits on what could be placed on Web servers in the United States and prescribed penalties for those who violated these limits. In June 1997, the United States Supreme Court declared the CDA unconstitutional on the basis of the First Amendment, which guarantees freedom of expression. The failure of the CDA illustrates some of the difficulties in establishing legally enforceable limits on the sources of Web information, even when the attempt is limited to one culture and one country.

How then can we hope to put any controls on the dissemination of information across the Web? It appears that the only approach with a chance of succeeding is to apply controls not at the source of the information, but rather at its access points. Current efforts to do this focus on two related but distinct approaches: blocking software and access control through document content labeling. Figure 3.14 illustrates.

The basic function of **blocking software** is to prevent the downloading of a prohibited Web document based on one of several criteria. The simplest way to do this is to have the software consult site exclusion lists and block any sites found on these lists. These lists are prepared and updated by a third party, often the same company that sells the software. Another approach is to have the software block access to any site whose page names contain particular keywords that suggest its content may be undesirable. For example, the user may choose to block all pages where the word *sex* is used in the page names. With some blocking software, a more extensive filter can be employed to block any document in which certain words are used anywhere within the entire document. In each of these cases, the actual blocking is most often done by consulting a database of restricted Web sites and/or pages. Blocking software can also prevent certain kinds of outgoing data as well. For example, a parent might configure such software to block his or her child from sending telephone numbers or names over the network.

Blocking software can operate at one of several levels. The most common type of blocking software resides on the client machine; its advantage is that it can be tailored to the tastes and judgment of the machine owner. Its disadvantage is that children, students, or employees (or other blocking software targets) may be able to disable or otherwise circumvent the software because it is stored locally.

Blocking software can also be installed on systems that are connected to and serve the local machine. For example, the software could be installed and monitored by the online access provider or by the wide area network provider. Software installed and maintained at these levels is much less likely to be circumvented. There is a trade-off, though, because such arrangements may also reduce an individual's control over the parameters the software uses to decide which sites to block.

Perhaps the biggest problem with blocking software is the inherent difficulty in keeping the databases of objectionable material up to date and distributing updated copies in a timely manner. Any list of objectionable sites will no doubt change rapidly. New sites come onto the Web daily, and older sites may change their names and language to avoid being detected by the blocking software.

Another problem with such a broad-brush approach to censorship, from the user's perspective, is that a great many interesting, useful inoffensive sites might be blocked by the keyword filters used in blocking software. For example, in 1996, the telecommunications company NYNEX had all its pages about a new service blocked by several blocking programs because the Web page file names (which had been generated by a program) contained an offending sequence of letters.

An alternative approach to simple blocking software has been proposed recently. **PICS (Platform for Internet Content Selection)** is an attempt by the World Wide Web Consortium (W3C) to develop an infrastructure for the exchange of information about Web page content. The goal is a generally accepted system for labeling the content of docu-

FIGURE 3.14

One of two methods is commonly used to control pages being transmitted to a Web client. Blocking software utilizes a database of forbidden sites and pages. If a site or page is in the database, it will not be loaded. Access control methods depend on information stored with a page or site that rates its content. Access is denied depending on rating criteria specified at the client.

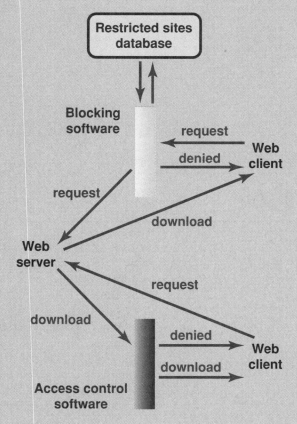

ments on the Web. PICS labels contain one or more ratings about a document's content. The creator of a page can provide his or her own rating when the page is created. In addition, third-party rating services can provide PICS ratings as part of their service. **Access control software** can use a PICS label to decide whether a document is allowable. This scheme may seem quite similar to simple blocking software, but it does have some distinct advantages. For example, it easily allows blocking on a document-by-document basis. In addition, it allows the user of PICS-based censoring software to get ratings from a number of different ratings services. The user can usually choose which rating services he or she wishes to give highest priority. Of course, there is no guarantee that PICS ratings will accurately reflect content, but if several rating sources are consulted, the chances of abuse of ratings categories are likely reduced.

PICS labels provide a very flexible system of content rating. Any document accessible on the Web (that is, with a URL) can be given a PICS label. PICS labels can be distributed as part of the document itself, or they may be generated by third-party rating services (or both). These labels can apply to a particular document, a collection of documents, an entire site, or even a collection of sites.

Labels can be interpreted by a browser or by some intermediate network blocking server, so the level at which access control is applied is also flexible. To avoid having PICS-based access control software bypassed by clever users on client machines, many parents, educators, and businesses are likely to prefer to use blocking servers at some level above the client in the network. For example, governments in countries like China might employ such access control on servers controlling all Web network traffic entering their country.

The promoters of PICS tout it as an open standard that can be a viable and workable substitute for otherwise unworkable censorship "at the source" methods and overly restrictive blocking software. Time will tell if PICS provides the level of comfort Web users and providers seek in controlling what information is delivered to their computer screens. One thing, though, is certain. The debate about Web censorship and freedom of expression isn't going to disappear soon (if ever); hence, this very likely won't be the last essay you read concerning these issues.

Social Themes

INTRODUCTION TO HTML

You now have experience in viewing, listening to, and otherwise interacting with Web documents. Perhaps it has occurred to you that the interest and attraction generated by the World Wide Web is in no small part due to the incredible variety and volume of information available through easy-to-use browsers like Internet Explorer and Netscape Communicator. What accounts for this staggering variety and volume? In large measure, they are a function of the relative ease with which anyone with a serious interest can create and publish his or her own World Wide Web documents.

As you have learned, World Wide Web documents are written in a language called HTML (for Hypertext Markup Language). World Wide

Web documents have three distinguishing characteristics. First, they are constructed to be **resolution independent**—that is, they can be interpreted and displayed on a large variety of display systems without modification. Second, in addition to text, Web documents routinely contain multimedia elements such as sounds, images, graphics, and even video clips. Finally, Web documents are by their very nature hypertext documents, meaning that they contain electronic links to other information published on the Web (by the same or different authors).

HTML is designed to implement each of these characteristics. The rest of this chapter will focus on exploring the basic features of this language. You will see that HTML was developed specifically to create documents that can be made available on the World Wide Web and that it is designed explicitly to take advantage of the Web's utilization of the distributed client/server computing model.

HTML: Philosophy and Design

The World Wide Web is the ultimate open systems environment. This means that its users employ and attach to it a wide variety of client computers—all makes, models, and operating systems. Consequently, the designers of HTML realized that HTML documents must be playable on a large and unpredictable variety of client computers.

In other words, insofar as possible, HTML designers wanted to create a language that defined documents in a way that would not depend on the type of display device used by the client system. This was accomplished by specifying in HTML only the basic structure of a document as opposed to its actual appearance on that display device. Once a definition of a document's structure is specified in HTML, the HTML document is stored on a Web server. When a client computer accesses the server and requests that HTML document, the stored document (specifying the structure and information separately) is transferred to the client computer.

After the document is transmitted to the client machine, the Web browser software interprets the structure and displays it on that machine's display device. The browser software makes any necessary decisions about how the document will look on the screen according to the characteristics and capabilities of the display device itself. As Figure 3.15 illustrates, an HTML document can look quite different when moved from one client browser/hardware combination to another.

Because Web documents make essential use of multimedia elements, the designers of HTML have also provided a convenient method for incorporating these elements into HTML documents. In fact, the same method is used to incorporate hypertext capabilities as well. A simple HTML command allows a document designer to establish a link to another Web document or resource file. When the linked file is another document, that document is fetched and displayed when the link is activated. When the linked file is an image, sound, or video, the browser displays (or plays) the file if it can handle information of that type.

Not surprisingly, different browsers have varying capabilities to play such files themselves, but most initiate a search for appropriate player/display software on the client machine. When such software is available, its use is generally transparent to the browser user. Notice again how the client/server model is exploited. The HTML document

FIGURE 3.15
An HTML document resides on a Web server. It stores only information about the structure of a document—not its appearance. When a particular client accesses the HTML file, its browser software formats the document for display on the client's display device. The same HTML document can look quite different on different client displays.

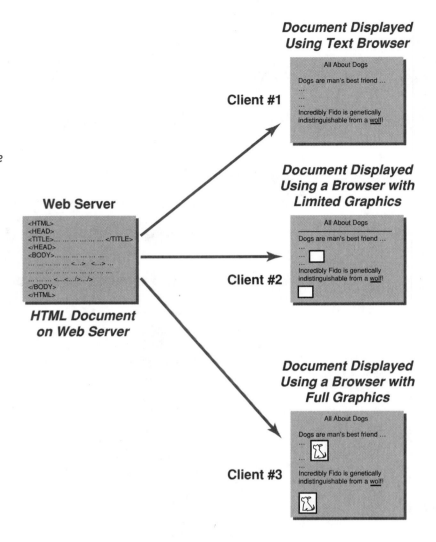

supplied by the server contains only the reference to the appropriate multimedia file. The burden of interpreting this file (displaying an image, playing a sound or a video) resides entirely with the client software and hardware.

What Is a Markup Language?

The name *Hypertext Markup Language* is actually a good starting point for understanding HTML. We've already mentioned, and you have observed in your own Web excursions, how essential hypertext links are to Web documents. Hence, the *Hypertext* portion of the name HTML should come as no surprise. The term *Markup* is borrowed from the publishing industry. Before the advent of electronic typesetting in this industry, plain-text proof pages were typically *marked up* with a variety of typesetting codes to illustrate how the text was to appear when it was actually printed. HTML borrows this idea, and an HTML document consists of marked-up plain (or unformatted) text, with the special markings indicating how the text is to be treated when it is "published" (that is displayed) on a Web client machine. Hence, an HTML file consists of regular text interspersed with special markup codes called

tags. Learning to write HTML is a simple matter of learning to use these tags to produce desired effects in the published document.

As we have already emphasized, HTML focuses on the basic structure of a document rather than its exact appearance when viewed. Of course, there is a relationship between the structure and appearance of a document, but they are not one and the same. Documents written in HTML are in plain text; they contain no formatting whatsoever—no tabs, no different fonts, no italics or bold text, and so on. These documents contain two things: the text you want to display and the HTML tags that indicate document elements, structure, formatting, and hypertext links to other Web documents or included media. Web browsers use these tags to format and display the text we provide.

Obviously, our task is to learn how to use HTML tags to create the effects we desire when a Web browser interprets and displays our document. Let's examine the format of a typical HTML tag:

```
<tag identifier>text affected by the tag</end tag
identifier>
```

Many (but not all) HTML tag types have beginning and ending tags surrounding the affected text, as shown above. We will refer to these as **paired tags.** The closing tag generally has a slash (/) followed by the tag identifier. *All HTML tags are case insensitive,* so any mixture of upper- and lowercase may be used to express them. We will adopt the convention of placing tag identifiers in all uppercase to help distinguish the tags from the surrounding plain text.

HTML: General Document Structure

A small number of general structure tags are included in every HTML document. For example, paired <HTML> tags must surround the entire document, paired <HEAD> tags surround the heading material, paired <TITLE> tags enclose the document title, and paired <BODY> tags bracket the body of the document. The heading material can include a number of items, but the only one the browser displays is the document title.

Figure 3.16 illustrates a simple HTML document. We've placed the various document structure tags on separate lines for emphasis, but this is not at all necessary. Carriage returns (and all other ordinary formatting information) have no meaning within an HTML document.

FIGURE 3.16

A simple Web page description demonstrates the basic structure of an HTML document. The various components of the document are colored differently for clarity.

```
<HTML>
<HEAD>
<TITLE> Our Own Page About Dogs </TITLE>
</HEAD>
<BODY>
It is no accident that dogs are known as man's best friend.
On this page we will explore some interesting facts about
dogs.
</BODY>
</HTML>
```

If you examine the example HTML document, you can probably guess what it will look like when displayed by a Web browser. When this document is displayed by Internet Explorer, we get the results shown in Figure 3.17. Observe the title in the browser window title bar. Note that the text that appears there is exactly the text surrounded by the <TITLE> and </TITLE> tags in the HTML document. Notice also that the body text is wrapped to fit the browser window and that this wrapping is different from that shown in the HTML file—another reminder that any formatting in the actual HTML file is ignored.

Admittedly, our example document is not very exciting yet, but we're on our way! Let's spruce the document up a bit. Clearly our text could use a heading of some sort, that is, some text in a larger font size to appear at the beginning of the page. Notice that the title we specified between the <TITLE> and </TITLE> tags does not serve this purpose. It is for display in the browser title bar only.

HTML allows six levels of headings using paired tags <H1> through <H6> to specify the particular level you desire. A large font will be used for H1 headings, with decreasing font sizes as we move through H2 headings, H3 headings, and so on. The browser will decide the exact font sizes when the page is displayed; we can be sure only of the relative sizes. This trait highlights a central feature of HTML—it does *not* support precision text formatting. An HTML author must keep in mind that the exact format for his or her Web pages will be determined by the particular browser and client machine on which the pages are displayed, not by the HTML supplied in the document. Hence, as authors, we should not become too focused on exact formatting, but rather must settle for the general "guidelines" that HTML tags provide for the various browser/client machine combinations.

Perhaps we'd also like a horizontal line separating the heading from the rest of the text. Horizontal lines are coded in HTML using the unpaired tag <HR> (for *horizontal rule*). The HTML document shown in Figure 3.18 now includes both an H1 heading and a horizontal rule. The new HTML lines are shown in red. Note that the <HR> tag stands on its own—it has no matching closing tag. The revised document viewed using the Netscape Communicator browser is shown in Figure 3.19.

FIGURE 3.17

Our simple HTML document is displayed using the Internet Explorer 4.0 browser.

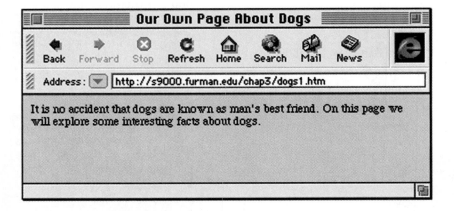

FIGURE 3.18

Our HTML document with two new lines added (shown in red). These insert a document heading (at the H1 level) and a horizontal rule before the opening paragraph.

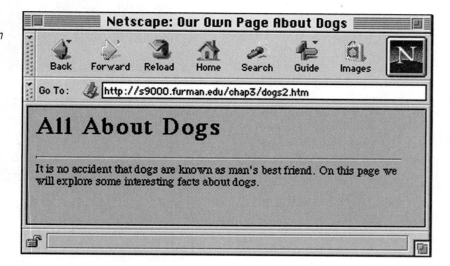

```
<HTML>
<HEAD>
<TITLE> Our Own Page About Dogs </TITLE>
<BODY>
<H1> All About Dogs </H1>
<HR>
It is no accident that dogs are known as man's best friend.
On this page we will explore some interesting facts about
dogs.
</BODY>
</HTML>
```

FIGURE 3.19

The modified HTML document is viewed in the Netscape Communicator 4.0 browser.

Netscape: Our Own Page About Dogs

Back   Forward   Reload   Home   Search   Guide   Images

Go To: http://s9000.furman.edu/chap3/dogs2.htm

All About Dogs

It is no accident that dogs are known as man's best friend. On this page we will explore some interesting facts about dogs.

HTML: Lists

Now that's more like it! But, of course, we're not done. We want to spruce our page up with more features. Very often we tend to organize information, on the Web or in traditional publications, into lists. Several different kinds of lists are available in HTML. We'll illustrate an **unordered list,** often called a bullet list. Later, in Chapter 18, we'll describe the other kinds of lists available in HTML.

Let's add to our page a list of topics we'll explore. Suppose we want a topic list that includes the following four topics: *Choosing the Right Dog, American Kennel Club, Dog Behavior and Training,* and *Wolf Behavior and Dogs.* We will need two kinds of tags for the list. The paired tag <UL> (for *u*nordered *l*ist) is used to surround the entire list, and then each item in the list is preceded by the unpaired tag <LI> (for *l*ist *i*tem). The revised HTML document is shown in Figure 3.20 with the new lines shown in red to make them easy to pick out.

The new document is displayed in Internet Explorer in Figure 3.21. Notice the bulleted list items. The browser provides the bullets automatically—this is its way of displaying unordered lists. Other browsers might implement unordered lists with a slightly different appearance.

FIGURE 3.20

The example HTML document is modified to include an unordered list containing four elements. The new code describing the list is shown in red.

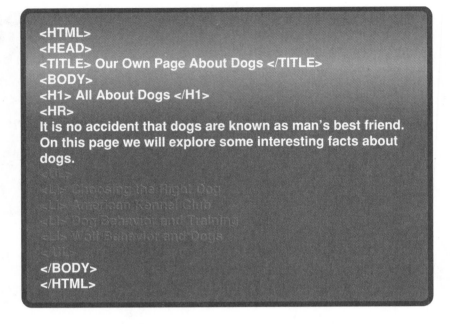

```
<HTML>
<HEAD>
<TITLE> Our Own Page About Dogs </TITLE>
<BODY>
<H1> All About Dogs </H1>
<HR>
It is no accident that dogs are known as man's best friend.
On this page we will explore some interesting facts about
dogs.
<UL>
<LI> Choosing the Right Dog
<LI> American Kennel Club
<LI> Dog Behavior and Training
<LI> Wolf Behavior and Dogs
</UL>

</BODY>
</HTML>
```

FIGURE 3.21

Our modified HTML is displayed in Internet Explorer 4.0. Compare the unordered list now included to the HTML code in Figure 3.20.

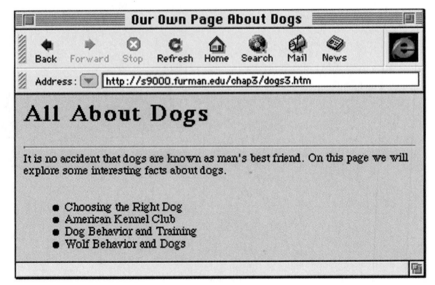

By the way, we've summarized all the HTML tags we introduce in the text in Appendix A, so don't worry about memorizing them all as we go. Instead, concentrate on understanding how the desired document structure is encoded using the various tags in an HTML document. At each stage of the development of our example Web page, compare the HTML document and the displayed page carefully.

HTML: Images

Web pages are often enhanced by adding images. You saw in Chapter 2 that an image is digitized by breaking it into pixels and storing the numerical values that represent each pixel. The actual encoding of pixel values can be done in one of several different ways, and these different methods define a number of different **image file formats.** The software used to display a stored image file must be tailored for the kind of file format used to create that file. Hence, we must choose the type of image files we use in our Web page designs carefully because readers of our pages will be able to see only those images for which they have appropriate viewer software.

Most of today's browsers have built-in capability for displaying files in either of the two image file formats whose suffixes (file extensions) are abbreviated as **gif** and **jpg.** You'll learn more about these and other file formats in Chapter 11. For now, it is enough to be aware that different file formats exist and to know that these two formats are the ones most commonly used for Web work. Generally, it is best to limit images for Web pages to either of these two types.

Images in Web pages fall into two categories: inline images and external images. We will examine inline images here and postpone the treatment of external images. **Inline images** appear on the Web page when it is loaded by your browser—unless you have a nongraphical browser or have chosen your browser's option to suppress the images on displayed Web pages. Ideally, the browser will be able to recognize and display the inline image files directly, without appealing to additional software.

Let's see how to place an inline image in our example Web page. Suppose we have an image stored under the file name *springer.gif.* The <IMG> tag (for *im*age) places the image on our Web page. The tag <IMG> is not a paired tag, but it does require us to supply additional information for its use. In particular, we place the image source file name, enclosed in quotation marks, inside the tag itself, as follows:

```
<IMG SRC="springer.gif">
```

The SRC stands for *source* file. In this case, the *gif* suffix in the file name indicates the image file format. This suffix triggers the browser to use the corresponding viewer to display the image found in the file.

In our example, we place this tag within the existing <H1> tag pair to include the image as part of the heading. We also add a phrase inside the tag to align the image vertically relative to any text that appears on the same line. Let's suppose that we want the text to appear in the middle of the vertical dimension of the image. Figure 3.22 shows the new line of HTML replacing the previous H1 heading tag. The resulting Netscape-interpreted page is shown in Figure 3.23.

A second category of Web page images, **external images,** are downloaded only at the Web page reader's request and are sometimes played by a viewer program outside the browser itself. Hence, if the client machine has the appropriate viewer software, the format of external images will not be a problem. You'll learn how to accommodate external images in your Web pages in Chapter 18.

HTML: Hyperlinks

Hyperlinks are the primary feature that drives the World Wide Web. Hyperlinks are often associated with text words or phrases, but they can also be associated with inline images as well. The links they implement often connect to information stored on a different computer (and frequently created by another author). We can also link to our own separate HTML files, image files, sound files, and so on, or even to a separate location within the same HTML document. Indeed, we have the ability

FIGURE 3.22

An inline image is added to the heading in our Web page. The revised line of HTML is shown in red. Note that the <IMG> tag is inserted inside the paired <H1> tags. The ALIGN attribute is set to the value MIDDLE, meaning that any text on the same line with the image is to be displayed in the middle of the image's vertical dimension.

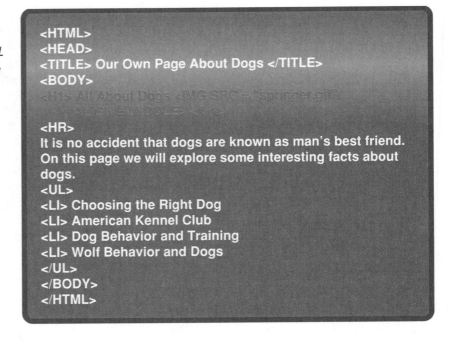

```
<HTML>
<HEAD>
<TITLE> Our Own Page About Dogs </TITLE>
<BODY>
<H1> All About Dogs <IMG SRC = "springer.gif"
ALIGN = MIDDLE> </H1>

<HR>
It is no accident that dogs are known as man's best friend.
On this page we will explore some interesting facts about
dogs.
<UL>
<LI> Choosing the Right Dog
<LI> American Kennel Club
<LI> Dog Behavior and Training
<LI> Wolf Behavior and Dogs
</UL>
</BODY>
</HTML>
```

FIGURE 3.23

The example page with the new inline image is displayed in Netscape Communicator 4.0. Generally, inline images should be in .gif or .jpg format to ensure that any image-capable browser will be able to display the image.

to weave a "web" of information as tightly or as far-flung as we desire by using hyperlinks.

Let's investigate how to place hyperlinks on our example Web page. Suppose we have located a Web page that we would like to access to expand the *American Kennel Club* bullet in our Web page unordered list. In particular, suppose we wish to link to the page shown in Figure 3.24. Notice that its URL is *http://www.akc.org.*

The <A> paired tag (for *anchor*) implements this hyperlink. Within the tag we supply two things: the URL for the page and the text we wish to have used as the hyperlink. In our example, we place this tag within the existing <L1> tag for *American Kennel Club,* and we move the text for the list item inside the tag to make it the hyperlink. Figure 3.25 shows the new HTML document, with this change in red.

Notice several things about the paired <A> tag. The URL for the page we wish to link is given as part of the first tag (HREF = "..."). HREF stands for *hypertext reference.* After closing the first tag, we give the text that will serve as the hyperlink, then close the paired tag with </A>. Figure 3.26 displays our handiwork. The text associated with the new hyperlink (*American Kennel Club*) is now shown in a different color and underlined. The browser pointer is over the new hyperlink. In the status bar at the bottom left of the window, you can check the address that will be requested if we click. Clicking the link would of course, cause the page shown in Figure 3.24 to be loaded.

FIGURE 3.24

This is a page from the American Kennel Club Web site. We can link pages such as this as our own hyperlink destinations by encoding their URLs (taken from the URL display) inside an <A> tag.

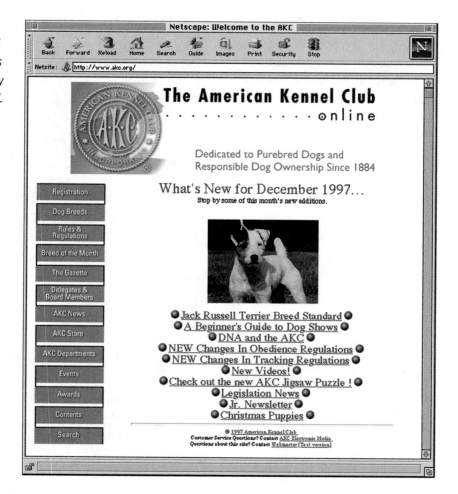

FIGURE 3.25

The HTML document now has the new hyperlink inserted. Note that we used the text in the list item as the actual link.

```
<HTML>
<HEAD>
<TITLE> Our Own Page About Dogs </TITLE>
<BODY>
<H1> All About Dogs <IMG> <SRC = "springer.gif"
     ALIGN = MIDDLE> </H1>
<HR>
It is no accident that dogs are known as man's best friend.
On this page we will explore some interesting facts about
dogs.
<UL>
<LI> Choosing the Right Dog


<LI> Dog Behavior and Training
<LI> Wolf Behavior and Dogs
</UL>
</BODY>
</HTML>
```

FIGURE 3.26

Our page is viewed by Internet Explorer 4.0 with the new hyperlink implemented. Note that the text associated with the hyperlink is now shown in a different color and is underlined. The American Kennel Club home page is just a mouse click away!

Inline images can be used as hyperlinks as well as text. If you include an <IMG> tag inside a paired <A> tag, the image becomes part of the clickable hot spot for the hyperlink. For example, the following construction makes the image *springer.gif* the hyperlink for accessing the HTML document *springer.html:*

```
<A HREF="springer.html"><IMG
SRC="springer.gif"></A>
```

Lab Activity

When the page is loaded the image *springer.gif* is displayed and bordered in a different color as a hypertext link. When the mouse is clicked over the image, the document *springer.html* is loaded.

CREATING YOUR OWN WEB PAGE

In this exercise you will create your own Web page. You will need access to a text editor that allows you to save text files in *text-only* format. Any standard word processor will certainly work, as will the simple text editors that typically come preinstalled with the Macintosh and Windows operating systems. We assume that you know how to save and open documents.

Remember that every HTML document must contain certain structural tags (for example, HTML, HEAD, TITLE, and BODY tags). Let's begin your page by including just these elements and a minimal amount of text. Replace Mary Smith's name with your name in the instructions that follow.

1 Open your text editor and type the following HTML code into the editor's window. Note that we have indented and included some blank lines to illustrate better the structure of the HTML document. You need not worry about this kind of formatting when you type your document. Remember that all formatting will be ignored when your browser interprets this HTML document. Only the tags and raw text are relevant for the browser.

```
<HTML>

<HEAD>
    <TITLE>
    Mary Smith's Home Page
    </TITLE>
</HEAD>

<BODY>
Welcome to Mary's Home Page
</BODY>
</HTML>
```

2 Save this document and name it *page1.htm*. If your text editor gives you a choice of file types, choose *text only*. Leave your text editor open, and open your browser (Netscape Communicator, Internet Explorer, or other). Open your *page1.htm* file as a Web page in the browser—Netscape Communicator and Internet Explorer instructions follow.

Netscape Communicator: Select the *Open Page* command from the **File** menu. Then find and open the file.

Internet Explorer: Select the *Open File* command from the **File** menu. Then find and open the file.

3   You should see your page displayed. Figure 3.27 illustrates how the page would appear in Netscape Communicator. Check to make sure the document title appears as the title of the browser window and that your welcome message is displayed in the window itself. If there is a problem, review steps 1 and 2, checking your HTML code carefully.

4   Let's add some more elements to your page. Start by making your welcome message appear larger. Leave the browser and return to your text editor document. Enclose the text in the BODY part of the document with a paired H1 tag as follows:

```
<H1>Welcome to Mary's Home
Page</H1>
```

Save the modified file. Leave the text editor open, and return to the browser. Click the Reload button on the browser's tool bar; your page should reappear with a larger welcome message. If this does not happen, check your HTML code carefully, then try again. Don't forget to save your HTML document; otherwise, you're just reloading the old document in your browser.

5   Let's add a list to your page. Leave the browser, and return to your text editor document. Let's place a horizontal line just after your welcome message. Do this by putting a <HR> tag in the document just after your line of text. Next let's include a bulleted (unordered) list with two items. The two items will be *My Favorite Web Site* and *Another Cool Web Site.*

Remember that unordered lists are enclosed by paired <UL> tags, and inside these, the list items are each preceded by an unpaired <LI> tag. Your modified HTML code inside the <BODY> tags should now look like the following (again, the indentation is to make the structure clearer—you needn't worry about it):

```
<H1>Welcome to Mary's Home
Page</H1>
<HR>
<UL>
   <LI>My Favorite Web Site
   <LI>Another Cool Web Site
</UL>
```

FIGURE 3.27

This example shows how the first version of your Web page should look. This page is displayed in Netscape Communicator 4.0, but it will look essentially the same in Internet Explorer 4.0.

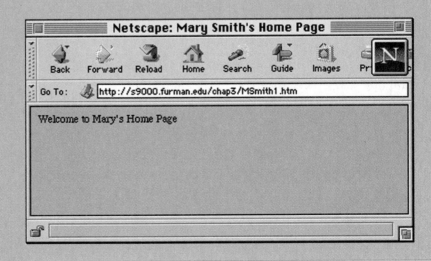

6 Save the modified file. Leave the text editor open, and return to the browser. Click the Reload button on the browser's tool bar; your page should reappear with the added horizontal rule and list. If this does not happen, check your HTML code carefully, then try again.

7 Obviously, the list on your page is intended to be a list of hyperlinks to take the viewer to the appropriate Web sites. Let's implement the first link. Of course, the URL for your favorite Web site is:

```
http://s9000.furman.edu/DD
```

(Humor us here!) We can include this as the destination for the first link in the list. We do this by changing the appropriate line in the HTML. Return to the text editor (leaving the browser open), and replace the first item in your list with the following (review the <A> tag structure if necessary):

```
<LI><A HREF="http://
s9000.furman.edu/DD">My
Favorite Web Site</A>
```

8 Save the modified file. Leave the text editor open, and return to the browser. Click the Reload button on the browser's tool bar, and your page should reappear with the new list item underlined and in a different color, as illustrated in Figure 3.28 using Internet Explorer.

If this does not happen, check your HTML code carefully, then try again. Assuming your new link does appear as it should, test it. Click the link to see if it takes you to the *Exploring the Digital Domain* Web site. Return to your page using the Back button.

9 Finish the exercise by locating a Web site of your choice to use as the link for your second list item. Change the HTML to implement that link, then test it to make sure it works. (Review steps 7 and 8 if needed.)

10 Now that you've seen how easy it is to create your own Web pages, you no doubt can think of other elements you'd like to add to your page. Of course, you're welcome to experiment on your own right now.

FIGURE 3.28
This is what your Web page should look like after adding a hyperlink within your unordered list. This page is displayed in Internet Explorer 4.0, but it will look essentially the same in Netscape Communicator 4.0.

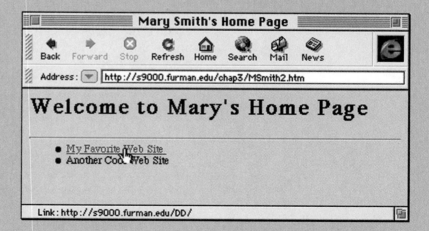

Social Themes

Commerce on the Web

Businesses have become increasingly aware of the Web as an advertising venue; therefore, a Web presence is a given for many companies. Hardly a magazine, newspaper, or television advertisement appears without an accompanying Web URL these days. For many companies, the merits of electronic commerce—that is, electronic transactions conducted over the Web—are still under scrutiny. Reluctance toward electronic commerce is beginning to fade, and commerce over the Web is well on its way to becoming an accepted means of transacting business. The Web commerce market research firm ActivMedia Inc., in its *1997 Real Numbers Behind Net Profits* report, predicts Web sales of products and services of $1.5 trillion worldwide by 2002. And Forrester Research, Inc. predicts Web commercial software revenues to grow from $20 million in 1996 to more than $3 billion by 2000.

There are two basic types of electronic commerce: business-business transactions and business-consumer transactions. The former is the more developed form of electronic commerce currently, but it is business-consumer commerce that promises to revolutionize the way we do business in the next century. A number of markets are already emerging in this category; these include Web auctions, malls, single-vendor outlets, and electronic software delivery. Each of these markets has differing technical needs. For example, an electronic auction must be able to co-ordinate bids among participants. Internet malls sell products from multiple vendors; hence, they need to track percentage splits and payments made to various vendors. Some electronic malls are personalized for a particular company or organization. For example, CyberSystem Technologies, Inc. developed IntraMall for the National Institute of Health. IntraMall allows NIH scientists to skip the procurement process and shop from government-approved vendors directly.

Of course, an individual company can simply offer its goods or services as part of its Web site. To do this, the site needs to implement and track the order-entry process and the shipment of goods, offer consumers a way to check on their orders automatically, and provide a method for payment. Payment is most frequently accomplished by the use of credit cards, and this has been one of the limiting factors in the rate of growth of electronic commerce. In a recent survey by the Silicon Valley–based company World Research, 70 percent of respondents did not feel that security measures had made Web transactions safe. Actually, experts in credit card fraud indicate that these transactions are as safe, if not safer, than giving your credit card number over the phone or using it in a restaurant. The Web search directory Excite guarantees credit card transactions with an Excite Certified Merchant—J. Crew and Wal-Mart are just two examples. Excite will reimburse the electronic shopper for up to $50 (the maximum amount for which a consumer is normally held responsible) in the event of credit card fraud.

Contrary to popular belief, securing an electronic transaction is not that difficult. Netscape Communications Corp. has developed a protocol for electronic transactions called **Secure Sockets Layer (SSL)**. Although SSL isn't the only solution created for securing electronic commerce, it has become the de facto standard. SSL is included with every commercial Web server today, and it is supported by all major Web browsers. Commercial Web sites using SSL encode your sensitive payment information before transmitting it over the network. Once this encoded information reaches their server, it is decoded there. Even if someone intercepts the transmission, he or she would have to crack the code before being able to use the intercepted information.

There is more to electronic commerce security, however, than simply ensuring secure transmissions. Web-based merchants, like their nonelectronic counterparts, must ensure that sensitive customer information isn't abused by employees. Employee abuse is, in fact, the most common way that credit card information is misused, according to CommerceNet, an electronic commerce consortium in Palo Alto, California. Of course, electronic commerce systems should never store or print decoded credit card information. Web-based merchants should always include messages that explain credit card fraud legalities and limits and the security methods in place for the transaction. Once customers have such information, they will likely become more confident about transmitting credit card information over the Web.

Most purchases made on the Web today are traditional credit card transactions. This is natural because merchants had mechanisms for handling credit card purchases long before electronic commerce became an issue. We can expect to see alternative payment methods implemented as electronic commerce becomes more commonplace. There are several reasons for this. One is to reduce the cost of electronic transactions. A credit card transaction costs between 25 and 75 cents, and the merchant pays a 2 to 3 percent service fee in addition. We can expect to see new electronic payment options with per-transaction costs of only a few pennies. Another reason for alternatives to credit card payments is to insure the anonymity of the customer. To process a credit card, the merchant must know the customer's name and account number, and perhaps his or her address. Many potential Web customers are reluctant to give out their names and addresses, and anonymous payment schemes would probably increase Web sales. A third reason to seek alternatives is to broaden a merchant's customer base. Many potential customers may not have a credit card—either by choice or because they do not qualify for one.

What alternatives to traditional credit card payment are likely to emerge? It's too early in the history of electronic commerce to make a confident prediction about this, but a number of possibilities are emerging. We'll quickly survey some of the more promising electronic payment systems.

DigiCash is an electronic payment system developed by David Chaum in Amsterdam. The system is based on digital tokens, called digital coins. Each digital coin is created by the consumer and then certified by the DigiCash mint, operated by a government or bank. This certification is done by adding to the digital coin something called a digital signature—you will learn about digital signatures in Chapter 18. Of course, digital coins exist only in cyberspace. These are not physical objects, just blocks of bits to be exchanged via the Web. To enroll in the DigiCash system, a consumer must download the DigiCash software and establish an account with a bank or other financial institution that can both mint and receive digital coins. DigiCash accounts consist of a deposit account with the financial institution and an electronic wallet maintained on the consumer's computer. DigiCash provides for consumer privacy. The consumer knows the identity of the merchant, but the merchant will know the identity of the consumer only if the consumer tries to double spend a digital coin.

A company called First Virtual Holdings has introduced a system called **Virtual PIN** for making credit card charges over the Internet without transmitting credit card numbers. In this system, the consumer needs no special software. First Virtual holds the consumer's credit card number and issues the consumer a Virtual PIN (a number). The Virtual PIN purchase cycle then goes as follows. The consumer sends his or her Virtual PIN to the merchant. The merchant submits the Virtual PIN with a potential charge to First Virtual Holdings. First Virtual Holdings e-mails the consumer asking for authorization. When the consumer gives authorization, First Virtual Holdings charges the consumer's credit card and notifies the merchant that the charge was approved.

Virtual PIN gives the consumer anonymity (all the merchant gets is your Virtual PIN). Because each transaction must be manually verified via e-mail, the consumer is protected from fraud at the merchant's end as well. A disadvantage is the slight nuisance of having to authorize all your electronic purchases by returning an e-mail message to First Virtual Holdings.

CyberCash is a payment system similar to Virtual PIN, but it uses encoded credit card information instead of PINs. To use CyberCash, a consumer must download the CyberCash wallet software to his or her machine. The wallet maintains a database of authorized user's credit cards and other payment instruments. To use the system, the CyberCash wallet sends an encoded payment order to the merchant. The merchant can decode part of the order information but not all of it. The merchant adds encoded payment information to the order and sends the order to the CyberCash gateway for processing. The gateway then checks the order for validity (checking that the consumer's and the merchant's versions agree) and sends the credit card payment information to the bank issuing that credit card. Once the bank authorizes the transaction and sends this information back to the gateway, the information is transmitted to the merchant, who then processes the order. The strength of this system is that the merchant never has access to the customer's credit card number or other sensitive information. The CyberCash gateway acts as an intermediary between the merchant and the appropriate bank.

A CyberCash customer can also create something called a **CyberCoin** account by transferring money from a credit card or checking account using the Automated Clearing House (ACH) electronic funds transfer system. The CyberCoin account can then be charged for an electronic order in a way very similar to that used for credit card purchases. The transaction will be faster because no exchange of information between the CyberCash gateway and a bank is necessary.

From the consumer's perspective, a system called **SET** (for **Secure Electronic Transaction**) works in a way very similar to CyberCash. The difference is that the SET standard is being jointly developed by MasterCard, Visa, and others, and it will likely be readily acceptable to a great many merchants.

No doubt additional digital payment systems will evolve and those described will be improved if the volume of electronic commerce increases dramatically over the next few years as predicted. It is very likely that commerce on the Web will become as commonplace and accepted as placing credit card orders by mail and telephone is today. The good news is that such electronic transactions are faster and actually safer. There will be less danger of anyone intercepting your sensitive information. Likewise, electronic commerce will have excellent built-in protections from traditional forms of credit card fraud.

Social Themes

HTML TAG EDITORS AND GENERATORS

So far in this chapter you have learned that Web documents must be written in HTML, and you've been introduced to a few of HTML's features. And, assuming you did the second "At Your Computer" activity, you've actually constructed your own HTML document. As Web publishing has become more and more popular, software products have been introduced to make the process of constructing HTML documents easier. These products are generally referred to as HTML editors. The first generation of HTML editors, sometimes called **tag editors,** made creating and working with HTML documents more user friendly. HTML Assistant and BBedit are two of the older but still popular tag editors, and there are many others from which to choose. Such products offer a number of conveniences in constructing HTML code. For example, tags can be inserted by clicking buttons on a tool bar, and tags are sometimes shown in different colors from the plain text to make the HTML structure stand out more clearly. Most of these products do some simple syntax checking as well, such as making sure that all paired tags are properly closed. A user of a tag editor still works directly with the HTML code, but the editor makes this work much easier and less error-prone.

More recently, a second generation of HTML editors, which should more properly be called **HTML generators,** have become popular. HTML generators allow their users to describe and construct Web pages in a more natural way than by constructing HTML directly. Instead of actually writing the HTML code, you lay out the features and appearance of a Web page as you want it to appear in a browser. The HTML generator software then automatically derives the underlying HTML document that will produce the browser interpretation you have specified.

Such software can be a great time saver, and it is certainly good to know at least one such package. We believe it is a great advantage for a user of HTML generators to understand HTML coding. The HTML generator approach is sound and certainly attractive, but there are some shortcomings in these products. The HTML generated doesn't always produce exactly what you originally had in mind when the pages are displayed in a browser. One problem is that HTML changes rapidly, so these products often will not have the latest HTML features available. On the other hand, if you have some knowledge of HTML, then you can fix the generated code directly to produce more satisfactory results. This is exactly why we introduced "raw" HTML before we discussed these higher-level editors.

A good analogy might be drawn to cars. Although it is possible to drive a car and know absolutely nothing about what actually goes on under the hood, in a great many situations even a little knowledge about the underlying functioning of the car can be very beneficial. This is especially true for troubleshooting when everything doesn't go according to plan. We believe the same is true for Web authoring.

Perhaps the best way to use HTML generator software is as a quick approach to laying out the basic features of a Web page. Once the HTML file has been generated, the knowledgeable user can adjust the HTML directly to achieve optimal results. In this section we will describe the general features of HTML generators. Quite a number of such products are available, and they all have distinctive interfaces and their own individual organizations. We will not attempt to teach the particulars of any of these, but rather to give an impression of their common capabilities. Check the *Exploring the Digital Domain* Web site for detailed tutorials on several of the most popular of these packages.

You can type plain text directly into the HTML generator window, then format it later. For example, you might type in the text that will serve as the page heading, then declare it be an <H2> head. The generator will surround the text with paired <H2> tags when it produces the HTML document. Typically, you would make this declaration by selecting (highlighting) the text, then selecting the <H2> heading characteristic from a pull-down menu or tool bar button. You can also center the heading on the screen if you like with some similar actions. Changing the color of the text is accomplished in essentially the same way as well. Figure 3.29 shows a simple page heading being configured in the HTML generator Claris Home Page. Note there that a horizontal line has been added after the text. This is done by positioning the cursor at the point you wish to insert the line and clicking a button on the tool bar.

Other text formatting is done in a very similar way. For example, simply select the text to be made bold (or italic) and click the appropriate menu selection or tool bar button. Lists can be generated by first typing out the list in plain text, then selecting the text and declaring it to be a certain kind of list. Individual list items can be designated in a similar way.

Inserting graphics using a HTML generator is easy. The process is essentially the same as inserting a horizontal rule. Position the cursor where you wish to insert the graphic, then click the appropriate button on the tool bar (or select the appropriate command from a pull-down menu). A dialog box is presented in which you can choose the image file you wish to insert. The generator takes care of constructing the corresponding <IMG> tag. Placing hyperlinks in the document is also

FIGURE 3.29

A page heading (an H2 level heading) in the Claris Home Page HTML generator is shown. Notice the toolbar buttons that give immediate access to a number of standard HTML features.

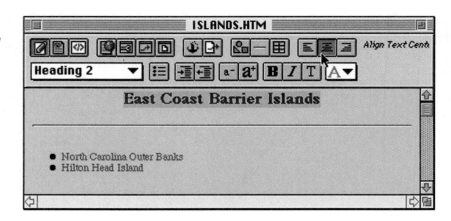

FIGURE 3.30

A hyperlink is defined in the HTML generator Microsoft FrontPage 97.

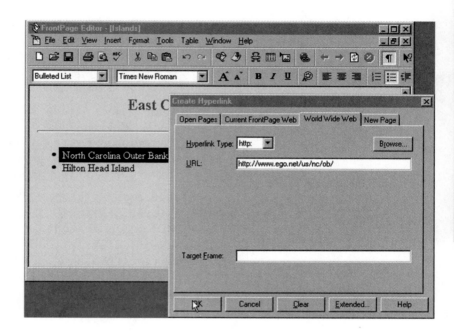

straightforward. First type in the text you wish to serve as the link. Then, with the text selected, choose the link tool from a menu or from the tool bar. A dialog box appears into which you type the URL for the page or resource to be linked. Figure 3.30 illustrates this process using the HTML generator Microsoft FrontPage.

In addition to products like Home Page and FrontPage, which are specifically designed to generate HTML, some of the latest generation of application software, like word processors and presentation software, allow documents produced in those packages to be converted to HTML documents. These conversions sometimes fail to capture the exact intent you had when you created the original document, but they will no doubt improve in the future.

It is a great time to be learning about Web publishing. Armed with a basic knowledge of HTML and the latest HTML generation software, you can create Web pages with a minimum of effort. And this process will only get easier in the future. The technical details of creating Web pages can truly be mastered by most anyone. Just because you can create Web pages, however, doesn't about mean the Web pages you create will be effective, eye-catching, and informative. To produce really great-looking and informative Web pages requires a mix of creative and technical skills. This is why professional Web publishing is often a team effort, involving content experts, graphic artists, and technical experts. You should not be discouraged by this. Creating Web pages for yourself can be both fun and easy. And the more of this work you do, the better at all the requisite skills you become.

Lab Activity

MORE ABOUT HTML

In this chapter, you've seen just how easy it is to build your own hyperlinked Web pages. Of course, we haven't covered everything there is to know about HTML. And HTML is constantly changing. New features and capabilities are added to it regularly. Nonetheless, you've learned the basics, and you are ready to create your own distinctive Web pages.

You should know about a number of additional features of HTML. These too are easily mastered. In the section on HTML in Chapter 18, we will cover the basics of some additional features, including the following:

- Linking external resources to your Web pages
- Four additional kinds of HTML lists
- Paragraph and text formatting in HTML
- HTML tables
- Using frames on Web pages

In fact, you can go directly to that section now if you wish. You'll also find expanded coverage of all the HTML features discussed in the HTML tutorials accessed from the *Exploring the Digital Domain* Web site. Remember also that Appendix A contains a summary of the most commonly used HTML tags.

SUMMARY

The World Wide Web provides connectivity for the digital domain. Organized on the client/server model of computing, the Web is an open, distributed repository of hypermedia information. Thousands of Web servers offer relatively easy access for posting materials on the Web. Many more thousands of Web client machines are attached to the Web and provide access to the Web's resources for millions of people.

Computers with many different scale and performance capabilities can attach to the Web because all Web communication is handled through the set of standard Web protocols (or communication rules): URL, HTTP, and HTML. A URL (for *Uniform Resource Locator*) is the agreed-upon protocol for specifying the address of a Web page or resource available on a Web server. The set of rules governing the exchange of information between Web clients and Web servers is HTTP (for

Hypertext Transfer Protocol). And Web documents are encoded using the HTML (*Hypertext Markup Language*) standard.

Browser programs, such as Internet Explorer and Netscape Communicator, running on client machines, interpret and display HTML documents for a specific client environment. Web search engines and searchable directories make finding information on the Web relatively easy. HTML employs tags to mark a plain-text document for formatting and display by a browser. HTML is not difficult to master, and anyone with a serious intent can learn to use it effectively to construct Web pages. High-level HTML editor software makes this task even more straightforward. Employing such editors, you can format a Web page as you would like it to appear, and the editor will create the appropriate HTML code to implement the design.

PROJECTS

1 Use a Web search tool to look for Web pages that contain your name (first and last). Did you find any? How many? If you found none, try a search on just your last name. Check out a few of the returned pages.

2 Employ a Web search tool to find out the population of Boston. Don't be satisfied with the first answer you find. Continue searching until you have located multiple sources for this information. Do these sources agree with each other? If not, which do you believe? Explain your last response.

3 Repeat project 2, but this time try to find an estimate for the mass of the moon. Find at least three sources for this information. Which is the most reliable? Why?

4 Review the features of the AltaVista search engine discussed in the "Focus" box earlier in the chapter—this project extends that discussion to some hands-on activities. Start your Web browser and access AltaVista (see the first "At Your Computer" activity in this chapter if you need to review how to do this). Perform all the searches for information about Yellowstone Park and wolves one by one, just as they are given in the "Focus" box. For each search, note the number of sites returned. Compare the numbers of sites for related search criteria. Explain the differences you observed. Check out some of the sites returned to see if you can find relevant and useful information about the project to reintroduce wolves into the Yellowstone ecosystem. List the URLs for the three sites you think have the best summary of the status of the project.

5 Use AltaVista or another Web search engine to get additional information about the Communications Decency Act (see the first "Social Themes" section in this chapter). Write a one-page essay summarizing the background of the act and what happened to it once it passed Congress. Can you find the complete text of the act? If so, record the URL for that site.

6 Use a Web search engine to find out more about PICS (Platform for Internet Content Selection). Try to find some evaluation and/or discussion of the pros and cons of PICS. Based on your findings, write a brief essay describing what PICS is and how it might affect censorship on the Web. Be sure to cite the sources (give URLs) you used in writing the essay.

7 Design and create a Web page that will serve as an informative introduction to Ayers Rock, Australia. Create the HTML document in a text editor. In other words, do not use an HTML tag editor or generator. Your page should contain at least the following elements:

- An introductory paragraph detailing some essential facts about Ayers Rock
- Links to at least four other Web pages giving more details about Ayers Rock
- A link to a map that shows the location of Ayers Rock
- Several links to pages containing some images of Ayers Rock

If necessary, review the instructions for creating your own Web page in the second "At Your Computer" activity in the chapter. Use the bookmarks you saved in the Web search activity on Ayers Rock in the first "At Your Computer" activity.

8 Conduct some Web-based research to learn more about electronic commerce. Look for sites on DigiCash, CyberCash, Virtual PINs, and SET, but do not limit yourself to just these subtopics. Bookmark any particularly informative sites you find. Write a brief essay about your findings.

9 Design and create a Web page that will serve as an informative introduction to Web commerce. Use the links you bookmarked in project 8. If you have access to an HTML generator, such as Home Page or FrontPage, use it for this project. If not, use a tag editor if one is available. If neither an HTML tag editor nor an HTML generator is available, construct the HTML directly using a text editor.

Key Terms

access control software	Hypertext Markup Language (HTML)	protocol
blocking software		resolution independence
bookmark lists	Hypertext Transfer Protocol (HTTP)	search engines
browse tool		Secure Electronic Transaction (SET)
browser (Web)	image file format	
client (Web)	index sites	Secure Sockets Layer (SSL)
CyberCash	inline images	server, Web
CyberCoin	Internet Explorer	session, browser
DigiCash	loading, Web page	surfing, Web
home page	Mosaic	tag editor
HTML generator	Netscape Communicator	tags
HTML tags	page, Web	Uniform Resource Locator (URL)
hyperlink	paired tags	unordered list
hypermedia document	Platform for Internet Content Selection (PICS)	Virtual PIN
hypertext		World Wide Web Consortium (W3C)

QUESTIONS FOR REVIEW

1 Describe the basic organization of the World Wide Web.

2 Describe the role of hypertext in the Web.

3 What is meant by the client/server model? Relate this to the Web.

4 What is a browser? Relate this concept to the client/server model.

5 What is meant by the term *protocol?*

6 What does URL stand for? What is the function of a URL?

7 What does HTTP stand for? Why is it important?

8 What does HTML stand for? What is its significance?

9 What do we mean when we say that the Web has resolution independence?

10 Give an example of an actual URL and explain what its various parts represent.

11 How would you go about finding information about Arabian horses on the Web?

12 What are bookmarks in a Web browser? Why are these useful?

13 What are tags used for in HTML?

14 List some HTML paired tags and describe their use.

15 List some unpaired HTML tags and describe their use.

16 What is a tag editor?

17 What is an HTML generator?

18 Describe some of the main functions available in a browser tool bar.

19 How do the Netscape Communicator and Internet Explorer tool bars compare? Which buttons are common to both?

20 What is a search engine? How do search engines work from a user's perspective?

21 What is blocking software?

22 What does PICS stand for? What is its significance?

23 Do you think the use of PICS involves censorship? Explain.

24 What is the Secure Sockets Layer (SSL) protocol used for?

25 Give examples of two electronic payment systems and explain their use.

26 Would you feel safe sending your credit card number over the Web? Explain why or why not.

PART 2

INSIDE COMPUTERS

Vasily Kandinsky, *Improvisation*, June 1923. Solomon R. Guggenheim Museum

The modern-day computer is an electronic digital processing system. Our main interest is helping you learn how to exploit such systems to enhance your abilities to create, store, retrieve, analyze, and communicate information in a variety of media. To do these tasks well and to adjust effectively to the rapidly changing computing landscape you will encounter in your lifetime, you must have a depth of understanding that goes beyond the use of the latest software and hardware.

This is the first of four chapters that explore the basic structure and workings of the modern computer in some detail. In this chapter, we will focus on a major component of the hardware of the modern computer system: the processor. The processor is often referred to as the "mind" or "brain" of a computer system. Even though such metaphors tend to overstate the abilities of the modern computer (it is not a *thinking* entity), they do correctly emphasize the importance of the processor to the computer's operation. You will learn in this chapter how the processor controls and manages the functions of the computer and how it directs the computer's operations according to programs stored in its associated memory.

The modern computer is an engineering marvel, and we could spend many chapters (or books, for that matter) exploring the intricacies of its construction and operation. Of course, such a study is well beyond the goals of an introductory text; our focus is instead on the basic concepts upon which the organization of the processor is based. And because we believe this information is best appreciated when presented an historical context, we include a brief history of the development of modern computers and their underlying logical organization.

OBJECTIVES

- The basics of computer system organization

- The history and development of computing machines

- The stored program concept and the computer as a general-purpose programmable device

- How the computer's main memory is organized to manage data storage and retrieval

- Types of instructions a typical processor can perform

- Scale and performance factors of the current generation of computers

CHAPTER 4

THE DEVELOPMENT AND BASIC ORGANIZATION OF COMPUTERS

Vasily Kandinsky, *Improvisation*, June 1923. Solomon R. Guggenheim Museum

COMPUTER SYSTEM COMPONENTS

A computer system is a combination of physical devices, called hardware, and programs, called software, that direct the operations of these components. The **hardware** of a typical system consists of a number of devices: a processor that carries out the detailed instructions defining the computer's activities; a mouse, keyboard, printers, and monitor that allow our communication with the machine itself; and memory devices used to store information in electronic form. **Software** is the term used to describe all the programs we use when we employ the computer for some task. Software is usually delivered to us on either one or more small magnetic disks or CD-ROMs.

There are two basic categories of software: system software and application software. **System software** consists of the programs that manage our operation of the computer. As you will learn in Chapter 7, such programs are collectively referred to as the computer's operating system. These programs allow you to start up and shut down the computer, save your work as files, retrieve that work later, print documents, and so on. We would be helpless in front of our computer screen without the system software that enables us to direct and interact with the computer's hardware.

On the other hand, **application software** consists of the programs that allow us to work on higher-level tasks. For example, when you write a letter using the computer, you employ application software known as an editor or word processor. When you play a game, you employ application software designed specifically to make the computer behave as a game machine. In fact, most of the interesting things we do with computers are made possible by application software packages. These are the programs that line the shelves of your local electronics store; the range of activities they enable is truly impressive. Tasks like writing letters and term papers, playing interactive games, computing taxes, recording and playing digital music, sending and receiving electronic mail, and a myriad of others depend directly on having the appropriate software available.

Computer hardware by itself is capable of surprisingly few basic operations. If we have the right application software, the computer can perform an absolutely amazing range of feats. It is the hardware that carries out these low-level instructions, but the software that defines, organizes, directs, and orchestrates the complex sequences of instructions that produce something meaningful for us.

As illustrated in Figure 4.1, the user interacts with the hardware only indirectly through a user-friendly interface provided by application software. Requested tasks are interpreted for the hardware, which carries them out and returns the result—once again, through the software. The system software acts as an intermediary and complement to the application software. The computer hardware, system software, and application software combine to make the computer a useful and indispensable tool for the user. In this and the next two chapters you will explore in some detail how this combination works. We begin in this chapter by considering the history of the development and organization of the modern computer processor.

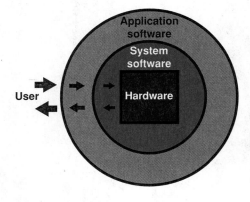

FIGURE 4.1

A computer system consists of both hardware and software. The software provides the interface the user employs to communicate his or her task for the machine; the hardware carries out the instructions that implement that task.

THE DEVELOPMENT OF COMPUTING MACHINES

We tend to think of the computer as a recent invention. Certainly, electronic digital computers are very new in the big picture of civilization—the first devices appeared less than a half century ago. On the other hand, these electronic versions are not the first computing devices. In fact, the quest for automatic calculating or computing devices has a very long history. A survey of this history will help you understand the capabilities and organization of the modern computer. Note that what follows is not intended as a history of the entire field of computer science, but rather a more focused history of the development of the modern computer itself.

Humans invented mathematics, but we are—on the whole—ill equipped to perform consistently accurate mathematical computations. Throughout history, people have been highly motivated to create devices that improve or extend human computational performance. Indeed, nearly all cultures and civilizations expended some efforts on devising tools that aided calculation. These efforts have culminated in the invention of the modern computer, the most successful calculational tool yet developed.

Computing or calculating machines may be either analog or digital devices. Analog computers employ continuous forms for representing their data as well as mechanisms based on analog methods. Analog devices are usually special-purpose machines dedicated to very specific tasks. Digital computers are discrete state machines. Not only is their data represented discretely using digital encoding, but their processing is defined by a series of separate or distinct events or states. Digital computers, as we will soon see, have more flexibility. Unlike analog computers, digital computers may be general-purpose machines.

There is a long history detailing the invention of computing and calculating machines. The earliest recorded calculating device is the abacus. Used as a simple computing device for performing arithmetic, the **abacus** most likely appeared first in Babylonia (now Iraq) over 5000 years ago. Its more familiar form today is derived from the Chinese version pictured in Figure 4.2. Our interest in this survey, however, is primarily with the development of modern digital devices. Accordingly, we will move rapidly down the timeline to seventeenth-century Europe.

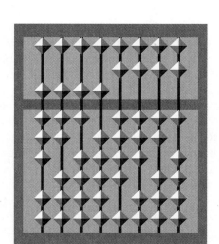

FIGURE 4.2

The modern version of the abacus is a frame holding rows of beads suspended on metal rods. Each row represents a power of ten in calculations.

Early Digital Computational Devices

The inventor of the first mechanical (digital) calculating device was a German professor named **William Schickard** (1592–1635). Not a great deal is known about either Schickard or his mechanical device. We do know that the device was composed of rotating rods and gears. The rods represented columns of numbers, and the gears moved the rods to display the proper results. Basically, the machine performed the arithmetic operations of addition and subtraction, though it could apparently assist in performing multiplication and division. Unfortunately, most of the information about Schickard's invention was lost to history with his death from the plague in 1635.

FIGURE 4.3
A box-shaped device, the Pascaline—as it came to be known—displayed a row of digits on the front. Number dials allowed its user to enter the operands, and the gears inside the machineworks moved the short rods to display the result in the answer windows.

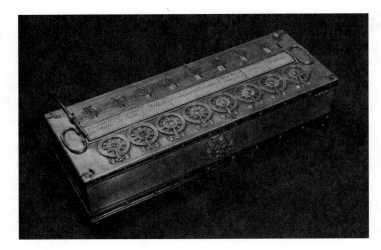

For years historians considered the inventor of the first mechanical calculator to be the French mathematician, philosopher, and apologist **Blaise Pascal** (1623–1662). To assist his father's work as a tax collector, the 19-year-old Pascal created a mechanical device that performed simple addition and subtraction. Even though the machine brought Pascal some notoriety, it was a commercial failure. See Figure 4.3.

The German scientist, mathematician, and philosopher **Gottfried Wilhelm von Leibniz** (1646–1716) is the next notable figure in our story. He is the designer of the Stepped Reckoner, the first fully featured arithmetic calculator capable of performing both multiplication and division as well as addition and subtraction. Its chief feature was the so-called "Leibniz wheel," a gear-shaped metal cylinder that served as a mechanical multiplier. A crank rotated the collection of cylinders, which turned the wheels that displayed the digits of the answer. However, Leibniz's prototype device never quite worked properly. Consequently, the machine is more important for its historical influence than as a practical device.

Although the Stepped Reckoner was a decimal device, it is interesting to note that by coincidence, Leibniz was the first mathematician to investigate the properties of base-2 or binary numbering. As you read earlier, binary coding is the native tongue of computers today.

Developing a Programmable Computing Device

The first truly modern pioneer in the history of computing is the Englishman **Charles Babbage** (1791–1871). See Figure 4.4. Babbage designed not one but two very different automated calculating machines. Unfortunately, his ideas were so modern that they far outstripped the capabilities of nineteenth-century technology. As a result, he was never able to realize them fully; consequently, many of these ideas were lost to posterity.

Much of the mathematical computations done in Babbage's day depended on consulting mathematical tables. Thus, enterprises such as navigation, science, and commerce relied heavily on the accuracy of these tables to aid the human "computers" who used them. The process of creating and publishing these tables was not always reliable, though. As might be expected, errors could result from either commission or transcription. The individuals doing the original computations might commit errors, and the publishing process might introduce others.

FIGURE 4.4
The English mathematician and inventor Charles Babbage pioneered the concepts of the modern computer.

Babbage reasoned that if a machine could be constructed to automate both of these processes, it would also bypass these sources of errors. He designed such a device, which he dubbed the Difference Engine. The **Difference Engine** not only calculated tables of figures but also prepared plates for printing them. Unfortunately, the mechanical technology of the day was not suitable for the kinds of specifications needed to realize a fully functional device. That Babbage was a perfectionist who continually changed its design did not help matters either.

All in all, for its day, the Difference Engine was an amazing conception. Yet as an automated calculating device, it represents a small step backward from machines like Leibniz' Stepped Reckoner in that it was a very special-purpose machine. The machine could perform a complicated series of computations for a given set of values. The results would be determined, of course, by both the original values and the process used to make the calculations. Unfortunately, the machine could perform just that process and nothing else. To be able to perform another type of computation would require redesigning and building an entirely different machine. By contrast, the Leibniz calculator performed only simple arithmetical computations, but the user could control the order in which they were done. Such a calculator is a little more flexible, but still only a special-purpose machine because it can do nothing other than the simple arithmetic operations built into its hardware.

You know that today's computers are not so limited. In fact, it is likely that you have used one computer to perform a variety of tasks. For example, you may have employed a computer as a word processor to create text documents, as a calculator to do mathematical computations, or as a game machine for entertainment. Today's computers are **general-purpose computers** (see Figure 4.5). But how is this possible? This very

FIGURE 4.5

A computer produces results or output by transforming its input by means of steps defined by its process. Like most machines, special-purpose computers are designed to perform one type of process. The input may be altered, but the output is always determined by that same process. On the other hand, a general-purpose computer has both a variable input and a variable process. Its mechanism is defined by the instructions of a program. The program therefore defines what process will be performed.

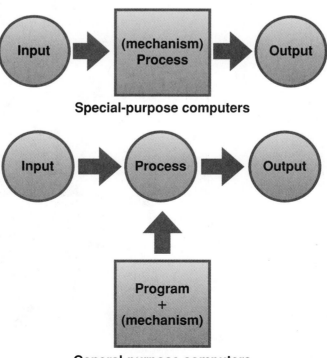

problem occupied Babbage during one of his breaks from work on the Difference Engine in 1833.

The idea that unlocked the solution to the problem was, surprisingly, the contemporary invention of the Jacquard loom. J. M. Jacquard developed a device that attached to a loom to help automate the process of weaving. Jacquard's invention automated the action of the weaving needles to achieve a desired design by using a series of punched cards that directed, or **programmed,** this process. That is, the punched cards contained the instructions or **program,** written in a manner the weaving loom could understand, to direct the weaving. See Figure 4.6.

Babbage recognized that computation in general could be organized in just this manner: The computational process could be programmed. The key is that the program does not have to be hardwired into the machine but fed into it much like the values processed. The advantages are enormous. Such a machine could not only vary *what* it processes but also vary *how* it processes. A programmable machine would be general purpose rather than limited in its capabilities. Changing the controlling program would enable the machine to perform an entirely different computational process.

Babbage called his design for such a machine the **Analytical Engine.** The computations were directed by punched cards. Some of these cards specified the actual steps of the process to be performed; others specified the particular values or data to be used by the process. Babbage later recognized that other means could be used instead of punched cards to program a machine, but Jacquard's punched cards sparked his original insight. Babbage was assisted in this work on the Analytical Engine by Lady **Ada Lovelace,** who is sometimes referred to as the first

FIGURE 4.6

This vintage illustration shows the Jacquard loom powered by the human operator. Across the top, a series of connected punched cards direct the weaving process.

computer programmer and in whose honor the recently developed programming language Ada was named.

Had he been able to realize the Analytical Engine as a functioning device, Babbage would have created the first general-purpose programmable computing machine. But, like the Difference Engine, it had little life beyond the drawing board. In retrospect, we must marvel at Babbage's ingenuity but regret that his accomplishments were known to so few and had so little influence on later generations who would struggle with the same enterprise.

From the end of the nineteenth century through the beginning of the twentieth, the effort to develop better and more efficient calculating machines continued. In the United States, **Herman Hollerith** (1860–1929) reinvented the punched card as a means for storing numerical information that mechanical calculators could use. The punched card tabulator was first used for processing the U.S. census in 1890. Hollerith also launched the Tabulating Machine Company that later would merge and evolve into the computing giant, International Business Machines (IBM).

The title of inventor of the first general-purpose programmable digital computer goes to the German engineer, **Konrad Zuse** (1910–1995). See Figure 4.7. Zuse developed a series of computing machines between 1936 and 1943 that employed electromechanical telephone relay switches to represent and store numeric values. These relays offered speed that could not be matched by purely mechanical devices. Electrical relay switches could shift hundreds of times per minute. Because an electrical switch can be set reliably to only two separate positions, *on* and *off,* numeric values had to be coded internally using a two-value digit system, that is, binary numbering. Zuse used punched holes on discarded 35mm motion picture film to encode the machine's program instructions.

FIGURE 4.7

The German engineer and inventor Konrad Zuse (pronounced "Zoo-zah") invented the first general-purpose programmable digital computer.

Electronic Computers

In the meantime, in the United States, **John V. Atanasoff** (1903–1995) was hard at work designing the first *electronic* digital calculating machine. He was, of course, quite unaware of Zuse's machines because the world's political climate had effectively shut down the normal free exchange of scientific ideas.

Like most of the inventors involved in the development of the computer, Atanasoff had a practical need for calculations that existing technology simply could not satisfy. As a physicist and mathematician, he was interested in a faster and more reliable way to solve large sets of simultaneous equations. Mechanical calculators were too slow. Special-purpose analog calculators called differential analyzers were built to handle these sorts of computations but were difficult to use. Atanasoff thought that a digital machine would perhaps be a better approach. He also recognized the practicality of using a binary numbering system for representing information, and he decided to use electronic technology in his machine. Electricity could switch a mechanical relay hundreds of times per minute, but a purely electronic relay, like a vacuum tube, in which only electrons move could switch on and off much faster.

With the assistance of graduate student **Clifford Berry,** Atanasoff built the prototype ABC (Atanasoff Berry Computer) at Iowa State College in 1939. It was the first machine to perform arithmetic electronically.

See Figure 4.8. It was neither entirely automatic nor general purpose. An operator had to administer each stage of the computation, and, not surprisingly, it was designed for the specific purpose of solving simultaneous equations. The ABC also had other problems due to a faulty input device; consequently, it was never fully operational. Still, Atanasoff rightly believed that he and Berry had demonstrated the practicality of electronic digital computing machines. So convinced was Atanasoff that he invited the physicist John Mauchly to inspect the ABC in 1941.

Mauchly was apparently inspired by what he saw. As he wrote later, he was indeed impressed by it, but he was also disappointed by the ABC's shortcomings. Upon his return to the Moore School of Engineering at the University of Pennsylvania, he proposed to build an electronic computing device of his own. **John Mauchly** (1907–1980) and his colleague **J. Presper Eckert** (1919–1995) were able to convince the U. S. Army of the utility of such a device. They won a contract in 1943 to build what would

FIGURE 4.8

The ABC built by Atanasoff and Berry was a special-purpose computer for solving differential equations. Unlike analog devices of the day, the ABC was an electronic digital calculating machine.

FIGURE 4.9

This photo shows some of the detail of one of the numerous panels that comprised the ENIAC.

© 1993 Smithsonian Institution

FIGURE 4.10

This U.S. Army publicity photo shows the ENIAC in operation.

FIGURE 4.11

The English mathematician and logician Alan M. Turing was instrumental in the development of the Colossus code-breaking computer.

be the first operational, general-purpose, programmable electronic digital computer called **ENIAC** (for *E*lectronic *N*umerical *I*ntegrator *a*nd *C*alculator). It was completed three years later but too late to help calculate the ballistic firing tables for which it had been intended.

Even so, the ENIAC was quite a marvel—both in scale and complexity. It was composed of 40 panels arranged in a U-shaped pattern that extended 8 feet by 80 feet and weighed nearly 30 tons! See Figures 4.9 and 4.10. ENIAC contained more than 17,000 vacuum tubes, 70,000 resistors, 10,000 capacitors, 1,500 relays, and over 6,000 manual switches. It had an operating capacity of 100,000 pulses per second, which meant that it could multiply 333 ten-digit numbers in 1 second. A single ballistic trajectory could be computed in 20 seconds compared to the 30 minutes needed when using other conventional mechanical calculators.

On the other hand, programming the ENIAC was a nightmare. Thousands of switches and hundreds of cables had to be connected by hand. The programmers (a number of young women in the Army) quite literally had to reconfigure the machine's circuits manually to change its operation. On the average, it took about two days to set up ENIAC to execute a single program that might run for a few seconds at a time. Manual programming proved a serious liability to its productive use. Still, it was a remarkable achievement and a significant watershed in the history of modern computing machines.

Researchers in Great Britain were also making strides in the development of computing technology. During World War II, the Germans had constructed a mechanical enciphering system, called the Enigma machine, that was so complex they believed it unbreakable. A group of Britain's "best and brightest," the most notable of whom was **Alan M. Turing** (1912–1954), were assembled to work on the ULTRA project, whose goal was to break the code for the Enigma machine. See Figure 4.11. With the help of vital operating information received from espionage sources, Turing and his colleagues were able to construct machines that would not only break the code but also automate the process. The most notable of

FIGURE 4.12

Colossus was employed to decrypt codes generated by the German Enigma machines during World War II.

these code-breaking computers was the **Colossus,** shown in Figure 4.12. It became operational in 1943—a full three years before ENIAC. Colossus, like ENIAC, was an electronic device, containing 2400 vacuum tubes. Its operational details are still classified even today, but historians have noted that the code-breaking intelligence generated by ULTRA was decisive in the Allied war effort.

MODERN COMPUTER DESIGN—THE VON NEUMANN MACHINE MODEL

Even before the ENIAC project was completed, Mauchly and Eckert had recognized that its design had limitations that would restrict its widespread use. In August 1944, while the final components of ENIAC were being assembled, the idle project design engineers set out to plan an improved machine. One important goal was to overcome the problem of manual programming. And, as luck would have it, the renowned mathematician John von Neumann visited Mauchly and Eckert at the Moore School in Philadelphia at the same time. Having heard about the project, von Neumann was curious about its progress.

The Designer

John von Neumann (1903–1957) was born in Budapest, Hungary. Educated in Europe, he came to the United States in 1930 and eventually accepted a post at the newly created Institute for Advanced Study at Princeton, New Jersey. See Figure 4.13. His career was marked by significant achievements in a number of fields: set theory, mathematical logic, game theory, quantum mechanics, hydrodynamics, cybernetics, and more. He even helped to devise the implosion scheme used in the first nuclear bomb. Eclipsing all of these achievements, his name has come to be synonymous with the basic design of the modern generation of electronic digital computing machines.

FIGURE 4.13

John von Neumann is pictured here alongside the Princeton Institute for Advanced Study (IAS) computer.

As an informal member of the Moore School team, he helped to create a new design for the machine that later would be dubbed **EDVAC**— for *E*lectronic *D*iscrete *V*ariable *C*omputer. A central feature of its design provided for an encoded, **stored program.** The machine could be freed of manual programming and operation if the instructions of the program might be encoded and stored within it, much like the data on which it operated. The idea is so simple and natural that we may find it difficult to appreciate how significant it was at the time. There is still some controversy as to the true originator of the idea, but there is little doubt von Neumann crystallized and championed it.

The Machine Design

Von Neumann proposed a new logical organization, or **architecture,** for the computer. Machines based on this architecture came to be called von Neumann machines. Several points are especially noteworthy about the von Neumann architecture. First, the von Neumann model clearly separated the logical design from the engineering details. In other words, the descriptions of the components are based on their function and not merely the mechanism that achieves that function. A computer could now be understood in terms of its architecture rather than in terms of engineering its devices. Employing this approach, the technology behind computing machines may change, but the logical design or architecture would remain much the same.

The chief elements of the von Neumann machine architecture are illustrated in Figure 4.14. Of course, this architecture is designed to implement the stored program concept. It employs a binary internal coding scheme like the calculating machines of Zuse and Atanasoff. The binary code, however, serves to represent not only the data that the machine processes but, just as importantly, the program that dictates that processing.

FIGURE 4.14

The modern electronic digital computer is composed of two major subsystems: a processor and its subordinate input/output system. The processor consists of a main memory device that services a central processing unit (CPU). The input/output subsystem consists of devices dedicated to input, output, and storage of data.

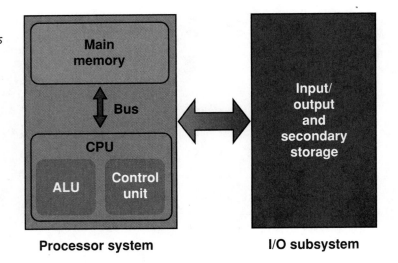

Processor system   **I/O subsystem**

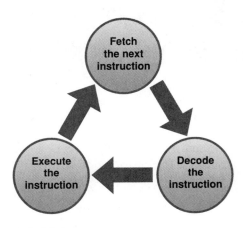

FIGURE 4.15

The stored-program concept requires that each instruction be encoded like data and stored in a memory device for subsequent use. When a program is executed, each instruction must be fetched, one by one, from that memory store, decoded, and then executed. The process of interpretation continues step by step until the last instruction of the program has been executed.

Both data and instructions are stored in a **main memory unit. A control unit** manages the fetching, decoding, and executing of the encoded instructions of the stored program. The design also includes a unit, called the **arithmetic-logic unit (ALU),** dedicated to the performance of the machine's built-in arithmetic and logical functions. These built-in operations are referred to as the **machine instruction set,** which varies from one computer model to another. The control unit and ALU together are known as the **central processing unit (CPU).** Together the CPU and the memory unit are known as the **processor.**

Devices devoted to managing the exchange of information between a human user and the processor, known as **input and output devices,** are also included in the design. Finally, a memory device, called **secondary memory,** is included to archive data and instructions when they are not in use.

Von Neumann's design also described a simpler and more efficient means for implementing the stored program concept. Whereas the ENIAC performed a number of tasks simultaneously or in parallel, the von Neumann machine is a **serial uniprocessor:** a single machine that performs a series of instructions and tasks one at a time. The tasks of fetching, decoding, and executing the encoded instructions of the stored program performed by the control unit are repeated over and over as long as there are program instructions to be carried out. This repeated cycle is called the **instruction-execution cycle** and is illustrated in Figure 4.15. This concept of sequential operation simplified engineering design and actually increased the speeds at which a machine could execute programs compared to the more complicated ENIAC design.

The von Neumann architecture has become synonymous with electronic computing machines featuring the following:

- Automation based on stored-program execution
- Logical design composed of the principal functional units: a central processor, a memory unit, input/output devices, and secondary memory devices
- Internal binary coding for data and instructions
- Serial uniprocessor operation

Between 1946 and 1951, von Neumann and his colleagues at Princeton engaged in the task of building a machine that used this new architecture. This machine, shown in Figure 4.13, was known as the **IAS computer** because it was built for the Institute for Advanced Study. The distinction of actually realizing the *first* operational stored-program, general-purpose electronic digital computer system, however, goes to **Maurice Wilkes** (b. 1913). Wilkes and his Cambridge University design team in Great Britain based the EDSAC (*Electronic Delay Storage Automatic Calculator*) on the published proposals of both von Neumann and the EDVAC of Mauchly and Eckert. EDSAC executed its first program in 1949—a full two years before the IAS machine and three years before EDVAC.

A special feature of the EDSAC was its ability to interpret programs written in an elementary symbolic programming language. These symbolic instructions could be translated to the binary coded instructions for execution. The instructions were punched on paper tape and read into the EDSAC, which converted them automatically to binary instructions. This symbolic form of programming is much easier for human programmers to manage; it later came to be known as **assembly language.**

This completes our historical sketch of the development of the modern computing machine. Of course, a lot has taken place over the past fifty years in the fabrication, performance, and technology of computers. Strange as it may seem, though, most of the machines today do not differ radically from the stored-program machine model outlined here. Computers have changed significantly in their speed, size, and capabilities; on the other hand, most computers today are faithful to the basic architecture as envisioned by von Neumann and others. In the next section, we will examine this basic design more closely.

More information

COMPUTER ORGANIZATION

As you have learned, the modern general-purpose electronic digital computer is based on the von Neumann architecture and its stored-program concept. In this section, we will examine in more detail how the basic components of a typical computer system are organized and how this organization lends itself to the implementation of a computer's programs.

As Figure 4.14 illustrates, we can think of the standard computer system as composed of two fundamental subsystems: the processor and the input/output (or I/O) systems. The processor is organized to implement the von Neumann instruction-execution cycle much as an agent carries out your instructions to perform some task. The input/output system is usually a collection of devices, including a mouse, a keyboard, a monitor, one or more printers, and so on, loosely designated as **peripherals.** As the name suggests, input devices convert information that is understandable to you and me into machine-readable data, that is, an electrical binary representation. Output devices accomplish the opposite process: they convert machine-readable data to a form that is useful to us (text, graphics, sounds, and so on). The I/O system has two main functions. First, it serves as a translator in communications between the user and the processor. Specifically, it facilitates input and output operations. Secondly, the I/O system provides access to secondary memory devices where both programs and data can be stored when they are not being used by the processor.

The I/O system is usually a collection of a variety of devices. In fact, the actual hardware for individual computer systems differs more in this category than any other. These devices are very much like the options you select when you purchase an automobile. In other words, most computer users tailor their system to their needs by adding these peripherals to the basic processor. For this reason, we will treat the variety of devices that qualify as the options of the I/O system separately in the next chapter. In this chapter, we concentrate on the "standard equipment"—the processor system.

As described earlier, the processor system is also a collection of devices or components. From an architectural standpoint, it consists of two major units: the CPU and the main memory unit. The CPU manages the instruction-execution cycle, and main memory is a fast storage device for holding binary instructions and data. These are connected by a signal pathway called a **bus,** as illustrated in Figure 4.14. When the processor is operating, bits are moved rapidly across this bus. The number of bits that can be moved simultaneously across the bus (32 bits for most modern desktop computers), called the **bus width,** is an important factor in determining the speed of the computer system.

MANAGING DATA: MAIN MEMORY

As we have stated, the primary function of main memory is to store data and instructions for use by the CPU. There are, in fact, several types of main memory, but all varieties are organized in the same manner. As you have already learned, the *lingua franca* of all computer systems is binary. But a single bit doesn't provide much latitude for expressing information. We could use a "0-1" coding scheme to represent things like "yes-no," "dark-light," and so on. But two-valued representations are very limited. Instead, we need strings of bits to represent more potential values. Consequently, memory is usually divided into uniform-sized units that contain a sequence of binary digits.

These sequences of bits are treated as single units of information. Each of these units is known as a **memory word,** the smallest meaningful unit for representing information. A memory word is denoted by a unique number called its **address.** Just as your street address locates your home, a memory word's address locates its unique position in main memory. Thus, we can conceive of memory as a collection of standard-length, addressable words. See Figure 4.16. Most processors today use a memory word size of one byte (remember, a byte is eight bits). This does not mean that the processor cannot handle larger or smaller configurations of bits—just as you and I can process sentences as well as letters. It means only that the standard package for data processing and transfers is based on bytes.

Because we often have occasion to deal with very large numbers of bytes of memory (millions or even billions of bytes), terms to express these quantities have become common. For technical reasons, memory is actually manufactured to contain quantities of bytes measured in powers of 2.

Memory address space

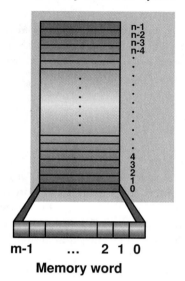

m-1   ...   2 1 0

Memory word

FIGURE 4.16

Main memory is divided into fixed-sized units called words. Each word has m bits or binary digits. Accordingly, these bits are addressed from 0 to m − 1. Each of these words holds data or instructions and can be fetched by its address. Word addresses are also numbers. For n addressable words of memory, the addresses range from 0 to n − 1.

FIGURE 4.17

Dynamic RAM for most desktop computers today is based on microchip integrated technology. Pictured here are two types of memory units: single in-line memory modules (SIMMs) and dual in-line memory modules (DIMMs).

For example, 2^{10} (=1024) bytes is called a **kilobyte** (abbreviated **K** or **KB**). For estimates, we can and usually do think of a kilobyte as 1000 bytes because 1024 is very close to this value. A thousand kilobytes (approximately 1 million bytes) is referred to as a **megabyte** (abbreviated **MB**), and a thousand megabytes (approximately 1 billion bytes) is referred to as a **gigabyte** (abbreviated **GB**). On rare occasions, you may see mention of a thousand gigabytes (approximately 1 trillion bytes); this is dubbed a **terabyte.**

The two most important forms of main memory are called **random access memory (RAM)** and **read-only memory (ROM).** ("RAM" is something of a misnomer because read-only memory is randomly accessible too.) The larger amount of main memory is devoted to RAM. These days, the amount of RAM in a typical desktop system is somewhere between 16 and 64 megabytes. ROM is more often in the 4–8 megabyte range. **Reading** a memory item means consulting its contents, while **writing** an item means storing something in its address. Reading is nondestructive because a *copy* of the contents is transferred from the memory unit, but the original contents remain unchanged. On the other hand, writing is destructive because the original contents are *replaced* by the new data. RAM units are sometimes referred to as readable-writable because they can both send and receive items. They are called "random access" because each memory word is accessible immediately by its address. For example, to read from memory, the CPU can signal which items it needs by specifying their addresses. Main memory fetches those items without having to start at the beginning each time and look at the contents of each memory word.

Most RAM units today are volatile, meaning that they require a constant source of electrical energy to maintain their contents. These are called **dynamic RAM** (or **DRAM**) chips. See Figure 4.17. Although DRAMs are reasonably fast and comparatively economical, their volatility is a liability. When system power is interrupted—by power surges, brownouts, or simply shutting down the computer—the contents of RAM are lost. This is why it is important to have a nonvolatile source of secondary memory that can be used to back up programs and data.

Main memory is designed to provide the fastest possible access to data and instructions for the processor. Several factors determine data transfer speeds between the central processing unit and memory. First, the memory device itself has a rated capacity for data transfers. Typical DRAM chips found in many desktop systems today are rated at 80 **nanoseconds** (one-billionth of a second) or better. This means that their response time can be as fast as 80-billionths of a second. In this instance, "response time" means the delay between the memory unit receiving the address and either sending the appropriate data back to the CPU or storing new data in memory. Another factor is the overall speed of the computer system. Memory transfers are synchronized to the speed of operation of the CPU. For example, a fast-response memory chip may be wasted in a system whose speed cannot support it. Of course, the opposite condition is undesirable as well. The final factor, as mentioned earlier, is the bus width or how much data can be transferred between the CPU and main memory at once.

Like RAM, ROM is also randomly accessible; however, it differs from RAM in several ways. ROM is not writable. ROM is also nonvolatile; its contents do not disappear when the power supply to the computer is shut off. ROM usually stores proprietary instructions that the manufacturer has written for basic system functions such as starting the computer system, I/O operations, and the like.

Main memory is an essential component of the computer system. The amount of memory available to the processor and its access speeds can affect the overall performance of the system significantly. Modern application programs place enough demand on a computer's main memory capacity that we might be tempted to modify the old saying, "You can never be too rich or too thin—or have enough RAM."

INSIDE THE CPU

Taking a closer look at the CPU, we find several important components that define its operation. As we explained earlier, the two main functional units of the CPU are the control unit and the arithmetic-logic unit (ALU). Recall that the control unit manages the instruction-execution cycle, and the ALU is a collection of circuits that actually perform the processing instructions dictated by the program. There are also several special memory units called **registers** that help the CPU keep track of its work: a memory address register, a memory data register, a program counter, an instruction register, and one or more general registers.

Managing the Instruction-Execution Cycle

To illustrate how all these components are coordinated, we will document a single instruction-execution cycle of a typical processor. Figure 4.18 illustrates the various components referenced.

Fetching the instruction
1   The previous cycle has left the address of the next instruction stored in the program counter (PC) register. The control unit now signals for

FIGURE 4.18

The illustration represents a functional diagram for the components that make up a simplified CPU design. It depicts the fundamental units and how they are interrelated—though not how they are arranged geometrically on an actual processor chip.

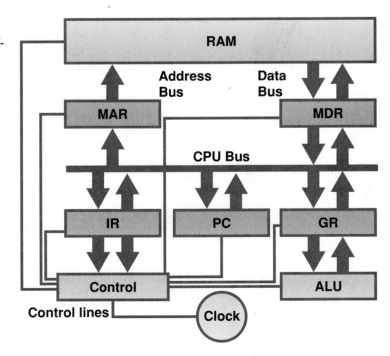

a copy of that address to be sent to the memory address register (MAR) over the CPU bus.

2   The value of the address in the program counter (PC) is then incremented to reflect the correct location of the *next* instruction in main memory (in preparation for the next cycle).

3   The instruction, whose address is now stored in the memory address register (MAR), is now copied to the memory data register (MDR) over the data bus. The MDR serves as temporary storage for such transfers from RAM.

Decoding the instruction

4   The instruction is next copied over the CPU bus from the MDR to the instruction register (IR) for decoding. The IR has special circuits that break the instruction down into its meaningful components.

Executing the instruction

5   Once the instruction is deciphered in the IR, the control unit sends the appropriate signals to commence its execution. This execution is usually carried out by the arithmetic logic unit (ALU), which may also employ one or more of the general registers (GR).

6   Once execution of the instruction completes, the CPU returns to step 1 and repeats the entire process

The entire instruction-execution cycle is governed by the cadence of the **system clock.** Each stage takes a certain number of clock cycles. And the system uses its clock cycles to ensure that all its components are properly sequenced. The clock, however, keeps an incredibly rapid beat—clock cycles are usually measured in **megahertz (MHz),** where a megahertz is one million cycles per second. Processors in today's desktop computer systems have clock speeds of 200, 300, 400 MHz, and higher. A 400-MHz processor has a clock speed of 400 million cycles per second. A single instruction may take several cycles to complete. Nonetheless, such a processor can perform, on average, millions of instructions per second.

More information

Social Themes

Hardware Designs Are Not Infallible

In this chapter, you have seen that the processor is at the heart of a computer system. The processor's CPU manages and carries out all the computer's digital computations and transformations. Intel Corporation manufactures the processors used in the vast majority of all microcomputers in the world today. Intel has produced a succession of very popular chips, including the i286, i386, i486 chips and several generations of the Pentium chip. The "Intel Inside" label adorns millions of personal computers worldwide, including those made by IBM, Gateway 2000, Compaq, Dell, and a host of other computer manufacturers.

A remarkable sequence of events surrounding Intel's Pentium chip began in late October 1994, when a mathematics professor announced that he had discovered an error in the chip's arithmetic. Dr. Thomas Nicely, professor of mathematics at Lynchburg College in Lynchburg, Virginia, discovered the error in some calculations related to his theoretical research on prime numbers. He found that the Pentium chip returned erroneous values for certain division operations. Nicely announced his results on the Web and offered his programs for others to double check. This posting produced a flurry of activity on the Web during the first two weeks of November 1994, as others confirmed Nicely's results, found even more troublesome examples of the error, and offered "work-arounds" to protect computations being made with the flawed chip.

Perhaps the most dramatic example of the type of error the chip produced was offered by Tim Coe of Vitesse Semiconductor. One form of his example follows.

Let $a = 4,195,835$ and $b = 3,145,727$.

Now formulate the following calculation for the value of c.

$$c = a - (a/b) \times b$$

With an exact computation, the result for c would be zero. But, as you will see in Chapter 8, numerical calculations on the computer are almost always approximate. What we hope to do is make the approximation errors as small as possible. Industry standards specify how small these errors should be for simple arithmetic operations like division and multiplication. These standards specify that the calculation for c in the above formula should be very, very close to zero. Indeed, when the above calculation is made using computers with Intel's i286, i386, and i486 chips, the result *is* zero in each case. When this calculation is done on the flawed Pentium chip, the result is not zero; it is 256—a nontrivial error in almost anyone's book.

Many computer owners and users were dismayed that it took Intel almost a month after Nicely's announcement to make an official response acknowledging the Pentium chip's flaw. Some were further discouraged to find out that Intel had known about the flaw for several months prior to Nicely's discovery but had made no mention of it. Even after the public admission of the problem, Intel did not immediately offer to replace the flawed processors. The offer it did make placed the burden on the customer: Intel would consider a replacement for anyone who could make a case that their computer use involved numerical computations intense enough to put their results at risk. Intel went on to estimate that the average spreadsheet user could expect to see this error only about once every 27,000 years.

Others disagreed not only with Intel's response to its customers but also with their estimates of the risks involved for an "average" spreadsheet user. IBM conducted tests at its Thomas J. Watson Research Center and concluded that an error could occur as often as once every twenty-four days for an average spreadsheet user. In early

December 1994, IBM announced it was suspending sales of all computers with the faulty chip. Additional occurrences of the error were reported toward year's end. A major New York bank reported calculation errors it attributed to the flawed chip; a multimedia software and training company on Long Island claimed the chip caused a miscalculation in a graphics program it had developed; and *Newsday* reported that scientists at the Brookhaven National Laboratory on Long Island got wrong answers in calculating the impact of colliding subatomic particles.

Finally, on December 20, bowing to public pressure and general concern about the chance for errors from use of the chip, Intel announced that it would exchange flawed chips for the updated and corrected version at no cost to any customer anytime during the lifetime of his or her computer. It also issued a public apology for its handling of the situation. In the same announcement, Intel reasserted that its own assessment of the problem indicated that it was an "extremely minor technical problem."

This is not the only example of a flawed computer chip. Indeed, the earlier i386 and i486 Intel chips had been discovered to have arithmetic flaws, but these problems had been caught early enough to minimize their impact. Sun Microsystems acknowledged a division error in one of its chips in the early 1990s. And the Pentium II chip, introduced in May 1996, was discovered to have a flaw similar to the one discovered in its predecessor Pentium chip.

The moral of the story is simple but important. Hardware designs are not, nor are they ever likely to be, infallible. As you will learn in Chapters 6 and 8, software is even more error-prone—many times over, in fact. When humans build computer systems—hardware and software—there is always a risk that these complex systems contain errors and will malfunction at times. For this reason, we must take great precautions when we place our own lives and the lives of fellow citizens in the hands of such systems. Make no mistake that we do this all the time. Air traffic control systems, modern medical procedures, nuclear power stations, and even our automobile control systems all depend heavily on—indeed are impossible without—computer systems. Hence, the important lesson is that we must engineer these systems with the best safeguards within our knowledge, including redundant systems where appropriate and possible. As our society becomes ever more dependent on complex computer systems, we must never lose sight of the risks inherent in these systems.

Another interesting observation can be made from the Intel Pentium episode. In this situation, the World Wide Web proved its worth as an incredible resource for bringing important information, especially highly technical and complex information, to the attention of a community that can validate it and explore its consequences effectively. After Professor Nicely posted his findings, the Pentium problem was common knowledge almost overnight in the computer science and mathematics communities. And everyone who wished to do so had an opportunity to test the reported errors and offer suggested fixes for those using the flawed chip. The traditional press could never have produced such a rapid and and timely international debate. Thanks to the Web, the age of global and immediate communication is here.

Social Themes

Machine Languages

As noted before, the built-in set of operations a particular computer model is capable of is referred to as its instruction set. A particular set of codes that implement all the operations in its instruction set is called the **machine language** for that type of computer. These languages, of course, are arbitrary in that the designers of the processor have created the underlying instruction set, and the many engineering decisions about how to implement basic operations vary considerably from one processor to another. Thus, programs that are written for a particular processor cannot be executed on a different one. This is why software created for a computer based on an Intel processor, for instance, cannot be executed on a Macintosh. The underlying processors speak very different machine languages, and you must match the software with the appropriate processor.

What kind of operations does a typical commercial processor perform? Basically, there are three groups. **Data movement operations,** as the name implies, move data. These operations include the following:

- Transferring data from memory to CPU (and vice versa)
- Transferring data from memory to memory
- Performing input and output operations

Arithmetic and logical operations perform mathematical operations such as these:

- Adding, subtracting, multiplying and dividing numbers
- Comparing two quantities for equality, greater, lesser, and the like
- Shifting or rotating bits in a quantity
- Testing, comparing, and converting bits

Program control operations manage the execution of a program, with such actions as these:

- Starting the execution of a program
- Halting the execution of a program
- Skipping automatically to other instructions in the program
- Testing a data item to decide whether to skip to another instruction in the program

As the list attests, a typical processor performs very basic, even primitive types of operations. The ALU has circuitry that can implement the basic data processing steps, but these steps are limited to operations with no more than two quantities at a time. How, then, can a processor accomplish some of the very sophisticated tasks that we have used it for? After all, simple arithmetic and some bit operations seem a far cry from using the computer to do accounting, edit documents, record and edit a musical piece, and so on. The short answer is that the speed and reliability of the processor mean that the system can achieve higher-order results from thousands and sometimes millions of much simpler steps. Ants, for example, can move mountains one grain at a time. By the same token, the computer can achieve impressive results by sheer speed and persistence. The complexity is built into the program or list of instructions, not into the processor that performs these instructions.

AT YOUR COMPUTER

SIZING UP YOUR COMPUTER

In this chapter, we have identified some of the basic performance factors and characteristics of modern computer systems. What about your computer? How much RAM does it have? What system software does the computer use, and how much RAM does this software require to operate? What kind of processor does the machine have? You can easily get the answers to these questions from the source itself—your computer. Follow the instructions appropriate for the type of computer you're using.

Sizing Up Your Windows 95 Machine

Access the *Control Panel* command under the **Settings** submenu found in the **Start** pull-up menu, as illustrated in Figure 4.19. The **Start** menu is normally in the lower left corner of your screen when you are operating at the desktop level (that is, when you're not currently using an application program). When you select the *Control Panel*

command, look for the *System* icon in the window that is displayed. Double-click this icon and you should see a box similar to the one shown in Figure 4.20. In that box, the user learns that the computer is equipped with a Pentium processor and that it has 32 MB of main memory. In addition, the user is also informed that the system software currently being used is Microsoft Windows 95 version 4.00.950. You should get comparable information about your own computer.

If you would like to see how much RAM is being used by the programs currently running on your system, click the *Performance* tab near the top of the displayed window. The resulting box tells you the percentage of system resources that are free. From this statistic you can easily compute the amount of RAM being used. For example, if you have 32 MB of main memory and 70 percent is free, then your system software is using 30 percent of 32 MB, or 9.6 MB.

FIGURE 4.19
You can access the Control Panel *command in Windows 95 by choosing the* Settings *command from the* **Start** *menu.*

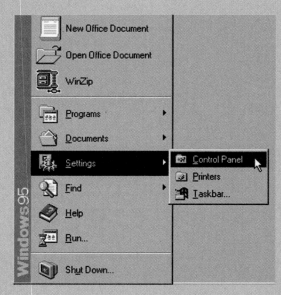

FIGURE 4.20
This dialog box displays system infor-mation for a Windows 95 machine.

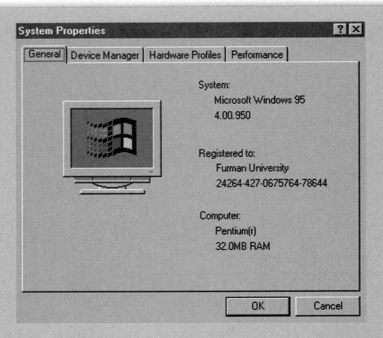

Sizing Up Your Macintosh

To find out about your processor, main memory, and the version of the Macintosh system software you're running, access the *About This Macintosh . . .* command under the **Apple** pull-down menu. This menu is normally in the upper left corner of your screen when you are operating at the desktop level (that is, when you're not actively using an application program). When you select this command, a box similar to the one shown in Figure 4.21 appears. In that box, the user learns that the computer is equipped with a PowerPC processor and

that it has more than 65 MB of main memory, of which approximately 48 MB is currently unused. In addition, the user is also informed that the system software is currently using almost 10 MB of memory, that the application software Microsoft Word is running and using nearly 7 MB of memory, and that the machine is running version 7.5.3 of the Macintosh system software. You should get analogous information about your own Macintosh.

At Your Computer

FIGURE 4.21
This dialog box displays system infor-mation for a Macintosh machine.

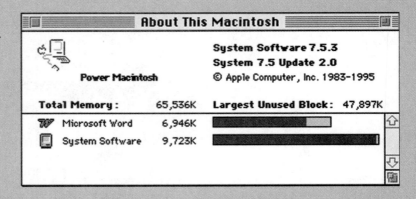

SCALE AND PERFORMANCE FACTORS

The earliest computer systems were monstrosities by current standards. Processors such as the ENIAC, the EDSAC, and the IAS machine, for example, were large enough to fill up most of a room. Today, of course, computer systems fit neatly on a desk with room to spare. The processors, in fact, are considerably more tidy. Most are confined to a chip no larger than a matchbook. And they are much more powerful than those early computers as well.

While the architecture, that is, the logical functions, of processors has changed little over the past fifty years, the technology used to construct them has changed drastically. In this section, we will consider some of the more important technological developments that have affected both the scale and performance of computers today.

Computers today span the spectrum from small, special-purpose processors that control functions in our automobiles and appliances to those that occupy rooms and perform such tasks as predicting the weather and managing complex transportation systems. The traditional classification of computers associated the size of the processor with its overall speed and performance. This older taxonomy divided computers into three groups: microcomputers, minicomputers, and mainframes. **Mainframes** were the largest systems; they served a large number of users, usually had a wide range of peripherals, and had hefty price tags, too. See Figure 4.22. **Minicomputers** were smaller and capable of serving a smaller number of users (dozens rather than hundreds). **Microcomputers** were so named because they contained **microprocessors**—an entire processing unit integrated on a single chip. Microcomputers were personal or single-user computers that were relatively inexpensive, and they had performance capacities considerably less than those of their larger counterparts.

This terminology persists to some extent today, but the distinctions on which it is based have all but disappeared. Almost all processors to-

FIGURE 4.22

Mainframes are the computing equivalents of the dinosaurs. These large, ponderous systems are virtually extinct today. Pictured here is a typical mainframe system circa 1960. Note the various cabinets and consoles that constitute the complete computer system.

day are designed and fabricated using the very-large-scale integration (VLSI) methods, which integrate the entire processor on a single microchip. See Figure 4.23. The physical size of the computer system tells very little about its processing speed and capacities.

Today, it is more useful to differentiate two classes of systems: single-user and multi-user systems. Even though the capacity to serve only one or multiple users is actually a function of the system's software (as you will learn in Chapter 7), the hardware must be sufficient to support it. Single-user systems come in two varieties based on scale and performance: desktop systems and workstations. **Desktop systems** are personal systems that are relatively inexpensive, general-purpose machines used for a variety of applications in the home and office. In size, they range from portable notebook and laptop systems to those that fit neatly on a desk or table. **Workstations** are higher-performance single-user systems that carry a higher price tag as well. Besides having greater processing speed and larger main memory capacities, they usually have specialized peripherals such as high-resolution graphics video displays. Professionals employ workstations in software development, graphic design, computer-assisted manufacturing (CAM), and a host of other activities that have specialized processing requirements. In appearance, however, they appear similar to a typical desktop system.

As single-user systems become more and more sophisticated, the distinction between desktop computers and workstations is beginning to blur. As you might suspect, the term "workstation" has a snob appeal that is favored by advertisers and others trying to impress you with their systems, but in truth, the difference between a workstation and a

FIGURE 4.23
VLSI methods reduce the components of the central processing unit to a single microchip. Pictured at actual size is the Motorola 604 PowerPC chip.

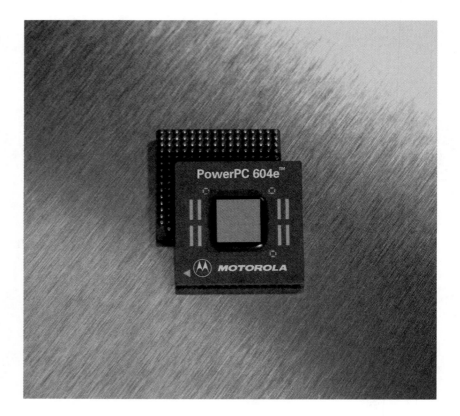

high-end desktop system (that is, personal computer) can be difficult to articulate.

Multi-user systems encompass a great variety of systems that range in size, capacity, and price. Such systems employ one or more **servers,** which in this context are powerful computers running software allowing the connected machines (called **clients**) to communicate. Servers may also be repositories for shared software and data. Figure 4.24 illustrates. Smaller systems may support ten or twenty users who communicate via a network of terminals (a monitor and keyboard) and single-user systems. Larger systems serve a much greater number of users and often distribute processing among several machines.

A special class of multiuser systems is that of **supercomputers,** very high-performance, specialized computers used primarily for scientific applications that require intensive numerical calculations. See Figure 4.25. Supercomputers often break tasks into subtasks that can be accomplished in parallel to boost processing speed and performance. They are used for a variety of tasks such as meteorological forecasting, modeling of physical systems, and graphics and image processing.

More information

FIGURE 4.24

In a typical multiuser system, a central computer system is connected to terminals, peripherals, and other computer systems over a local area network.
Connecting points over the network are called nodes. The multiuser computer system acts as a server providing processing for its client machines via the network.

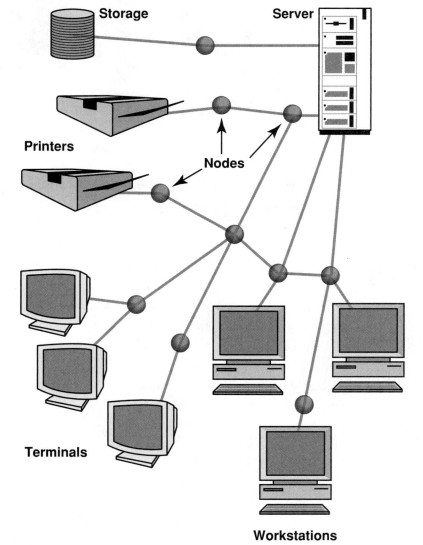

Storage   Server

Printers   Nodes

Terminals   Workstations

FIGURE 4.25
The Cray T3D is an example of the current generation of supercomputers employed for intensive numerical and graphic computations needed for scientific applications.

SUMMARY

A computer system is a combination of hardware and software. The hardware consists of the devices of the machine: a processor that carries out the detailed instructions defining the computer's activities, peripherals that allow our communication with the machine itself, and secondary memory. Software directs the operations of these components. Computer hardware by itself is capable of surprisingly few basic operations, but driven by application software, the computer can perform a wide range of functions.

A long history details the invention of computing and calculating machines, leading to the first modern electronic computers in the 1940s. Today's machines are based on an architecture, first proposed and articulated by John von Neumann, that clearly separates the logical design from the engineering details. Employing this approach, the technology behind computing machines may change, but the logical design or architecture will remain much the same.

The von Neumann machine model consists of a number of relatively distinct units. Both data and instructions are stored in a main memory unit, and a control unit manages the fetching, decoding, and execution of the encoded instructions of the stored program. The arithmetic-logic unit (ALU) implements the machine's built-in arithmetic and logical functions. These built-in operations are referred to as the computer's machine language, and this language will vary from one computer model to another. The control unit and ALU together are known as the central processing unit (CPU). Together the CPU and the memory unit are known as the processor. Input and output devices devoted to managing the exchange of information between a human user and the processor are also included in the design. Finally, secondary memory archives data and instructions when they are not in use.

In this chapter we concentrated on a study of the processor and its two major units: the CPU and main memory. The CPU manages the instruction-execution cycle, and main memory is a fast storage device for holding binary instructions and data. These are connected by a signal pathway called a bus. The two most important forms of main memory are called random access memory (RAM) and read-only memory (ROM), with the larger amount of main memory devoted to RAM. The processor is the most essential component of a computer system, and its speed and amount of memory are two of the most important factors in determining the overall performance of the system.

PROJECTS

1 Take an inventory of the computer systems that are part of the lab(s) you are using to complement this study. List the clock speed (in MHz) and the amount of main memory (in MB) those machines have. Your lab manager or lab assistants should be good sources for this information.

2 Compare clock speeds and amounts of memory for some of today's latest desktop computers. Consult the suggested computer vendor links found on the *Exploring the Digital Domain* Web site to conduct the necessary research. Report your findings in a table, comparing various computer models.

3 Using AltaVista or a similar search engine, conduct some Web-based research on the ULTRA project and the Colossus code-breaking computer. Try to find information to help you assess what impact this project had on the outcome of World War II. Write a brief report on your findings. Be sure to cite the URLs of your sources.

4 Using AltaVista or a similar search engine, conduct some Web-based research on the development of the integrated microcomputer chip. Try to find answers to the following questions. Who is given credit for the chip's invention? Approximately when was the first chip developed? Approximately how many components (transistors) were on the early chips? How does this number compare with that for today's chips? What roles do Motorola and Intel play in today's chip marketplace? What does a typical microcomputer chip cost today? Write a brief report on your findings. Be sure to cite the URLs of your sources.

5 *Time* magazine named Andrew Grove, chairman and CEO of Intel Corporation, as its "Man of the Year" for 1997. Get a copy of the December 29, 1997, issue of the magazine, read the lead articles, and then write a brief report on why you think that particular choice was made.

Projects

Key Terms

abacus	general-purpose computer	peripherals
ABC	gigabyte (GB)	processor
address (memory)	hardware	program, programmed
Analytical Engine	Hollerith, Herman	program control operations
application software	IAS computer	random access memory (RAM)
architecture	input/output (I/O) system,	read-only memory (ROM)
arithmetic and logical	devices	reading (memory)
operations	instruction-execution cycle	registers
arithmetic-logic unit (ALU)	kilobyte (KB)	Schickard, William
assembly language	Leibniz, Gottfried Wilhelm von	serial uniprocessor
Atanasoff, John V.	Lovelace, Ada	server
Babbage, Charles	machine instruction set	single-user computer system
Berry, Clifford	machine language	software
bus	mainframe	stored program concept
bus width	Mauchly, John	supercomputer
central processing unit (CPU)	megabyte (MB)	system clock
client	megahertz (MHz)	system software
Colossus	memory unit	terabyte
control unit	memory word	Turing, Alan M.
data movement operations	memory, main	von Neumann architecture
desktop computer systems	memory, secondary	(machine model)
Difference Engine	microcomputer	von Neumann, John
dynamic RAM (DRAM)	microprocessor	Wilkes, Maurice
Eckert, J. Presper	minicomputer	workstation
EDSAC	multiuser computer system	writing (memory)
EDVAC	nanosecond	Zuse, Konrad
ENIAC	Pascal, Blaise	

QUESTIONS FOR REVIEW

1 When did the first digital mechanical calculating devices appear? Who is credited with their invention?

2 Contrast a special-purpose computer and a general-purpose computer. How does the concept of a *program* arise within this context?

3 Describe the work of Charles Babbage and its significance for the development of modern computers.

4 How was Babbage's work influenced by the Jacquard weaving loom? How did Babbage's work extend the concepts inherent in the loom?

5 What is the significance of Babbage's Analytical Engine?

6 Who was Konrad Zuse? Summarize his role in the history of computing.

7 Who was John Atanasoff? Summarize his role in the history of computing.

8 Identify John Mauchly and J. Presper Eckert and their significance in the development of the modern computer.

9 What was the ENIAC? What does the acronym stand for?

10 Describe the major contribution John von Neumann made to the development of the modern computer.

11 Identify the distinguishing characteristics of the von Neumann computer architectural model.

12 Why is the stored-program concept important for general-purpose computing?

13 Describe the von Neumann instruction-execution cycle.

14 What does the acronym CPU stand for? What is its significance?

15 Describe the function of the I/O subsystem in a modern electronic digital computer.

16 Describe the function of the processor subsystem in a modern electronic digital computer.

17 What do the acronyms RAM and ROM stand for? Explain what they mean and how they differ.

18 Describe the overall structure of a computer's main memory.

19 What is meant when we say that RAM is volatile?

20 What is meant by a "word" of main memory?

21 What does the computer system clock do? Why is its speed so important?

22 Explain what a machine language is.

23 Define and compare the terms "microcomputer," "minicomputer," and "mainframe" computer. What relevance do these terms have in today's computer domain?

24 Compare and contrast single-user and multi-user computer systems. How do they differ with respect to scale and performance?

In the previous chapter, we focused on the organization and workings of the basic processor. As you recall, the processor is composed of two chief components, the CPU and main memory. Main memory stores the data and instructions used in processing. The CPU manages the execution of programs stored in memory. A processor by itself, however, is neither very capable nor useful. First, it needs a great deal of supplemental storage to retain both data and programs not in current use. Moreover, the processor has little to do without some means of receiving data and producing it. These, of course, are the responsibilities of the input/output (I/O) subsystem. As introduced in the last chapter, the I/O subsystem is a collection of devices dedicated to secondary storage and the input/output functions of transferring data between the user and the system. In this chapter, we will consider the basic forms of secondary memory and examine the variety of ways in which input and output are performed.

OBJECTIVES

- *The operation of two classes of secondary memory devices: sequential access (magnetic tape) and direct access devices (magnetic and optical disks) and their respective storage media*

- *How primary and secondary memory are organized for typical processing tasks on a desktop computer system*

- *How data is organized and stored on magnetic tape, disks, and optical discs*

- *An overview of typical devices for the input and output of information including keyboards, display monitors, printers, and more*

CHAPTER 5

SECONDARY MEMORY AND INPUT/OUTPUT

Vasily Kandinsky, *Dominant Curve*, April 1936. Solomon R. Guggenheim Museum

SECONDARY MEMORY

We have seen that main memory comprises electronic circuits organized to store addressable strings of binary digits. Most of the memory in a processor is dedicated to readable/writable random access memory (RAM). While the speed of RAM is its chief asset, its capacity, physical size, and cost are its greatest liabilities. In terms of cost per bit, RAM is too expensive for all storage needs. Even if it were economical, the amount of space and the power supply needed to support it would be prohibitive. Also, without a continuous power supply, RAM is useless for long-term storage because its contents disappear every time the computer is turned off. For these reasons, computer systems require a source of secondary (sometimes called external) memory. **Secondary memory** satisfies two main objectives:

- Permanent storage in the place of volatile RAM
- Cheaper, mass storage for long-term use

Secondary memory is cheaper, has greater capacities, is nonvolatile, and usually is a more compact means of storage than RAM. On the downside, it has significantly slower access and retrieval times.

Types of Secondary Memory

Classifying forms of secondary memory by their access methods is convenient. There are two general classes: direct access storage devices and media, and sequential access storage devices and media.

Direct access storage devices (DASD) and media are organized to permit immediate access of data items without having to search the content of stored data. In this respect, these devices resemble how RAM works. The differences, however, are speed of access and retrieval times. Direct access technologies have mechanical components that are significantly slower than the electronic circuits employed in main memory.

Sequential access storage devices (SASD) and media are constrained by their linear physical organization. Linear organization means that items are stored on the medium one after the other from start to end. For this reason, data must be retrieved by traversing sequentially across the medium. Retrieval times for SASD can be significantly slower than even for DASD—especially if significant amounts of content searching or sequential searching are required.

The situation is very similar to audio playback devices for tape versus compact discs. Audio tape performs much like sequential access media, while digital audio CDs function like direct access media. To find a particular passage on an audio cassette tape, you must fast forward or rewind the tape to the appropriate location. This can often mean searching for the passage—listening to short bits of the tape to determine the desired passage. On the other hand, a compact disc supports direct access. You may go immediately to a given passage provided that it is indexed. In fact, you can program the CD player to play a collection of pieces in any arbitrary order. This is possible because the CD player can immediately locate the beginning of each piece without searching through the disc's musical content.

Magnetic tape is the most commonly used sequential access storage medium. It comes in a variety of formats and is used primarily for archiving large amounts of information. Direct access storage devices and media are more common. **Magnetic disks** are direct access media that come in two varieties. **Magnetic floppy disks** are used for storing modest amounts of data. **Magnetic hard disks** have much greater capacities for storing data and faster access speeds. Floppy disks are convenient, though, because they can be detached easily from their devices (called "drives") and stored apart from the computer system. Recently, removable hard disks have offered an alternative to lower capacity and slower access floppy disks. **Removable hard disks** are direct access media that have similar performance to conventional hard disks and the transportability of floppy disks. **Optical discs** are another class of direct access devices and media. Optical discs generally have much greater capacities for storing data than magnetic disks. They come in a variety of formats. Most are permanent forms of storage; data stored on these discs is not erasable. **Compact disc–read-only memory (CD-ROM)** is the most common type of nonerasable optical disc. Newer technologies for optical discs provide erasable, writable storage that functions much like traditional hard disks.

The differences between direct access and sequential access devices can be significant for information processing. Because most data is stored and retrieved from secondary memory, the choice of the type of storage device can be a crucial one. Factors such as overall response time and economy play important roles in these decisions.

The Memory and Storage Hierarchy

Faced with a daunting array of choices for storing data, it would be natural to ask, "Why so many types of memory?" The problem is that RAM is too expensive to be adequate for all processing needs. SASD and DASD technologies suggest alternatives to RAM that are more economical but they sacrifice speed of response. Secondary memory devices and media, however, differ considerably with respect to both cost and response time. It is customary to think of memory devices and media as building a hierarchy, as pictured in Figure 5.1.

The hierarchy is organized to represent the inverse relationship between cost and speed for computer storage. RAM is both the fastest form of memory available to the processor and the most expensive in terms of cost per bit.

At the next level are magnetic hard disks. These drives and their media are much more economical in their cost per bit than RAM but significantly slower. As you may recall, RAM access speeds are measured in nanoseconds—that is, billionths of a second. The fastest hard drives have response times measured in microseconds, or millionths of a second. To put this in perspective, consider this analogy. Our lives are measured in seconds, minutes, and so on. Suppose that you were a CPU waiting for data to be delivered from a magnetic hard disk. If the average response time for a fast magnetic hard drive is 10 microseconds, then (equating the CPU's nanoseconds to human seconds) you would have to wait over $2\frac{3}{4}$ hours to receive the data!

Removable magnetic hard drives and disks are at the third level of the hierarchy. These media have smaller capacities than comparably sized nonremovable magnetic hard disks, but their cost per bit is still more economical. In terms of performance, they are somewhat slower than the fastest magnetic hard drives.

FIGURE 5.1

The traditional storage hierarchy is intended to convey the relationship in cost and convenience of the various forms of storage available for a computer system. The top level is occupied by random access memory (RAM). The next four levels (colored in shades of blue here) are direct access devices and media. Finally, at the bottom is the only sequential access medium—magnetic tape. The pyramid is arranged so that, from top to bottom, it represents forms of memory that decrease in their relative cost per bit for storage. At the same time, the levels from bottom to top increase in their relative speed of access. For example, RAM has both the fastest access speed and the greatest cost per bit for storage. On the other hand, magnetic tape as a storage medium has the least cost per bit, but its sequential access makes it the slowest in access speed.

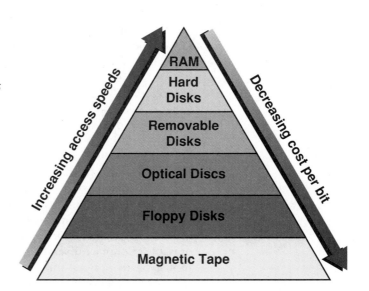

Optical drives and discs occupy the fourth level. These media usually have greater capacities than magnetic hard disks and a lower cost per bit. They are also slightly slower in response time compared to hard disks. Magnetic floppy disks complete the direct access category. Though floppies have low capacities, they are very inexpensive. On the other hand, they are significantly slower than other forms of direct access media.

At the bottom of the hierarchy is magnetic tape. Most tape formulations have very high data capacities; a great deal of data can be stored in a small amount of space. Tape is also very economical. Unfortunately, the limitations of sequential access render it the slowest medium.

The traditional storage hierarchy is useful for understanding the conceptual lay of the land, but what does all of this mean for practical applications? For the typical desktop computer system, there is a comparable version of the memory hierarchy. As shown in Figure 5.2, we can think of main memory (RAM) and different forms of secondary memory as arranged in a series of levels based on their roles in storing and processing information. Any data that is being processed currently must come from RAM. Just as the instructions of the program are loaded into main memory for execution, all data that these programs process must *at some time* be stored in RAM. This ensures that processing is both simpler and faster for the CPU. Not all data, though, can live permanently in RAM: there is simply not enough room to store it all. Information that is not currently being used must be transferred to another medium. Most computers are organized to handle this in an orderly fashion.

Figure 5.2 represents the memory hierarchy from an operational perspective. The levels in this context depict how data flows within the system during processing. Information that is currently being processed must be transferred to and stored in main memory. Data that is used often for processing or is about to be processed is usually transferred to and stored on magnetic hard disks. These disks service timely data well because they are continuously connected to the system and have the fastest response times among secondary memory devices. Magnetic hard disks are an important part of any desktop computer system, but they generally serve only as an intermediate form of storage. They seldom have enough capacity for all storage needs, and they are inconvenient for introducing data into the system.

FIGURE 5.2

From the user's standpoint, a more practical version of the hierarchy is shown here. Random access memory occupies the highest level because all processing depends on it for primary storage. Magnetic hard disks occupy the second level because nearly all data and programs are transferred to and from them as a part of normal processing. The second level serves as constant or online storage. But there is usually a third level of storage devices and media that are needed for either introducing data into the system or archiving it for security. These are offline forms of storage. At this level are optical discs, magnetic floppy disks that are popular means for introducing data into the system. Likewise, removable disks and magnetic tape are popular choices for archiving data—though floppy disks and optical discs may be used in this capacity as well.

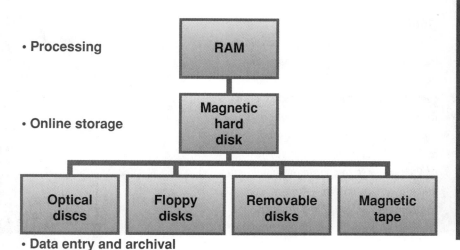

- Processing
- Online storage
- Data entry and archival

For these reasons, another level of devices and media is needed. Optical discs, removable hard disks, and floppy disks can serve as entry points for data into a system. For example, programs or software can be installed from floppy disks or optical discs, such as CD-ROMs. Removable hard disks can be used to transport large data files from one computer to another. Their data can be copied to a (nonremovable) magnetic hard disk for eventual processing.

Data can be read by the system from magnetic tape, too, though tape is normally used for copying data from other media. Copying the contents of the hard drive, for example, to a tape cartridge creates what is called a **system backup.** Copying or **archiving** data from a computer system and storing it separately is important for routine maintenance. Backups can be used to restore a computer system when data is lost. Floppy disks and removable hard disks can be employed as backups, too. Floppies, of course, are limited in capacity; removable hard disks are a much more expensive medium than tape. Nonerasable optical discs are not suitable for backups. Their permanence, however, does make them ideal for storing published data—such as permanent records—that we wish to keep secure.

Figure 5.3 illustrates an example of both how information is introduced into a system and how it migrates during processing. Suppose that you wish to install a program to execute on your computer. The program must first be introduced or "loaded" into the memory devices of your system. The software might be distributed on a floppy disk, which can be inserted into a floppy disk drive, as shown in Figure 5.3(a). A copy (b) of the program is transferred to the magnetic hard disk of your system. Installing the program on the hard drive makes it easier to load into RAM (c) for execution and means that it is readily available for reuse. When the program is executing, three copies of it coexist at the different levels of the memory hierarchy: in RAM (c), on the hard disk (b), and on the floppy disk (a). When the program terminates, the space in RAM is freed for other uses, and only the two disk copies (a) and (b) remain. If you perform a system backup and copy the entire contents of your hard disk to tape, another copy of the program (d) will be transferred to the backup tape. Thus, the program could be reinstalled if hard disk version (b) becomes corrupted and you misplace the original copy (a) on the floppy disk.

FIGURE 5.3

A program file may be introduced into the system by means of a floppy disk, as shown in (a). The file might be copied to the magnetic hard disk both for storage and faster installation (b). Once the program is installed and executing, a copy of the file (c) resides in RAM at least temporarily. Should you make a system backup—that is, copy the contents of your hard drive to magnetic tape—a copy of the program would also be stored on the tape cartridge (d).

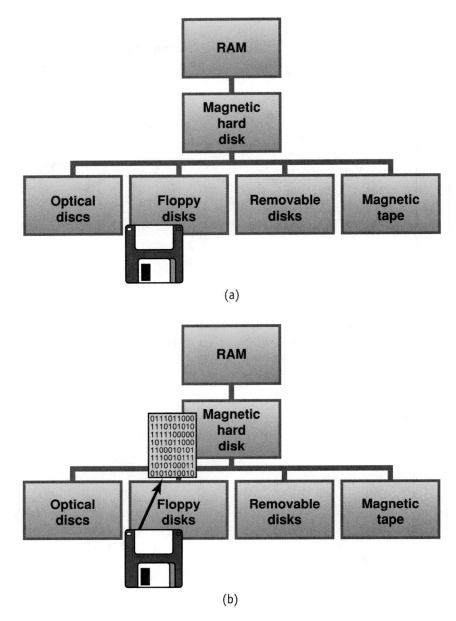

In a typical desktop computer system, the variety of processing performed dictates what sort of secondary storage will be required. All systems must have at least two levels of memory to function efficiently: RAM and readable, writable direct access secondary memory—usually a hard disk. An additional level adds functionality to the system by providing a means for introducing data to the system or archiving data from it.

How Much Storage?

How much data can secondary storage media hold? That depends, of course, on the device used. Capacities and actual amounts of data are typically expressed in the standard unit of bytes. In previous chapters, we

FIGURE 5.3—continued

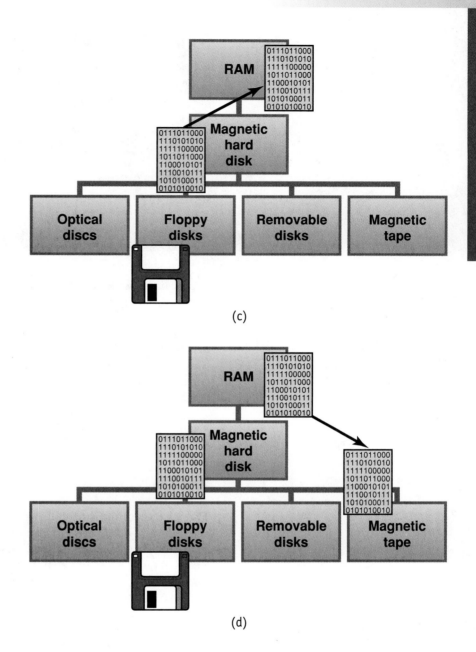

(c)

(d)

have referred to the byte as the fundamental unit of digital data. Bytes are organized in quantities to represent and store useful forms of information. Because binary numbering is the natural language for computers, it is convenient to express quantities of storage in powers of 2. For example, a **kilobyte** is 2^{10} bytes, that is 1,024 bytes. Kilobytes are often abbreviated as simply **KB.** Thus, 32K is actually 32×2^{10} or 32,768—which is approximately 32,000. This has led to the common practice of referring to kilobytes as roughly equivalent to thousands of bytes. Note that the term "K" has slipped into the vernacular and we often hear that an automobile, for instance, costs "32K." In this context, we would expect to pay $32,000 and no more. The moral of the story is that money is decimal, but for computers powers of 2 rule. Table 5.1 details the most common units of measure for computer storage.

More Information

TABLE 5.1

POWERS OF TWO FOR MEASURING STORAGE				
Unit	*Abbreviation*	*Power of 2*	*Quantity of Bytes*	
kilobyte	KB	10 =	1,024	(≈ 1 thousand)
megabyte	MB	20 =	1,048,576	(≈ 1 million)
gigabyte	GB	30 =	1,073,741,824	(≈ 1 billion)
terabyte	TB	40 =	1,099,511,627,000	(≈ 1 trillion)

MORE ABOUT SEQUENTIAL ACCESS STORAGE DEVICES AND MEDIA

Today magnetic tape is the last remaining form of sequential access devices and media still commonly used. Magnetic tape systems have been the workhorse for computer data storage since the early days of computing. Magnetic tape represents a form of **offline storage;** the media may be detached and stored separately, apart from the system. This contrasts with **online storage,** which is continually attached to and therefore constantly available to the system. Because tape may be taken offline, it is suitable for both mass storage and archiving information.

First, we will examine briefly how magnetic tape stores information. Then, we will consider some of the implications of its sequential storage and access for normal use.

How Data Is Stored on Tape

The tape medium is usually a plastic compound having several layers. See Figure 5.4. The top is composed of a thin coat containing magnetic particles. This layer is attached to a substrate for stability and sometimes a back coating. The thin coat in the top layer is typically based on ferrite alloys. Older formulations employ metallic oxide compounds; newer ones are composed of pure metallic particles. The atoms of these alloys

FIGURE 5.4

A cutaway of a strip of magnetic tape reveals several layers. The top coat is a polymer binder in which magnetic particles are suspended. One or two undercoats add stability to the medium. The total thickness, though, is still only about 500 microinches.

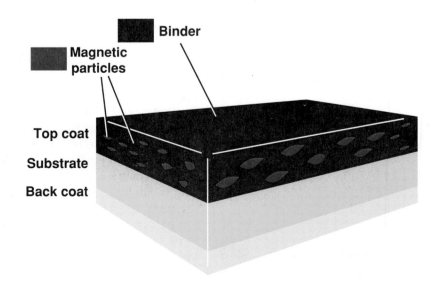

FIGURE 5.5

The polarity for magnetic particles on an unmagnetized medium (left) are arranged randomly. When magnetized, these domains (right) have a uniform polarity.

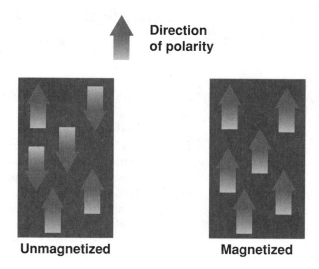

Direction of polarity

Unmagnetized　　　**Magnetized**

are easily magnetized. Atoms of elements such as iron, cobalt, chromium, and nickel behave like natural magnets and align themselves in microscopic clumps called **domains.** Usually, however, domains are randomly distributed. On the other hand, when a strong magnetic force is applied to them, the domains can be polarized or realigned. See Figure 5.5.

The magnetic tape is fed through a device called a **tape drive,** which can wind and unwind the tape, thereby exposing the surface to a sensing device called the **read/write head.** The read/write head contains an electrical coil that induces a magnetic charge. To write data on the tape, the coil is charged as the tape passes over it. This establishes a uniform polarity for the portion of the surface that it contacts. See Figure 5.6. The polarity—that is, the alignment of the domains—can also be reversed. This means that the tape is capable of storing a two-value coding scheme based on the transitions from one polarity to another. Consequently, there is a natural translation for binary data. The magnetic pattern stored on the tape is relatively permanent until altered by another magnetic source—such as overwriting the tape.

When the magnetizing current is turned off, the same coil that wrote the tape can be used to read it by sensing the magnetic properties of that portion of the tape that passes over it. Specifically, changes in polarity on the tape cause a current in the magnetic coil of the read/write head.

FIGURE 5.6

In this idealized depiction of magnetic recording, the write head is shown magnetizing the surface of the tape recording medium. A current passing through the coil causes the head to magnetize regions of the tape as it passes under. The resulting signal may be read by the same head when the current is off, though newer technologies employ a separate, more sensitive, read head.

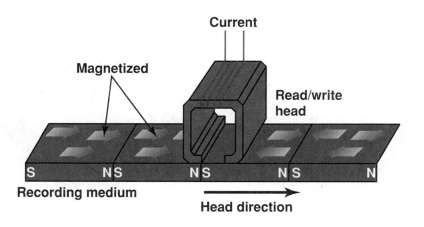

Current

Magnetized

Read/write head

S　　N S　　N S　　N S　　N

Recording medium

Head direction

How Data Is Organized on Tape

Next, we will consider how information is actually organized on the tape. As mentioned, data on tape is stored and accessed sequentially. The magnetic information is laid down in parallel paths called **tracks** along the length of the tape. The number and arrangement of tracks vary. In general, there are three basic track formats: longitudinal, serpentine, and helical scan, depending on the type of tape used. Figures 5.7, 5.8, and 5.9 illustrate the different geometries of arranging tracks on magnetic tapes.

Longitudinal tracking means that the tracks are arranged along the entire length of the tape. In its conventional form, it also means that the data for a single byte is stored in multiple parallel tracks. Multiple heads, therefore, allow for the bits to be read simultaneously as the tape passes through the head assembly. **Serpentine tracking** is similar geometrically, but the data is stored sequentially in a single track. A single tape head could read the data by reading one track after another as the tape is wound back and forth. **Helical scan tracking** is derived from videotape

FIGURE 5.7

Nine-track blocking is a popular form for longitudinal track formats. As shown here, each track is written parallel to the tape edge. A single byte of data is the combination of parallel bits from all nine tracks in the same position. (The ninth bit is used for error detection.)

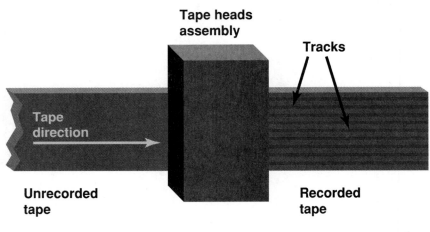

FIGURE 5.8

In the serpentine format, all tracks are arranged longitudinally; however, the bytes of data are written continuously on a single track. At the end of the tape, the track direction is reversed. This is a popular format used for archiving data.

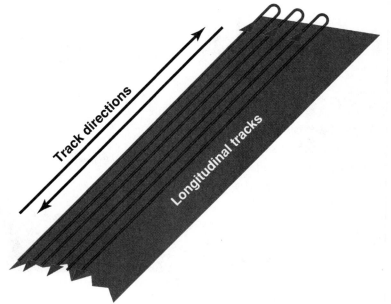

FIGURE 5.9

Helical scan formatting applies the same geometry used for VCR and other video tapes. Tracks are arranged in a helix or spiral rather than longitudinally along the tape.

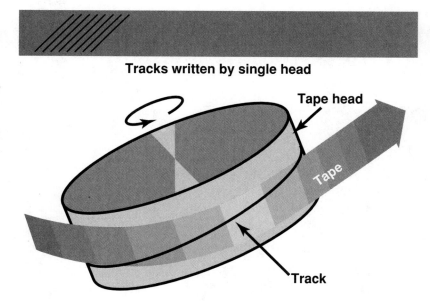

Tracks written by single head

Tape head

Tape

Track

FIGURE 5.9

Helical scan formatting applies the same geometry used for VCR and other video tapes. Tracks are arranged in a helix or spiral rather than longitudinally along the tape.

technology. The tracks are arranged in a spiral that supports a greater data density per square inch compared to the other formats.

Varieties of Tape

Tape comes in two general forms: reel tape, which is an older and more traditional method of mass storage, and cartridge and cassette tapes, which are used commonly as inexpensive means of copying or archiving other sources of secondary memory in a computer system. Reel-to-reel tape systems were the mainstay of data storage for several decades. These systems typically employed half-inch-width tape with seven or nine longitudinal tracks. Tape drives the size of refrigerators were equipped with multiple read/write heads positioned over each track in parallel. In nine-track format—sometimes called **nine-track blocking**—nine heads could read or write nine bits of information simultaneously. See Figure 5.7. As you know, eight bits represent a byte of information, and the ninth bit, called the **parity bit,** is used for error detection. Today reel-to-reel tape systems have largely been replaced by cartridge systems. Tape cartridges enclose the tape on a single take-up reel within a protective case. Even so, a significant amount of archived data remains in the older reel tape formats.

Magnetic tape is predominantly used as an economical means of archiving data stored on other forms of secondary memory. These backup tapes are used to rebuild the data and programs stored on a computer system if there is a system failure.

A popular format for desktop systems is **quarter-inch cartridge (QIC)** tapes. QIC employs the serpentine track format in which bytes of data are written sequentially on a track from end to end (see Figure 5.8). This method is sometimes called **streaming tape** because the tracks store bytes contiguously along the track in a continuous stream of data. A typical tape density is 120 tracks per inch of width, though a new high-capacity formulation boasts 770 tracks per inch.

Digital linear tape (DLT) cartridges also use a serpentine track format. These are designed for larger-capacity systems, such as workstations,

DATA PROCESSING WITH MAGNETIC TAPE

In some business environments, computing still involves processing data stored on magnetic tapes. A single byte usually represents a small piece of information, such as a letter of the alphabet or perhaps a piece of a digital picture. Larger segments of information are blocked together as contiguous bytes forming what is called a **record.** Records may be of variable length or uniform size. A **file** is a collection of related records; a single tape may store numerous files.

Suppose that a file of records is stored on tape representing information on students attending your school. From time to time, the information would have to be processed and updated. What would be the most efficient way to do this? Would it be better to process the records at random as needed? Or would it be better to process them in some specific order? Assuming variable-length records, how should the tape be updated?

Random processing would be time consuming because the tape would have to be searched back and forth to find the record of the particular student needed. Instead, it makes better sense to process the records in the order in which they are stored on the tape. This would mean that the update data, of course, would have to be rearranged to reflect the tape's ordering, but the processing would be more efficient. This approach is called **sequential processing;** that is, groups of similar transactions are processed together in sequence.

Because we assumed that files and records are variable in length, then updating or rewriting them in place on the original tape may cause some data loss, due to overwriting. For example, if a new student is added to the middle of a file containing student records, the new record would overwrite the previous one stored in that location. For this reason sequential processing usually involves at least two tapes: a **master tape,** which contains the original data that serves as input, and an **update tape,** which is the result or output from that process. See Figure 5.10.

FIGURE 5.10

In sequential data processing, the data stored on an original master tape is fed as input into the CPU for processing en masse—one item after the other until completed. The output is written sequentially to a different update tape. At the end of processing, the updated tape replaces the old master tape. Sequential processing minimizes the liabilities of storing data on SASD and media.

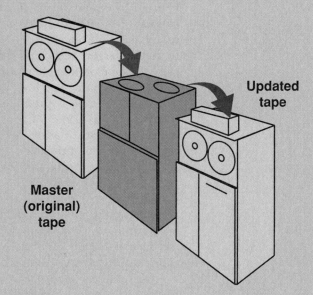

Updated tape

Master (original) tape

systems that support local area networks, and mainframes. Most DLT cartridges house half-inch-width tape. Unlike QIC, though, these drives usually contain a multiple head assembly that can read or write two or more tracks simultaneously. For example, in a two-head drive, the first head might be reading from the first track, while the second is positioned simultaneously over the 55th track, thus doubling the data transfer rate.

Larger systems may also employ 4 mm and 8 mm cassettes for backup. These are based on the helical scan technology employed in audio and video applications. Helical scanning means that the head and tape are angled so that the data is recorded as diagonal stripes on the medium (see Figure 5.9). The resulting tracks have a nonlongitudinal organization and form instead a spiral or helix if we were to connect them from edge to edge. Multiple heads can record additional tracks in an opposing crisscross pattern. Naturally, this doubles the data density per square inch. **Digital audio tape (DAT)** is another name for 4 mm magnetic tape. Tapes based on helical scanning have the advantage of very high data density and compact storage. A single DAT cassette used for computer storage, for example, fits easily into the palm of your hand and yet can archive up to 2 gigabytes of data. Because the media are adapted from existing technologies, they are relatively economical. Even larger tape formats are available that are based on helical scan technology. These serve as mass storage for very large computer systems and networks.

Table 5.2 summarizes standard specifications for various forms of magnetic tape. **Data density** is the potential number of bits per square inch, taking into account both the number of tracks and bit density for the format. The **transfer rate** specifies how fast data can be transferred from the tape to the computer once it is located on the tape. Finally, **capacity** refers to how much raw or uncompressed data can be stored. The latter figures express a range of values that account for different versions or products.

TABLE 5.2

COMPARING MAGNETIC TAPE FORMATS			
Format	**Data Density**	**Transfer Rate**	**Capacity**
(longitudinal)	(bits per square inch)	(per second)	(min.–max.)
9-track reel	110.0 K	625 KB	40–400 MB
QIC	1.4 M	122 KB	40–400 MB
0.5-inch cartridge	2.7 M	3 MB	200–400 MB
DLT	9.5 M	1.5 MB	6–100 GB
(nonlongitudinal)			
DAT (4 mm)	4.3 M	180 KB	1.3–2 GB
8 mm	1.3 M	500 KB	2.3–50 GB

In spite of the liabilities of sequential organization, magnetic tape has several attractive features. It is an easily reusable medium that is suitable for offline storage or archiving. Tape is also very economical as mass storage. Its high data density means that its cost per bit is very low compared to other forms of secondary memory. In addition, the supporting technology is well established and relatively inexpensive.

More Information

MORE ABOUT DIRECT ACCESS STORAGE DEVICES AND MEDIA

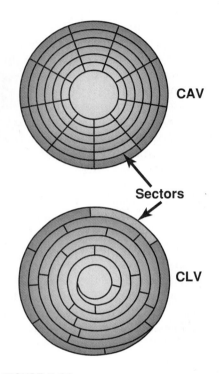

FIGURE 5.11

CAV format distributes tracks in concentric circles, as shown here. The physical size of a sector varies, depending on its location on the disk. Sectors on the outside are larger than those inward and closer to the center or hub. In spite of this, the amount of data stored on a track in a given sector is the same. Because the rotational speed of the disk is also constant, some compensation must be made to ensure that data transfers are uniform. Consequently, the density of data per track—the amount of bits per linear inch—varies from track to track. Bits of data are stored more sparsely on the outer edges of the disk than inward.

CLV has a uniform data density, and all the sectors are the same size. To achieve uniform data transfers, the disc must vary its rotational speed to compensate.

The chief drawback to magnetic tape as an online storage medium is its need to store and access data sequentially. In contrast, direct access methods eliminate the need for extensive sequential searches. For this reason, most computer systems employ direct access devices for their chief online secondary memory sources. In addition, DASD is often favored over tape for offline storage in some specialized applications as well.

There are two general types of direct access devices and media: magnetic disks and optical discs. Magnetic disks come in two varieties, floppy and hard disks. On the other hand, there are several types of optical discs: CD-ROM, CD-R, WORM, and readable-writable magneto-optical discs. We will survey each of these technologies and consider how they are best employed. But before we do, it will be useful to point out some general features about the geometry of direct access media.

All direct access disks store data on circular paths called **tracks.** Each track is divided into segments called **sectors.** Magnetic disks, for example, often arrange data in concentric circular tracks and store uniform quantities of data in sectors. The physical area of a sector actually shrinks as the tracks move closer to the center. Because the amount of data stored is constant regardless of the sector, the data is simply stored more densely on the interior tracks. This format is called **constant angular velocity (CAV)** because these types of drives maintain a constant rotational speed. At fixed speeds, the variance of its data density allows for constant data transfer rates regardless of its physical location on the disk. See Figure 5.11.

In contrast to the CAV format, the CD-ROM disc actually contains only one track that spirals continuously from the outer edge to the center. This is very much like the grooves of a phonograph recording. To transfer data stored in sectors at a constant rate, the drive varies the spin rate of the disc. Thus, this format is called **constant linear velocity (CLV).** Although it requires more complicated drive mechanisms, the CLV format has much greater overall data density than comparably-sized CAV disks. The latter format wastes a great deal of space on the outer edges of the disk. See Figure 5.11.

A new format recently introduced is called **ZCAV** for **zoned CAV.** A number of zones are defined on a ZCAV disk. The number of sectors per track depends on its zone. In this manner, binary data can be packed more densely and uniformly than the normal CAV format. The ZCAV format, however, sacrifices uniform data transfer rates to accommodate higher data densities while maintaining constant rotational speeds. Disks using the ZCAV format offer much greater data capacities than similarly sized disks based on the older CAV format. Many new magnetic hard disks and some magneto-optical discs employ the ZCAV format.

Magnetic Floppy Disks and Drives

Magnetic floppy disks (also called diskettes) are pliable disks usually composed of mylar plastic coated with one or two polished magnetic surfaces. The disk is stored in a jacket that itself may be either pliable or somewhat rigid. Floppy disks are an offline form of storage because they may be inserted into and removed from floppy disk drives. See Figure 5.12.

All magnetic disks, including floppy disks, use basically the same technology for storing data as that of magnetic tape. Bits are encoded by

FIGURE 5.12

The 3¹/₂-inch-diameter floppy diskette is enclosed inside a rigid plastic case. The diskette is pictured here from front (left) and back (right) views. A metal disk cover slides back inside the floppy drive to reveal the disk surfaces. A write-protect tab can be engaged to prevent the drive from overwriting any stored data. High-density (HD) diskettes have an extra guide hole so that the drive can distinguish them from older, lower-density formats.

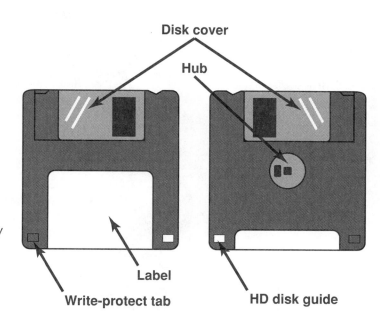

magnetizing microscopic particles embedded in the surface of the disk. The chief difference, of course, is that their media are based on a different geometry than that of magnetic tape. A typical floppy disk uses the CAV format. Information is stored magnetically along circular tracks. The size and number of tracks vary. The sectors are numbered by the system and therefore divide the tracks into addressable units called **data blocks.** Each data block is identified by unique track and sector numbers. Data blocks contain a uniform amount of data—even though the sectors they occupy may be different physical sizes.

In some cases, data blocks may be connected logically. On a double-sided floppy disk, for example, the same sectors on opposite sides of the disk are accessed by the read/write heads simultaneously. Thus, a data block is composed of the contents of identically positioned sectors on both sides of the disk. Ultimately, the size of a data block and its configuration are determined by the system software (the operating system, in particular), not by the hardware itself. (We will address these issues in Chapter 7.)

We can now see exactly how direct access works for magnetic disks. A disk in a drive revolves at a constant rate of speed. The drive contains read/write heads that are used in a manner similar to those in magnetic tape drives. The read/write sensor must locate the proper data block by finding both the right track and sector. First, the disk drive must find the proper track. The amount of time this takes is called the **seek time.** Next, to find the proper block, the disk controller must wait until the read/write head is aligned with the desired sector on that track. This is called the **latency time.** Once positioned over the proper sector, the sensor can read or write the data block. This is called the **read/write time.** See Figure 5.13. The latter is relatively constant, but seek and latency times are variable. They depend on the random factor of where the read/write head is when the process begins. Consequently, direct access transfer speeds are not constant, though the variability of the times is small enough to be significant only to the computer system, not to us.

Floppy disks come in a variety of sizes and capacities. An older format uses 5¼-inch disks; these have largely been supplanted by 3½-inch disks. The former is housed in a flexible jacket and has a capacity up to 1.2 MB, while 3½-inch disks are enclosed in a hard plastic case. Common

FIGURE 5.13

Accessing the disk information involves three stages to accommodate its geometry: the seek time is the interval needed to locate the proper track, latency is the amount of time it takes for the sector to rotate under the read/write head, and the read/write time is the normal transfer rate once a data block is located.

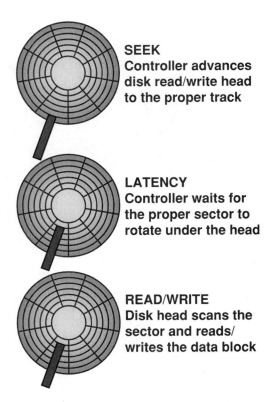

SEEK
Controller advances disk read/write head to the proper track

LATENCY
Controller waits for the proper sector to rotate under the head

READ/WRITE
Disk head scans the sector and reads/writes the data block

capacities include 1.44 MB (the so-called high-density, or HD, format) and 2.88 MB (or 2HD). More recent versions of the 3 ½-inch disk offer even greater data densities, from 4 up to 21 MB. These disks, however, require their own proprietary drives that do not support earlier formats.

Floppy disks are relatively inexpensive, but they have much lower capacities for storing data compared to other media. They are a convenient form of offline storage for data and programs that fit these capacities.

Magnetic Hard Disks and Drives

As mentioned, there are two varieties of magnetic disks: hard disks and floppy disks. Hard disks are so called because they are ferrite alloy–coated surfaces on a rigid disk made of aluminum alloy, hard plastic, glass, or some other nonmagnetic substance. Hard disks are usually permanently sealed in a disk drive mechanism to protect them from contaminants in the environment. In this configuration, hard disks can serve only as online storage.

Magnetic hard disk drives and media differ from their floppy disk counterparts in several important ways. First, hard disk drives have rotational speeds that are much greater than floppy drives. For example, a typical hard disk drive in a desktop computer rotates its disks at a speed of 3600 revolutions per minute (rpm) and higher. Floppy drives in the same system typically rotate their disks at only 600 rpm. The read/write heads in a hard disk drive never actually touch the surface of the disks; the friction would be too great. Instead, the head floats on a microscopic cushion of air. For this reason the disks and drive are self-contained or sealed. Contaminants such as human hair, dust particles, and so on could actually cause the head to rebound and bounce off the surface of the disk. This would destroy the disk surface—or "crash" the disk. See Figure 5.14.

FIGURE 5.14

Pictured here is a typical external hard drive assembly for a desktop computer system. With its cover off, you can see the multiple disks and the actuator arm that houses the read/write heads for the unit.

Hard disks usually contain fixed multiple disks that rotate together. Thus, the sectors on each disk are accessible at the same time to aligned read/write heads. Consequently, the sectors create logically what is called a **cylinder**—that is, multiple sectors vertically associated. Cylinders may constitute large data blocks for some systems. See Figure 5.15.

Magnetic hard disks have a much higher data density than floppy disks, too. Hard drive technology permits both a greater number of tracks and a greater number of bits per square inch than floppy disks. A typical 3½-inch hard disk platter has roughly 3000 tracks per side. Hard disks employing the ZCAV format can pack even more sectors onto the same size disk and thus increase capacities by as much as 25 percent.

New higher-performance drives improve response time by increasing disk rotational speeds—some run as high as 7200 rpm. Faster rotational speeds affect both latency and read/write response, although improvements in these specifications may not always translate to significant improvements in the overall performance. Figure 5.16 shows how these and other factors affect how fast data is retrieved in practical circumstances.

With increasing demands for hard drives with larger capacities and faster response, the industry has pushed the technology envelope at an incredibly rapid rate: each year new drives feature more than double the capacities of last year's even as their prices continue to drop.

From the user's standpoint, data and programs are stored and retrieved on hard drives as **files.** A file is a sequence of bytes representing

FIGURE 5.15

Most hard disk drives have multiple platters fixed to a central hub. The drive rotates the disks in unison, and multiple read/write heads move in and out perpendicular to the hub. It is possible, therefore, for the sensors to be positioned on precisely the same track and sector on both sides of each of the platters simultaneously. Thus, a data block may be distributed across several disks and yet be read or written much faster than when stored on a single side of one disk. This configuration is called a cylinder.

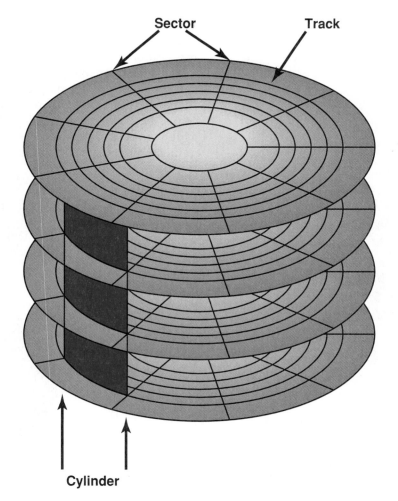

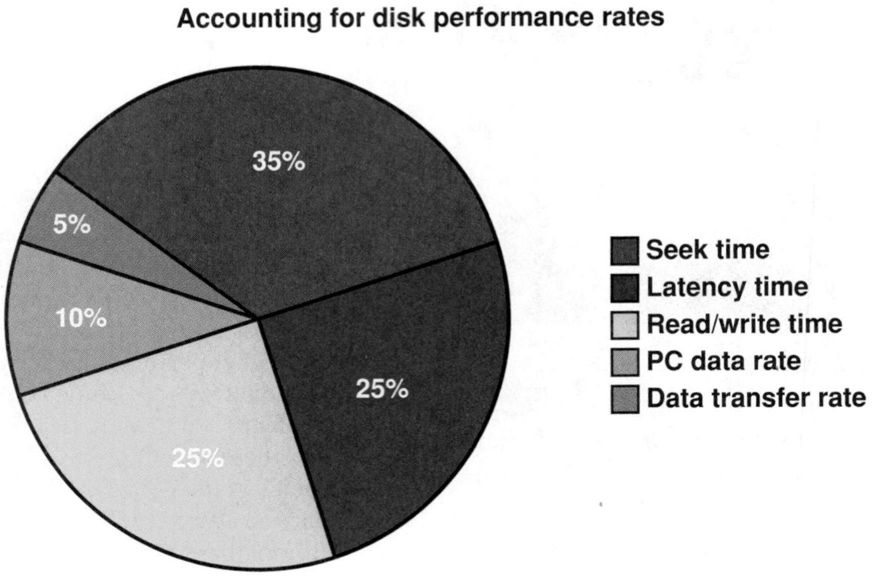

FIGURE 5.16

The seek, latency, and read/write times are significant factors in how fast a random I/O transfer from a hard disk occurs. Other factors come into play as well. How fast data is transferred over the I/O bus (data transfer rate) and the speed at which the CPU can handle data sent to it (CPU data rate) are important, too. The chart shows the relative contribution of each factor to the overall equation. Mechanical elements of the disk drive (seek, latency, and read/write) count for 85 percent, but the rest is determined by associated electronics in the system.

Accounting for disk performance rates

35%

5%

10%

25%

25%

- ■ Seek time
- ■ Latency time
- ☐ Read/write time
- ■ PC data rate
- ■ Data transfer rate

data or a program that is recognized by a unique file name. Disks—whether hard or floppy disks—store data in blocks on tracks in sectors, though. How then does the disk system handle requests for reading and writing files?

The outermost track on the disk is usually reserved for the directory. It serves as both a listing of all the names of files stored on the disk, including their sizes, as well as a **file allocation table (FAT).** The FAT lists the locations of the various sectors belonging to the file. See Figure 5.17. Disk systems, unlike tape, do not store parts of a file serially. For example, when a change is made to a file stored on disk, the disk controller simply finds the next available sector and writes the insertion there. The result, then, is that files are often distributed throughout the disk. When a file is deleted by the user, the controller simply sets the directory entry in the FAT to empty rather than erasing the file's contents elsewhere on the disk.

FIGURE 5.17

The file allocation table indicates which physical sectors belong to which files. A single file can have data blocks at various locations throughout the disk. The more disconnected these blocks, the more fragmented the disk.

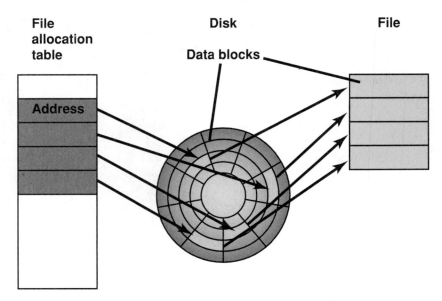

File allocation table

Address

Disk

Data blocks

File

RAID

In spite of the continual improvements in hard disk drive technology, there are still limitations that have practical significance for their uses. First, no electromechanical device is totally immune to failures. The latest technology employs clever strategies to preserve and protect data from local failures such as bad sectors on a given disk. Larger-scale faults can and do happen. Another limitation is the real-time response of disk drives. For example, capturing and recording digital video places tremendous demands on the system for writing large amounts of data to a disk rapidly. If the disk cannot keep up with this demand, valuable data may be lost. (See Chapter 14 for more about digitizing video information.)

A new scheme for hard drive systems has been introduced to handle these and other performance issues. Called **RAID drives** for **redundant array of inexpensive disk drives,** these are systems that combine two or more disks and drives into a single functioning system. The terminology was introduced in 1987 by three researchers from the University of California but since that time has expanded to cover a variety of arrangements and schemes for distributing data among the disks and drives. RAID systems offer improvements in three areas: data protection, performance, and capacity/cost ratios.

When data is distributed redundantly among several disk drives, it is less susceptible to loss when one drive fails. A simple type of redundancy would be to mirror the contents of one disk on another one. This is expensive, though, because it doubles the cost of storing the same amount of data. RAID systems employ more sophisticated techniques for protecting data while enhancing performance and reducing costs.

Distributing data among several disk drives can increase the overall throughput of the system, too. For example, if each bit of a byte of data can be written simultaneously to one of eight separate drives in parallel, then the overall response increases by a factor of 8. RAID systems employ schemes like this one to improve speed for critical applications such as capturing digital video.

Finally, RAID systems combine a number of economical, smaller drives with an intelligent controller that makes them appear as one single drive to the computer system. This strategy is a less expensive way to increase overall drive capacity compared to the cost of building larger single-drive systems.

Reading files from the disk employs a similar process. The disk controller finds the location of the blocks that constitute the file from the directory FAT. Reading these blocks may require performing a number of seeks to different sectors if the file is large and distributed throughout the disk.

The moral of the story is that files, file names, and the like belong to an abstract world created by software—the operating system, in fact. (The operating system is the topic for Chapter 7.) At the level of hardware, data is stored on disks and tape in data blocks and sectors. The two worlds are connected, of course, but they have separate realities.

The chief advantage of magnetic disks is their direct access capability. Magnetic hard disks also have the fastest response times of any current secondary memory technology. This is why the technology is especially suited for transactional processing. In **transactional processing,** the computer system *interacts* with a user or another system, usually through a series of interchanges. To do so, the system must be capable of responding to requests for processing and information on demand. For example, applications such as automatic teller machine transactions, library database queries, and airline and hotel reservations are tasks whereby the events of the process can be affected by the latest, up-to-date information stored in secondary memory. Magnetic hard disks have the response time and capacities suitable to support such work.

Hard disks also have very large capacities for readable/writable nonvolatile mass storage. There are some liabilities to consider, though. First, magnetic disk media are vulnerable to heat, magnetism, and some environmental contaminants. Hard disks have higher data density and faster response times, but they are still more expensive than other forms of storage. In addition, because most hard disk systems are fixed (nonremovable), data stored on them should be archived or backed up for security.

Removable Magnetic Hard Disks and Drives

A significant liability for magnetic hard disk systems is the fact that they support online storage exclusively. Thus, there is little reprieve when a hard disk fills to its capacity. The user is forced either to erase some of the data or to replace the drive with a larger one. Of course, data may be archived to magnetic tape, if such a system is available. Tape is not convenient, though, for handling data that is used often. For these reasons, the computer industry has developed magnetic hard disk systems that contain removable disks.

CARE AND CLEANING OF YOUR SYSTEM'S DISKS

The physical reality of how data is stored on magnetic disks is very different from how it appears to us in use. Several practical consequences are worth considering in this connection. Understanding these facts may prove extremely useful in particular circumstances.

For example, you may receive a message that your disk is unreadable or uninitialized when you know that it contains data that you have saved

previously. A disk that appears damaged or erased may actually have sustained damage to the FAT. And it is very likely that only the directory is corrupt. **Disk utility programs** are available that can read the sectors of a disk even when the FAT is damaged.

By the same token, when you believe that you have erased a file on a floppy or hard disk, the truth is that you have only released the disk space for other use. This means that the data can be retrieved as long as it has not been overwritten by some other file changes. Depending on the circumstances, this can be a plus or negative. For example, if you have accidentally deleted the file and need its contents again, a disk utility program can retrieve it. On the other hand, this can be a negative if the data is sensitive and you don't wish anyone to retrieve it; after all, the same type of utility program will permit someone else to read the data even though you intended to erase it. Special programs are available to handle this situation, too, that overwrite the sectors of the disk, thereby effectively erasing the original data.

As mentioned, a file can be distributed across the disk in many different sectors. In fact, as the disk fills, the system must look about for vacant sectors to add new files or update old ones. When files are spread out over too many sectors, the disk becomes **fragmented.** Reading fragmented data, naturally, is slower because the controller must jump around from track to track to find the right blocks. Utility software can be used to reassign disk contents by reducing fragmentation, which usually improves performance. Performing routine maintenance on your system's hard disks using utility programs can help improve their performance and prevent problems. Figure 5.18 shows how the sectors of a fragmented disk may be redistributed to optimize its performance.

FIGURE 5.18

(a) The dialog box illustrates the extent of fragmentation for data stored on a hard disk. The map shows how data is distributed on the disk. Black areas are empty; the lighter shaded blocks signify fragmented files. The table on the left lists the file names of some of the larger fragmented files. (b) After running a disk utility program to reconfigure the data on the disk, the map shows that the disk no longer has fragmented files. This is called optimizing the disk, which improves its overall response time.

(a)

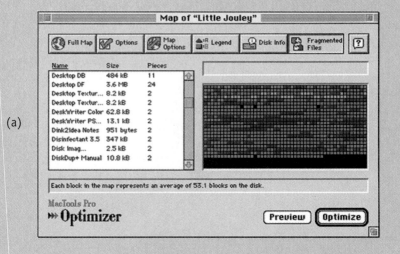

(b)

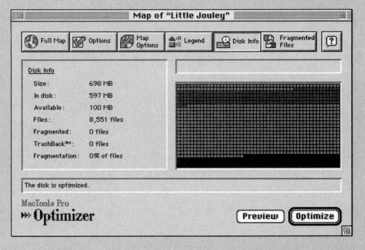

The original format for removable magnetic disks was based on patented Bernoulli® technology. A flexible magnetic disk is encased in a cartridge that is protected from outside contaminants and engineered to prevent head crashes. Though the disk is flexible, the rotational speed causes an air cushion that renders the disk rigid for reading and writing. The original 5¼-inch disk format yielded capacities of 44 and later 88 MB. The current Bernoulli drives handle cartridges with capacities ranging from 20 to 230 MB. Though the disk cartridges are a convenient form of offline storage, they are significantly slower in both access speed and data transfer rates than conventional hard drives.

Competing manufacturers have since introduced other removable magnetic disk technologies. These have capacities similar to those of Bernoulli cartridges, with even better performance. For example, 100 MB removable disks are a very popular format (see Figure 5.19). A recent version has 1 GB of available storage on a single 3½-inch disk with access speeds and transfer rates that rival those of some fixed hard disk systems.

Removable disks provide high-capacity offline storage that is ideal for a number of applications. For example, desktop publishing (composing and formatting published materials) requires storing large data files containing texts, graphics, and images. Graphic designers also create data files that take up large amounts of storage. A removable disk is a convenient means for storing and transporting such data. Desktop publishers and graphic designers can prepare press-ready files, store them on removable disks, and send them to publishers or commercial printers for publication. Of course, the recipients must have compatible drives to accommodate these disks.

In sum, removable disks offer secure offline storage for sensitive or important data. Although they are convenient, removable disks have some liabilities. As online storage, removable disks are usually considerably slower than fixed magnetic hard disk systems. In addition, the media costs are much higher than those for magnetic tape or diskettes.

More Information

FIGURE 5.19

The popular Zip disk is a removable magnetic disk that holds up to 100 MB. These disks are extremely useful for transporting files and data that are significantly larger than floppy disk capacities. Newer formats hold even more data. (The Iomega 100MB Zip® disk — The SuperFloppy Preferred by Millions™ Copyright ©1998 Iomega Corporation. Iomega, Zip, and Bernoulli are registered trademarks and The SuperFloppy Preferred by Millions is a trademark of Iomega Corporation.)

CD-ROM (Compact Disc–Read-Only Memory)

As a medium for secondary memory, CD-ROM is based on the earlier technology of compact disc digital audio. The compact disc used for audio playback is a 120-mm-diameter disk capable of storing up to 650 MB of data. Using a CLV format, it has nearly three miles of recordable track space, which counts for almost 400 times the capacity of a standard floppy disk! Data stored on a compact disc, however, is permanent or read-only memory. For this reason, CD-ROM is useful only for established or published information because it cannot be edited without replacing the disc entirely.

That CD-ROM is a permanent form of secondary storage can be both a strength and a liability. For some applications, permanent data is both acceptable and even desirable. For example, archiving information such as annual records is perfectly suited to CD-ROM. Obviously, these documents are unlikely to change. On the other hand, data and programs that must be edited or modified on a regular basis would be unsuitable for CD-ROM because pressing discs is costly unless very large quantities are produced. In fact, the economy of CD-ROM depends mostly on publishing a great many discs from the same mastering. Even for permanent records, if only a small number of discs is required, there are usually better choices than CD-ROM for storage.

It is useful to take a closer look at the optical technology employed by CD-ROM drives and discs because all other forms of optical drives and media have similar components and features. See Figure 5.20. The lacquered plastic disc encases a thin sheet of reflective metal—usually aluminum—that covers a plastic base that has been stamped permanently with a series of embossed pits of microscopic size. Viewed from the top, as depicted in Figure 5.21, the **pits** are depressions surrounded by reflective areas called **lands.** The pits themselves vary in length but are typically the size of a bacterium, averaging around 0.6 microns (a **micron** is one-millionth of an inch). The pits are arranged in tracks at a density of nearly 16,000 per inch.

FIGURE 5.20

The bottom side of the CD-ROM reveals the highly reflective surface covered by layers of protective plastic for stability. The disc is read using a focused beam of a low-intensity laser. Reflective energies from the surface are interpreted as the binary encoding.

FIGURE 5.21

A graphic rendering of a microscopic cutaway of the encoded layer of a CD-ROM disc reveals a series of indentations dubbed "pits" and smooth areas called "lands." Pits and lands have different reflective energies, and the transitions between a pit and land signify changes in bit signals. These are organized to form tracks, which are read by a focused laser beam.

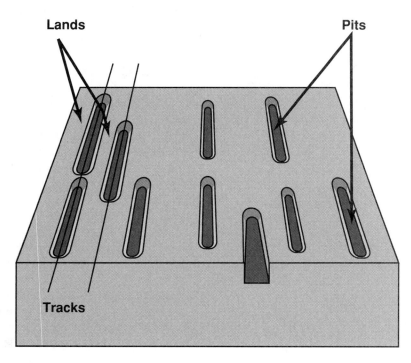

A laser beam is projected across the bottom of a spinning disc. The beam is controlled by a drive mechanism that can pick out single tracks for reading. A photodetector senses the reflective properties of the focused beam on the disc. From the bottom, pits are actually protrusions that scatter the light. The land areas reflect light straight back to the detector. Consequently, pits and lands differ in reflective intensity. Just as the coding of magnetic media is based on reading transitions between polarities, the optical sensor signals the changes or transitions in intensity rather than the amount of reflectivity itself. This works very well for a two-valued coding scheme like that of binary because detecting changes is easier and more reliable than measuring exact values.

Compared to magnetic disk technology, CD-ROM drives have a higher data capacity but slower access and transfer rates. If you have ever used a CD-ROM drive with your system, you have likely had to wait several seconds for information to be read and processed. For example, a standard transfer rate of 153.6 KB per second is required for reading information such as audio. The earliest drives had spin rates between 200 and 500 rpm, which are sufficient to maintain this minimum constant transfer rate. (Remember that constant linear velocity necessitates varying the actual rotational speed of the disc.) These so-called single-speed drives have been surpassed in performance by an increasing array of multispeed drives: double-speed (2X), quadruple-speed (4X), 12X-speed, 16X-speed, 20X-speed, and even higher.

The nomenclature is a little unfortunate because it more accurately denotes the maximum *capacity* for data transfer rather than the actual continuous drive speeds. A double-speed drive, for example, has the capability to achieve transfer rates as high as 300 KB per second—twice that of single-speed drives. To achieve this transfer rate, of course, it must be capable of spinning up to twice as fast as the so-called single-speed drive.

The faster transfer rate is fine for some forms of data, such as large images or video; however, these newer drives automatically shift down to lower rates of transfer for other forms of data. Consequently, having a 4X- or 8X-speed drive generally means that performance is better, but not in every instance. For example, when the data must be fetched in smaller chunks, multispeed drives do not perform much better than slower drives.

CD-R (Compact Disc–Recordable)

CD-R or **compact disc–recordable** is a good choice when only a few published discs are needed. CD-R discs do not have to be pressed or mastered; instead a drive may be used for writing the data permanently. Once written, the data is permanent and can be read by most conventional CD-ROM drives as well. Today, consumer models are very affordable and improve in performance each year.

CD-R media are similar to their CD-ROM cousins with a few notable differences. The normal CD has a single aluminum reflective layer that is sandwiched between a plastic substrate and protective coatings. CD-R discs, in contrast, have a gold reflective layer with an additional dye layer underneath it. Rather than pits or physical depressions, CD-R discs use microscopic dye spots to encode data. The disc is written by activating the dye using higher-intensity laser beam in the CD-R drive. See Figure 5.22.

Writing a CD-R disc is not a trivial task. Besides the CD-R drive, you must have appropriate hardware and software to support the publishing process. CD authoring software is needed to manage organizing and for-

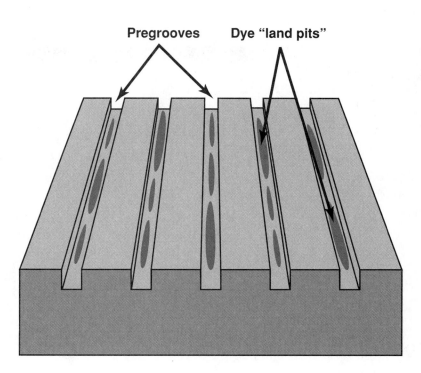

FIGURE 5.22

A CD-recordable disc differs from the normal CD-ROM in two ways. First, beneath the reflective layer is a layer of chemical dye. Second, a series of pregrooved tracks is imprinted on the bottom layer, as shown in the cutaway illustration of the disc. The high-intensity laser beam causes the dye layer to deposit spots on the pregrooves. These act much like the land and pits of traditional CDs. When a lower-intensity beam is focused on the track (from the bottom), it senses the transitions between dye spots and land by their different reflective energies.

matting the data. The computer system must be fast enough to transfer data to the CD-R drive on a continuous basis during the actual writing. This also means that the written data must be initially stored on a magnetic hard drive with enough capacity and throughput speed to match the CD-R drive. Usually, the data is written continuously to the disc nonstop; some drives and authoring software permit writing it in stages. Either way, errors occurring in the original data or during the writing process cannot be corrected because the medium is permanent.

CD-R media have the same capacity as CD-ROMs and can be read by the same drives. This is an important advantage, because most other forms of writable optical storage are based on proprietary equipment with little or no compatibility. Another plus is that media costs are falling. On the other hand, publishing with CD-R requires supporting hardware and software that add to the total cost. It is also a time-consuming process. Even so, for some applications, CD-R represents the best choice for offline data storage.

WORM (Write-Once, Read-Many) Discs

An alternative to CD-R is the older technology of **WORM** or **write-once, read-many** optical discs. These discs do not have to be mastered or pressed either; instead, a single drive may be used for both writing and reading data. A WORM drive permanently writes data to unused portions of its disc. Afterward, it can be read by the drive anytime when needed. When the disc is filled to capacity, it can be removed and replaced by another. Of course, archived discs can be mounted when needed to retrieve data.

WORM discs are also usually larger than CD-R discs. A 12-inch-diameter disc is a popular format. These discs have huge data storage capacities ranging from 6.5 GB to as much as 15 GB. The chief drawback to WORM discs is their incompatibility. Drives from different manufacturers use proprietary technology and formats. Consequently, discs cre-

DVD-ROM

The new kid on the block for optical storage is the DVD format. **DVD,** which stands for **digital versatile disc,** is an optical storage medium based on older CD-ROM technology. The disc has the same diameter and thickness as that of compact discs. See Figure 5.23. DVDs have a substantially greater storage capacity than traditional CDs. They achieve this increased capacity in several ways. Unlike a CD, which has a single layer of encoded data, a DVD can have up to two dual-sided readable layers bonded within the same disc. Each of the layers has narrower tracks and smaller pits than those of a CD-ROM, yielding a greater data density for even single-layer versions. A single-sided, single-layer disc can hold up to 4.7 GB of data. This is over seven times more information than CDs. Two-sided, single-layer discs double this capacity. A two-layered, two-sided disc can store up to 17 GB of data—the equivalent of more than 26 CDs!

The second layer is read by focusing the laser through the top layer. To help compensate for some of the potential errors caused by this process, the bottom layer has a lower data density than the top layer. This accounts for the slightly reduced total capacity for a four-sided disc. Today, two-sided, two-layered discs are rare because of the difficulties in manufacturing. They are expected to become more common in the next several years when the technology improves and the commercial market grows.

The earliest application for DVD has been consumer video. DVD video players were introduced in 1996. DVD video exploits digital methods to produce an improved picture and multichannel sound that surpasses that of analog sources such as VHS videotape and even laserdiscs.

Computer-driven DVD-ROM drives will soon begin to replace the ubiquitous CD-ROM drives found on desktop computer systems. These drives will be backwardly compatible, which means that

FIGURE 5.23
DVD or digital versatile disc represents a new generation of optical technology that will likely supplant the older CD-ROM format.

they will be able to read standard CD-ROMs as well as the new DVD-ROMs. The earliest models offer 8X, 10X, and 12X transfer speeds. Greater data density and high-speed data transfer will mean that DVD-ROM can support full-screen video in a manner impossible for the older CD-ROM technology. Though the future of the DVD format is still unclear at the moment, experts have predicted that it will supplant CD technology in the computer industry as early as 2000.

ated on one type of drive can be read only by similar drives from the same manufacturer. Today, WORM discs occupy only a 3 percent share of the market for optical storage. With CD-R technology improving, this share will likely dwindle even more in the future.

Erasable Magneto-Optical (MO) Discs

In spite of their advantages, CD-ROM, CD-R, and WORM optical discs are not erasable. Data stored on them is permanent. The newer magneto-optical technology combines magnetic and optical methods to create an erasable disc that is readable, writable, and erasable.

A **magneto-optical (MO) disc** is composed of several clear layers encasing a metal alloy interior. See Figure 5.24. Ordinarily, the metal platter is stable and not subject to magnetization except when heated to very high temperatures. To write data, the MO drive focuses a powerful laser beam on spots on one surface of the disc. At the same time, a magnetic source from the other side of the disc changes the polarity of the heated spots to encode 1s and 0s. This is typically done in two passes. On the first pass, the magnet erases the data currently on the track by writing all 0s. During the second pass, the new data is written. When cooled, the data remains fixed until the spot happens to be reheated during another writing. The drive reads its data with a lower-intensity laser using conventional optical methods.

MO discs are removable, unlike most hard disk media. In addition, MO media usually have greater data capacities compared to similarly sized

FIGURE 5.24

The external MO drive pictured here holds removable MO cartridges with a data capacity of 5.2 GB.

magnetic hard disks. The current generation of MO discs and drives, however, is somewhat slower than hard disks. The chief reason for slower performance is the two-pass method required for writing data.

Standards for higher-capacity MO discs are still evolving. A typical 5¼-inch disc based on a ZCAV format can hold up to 2.6 GB of data. The drive rotates the disc at 3600 rpm, and the average access speed is about 25 microseconds. Faster drives have been introduced recently. This newer optical technology achieves higher performance by eliminating the need for a second writing pass.

Comparing the Cost of Secondary Memory

More Information

Before we complete our survey of secondary memory devices and media, it may be useful to put these various forms of storage into some perspective. Table 5.3 compares the current costs for storing data on different forms of media. (Keep in mind, though, that these amounts reflect the cost of the media only; production and maintenance expenses are not included.)

TABLE 5.3

COMPARATIVE COSTS FOR STORING DATA

Medium	Cost per MB
Fixed magnetic hard disk	$1.36
Removable hard disk	0.96
QIC magnetic tape	0.50
Floppy disk	0.33
MO disc	0.08
CD-R	0.03
WORM	0.03
CD-ROM	0.02
8 mm tape	0.006

focus   ROMS AND P-ROMS

An interesting feature of newer high-capacity MO disc formats is that they can combine the capabilities of CD-ROM and erasable discs into a single medium. (Fujitsu, Sony, and a few other companies are researching these hybrid media formats.) Called **partial-ROMs (P-ROMs),** these discs have both read-only and rewritable partitions. See Figure 5.25.

The P-ROM can store software used for operating a computer system in the section permanently written on the disc. Another area of the same disc can be reserved for personalized

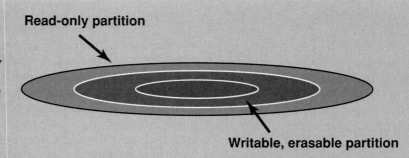

FIGURE 5.25
The partial-ROM disc combines both permanent data storage and erasable, writable optical storage. As shown here, the disc is partitioned into ROM and reusable segments.

information about an individual's working preferences for the system. Such information would vary from person to person and could be updated as needed. A person equipped with such a disc could move from machine to machine, taking along his or her computing environment. Thus, computers at home and office could look and function identically. P-ROMs would thereby create personal computing environments that supersede the boundaries of personal computers.

Software publishers could also employ P-ROMs to publish applications software. The software could be permanently written to the disc and still allow the user to store working data on it, too. The publisher would take advantage of the P-ROM's copy protection. The user would be able to employ the software without the fuss of installation.

P-ROM offers some interesting possibilities for dramatically changing our personal computing environment. Whether the technology is embraced by the industry and consumers remains to be seen.

INPUT AND OUTPUT DEVICES

So far our survey of hardware for the computer system has omitted one vital ingredient: the ability to communicate with the user. Computers have nothing to do if they cannot receive data from the user to process. At the same time, the results of processing are useless if they cannot be converted to a form meaningful to the user. Consequently, input and output functions are very important for any practical computer system.

Yet, in spite of their importance, input and output needs vary considerably from one user to the next. For this reason, a wide assortment of devices is dedicated to these functions. And, as mentioned in the last chapter, the choice of I/O devices or peripherals is usually what distinguishes one system from another. In this section, we will sample some of the more notable types of I/O devices. First, we begin with devices used exclusively for input.

Input Peripherals

You will recall that **input** means translating information that is understandable to you and me into machine-readable form. In short, input devices convert human forms of information into binary encoded data. There are a wide variety of forms for communicating information to the computer system and, naturally, an assortment of devices that accommodate these forms. We will examine a few of the most commonly used input devices.

● **Keyboard.**   Certainly the most common form of input is text. The standard device for communicating text information to the computer is by way of the **keyboard,** a set of keys organized and employed like those of a typewriter. The user presses the keys to signal individual symbols called **character codes** that are transmitted electronically to the computer system. (For a closer look at character coding, see Chapter 9.)

Most keyboards are based on the American standard "QWERTY" arrangement (taken from the second row of keys). Many keyboards, however, are programmable and can be rearranged to suit personal preferences and character sets. Most keyboards also contain a number of special keys for computers—keys not found on typewriters. For example, you will likely find Escape and Control keys, cursor movement keys, a numeric keypad, and sometimes special function keys on your keyboard in addition to the regular characters and numerals.

● **Mouse.**   Conceived by Doug Engelbart, the **mouse** is a hand-held device that is rolled around a small area of the desktop (or a pad especially designed for its use). His goal was to create an input device that would operate simply and intuitively, like pointing to indicate choices and actions. The mouse is used in conjunction with a graphic-oriented interface for communicating with the computer system. Specifically, it is employed to control pointers or icons on the video display monitor. The mouse contains a trackball and electrical contacts that measure the direction and extent of your hand movements. These are transmitted as coordinates that are used by the system to plot the pointer movements on the screen of the video display monitor.

The mouse has one or several buttons on top that are pressed to indicate specific actions while pointing. For example, the Macintosh employs a one-button mouse, while most computers running Windows employ a two-button mouse. The three-button mouse shown in Figure 5.26 is used with workstations such as those made by Sun Microsystems.

● **Scanner.**   Drawings and photographs can be digitized using an image **scanner.** The most common form for desktop computing is a flatbed scanner. Similar to the way you use a copier, you place the image face down on a sheet of ruled glass. With the cover closed, a horizontal light bar passes down the image. Photoelectric cells sample the reflected light from the image row by row as the bar passes over it. See Figure 5.27. The user can select both image size (how much area to scan) and resolution

FIGURE 5.26

The mouse is used as a pointing device for manipulating objects in a graphical user interface. The three buttons at the top are pressed to indicate specific actions.

FIGURE 5.27

The flatbed scanner has a glass platen on which the image source is placed. The mechanism beneath the platen illuminates the source in a scanning motion.

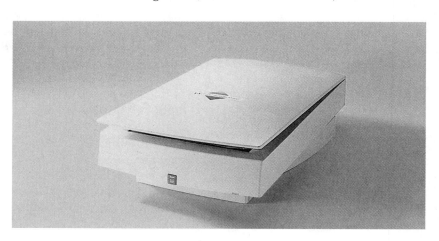

(how much detail) before scanning a final copy. Flatbed scanners have resolutions measured in dots per inch (or dpi). Resolutions range from 72 dpi to 600 dpi or higher. Some scanners produce only black-and-white or grayscale digital images. Color scanners create images capable of display on a color video monitor.

Scanners come in other varieties as well. Hand-held scanners are operated manually. These, however, are usually limited to scanning text rather than detailed graphics or images. See Figure 5.28. Slide and drum scanners are employed in professional applications. A slide scanner converts 35mm slides to digital images at high resolutions—up to 1000 dpi. Drum scanners have even greater resolution (up to 3000 dpi) and are used primarily in high-end publishing.

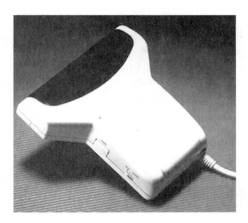

FIGURE 5.28

A hand-held scanner is operated manually for capturing and digitizing information. With the aid of software, these scanners can help translate printed text to an electronic format suitable for editing or transmitting over a network.

● **Digital Camera.**   You can simplify the two-step process of producing a digital image from a scanned analog photograph by employing a digital camera instead. A **digital camera** uses conventional analog optical methods to capture a scene but automatically samples and converts it to digital form. The digital images are produced as files that may be transferred directly to the computer's memory or stored on microdisks or some other type of memory device supplied with the camera.

Consumer versions of these cameras produce color images at both high and low resolutions that are suitable for use with video display monitors (for multimedia applications) and noncommercial publishing. See Figure 5.29.

● **Sound Digitizer.**   A **sound digitizer** is a board that plugs into the expansion slot of your machine. It is usually assisted by some software to capture and process sound in digital form. The original sound can be generated from a variety of analog sound sources; microphones, audio tape, and CD playback are a few examples. The digitizer converts the source to a digital format according to the sampling rate selected. A sound digitizer may offer several sampling rates from a low sampling frequency for voice and acceptable sound to a high sampling frequency for high-fidelity sound. The resolution for sound digitizers is also adjustable. Higher resolution translates to greater dynamic range and higher fidelity. Some computer systems have sound digitizing hardware as standard equipment. (You can find more about digitizing and processing sound in Chapter 13.)

● **Musical Instrument Digital Interface.**   Musical instruments may be recorded and digitized using microphones and a sound digitizer, as just described. In contrast, some instruments are capable of producing electrical signals that can be recorded directly without the typical analog-to-digital conversion. These instruments require hardware and software that implement a protocol called **musical instrument digital interface (MIDI)** to control the communication.

MIDI information is not sampled digitized sound but rather instructions for reproducing a given sound. Because these files are encoded as instructions rather than digitized sound waves, they are much smaller than those of sampled sound.

MIDI instruments are specially designed instruments that are combined with hardware and software to transform analog electrical signals to the coded instructions for MIDI files. Special hardware and software are also needed to play these files. When a computer system is employed in the MIDI process, a dedicated interfacing device must be used to convert MIDI signals to a form suitable for handling by the computer.

FIGURE 5.29

A consumer version of a digital camera is shown here. The camera is equipped with a 3X zoom lens and built-in flash. Pictures are stored on a removable 4 MB storage card.

● **Video Digitizer.** Like audio, video information may be acquired from a number of sources but must be digitized to be used by a computer system. Broadcast video, video cassette recordings, video cameras, and video disc playback may supply appropriate (analog) video signals for digitizing. **Video digitizers** are hardware/software combinations similar to those of sound digitizers. A special hardware board often must be added to an expansion slot or interface in your computer. With this board and additional software, video signals can be digitized, stored, and processed on your system.

Most video digitizers have compression capabilities, too. They can convert the digital video signal to a compressed format that is smaller and easier to transmit and store. (For more details about digital video and data compression, see Chapters 14 and 15.)

● **Digitizing Tablet.** Suited to artistic applications, a **digitizing tablet** is a pressure-sensitive electronic pad that converts drawings to digital form. The user employs a stylus to either draw or trace lines and curves on the tablet. The tablet permits greater control and finer detail compared to other drawing techniques using a computer. See Figure 5.30.

Some tablets have software that translates handwritten text and special movements as commands for operating the user interface as well. For example, equipped with a tablet plus this special software, you may edit text documents using conventional editing markings like those used on printed copy.

We have examined only a few of the many types of devices whose function is to translate human representations of information into binary encoded forms for processing by the computer. Besides these there are a variety of others. Many are similar or closely related in function to those listed. For example, the mouse has its cousins, the trackball and joystick, also used for hand manipulations. The digitizing tablet is related to touch-sensitive and light-sensitive screens. Some very specialized input peripherals provide access to individuals who have physical limitations that prevent them from using more conventional tools.

Output Peripherals

The utility of computers depends also on having machine-generated data translated to forms that are useful for us, the computer users. This, of course, is the function of output devices. Let's list some examples of the most commonly used output peripherals.

FIGURE 5.30

Drawings and artwork can be converted to digital form using a digitizing tablet. The tablet interprets lines and curves drawn using a special pen or stylus.

FIGURE 5.31

A video display monitor has a viewing screen that is typically powered by a cathode ray tube similar to those used in television monitors. Most monitors today are capable of displaying both text and graphics.

● **Video Display Monitor.** The **video display monitor** is a television-like device attached to most computer systems. The chief component of the video display monitor is the **cathode ray tube (CRT),** much like the picture tubes used in standard televisions. See Figure 5.31. The CRT consists of a screen composed of phosphorescent dots or **phosphors.** The phosphors, which are too small to be seen individually, are combined to represent visually the individual elements or pixels that make up digital images and graphics. When the phosphors are excited by an electron gun at the end of the tube, they glow at an intensity that is a function of the voltage levels fed to the gun. Each phosphor, however, can glow at this intensity for only a short period of time. Consequently, the electron gun must scan the phosphors at regular intervals to refresh them. The **refresh rate** is the number of times per second the phosphors are refreshed by the electron guns. Refresh rates are usually expressed in **Hertz (Hz),** or cycles per second.

Most monitors use a horizontal scanning pattern to refresh phosphors, and they scan every line top to bottom. This is called raster scanning, as shown in Figure 5.32. Video display monitors used for computer systems have a refresh rate of 60 Hz or higher; this means that the entire screen is

FIGURE 5.32

The phosphors in a CRT are luminescent, but they will continue to glow only momentarily. They must be refreshed by repeated scans of the electron beams to maintain the image. The electron gun sweeps the phosphors line by line in the pattern depicted in the diagram. This is called raster scanning. The time that it takes to perform a complete sweep is called the refresh rate.

Raster scanning

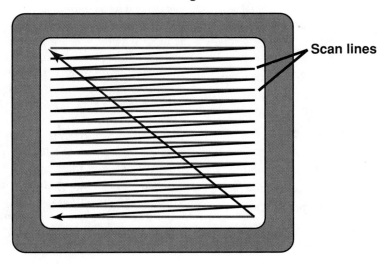

Scan lines

Electron guns

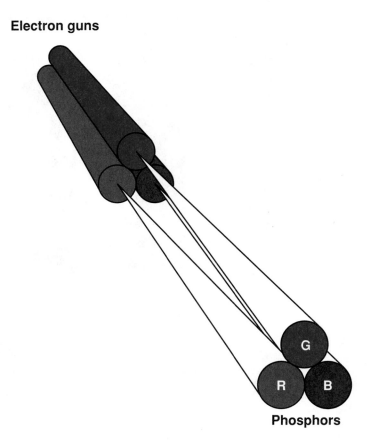

Phosphors

FIGURE 5.33

A color display is powered by three coordinated electron guns; each focuses a specific amount of energy on a single type of phosphor. The red, green, and blue phosphors are materials that coat the inside of the screen and glow when struck by electrons. If all three phosphors in a triple are struck by energies of the same high intensity, then the viewer sees a dot of white light. Different perceived colors are created by varying the intensities of the three electron beams.

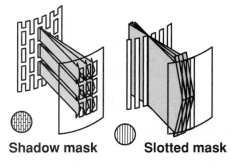

Shadow mask   Slotted mask

FIGURE 5.34

The beams from the CRT's electron guns are focused more precisely by masking. In shadow masking (left), a metal plate with a series of holes helps to align the electron beams precisely on each phosphor triple as the guns scan the line. This prevents bleeding or blurring of the image and loss of detail. Trinitron technology uses masking, but these phosphors are arranged as parallel slots (right) instead of holes.

scanned, line by line, 60 times or more each second. Higher refresh rates are customary for the more expensive, higher-resolution monitors. Televisions often use a different scanning method called **interlacing** that scans and refreshes all even scan lines followed by all odd lines. The result is a slower refresh rate of 30 times per second. This is one reason why ordinary televisions are not suitable as computer video displays.

A **monochrome** monitor has a single color phosphor, usually white. Color video display monitors are more complicated in that each dot that makes up an image is actually a combination of three phosphors: the additive primaries of red (R), green (G), and blue (B). (See Figure 5.33.) Each triplet of phosphors is too small to be seen individually. Instead, we perceive it as a single colored pixel based on its combined intensities for each of the three primary colors. A color display monitor has three electron guns that are fed various combinations of voltages continuously while focusing their beams on the primary color components of a single pixel simultaneously as they sweep across the scan pattern.

Most monitors produce crisper images by using a focusing method called **masking.** The mask is a screen that focuses the beams from the three electron guns and helps to converge their energies more precisely on the intended phosphor in the triple. See Figure 5.34. The display's fineness of dots for these types of CRTs is typically measured in pitch. The **pitch** is the distance between mask apertures and ranges from 0.6 to 0.2 millimeters. All other things being equal, a smaller dot pitch means a crisper image. Tubes having less than 0.3 mm pitch are considered high quality.

Pitch and screen size determine the **display resolution** of the monitor, which should not be confused with image resolution (as introduced in Chapter 2). Image resolution refers to the number of picture elements or pixels that make up a digital image. A monitor must have sufficient display resolution (dot fineness) to represent an image's resolution (pixels) accurately. Most monitors today have display resolutions between 72 and 75 dpi. This resolution, however, does not fully convey the graphic-handling capability of the monitor. High-resolution graphics, for example, require monitors with a high number of dots per inch and enough usable screen area to accommodate them. Consequently, the monitor's resolution will sometimes be described in terms of the maximum number of pixels per scan line that it is capable of displaying and the number of horizontal scan lines available. For example, a monitor with a resolution of 1024 × 768 has the capability of displaying 1024 pixels per line and 768 lines on the screen. Even so, because digital data is scalable, monitors with lower display resolution can still display higher-resolution graphics although with some loss in accuracy and detail.

The extent to which the resolution of a monitor is usable depends on the dynamics of the monitor with its video adapter. The **video adapter** is hardware that serves as an interface between the computer system and the display device. The video adapter translates the graphic information stored in main memory to a video signal. Video adapters usually have specialized memory units called **video RAM (VRAM),** which is fast access memory that stores a direct digital representation of the graphic image intended for the display. Standard RAM in the computer system does the necessary numerical calculations to determine what type of image is displayed; the results are transferred to VRAM, which serves as a middleman in the exchange. The adapter also converts the contents of VRAM into an electrical signal that drives the monitor's electron guns. See Figure 5.35.

Video display resolutions are often characterized by labels such as EGA, VGA, SVGA, and XGA. These refer primarily to the video adapter hardware, but they have come to connote the maximum display resolution that these hardware components support. One of the oldest is **EGA,** which stands for **enhanced graphics adapter.** It supports a maximum resolution of 640 × 350. **VGA** (for **video graphics array**) has a maximum resolution of 640 × 480. **SVGA (super VGA)** supports up to 800 × 600. The newer **XGA** standard **(extended graphics array)** has a resolution of 1024 × 768.

Many of the current generation of monitors can switch image resolutions on the fly—without the need to restart the computer system. These

FIGURE 5.35

Video images displayed on a monitor are created in several stages. The process converts digital image data to an analog form appropriate for the display device. The pixels that make up the image are initially created and stored in main memory. Most systems employ VRAM for the rapid transfer of video image data. The data is shuttled from RAM to VRAM, where it is processed by the DAC. The DAC produces the electrical signals that create the on-screen display.

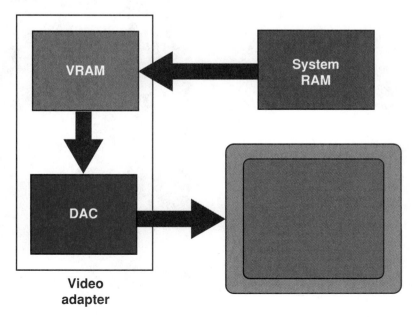

so-called **multiscanning video monitors** (or sometimes, **multisync**) are equipped to handle video signals requiring different resolutions and refresh rates. Thus, these monitors offer more versatile performance while costing only a little more than fixed-scanning models.

● **Flat-panel Display Monitors.** CRT video monitors are very common, but they do have the liabilities of imposing physical size and high power requirements. In recent years, new technologies have been utilized to produce **flat-panel displays** that feature a smaller volume and weight while having more modest power demands. The most popular of these alternative technologies is that of **liquid crystal displays (LCDs).** LCDs are commonly used in notebook and laptop computer systems, but recently larger desktop versions have been introduced. LCDs offer the advantages of full-color display with low power consumption and compact size. The current generation of LCDs have lower contrasts and accommodate a narrower viewing angle compared to CRT monitors. See Figure 5.36.

● **Printer.** In spite of claims about the epoch of the electronic office, printed text remains a popular form of computer output. In fact, computers probably generate even more paper today than before their introduction to the workplace. And because printed text is so prevalent in so many endeavors, printers themselves come in a wide assortment of sizes and kinds. Separating printers into three classes based on how they compose text is a convenient approach:

- Character printers
- Line printers
- Page printers

Character printers produce text by forming each individual character separately. **Dot matrix printers** were among the earliest character printers used widely in desktop computing. The dot matrix printer is an impact printer, which means that it forms symbols by moving the print head across the width of the paper and striking a ribbon to paper. Characters are formed by creating dot patterns. See Figure 5.37. The quality of the output

FIGURE 5.36

Flat-panel displays are an alternative technology to that of CRT monitors. Pictured here is a liquid crystal display (LCD) monitor, which features high-resolution and full-color display. LCDs are smaller and weigh less than comparable CRTs.

FIGURE 5.37

Dot matrix printers are so called because they produce text and graphics composed of patterns of dots. A close-up of the printed letter "A," for example, reveals its pattern.

largely depends on the resolution of the matrix (how many dots). Other methods such as overstriking or duplicated printing can be used to improve quality. Besides text, these printers can be used to produce graphic drawings. Although dot matrix printers fail to produce high-quality text output, they have been favored for their economy and flexibility.

Another type of character printer is the **inkjet printer.** As in dot matrix printers, the print head of an inkjet printer glides across the width of the page. But rather than impacting the page, the print head in an inkjet printer sprays a fine stream of ink that forms small dots on the page. The individual dots are much smaller than those of impact printers, so the quality of the resulting text or images is better. Inkjet printers typically have a print quality of 300 dpi and higher. Today even color inkjet printers are only slightly more expensive than dot matrix printers, so they are usually the choice for desktop systems.

Because these printers produce the page one character at a time, they are generally slower than other printing technologies. For a number of years, line printers were the mainstay of data processing centers that needed to print thousands of pages of text a day. **Line printers** print the text for a page line by line. **Drum printers** are line printers composed of bands that can be individually rotated to align the proper character type in each column. The drum then impacts a ribbon that leaves an impression of the entire line at once. Line printers naturally print much faster than character printers, but they are limited to text output exclusively.

A **page printer** composes the entire page at once for output. **Laser printers** are the most popular type of page printer used in desktop computer systems. A laser printer creates its image by borrowing a technology similar to that employed by photocopying machines. The entire page is composed by a coordinated process that first employs a focused laser beam that electrically charges a sequence of lines of extremely small spots or dots on a rotating drum. The pattern of electrical charges is transferred to the paper page as it rolls across the drum. Subsequently, toner is fixed to the electrical charges on the page. Laser printers have high-quality output due to their high resolution. Consumer models, for instance, have resolutions of 300 and 600 dpi. Laser output is generally superior in quality to inkjet output—even at comparable resolutions. The dot pattern in laser printed output is more precise than that of inkjet printers. In fact, the printed output from laser printers can rival the quality of typeset printing technologies.

● **Sound and Voice Output.** For multimedia applications, the computer system should be equipped with the capability to produce sound output. This reverses the process of digitization by converting the binary coding of sampled sounds to an electrical signal suitable for the speakers. The analog signals are boosted by amplifier circuits that match the power requirements of the speakers.

Some systems do not have the built-in capability of handling sound for output. In these instances, the conversion of digitized sound is usually handled by a **sound card,** which is added to an expansion slot inside the computer case. Most systems have a built-in speaker, but it is usually very small and not suitable for stereo or higher-fidelity sound. For more faithful reproduction of sounds, you may add a powered speaker pair to your system. These combine amplifiers with the speakers for producing better-quality stereo sound. (Most desktop systems have a sound output port for connecting such speakers.) For more about digital sound, music, and voice, see Chapter 13.

MIDI Synthesizer. As discussed earlier, MIDI is a protocol for communicating information about musical sequences. MIDI information, of course, is digital, but it is not a sampling of musical sounds. Instead, it contains instructions on how to make musical sounds. These instructions specify what notes to play and how long to play them. In addition, they describe the volume and modulation for the notes as well. MIDI information may also indicate what sort of musical voice should play these notes. For example, it may specify several voices including synthetic or artificial sounds like those of strings (violins and cellos) or percussion. (For more about musical synthesis, see Chapter 13.)

To play MIDI-generated music, you must employ a **MIDI synthesizer,** which converts the MIDI instructions to electrical signals that can be amplified and reproduced as musical sounds through conventional audio equipment. Often MIDI synthesizers are combined with instruments such as a piano keyboard for both input and output of music.

These are but a sampling of the great variety of peripherals dedicated to I/O functions in a computer system. The choice and configuration of input and output devices for a particular system depend, of course, on the type of tasks performed with the system.

More Information

SUMMARY

There is not enough main memory in a typical computer system to meet all its storage needs. Even if there were, the volatility of most RAM would necessitate backing up the programs and data to prevent their loss. For these reasons, secondary memory devices and media have been developed to serve as a cheaper and more plentiful source for storing digital data. These devices and media are often distinguished according to the manner in which data is retrieved from them. Sequential access storage media are those in which the data is arranged in a linear sequence. Each item is fetched by traversing all the items that come before it in that sequence. Direct access storage media permit the data to be fetched directly without the need for sequential searching.

Magnetic tape is a sequential access medium that is used primarily for archiving system information and large amounts of data. Magnetic hard disks and floppy disks are popular direct access storage media. Hard disks serve as the chief source of online secondary storage on a typical computer system. Floppy disks are used to enter data into a computer system as well as to copy or archive small amounts of it. Removable magnetic disks come in a variety of sizes and speeds. These are often employed as substitutes for hard and floppy disks, when greater capacity and/or portability are important. Optical discs are likewise direct access storage media. CD-ROMs are used for publishing large amounts of data. Magneto-optical discs and drives are emerging as a high-capacity substitute for hard disks.

Input/output devices are used to translate information from human-readable forms to those that may be employed by the computer system. Input devices translate discrete or analog forms of information to a digital representation. Output devices convert digital data to a form that the user can understand. There is a wide variety of I/O devices; each is suited to the specific requirements for the form of information that it handles.

PROJECTS

1 Complete an inventory of the secondary memory and input/output devices that are part of the computer systems in your lab. For each of the secondary memory devices, indicate how it is used in these systems: online storage, introducing data to the system, or archiving data. For each of the I/O devices, describe what function it serves.

2 Earlier in Chapter 2, it was estimated that a typical book contained approximately 1 million symbols. To recap: suppose that there are 70 symbols per line (counting blanks, punctuation, etc.) and that there are 50 lines per page. If the average size of a book were 300 pages, there would be 1,050,000 symbols in it. Suppose also that each symbol requires a single byte of storage. Then it would require 1,050,000 bytes to store the contents of a single book.

Find out how many volumes are stored in your university or college library. Based on this estimate, how many megabytes would be required to store your library's collection? How many gigabytes? How many terabytes? (Consult Table 5-1 for these units of measure.) How many CDs would be required to store the entire collection?

3 Consult the system manager/staff for your computer laboratories at your college or university. Find out what sort of system backups are performed on the computers that they service. Specifically, what types of media are employed for system backups? How often are these backups performed?

4 Write a short report on the special I/O devices needed or recommended for the computer system used to support one of the following professionals: graphic artist, desktop publisher, musician, or photographer. Explain how each device would be useful for some type of work performed in that profession.

5 Now that you have learned about all of the types of devices that make up a typical desktop computer, try to put this knowledge to practical use. Given a budget of $2,500 (excluding taxes), assemble an itemized list of equipment for a desktop system that has a useful array of I/O devices and secondary memory storage, in addition to a basic CPU with main memory. For each item, list its price and performance features (for example, speed, capacity, etc.). Consult the suggested links found on the *Exploring the Digital Domain* Web site for researching more about actual costs and performance features of current hardware.

Assemble a similar itemized list of equipment for a system budgeted at $5,000. What improvements does it have over your lower budget system?

Projects

Key Terms

archives, archiving	compact disc–read-only memory	data density (linear, area)
capacity, data	(CD-ROM)	digital audio tape (DAT)
cathode ray tube (CRT)	constant angular velocity (CAV)	digital camera
character codes	constant linear velocity (CLV)	digital linear tape (DLT)
character printers	cylinder	digital versatile disc (DVD)
compact disc–recordable (CD-R)	data blocks	digitizing tablet

direct access storage devices,
    media (DASD)

disk utility programs

display resolution

domains

dot matrix printer

drum printer

EGA (enhanced graphics adapter)

file

file allocation table (FAT)

flat-panel display

fragmented disk

gigabyte (GB)

helical scan tracking

Hertz (Hz)

inkjet printer

input

interlacing

keyboard

kilobyte (KB)

lands

laser printer

latency time

line printers

liquid crystal display (LCD)

longitudinal tracking

magnetic disks

magnetic floppy disks, drives

magnetic hard disks, drives

magnetic tape

magneto-optical (MO) discs, drives

masking

master tape

megabyte (MB)

micron

monochrome monitor

mouse

multiscanning video monitor

musical instrument digital interface
    (MIDI), synthesizer

nine-track blocking

offline storage

online storage

optical discs, drives

page printers

parity bit

partial-ROM (P-ROM)

phosphors

pitch, monitor

pits

quarter-inch cartridge tapes (QIC)

RAID disks, drives

read/write head

read/write time

record

refresh rate, monitor

removable hard disks

RGB color video monitor

scanner

secondary (external) memory

sector

seek time

sequential access storage devices,
    media (SASD)

sequential processing

serpentine tracking (streaming tape)

sound digitizer (sound card)

streaming tape

SVGA (super VGA)

system backups

tape drive

terabyte (TB)

tracks

transactional processing

transfer rate, data

update tape

VGA (video graphics array)

video adapter

video digitizer

video display monitor

video random access memory
    (VRAM)

write-once, read-many discs, drives
    (WORM)

XGA (extended graphics array)

zoned constant angular velocity
    (ZCAV)

QUESTIONS FOR REVIEW

1   What is meant by secondary memory? How does it compare to RAM?

2   Compare direct access and sequential access storage devices.

3   Give an example of how magnetic tape drives are used in today's computing environments. Why might they be preferable for some uses to magnetic optical discs?

4   Compare and contrast the disk geometries of CAV, CLV, and zoned CAV. What are the strengths of each format?

5   Explain the terms *track, sector,* and *cylinder* relative to the geometry of direct access storage devices.

6   Describe seek time, latency time, and read/write time for magnetic disks. How do they affect the amount of time it takes to transfer data from the disk to the system?

7   Compare hard disk drives and floppy disk drives with respect to storage capacity, performance, and method of operation.

8   What are RAID systems? What advantages do they have over ordinary hard disk drives?

9   What is a file and what role does it assume in data storage?

10 What is the function of the directory tracks on a storage disk?

11 What is the purpose of the file allocation table within a disk's directory tracks?

12 What are disk utility programs used for?

13 What is meant by a fragmented disk?

14 Compare CD-ROM technology with hard disk drive technology. Which is preferable? Explain.

15 Give a brief description of the encoding scheme used for CD-ROM disks.

16 Describe the differences between CD-R and ordinary CD-ROM drives. What advantages does CD-R have over WORM?

17 How does the current generation of magneto-optical disc technology compare with hard disk technology? With CD-R technology?

18 What does the acronym DVD refer to? What is its significance?

19 Describe a variety of computer input devices and the specific purposes for which they are designed.

20 What does the pitch of a monitor represent? Is a larger or smaller pitch value preferred?

21 Define the acronym VRAM and describe its role in displaying computer output on a monitor.

22 How is monitor resolution usually described?

23 What do the terms EGA, VGA, SVGA, and XGA refer to? What performance characteristics of a video monitor are normally associated with these terms?

24 Contrast the way dot matrix, inkjet, and laser printers operate.

25 What does MIDI mean? How are MIDI musical files different from digitized sound?

As you learned in Chapter 4, hardware provides the platform for information processing with a computer. Without a program to direct this process, however, the hardware is simply inert. Programs, of course, are collectively called software. The hardware of the modern computer system is organized to function as a general-purpose information processing machine. You and I, though, use computers for specific tasks. We write letters, draw pictures, send mail, play games, and the like. The key is software: Software is responsible for defining exactly what sort of machine the computer becomes.

As computer users, we employ application software to perform work with our machines. When you use your computer to compose a paper, word processing software orchestrates that process. While that program is executing, your computer behaves like a document processor. Should you use your system to compose and record music, the software dedicated to this task converts your machine to a digital recording studio, complete with editing and mixing capabilities. Thus, the instructions of a program transform our computers into the types of machines that aid us in our work.

Programs, of course, are written by people who speak and think in natural languages such as English. On the other hand, computers are fluent only in binary. How then do programmers write instructions for computers? Fortunately, over the past forty years computer scientists have developed special languages that allow programmers to communicate with computers by meeting them halfway. These programming languages are symbolic, much like natural languages. They differ from natural languages in that they are organized in ways that make directing the computer's work easier.

In this chapter, we continue our picture of how computers function from the standpoint of how software is developed to direct their work.

OBJECTIVES

- *The basics of the programming process*

- *The development of programming languages to improve software development*

- *Programming languages that the average user can employ to enhance working with a computer*

CHAPTER 6

PUTTING COMPUTERS TO WORK: SOFTWARE

Vasily Kandinsky, *In the Black Square*, June 1923. Solomon R. Guggenheim Museum

UNDERSTANDING THE PROGRAMMING PROCESS

Software is composed of programs. A **program** is a list of instructions that directs the steps of the computer's process. We saw in Chapter 4 that the processor acts as a single instruction interpreter: It fetches the next binary-encoded instruction of the program, decodes it, and executes it.

The fetch-execute cycle is performed over and over until the process is instructed to halt. From this perspective, the computer system is like an incredibly single-minded agent that concentrates on only the current activity and proceeds relentlessly to complete the overall task. It is up to the instructions—and this means the author of the instructions—to provide overall guidance and strategy for the process. The programmer is like a playwright who not only creates a premise or plot for the drama but also supplies all the words and actions that the actors will perform. The actors, of course, bring the play to life, but the playwright has determined in advance what that life will be. The hardware brings the program to life as a process, but the programmer makes all of this possible.

The earliest programs were conceived and created as lists of binary-encoded machine language instructions. Recall that these instructions are the types of primitive operations that the processor is designed to perform. The first symbolic programming languages mimicked the structure and organization of these machine languages. Called **assembly languages,** they simply replaced the binary encoding with sets of mnemonic symbols. Thus, an assembly language program is virtually a 1–1 representation of the machine language version that is executed on that processor. Because they replace binary strings with symbols, assembly languages are more convenient for programming. Even so, programmers still must manage some of the difficulties they faced when using machine languages. In short, the instructions are primitive, which means that even the simplest tasks require a great many steps to complete. Also, assembly language programs can be executed only on processors that share the same machine language. This lack of **portability**—the capability to execute programs on different hardware platforms—means that commercial programs written in assembly language must be rewritten for computers with different processors.

More Information

Today, however, programmers do not have to think and write their programs in such low-level languages. Instead, a variety of symbolic programming languages allows the programmer to express a process in more convenient and abstract ways. These higher-level programs must be translated to the appropriate machine language instructions before they can be executed on a given processor. But this is done automatically by system software called **translation programs,** which convert a program written using a symbolic programming language into binary-encoded instructions that can be executed on the intended processor. Programmers are free to choose an appropriate programming language as their vehicle for expressing the processing task, provided they have the capability to convert it to a form that can be handled directly by their computer.

A Sample Program

Let's illustrate how programs are organized to direct a process. Our example is a short program for adding some special effects to a Web page. From your experience with the World Wide Web, you know that your browser can display both text and graphics on a page. Suppose that we wish to create a page that displays a sequence of pictures that change when the user chooses. To do this, we will employ a programming language called JavaScript.

JavaScript is a scripting language employed to add interactivity and functionality to Web pages. A **scripting language** is an interpreted programming language. It is executed in a manner very similar to the way the CPU processes the instructions of a machine language program. Each instruction in a JavaScript program is fetched or downloaded as text. The JavaScript interpreter that is part of your browser program decodes it and generates the necessary instructions to execute it. The difference, of course, is that JavaScript instructions are much more abstract than typical low-level processor instructions. We will have more to say about these issues shortly. For now, examine the program in Listing 6.1.

LISTING 6.1

A JavaScript program is embedded within a simple Web page. The program (in blue) allows the user to display a series of images by clicking on it.

```
<HTML>
<HEAD>
<TITLE>image script</TITLE>
<SCRIPT LANGUAGE="JavaScript">                    (1)
<!--HIDE                                          (2)
var counter = 0                                   (3)
function changer() {                              (4)
counter += 1                                      (5)
   if (counter == 4) {
      counter = 0                                 (6)
   }
   document.images[0].src = counter + ".jpg"  (7)
}
//STOP HIDING--</SCRIPT>                           (8)
</HEAD>
<BODY BGCOLOR="#FFFFFF">
<P>Click on the image to change it.</P>
<P>
<A HREF="#" onClick="changer()">                 (9)
<IMG SRC="0.jpg" WIDTH=279 HEIGHT=184 BORDER=0
ALIGN=bottom>
</A>
</P>
</BODY>
</HTML>
```

The actual JavaScript portion of the listing is restricted to the statements represented in blue, with each step numbered for convenience in red. As you learned in Chapter 3, the remaining parts of the listing define formatting controls for the Web page's content.

The script defines a program module called a function. Among other uses, JavaScript functions may be assigned to specific events. In this instance, the event is a mouse click. Statement (9) assigns the function *changer* to the occurrence of a mouse click. Specifically, anytime the user clicks on the image displayed on the page, the function *changer* will be executed.

Let's dissect the instructions of the program. Statements (1), (2), and (8) act like punctuation. These simply tell the browser program where the JavaScript program commences and ends. The actual executable portion of the program are statements (3)–(7). Statement (3) defines a data object called a variable. **Variables** are objects storing values that may change in the course of processing. In this case, the variable named *counter* stores an integer value that is initially set to 0. Statements (4)–(7) define the function *changer*. Statement (4) specifies the beginning of the function and its name; the opening bracket in line (4) and the closing bracket after line (7) signify its scope. The function's instructions are composed of only three statements. The first instruction is statement (5), which increments the variable *counter* by a value of +1. In other words, the current value of *counter* is replaced by the sum of that value plus 1 more. Statement (6)

```
if (counter = = 4) { counter = 0 }
```

resets the value of *counter* to 0 when it reaches 4. This structure is a conditional statement. **Conditional statements** cause the program to choose between courses of action based on the current conditions of the process. In this case, the condition is when the value of *counter* reaches 4. The result is that the value of *counter* is reset to 0. Should the value of *counter* be anything other than 4, it will remain the same. The intent here is to constrain the value of *counter* so that it cycles from 0 to 4 only.

JavaScript stores all the details about the browser in a collection of programming entities called **objects.** One of the objects that it defines is the *document* object, which contains all of the links, images, and more that make up a given Web page. To identify a particular image, you must refer to it as

```
document.image[n]
```

where *n* is the number of the image. The images are numbered starting from 0 as they are listed on the coded page. This page displays only one image at a time so it is signified by

```
document.image[0]
```

Most objects have **properties;** these are attributes or features normally associated with the object. Images have properties such as width, height, and a source. For example,

```
document.image[0].src
```

addresses the source or name of the file of the first image on the page. Thus, statement (7) assigns a new source for the image. In this instance, the source is made up of the current value of *counter* with the suffix ".jpg." For example, when *counter* equals 1, the image source is assigned the image "1.jpg." When *counter* is 2, the image is "2.jpg," and so on. The program, therefore, allows the user to click on the image and cycle through the series of four images, 0.jpg through 3.jpg.

The accompanying diagram in Figure 6.1 shows how the steps of the program could be conceived as it executes. Trace through the steps to understand how the program works.

More Information

FIGURE 6.1

The diagram depicts the sequence of events for the process defined by the JavaScript program in Listing 6.1.

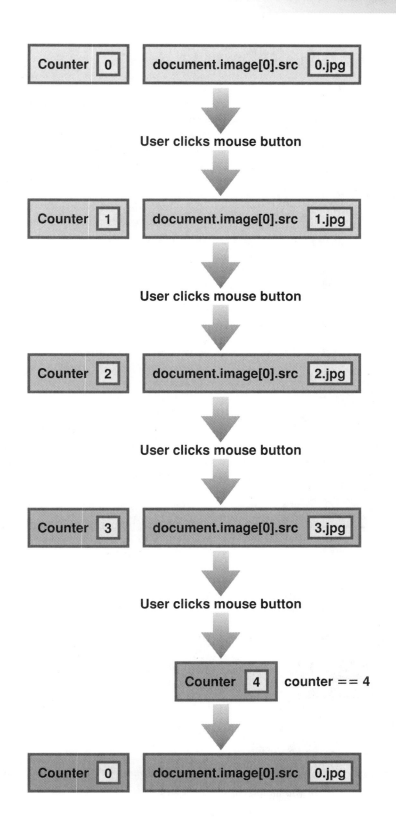

THE SOFTWARE DEVELOPMENT CYCLE

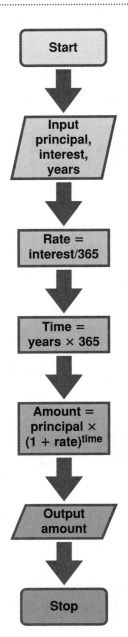

FIGURE 6.2

This flowchart shows the algorithm for calculating compounded interest on an investment. The rounded rectangles signify the end points for the algorithm. Slanted boxes denote input or output steps, and rectangular boxes represent processes. Each step is labeled accordingly. The arrows depict the flow of control for the execution of the steps.

The example illustrates how a program organizes a simple task. The example is an already finished program—all of the planning and work of the programmer have been done. How would the programmer approach the problem from the beginning? What steps would he or she take to complete it?

The basic software development process involves at least four stages:

- *Analyzing and understanding* the problem or task to be performed
- *Devising a plan* to solve the problem or model the task
- *Creating an executable program* that implements the plan
- *Testing and correcting* the program

Analyzing the Task

We write programs so that the computer can perform work that is useful to us. Consequently, the first stage of producing a program is to understand better the nature of the task we want the computer to do. Many processing tasks can be conceived as finding the answers to an informational problem: Given such-and-such information, what is a satisfactory or correct result? For example, suppose that we wish to create a program that calculates the compound interest earned on a savings account. Most practical processing problems are a great deal more complicated than this one, but it will do for the sake of illustration.

To create a program to calculate compound interest, the programmer must understand precisely what is called for. In a sense, he or she must know not only all the questions, but all the answers as well, and in advance. Only by foreseeing the entire process can the programmer create the script that can model it. Usually a program treats a general class of problem instances rather than a single case. This means that the programmer must often think of the task in very general terms to envision what sequence of events might be possible for trying to solve a variety of instances.

In this case, the problem involves calculating the total amount of an investment, given interest payments compounded periodically over a known period of time. To solve the problem, we must specify several pieces of information: the initial or *principal* amount of the investment, the periodic interest *rate,* and the amount of *time* over which the interest is compounded. Given these values, we could calculate the resulting amount using the well-known formula

$$amount = principal \times (1 + rate)^{time}$$

Each of these values, of course, could vary. We would have to know what these specific values are to solve for an individual instance.

Devising a Plan

After he or she understands the problem and its solution, the programmer must devise a plan that the computer can use to produce the desired results. The program plan is called an **algorithm,** and it should express the following:

- What information is needed to perform the task
- Exactly what events are needed to complete the task
- The precise sequencing of these events to complete the task reliably

The algorithm must also be conceived in a manner that is suitable for the computer to perform. In other words, the events or actions must be the type that the computer is able to complete.

Suppose that we ask the user of the program to specify the information that we need to calculate the amount of investment. Usually, savings accounts are compounded daily; this means that there are actually 365 periods per year and that the periodic interest rate is the daily interest rate. Even so, most interest rates are quoted based on their annual percentage rate (APR). The point is that we should ask the user to specify the interest rate in terms of APR and the span of the investment in terms of years. Our algorithm would have to adjust these values for periodic rate and the corresponding amount of time.

Algorithms may be expressed in a variety of ways. Some are charted graphically using **flowchart** symbols that show the sequencing of important events that constitute the overall process. Figure 6.2 shows how a flowchart for calculating compound interest would be designed. Others are written in an English-like manner called *pseudocoding.* Listing 6.2 contains a pseudocoded algorithm for calculating compound interest. This technique is like outlining; it allows the programmer to focus on the task and ignore the details of how the actual instructions or statements must be phrased and written. Various other methods can be employed as a vehicle for writing the algorithm. The goal is to have a clear idea of what the program must do.

LISTING 6.2

This code is a pseudocoded version of the algorithm for calculating compound interest. Similar to flowcharting, pseudocoding is another method used by programmers for expressing algorithms without attending to the details required by actual programming languages. The left-arrow symbols signify assigning a value. Specifically, the value of the expression on the right side of the arrow is assigned to the variable on the left side.

```
begin
    input principal, APR, years
    rate ← APR/365
    time ← years × 365
    amount ← principal × (1 + rate)^time
    output amount
end
```

Coding the Program

Only after the algorithm is complete does the programmer actually try to convert that plan into a form that the computer can execute. Translating an algorithm to an executable program is called **coding.** It involves expressing the algorithm in a programming language that the computer understands. Programming languages have very precise rules for forming statements or instructions.

Most programs today are coded using high-level programming languages, as illustrated by the JavaScript example. These languages are symbolic and more abstract than the binary-encoded instructions that the processor actually executes. They differ not only in their modes of expression but also in their suitability for various types of problem solving. In a later section, we will survey the landscape of programming languages available to the programmer.

Testing and Correcting the Program

After an executable version of the plan has been created, it must be subjected to rigorous testing to ensure that it performs reliably. If a program is general enough, it has many sets of input data that can be computed. Even in the compound interest example, there are an indefinitely large number of possible legitimate values. But what happens if the input values for years or APR are negative? Will the algorithm work correctly? In fact, the results would be incorrect.

Cases like these are often revealed only by testing. Most programs are not as simple as the compound interest problem, though. They are too complicated to comprehend at once all the possible eventualities. Programs therefore must be tested with many sets of real-life, concrete data. In addition to routine testing, commercial software developers will often recruit customers and other users to test prerelease or "beta" versions of programs to find out what sort of errors result from actual use.

When errors (called **bugs**) are found, the programmer must determine whether they are the result of misunderstanding the problem, a faulty plan, or mistakes in coding. Identifying the source of the error means going back to that stage to fix it. The process of testing, returning to earlier stages to debug the program, can often cycle many rounds. See Figure 6.3.

Unfortunately, most programs can never be tested completely because they have too many possible problem instances. Even for our simple compound interest program, testing all possible sets of values is not practical. This means that testing is almost always an art rather than a definitive process. As computer scientist E. W. Dijkstra succinctly put it,

FIGURE 6.3

The development of software normally proceeds in a predictable cycle. After the task is studied and specifications for its solutions are written, the program is planned in the design stage. From plans or algorithms, the code is written and thoroughly tested. At any time, it may be necessary to revert to an earlier stage of the cycle to correct problems encountered.

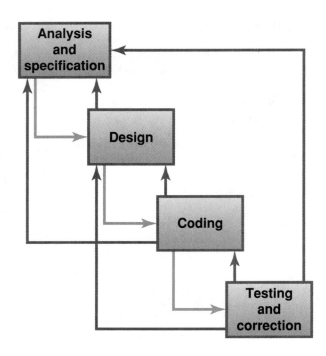

"Program testing can be a very effective way to show the presence of bugs, but it is hopelessly inadequate for showing their absence."

After a program has been tested and shown to perform reliably, it is then released for general use. Most commercial software is continually revised and modified to fix bugs discovered after its release and to incorporate new features that are desirable. Thus, the life cycle of software continues until the program becomes outdated and obsolete.

Social Themes

Software Risks

Most useful programs for large-scale automated systems are composed of thousands, sometimes millions, of instructions, and they are written by teams of programmers. Each individual is responsible for small segments of the final program. The sheer size and complicated nature of such systems outstrip the capability of a single individual to comprehend them entirely. As expected, these programs can never be fully tested or certified for correctness or even reliability. Yet these systems are used in important and serious circumstances. Unfortunately, they can cause accidents, mishaps, or mistakes due to faults or bugs that are discovered only during their use.

Here is just a partial list of some of the most dramatic instances of the failure of software systems.

○ The United States' efforts in space exploration and manned space flight have suffered a number of setbacks and disasters due to software faults. A simple programming error caused Mariner 1's Atlas booster to fail during launch; the total loss was nearly $18 million. Another one-line programming error caused the Mariner 8 interplanetary probe to be lost in space. During a five-year period (1981–1985), the Space Shuttle program logged more than 700 computer anomalies. Many were minor; a few were potentially serious. The Hubble space telescope was nearly rendered useless by the failure to detect a manufacturing error of 1 millimeter in the monitor program for mirror polishing.

○ The computerized Therac 25 radiation treatment system malfunctioned in a Texas clinic from 1985 to 1986. Lethal doses of X-rays caused by a software error killed three persons and burned several others before the fault was found.

○ The USS *Vincennes* accidentally shot down an Iranian commercial airliner, killing 290 people. The accident was attributed to human error that was provoked by a confusing computer interface used by operators on the *Vincennes*.

○ During the Gulf War, so-called "smart weapons" were often applauded for their successful deployment during the war. It was eventually discovered that the effectiveness of the Patriot missile defense system was less than 10 percent due in part to a software error in the system's clock that caused the missile to fail in real-time tracking of targeted missiles. (You will learn more about this in Chapter 8.)

◯ More than 250 accidents—including two fatalities—have involved the Audi 5000 automobile. Its computer-controlled system apparently failed to cut off fuel flow when the brakes were applied and the automatic transmission manually shifted. The result was a sudden, unexpected acceleration that caused these accidents.

◯ The stock market crash of 1987 was due in large part to the uncontrolled selling of stocks prompted by automated trading by computers. In its aftermath, Congress enacted legislation to curb the impact of program trading on the market.

◯ The opening of the $200 million Denver airport was delayed due to a software malfunction in its automated baggage system.

◯ After several years and more than $4 billion in development, the IRS abandoned its efforts to replace its older software system for processing taxes.

◯ Much of the software used by businesses, government, and institutions for several decades will become instantly obsolete on January 1, 2000. The root of the problem is the simple choice of representing dates with a two-digit value for the year. For many years, this was an acceptable simplification that conserved precious space. What seemed acceptable then is certainly not today. For example, if you were born in 1981, your current age would be calculated by subtracting 81 from the current year. But in 2000, the computer system will incorrectly deduce that you are −81 years old! You can imagine the kind of havoc that will result from these kinds of errors. The "Millennium Problem" poses a serious challenge to all enterprises that rely on information systems for their basic work.

These are just a few of the many risks due to the faults and failures of various software systems. The obvious question, then, is why have there been so many errors and difficulties? The problem is not due to a lack of dedication or skill among software developers. To put it plainly, developing large-scale software systems is extremely difficult. Although there have been rapid—almost breathtaking—advances in the design and manufacture of computer hardware components, the development of software has not had such breakthroughs. The complexities and intricacies in creating large-scale software systems seem to be embedded in the enterprise itself and not just the result of our admittedly incomplete knowledge of the process involved.

Social Themes

DEVELOPING RELIABLE SOFTWARE

In spite of earnest efforts, software systems almost invariably exhibit errors and breakdowns. Even the most casual computer user has experienced the annoyances of faults and system crashes that result from software bugs. Why is creating a reliable software system so difficult? There are two reasons. First, creating a software system, regardless of scale, involves inherent complexities. Second, most modern software systems are composed of thousands and even millions of lines of code. Their scale increases the inherent complexities many times over.

The Inherent Complexities of Developing Software Systems

Some of the inherent complexities in devising reliable software systems include difficulties attributable to their problem domains, the processes used to create them, and the very nature of the products themselves.

Over the years, computer hardware has become more and more powerful. Even desktop systems today outstrip the performance of the early behemoths that cost considerably more. We have come to expect our computers to be capable of performing more and more complicated tasks. After all, what is the point of paying for all that power if it means no added capability? As a result, the sort of problems that software systems seek to solve have become more and more sophisticated.

The plain fact remains that devising software systems is an intellectual exercise. To solve a problem using a computer, the programmer must first understand the nature of the problem. The more sophisticated the problem, the more difficulties there are in analyzing and understanding it. For example, creating a system that recognizes voice commands and responds to them is rife with intellectual difficulties. (This is why you shouldn't expect to purchase a computer that converses with you anytime in the near future.) The problems are many and deep. There are difficulties in translating voice (speech) to language (words). Specifically, there are significant speech differences among speakers, and even speech differences for the same speaker under different conditions. Once speech is converted to written language, there are inherent difficulties in understanding the meaning as well. The point is that these are intellectual problems that have little to do with computers per se. We must solve these problems before we can instruct computers to handle them.

Even when the problem is well understood, devising software solutions for it can yield other difficulties. The process of composing programs is a case in point. The JavaScript program example developed earlier illustrates the nature of the process. The idea behind that program is relatively simple and straightforward: The images appear one by one, as controlled by the user. The problem, however, is that this idea must be transformed to a mechanism that the computer can implement. This means that the programmer must pose the process in terms that are functionally effective for computers. For example, the computer can pay attention to mouse clicks and can count quite capably. Thus, the solution for the task could be cast in these terms. The point, then, is that programmers must always recast the way that humans think about doing things into forms that the computer can handle.

Software systems pose some potential difficulties by their very nature. Unlike natural or analog systems whose processes are continuous, we know that programs are executed on computers discretely, one step at a time. Consequently, software systems can behave quite differently from their analog counterparts. For example, in a normal mechanical braking system for an automobile, we would expect that faults in the system would be attributable to the components that make up that system. We would examine the brake pedal, the brake drum, and the various connecting links for malfunctions. No one would investigate the headlights or, perhaps, the radio to find the cause of the breakdown. In analog systems we expect that effects have "proximate" causes. In a software system, all bets are off: Anything might potentially interact with anything else—if the instructions permit it. It is not so fantastic that the computer-controlled braking system of the Audi 5000 could have the problem of sudden acceleration. Designers had failed to anticipate and prevent the interaction of fuel flow with braking and manual shifting.

Developing Modern Large-Scale Software Systems

The difficulties attributable to problem domain, process, and product are multiplied when the scale of the software system increases. Imagine, for example, software systems that manage an airline reservation system, a nuclear power plant, or a long-distance telephone switching network. These are software systems whose sheer scale may require thousands and even millions of lines of code. Even software for desktop systems such as office productivity programs and the operating systems that manage these computers can be formidable projects for commercial developers.

Large-scale systems cannot be physically managed by a single programmer but require teams of programmers to complete them. The division of labor among programming teams is often very precise. **System analysts** are responsible for the planning, design, and oversight of software development projects. **Programmers** work in groups to implement or code the components that make up the overall design of the project. In the case of large-scale projects, programming groups are responsible for only very specific portions of the project, just as assembly line workers concentrate on individual components of a manufactured product. Usually, a separate team is engaged to conduct testing of the project at various phases. This **software quality assurance** group is often managed separately or independently from the development team.

Many development projects go through various phases or releases of the product. An **alpha version** is the prototype of the software that is usually completed early in the project's development schedule. It is typically restricted to "in-house" testing to assess whether the design meets the basic requirements. Later, **beta versions** are releases of the product that have met the minimum testing standards. These are often tested by actual users who are willing or contracted to report problems that they encounter in everyday use. The final release, which has benefited from several stages of in-house and beta testing, is often periodically reviewed and modified. Purchasers of software applications are well aware of the steady stream of updates and revised versions for commercial products that they have purchased. Some of these updates are fixes for errors or difficulties encountered after the product has logged more hours of actual use. Others are revisions that add new and desired functionality to the system.

Given a system's scale and the division of labor, it is extremely unlikely that any one individual has a complete understanding of all the details that constitute such a system. And, as these systems become more and more sophisticated, it is even less likely that any one person could ever master a comprehensive understanding of them. Developing effective, productive large-scale software systems has become perhaps our civilization's greatest intellectual achievement and its most difficult intellectual challenge.

Liabilities and Responsibilities. The development of large-scale software systems must always involve some risk. Because only the most trivial of systems can be validated for correctness, the best that can be hoped is that thorough planning, disciplined implementation, and diligent testing can warrant some measure of reliability for software products. Thus, software professionals bear some responsibility to weigh the potential risks that their products may engender. Of course, the risks of software vary widely. A bug that "crashes" a desktop computer system is annoying, but it pales in importance to software faults that cause economic hardships or threaten lives.

Social Themes

Software Responsibilities

As you have learned, software systems—especially large-scale systems—almost always involve some risk due to errors and faults. The faults in software range from minor to extremely serious. Minor bugs may inconvenience us as we work; significant faults can cost us money or perhaps our lives. Who is responsible when these errors have serious consequences? What can be done to improve the quality of software production?

In recent years, the computing field has recognized its responsibilities to both clients and society by devising and supporting professional codes of ethics. These codes reflect a trend toward "professionalizing" the career of computing.

Two of the most influential professional societies are the **Association for Computing Machinery (ACM),** founded in 1947, and the **Institute of Electrical and Electronics Engineers (IEEE),** founded in 1963. They have recently introduced a joint provisional *Software Engineering Code of Ethics* to elucidate more precisely these areas of responsibility. (Consult the Web site for this book for the entire *Code* and more commentary.) There are eight chief divisions: responsibilities for product, the public, judgment, client and employer, management, profession, colleagues, and self. Here is a summary of its tenets.

The software professional should do the following:

- Ensure that his or her work is useful and of acceptable quality to the public, the employer, the client, and the user
- Act only in ways consistent with public safety, health, and welfare
- Protect the independence of his or her professional judgment
- Act in professional matters as a faithful agent and trustee of his or her client and employer

- In management or leadership capacity, act fairly and encourage those whom he or she leads to meet their own obligations
- Advance both the integrity and reputation of the profession
- Treat all coworkers fairly
- Strive to enhance his or her own abilities to practice the profession

On their own, these prescriptions seem both defensible and desirable. Potential conflicts in attempting to mediate all of these demands may arise though. A more serious flaw, however, is a lack of enforcement for the *Code*.

Even though software professionals may belong to professional societies such as the ACM and IEEE, the profession has no licensing bodies, such as those for doctors, lawyers, and some engineers. Software professionals who do not adhere to ethical codes of conduct do not face the consequence of losing their licenses to practice as members of these other fields do. Moreover, mediating the demands for loyalty to one's organization with broader social responsibilities can be extremely difficult. For example, a consultant warned the Department of Defense that the accepted analyses of the effectiveness of the Patriot missile were flawed. Instead of being commended for his commitment to high standards, he was ostracized and removed from the project. Only later were his warnings heeded. There can be little incentive to make a stand and "blow the whistle" on a client or organization if the professional has everything to lose and nothing to gain.

Social Themes

Computing—and especially software—professionals have raised their social consciousness by supporting professional codes like those of the ACM and IEEE. In spite of this progress, a number of very real problems remain. Consult the Web site for this book for case studies that illustrate the sort of problems encountered.

HIGH-LEVEL PROGRAMMING LANGUAGES

Even though a computer can execute only programs that are written exclusively for its processor, modern programming is seldom done in binary-encoded machine languages. The program at the beginning of the chapter, for instance, was written in JavaScript, which is an example of a high-level programming language. A **high-level programming language (HLL)** is a set of rules for expressing programs as symbolic sets of instructions that resemble English—unlike machine-language instructions, which are sequences of 0s and 1s.

As we stated earlier, high-level language programs must be translated to machine-language instructions before they can be executed on a given processor. HLLs are translated in one of two ways: *interpretation* or *compilation*. An **interpreter** is a program that simultaneously translates and executes the instructions of an HLL program one by one. It functions much like a foreign language interpreter who provides a simultaneous translation on the fly as the person speaks. In contrast, a **compiler** is a program that prepares a complete translation of the HLL program into the processor's machine code that can be run later as a stand-alone executable program. Interpreters are usually uncomplicated and therefore inexpensive. Because interpreters must repeatedly translate a program every time it is used, the execution of interpreted programs is generally slower. Compilers offer faster executable versions of the program because the translation is done only once and prior to execution. When a compiled program is modified, though, it must be recompiled to update the changes in the translated version. Compilers are also generally more expensive.

High-level programming languages are preferred over machine languages for software development because they have these basic characteristics:

- They are more abstract, relieving the programmer of machine-related details of execution.
- They produce programs that are more concise than their machine-language counterparts; HLL instructions have a one-to-many relation to processor instructions: A single instruction in an HLL translates to many instructions in lower-level languages.
- Their programs are portable to other processors, provided a translator is available for programs of this type.

High-level programming languages come in a great variety. Most programming languages are general purpose; that is, they are intended for use in solving a wide range of problems. In spite of this fact, designers of programming languages are typically motivated to create a language to handle a specific kind of problem domain or offer some special features. Although the programmer has a wide range of choices, the kind of problem to be solved usually helps determine the choice of language. Even though hundreds of different HLLs has been developed over the past forty years, thankfully there are only a few paradigms to which they belong. A programming **paradigm** defines the basic model by which the language expresses a process. The most common is the imperative procedural paradigm. A variation of this is the object-oriented paradigm. Some programming languages have characteristics and features that are decidedly different from the norm; these are nonprocedural languages.

Imperative Procedural Languages

The **imperative procedural paradigm** defines a class of languages that divide a program into units or modules called **procedures.** Each procedure usually defines a smaller task to be done. The sequence of smaller tasks or subtasks makes up the main process. Procedural units can be adapted for use in other programs as well. Thus, programmers save time and effort when they can call on libraries of procedures to perform basic tasks required in a larger program.

Statements in a procedural language are understood as instructions. They take the imperative form: "Do this," "Do that." In other words, each statement usually defines an action or operation performed on some data. The order or sequence of statements in a procedural language program is critical. As you might guess, imperative procedural languages closely resemble the manner in which machine languages express processes. Of course, they offer greater abstraction and efficiency than processor instructions.

A great many languages from this group are in use today. Pascal, BASIC, C, COBOL, and Ada are just a few examples. Listing 6.3 contains a short Pascal program that solves the compounded interest problem. As you can see, it resembles the pseudocoded version of the algorithm in Listing 6.2. Pascal lacks a built-in operation for raising a number to a given power, so it is created here as a special type of procedure called a function. **Functions** are procedures that return a value to the portion of the program that invoked them. Raising a value to a given power is achieved by a standard technique called **repetition** or **looping.** The value is computed by repeatedly multiplying the number times the previous

LISTING 6.3

This is a Pascal version of the algorithm for calculating the amount of an investment whose interest is compounded daily.

```pascal
{ a Pascal program that calculates the amount of an
  investment whose interest is compounded daily for
  a given number of years   }
program Compound (input, output);
var   { variables }
  APR, rate, amount, principal: real;
  years, time: integer;

{ Pascal does not have a built-in exponentiation
operator, so it is devised here }
  function power (num: real; exponent: integer): real;
  var
    total: real;
    i: integer;
  begin
    total := 1.0;
{ loop accumulates power of num raised to exponent }
    for i := 1 to exponent do
      total := num * total;
    power := total
  end; { power }

{ main }
begin
  writeln('Enter the values as numbers only.');
  writeln;
  writeln('Press Enter after each number.');
  write('Enter starting amount of the investment:');
  readln(principal);
  write('Enter the annual rate of interest (as
    decimal fraction):');
  readln(APR);
  write('Enter the number of years for earned
    interest:');
  readln(years);
  rate := APR / 365;
  time := years * 365;
  amount := principal * power((1.0 + rate), time); {*}
  writeln;
  writeln('The resulting amount of the investment
    is $');
  writeln (amount : 1 : 2)
end. { main }
```

FIGURE 6.4

The Pascal version of the compound interest program is executed here. The user is prompted to enter the needed data and the results are displayed in the text box.

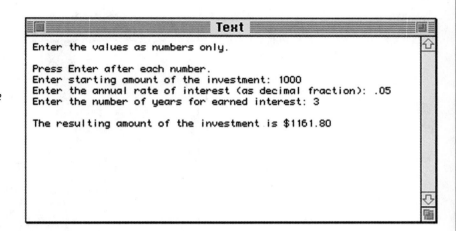

```
Text

Enter the values as numbers only.

Press Enter after each number.
Enter starting amount of the investment: 1000
Enter the annual rate of interest (as decimal fraction): .05
Enter the number of years for earned interest: 3

The resulting amount of the investment is $1161.80
```

product. The *power* function is invoked by the main program in the step labeled [*]. The function is designed to be general enough so that it might be used in other programs that require the same operation.

To see how the program works when executed, examine the instance in Figure 6.4. The values are entered by the user from the keyboard, and the result is displayed in a text box on the screen.

Object-Oriented Languages

Object-oriented programming languages divide a program into units like procedural languages; however, the units describe entities or objects with specific attributes or capabilities. A program defines a process that is populated by a group of objects; objects interact in various ways to perform the process. Objects have methods or specific actions that are natural for them to perform. Objects also send messages to and receive messages from other objects in the course of a process. For example, a file-processing object might send a message to a printer controller object to request permission to transmit a document to the printer for output.

The object paradigm has several advantages over traditional procedural programming. First, the concept of an object is more intuitive than the imperative elements of conventional languages. Many of the processes that programmers seek to model can be described more naturally in terms of different objects interacting with one another. Object-oriented languages also offer features that make their programs more secure and predictable in their behavior. To create objects, the programmer defines object classes with characteristic properties and methods. These classes make it easier to duplicate objects as well as reuse and modify them in other programs. Newly defined classes may also inherit the features and capabilities of other predefined classes.

Proponents of object-oriented programming tout its greater abstraction and ease in recycling reliable, developed code into new programs. SmallTalk, Java, and C++ (pronounced "see-plus-plus") are popular examples of programming languages that support the object-oriented paradigm. Listing 6.4 is a Java version that solves the compound interest problem. The program creates a new class called *Interest*

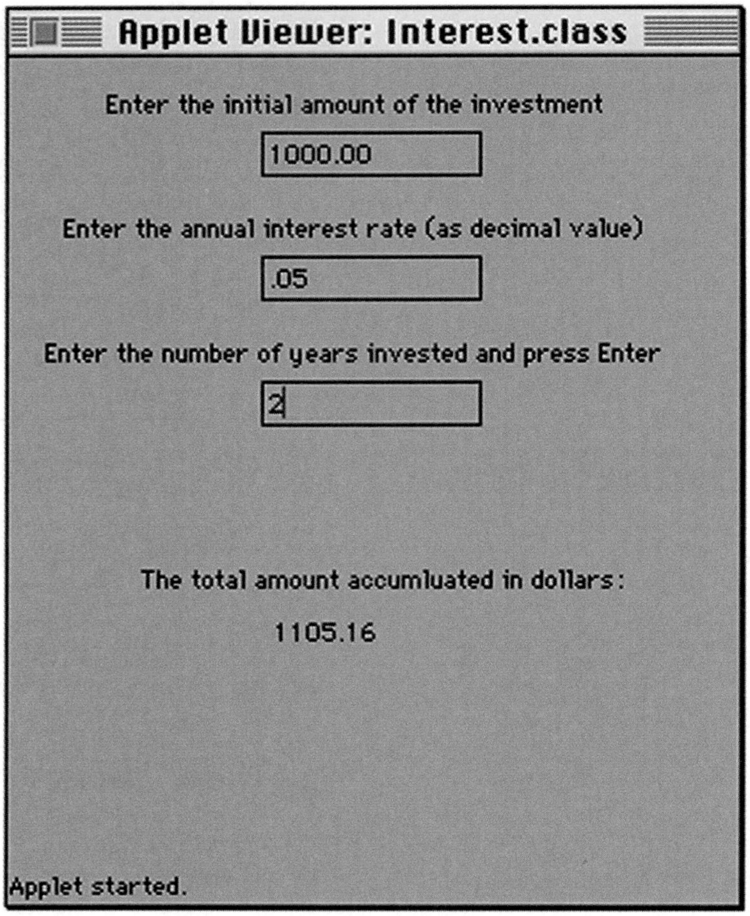

FIGURE 6.5

A Java applet executes the program in Listing 6.4. The user enters the required values in the labeled boxes, and the result is calculated and displayed.

Applet Viewer: Interest.class

Enter the initial amount of the investment

`1000.00`

Enter the annual interest rate (as decimal value)

`.05`

Enter the number of years invested and press Enter

`2`

The total amount accumluated in dollars:

1105.16

Applet started.

that is a subset of the predefined generic class *Applet*. Java **applets** are programs that specially equipped World Wide Web browsers can execute. *Interest* employs three methods to complete the task. The method *init* manages the graphical components for entering input values while the method *action* interprets these values. Finally, the method *paint* calculates and displays the results. Consult Figure 6.5 for an example of the applet's execution.

More Information

LISTING 6.4

A Java version of the algorithm calculates the amount of an investment whose interest is compounded daily.

```java
//Calculating compound interest
import java.awt.*;
import java.applet.Applet;

public class Interest extends Applet {
    Label prompt1;      // prompt user to input
                        // principal
    TextField input1;   // input value for
                        // principal
    Label prompt2;      // prompt user to input
                        // APR
    TextField input2;   // input value for APR
    Label prompt3;      // prompt user to input
                        // years
    TextField input3;   // input value for years
```

```
    double principal, APR;
    int years;

// setup graphical user interface
public void init ( )
{
    prompt1 = new Label( "Enter the initial amount
        of the investment" );
    input1 = new TextField( 10 );
    prompt2 = new Label( "Enter the annual
        interest rate (as decimal value)" );
    input2 = new TextField( 10 );
    prompt3 = new Label( "Enter the number of
        years invested and press Enter" );
    input3 = new TextField( 10 );
    add( prompt1 );     // put prompt1 on applet
    add( input1 );      // put input1 on applet
    add( prompt2 );     // put prompt1 on applet
    add( input2 );      // put input1 on applet
    add( prompt3 );     // put prompt1 on applet
    add( input3 );      // put input1 on applet
}

// process user's action on the input text fields
public boolean action( Event e, Object o )
{
    if ( e.target = = input3 ) {
        Double val1 = new Double ( input1.getText( ) );
        principal = val1.doubleValue( );
        Double val2 = new Double ( input2.getText( ) );
        APR = val2.doubleValue( );
        years = Integer.parseInt ( input3.getText( ) );
        repaint ( );
    }
    return true;         // user's action is
                         // processed
}

// calculate and display the results
public void paint ( Graphics g )
{
    double amount, rate, days;

    rate = APR/365.0;    // daily interest rate
    days = years * 365.0;      // term of the
                               // investment
    amount = principal * Math.pow( 1.0 + rate,
        days);
    g.drawString ( "The total amount accumulated
        in dollars:", 50, 200);
    g.drawString( Double.toString( amount ), 100,
        220 );
    }
}
```

Nonprocedural Languages

Another group of languages supports a **nonprocedural programming paradigm.** These programming languages are based on very different models and concepts, but they do share one common feature. Their programs are composed of statements that are *not* interpreted procedurally. In other words, the order of the statements in the program does not necessarily define a sequence of events or actions. Examples of nonprocedural programming languages include LISP (a list processing language), Prolog (a logical or declarative language), and FP (a functional programming language). In addition to standard developmental uses, LISP and Prolog are also popular languages for the discipline of **artificial intelligence (AI).** AI researchers seek to understand the nature of intelligence by creating systems (programs) that model or simulate its performance. Chapter 20 treats the field of artificial intelligence and some of its applications.

A short Prolog program is given in Listing 6.5. The program can be thought of as a collection of statements about generalities and particulars. As shown in Figure 6.6, the user can query the program to find out facts about the "world" that it describes. When a query is executed, only those statements in the program that are relevant to answering it are consulted. For example, the variable "Who" is instantiated with the value "henry_wingo" because it is satisfied by the first fact in the program. On the other hand, the second query involves applying several rules to deduce whether Tom and Luke are brothers. First, brothers are males and siblings. And, siblings share at least one common parent. The Prolog inference engine verifies these from the appropriate rules and facts and responds "yes."

LISTING 6.5

This Prolog program documents the relations among the literary Wingo family. Besides defining facts, the program expresses generalities such as how one identifies brothers and sisters.

```
% wingo family facts

father(henry_wingo, tom_wingo).
father(henry_wingo, savannah_wingo).
father(henry_wingo, luke_wingo).
mother(lila_wingo, tom_wingo).
mother(lila_wingo, savannah_wingo).
mother(lila_wingo, luke_wingo).
father(amos_wingo, henry_wingo).
mother(tolitha_wingo, henry_wingo).

male(henry_wingo).
male(tom_wingo).
male(luke_wingo).
female(savannah_wingo).
female(lila_wingo).
female(tolitha_wingo).
male(amos_wingo).

parent(X,Y) :- father(X,Y).
parent(X,Y) :- mother(X,Y).

sibling(X,Y) :-
    parent(Z,X),
    parent(Z,Y).
```

```
brother(X,Y) :-
   male(X),
   sibling(X,Y).
sister(X,Y) :-
   female(X),
   sibling(X,Y).
```

FIGURE 6.6

When using a Prolog program, the user enters queries that are answered by deducing the facts from the database created by the program. The first query asks, "Who is the father of Tom Wingo?" The second asks whether Tom and Luke Wingo are brothers.

```
% Queries

Yes
father(Who, tom_wingo).
Who = henry_wingo

Yes
brother(tom_wingo, luke_wingo).
Yes
```

PROGRAMMING LANGUAGES FOR THE REST OF US

In recent years, a new class of programming languages has evolved for use by nonprofessional programmers. These languages allow casual users to write programs that create new applications or add functionality to existing ones.

End-user programming languages are languages designed for average users to create programs without the normal fuss and complications of professional software development languages. They are easier to use because they have a simpler, more intuitive structure and organization. End-user programming languages often have ready-made components that can be incorporated into programs to produce sophisticated results. Many are scripting or interpreted languages whose programs are also easier to implement on a variety of platforms without expensive translation software. In addition, some are supported by tools that make composing and assembling programs easier as well.

Languages for Internet Applications

One group of end-user programming languages is those dedicated to World Wide Web and Internet programming. At the beginning of the chapter, you were introduced to JavaScript, which is a popular end-user programming language for Internet applications. Based on the object-oriented language Java, JavaScript programs add functionality to Web pages. Unlike Java programs, which are compiled, JavaScript programs are embedded in the formatting code used to define Web pages. (See Listing 6.1 earlier.) Not all browser programs are equipped to interpret JavaScript programs, though. When a capable browser encounters JavaScript instructions, they are translated and executed on the computer running the browser program.

Though it shares the object-oriented paradigm with its predecessor Java, JavaScript is primarily an event-handling language. An **event-handler** is a special program component that is associated with the occurrence and detection of a particular event. In other words, programs are designed to react to a specific set of events that might take place during their execution. The user might click the mouse, use the mouse to roll over an object, press a button, or enter text from the keyboard. In addition, other events may occur that are not caused by the user: A transmission may be completed or interrupted; a time limit may be exceeded; and so on. JavaScript event-handlers can be devised to respond to these events in various ways. Event-handlers can add interactivity to Web pages, perform calculations, manage animation and special effects, collect data and perform error-checking, cater to browser differences, and so on.

One of its most appealing features is that JavaScript is not tied to a particular hardware platform. JavaScript programs can be incorporated in a Web page and executed by any processor that runs a browser program that can interpret its instructions. The programmer does not have to be concerned about the machine-dependent details of the types of computers that may be used to view his or her page.

Besides JavaScript, several other scripting languages are employed for Internet applications. These include VBScript (see Visual Basic below), JScript (a Microsoft variant of JavaScript), and Python.

Languages for Extending and Making Applications Work Together

Another class of end-user programming languages is intended for creating new applications, modifying or extending existing ones, or causing applications to cooperate or communicate with one another. From this category, Visual Basic is a popular choice for working with applications in the Microsoft Windows family of programs.

Visual Basic is a successor to the venerable language BASIC (for *Be*ginner's *A*ll-Purpose *S*ymbolic *I*nstruction *C*ode), which was the first end-user or consumer programming language. Today Visual Basic has inherited the procedural structure of BASIC, object-oriented features of later languages, and a visual programming interface.

Visual programming incorporates tools for creating and manipulating graphical or pictorial elements in the solution of the program. In Visual Basic, the programmer may exploit graphical tools for building program components such as forms, dialog boxes, buttons, menus, text boxes, and more. Even so, Visual Basic remains a symbolic or textual programming language: Its primary components are procedures composed of symbolic instructions. These instructions are written to tie together the graphical components of the program.

Figure 6.7 shows the results of a Visual Basic application that solves the savings account problem introduced earlier. The window—called a "form" in Visual Basic terminology—is created using graphic tools that

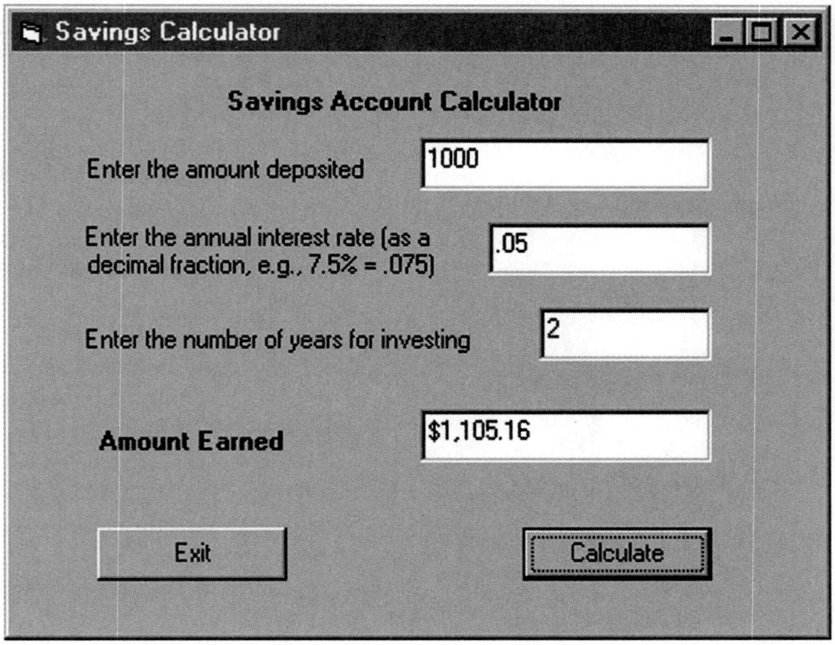

FIGURE 6.7

The Form window is produced by running the program in Listing 6.6. The user enters the required values, and the result is calculated and displayed.

define its size and appearance as well as its components such as text boxes, labels, and command buttons.

The user enters values and presses the Calculate command button to cause the results to be revealed. The command button is programmed by a special event-handler that prescribes how the computation is carried out and displayed in the *Amount Earned* text box. Listing 6.6 is a Visual Basic event procedure for solving the savings account problem. Compare its structure with that of the original algorithm expressed in Listing 6.2.

LISTING 6.6

This Visual Basic program solves the familiar compound interest problem.

```
Private Sub cmdCalc_Click()
'calculate the total amount
'earned on an investment with
'a fixed rate of interest
'compounded daily
   Dim Amount As Single     'amount invested
   Dim APRate As Single     'annual int rate
   Dim PerRate As Single    'periodic rate
   Dim Term As Integer      'number of years
   Dim Periods As Integer   'number of days
   Dim Total As Currency    'amount earned

   Amount = txtAmount.Text
   APRate = txtInterest.Text
   Term = txtYears.Text

   PerRate = APRate / 365
   Periods = Term * 365
   Total = Amount * (1# + PerRate) ^ Periods

   txtTotal.Text = Format(Total, "$###,##0.00")
End Sub
```

In addition to creating a new application, as in this example, Visual Basic programs can be designed to add special functions to existing programs. For example, Visual Basic programs can interact with other programs such as word processors and spreadsheets to perform specific tasks. In this manner, application programs can be tailored or customized for individualized use without having to design and create an entirely new software system.

Several other languages may be enlisted to create or extend applications. Microsoft has incorporated the visual programming environment to languages such as Visual C++ and Visual J++, based on object-oriented languages C++ and Java, respectively. AppleScript, a scripting language that allows the programmer to create customized applications by modifying and combining existing ones, may be employed on Macintosh platforms for similar purposes. For example, scripts can be designed to cause two or more applications to communicate and share data. Thus, one application could be used for entering data; this data can be sent to, stored, and processed by another program. AppleScripts can also be used to automate routine tasks such as sorting electronic mail, making copies of valuable documents, and so on.

Languages for Specialized Applications

Some application programs have their own built-in programming languages that users may employ to add functionality to their products. These proprietary languages are especially tuned to the characteristics and features of their applications' environments. A good example of this class is Lingo, the programming language of the multimedia authoring program Director. **Multimedia authoring programs** make it easier to produce electronic documents that organize and incorporate multimedia elements in effective ways.

Lingo is an event-oriented scripting language that allows authors of Director documents (called "movies") to add special effects and greater interactivity to their creations. Listing 6.7 illustrates a Lingo script that creates a special dialog box activated by the user. The user presses a button that spawns a special event called "showDialog." See Figure 6.8. When this happens, the event-handler *on showDialog* is executed. The handler uses the so-called "movie-in-a-window" (MIAW) technique; it simulates the dialog box by actually running a separate Director movie within a smaller window within the main movie. As you can see, Lingo instructions read somewhat like ordinary English commands. (The comments preceded by "—" were added to improve their readability.)

LISTING 6.7

The Lingo script produces a dialog box on the user's screen. This is actually done in the event-handler on showDialog by opening a second Director movie in a smaller window on top of the main movie window. The size of the window is calculated and then opened.

```
—by Alan Levine, Maricopa Community College, who
—maintains Director Web
—http://www.mcli.dist.maricopa.edu/director/
on startMovie
    set the volume of sound 1 to 140
end startMovie


on stopMovie
    disposeWindow
end
```

```
on doQuit
   go to frame 1
end

on showDialog
   —create MIAW using the movie "dlog.dir"
   —which needs to be in the same directory as
      this movie
   global dlogWindow
   —dispose window if it exists
   disposeWindow

   —calculate window position to be centered on
      screen
   set centerH to (the stageRight — the
      stageLeft)/2 + the stageLeft
   set centerV to (the stageBottom — the
      stageTop)/2 + the stageTop
   set dlogW to 323   —width of dialog window
   set dlogH to 152   —height of dialog window
   set dlogLeft to centerH —dlogW / 2
   set dlogTop to centerV —dlogH / 2
   set dlogRect to rect (dlogLeft, dlogTop,
      dlogLeft + dlogW, dlogTop + dlogH)

   set dlogWindow to window "dlog.dir"
   —This uses the file "dlog"

   set the windowType of dlogWindow to 1
   —modal alert
   set the modal of dlogWindow to true
   set the rect of dlogWindow to dlogRect
   open dlogWindow
end

on disposeWindow
   —get rid of MIAW
   global dlogWindow

   if objectP(dlogWindow) then
      forget dlogWindow
   end if
end
```

Other examples of end-user programming languages for applications include HyperTalk, HyperLogo, and OpenScript. HyperTalk is a scripting language used to add functionality to hypermedia documents produced using the application program HyperCard. **Hypermedia** are multimedia documents organized and linked so that the user can navigate them freely. HyperLogo and OpenScript are alternative scripting languages for similar, competing hypermedia applications. HyperLogo is the proprietary scripting language for the program HyperStudio. It is a distant cousin of the instructional programming language Logo. OpenScript is the built-in programming language for the software pack-

FIGURE 6.8

The dialog box is created by the Lingo script in Listing 6.7.

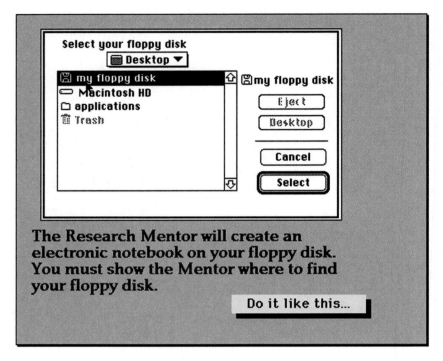

age Multimedia Toolbook. All three languages provide the means for creating sophisticated effects and more precise control of hypermedia documents. You can find out more about multimedia authoring and hypermedia programs in Chapter 19.

End-user programming languages have not yet brought programming to the masses; they still require study and practice to use effectively. Nonetheless, they offer considerable advantages over conventional languages in both ease of use and power of expression. They are clearly the fastest growing segment of high-level programming languages available today.

More Information

SUMMARY

Software or programs are lists of instructions that direct the steps of processing conducted by the computer system's hardware. Even though all processors execute binary-encoded programs stored in their main memories, few programs today are written by humans in this machine-language form. Instead, programmers employ symbolic programming languages that simplify the process of devising and developing programs.

The basic software development process involves several stages: analyzing the problem or task that the software is intended to perform; de-

vising a plan to solve the problem or model that task; creating an executable program that implements the plan; and testing and correcting the program.

Most software systems—and especially large-scale systems—are too complex for testing that could prove their validity in all circumstances. Besides scale, software systems involve a number of other inherent complexities. The problems that they attempt to solve often are not well understood. There are difficulties attributable to the process by which these systems are created. Finally, as discrete systems, they perform very differently than other types of engineered systems.

High-level programming languages (HLLs) are symbolic programming languages that are more abstract than machine-language programs. In addition, HLLs produce programs that are more concise and portable than their machine-language equivalents. Even so, HLL programs must be translated to the appropriate machine language to be executed on a given processor. HLLs usually employ one of several different paradigms or models to express processes. These paradigms form distinct families of languages. The members of a given family of programming languages will share certain common features in spite of the many individual differences among them.

PROJECTS

1 Modify the JavaScript program in Listing 6.1 to display a sequence of six pictures instead of four. Specifically, how would the function *changer* have to be altered to effect these changes? How would the additional images have to be prepared to work effectively in this solution? (Adventurous readers can test their solution in an actual Web page.)

2 The algorithm expressed in Listing 6.2 solves the problem of computing compounded interest for normal values supplied by the user. Can you think of any sorts of input values that would result in incorrect calculations? How could the algorithm be improved to handle these types of exceptional input data?

3 Write an essay that recounts the types of faults or bugs encountered by real users employing software applications. Interview some of the students in your class to gather information about their experiences using specific software applications. How serious were the problems they encountered? How pervasive were these problems? To what extent did these faults arise from misuses of the system (problems with documented incompatibilities, failure to follow operating instructions, etc.)?

4 Find out more about the so-called "Millennium Problem." In addition to consulting the resources listed on the Web site, research what your college or university has done to combat some of the potential problems that will affect the information systems they employ after the year 2000.

5 Study the *ACM Code of Ethics and Professional Conduct* (as cited on the Web site). This, unlike the *Software Engineering Code of Ethics,* is a general code for all computing professionals. Analyze each of its regulations based on the following considerations. Give a brief justification or defense to support it as general rule or practice. Identify whether the code is derived from the special responsibility of practicing the profession per se or whether it is derived from a broader moral responsibility to the interests of society. Finally, cite how the code could be (practically) enforced.

6 Conduct some research on programming languages used by developers for creating commercial software. Specifically, create a table that lists the names of at least five programming languages not mentioned in the chapter. Find out when the language was first introduced. Label each language according to which programming paradigm it belongs to, and specify the kinds of tasks that it is especially suited for handling. Here is an example entry:

Language	Origin	Paradigm	Specialty Applications
FORTRAN	1950s	imperative procedural	scientific applications

Key Terms

algorithm	flowchart	object, property
alpha version	function	paradigm
applets	high-level programming	portability
artificial intelligence (AI)	languages (HLLs)	procedure
assembly language	hypermedia	program
Association for Computing	imperative procedural paradigm	programmer
Machinery (ACM)	Institute of Electrical and	repetition, looping
beta version	Electronics Engineers (IEEE)	scripting, scripting language
bug	interpreter	software (program)
coding	multimedia authoring program	software quality assurance
compiler	nonprocedural programming	system analyst
conditional statement	paradigm	translation program
end-user programming language	object-oriented programming	variable
event-handler	language	visual programming

QUESTIONS FOR REVIEW

1 What is a symbolic programming language? Contrast it with a machine language.

2 What is an assembly language? How is it related to a machine language for the same processor?

3 What are variables? What roles do they play in programs?

4 Two of the structures found commonly in many programming languages are conditional statements and repetition. Both are similar in that they interrupt the normal sequential or step-by-step flow of the execution of instructions. Both are different in how they do this. Describe how they affect the flow of the execution of instructions in a program.

5 Describe the four basic stages involved in the software development process.

6 What is an algorithm? Describe several methods for expressing algorithms.

7 What are flowcharts? What are they used for?

8 Software systems can seldom be validated. Instead, they can be shown to be reliable by testing. Explain what "validity" and "reliability" mean in this context.

9 Identify the types of difficulties facing software developers in the design and implementation of reliable software systems.

10 How does the behavior or performance of software systems differ from those of their analog counterparts? Why does this make them more difficult to develop reliably?

11 Describe the responsibilities of the following roles in a software development project: systems analyst, programmer, software quality assurance group.

12 What are the differences between the alpha and beta versions of a software product?

13 What is meant be the term *higher-level language?* How are assembly and machine languages related to these languages?

14 Define and compare an interpreter and a compiler.

15 What is a programming paradigm?

16 What are procedures? How are they employed to define a process?

17 What are the chief characteristics of programming languages that belong to the imperative procedural programming paradigm?

18 What are objects? Describe the roles of properties, methods, and messages in defining an object class.

19 What is an applet?

20 What are the chief characteristics of programming languages that belong to the object-oriented programming paradigm?

21 Nonprocedural programs are composed of statements that are not organized sequentially. What does this mean?

22 What are the chief characteristics of programming languages that belong to the nonprocedural programming paradigm?

23 What is an event-handler?

24 What is visual programming? How does it make programming applications easier?

25 What are scripting languages? Give several examples of programming languages that belong to this category.

FOR FURTHER READING

To find out more about the topics discussed and cited in this chapter, consult the following.

Abernethy, Ken and J. Thomas Allen. "Developing Program Solutions" in *Exploring the Science of Computing: A Laboratory Approach with Pascal.* Boston: PWS Publishing, 1994, 204–207.

Brooks, Frederick P. "No Silver Bullet: Essence and Accidents in Software Engineering" in *Information Processing '86,* edited by H.-J. Kugler. New York: Elsevier Science Publishers, 1986. [Reprinted in *IEEE Computer* 20 (April 1987), 10–19.]

Dijkstra, E. W. "The Humble Programmer." *Communications of the ACM* 15 (October 1972), 859–866.

Gotterbarn, Don, Keith Miller, and Simon Rogerson. "Software Engineering Code of Ethics." *Communications of the ACM* 40 (November 1997), 110–118.

Parnas, David. "Software Aspects of Strategic Defense Systems." *Communications of the ACM* 28 (December 1985), 1326–1335.

Application programs perform the specific tasks for which we employ our computers. Even these programs would be powerless to perform our bidding without the aid and assistance of another type of software—the computer's operating system. The operating system is a collection of programs that actually manages the basic functions of a computer.

These programs assist us in many of the fundamental tasks that we require to maintain our systems. To copy and print files, to format disks, and even to execute applications, we need the assistance of operating system software. Operating systems help by managing many of our hardware resources such as main memory and secondary storage. They provide useful services such as organizing files and printing. This software also creates and maintains the interface by which we direct and communicate with the system. In fact, the operating system software has a much greater impact on the look and feel of our computers than the hardware devices that make up the system. Most computer users can become quite passionate when it comes to their operating systems, but few even know or care what type of CPU or hard disk drive their system employs.

In this chapter, we will complete our picture of how computers function from the standpoint of how software directs the inner workings.

OBJECTIVES

- *How system software and operating systems run the show*
- *The special functions of single-user and multiuser operating systems*
- *Graphical user interfaces for desktop computer systems—Windows 95/98 and NT, plus the Macintosh OS*

CHAPTER 7

OPERATING SYSTEMS: SOFTWARE THAT RUNS THE SHOW

Vasily Kandinsky, *Graceful Ascent*, March 1934. Solomon R. Guggenheim Museum

MANAGING THE SYSTEM

Software can be divided into two categories: applications and system software. **Applications** are end-user programs designed to perform specific tasks such as preparing documents, creating graphic images, or sending and receiving electronic mail. **System software** refers to programs that help manage the operation of computer systems. This category also includes development tools such as compilers and interpreters, which are used to create programs that run on computers. The most fundamental type of system software is the operating system. An **operating system (OS)** is a collection of resident programs that manages the computer's resources, supervises the execution of user processes, and provides useful services and security for the computer system. As users, we often feel as if we control what goes on with our computers, but this is not entirely accurate. The operating system, in fact, is in control of our computer systems at all times when they are in use.

Managing the details for operating a computer system can be an arduous and complicated task. Suppose, for example, you wish to edit a document that you created previously using a word processor. If you have ever used a computer system for word processing, you know that to open a file you enter a simple command. In fact, a lot of things are going on behind the scenes. First, the document has to be located. Text documents are stored as text files; a **text file** is a sequence of symbols that are treated as a unit and usually stored externally on a secondary storage medium, such as a disk. Files have names and locations. Once the file is found, it must be transferred—at least in part—to main memory for editing. The transfer from secondary memory to main memory is what is meant by "opening" the file. But, first, memory must be allocated for this use. Care must be exercised to prevent the incoming data from conflicting with the program and other segments of memory currently in use. After memory is set aside for the document, a copy of the file must be transferred from its location on your disk to the reserved segment of main memory. A pathway must be cleared, and the details of the transmission should be overseen to ensure that all goes well. Finally, your word processing program is ready to respond to editing actions and commands.

Sound complicated? In fact, this is just the big picture; we have left out a lot of the details. The point of the story is that if we had to manage all these details, very little productive work would get done. Instead, we would spend most of our time and effort on simply trying to operate our computers. We would very likely make a lot of mistakes, too. Under these circumstances, only the most knowledgeable and patient of users would be able to get anything done at all.

Fortunately, the operating system manages most of these details automatically. Most operating systems are designed as a suite of smaller programs or services that control various aspects of the operation of our system. Some of these smaller programs are always resident in main memory. In other words, every time the computer system is powered on, specific portions of the operating system program are loaded into memory.

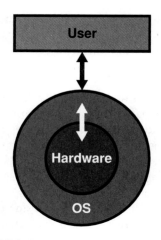

FIGURE 7.1

The operating system functions as the go-between for the user and the computer's raw hardware features. This shields the user from the complicated, tedious details of the hardware's operations and likewise protects the hardware from inadvertent errors committed by users.

In this manner, the operating system actually controls the computer system at all times. We often think that we are operating the computer; in reality, our actions are requests to the operating system to do such and such. In this manner, the operating system serves as a buffer between the user and the computer system's hardware. See Figure 7.1.

This role has advantages in two ways. First, it relieves us of handling the myriad of details necessary for managing the system. In fact, the operating system creates powerful services that provide an abstract view of the computer's capabilities. Launching applications and storing data in files are two of the kinds of abstractions made possible by the operating system. We will delve into these and other services shortly.

Application programs can exploit the services of the operating system by executing specific system calls. A **system call** is a particular request to the operating system to perform a needed service. The example of editing a document involves several system calls: Finding the file, allocating some memory to store a working copy of the file's contents, copying the disk file to memory, and so on are just a few of the operating system services employed by the word processing program. Without this assistance, our application programs would have to be much larger and more complicated to handle all these details directly. The bottom line is that applications would be much more expensive because they would have to be tailored to the many versions of systems commercially available.

In addition to making it easier for our application programs to run on our computers, the operating system also protects the computer system from errors committed by users or by their processes. Even when a program is executing, the operating system can interrupt that process if the program commits an illegal condition called an exception. For example, division by zero is undefined by most processors, and a program that attempts this can generate a system error. A system error is a special message issued by the operating system in response to exceptions. In these circumstances, the operating system often causes the offending program to be terminated prematurely.

The operating system can also prevent us from performing actions that might have undesirable results. It monitors our commands and accepts some, asks for verification of some, and rejects others. Thus, the operating system offers some security and protection for the system.

It is difficult to overestimate the importance of the operating system for your computing environment. In fact, the choice of operating system is a greater factor in determining how your computer performs—its look and feel in use—than any of its hardware. Some computers with different processors will seem indistinguishable to you when they run the same operating system. For example, Windows 95 will look the same whether the underlying computer is powered by a 486 processor or a Pentium processor. The Macintosh OS on 68040 processors runs much the same as on newer PowerPC processors. Moreover, computer systems with the same processor but running different operating systems will perform very differently. As an example, the same PowerPC processor is used both by Apple for the Macintosh computer running the Macintosh OS and by IBM for PCs running the operating system OS/2. Users, though, would hardly recognize this fact because of the differences in their operating systems.

We can divide operating systems generally into two groups: those that support single-user, single-programming operation and those that allow for multiuser, multiprogramming operation. (Recall the discussion earlier in Chapter 4.) On the surface, the difference is whether the operating system supports one or many users on a given computer system simultaneously. The fundamental difference in these types of systems is whether the operating system is equipped to manage a single process at a time or multiple processes over a span of time. The latter is called **multiprogramming** or **multitasking;** this is the ability of the computer system to attend to the execution of several programs concurrently. First, we will consider in some detail what services a single-user system provides and how these services are organized. Afterward, we will examine briefly multiprogramming and how the operating system manages it.

ANATOMY OF A SINGLE-USER OPERATING SYSTEM

The hallmark of most **single-user, single-programming operating systems** (usually shortened to **single-user operating system**) is that they afford the execution of only one process at a time by one user at a time. Whether the process is a system or application program, the single-user operating system is designed to manage one task at a time. This is quite natural, however, because we know that most CPUs are serial uniprocessors anyway. This means that they can execute only one instruction from a program at a time. Single-user systems are simply organized to complete the instructions from a single process before going on to the next one.

Single-user operating systems are usually designed into functional units. Each unit has a specific set of responsibilities. This division of labor has advantages. Because each unit is restricted to limited tasks, the size and number of system programs that must be loaded concurrently in memory are smaller. Functional separation also makes the OS easier to design and maintain.

Although the actual organization of single-user systems varies considerably from one vendor to another, they all share some common denominators. A typical single-user operating system will have the following functional units or components:

1 Supervisor
2 I/O control drivers
3 Memory manager
4 File manager
5 User interface

Supervisor

Perhaps the most important task for the operating system is managing user processes and requests. For most users, their chief interest in computing is to employ application software such as word processing, drawing and painting programs, electronic mail, and the like. As we know, programs must be loaded into main memory and their execution commenced. It is the job of the **supervisor** to oversee and control these and other processes. See Figure 7.2.

Besides user programs, the supervisor manages special requests for services made both by users and user processes. For example, when we request to print a file, a system call is made to a special routine that performs the task. The supervisor accepts the request and oversees the loading and execution of the operating system program that actually does the work. User programs can also make system calls for operating system services. Again, opening a file is a good example. The user program makes the request for the file and is interrupted while the supervisor handles these details. After the file is located and allocated some memory space, the user program is commenced again.

I/O Control Drivers

As you learned in earlier chapters, the physical organization of data varies depending on the type of device that stores or transmits it. The **I/O control drivers** are primitive input/output routines that manage the details of transfers between I/O devices and the CPU. For example, to access information stored on a magnetic hard disk, it is necessary to do the following:

- Seek the track
- Identify the sector
- Read/write the data block

To complete these tasks, the system must issue several commands to the appropriate disk controller. And, in addition to these commands, the transfer must be synchronized properly. The devices, therefore, must also exchange signals to ensure that the timing is right, too. As you can imagine, all of these details—though simple-minded—are very tedious. To make matters worse, they differ from one peripheral to another. In

FIGURE 7.2

The supervisor oversees the work of your system by converting programs to actual executing processes. When you launch an application program, for example, the file containing its instructions must be loaded into main memory and the processor must be directed to commence its execution. The operating system supervisor handles the details and turns over the control of the processor to the newly loaded program for execution.

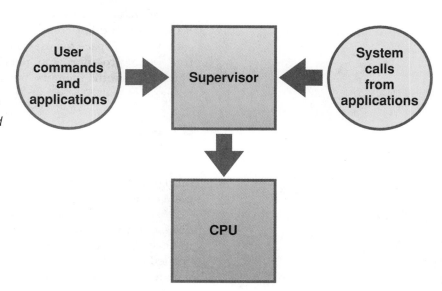

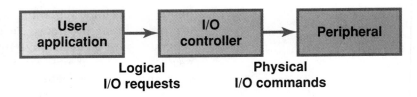

**Logical
I/O requests**

**Physical
I/O commands**

FIGURE 7.3

The application program makes requests for input and output that are abstract in that they specify logical entities such as files, buffers, and the like. The I/O control driver translates these requests to specific commands that are transmitted as signals to the I/O device.

other words, your magnetic hard disk has different signals and timing than your CD-ROM drive.

I/O service routines simplify transferring and storing data on the system. An application program makes a *logical* I/O request in the form of a system call. The logical request is abstract in that it specifies the data apart from its physical organization and location. The request is transferred to the I/O control driver, which interprets it and issues a series of commands and signals to the peripheral. See Figure 7.3. For example, the CPU may be copying a file from a disk. The CPU can simply ask for a block of data and allow the I/O driver to handle the details of translating that logical request into the physical commands of finding the track, sector, and block.

These services also shield user programs from the machine-specific details that are necessary to implement input and output. I/O transfers are not only more efficient but also more reliable than they would be if user programs had to handle them directly.

Memory Manager

Instructions and data are stored in random access memory (RAM) during program execution. Even in a single-user system, the demands for memory can be complicated. Some portion of the operating system must reside continually in memory. User application programs, of course, must be afforded memory space to execute. This often means finding room for the data created by these applications, too. If we are switching between applications, the programs will often be loaded concurrently in main memory, even if only one can execute at a time.

The **memory manager** has responsibility for allocating segments of RAM to these often competing processes. The memory manager allocates memory space for user processes and protects the system from errors when programs and data might overlap in RAM. Figure 7.4 illustrates how the memory manager segments main memory for different uses.

File Manager

An important contribution of the operating system is to provide abstract or logical services that make computing easier and more convenient. A good example of this is the file system.

As you know, data is stored in physical units that are blocked on disks, CD-ROMs, tape, and so on. The size of these data blocks is usually uniform for that peripheral and medium. On the other hand, data created by user programs is seldom uniformly sized. Think of a text document created by a word processing program. The number of paragraphs, sentences, words, and letters can vary considerably from one

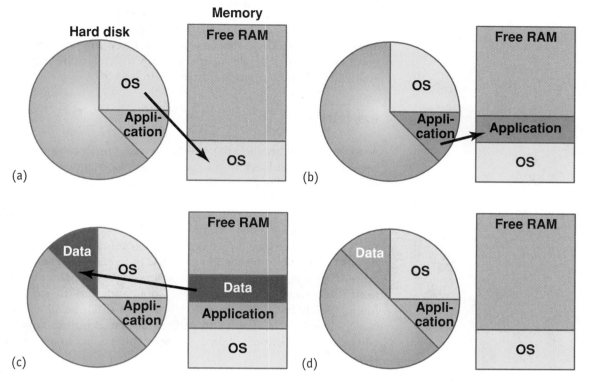

FIGURE 7.4

The memory manager allocates space for the operating system and applications that run on a single-user system. This also means protecting data and processes by ensuring that the memory partitions do not overlap. (a) When the system boots, a portion of the operating system is loaded into RAM. (b) Later, the user launches an application; the memory manager allocates space in RAM for its execution. (c) The application creates a data file, which is also allocated space in RAM and later copied to disk. (d) When a process is done, the memory manager frees the space for new uses.

document to the next. The point then is that a single document created by a user application may require a variable number of blocks to store it externally in secondary memory. And, of course, the number of blocks will also depend on the medium used for storage.

The operating system creates a convenient fiction to hide these messy details from us. Data is organized in entities called files. A **file** is a sequence of items treated as a single unit and identified by the system with a unique name. Text files are files of characters or symbols, but there are other types of files, too. A file may contain the instructions of a program, or a file may be a sequence of records. The **file manager** creates and maintains the set of files stored on a specific system. Operating systems have naming conventions for files and usually provide a series of services for managing them. It is the job of the file manager to translate logical requests for file services into those that the system can handle.

Most operating systems provide an abstract structure or organization for locating and storing files. Again, this is a convenient fiction. Data is stored in physical blocks, but file systems can have more complicated structures. Today, most operating systems offer a **hierarchical file structure (HFS).** A hierarchy is a series of levels. A device such as a hard disk is conceived as having a series of levels where files may be stored. Levels have locations called "directories," "folders," or some other system-dependent term. These locations are also given unique names to distinguish them. Figure 7.5 shows how a floppy disk might be organized hierarchically using the operating system Windows 95.

User Interface

As we mentioned earlier, the operating system maintains control of the system continuously while the power is on. Consequently, to make the computer system perform tasks that are useful for us, we must communicate our desires as requests or commands to the operating system. The **user interface** is a program that runs almost continuously to interpret our commands for work.

The user interface is the medium for communication. The mode or means for this communication can vary. In fact, some systems may offer more than one user interface for processing user/system communication. Some are primarily text-based. Commands and messages are communicated by text. Most are visual or graphical. These allow the user to manipulate objects, icons, and gadgets displayed on the monitor to facilitate communication. We will consider these issues in more detail in a separate section.

Let's take a simple example to illustrate how these operating system functions come into play in normal use. Suppose that you wish to launch or start the execution of an application—perhaps a drawing program for creating graphics. From the user's standpoint, the operation is simple. Locate the file icon in the appropriate directory; issue the command to

FIGURE 7.5

Windows 95 employs a hierarchical filing system. The window portrays several levels of the filing system for a desktop computer. On the left side, all devices and folders are shown by their respective levels. Notice the contents of the floppy disk drive. A disk is identified by the device to which it is connected. In this case, the floppy disk is located in drive A.

The disk itself is organized into a series of folders that contain files and other folders. At the topmost level are two folders, Documents *and* Pictures. Documents *contains another folder called* chapters. *The contents of that folder are shown on the right side. It is composed of several text files,* Chapter1, Chapter2, Chapter3, *and* Chapter4. *Note also that the folder* Pictures *contains two other folders,* objects *and* screens.

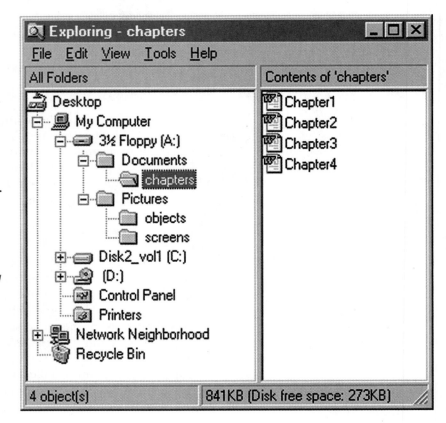

FIGURE 7.6

Behind the scenes, an application is launched for execution. Whenever you choose to run a program such as a game or perhaps a text editor, a lot of activity is going on behind the scenes. Here is a typical (generalized) sequence of events to execute what appears to be a simple step to the user. (a) The command to run the program is interpreted by the user interface. The user interface notifies the supervisor. (b) The supervisor, in turn, directs the file manager to locate the file. The disk I/O controller is enlisted to perform the actual transfers of data blocks that constitute the file. Finally, (c) the supervisor signals the memory manager to load the program file into a segment of memory. The supervisor then signals the start of the execution of the program. The user interface, of course, relays system calls from the program as its window opens and operation commences.

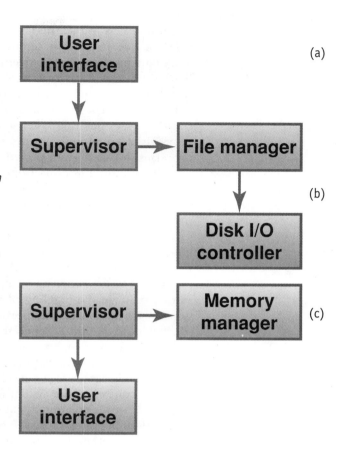

open; and, after a short delay, start using the program. But what is going on underneath? Here is an overview of the process. (Details will vary depending on the operating system.)

1. The user interface translates the user's actions to signify launching an application.
2. The file manager resolves the location of the data that makes up the program.
3. The memory manager allocates a segment of main memory for loading the program.
4. The I/O control driver manages the transfer of a copy of the program from the physical device to memory.
5. When the transfer is complete, the supervisor passes the control of the processor to the first instruction of the program.

Of course, these tasks are executed by a series of system calls that coordinate and manage the details. Figure 7.6 illustrates the process.

ANATOMY OF A MULTIUSER OPERATING SYSTEM

Most desktop computers employ single-user operating systems (Microsoft Windows and the Macintosh OS are the primary ones). The entire computer system is physically small enough to fit on a portion of your desk at home or office. Desktop computers are convenient and economical, but as you learned in Chapter 4, they do not offer the highest performance. In contrast, some computing environments are composed of a single machine that services a group of users. Though the extent of the hardware is not significantly greater, these machines offer higher speed and increased performance. However, the hardware is only part of the picture. These systems serve more than one user because they are controlled by operating systems that support multiprogramming.

Multiprogramming means that the system can execute several processes during a given period of time. (Note that we avoided saying "simultaneously.") Multiuser operating systems are usually based on serial processors. Of course, a serial processor can execute only one instruction at a time. How then can a serial processor execute several processes? The short answer is by switching back and forth from one program to another. Processors are not picky: One instruction is very much like another. So, too, are programs. It does not matter whether the next instruction for the CPU comes from the same or a different program. On the other hand, processors are not "clever" either. They cannot manage the juggling of programs required for multiprogramming. The **multiuser, multiprogramming operating system** (usually shortened to **multiuser operating system**) creates and manages the multiprogramming environment.

A multiuser system can handle a number of users at the same time because the hardware is fast enough to make it appear that each user has exclusive control of the system for his or her processes. For example, while one user is creating a text document using a word processor, another might be using a spreadsheet to perform some numerical calculations. Still another user might be reading his electronic mail, and another might be compiling a program that she has written. The multiuser operating system creates the illusion that each of these processes has the system's undivided attention. In reality, though, the operating system instructs the processor to switch back and forth between these in an orderly manner.

A multiuser operating system often means the system is being utilized more efficiently than with a single-user operating system. Most programs can be analyzed into segments that are dominated by CPU instructions and those that are dominated by I/O operations. When the process is dominated primarily by CPU instructions, we can say that the system is **CPU bound.** In contrast, when the process is fixed on performing I/O operations, we can say that the system is **I/O bound.** We have seen that the speed of typical CPU instructions is measured in nanoseconds (one nanosecond is one-billionth of a second). On the other hand, I/O operations that involve peripherals are usually measured in microseconds or even milliseconds. This means that while the CPU is waiting for an I/O operation to complete, it is wasting a lot of time that might be used on other tasks.

Consider the simplified example illustrated in Figure 7.7. Two processing jobs are first executed consecutively. Both jobs contain several segments of predominantly CPU activity and predominantly I/O activity. The top line depicts how long it would take the two processes to complete when run consecutively. Suppose, instead, that we could switch from one program to another whenever the CPU becomes idle while I/O operations are performed independently of it. In this instance, the CPU is utilized more efficiently with less waiting time spent for I/O operations to complete. Separating the CPU instructions and I/O instruc-

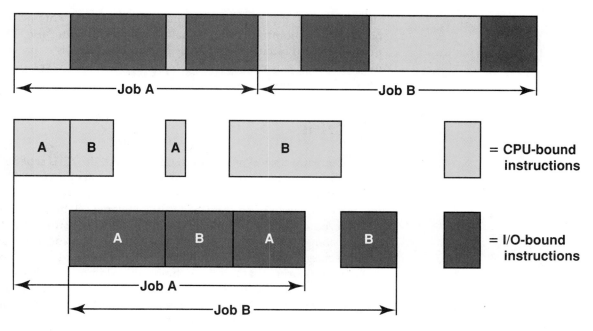

FIGURE 7.7

Timelines for serial, sequential processes and for multiprogramming are shown here. The upper timeline shows the length of time it takes for two jobs to run consecutively. In the bottom timeline, the programs are executed on a multiprogramming system that permits switching back and forth between processes while the I/O operations are performed independently of the processor. Because of multiprogramming, the total amount of time in the second case is reduced.

tions from each process and executing them separately while combining more than one process would reduce the total amount of time required to complete the two jobs.

This example is somewhat simplistic, but it conveys the basic idea behind multiprogramming in a multiuser operating system. A multiuser operating system can accommodate a number of users and maximize the use of the system's resources. This is why many businesses employ multiuser systems over single-user desktop computing systems.

To support multiprogramming and multiple users, a multiuser operating system must have functions or features in addition to those outlined for the single-user OS:

1 Context switching by the supervisor
2 CPU scheduler
3 Virtual memory by the memory manager

Context Switching

In a multiuser operating system, the supervisor has the responsibility not only for initiating processes but also for overseeing the transition between processes. In particular, the supervisor handles the details of changing between processes that are interrupted and those that are continued; this is called **context switching.** In effect, the operating system takes a snapshot of the current process at the moment that it is interrupted. All of the relevant information needed to commence that process at the point where it was halted is stored for later use. The new process—which often is a previously interrupted one—is reinstated into main memory and execution commences. All of this takes place in a fraction of a second.

CPU Scheduler

When there are several processes to be executed, the **CPU scheduler** decides which process will be next in line when a context switch takes place. The scheduler maintains a list of waiting processes that are ready for execution and orders them according to some established criterion.

The criteria for determining priority varies with the system. The round-robin method, for example, divides a processing interval into equal segments so that all waiting processes get an equal amount of processing time during that interval. The round-robin method is a very simple one that attempts to ensure that all waiting processes are treated fairly. Other types of scheduling are more complicated and take into account factors such as the importance or priority of processes, how much time a process has previously had, and the type of activity.

Virtual Memory

Most multiuser systems (and some single-user systems, too) often lack sufficient main memory to support processing. There is simply not enough RAM for the operating system and executing processes and their data. For example, to serve a number of users, their programs should be stored concurrently in memory to allow for faster context switching.

These operating systems create and support an expanded memory space called **virtual memory.** The operating system establishes a memory address space that is much larger than actual physical main memory. (See Figure 7.8.) Additional space is usually borrowed from one of the system's hard disk drives. The operating system maintains this virtual address space by shuttling data back and forth between secondary and primary memory as needed. As far as the CPU is concerned, the actual location of data is transparent.

Virtual memory creates the illusion of a much greater memory store. In this way, the system can support processes with large data demands as well as sufficient space for multiple processes. Executing processes and their data are still stored in RAM, while unused data is moved to secondary storage until needed again.

The services of virtual memory are not without cost, though. Locating data and moving it between primary and secondary physical memory slow down the system's overall performance. The cost in time is usually worth the benefits of increased processing capacity.

Multiuser operating systems vary considerably in both design and features. Some prominent examples include the proprietary systems of DEC VMS, IBM OS, and AT&T UNIX.

Even though most desktop computer systems employ single-user operating systems, a number of them have evolved to include multiprogramming capabilities. IBM OS/2, the most recent versions of Microsoft

FIGURE 7.8

Virtual memory is created by the operating system by combining segments of physical RAM with those of secondary storage. An operating system may employ several types of schemes to create a virtual memory space. In the illustration, the operating system divides programs and data into a series of uniformly sized units called "pages." When the CPU requests an item for a specific process, the operating system translates its virtual address into a physical one. If it is currently stored on secondary memory, the operating system fetches that page and swaps it with one currently in physical RAM. If the page is already in physical memory, the transfer is immediate. Using this juggling act, the operating system is able to maintain the illusion of a much larger memory space than that provided by the hardware's RAM.

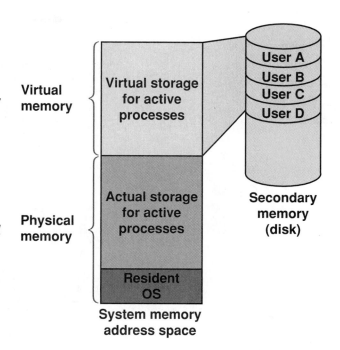

Windows—95/98 and NT—and Macintosh OS 8 support multitasking. For example, you may copy a file to disk or send it to the printer, and while the system is managing this, you can work with another application. These single-user systems likewise support some of the features normally expected in larger multiuser systems such as virtual memory.

HUMAN-COMPUTER INTERACTION: TEXT-BASED INTERFACES

As mentioned, the user interface is the medium through which we communicate our wishes to the operating system. Consequently, the form and style of that communication are the most important factors in how the system looks and feels. One type of user interface is text-based. With a text-based user interface, the user expresses commands as a series of short text strings typed at the keyboard. The syntax or rules for the formation of these commands are usually very precise. Text-based interfaces are often **command line interpreters,** which means that the command processor interprets only one command at a time. Commands are entered when the system signals its readiness to the user with a symbol called a **prompt sign.** Figure 7.9 contains a sequence of commands issued using the command line interpreter for the UNIX operating system. The prompt sign is the "$" symbol. The text that follows the "$" on the same line is a single command. System responses to these instructions follow them. Although the previous commands are visible on the screen, the interface processes only the current command.

As you can see, each command is terse and cryptic. Consequently, the burden of communication is entirely on the user. You must know the commands and their syntax to get an appropriate response from the system. Text-based interfaces are not always easy to learn and use. Some text-based interpreters are not at all for the faint of heart. They offer few safeguards and almost no error protection. If you inadvertently tell the

FIGURE 7.9

A sample session of entering commands using the text-based interface that is standard for the UNIX operating system is shown. Explanations of the commands and responses are added.

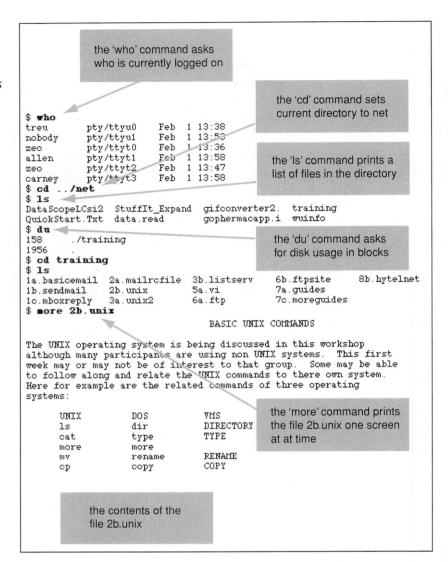

system to erase your file or a disk, it will assume that you know what you are doing and carry out the command immediately.

An advantage to using a text-based interface is that many of them permit scripting. A **script** is a sequence of commands, similar to a program listing, that the interface interprets much like a program. Commonly used sequences of commands can be effected automatically simply by executing the script.

GRAPHICAL USER INTERFACES

Graphical user interfaces take a very different approach from that of their older cousins, the command line interfaces. A **graphical user interface (GUI)** employs visual elements on the display monitor such as icons, windows, and other gadgets that the user manipulates to facilitate communication. GUIs are intended to be intuitive, easy to use, more friendly and helpful environments.

FIGURE 7.10

*Shown here is the desktop for the graphical user interface for Windows 95. The entire screen is organized as a workspace called the desktop. On the desktop are a number of elements that the user can manipulate with the mouse pointer. On the left of the desktop is a series of icons that represents the computing environment. **My Computer** denotes the resources for your system, and **Network Neighborhood** contains the computer systems with which you may communicate over a computer data network. The **Inbox** is a message system for sending mail and facsimiles. The **Recycle Bin** acts as a trash bin for discarded files; the **Internet** icon connects you to your Web browser program. The contents of **My Computer** are shown in the window. Windows usually have menus and a series of tools to help the user work with their contents. Besides several secondary storage drives, the user can access printers and general resources through the Control Panel. Across the bottom of the desktop is the taskbar, which displays information about the current working environment, including the programs and windows that are open.*

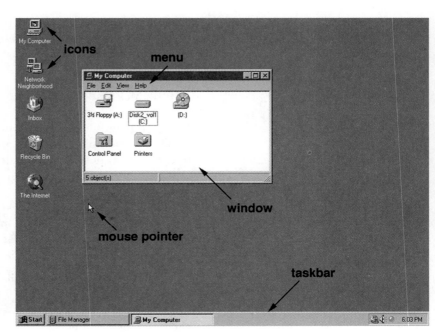

Consider the screen shown in Figure 7.10, which illustrates the graphical user interface of the Windows 95 operating system. The full screen is configured as a workspace called a **desktop** in which various documents, icons, and gadgets are available for use. **Icons** are small pictures depicting devices, files, programs, and the like. Documents and icons are displayed inside rectangular frames called **windows.** Tools and gadgets are used to perform various tasks associated with these desktop windows and other objects. Rather than relying exclusively on language, the chief metaphors for communicating in a GUI are hand actions and pointing. The user manipulates icons and windows with a graphical element called a **pointer,** which is usually controlled by a mouse. The pointer icon typically appears as an arrow, but it may take a variety of shapes depending on the context of its use. Text information is provided using the keyboard, but many of the actions are dictated by mouse manipulations, including the selection of commands from a listing called a **menu.**

The purpose of the desktop metaphor is to make the manipulation and use of the computer more natural by emulating the way we move, store, and dispose of paper products on our desks. Think of the screen as your desktop, disks as filing cabinets, the pull-down menus as a shorthand list of frequently employed procedures, and the mouse and keyboard as your personal assistants in manipulating all of these.

The advantages of a GUI are obvious. Because the burden of communication is shifted to the machine rather than the user, GUIs are easy to use and easily learned. They are also usually designed to provide a number of safeguards to protect the user from disastrous mistakes. On the downside, they are not very efficient. These protections, safeguards, and easily visualized actions take some time, and experienced users of text-based interfaces can become impatient with the steps required to achieve relatively simple actions. Most likely, the computer that you are using employs a GUI—either a version of Microsoft Windows 95, 98, or NT, or the Apple Macintosh OS. We will discuss these operating systems in more detail a little later, but first let's consider the basic common features that the interfaces for these popular desktop computer operating systems share.

Menus and Dialog Boxes

Most commands are executed by selecting them from menus. Whether using the desktop or within an application, menus are usually accessible to execute a variety of commands or actions. Menus change depending on what application you are running and the context in which you are using it.

Most GUIs support several types of menus: pull-down, pop-up, contextual, and submenus. Some menu commands require additional information to complete the actions prescribed. In these instances, dialog boxes are used as forms that the user may fill out to specify the details.

● **Pull-Down Menus.**   A **pull-down menu** appears as a list of items in a horizontal menu bar. Figure 7.11 illustrates a pull-down menu within the Windows 95 Control Panel window. To choose a command, the user clicks the menu name. The pull-down menu reveals a list of commands. Commands that are not currently available will be dimmed (will appear as light gray). Otherwise, individual commands may be selected by pointing and clicking them. The menu disappears in a few seconds or immediately after selecting a command.

Figure 7.12 shows a typical menu bar from the Macintosh desktop. In the latest version of the Macintosh OS, pull-down menus work exactly the same way as those in Windows. This new feature is called *sticky* menus. Experienced Mac users can still manipulate them using the classical method: by pointing to a menu name and *holding the*

FIGURE 7.11

*The **View** menu from the Control Panel window in Windows 95 is shown here. The user may select a command by pointing to it and clicking the right mouse button. In this case, the* Options *command is highlighted, indicating that it is selected.*

FIGURE 7.12

*The desktop menu bar is for the Macintosh OS. The user has pulled down the **File** menu and dragged to the Find command. Releasing the mouse button completes the selection of the command.*

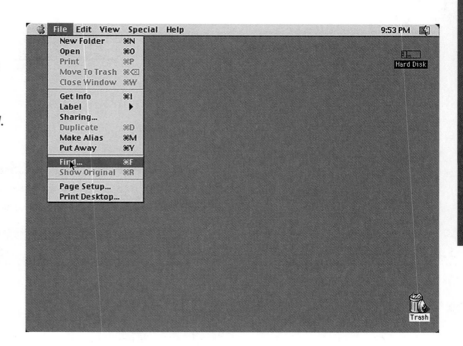

mouse button down to reveal a list of commands. A particular command is then selected by dragging to it and releasing the mouse button. In Figure 7.12, the **File** menu is pulled down and the *Find* command is selected.

● **Dialog Boxes.** When a menu choice appears followed by an ellipsis (three dots), this signifies that the selection of the command will be followed by the presentation of a dialog box. A **dialog box** is used to collect additional information from you before the command is actually carried out. For example, if you select the *Print* command from the **File** pull-down menu, a dialog box like the one shown in Figure 7.13 appears. It asks you to specify particular information about the print job. Do you

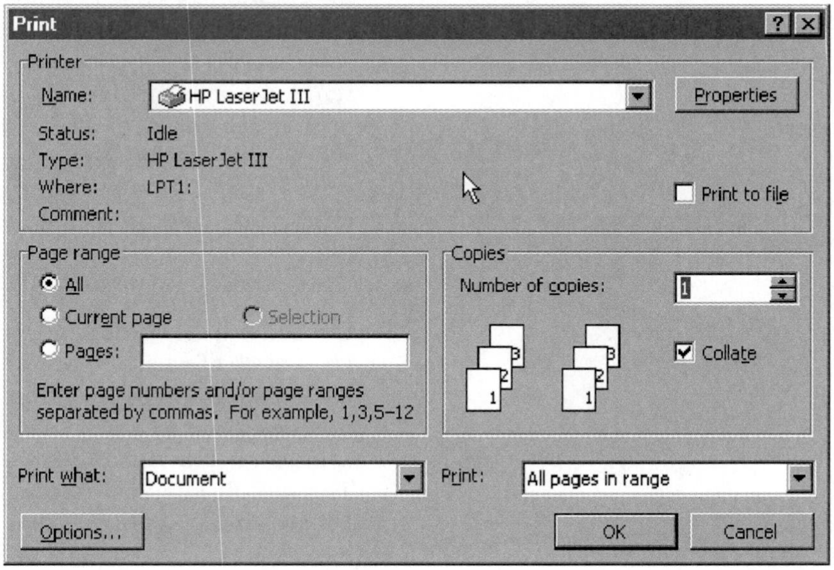

FIGURE 7.13

The Print dialog box in Windows 95 is shown here. The user may designate which printer to use, what pages to print, the number of copies, and several other options. Dialog boxes like this one allow you to tailor commands to suit your specific needs.

FIGURE 7.14

The Save As *command dialog box from Windows 95 is shown here. Saving a file means copying the contents of the file to some location such as a disk. In (a), the current location (in the box) is the directory Winword. The user may choose an alternate location by pressing the arrow for a pop-up menu. In (b), the pop-up menu lists the other locations that may be selected.*

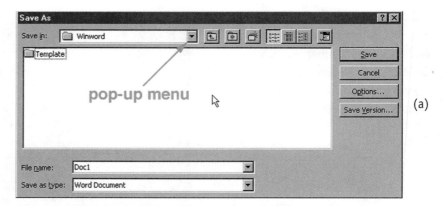

(a)

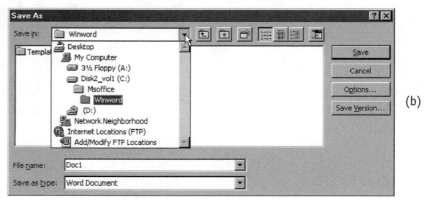

(b)

want to print one page or a whole document? How many copies would you like to print? Which printer do you intend to use? A dialog box provides you the opportunity to select the particular options you wish to set for the command the computer is about to execute.

● **Pop-Up Menus.**   In some instances, you might need to choose one among several alternatives. These are typically organized in a GUI by means of a pop-up menu. The **pop-up menu** contains a list of alternatives or settings—one of which must be selected. For example, as shown in Figure 7.14(a), the *Save As* command dialog box in Windows 95 allows you to designate the location to save the file. In this instance, the current location is the directory Winword. But, as shown in Figure 7.14(b), pressing on the arrow gadget reveals a pop-up menu that lists other locations that may be selected in addition to the current one.

Figure 7.15 shows the *Save* command dialog box from the Macintosh OS. As you can see, the only difference is that the pop-up menu is indicated by a double arrow. Pressing on the double arrow likewise reveals a pop-up menu of locations for saving the file.

● **Contextual Menus.**   Most modern GUIs are intelligent enough to keep track of what you are doing while you work. For example, as you move the mouse pointer from one icon to another, the GUI internally notes which objects are indicated. **Contextual menus** are special lists of commands that appear in the context of pointing to specific objects. The specific commands will likely vary depending on what you are doing and the object in question. GUIs differ according to how contextual menus are triggered. In Windows 95, for example, clicking the right mouse button signals a contextual menu. An example is shown in Figure

FIGURE 7.15

The Save *command dialog box from Macintosh OS is shown here. In (a), the current location (circled for emphasis) is Correspondence. The user may choose an alternate location by clicking the double arrow for a pop-up menu. In (b), the pop-up menu lists the other locations that may be selected.*

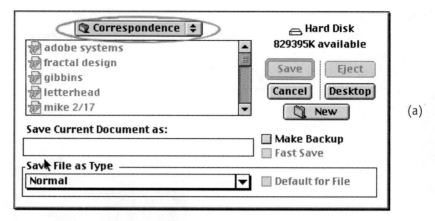

(a)

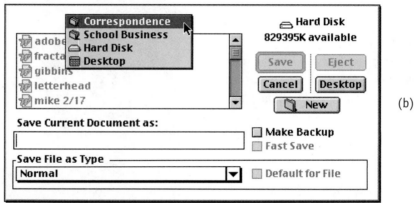

(b)

FIGURE 7.16

The contextual menu from Windows 95 is revealed by clicking the right mouse button. In this instance, because the icon happens to denote a printer, the menu displays commands that are relevant to using the printer.

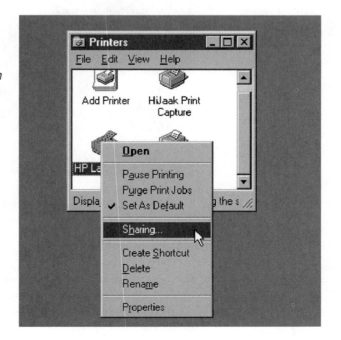

7.16. For the Macintosh OS, you click the mouse button while holding down the Control key. See Figure 7.17 for an illustration.

● **Submenus.**   Sometimes a command has a range of available choices or variations. These are often organized as a subordinate menu, or simply

FIGURE 7.17

The contextual menu from the Macintosh OS is triggered by clicking on the object while holding down the Control key. The object in question is a folder that contains files and possibly other folders. Consequently, the commands shown in the contextual menu are relevant for manipulating a folder.

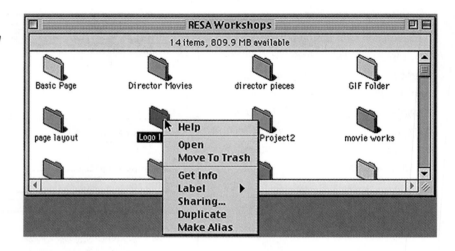

FIGURE 7.18

The Programs *command in the* **Startup** *menu for Windows 95 has an extensive submenu that contains all the program groups currently installed on your system. Clicking the right arrow reveals the submenu. Many of these submenus, in turn, have submenus. On the system pictured here, WinZip (an application for compressing and decompressing files), for example, contains its own submenu listing several additional choices.*

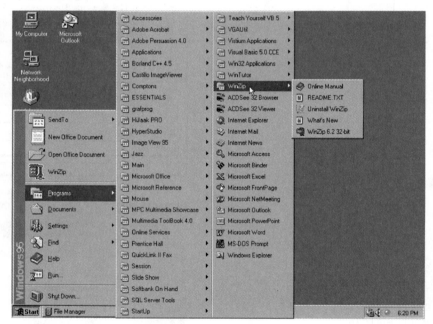

a **submenu.** Submenus are indicated by triangular arrows after the command. For instance, in Windows 95, the *Programs* command has a submenu listing the range of program groups available to the user. See Figure 7.18.

Managing Files

Both Windows and the Macintosh OS provide hierarchical file structures for storing information. Files are located at different levels of the hierarchy. A disk or device is always the topmost level. These usually contain file folders or directories. **Folders** (or **directories**) contain other files and additional folders. The user, therefore, can create new folders to define a new level belonging to the current one. In Figure 7.19, the disk inserted into the floppy drive is opened to reveal three objects: a program file and two folders. Suppose that you opened each of the folders to examine its contents and continued this process until all items were revealed. The result would be a series of levels, as illustrated in Figure 7.20.

FIGURE 7.19

The disk inserted into the floppy drive (named "A:") is opened. Its topmost level contains the program Pkunzip and two folders, Documents and Pictures. You may open these folders to reveal their contents as well. The contents of each folder would be displayed in a separate window.

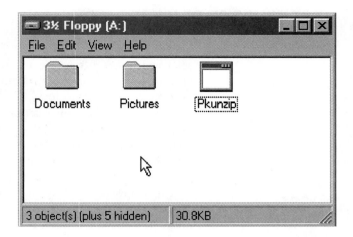

FIGURE 7.20

It is sometimes more convenient to think of the folders as being arranged in a series of levels, as depicted here. At the origin is the disk or device; each of the succeeding levels may, in turn, have successors. In this case, at the top level of the disk are three objects: the folders Documents and Pictures, and an application file named Pkunzip. The folder Documents contains two files, cmdCalc and letter, as well as a folder called chapters. The folder chapters holds four text files. The folder Pictures stores two more folders, objects and screens. Each contains several image files, as shown.

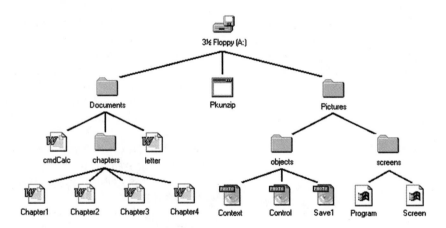

In Windows and the Macintosh OS, the actual address of a file is written as the sequence of levels that must be traversed to arrive at the point occupied by the file. These sequences are called **pathnames.** For example, to locate the file *Control,* as shown in Figure 7.20, you would need to start at the top level and traverse a distinct path through three succeeding levels. The pathname would be written as

```
A:\Pictures\objects\Control
```

In this way, the full name of the file includes the distinct path that locates it. That is why it is possible to have two files with the same (short) name on the same disk. As long as they belong to different folders, they actually have different full pathnames.

As this discussion demonstrates, the Windows and Macintosh GUIs are organized to make them easy and intuitive to use. After learning a few simple concepts and techniques, you are able to perform a wide range of operations. There are a number of built-in safeguards as well. It is difficult to commit errors from which you cannot recover. You can feel free to experiment with the interface confidently, knowing that you can't do a great deal of damage.

Although they differ in some details of appearance and operation, these operating systems are really quite similar. If you become an accomplished user of either of these operating systems, it will take you only a fraction of the effort to master the other.

A CLOSER LOOK AT WINDOWS 95/98 AND NT

Microsoft currently supports a number of versions of its Windows operating system. The most recent ones are Windows 95, Windows NT, and Windows 98. Windows 95 and NT share the same basic graphical user interface. This means that for most users, 95 and NT would appear almost indistinguishable. In fact, they differ in significant ways in terms of their internal design, organization, and performance. Windows NT occupies less memory and offers greater security, enhanced networking capabilities, and better performance for the hardware that it supports. On the other hand, Windows 95 supports a greater range of hardware platforms and best fits the individual user environment. Recently, Windows 98 appeared as an updated and enhanced version of Windows 95.

The Windows 98 GUI differs from that of its predecessor in minor ways. Windows 98, however, breaks new ground with several other features. *Active Desktop* allows you to add active content to the desktop such as updated headline news, weather, sports scores, a video camera image, or a host of other items. In essence, your desktop becomes like a Web page. Besides icons signifying links to resources, you may add elements from the Internet that are updated regularly on your system. Weather maps, stock tickers, and headline news are just some of the choices available.

The Internet Explorer browser is more tightly integrated into the operating system. In fact, you may customize the user interface to integrate views of files, programs, and resources that look very much like those presented in the browser itself. Users may also modify the look and feel of the interface in other useful ways: adding multiple monitors, changing screen resolution, and customizing colors and fonts.

Windows 98 also expands the basic functionality of your system with added software and utilities. It contains a range of utilities that enhance the day-to-day operation of your system. For example, *Windows Tune Up Wizard* steps you through diagnostic checks that help fine-tune the performance of your hardware and software. Other software such as *Sound Recorder, Media Player,* and *TV Viewer* make it easy to record and play back multimedia content. Windows 98 is likewise fully equipped with applications that can assist you in creating, maintaining, and publishing your own Web materials as well.

Our discussion of the Windows GUI will be general—Windows 98 differences will be treated where appropriate. The start-up screen for Windows is the desktop shown earlier in Figure 7.10. At the bottom of the desktop is a taskbar containing a Start button. By clicking the Start button, you bring up a menu containing some of the most frequently used commands. For example, when the *Run* command is selected, a dialog box is presented for choosing or specifying the particular application you wish to run. Not surprisingly, the *Help* command brings up the system Help files, and the *Shutdown* command safely turns off your computer. Each time you start an application or open a window in Windows, a button representing the program or window appears in the taskbar at the bottom of the desktop. See Figure 7.21. To switch between windows and applications, you just click the button in the task bar for the window or program you want.

FIGURE 7.21

The taskbar contains several icons denoting windows and programs that are currently opened. The game Solitaire is open, but several other windows are also available. The active window or program is highlighted in the taskbar; the user can switch between windows simply by clicking another icon in the taskbar.

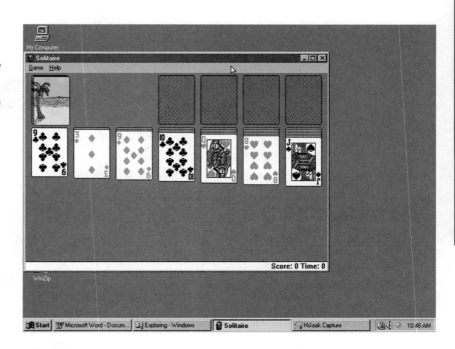

Desktop Windows in Microsoft Windows

As we have mentioned earlier, the most common workspace for a GUI is the window object. Some windows depict the contents of disks; other windows display a portion of a file or document created by an application program. Regardless of their origin, the windows in Microsoft Windows typically have a consistent structure and organization. In addition to gadgets or tools around their borders, windows contain a group of objects. How many are visible depends not only on the contents but on the size of the window as well. It may not be possible for all objects to be visible at once on the screen. In this case, the window provides only a partial view of its contents. To see other parts, you must either change the point of view or the size of the view. You do this by manipulating the window tools.

The diagram in Figure 7.22 illustrates the major components, tools, or gadgets associated with windows in Microsoft Windows. Here are a listing and a brief explanation of these common features.

●   **Title Bar.**   The **title bar** is the top line of the window. Inside the title bar is the name of the disk, folder, program, or document whose contents are contained in the window. The entire window can be moved around on the desktop by pointing to the title bar and dragging it. When you release the mouse button, the window remains in its new position.

●   **Control Icon.**   Though the look of the icon changes with the type of the window, the **control icon** may be clicked to allow you to manipulate the window from the keyboard rather than from the mouse pointer.

●   **Minimize, Maximize, Restore, and Close Buttons.**   The size of the window may be controlled by the Minimize and Maximize buttons. You can click the **Minimize** button to remove the window from view. This is useful when you may later need to return to the window but do not require it on the desktop. The **Maximize** button is used to enlarge the window to full-screen size. When it is pressed, the button transforms to the

FIGURE 7.22

A typical window in Microsoft Windows is shown here. In the title bar is the name of the disk, folder, document, or program. A control icon signifies the type of item; in this instance, the open folder icon denotes that the contents of a folder are revealed. On the right side of the title bar are buttons for controlling the size of the window. At the bottom is the status bar, which contains information about the window's contents. At the right side of the status bar is the sizing corner, which may be dragged to resize the window by hand. The scroll tools allow you to move the window to display other portions. Inside the window is a variety of icons signifying different types of objects: files, programs, and other folders.

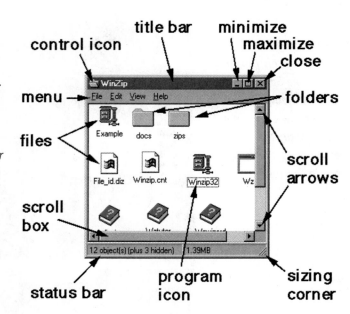

Restore button (not pictured), which can be clicked to reinstate the previous size. The Close button may be pressed to close the window and remove its icon from the taskbar as well.

● **Menu Bar.** Most windows have a **menu bar** that contains pull-down menus for exercising commands associated with the window. (Some windows may not have a menu bar.)

● **Status Bar.** Useful information is displayed in the **Status bar.** In Figure 7.22, the number of objects contained in the folder is displayed. The content of the Status bar changes, however, with the context of your actions. For instance, short descriptions of the meaning of your actions appear in the Status bar when you point to menu commands.

● **Explorer Bar.** A third optional bar, for Windows 98 only, is the **Explorer bar,** which contains a set of tools and buttons for manipulating files, searching, and finding links. See Figure 7.23 for an example.

● **Scroll Box.** The **scroll box** shows the amount and relative position of the window in the scene. The size of the box indicates the relative portion of the contents that is visible. The larger the box, the less that is obscured from view. The position of the box tells you what portion of the contents is visible—top or bottom, left or right. You may drag the scroll box to change the portion that is visible.

● **Scroll Arrows.** A window has up to four **scroll arrows:** two each in the vertical and horizontal scroll bars. These are used to move the window to a new location in the scene. For example, the upward-pointing scroll arrow at the top of the vertical scroll bar can be used to move the window upward (i.e., in a backward direction) in the scene. Pointing and clicking the arrow advances the window in that direction in small intervals. If you press and hold down the mouse button, the window continues to advance until you release the button.

● **Sizing Corner.** The **sizing corner** may be dragged in different directions to change the size of the window by hand. Releasing the mouse button causes the window to remain at the current size.

FIGURE 7.23

New to Windows 98 is the optional Explorer bar. The Explorer bar can be set by the user to add useful tools or features to windows. In this example, a listing of Favorites is added to the My Computer window in the Explorer bar. The user can quickly consult locations recently visited using this regularly updated index.

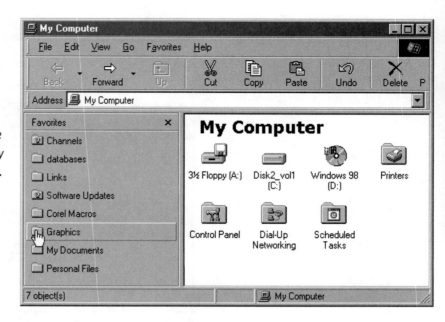

● **Multiple Windows.** Having more than one window visible on the desktop at once is often useful. This can be done by simply opening and repositioning the windows as needed. You may also use special commands to arrange the windows. Pointing to the taskbar and pressing the right mouse button reveals a pop-up menu in which these commands may be found. **Cascading windows** means to arrange them one on top of the other, as shown in Figure 7.24. An alternative arrangement is that of **tiling** windows, which means to make them all visible by arranging them either vertically or horizontally. See Figure 7.25.

Only one window at a time can be active. When a window is active, all commands and actions are assumed to be directed to that window

FIGURE 7.24

A group of windows is cascaded on the desktop. Clicking the right mouse button on the taskbar causes a pop-up menu to appear. To arrange the windows in this fashion, choose the Cascade *command from the menu.*

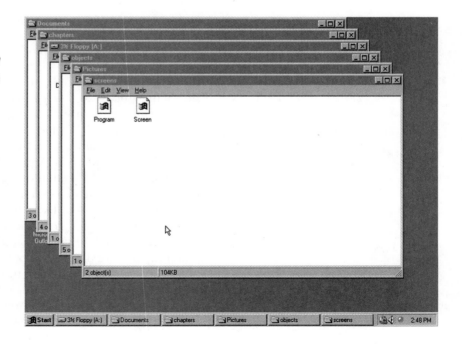

FIGURE 7.25

The same group of windows is tiled on the desktop. In this instance, the Tile Horizontal *command was chosen from the same pop-up menu mentioned in Figure 7.24.*

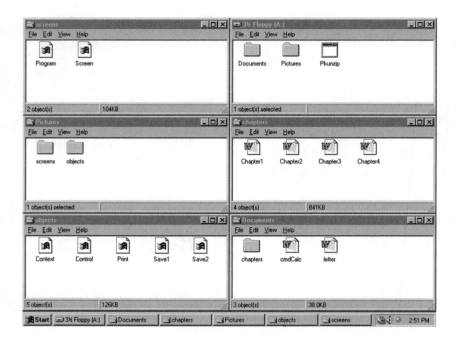

and its contents. The active window is indicated by the bright coloring in the title bar. To activate another window, you need only point and click inside it or click its icon in the taskbar. Immediately the window will move to the front if it is partially hidden.

Managing multiple windows does take up system memory. Consequently, it is often advisable to close or minimize those windows that are not needed both to clear some of the desktop clutter and to speed up system response.

Managing Files with Windows

The GUI in Windows offers several ways for you to manipulate the files and folders stored on your system. In Windows 95 (and earlier versions), File Manager provides a means for viewing the folder structure of disks and devices. Windows Explorer, however, has largely supplanted the older File Manager view.

In Windows Explorer, the window is divided into two panes, as shown in Figure 7.26. The left pane displays the computer's resources as a hierarchical structure. The right pane shows you the contents of the specific item selected from that hierarchy. You may resize both the window and its panes as needed. In addition, you can modify the manner in which the information is displayed to suit your needs. In this case, the right pane shows detailed information about the files according to their type and origin. The plus or minus signs associated with the icons in the left pane can be clicked like a switch to reveal (+) or conceal (−), the hierarchy that belongs to that icon.

From within the Explorer view, files may be moved and copied from folder to folder or disk to disk by dragging the icons. (See "At Your Computer" later in this chapter for more details.)

Files and folders may also be manipulated from the desktop through the My Computer window. The My Computer icon is shown earlier in Figure 7.10. Opening it reveals the set of resources that belongs to your system. By opening these devices and folders, you may

FIGURE 7.26

The Explorer window displays both the hierarchical structure of information stored on your computer and the contents of devices and folders.

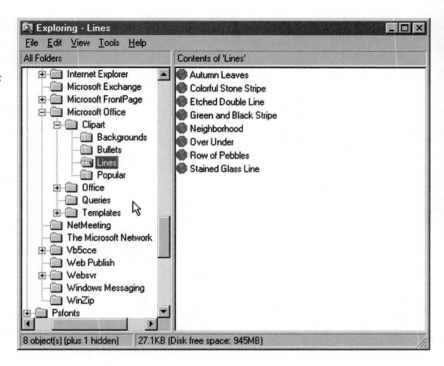

work with the folders and files directly on the desktop, as shown in Figure 7.27.

In Windows 98, you may employ still another view for managing the files and folders on your system. Internet Explorer 4 may be employed both as a Web browser and as a means of viewing and manipulating the contents of your computer. Figure 7.28 shows the contents of a folder much in the same manner as they might appear on a Web page. This integrated approach makes working with information a more seamless experience—regardless of its source. In fact, Windows 98 provides even more opportunities for customizing both Windows Explorer and Internet Explorer to suit personal needs or tastes.

More Information

FIGURE 7.27

Disks and folders may be manipulated directly from the desktop. Here the My Computer *window is open, revealing the resources available to the system. The floppy drive icon is selected and opened, too, to display its contents.*

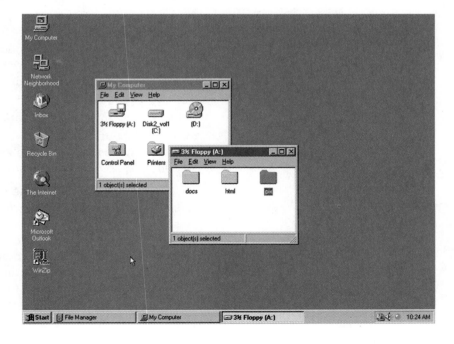

FIGURE 7.28

Windows 98 may be configured to view the contents of your disks and folders much in the same manner as you would a web page. Here the contents of My Computer are shown with devices and folders displayed like hyperlinks. Each link may be clicked to reveal its contents in the same window, much like your web browser would display pages.

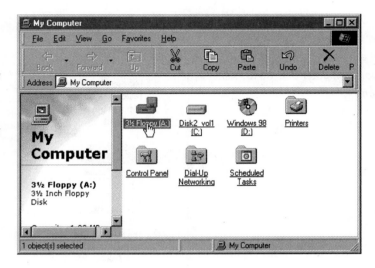

A CLOSER LOOK AT THE MACINTOSH OS

The Macintosh operating system graphical user interface is called the Finder. In this section we will investigate the Finder in more detail, exploring some of its characteristics that are a bit different from the analogous functions in the MS Windows operating systems.

Desktop Windows in the Macintosh OS

Naturally, windows are a prominent feature of the Macintosh Finder interface. Figure 7.29 illustrates the major components, tools, and gadgets associated with Macintosh windows. Here are a listing and brief explanation of these common features.

● **Title Bar.**   The title bar is the top line of the window. Inside the title bar is the name of the disk, folder, or document whose contents are contained in the window. The entire window can be moved around on the desktop by pointing to the title bar and dragging it. When you release the mouse button, the window remains in the new position. The title bar is also used to indicate when the window is active, signified by the horizontal striping, as shown in Figure 7.29. The striping disappears when the window is no longer active.

● **Header.**   Just below the title bar a space is usually reserved for information about the window's contents. Called the **header,** this space typically contains the total number of items in the window as well as the amount of space available for storing additional material.

● **Close, Zoom, and Collapse Boxes.**   Along the title bar are several gadgets used for manipulating the window. On the left side, the close box is used to close the window, removing it from view on the desktop. On the right side are two more tools. The **zoom box** (see Figure 7.29) may be toggled like a switch to change the size of the window on the desktop from its original to maximum size. The **collapse box** (see Figure 7.29, again) acts to minimize the size of the window on the desktop. Pressing it reduces the window to a mere title bar.

FIGURE 7.29

A typical window in the Macintosh OS is shown here. In the title bar is the name of the disk, folder, document, or program. A header usually offers information about the contents of the window. On the left side of the title bar is a tool for closing the window. On the right side of the title bar are buttons for controlling its size. At the bottom of the window and on the right side is the size box, which may be dragged to resize the window by hand. The scroll tools allow you to move the window to display other portions. Inside the window may be a variety of icons signifying different types of objects: files, programs, and other folders.

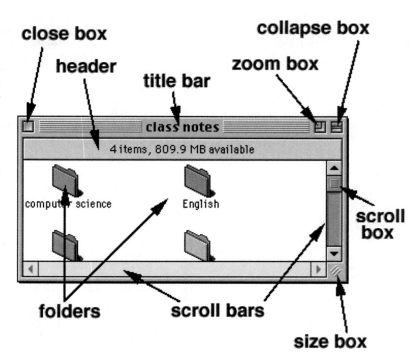

Scroll Bars.   The scroll bars allow you to position the window's view so that you can see a different part of the underlying scene. Elements in the vertical scroll bar allow you to move through the scene vertically. Using the horizontal scroll bar elements, you can look at parts of the scene that are too wide to fit on the screen at once. The scroll bar is shaded to indicate that the underlying scene is larger than the current window. When the scroll bar is not shaded, this means that the entire scene is visible in that dimension. If neither is shaded, all objects are visible.

Scroll Arrows.   A window has up to four scroll arrows: two each in the vertical and horizontal scroll bars. These are used to move the window to a new location in the scene. For example, the upward-pointing scroll arrow at the top of the vertical scroll bar can be used to move the window upward (i.e., in a backward direction) in the scene. Pointing and clicking the arrow advances the window in that direction in small intervals. If you press and hold down the mouse button, the window continues to advance until you release the button.

Scroll Box.   The scroll box shows the relative position of the window in the scene. For example, if the scroll box is positioned at about the middle of the scroll bar, the window is near the middle of the scene. The scroll box can be moved by dragging it. This will cause the window to scroll quickly to that relative position.

Size Box.   In the lower right corner of the window is the size box. The **size box** may be dragged to increase or decrease the size of the window on the desktop.

Viewing Objects.   Windows often contain graphic icons that represent the objects contained within that disk or folder. The Macintosh OS permits you to choose how to view these objects within a given window: as a list, as normal icons, or as buttons. Figure 7.30 displays the same window contents in these three different views. The list view arranges the

FIGURE 7.30

Several views of the contents of a Macintosh window are shown here: (a) the normal icon view; (b) the list view; and (c) the button view.

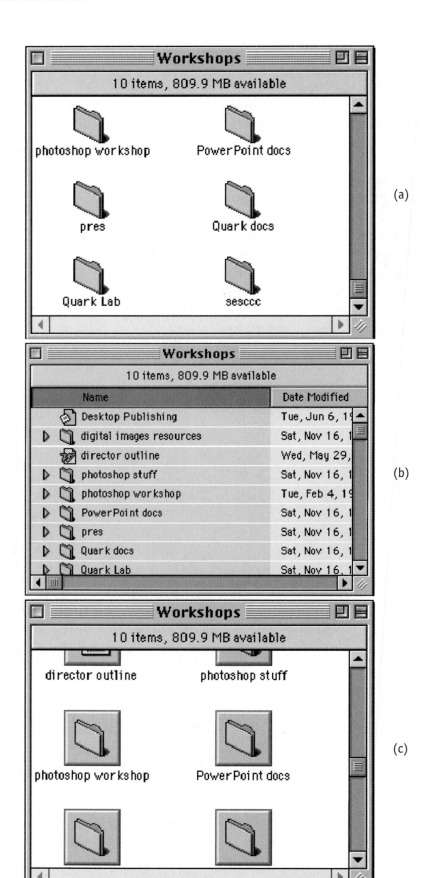

items in some specified order—by name, date, size, and so on. The icon view depicts the objects by the familiar graphic figure. You may control the size and arrangement of the icons. The button view renders the objects as clickable buttons much like those found in a Web browser.

● **Multiple Windows.** Having more than one window visible on the desktop at once is often useful. This can be done by simply opening and repositioning the windows as needed. Only one window at a time, however, can be active. When a window is active, all commands and actions are assumed to be directed to that window and its contents.

In Figure 7.31, portions of three windows are visible, but only the *chapter 7* window is active. To activate another window, you need only point and click inside it. Immediately the window moves to the front if it is partially hidden. Although resizing and moving windows at will around the desktop are easy, managing windows does take up memory. Consequently, it is often advisable to close or collapse those windows that are not needed both to clear some of the desktop clutter and to speed up system response.

Macintosh Finder has still another feature to help manage the clutter of multiple windows on the desktop. You may convert a normal window into what is dubbed a pop-up window. **Pop-up windows** appear as labeled tabs at the bottom of the desktop; when activated, they pop up to reveal their contents. See Figure 7.32 for an example.

Managing Files with the Macintosh OS

In Macintosh Finder, you have learned that there are several ways to view the hierarchy of any given disk. The list view, however, offers some advantages not found in either the icon or button view. In the list view, you can examine the entire contents of a disk or folder, including its interior levels, easily. The hierarchy is represented as an outline. Files or folders that belong to a folder are listed below it but indented to show their de-

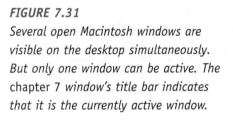

FIGURE 7.31

Several open Macintosh windows are visible on the desktop simultaneously. But only one window can be active. The chapter 7 *window's title bar indicates that it is the currently active window.*

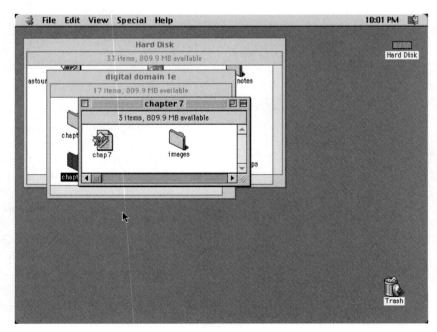

FIGURE 7.32
(a) The folder chapter 7 *is shown in a pop-up window. (b) The tab can be clicked to reveal the normal window view.*

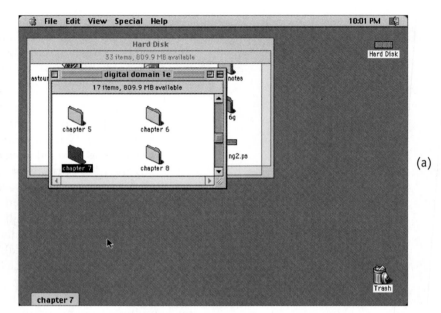

(a)

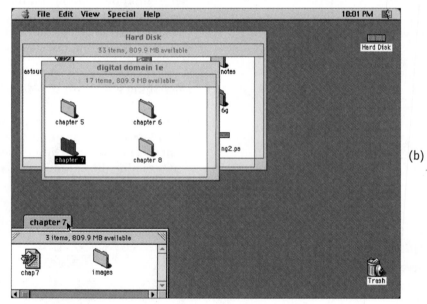

(b)

pendency. The triangles in the leftmost column act as switches for displaying the levels that belong to their associated folders. When you point and click on one, it either reveals the contents of the succeeding level or hides the contents. When a triangle points downward, it signifies that the succeeding level is shown; if it points rightward, it signifies that you are viewing the compressed or hidden view. Figure 7.33 reveals the contents of the folder *Sound Apps* including its hierarchy of folders and files.

Manipulating files and folders in Macintosh Finder is very simple and convenient using the so-called **drag-and-drop** operation. To move a file or folder from one level to another, you need only drag it from its original place to the desired location. When you release the mouse button, the object will be transferred to (i.e., "dropped in") the new location immediately. The folders themselves spring open to help you in relocating or copying files and other folders.

The outline view can display the entire contents of the folders in a disk or folder. Here the folder Sound Apps *is opened to reveal several levels of folders and files within.*

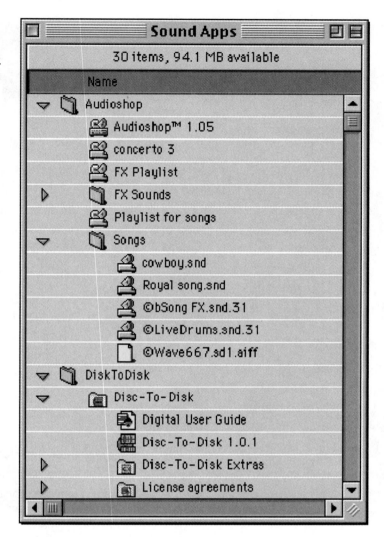

Copying disks, folders, or files to another disk is also a drag-and-drop operation. Copying files within the same disk can be done similarly. (For details, see "At Your Computer" later in this chapter.) In addition, the operating system and many Macintosh applications permit using drag-and-drop to exchange information between them. For example, you can print the contents of a word processing document by simply dragging and dropping it on the icon of the printer on the desktop. This is faster and more convenient because the word processing program does not have to be launched or opened to print the file.

The interface in the Macintosh OS offers a number of features that also allow the user to personalize his or her computing environment. These options are exercised from user dialog boxes managed by the system's Control Panels. The *Appearance* Control Panel lets you specify colors, fonts, and window options. The *Desktop Pictures* Control Panel allows you to choose from a selection of patterns, colors, or scenes to serve as the desktop background. You can keep a list of your favorite applications ready for immediate use with the *Launcher* Control Panel. Several other Control Panels add functionality to your system by managing sounds, monitors, the mouse, keyboard, and other components.

More Information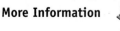

SIMPLE FILE MANAGEMENT WITH YOUR OS

As you have learned, operating systems offer useful services for managing information on your computer. In this activity, you will learn firsthand how to format a disk, create folders, and move and copy files. These are some of the basic tasks that every operating system affords. To complete the activity as described, you will need a new, unformatted disk.

For Windows users:

1 Start your computer system if it is not already running. Press the Start button on the left side of the taskbar (at the bottom of the desktop). Select the **Programs** menu command and *Windows Explorer.*

2 Place the new unformatted disk into the floppy disk drive. Click the icon for the drive in the Explorer window (it is probably labeled "A:"). You will see a dialog box similar to the one shown in Figure 7.34. Click the Yes button to start the disk format process.

3 Another dialog box will appear very much like the one shown in Figure 7.35. Make sure that

you select the Full Format radio button and enter your last name into the label box. (Figure 7.35 is labeled *"My Disk."*) The operating system attaches the label to the disk for identification. When you are ready, press the Start button to begin the formatting.

It will take several minutes for the system to format the disk. The operating system will create a sequence of magnetic marks on the disk to signify sectors and blocking for the disk. At the same time, it will create a space for storing information about the directory structure of the disk. Each operating system employs its own proprietary format. This is why (ordinarily) disks formatted for one operating system are not readable on computers employing a different operating system. When the process is complete, you should see a summary of the results. On a normal 3½-inch disk, the Windows operating system will create data blocks that are 512 bytes per block, for a total of 2,847 blocks per disk.

4 Select the floppy drive icon once again from the Explorer window. Choose the *New* com-

FIGURE 7.34
The Windows dialog box for formatting a floppy disk.

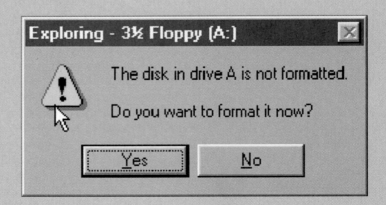

FIGURE 7.35

The dialog box assembles the needed information for completing the format process. The user may choose the type of disk format, a volume name, and other options.

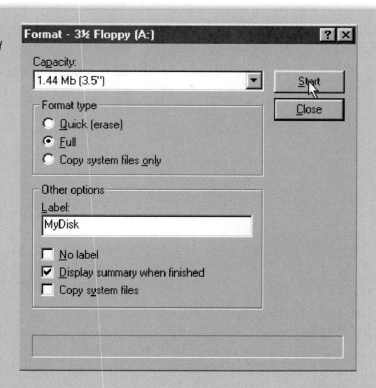

mand from the **File** menu and *Folder* from the submenu, as shown in Figure 7.36. (We will write command sequences such as this one as **File/New/Folder** for convenience.) When the folder icon appears in the right-hand window, type in the name "*docs.*"

5 Repeat the process and create two more folders named "*pix*" and "*html.*" When you are fin-

ished, your disk should be organized similarly to the one shown in Figure 7.37.

6 Next, create a text file for storing in the *docs* folder. Choose the Start button in the taskbar. Select **Programs/Accessories/Notepad.** The Notepad is a utility program for creating simple text files. It functions much like a word processing program. In this instance, you are interested

FIGURE 7.36

*Creating a new folder is shown here. The user may create a variety of special objects from the New command in the **File** menu. The submenu reveals a variety of choices. In this case, a new folder is chosen.*

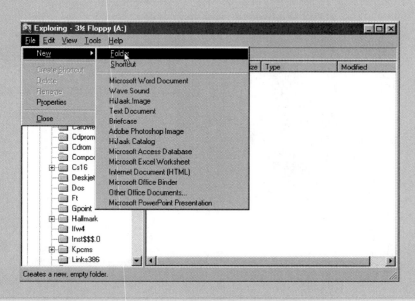

FIGURE 7.37
The three folders on MyDisk are shown in the Windows Explorer view.

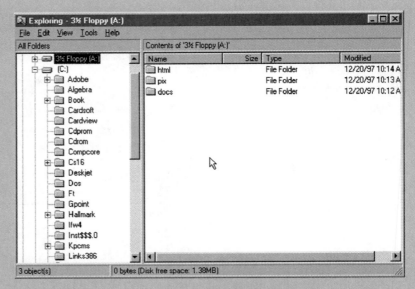

only in creating a file for further use. Type in a sentence or two and choose the command sequence **File/Save As.** Next, you will navigate through the system hierarchy. Click the up-arrowed folder until you reach the desktop. From there you can select the 3½-inch floppy icon to open your disk. Click the *docs* folder to open it. Type in the file name "note." Your Save As dialog box should look like the one in Figure 7.38. Press the Save button to copy the file to the *docs* folder on your disk. You can quit the Notepad program. (Choose **File/Exit.**)

7 In the Windows Explorer window, find the *note* icon inside of the *docs* folder. Drag the *note* icon to the *html* folder in the left window and release the mouse button when the folder darkens. The process box will show that the file *note.txt* has moved from the folder *docs* to *html*.

8 Open the *html* folder. There you will find the *note.txt* file. This time, hold down the Ctrl key and drag the *note* file icon back to the *docs* folder. As you can see, the process box tells you that the file is copied to the folder. Thus, both folders contain copies of the same file. Ordinarily, dragging the icon from disk to disk copies the item; on the same disk, though, you must hold down the Ctrl key to copy.

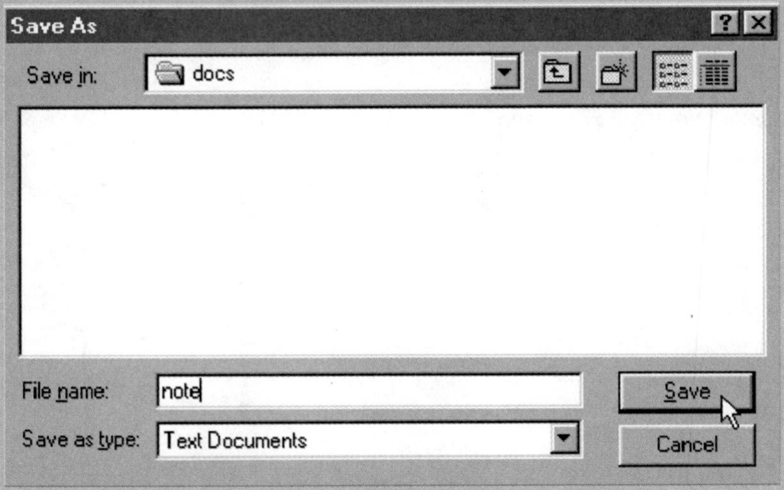

FIGURE 7.38
The Save As dialog box in the Notepad application asks the user to (1) name the file and (2) locate where the copy will be stored. In this case, the file note *will be saved to the* docs *folder.*

For Macintosh users:

1 Start your computer system if it is not already running. Place a new unformatted disk into the floppy disk drive. If the disk is unformatted, you will see a dialog box similar to the one shown in Figure 7.39. Enter your last name into the name box. (Figure 7.39 is labeled "*My Disk.*") The operating system attaches the name to the disk for identification. When you are ready, click the Initialize button to begin the formatting. This will be followed by a safety check (see Figure 7.40) to make sure that you realize that the formatting process will erase the current contents of the desk. That is precisely what we want to do. Press Continue to start the formatting process.

It will take several minutes for the system to format the disk. The operating system will create a sequence of magnetic marks on the disk to signify sectors and blocking for the disk. At the same time, it will create a space for storing information about the directory structure of the disk. Each operating system employs its own proprietary format. This is why (ordinarily) disks formatted for one operating system are not readable on computers employing a different operating system.

2 When the process has completed, an icon representing the disk will appear on the desktop. It will look similar to the icon in Figure 7.41. Double-click the icon to open the disk's window.

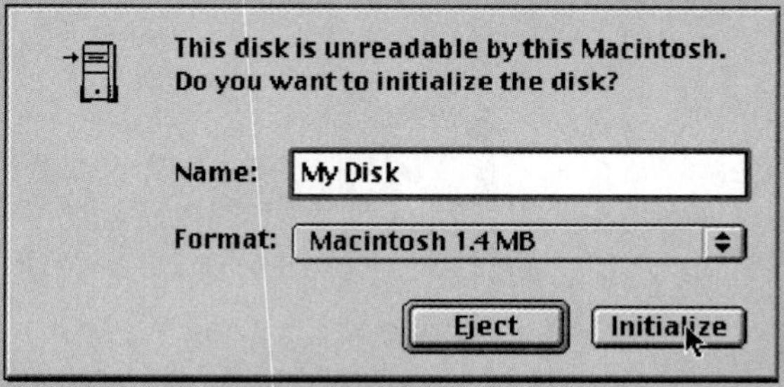

FIGURE 7.39

The Initialize dialog box is shown here. You name the disk volume and choose among several disk formats. When ready, the Initialize button will commence the process of formatting the disk.

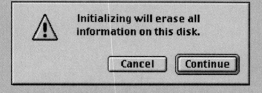

FIGURE 7.40

As a precaution, a safety check is issued by the OS to remind you that formatting the disk will erase its current contents.

FIGURE 7.41

When the formatting is done, the disk icon will appear on the desktop, as shown here. At this point the disk may be used to store files.

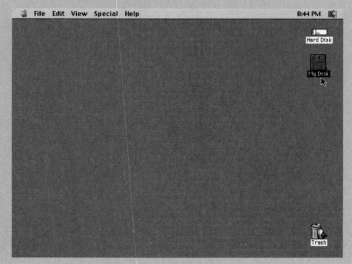

3 Next, create several new folders on the disk to hold files. Choose the *New Folder* command from the **File** menu, as shown in Figure 7.42. (We will write command sequences such as this one as **File/New Folder** for convenience.) When the folder icon appears in the window, type in the name "*docs.*"

4 Repeat the process and create two more folders named "*pix*" and "*html.*"

5 Now, create a text file for storing in the *docs* folder. Choose **File/Find. . . .** This will cause the Find utility dialog box, as seen in Figure 7.43, to appear. Enter the phrase "Simpletext," as shown in the figure. Click the Find button. In several moments, at least one icon representing the program will appear in the Find

window. You can double-click one of these icons to start the application.

6 SimpleText is a utility program for creating basic text files. It functions much like a word processing program. In this instance, you are interested only in creating a file for further use. Type in a sentence or two, and choose the command sequence **File/Save As.** Next, navigate through the system hierarchy. Click the Desktop button to show the contents of the desktop. From there you can select and open your disk. Double-click the *docs* folder in the window to open it. Type in the file name "note." Your Save As dialog box should look like the one in Figure 7.44. Click the Save button, and the file will be copied

FIGURE 7.42

When creating a new folder, the user chooses the New Folder *command in the* **File** *menu.*

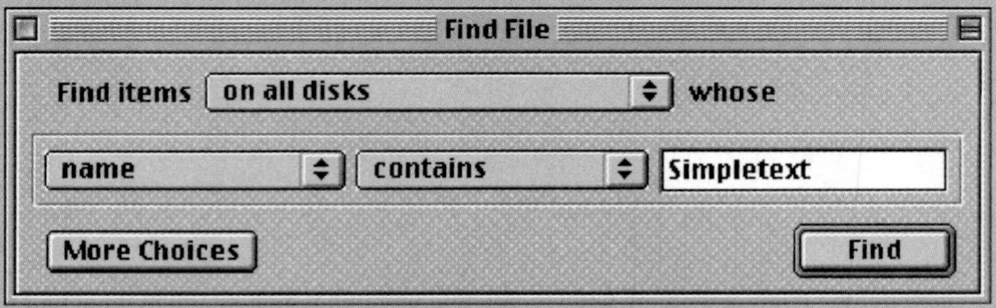

File	
New Folder	⌘N
Open	⌘O
Print	⌘P
Move To Trash	⌘⌫
Close Window	⌘W
Get Info	⌘I
Label	▶
Sharing...	
Duplicate	⌘D
Make Alias	⌘M
Put Away	⌘Y
Find...	⌘F
Show Original	⌘R
Page Setup...	
Print Window...	

FIGURE 7.43

The Find File utility can be used to locate files by name, date, type, and combinations of these and other criteria. In this instance, you are searching for the location of the application SimpleText on any of the disks in the system.

Find File

Find items [on all disks ⬍] whose

[name ⬍] [contains ⬍] [Simpletext]

[More Choices]   [Find]

to the *docs* folder on your disk. You can quit the SimpleText program. (Choose **File/ Quit.**)

7 With your floppy disk window active, choose **View/As List.** In the disk window, click the triangle next to the *docs* icon to reveal the *note* icon inside the *docs* folder. (It should be in the down position to indicate that the subordinate levels of the folder will be displayed.) Drag the *note* icon to the *html* folder and release when the folder darkens. If necessary, click the triangle next to the *html* icon to reveal its contents. As you can see, the file *note* has moved from the folder *docs* to *html*.

8 This time, hold down the Option key and drag the *note* file icon back to the *docs* folder. The Copy box tells you that the file is being copied to the folder this time. Thus, both folders contain copies of the same file. Ordinarily, dragging the icon from disk to disk copies the item; on the same disk, though, you must hold down the Option key to copy. The window should look similar to the one in Figure 7.45.

You have completed the activity. These simple steps reveal how easy it is to format disks, create folders, and move and copy files. The graphical user interface makes these tasks direct and intuitive.

FIGURE 7.44

The Save As dialog box in the SimpleText application asks the user to (1) name the file and (2) locate where the copy will be stored. In this instance, the file note *will be saved to the* docs *folder.*

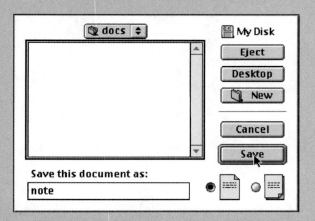

FIGURE 7.45

In the List view, you can see that the disk contains three folders and that two copies of the file note *are in the* docs *and* html *folders.*

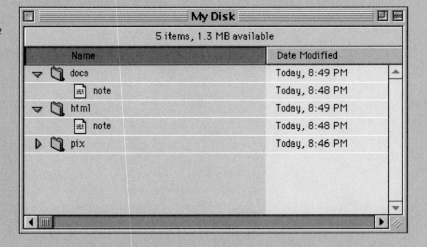

Social Themes

Software Piracy?

Ask anyone whether removing a printer or a video monitor from another's home or office constitutes theft, and there would be no hesitation in his or her answer. Everyone would agree that it does. Yet, ask whether copying a program or software from one machine to another amounts to theft, and the matter is perceived very differently. Perhaps it is wrong, but it is not a "serious" wrong. Somehow, the seeming "immateriality" of software and programs relegates them to another realm entirely.

Some software companies are apparently not immune to this rationalization either. Over the past several decades, there has been a steady stream of legal actions against companies charged with stealing by creating copycat versions of successful commercial products. For example, only recently did Apple Computer agree to drop its long-standing litigation against Microsoft Corporation. Apple had alleged that Microsoft Windows was a Mac OS GUI look-alike. The two companies settled when Microsoft invested in Apple; the precise terms of their agreement, however, were not made public.

Is copying a program file the same as stealing it? Does mimicking its "look and feel" amount to theft? If so, why are these forms of software piracy so widespread in the computing environment? As you will see, a closer look at the legal world of software reveals a number of interesting issues.

The Status of Software

Software is a list of instructions that direct the processing of a computer system. The hardware or components of a computer are certainly important, but without software, the hardware merely takes up space. Software has become big business, too; it has been estimated that software industry sales top $50 billion annually. Though they are a commodity, software programs have characteristics that make them different and more difficult to manage than other commodities.

Most products have a recognizable physical presence. Software, however, is a list of instructions that are encoded as a binary file and stored on a floppy disk, a tape, a CD-ROM, or a hard drive. In this form, software or programs are inert—they just sit there. A program, of course, must be loaded into the main memory of a computer system and executed by its CPU to be worth anything to anybody.

A crucial issue is this: What defines the software? To put it another way, what separates one program from another? Is it the list of instructions that make up the program, or is it what the program does when it is executed? If software is primarily a list of instructions, then it resembles other forms of intellectual property (books, plays, and so on) that are defined by their expression. On the other hand, if a program is best conceived by what it does, then software is defined by its functionality (like an invention or discovery) rather than its expression.

When presented such alternatives, we probably want to say that software concerns "both." The expression of software is important. Copying the list of instructions exactly certainly constitutes theft. But expression is not all. Programs, like other descriptions, can take on many different forms. It is quite possible to create a program listing that looks very different, yet prescribes the same kinds of operations. Certainly, conjuring the exact same functionality and appearance from an intentionally different set of instructions must also amount to piracy as well.

There are exceptions to both of these instances. Some tasks performed by computers are either so trivial or so commonplace that they belong to a software "public domain." No one could claim rights to these, and no one could be rightly accused of stealing them. Much of the fine details of how programs manage data or information falls into this category. On the other hand, the notions of "look-alike" and "work-alike" are not hard-and-fast concepts either. Does the fact that two GUIs employ graphical objects such as windows and icons mean that one copies the other? Sometimes the line is difficult to draw.

Naturally, issues like these have kept the legal profession busy for many years.

Legal Protections for Software

Traditionally authors, as the creators of intellectual property, are protected by a broad assortment of laws to protect trademarks, patents, trade secrets, and copyrights. **Trademarks** protect words, names, symbols, and logos normally used in commerce. **Patents** protect the rights of individuals who make discoveries or inventions. **Trade secrets** cover information, designs, and devices that companies wish to keep secret to retain commercial advantages from their creations. **Copyrights** protect authors of original works from damages caused by others who might improperly reproduce or use materials without their permission. Copyright laws are not extended to intellectual ideas or discoveries, to concepts and principles, nor to a process or procedure. In short, copyrights protect the expression of an idea, not the idea itself.

The development and distribution of software have attempted to incorporate all four of these legal protections. These efforts have met with different degrees of success.

Trademarks, of course, are the most obvious and least problematic. The name of the application and an identifying logo are often protected by trademark. "Windows 98," for instance, is a trademark of Microsoft Corporation. Its use is strictly prohibited without the permission of Microsoft.

Portions of a program may be classified as a trade secret. Trade secret protections allow a company to withhold information that may be significant for commercial reasons. Information is normally considered as a public resource, but trade secrets are not subject to disclosure. Programmers, for example, who work for a given company must sign nondisclosure agreements that they will not reveal specific information about their work even if they leave the employ of that company. Violations of trade secrets are treated as industrial espionage. Nonetheless, the great majority of case law has been accumulated to seek redress from violations of either patent or copyright law.

Patents are awarded to individuals who have made discoveries or inventions that "promote the progress of . . . useful arts." A patent holder has exclusive rights to manufacture and distribute patented goods as a reward for their usefulness, novelty, and "non-obvious" character. Patents are limited to a specific term—typically, 17 years.

For several decades, computer programs were ineligible for patents. Instead, programs were considered "mathematical algorithms," which are no more than a calculation of information. As mentioned, information per se is not patentable. Software may now incorporate patent protections, though. Recently, the law was amended to include "a series of steps to be performed on a computer" as a new category for potentially patentable products. Patent claims for software, however, are not automatic. The software must be classified into one of these three categories: (1) a manipulation of abstract ideas, (2) a solution to a mathematical problem, or (3) a process for transforming physical material or data into a different state to achieve a practical application. Only programs in class (3) are patentable.

Failing patent protection, most manufacturers seek to protect their products by appeals to copyright law. (See "Social Themes" in Chapter 2 for more background on copyrights.) Copyrights, however, protect the expression of ideas, not the ideas or information. This has proved to be a thorny issue for resolving disputes about software piracy. Copying software verbatim without permission—such as making disk copies of program files and distributing them—is an obvious infringement. On the other hand, a competitor might produce a program that performs like the original without actually copying the precise instructions of that original.

The landmark case for determining such violations was *Computer Associates International v. Altai, Incorporated* (1992). Computer Associates instituted a three-part test for deciding whether a commercial program infringed on the copyright protection held by another. This is the so-called "abstraction-filtration-comparison" test. First, the design and organization of the alleged copycat program are analyzed. Each of the components of its design is scrutinized. If any can be shown to be required for reasons of efficiency and operation or derived from the public domain of knowledge about programming, they are considered components not protected by copyright. Whatever is left after this filtering step is then compared with the original product. Significant similarities at this point may constitute a copyright violation. If the developer of the "work-alike" software had access to the original, then courts will almost always rule that copyright infringement did take place.

The industry practice of reverse-engineering is usually sufficient to prove access. As you learned in the last chapter, programs are often devised in a source language that is then compiled as machine instructions that are executed on a particular variety of processor. The source code program is not distributed with the software when purchased. Consequently, the user has no direct access to how the program was designed or written. Machine language programs can be decompiled—that is, translated back into a symbolic form that can be studied by professional programmers. A decompiled (or disassembled) program listing is not the same as the original source program listing. An experienced and knowledgeable programmer, though, can understand how the program works from this version. Creating another program based on analyzing a working version in this manner amounts to reverse-engineering.

For a number of years, decompiling and studying programs were considered acceptable practices. This is how programmers learned about the art. Copyright infringement cases have questioned the legality of such practices. Currently, the courts seem to decide these cases based on the extent that reverse-engineering played a part in the resulting product. This compares with other applications of the principle. A little bit of similarity is permissible; a lot is not.

Combating Software Pirates

Whether protected by trademark, patent, or copyright, the software developer cannot exercise these rights without legal action. In other words, violators must be brought to court. The results in these cases are never guaranteed, and they are always expensive. Recently, software developers have opted to protect their investments by using additional and other means.

Commercial developers often employ technology to help protect their products from piracy. Most commercial applications are protected by electronic serial numbers and online registration schemes. To install a copy of a program on a new computer system successfully, the user must possess a valid serial number. This number must be correctly entered to complete the installation process. The installation process may also involve an automatic electronic registration. The user is required to communicate information over a network connecting his or her computer system to the manufacturer's computer systems. These methods help to deter illegal copying of software.

Another common method is to employ copy protection on the media that store program files. A copy-protected program prevents additional copies from being installed on different computer systems.

A related strategy works in network computing environments. Some programs have so-called "network savvy." These programs are equipped with processes that search the network for copies of that program with the same registered serial number. If a program with that same serial number is currently running on another machine, the duplicate program will disable itself automatically.

Of course, none of these methods is fail-safe. But, like locks on doors, they tend to curb temptation among normally honest people. Someone determined to violate copyrights can always find a way to defeat these technological methods.

Licensing Software to Individuals

Software is commercially available to individuals in several forms. Some programs are considered freeware; others are shareware; most are licensed software. These differ in their manner of distribution and use.

● **Freeware.** A program is **freeware** when the author grants free access and use of the product to any user. A large number of individuals have contributed their time and energies to the creation of programs for general use and enjoyment. Most freeware is utility programs that add functionality to your system. Some, however, may be full-scale applications that rival the performance of commercial products.

Freeware programs carry no warranties or guarantees of performance. They may also be freely distributed from individual to individual and from computer to computer. Most freeware authors ask that you notify them if you adopt their product. This is considered an appropriate courtesy.

● **Shareware.** Some programs are considered **shareware** in that a user may try them out free of charge but is expected to pay a nominal fee for continued use of the product. Shareware software, however, depends on the honesty of its users. Its authors are willing for users to experiment and explore their products, but they do expect users to pay for the privilege of using them beyond these tryouts. Most shareware products lack any protection from copying or continued use. A user could easily appropriate the product without fear of detection.

Of course, if the majority of users fail to pay the nominal fees for shareware programs, then the authors will eventually go out of business. Users would be the ultimate losers because they would be deprived of the value of inexpensive yet useful shareware programs.

○ **Licensed Software.**   Most commercial products are licensed by the manufacturer for use by individuals or groups. **Software licenses** grant nonexclusive or limited rights of ownership to the user in exchange for the price of the software. The manufacturer grants the right to employ the software on one or more computer systems—though usually no more than one machine simultaneously. For instance, purchasing a word processing program might permit you to install it on your computer at school or the office as well as at home. It would not permit you to distribute the program to other machines or use these copies at the same time. The license may permit you to create an archival copy of the program for safe-keeping, too. On the other hand, it strictly prohibits making additional copies and distributing them to others. You may not sell, rent, or transfer the software to another person either.

The traditional single-user license is also a single-computer license—though there are exceptions, as noted above. Organizations that manage a large number of systems cannot afford to purchase single-user licenses for every computer system. Site licensing offers an alternative to single-user software licenses. Purchasing a site license entitles the organization to install up to a maximum number of copies of an application on any of the machines managed by that organization. Some site licenses may offer unlimited copies as long as they are restricted to machines within that organization. The fees are typically paid annually. Site licenses are expensive, but they are more economical than maintaining single-user ones. Another version of site licensing is for server-based software. The program is installed on servers within the organization that distribute copies to computers connected to the network. This approach offers the greatest flexibility. The software is distributed on an as-needed basis rather than sitting idly on computer systems that are not currently employing it.

Besides banning the copying and distribution of licensed software, the manufacturer usually prohibits any attempts to either modify or reverse-engineer the programs. Some manufacturers do not permit their software to be exported to specific countries—especially those that have violated international copyright agreements.

Failure to comply with these requirements voids the user's license. Of course, as we stated earlier, monitoring compliance and enforcing licensing regulations are very difficult. Why, then, should consumers take these regulations more seriously? The answer is one of simple self-interest.

The price of software is governed by the economics of supply and demand. Over the long term, a software manufacturer must charge a price per unit that meets at least the cost of production. Any less and the company goes out of business. Naturally, the manufacturer will try to charge more than the cost of production to ensure a profit; however, the dynamics of consumer demand will tend to curb overpricing. If the software is too expensive, no one will buy it. On the other hand, if the manufacturer must account for the illegal distribution of products as part of the economic equation, then the loss of sales will be absorbed in higher prices passed on to legal purchasers of these products. Thus, the cost of production must take into account illegal users. The price of software is artificially higher. Every time you pass along a copy of a program that you purchased to a friend, you are actually driving up the price you will pay for your next purchase. Ironically, curbing and controlling the illegal use of licensed software actually contribute to lowering the prices that you pay.

Software is a valuable commodity, and protecting that value is a matter for everyone, not just the developers and manufacturers of software.

SUMMARY

Users employ application programs to perform specific tasks such as preparing documents, creating graphics, browsing the Web, and so on. System software, in contrast, is the programs that you employ to control your computers and provide useful functions. The operating system is the most significant example of system software. Operating systems manage the resources of the computer system, supervise the execution of user processes, and provide important services for the user and his or her applications. The operating system actually controls all aspects of the computer's operation. The user communicates commands or requests that are executed by the operating system.

Operating systems are usually classified into two groups: single-user and multiuser systems. A single-user system is designed to manage one task or program at a time. Single-user operating systems traditionally support desktop or personal computers. A multiuser operating system is designed to support a number of users employing the computer's resources during the same period of time. Multiuser operating systems manage this feat by performing what is called multiprogramming—that is, executing several processes concurrently by switching execution among them.

The user interface for an operating system serves as the medium of communication between the user and the system. Text-based user interfaces allow the user to express commands as single-line text commands entered from the keyboard. The operating system responds in kind by providing text messages. In contrast, graphical user interfaces employ a more visual form of communication. The user employs a mouse or similar device to manipulate icons, windows, and other gadgets displayed on the video monitor.

The user selects commands from menus and provides any additional information needed by entering text into dialog boxes. Text-based user interfaces are concise and powerful. Graphical user interfaces are more intuitive and user friendly. Windows and the Macintosh OS are the most popular forms of GUIs for desktop computers.

Software is a form of intellectual property. Commercial developers often seek to protect their products by applying a variety of legal protections such as trademarks, trade secrets, patents, and copyrights. The most common defense against software piracy or theft is to prove copyright infringement.

PROJECTS

1 Find out how many different applications can be loaded simultaneously on your computer system. Open or start each program. After some simple operations, open another program without exiting (quitting) the previous application. Consult the operating system controls for information about current memory usage after each application is loaded. Eventually, you will reach a point where no further programs can be loaded. What and how many programs can your system support simultaneously? Is it a good idea to leave this many programs in main memory?

2 I/O control drivers are an important service supplied by your operating system. Discover what sort of print drivers your operating system provides. Why is it important to match the print driver with the specific device(s) employed by your computer system?

3 Multiuser operating systems employ virtual memory to expand the amount of storage available for users and user processes. Most modern single-user operating systems (Windows 95/98 and NT, and Macintosh OS) also support virtual memory schemes. Consult the documentation for your particular system to find out how virtual memory is controlled. Turn on the virtual memory system and conduct (or repeat) the experiment described in project 1 above.

Were the results different? Were these differences significant? (Be sure that you compare conditions when virtual memory is on versus conditions when it is off.)

4 Examine the file structure of your personal computer system's main storage device—pre-sumably your largest magnetic hard disk drive. Compose a diagram that details all the folders and their levels for that disk. (For simplicity, your diagram may ignore the files and depict only folders.) Are files and data organized conveniently for continued use? Are some folders unnecessarily cluttered? What improvements could you impose on this hierarchy?

Draw a second diagram that depicts an improved organization. Based on this plan, reorganize the directory structure of your disk. Note: Do not attempt this on a laboratory machine without the permission of the laboratory manager.

5 If you have access to both a Windows and a Macintosh computer, complete the "At Your Computer" exercises for both Windows and Macintosh systems. Compose an essay that compares and contrasts your experiences with these two different GUIs and operating systems. On the whole, are they significantly different or significantly alike? Explain.

6 Locate the software license agreements for several programs that you have purchased. (These are usually stored electronically with the software as well as printed with the documentation that accompanies it.) For each, find out what rights you are afforded as the owner of the software copy. Is it permissible to make copies of your copy of the program? Where and how may these copies reside? Is it permissible for you to transfer your ownership to another person? If so, under what conditions?

Compare these rights with those that you would enjoy owning an item of material property (such as an automobile, for example). How do they compare? In what ways do they contrast with normal property rights? Explain.

Key Terms

application software, programs	Close button (box)	command line interpreter
cascading windows	collapse box	context switching

contextual menu	icons	shareware
control icon	Maximize button	single-user operating system
copyright	memory manager	size box
CPU bound	menu	sizing corner
CPU scheduler	menu bar	software license
desktop	Minimize button	Status bar
dialog box	multiprogramming, multitasking	submenu
directory	multiuser operating system	supervisor
drag-and-drop	operating system (OS)	system call
Explorer bar	patent	system software
file, text	pathname	tiling windows
file manager	pointer	title bar
folder	pop-up menu	trade secret
freeware	pop-up window	trademark
graphical user interface (GUI)	prompt sign	user interface
header (bar)	pull-down menu	virtual memory
hierarchical file structure (HFS)	Restore button	window
I/O bound	script	zoom box
I/O control driver	scroll arrow, box, button	

QUESTIONS FOR REVIEW

1 Compare system software and application software. Which is more important? Explain.

2 Explain the overall role of the operating system in the functioning of a computer system.

3 Describe some particular functions and services provided by a single-user operating system.

4 What is meant when we say that an operating system employs a hierarchical file structure?

5 Describe the use of pathnames in identifying files in a hierarchical file system.

6 What is a user interface? How significant is it for determining how a computer appears to perform?

7 What does multiprogramming mean? Explain how it makes multiuser operating systems possible.

8 What is meant by the term "context switching"?

9 Describe some particular functions and services provided by multiuser operating systems—above and beyond those found in single-user systems.

10 Compare text-based and graphical computer user interfaces. Which would you prefer to use?

11 Explain how the desktop motif is intended to organize the way in which you work within a GUI.

12 Describe the use of windows within a graphical user interface. Specifically, what do they depict or contain?

13 Explain pull-down menus and their function within a graphical user interface.

14 What other sorts of menus help the user to direct and control the computer's operation?

15 What is a dialog box? Why are dialog boxes important? Explain.

16 What are submenus? How can you tell if a submenu is attached to a normal menu choice?

17 What are the most recent versions of Microsoft Windows? How do these versions compare generally?

18 Describe some of the basic features and gadgets associated with windows in Microsoft Windows.

19 What is the Windows Explorer? Explain its organization and major functions.

20 Describe some of the basic features and gadgets associated with windows in the Macintosh OS.

21 In the Macintosh OS, what are the practical differences among displaying files and folders by their icon view, button view, or list view?

22 How does software compare and contrast with typical products or commodities? Are these differences significant? Explain.

23 Explain the difference between copyrights and patents. How do these apply to the protection of commercial software?

24 What is reverse-engineering? Why is it a potential infringement on copyrighted software?

25 Explain the different categories of software: freeware, shareware, and licensed software.

PART 3

TEXT AND NUMBERS

Vasily Kandinsky, *Striped,* 1934. Solomon R. Guggenheim Museum

As you learned in Chapter 4, finding more reliable means for numeric processing motivated the invention of modern-day computers. Indeed, during the first three decades of electronic computers, numeric processing dominated their activities. The design of the electronic digital computer makes numeric processing, in many ways, easier to carry out than text processing because the fundamental arithmetic operations are part of the machine language of most computers. In addition, numeric problems are often easier to pose and solve than problems of a nonnumeric or nonquantifiable nature.

The numeric problems with which the early computers were occupied were problems whose solution methods were already known. What the computer added to the effort was its incredible speed and peerless accuracy. Numeric solutions that might take 10 people 2 weeks to work out could be solved on a computer in a matter of minutes.

Of course, today's computers do a great deal more than numeric processing, but numeric processing is still important. Mathematical models and numeric processing help us predict our weather; launch and track satellites and interplanetary space probes; design our telecommunication systems, highways, automobiles, and airplanes; maintain our military defensive systems; and undertake a host of other important tasks. In fact, a great many modern computing activities, such as image and sound processing and computer-aided design, which we ordinarily do not think of as numeric in nature, actually depend very heavily on numeric processing. It is fair to say that numeric processing is just as fundamental to the majority of today's computing applications as it was in the early days of computing.

OBJECTIVES

- *The way integers and decimal numbers are represented and stored in computers*

- *Limitations in the accuracy of numeric computations performed by computers*

- *Evolution of software tools to facilitate numeric processing*

- *Capabilities of spreadsheet software to perform numeric processing and modeling*

- *Overview of symbolic mathematical and visualization software*

CHAPTER 8
NUMERIC PROCESSING

MORE ABOUT BINARY NUMBER REPRESENTATIONS

As you already know, all information processed by a computer belongs to the digital domain. Consequently, any object that we wish to process must first be digitized, that is, converted to a discrete binary form or representation. At first glance, digitization might appear to be a natural and simple process for numbers. Generally, when we deal with numbers, we deal with them as individual, discrete entities. But a closer examination will reveal two difficulties with this naive assumption. These difficulties stem from the fact that the numbers are both infinite in number and continuously distributed along the number line.

For our purposes we can think of the number line as consisting of three categories of numbers: integers, numbers with a finite nonzero decimal part, and numbers with an infinite nonzero decimal part. **Integers** are made up of the whole numbers, zero, and the negatives of the whole numbers. Integers have no decimal part (or we could say a zero decimal part) and their conversion to a binary form is relatively straightforward, as you saw in Chapter 2. We will review this process momentarily. Numbers with a finite decimal part are a subset of all the fractions. The values $1/10 = .1$, $1/5 = .2$, and $5/2 = 2.5$ are examples. But not all numbers have finite decimal representations. For example, $1/3 = .3333333 . . .$ has an infinite decimal representation.

As you might guess, we would have difficulty converting an infinite fraction for storage on a digital computer, which by necessity has only a finite amount of memory available. We'll consider this issue in more detail shortly, but one point is worth mentioning here. Because the computer stores numbers (and all data, for that matter) in binary form, we will be interested in which fractions have finite and infinite *binary* representations. For some fractions, whether their representation is finite or infinite will depend on whether the representation chosen is binary (base-2) or decimal (base-10). You'll see some examples of this a little later. First we consider the representation of integers for digital storage.

The integers form a discrete and infinite subset of the number line, as illustrated in Figure 8.1. Their discrete nature means that every integer has a unique closed (finite) form. Computers are not only discrete machines, they are also finite machines. As a consequence, there will always be a practical limit to the number of integers that we can represent digitally. For example, many current computers allow exact representation only for integers in the range $-32,768$ to $+32,767$ (see Figure 8.2). You'll see why these particular limits are used shortly.

Let's review the representation of integers in the binary number system. When we write the number 235, how is it interpreted? If we read the number as two hundred thirty-five, we have almost answered this question. The notation 235 really means $(2 \times 10^2) + (3 \times 10^1) + (5 \times 10^0)$, assuming that we are using the decimal system (base-10 system) of representing numbers. As we saw in Chapter 2, each digit in the original number has a value that is determined by the value of the digit itself and the position it

FIGURE 8.1

The integers form a discrete, infinite subset of the real number line.

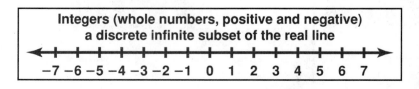

FIGURE 8.2

Because computer memory is finite, only a limited number range of integers can be represented.

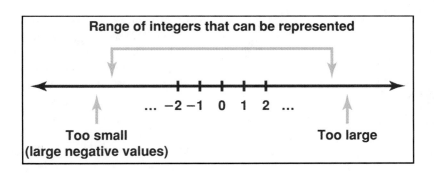

occupies in the number. The rightmost digit has its own value (remember that any number raised to the power of 0 is 1, so $10^0 = 1$), the next digit to the left has its own value multiplied by 10 (10^1), the next digit to the left has its own value multiplied by 100 (10^2), and so on. Each digit's value in the number is determined by multiplying its own value by a power of 10 equal to its position from the rightmost digit.

We saw that the binary number system is organized by exactly this scheme. The only difference between the binary and decimal systems is that we use powers of 2 rather than powers of 10 to compute the place value of digits. Consequently, the base-10 number 235 written in binary representation would be 11101011 or $(1 \times 2^7) + (1 \times 2^6) + (1 \times 2^5) + (0 \times 2^4) + (1 \times 2^3) + (0 \times 2^2) + (1 \times 2^1) + (1 \times 2^0)$. We will adopt the convention of writing 11101011_2 to indicate that the number represented is to be interpreted as a binary (base-2) number.

Let's review the process of changing a number's representation between decimal and binary. First, suppose the number is given in binary; how do we recover its decimal representation? That is easy. All we need do is perform the implicit calculation that is inherent in the number representation—sometimes we call this **expanding the number's representation**. For example, the number 11011011_2 would be expanded into a decimal number as follows:

11011011_2
$= (1 \times 2^7) + (1 \times 2^6) + (0 \times 2^5) + (1 \times 2^4) + (1 \times 2^3) + (0 \times 2^2) + (1 \times 2^1) + (1 \times 2^0)$
$= 128 + 64 + 0 + 16 + 8 + 0 + 2 + 1$
$= 219$

Similarly,

10110110_2
$= (1 \times 2^7) + (0 \times 2^6) + (1 \times 2^5) + (1 \times 2^4) + (0 \times 2^3) + (1 \times 2^2) + (1 \times 2^1) + (0 \times 2^0)$
$= 128 + 0 + 32 + 16 + 0 + 4 + 2 + 0$
$= 182$

Let's look at some examples of conversion in the opposite direction—decimal numbers to binary numbers. How will this be accomplished? Consider the simple example of converting the decimal number 14 to binary representation.

You can probably do the necessary work in your head to write $14 = 1110_2 = (1 \times 2^3) + (1 \times 2^2) + (1 \times 2^1) + (0 \times 2^0) = 8 + 4 + 2$. It isn't hard for us to figure out that we need an 8, a 4, and a 2 to "build" the decimal value 14 in the binary system. In fact, this is the process we always use: Find the necessary powers of 2 to build the given decimal number. Of course, it won't always be as easy as it was for the number 14, so we need to formalize our method a bit.

Let's consider the conversion of a larger number, say 176, to binary representation. The rightmost digit in a binary number is a value of either 0 or 1. When we converted the number 14, we might have started on the right of the binary representation by asking first "Do we need a 1 or a 0?" We could answer 0 immediately because 14 is an even number, and hence the "ones" digit must be 0. Moving left, we could ask "Do we need a 0 or a 1?" This is asking if we need the value 2 ($= 2^1$) in the representation. This is a tougher question, and, in fact, the answer isn't obvious until we investigate further.

A much better approach is to start with the leftmost digit of the binary number representation and move right digit by digit. But how do we know where the starting point is? The largest power of 2 that we will need is the largest power of 2 that is less than or equal to the number we are trying to represent.

In the case of 14, we can quickly decide that a 16 (which is 2^4) won't be needed because the value we're trying to represent is smaller than this value. But an 8 (which is 2^3) will be needed. Then we can proceed in a similar manner on the part of the original number left over. Let's illustrate the complete process for the number 176.

Step 1: Determine the largest power of 2 less than or equal to 176.

Now, $2^7 = 128$ and $2^8 = 256$, so the power of 2 we're looking for is 2^7. This means our binary representation will have the form

$$(1 \times 2^7) + (? \times 2^6) + (? \times 2^5) + (? \times 2^4) + (? \times 2^3) + (? \times 2^2) + (? \times 2^1) + (? \times 2^0)$$
$$= 1???????_2$$

Step 2: Next, we determine the largest power of 2 less than or equal to the original number less the number already represented.

The original number is 176. The first binary digit represents 128, so we now need to represent what's left.

$$176 - 128 = 48$$

So we must determine the largest power of 2 less than or equal to 48.

Now, $2^6 = 64$ and $2^5 = 32$, so the power of 2 we're looking for is 2^5 (we won't need a 2^6 term). This means our binary representation will have the form

$$(1 \times 2^7) + (0 \times 2^6) + (1 \times 2^5) + (? \times 2^4) + (? \times 2^3) + (? \times 2^2) + (? \times 2^1) + (? \times 2^0)$$
$$= 101?????_2$$

Step 3: Once again, determine the largest power of 2 less than or equal to the original number less the number already represented.

In this case we have already represented $1 \times (1 \times 2^7) + (0 \times 2^6) + (1 \times 2^5)$ or 160, so we must now represent

$$176 - 160 = 16$$

Clearly the power of 2 we're looking for now is *exactly* 2^4. Since there will then be nothing left to represent ($16 - 16 = 0$), the remaining binary digits will all be zeros. This means our final binary representation will have the form

$$(1 \times 2^7) + (0 \times 2^6) + (1 \times 2^5) + (1 \times 2^4) + (0 \times 2^3) + (0 \times 2^2) + (0 \times 2^1) + (0 \times 2^0)$$
$$= 10110000_2$$

More Information

In summary, we start with the largest power of 2 less than or equal to the original number and proceed step by step as indicated, continuing to derive digits in the binary representation left to right until we have the entire number represented.

INTEGERS AND LIMITED RANGE

From the previous discussion, it is clear that we can convert any integer to binary form. Hence, theoretically we could store any integer in computer memory. Of course, in practice we have only a finite amount of memory, and so there must be a limit on the size of the integers we are able to store. We cannot use all available memory to store a single number, so the limit on the amount of memory storage we allow for one number must be quite small. After all, we have to store lots of additional information in memory to do anything meaningful.

On many computer systems, 2 bytes or 16 bits are allocated for storage of integers. Admittedly, this is a somewhat arbitrary decision. This choice was made when most desktop computers were 16-bit computers (that is, they had 16-bit bus widths), and this no doubt influenced the choice. Today's computers are typically 32-bit computers, but the use of 16 bits of storage for integers has remained the convention. This is, however, nothing more than a convention, and in some workstation computers and larger systems, integers are represented using 32 bits or even 64 bits.

Let's assume that we are dealing with a computer that has a 16-bit storage size for integers. What is the largest integer we can store on such a machine? At first glance, it would seem to be $1111111111111111_2 = 2^{15} + 2^{14} + \ldots + 2^1 + 2^0 = 65{,}535$. But remember that integers can be either positive or negative, and we will need to store the sign of an integer as well as its absolute size. The usual convention is to use the first bit of the number to designate the sign, say, a 1 for $+$ and a 0 for $-$. This then leaves only 15 bits to store the actual number, and consequently the largest integer we could store would be $111111111111111_2 = 2^{14} + 2^{13} + \ldots + 2^1 + 2^0 = 32{,}767$.

This almost explains the range for stored integers we gave a bit earlier. But not quite. Recall we said that the range was from $-32{,}768$ to $+32{,}767$. Why the lack of symmetry? In other words, why not $-32{,}767$ to $+32{,}767$? This small discrepancy is a result of the particular method we actually employ to store integers, called twos complement. This method was developed because there is a serious problem with representing integers in the very straightforward way we described above. This problem is that the number 0 has two such representations: 1000000000000000_2 (positive) and 0000000000000000_2 (negative). Of course, zero is neither positive nor negative, so we would prefer it to have a single representation; in fact, allowing two different representations of the same number would cause many problems in implementing computer arithmetic.

The **twos complement method** is an integer storage scheme designed to encode a number's sign implicitly and hence eliminate the problem of dual representations of 0. As we noted earlier, this is not just a cosmetic issue. Twos complement representation makes it much easier to perform arithmetic operations with stored integers. The lack of symmetry for the range of integers we noted earlier is a direct byproduct of the twos complement method. The details of how the method works are beyond the scope of our brief treatment and needn't concern us here. Consult the *Digital Domain* Web site for more information if you are interested.

The usual range of integers stored in a computer is from $-32,768$ to $+32,767$. If the answer to a calculation involving integers is another integer outside this range, an error, called an **integer overflow error,** results. Such errors often cause the program being run to halt immediately. We'll see a way that sometimes gets us around this difficulty when we discuss decimal number representations next.

Let's summarize what we have learned about representing integers in a computer. Integer values can be represented exactly and without error in a computer's memory, provided they are within the computer's limited range of integer values. This range is typically from $-32,768$ to $32,767$ for personal computers.

More Information

DECIMAL NUMBERS—LIMITED RANGE AND PRECISION

Let's now turn our attention to decimal numbers, also called **real numbers.** Real numbers can have both a whole number part and a decimal fraction part. How are we to represent these numbers in a binary computer? Actually we can perform conversions to the binary system similar to those we performed with integers, but there is a complication. Let's examine a simple instance first where everything works out neatly. Consider the decimal number 14.75. We know that the whole number part (i.e., 14) represents $(1 \times 10^1) + (4 \times 10^0)$, just as before. What about the fractional part, that is, the .75?

This representation also uses the powers of 10—this time the negative powers of 10. Recall that $10^{-1} = 1/10^1 = 1/10$, $10^{-2} = 1/10^2 = 1/100$, $10^{-3} = 1/10^3 = 1/1,000$, and so on. Hence $.75 = (7 \times 10^{-1}) + (5 \times 10^{-2}) = 7/10 + 5/100$. Putting the entire expansion for 14.75 together, we get

$$14.75 = (1 \times 10^1) + (4 \times 10^0) + (7 \times 10^{-1}) + (5 \times 10^{-2})$$

or

$$14.75 = 10 + 4 + .7 + .05$$

Now back to the business of converting 14.75 to binary form. We saw earlier that 14 converts to 1110_2. But what about the fractional part? We need to represent .75 as an expansion in the negative powers of 2. In other words, in binary representation,

$$.75 = (? \times 2^{-1}) + (? \times 2^{-2}) + (? \times 2^{-3}) + \ldots$$

But $2^{-1} = 1/2^1 = 1/2$, $2^{-2} = 1/2^2 = 1/4$, $2^{-3} = 1/2^3 = 1/8$, and so on, and hence this becomes

$$.75 = (? \times 1/2) + (? \times 1/4) + (? \times 1/8) + \ldots$$

If we notice that .75 is actually the fraction 3/4, it isn't hard to see by inspection that we only need two fractions in its binary expansion

$$.75 = (1 \times 1/2) + (1 \times 1/4) = 3/4$$

or

$$.75 = .11_2$$

Putting the two binary representations together, we get

$$14.75 = 1110.11_2.$$

In this instance, we "eyeballed" the fractional part of the binary expansion; 3/4 is obviously 1/2 + 1/4. But there is a simple, step-by-step method for computing the binary expansion on the right-hand side of the point. We will illustrate the method by converting the decimal value .625 to a binary representation.

Step 1: Begin with the decimal fraction and multiply by 2. The whole number part of the result is the first binary digit to the right of the point.

Because $.625 \times 2 = 1.25$, the first binary digit to the right of the point is a 1.

So far, we have $.625 = .1??? \ldots _2$.

Step 2: Next we disregard the whole number part of the previous result (the 1 in this case) and multiply by 2 once again. The whole number part of this new result is the second binary digit to the right of the point. We will continue this process until we get a zero as our decimal part or until we recognize an infinite repeating pattern.

Because $.25 \times 2 = 0.50$, the second binary digit to the right of the point is a zero.

Now we have $.625 = .10??? \ldots _2$.

Step 3: Disregarding the whole number part of the previous result (this result was .50 so there actually is no whole number part to disregard in this case), we multiply by 2 once again. The whole number part of the result is now the next binary digit to the right of the point.

Because $.50 \times 2 = 1.0$, the next binary digit to the right of the point is a 1.

Now we have $.625 = .101?? \ldots _2$.

Step 4: In fact, we do not need a Step 4. We are finished in Step 3, because we had 0 as the fractional part of our result there.

Hence the representation is $.625 = .101_2$.

Let's double-check our result by expanding the binary representation.

$$.101_2 = (1 \times 1/2) + (0 \times 1/4) + (1 \times 1/8) = .5 + 0 + .125 = .625$$

More Information

At this point, you may be wondering why this method works. It seems a little mysterious to most people when they first see it. Be assured that it has a sound mathematical basis. To explain that basis here, however, would carry us too far afield. Consult the *Digital Domain* Web site for the details behind the method if you're interested.

Infinite Binary Fraction Representations

So far, so good, but what about the complication we alluded to earlier? It arises because there are decimal fractions whose binary representations require an infinite amount of space for storage. For example, the fraction 1/10 is 0.1 in decimal notation, but when converted to binary it has the following representation:

$$0.1 = (0.000110011001100110011\ldots)_2$$

where the pattern 0011 (which first begins in the second digit after the point) is repeated indefinitely.

We'll verify this representation momentarily, but first let's consider its significance. Clearly, no matter how much memory we have, we could never store the exact (and infinite) binary representation of 1/10. This seems undesirable; maybe we should abandon the binary number system and return to using the base-10 or some other system! Unfortunately, it wouldn't help us out of the difficulty. This problem is not unique to the binary number system; it occurs in every base system. As you already know, many fractions have no finite representation as base-10 fractions. For example, the fraction 1/3 has the infinite representation:

$$1/3 = 0.3333333333333\ldots$$

No matter what number system we use, there will always be values whose representations require an infinite number of digits. Unfortunately, the vast majority of numbers have this property, so the best we can do is to store some finite subset of numbers that will serve as reasonable approximations to the ones we've left out. This means that real numbers are, by necessity, represented in the computer with **limited precision.**

Actually, you are already familiar with a limited precision arithmetic system. Our monetary system represents all values with two-decimal precision. For example, if your favorite candy bar is on sale at three for a dollar and you decide to buy one bar, how much will you pay? Certainly not $1.00 divided by 3. Why not? Because this would mean a price of 33.33333 . . . cents, which is impossible in a finite monetary system. In all likelihood, you would pay 34 cents, with the .3333333 . . . amount being rounded up a full penny.

Let's return to our example and use the method you just learned to see that the binary representation of the decimal fraction 1/10 is, in fact, infinite. Recall our step-by-step process for performing this conversion.

Step 1: Begin with the decimal fraction and multiply by 2. The whole number part of the result is the first binary digit to the right of the point.

Because $.1 \times 2 = 0.2$, the first binary digit to the right of the point is a zero.

So far, we have $.1 = (.0???\ldots)_2$.

Step 2: Next we disregard the whole number part of the previous result (0 in this case) and multiply by 2 once again. The whole number part of the result is now the second binary digit to the right of the point. We will continue this process until we get a zero as our decimal part or until we recognize an infinite repeating pattern.

Because $.2 \times 2 = 0.4$, the second binary digit to the right of the point is also a zero.

Now we have $.1 = (.00???\ldots)_2$.

Step 3: We multiply by 2 once again. The whole number part of the result is now the next binary digit to the right of the point.

Because $.4 \times 2 = 0.8$, the next binary digit to the right of the point is again a zero.

Now we have $.1 = (.000?? \ldots)_2$.

Step 4: We multiply by 2 once again.

Because $.8 \times 2 = 1.6$, the next binary digit to the right of the point is a one.

So far we have $.1 = (.0001?? \ldots)_2$.

Step 5: We multiply by 2 once again, disregarding the whole number part of the previous result.

Because $.6 \times 2 = 1.2$, the next binary digit to the right of the point is a one.

So far we have $.1 = (.00011?? \ldots)_2$.

Step 6: We multiply by 2 once again, disregarding the whole number part of the previous result. Let's make an observation here. Notice that this next step to be performed (multiply $2 \times .2$) is exactly the same action we had in step 2. We are bound to repeat steps 2–5, then return to Step 2 again indefinitely. In other words, we will never get a 0 as the decimal fraction part of our result. Instead we will just cycle through steps 2–5 forever. This means we will obtain the sequence of digits generated in steps 2–5, namely 0011, over and over. The final binary representation will be

$$.1 = (.00011001100110011 \ldots)_2$$

The repeating pattern is more obvious if we add some spacing and underlining for emphasis, as follows:

$$.1 = (.0 \ \underline{0011} \ \underline{0011} \ \underline{0011} \ \underline{0011} \ \ldots)_2$$

FLOATING POINT REPRESENTATION

If we wish to represent infinite decimal fractions in our computer systems (and, of course, we do), a compromise very similar to our monetary example must be made. Recall that we "solved" the monetary problem by limiting the decimal precision to two decimal places in that system and rounding up any decimal fraction with more than two places. Of course, we'd like more than two-decimal precision for our computer representation because there are a great many calculations that require more accuracy than do monetary transactions.

To maximize the precision possible using a fixed number of bits of storage, real numbers are stored in the computer employing **floating point representation.** To convert a number to floating point representation, first the fraction must be normalized. To normalize a fraction, we place the first nonzero digit just to the right of the decimal point. This normalized fraction is then multiplied by the appropriate power of 10 to retain the original value. For example, in floating point notation, the decimal number 234.563 is written as 0.234563×10^3. Likewise, we would write 0.000435 in floating point notation as 0.435×10^{-3}. (Note: The remaining examples in this section will be numbers in decimal

FIGURE 8.3

Real numbers are stored in floating point format. In most desktop computers, 32 bits are used to store a real number—1 bit for the sign, 8 bits for the exponent, and 23 bits for the normalized decimal fraction or mantissa. By omitting the leading bit (which is always a 1) in the normalized fraction, we actually get 24 bits of precision.

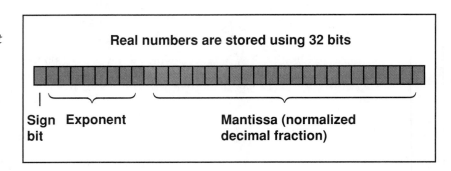

Real numbers are stored using 32 bits

Sign
bit   Exponent   Mantissa (normalized decimal fraction)

notation instead of binary for easier reading. The principles discussed here are exactly the same no matter what base number system we choose.)

Normalizing can achieve more places of accuracy because it avoids having to store leading or trailing zeros whose meaning can be captured with the exponent. For example, if we can store only seven digits, without normalization we would lose most of the meaningful digits in a number like 0.0000002346513. In fact, we would keep only the digit 2 because we waste storage on the six leading 0s. With normalization, we rewrite this number as $.2346513 \times 10^{-6}$ and preserve *all* the meaningful digits.

In floating point notation, a number is represented by two parts—the normalized fraction part, called the **mantissa,** and the **exponent** to correct for placing the value in normalized decimal form. Of course, we also need to store the sign of the number to indicate whether it is positive or negative.

The precision of real numbers stored using floating point representation is determined by the number of bits allowed for the decimal fraction. The standard convention employs 23 bits of binary representation. In fact, we can squeeze in 24 bits of precision by not storing the first bit, which will necessarily be a 1 because the fraction is normalized. This is the equivalent of about seven decimal places of precision in base 10. The first bit of storage is reserved for the sign of the number. The exponent occupies eight bits. See Figure 8.3. When a number has more digits in its representation than can be accommodated by this storage scheme, the number is usually rounded off (however, in some computers, the excess digits are simply chopped off with no rounding) to the nearest number that can be represented. The result is that there are lots of "holes" in the number line when we represent real numbers.

Obviously, this scheme is one with limited precision. The precision of the storage scheme determines how big the holes are, that is, the amount of spacing between the numbers we represent. This spacing will actually differ along the number line depending on the size of the numbers themselves. This occurs because the digits that are lost in rounding represent different values, depending on the size of the number being rounded. As an example, suppose we have a system that can accommodate five decimal digits. Then the number .334579 would be rounded to the nearest representable number, namely .33458. The actual difference between the true value .334579 and the value .33458 used to represent it would be .000001 in this case. On the other hand, suppose we wish to represent the value 334.579. The nearest number representable with five digits would be 334.58 and the difference this time is a larger value (by a factor of 1,000), namely .001. In other words, the spacing between

FIGURE 8.4

Three categories of numbers are by necessity left out when a floating point representational scheme is used. Some numbers are too small, others are too large, and the third group requires too many decimal digits of precision.

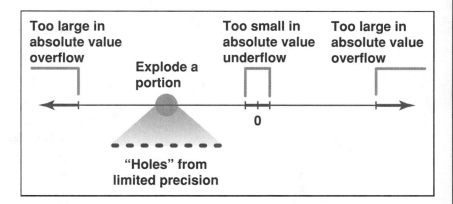

representable numbers is larger near 334.58 than it is around .33458. This spacing grows larger and larger as the absolute value of the numbers involved grows. Even such simple examples illustrate why the accuracy of arithmetic on a computer can be very unpredictable!

Some numbers will be too large in absolute value to be represented at all because we won't be able to use an exponent large enough. Remember we only have eight bits for the exponent. In these cases (as with integers), we have an **overflow error.** The largest number we can represent in the standard floating point scheme shown in Figure 8.3 is quite large—approximately 2^{127} or approximately 10^{38}—but this doesn't mean we won't ever encounter computations whose results exceed this value. Still other numbers will be too small in absolute value (i.e., too close to zero) to be represented because we won't be able to use a large enough negative exponent. In such cases we say we have an **underflow error.** We can represent the value 0 easily, but numbers too close to 0 can't be represented. For example, the very small number 10^{-40} ($= 1/10^{40}$) can't be represented for the same reason that the very large number 10^{40} can't be represented. In neither case can the exponent be represented in just the eight bits we have available for this purpose. Figure 8.4 summarizes all the difficulties involved in representing the number line in a computer.

Many computer systems offer greater precision and range for floating point numbers because they support 64-bit and even 128-bit representations. Even so, these only postpone rather than eliminate the problems of overflow, underflow, and limited precision.

Social Themes

Risks in Numeric Computing

As you learned in Chapter 6, it is not uncommon for software to contain errors. Indeed, it is almost expected that large, complex programs will contain one or more errors. For example, it is particularly difficult to ensure that software involving complex logic is error-free. Software that depends heavily on numeric computation is another class of software that is highly susceptible to subtle errors. This fact derives from the imperfect way we are forced to model decimal (real number) arithmetic using a computer. In fact, you may recall from Chapter 4 (see the "Social Themes: Hardware Designs Are Not Infallible" section) that even getting the prescribed arithmetic operations correctly designed in hardware chips is a very difficult problem. In this section we will examine two relatively simple numeric errors that led to the failure of complex software—resulting in the loss of many millions of dollars in one case and perhaps contributing to the loss of lives in another.

Arianne 5 Rocket Failure

On the morning of June 4, 1996, a French *Arianne 5* rocket, carrying a European Space Agency (ESA) satellite, was scheduled for its first launch in French Guyana. About 37 seconds into its flight, the rocket veered off its flight path, broke up, and exploded. A board of inquiry was immediately appointed by the ESA and CNES (Centre National des Etudes Spatiales).

The investigation examined telemetry data received on ground through 42 seconds after liftoff, trajectory data from radar stations, observations from infrared cameras, and the inspection of recovered debris. The origin of the failure was soon narrowed to the flight control system. Fortunately, the two primary computer-controlled inertial reference subsystems were both recovered, and after further investigation the source of the failure was determined to be a software error within these units.

Particularly, the error was traced to software controlling the alignment of the rocket's strap-down inertial platform. An integer overflow error occurred when the program attempted to convert a 64-bit floating point number to a 16-bit integer. The floating point number, which measured a quantity related to the horizontal velocity of the platform, was simply too large to be represented as a 16-bit integer. The *Arianne 5* software had been derived from the software for the previous generation *Arianne 4* rocket. The *Arianne 4* had a different initial trajectory that produced smaller horizontal velocity values. Hence, the larger values recorded during the *Arianne 5* flight were out of the range that the software was designed to handle.

The overflow error caused the computer in the primary inertial reference system to shut down and attempt to switch to the backup (redundant) system. Unfortunately, the redundant system had experienced exactly the same fault and had already shut itself down when the primary computer attempted to transfer control to it.

Had this problem been identified in preflight software testing, it could have been corrected very easily. Such is the case for many software errors. The smallest of problems can cause a program to crash or shut down. This is one of the reasons why it is so much harder to engineer reliable software than to engineer reliable bridges and other complex physical structures. An analogy might be that the failure of one very small bolt in a bridge could cause the entire structure to collapse—possible perhaps, but highly unlikely. Yet the failure of "small bolts" often causes software systems to collapse. Our next example provides further demonstration of this fact.

Patriot Missile Failure During the Gulf War

The American public was delighted to hear the Pentagon's estimates that approximately 90 percent of all Iraqi Scud missiles were being intercepted by the Patriot antimissile defense system during the Persian Gulf War in 1991. In the months following the end of the war, however, rumors about the Patriot's ineffectiveness began to surface. One critical failure of the system had already been observed during the war when a Scud missile hit a U.S. military barracks in Dhahran, Saudi Arabia, killing 28 U.S. soldiers.

A careful analysis after the war ended revealed that the earlier estimates of very high Patriot hit rates had been hastily constructed on the basis of insufficient data and that they were, in fact, inaccurate. An article in the February 15, 1992, issue of the *New Scientist* reported on findings by MIT professor Ted Postol, who reexamined the Patriot's war record at the request of a Congressional committee. Postol's basic conclusion was that Patriot missiles missed many of the Iraqi missiles that the United States thought had been shot down during the Gulf War, and that deploying the Patriot antimissile defense system did not reduce damage during Iraq's missile attacks on Israel and Saudi Arabia. One reason cited was that Iraq's modified Scud missile, called the Al-Husayn, was difficult to hit because it was so unstable that it broke into pieces when it reentered the atmosphere, creating a confusing barrage of debris. Although the debate about its effectiveness continues, most observers believe the Patriot hit rate was closer to 10 percent than to 90 percent.

In late March 1992, the U.S. General Accounting Office's report to Congress on the Patriot's problems was delivered. It identified a software error due to numeric calculations as the primary cause for the failure of the Patriot system. The report's own language provides a very succinct description of the problem, and so we quote a portion of it here.

> The [system's] prediction of where the Scud will next appear is a function of the Scud's known velocity and the time of the last radar detection. Velocity is a real number that can be expressed as a whole number and a decimal (e.g., 3750.2563 . . . miles per hour). Time is kept continuously by the system's internal clock in tenths of seconds but is expressed as an integer or whole number (e.g., 32, 33, 34 . . .). The longer the system has been running, the larger the number representing time. To predict where the Scud will next appear, both time and velocity must be expressed as real numbers. Because of the way the Patriot computer performs its calculations and the fact that its registers are only 24 bits long, the conversion of time from an integer to a real number cannot be any more precise than 24 bits. This conversion results in a loss of precision causing a less accurate time calculation. The effect of this inaccuracy on the [system's] calculation is directly proportional to the target's velocity and the length that the system has been running. Consequently, performing the conversion after the Patriot computer system has been running continuously for extended periods causes the [system's estimated Scud position] to shift away from the center of the target, making it less likely that the target will be successfully intercepted. [Excerpted from *Report to the Chairman, Subcommittee on Investigations and Oversight, Committee on Science, Space, and Technology, House of Representatives: Patriot Missile Defense—Software Problem Led to System Failure at Dhahran, Saudi Arabia, March 1992.*]

The error occurred when translating between integer and decimal number (floating point) formats. The error could become quite significant when the system was run for long periods without resetting. For ex-

Social Themes

ample, after 100 hours of continuous operation, the error in the estimate of the position of the target is almost 1/3 of a mile. We should note that the Patriot system software error had been discovered prior to the Dhahran barracks attack, and a software "patch" had been devised and shipped. Unfortunately, it arrived in Saudi Arabia the day after the Dhahran barracks attack.

NUMERIC PROCESSING AND SOFTWARE LIBRARIES

Admittedly, the preceding sections were more technical than most in this text. Even if you're not entirely comfortable with all the details presented there, however, the major point is easy to summarize. Storing real numbers with finite precision means that *every* computerized numerical operation using them is potentially in error. This follows from the fact that we can't even be sure the numbers themselves are stored without error—let alone the results of the calculations done on them. Consider, for example, the problem of calculating 0.1 + 0.1. We know in advance that the result will, in fact, contain a small error because we can't store .1 in binary form without rounding it off. In most ordinary calculations, such small errors would not cause us great difficulty. After all, how often do we need results to seven or eight decimal places? But in scientific and mathematical calculations, where arithmetic operations are performed sometimes thousands of times in one computation, these small errors can accumulate into significant—even preposterous—errors! We must always perform decimal calculations on computers with some degree of caution and skepticism for the results.

Here's a simple example to illustrate. Suppose we want to do the calculation 1000 × (.24456 − .24454). You can easily do the arithmetic using paper and pencil (or perhaps in your head). The result is 1000 × .00002 = .02. Now let's consider how a computer employing four-decimal place precision would make this calculation. The numbers .24456 and .24454 cannot be stored exactly in such a computer because they each have five decimal places, so each would be rounded. The number .24456 would be rounded to .2446 and the number .24454 would be rounded to .2445. When the subtraction is done on the rounded numbers, the result would be .0001. When multiplied by 1000 this gives .1 as the final result. Of course, .1 is not the same as .02—these answers differ by a factor of 5. Is this difference significant? It depends on what the result represents. If it represents the interest rate you're to earn on an investment, for example, there is a huge difference between 2% and 10%.

Because computations involving floating point representations of real numbers are likely to have inherent errors, computer scientists have studied the process of calculating with floating point numbers extensively. The main goal of this research is to design computational methods that reduce the size of the errors introduced because of limited precision. Often, the most straightforward way to do a calculation is not the way that minimizes the risk of large errors. This doesn't mean that every time such calculations are done, they produce large errors. Instead, they can produce large errors in special cases. Because we never know when one or more of these special cases might arise in practice, computer scientists have looked for methods that guarantee us some protection against large errors whenever possible.

During the 1950s through the 1970s, most calculations were done using high-level programming languages such as FORTRAN, BASIC, C, Pascal, and others. To make it easier for programmers to avoid creating calculations that might generate large errors, it became common to use methods that had already been tested against this outcome. These methods are stored in electronic form and collected into what are called **software libraries.** Consequently, when solving a complex numeric computation, such as approximating the solution to an equation whose exact solution cannot be derived, the wise programmer will employ the appropriate method from a software library. This is much safer than writing a new one because the methods stored in libraries have been carefully designed and tested to avoid common pitfalls that might generate large errors.

Even though many numeric computations are still performed by programs written in high-level languages, numeric application programs today provide more convenient access to powerful computational software libraries. Spreadsheet programs, for example, have made it possible for persons with little computer training to construct and exercise powerful and sophisticated mathematical models. As you will see shortly, spreadsheet programs mimic the way we do calculations with paper and pencil. But they add enhancements and capabilities that make it possible to extend such calculations well beyond what is possible with paper and pencil.

Symbolic computational programs also make computational methods more accessible to the nonprogrammer. Programs such as MATLAB, Mathematica, Maple, DERIVE, and others provide students, engineers, scientists, statisticians, and others with unprecedented opportunities to perform high-level mathematical procedures, graphical displays, and computations.

BASIC FEATURES OF SPREADSHEET SOFTWARE

Spreadsheet application software, or just **spreadsheets** for short, are especially designed for numeric processing. Spreadsheet software has been around for almost as long as personal computers. In fact, the first spreadsheet program, called VisiCalc, was an important incentive for consumers and a driving factor in the popularization of the personal computer in the early 1980s. Interestingly, spreadsheet software was available on personal computers several years before the first personal computer word processing software was developed.

Using spreadsheets, we can organize calculations in a natural and intuitive manner much as we might do on a sheet of paper. The bonus is that spreadsheets provide greater flexibility and power than pencil-and-paper calculations. Automatic updating of calculations with new data, charting or plotting calculations in a variety of ways, and employing built-in computational functions are some examples of this power and flexibility.

Today a large number of spreadsheet software products are available. Of course, the specific methods and techniques they employ to perform their calculations and charting differ from product to product. Three of the most popular are Lotus 1-2-3, Microsoft Excel, and Quattro Pro. Fortunately for us, all these products have a great deal in

FIGURE 8.5

The upper-left-hand portion of an opening Excel worksheet is shown here. Note that cell A1—the upper left corner cell—is highlighted to indicate that it is the active cell. In Excel (as in most other spreadsheets), the active cell is also indicated at the far left of the entry bar. The latter is the rectangle located just above the worksheet window.

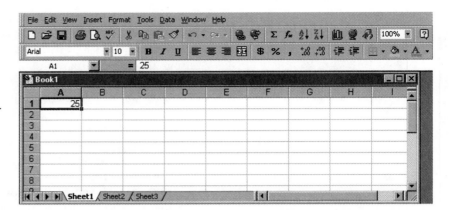

common—enough to motivate plagiarism lawsuits between several of the spreadsheet developers. As a consequence, knowledge and experience with one spreadsheet program translate easily to a different product.

In this section, we will introduce some of the important basic spreadsheet concepts. We will employ Microsoft Excel for all of our illustrations. We can assure you, however, that these concepts manifest themselves similarly in other spreadsheet programs. Common denominators for spreadsheets are the following:

- Column and row organization
- Entering data into a worksheet
- Performing calculations using formulas
- Copying formulas

Worksheet Organization

Spreadsheet documents are usually called **worksheets.** Worksheets are organized as a table of rows and columns. The columns are labeled with letters and the rows with numbers. Worksheets typically have a capacity for a great many rows and columns—so many that capacity rarely becomes a consideration in designing and carrying out spreadsheet computations. The intersection of a row and column is called a **cell,** and giving its column followed by its row identifies a particular cell. This combination of column letter and row number is called the **cell address.** For example, as shown in Figure 8.5, the cell in the upper left corner of the worksheet is cell A1—in column A and row 1. A rectangular block of cells is called a **cell range** and is denoted by the cell defining the block's upper left corner and its lower right corner. For example, the cell range B3:C4 includes the block of cells B3, B4, C3, and C4. Only one cell may be selected at a given time—the selected cell is referred to as the **current cell.** Each worksheet has an associated **entry bar,** which is the area where information (text, numbers, and formulas) is entered into the active cell. Again, Figure 8.5 illustrates.

Entering Data in a Worksheet

Typically, you can enter three kinds of information into a worksheet cell: text, numbers (including dates and times), and formulas to perform calculations. To enter information into a cell, you first select it as the current cell and then start typing. Formulas must begin with a special character (often = or @). This character signals to the spreadsheet that what follows is a formula. In turn, the spreadsheet examines the syntax of what is entered and checks it for correctness. Formulas can use any of the standard arithmetic operators: +, −, * (multiply), and /, or built-in functions.

Nonformula information is typed in directly. The spreadsheet automatically recognizes most of the standard date and time formats and treats such data accordingly. Dates and times are usually encoded as numbers no matter how they are displayed in their cells. Information not in one of these date/time formats will be interpreted according to its first symbol. If this symbol is a digit, an algebraic sign (+ or −), or a decimal point (period), the data will be interpreted as numeric; if it is a character other than these, the data will be interpreted as text.

Once data is typed into the entry bar, you can easily change the format in which it is displayed in the cell. For example, you may adjust the particular font, size, and style (bold, italics, etc.) of the characters and whether the entry is aligned to the left, the right, or centered in the cell. For numeric data, you may select the number of places to the right of the decimal, presence of dollar signs or commas, and other characteristics. Dates can also ordinarily be displayed in one of several formats. See Figure 8.6.

Using Formulas in a Worksheet

In the example shown in Figure 8.6, we would like to subtract all the values in the cells holding expenses (cells B6 through B10) from the figure in cell B5 to produce the net income value for cell B12. This is easily accomplished by entering a formula into cell B12, as illustrated in Figure 8.7. When this is done, the numbers to be employed in the calculation are referred to by their cell addresses rather than by value. This feature of using cell addresses like variables means that should we change one or more of the actual values later, the net income will automatically be updated. The automatic recalculation of formulas is one of the primary benefits of using worksheets.

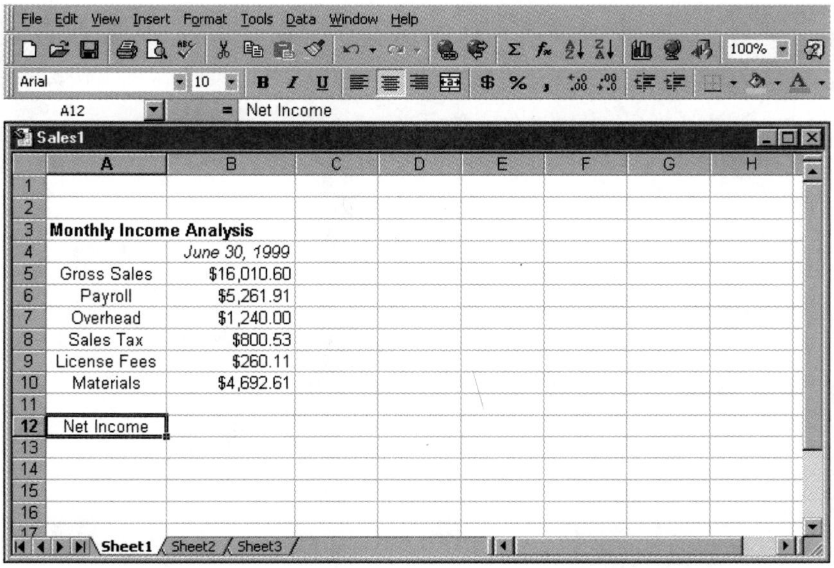

FIGURE 8.6

Entering text and numbers in a simple worksheet is shown. Note the different formatting that has been applied. The title "Monthly Income Analysis" is in bold type. The entries have been centered in column A beneath this heading. The numeric data in cells B5 through B10 has been formatted as currency.

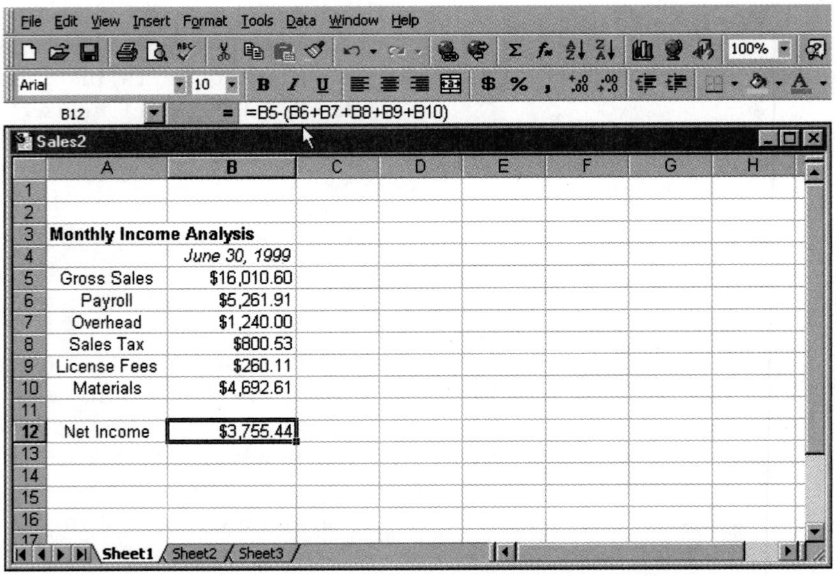

FIGURE 8.7

The figure illustrates defining an Excel calculation using a formula. Once the formula is entered, the value the formula computes is displayed in the cell itself, while the formula that produces the value is displayed in the entry bar. This is common among the various spreadsheet programs. When such a cell is selected, the cell displays the computed value; the entry bar shows the relevant formula that produced the cell's value.

Let's add another formula to our example. The sales tax figure appearing in cell B8 is no doubt related to the gross sales amount. We will assume that it is 5 percent of that amount. The way our worksheet is currently constructed, this calculation must be done separately, with the resulting value entered into cell B8. Why not let the worksheet do that calculation? This is accomplished easily by employing a formula to produce the value for cell B8. This formula will compute the appropriate percentage of the gross sales figure held in cell B5, as shown in Figure 8.8.

Copying Formulas with Relative Cell References

Besides the automatic updating of calculations, another important feature of spreadsheets is the automatic copying of formulas (this is sometimes referred to as formula replication) to perform similar calculations

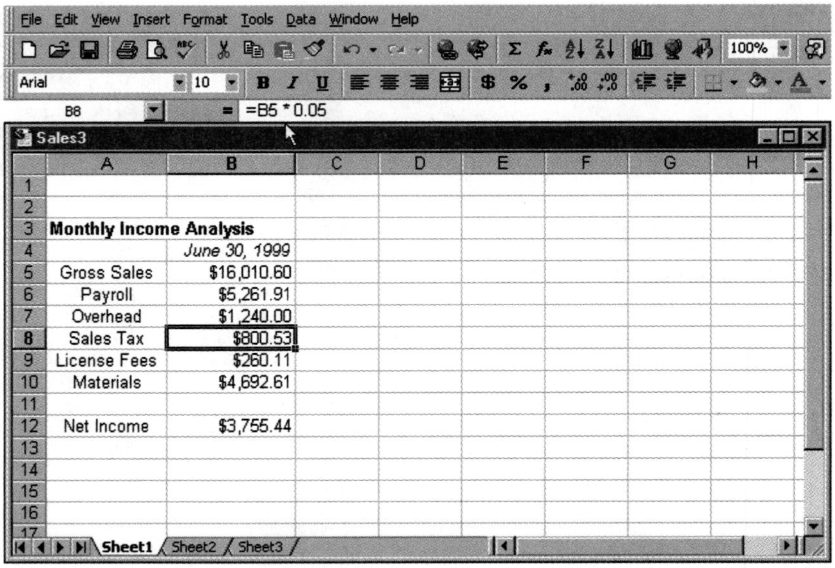

FIGURE 8.8

Using a formula to calculate the sales tax within the worksheet is shown. Here, we have assumed that the sales tax rate is 5 percent = 0.05. Note the reference in the formula to cell B5, where the gross sales value resides.

in another area of the worksheet. Often we wish to perform calculations on large data sets. The copying feature allows us to perform the calculation on a single instance within the data set, then copy the calculation automatically to the entire data set. Formula copying does not mean reproducing exactly the same formula in another location. To make copied formulas work correctly in their new cell locations, the cells referenced in the formula must be automatically adjusted for the new location. We can illustrate this by modifying our example worksheet to handle several additional months of income data.

Figure 8.9 illustrates what the worksheet might look like after adding data for July and August. Now let's extend our calculation of net income to include this new data. A straightforward way to accomplish this would be simply to select cells C12 and D12 one after another and enter the appropriate formulas directly into them, just as we did for cell B12. However, the formulas that we want are *nearly* identical to the formula entered in B12. The only difference is that the formulas should refer to data in columns C and D, respectively, rather than column B. Spreadsheets allow us to exploit this similarity by copying the formula in B12 to cells C12 and D12, adjusting the new formulas automatically to employ the appropriate columns in their cell references.

For example, in Microsoft Excel, we would select cell B12 as the anchor or model formula; drag to the right so that cells C12 and D12 are also highlighted; and then execute a *Fill Right* command: The spreadsheet then copies the formula in B12 to the corresponding cells (cells in the same row) highlighted to the right. The beauty of this operation is that the cell references in the new formulas are shifted automatically. See Figure 8.10.

Formula adjustment for copied formulas is accomplished by modifying the cell references in the original formula according to their relative positions to the cell holding the formula. The cell addresses in the new formula are calculated to be in the same *relative position* to the cell containing the formula as were the original cell references to the original formula cell. Consider again the example in Figure 8.10. In the original formula, cell B5, the first cell referenced in the formula, is seven cells above cell B12, the cell containing the formula. When the formula

FIGURE 8.9

The worksheet is modified to include two additional months' data. We now need to extend the calculational formula producing the value in cell B12 to compute values for cells C12 and D12.

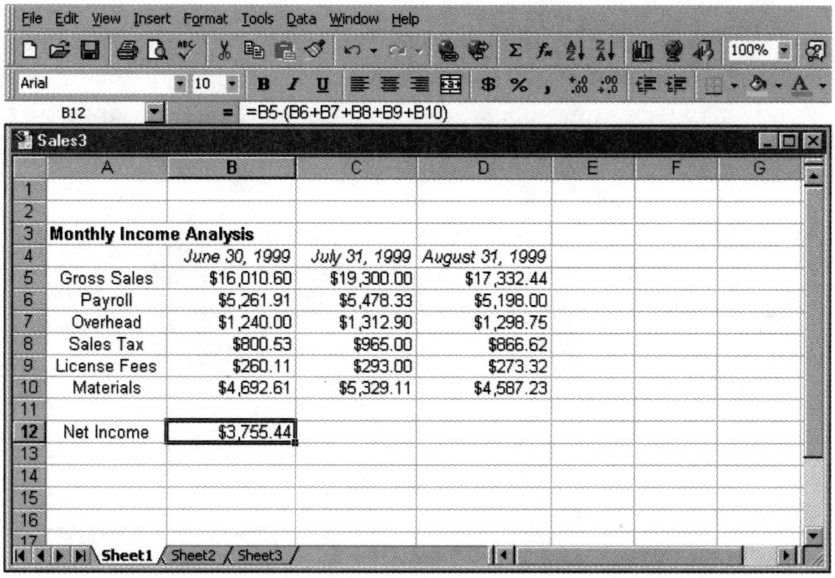

FIGURE 8.10

The formula of cell B12 has been replicated to cells C12 and D12. Note that the formula has been adjusted automatically so that the data referenced in cell D12 is in column D. In other words, all the references to cells in column B in the original formula have been changed to references to the corresponding cells in column D.

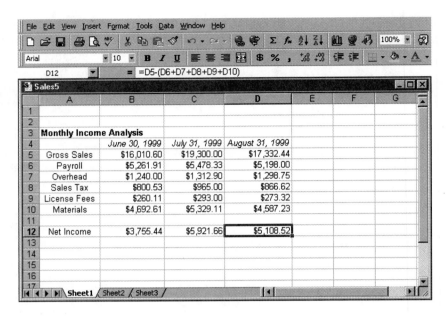

is copied to cell D12 as shown, the first cell referenced is changed to cell D5 because this cell is seven cells above the new formula cell. Unless we specify to the contrary, all cell references are treated in this manner in formula copying and, for that reason, are called **relative cell references.**

COMPUTING WITH SPREADSHEETS, PART 1

In this activity, you'll practice using a spreadsheet by constructing a solution to a sample problem. The problem is that of computing grades for a class of students. Suppose an instructor has the following grading policy. Three tests, five lab activities, and a final exam are the work to be graded during a term. Each of the three tests counts as 15 percent of the final grade average; the lab activities count 5 percent each, and the final exam counts 30 percent.

1 Sketch a layout on paper for a spreadsheet solution for the problem of computing the grades for a class based on the given grading policy.

Your layout should include a column for students' names, a column to record each of the grades received during the term, and, of course, a column holding the final course average.

2 Open your spreadsheet program and create headings for each of the columns you defined in your designed solution. Leave several rows at the top of the worksheet. Enter a title for your worksheet consisting of the (hypothetical) course number, term, and year. Save your spreadsheet now and after each of the following steps.

3 Make up a name and some grade data for the first student and enter this in the first row of your table.

4 Construct a formula to compute the weighted average that gives the course average for this student. In other words, multiply each test grade by .15, each lab grade by .05, and the final exam grade by .30. Enter the formula in the appropriate cell to complete the first row of the table.

5 Use your calculator (or do the computations by hand) to check the course average calculation that your formula performed. If the worksheet value doesn't match your computation, repeat the computation. If the worksheet value proves to be incorrect, find and correct the error in your formula.

6 Enter three more student names in the appropriate positions in the table. Now insert test, lab, and final exam grades for each of these students.

7 Use your spreadsheet's copy command *(Fill Down)* to copy the formula for computing the course average to the appropriate column in the three new rows. (This command is found under the **Edit** menu in Excel.)

8 Use your calculator (or do the computations by hand) to check the course average calculations that your copied formulas performed. If the worksheet values are incorrect, find and correct the error in your formula and its copies.

9 Select (highlight) all the course average data in your table. Now use the command appropriate to your spreadsheet to format this data to show only two places to the right of the decimal.

EXPLORING LIMITED PRECISION

In this activity, you'll use your spreadsheet's calculational capabilities to explore the concept of limited precision. Recall that the value $1/10 = 0.1$ has an infinite binary representation. This means that computations done with this value will have a small error. In this activity, you'll compare two computations that are identical when done with paper and pencil but that produce different results when done numerically on a computer.

In particular, you will compute the value N times 0.1 for a variety of values for N in two ways: by straightforward multiplication and by repeated addition. Consider the two calculations when $N = 100$. When you multiply 100 times .1 you get the result 10. When you add 0.1 to itself

100 times, you also get 10. In fact, if you do exact arithmetic (paper and pencil), these two methods always produce the same answer, because of the following simple identity.

$$N \times a = a + a + a + a + \ldots + a \; (N \text{ additions})$$

As you will see, things are different when you use a computer to do your calculations.

1 Consider the worksheet layout shown in Figure 8.11. Open your spreadsheet and label three columns as in this layout. Place the three headings in row 1 and in columns A, B, and C, respectively. In other words, the heading *N* will go in cell A1, the heading *Multiply* in cell B1, and the heading *Add* in cell C1. Save your spreadsheet now and after each of the following steps.

2 Next, you'll fill the first column with data, namely values of *N* from 1 to 100. You could do this by entering all this data, but it's much easier to construct a simple formula to do the work for you. Start by entering the value 1 in the first row under the column heading *N* (i.e., in cell A2).

3 Now enter the formula = *A2 + 1* in cell A3. The value in cell A3 should be 2. If it is not, find and correct your error.

4 Use the mouse to select cells A3 through A101 (click first in cell A3, then drag through cell A101 before releasing). Make sure you started at cell A3 and not A2; otherwise, click anywhere to deselect and repeat to select the range A3 through A101. With this range of cells selected (highlighted), choose the *Fill Down* command to copy the formula in cell A3 to the other selected cells. The first column should now contain the series of values 1, 2, 3, 4, . . . 100.

5 Now enter the formula = *A2 * 0.1* in the second column in cell B2. The value in B2 should be 0.1. Now select cells B2 through B101. Make sure you started at cell B2; otherwise, click anywhere to deselect and repeat to select the range B2 through B101. Use the *Fill Down* command to copy the formula in cell B2 to the other selected cells. The second column should now contain the series of values 0.1, 0.2, 0.3, 0.4, and so on.

6 Enter the value .1 in cell C2. Now enter the formula = *C2 + .1* in cell C3. The value in cell C3 should be 0.2. If it is not, find and correct your error.

7 Use the mouse to select cells C3 through C101. With this range of cells selected

FIGURE 8.11
The figure shows the layout for the calculations to explore floating point number precision.

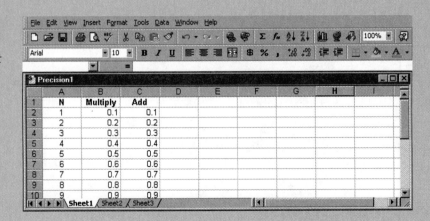

choose the *Fill Down* command to copy the formula in cell C3 to the other selected cells. The third column should now contain the series of values 0.1, 0.2, 0.3, 0.4, and so on.

8 Now we wish to see more decimal places in our results than the spreadsheet will display automatically. Find out how to change the width of a column in the spreadsheet you're using. Use the automated *Help* facility if one is available; otherwise, ask your lab assistant or instructor. Widen columns B and C considerably so they will display numbers with 20 decimal places.

9 Select the cell range B2 through C101 by dragging as before. With these cells highlighted, format the display to have 20 decimal places to the right of the decimal point. Your worksheet should look something like the one shown in Figure 8.12.

10 Now compare the values in the second column (calculated by multiplication) and the values in the third column (calculated by addition). They should be the same for the first few values (how many will depend on which spreadsheet software you're using). Eventually, these values should differ.

11 For what value of *N* do the computed values first differ? By how much do they differ? Note that this difference wouldn't show up if only a few decimal places were being displayed because the values that are in error would be rounded off to the correct values. Be sure your worksheet has been saved.

12 Can you think of a calculation where an error this size would be a problem? (Hint: Think of multiplying the computed values by another number.)

13 Note that every one of these calculated values actually has *some* error because 0.1 cannot be represented exactly in binary. Why do you suppose the addition method produces a *noticeable* error before the multiplication method?

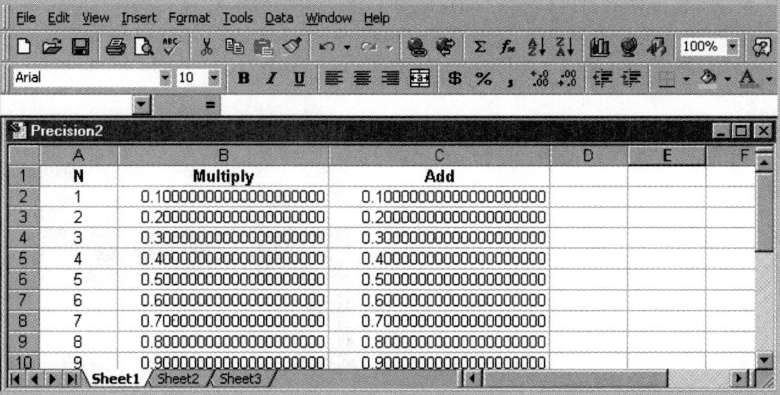

FIGURE 8.12

The worksheet explores limited precision for floating point number representations with calculations shown.

	A	B	C	D	E	F
	N	**Multiply**	**Add**			
1	N	Multiply	Add			
2	1	0.10000000000000000000	0.10000000000000000000			
3	2	0.20000000000000000000	0.20000000000000000000			
4	3	0.30000000000000000000	0.30000000000000000000			
5	4	0.40000000000000000000	0.40000000000000000000			
6	5	0.50000000000000000000	0.50000000000000000000			
7	6	0.60000000000000000000	0.60000000000000000000			
8	7	0.70000000000000000000	0.70000000000000000000			
9	8	0.80000000000000000000	0.80000000000000000000			
10	9	0.90000000000000000000	0.90000000000000000000			

ADDITIONAL FEATURES OF SPREADSHEET SOFTWARE

In the preceding section you learned the basics of using spreadsheets for computations. Of course, you have more to learn. In this section we continue our survey of important spreadsheet capabilities, including the following:

- Employing absolute references and problem parameters
- Using formulas that employ built-in computational functions
- Using formulas that employ built-in logical functions
- Displaying data and the results of computations as charts

Using Absolute Cell References

As we have emphasized, one of the major advantages of using spreadsheets for calculations is their automatic recalculation of results when data changes. To maximize the advantages of this feature, we must plan and design our worksheets carefully. Intelligent worksheet design involves identifying values that are subject to change; these are called **problem parameters.** Including problem parameters in our spreadsheet solutions makes them both easier to modify and more readable.

Let's consider our income analysis worksheet in this context. What values are likely to change in our simple computational model? A moment's thought suggests that the prime candidate value is the sales tax percentage. We assumed a 5 percent sales tax in our example. What happens if that changes to 6 percent?

We could edit the formulas for computing the sales tax in each cell in row 8 (see Figure 8.13). Alternately, we could change just the formula in one cell, then copy it to the other cells. This is preferable because there is less chance for error—we'd be editing only one formula. Either one of these methods is acceptable, but neither is ideal.

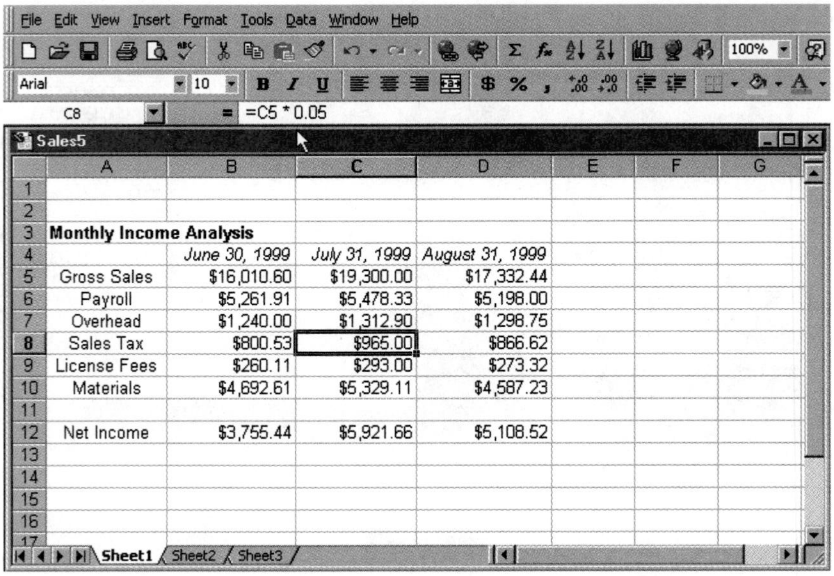

FIGURE 8.13

Changing the sales tax rate in formulas directly is shown.

File Edit View Insert Format Tools Data Window Help

Arial   10   B I U

C8   = =C5 * 0.05

Sales5

	A	B	C	D	E	F	G
1							
2							
3	**Monthly Income Analysis**						
4		*June 30, 1999*	*July 31, 1999*	*August 31, 1999*			
5	Gross Sales	$16,010.60	$19,300.00	$17,332.44			
6	Payroll	$5,261.91	$5,478.33	$5,198.00			
7	Overhead	$1,240.00	$1,312.90	$1,298.75			
8	Sales Tax	$800.53	$965.00	$866.62			
9	License Fees	$260.11	$293.00	$273.32			
10	Materials	$4,692.61	$5,329.11	$4,587.23			
11							
12	Net Income	$3,755.44	$5,921.66	$5,108.52			
13							
14							
15							
16							
17							

Sheet1 Sheet2 Sheet3

We can devise a better solution. What has actually changed in the three calculations? Only the percentage used to calculate the sales tax. If we make this change three times, the burden of the work is on us rather than on the spreadsheet. Wouldn't it be more desirable to design the worksheet so that a change in a single value could be implemented in the worksheet by changing only that value itself once?

This isn't difficult; it just requires some advance planning. As we begin, we recognize that the sales tax percentage is a likely candidate for later change (revenue-hungry governments being what they are). It makes sense to isolate this value on the worksheet and then have our formulas refer to its *address* rather than its value. For example, let's make cell B1 equal to 5 percent, then change the formula in cell B8 so that it references cell B1 instead of using the number .05. Figure 8.14 illustrates. When the sales tax rate goes up or down, we can change it directly on our spreadsheet only once. The formulas themselves will need no change because they will be revised when they are automatically recalculated.

When using problem parameters in a worksheet, it is often the case that we'd like to have some cell references remain fixed as we copy a formula. Our new formula in cell B8 for calculating the sales tax is a case in point. What happens when we copy the formula in cell B8 to cells C8 and D8? Due to relative referencing (remember, this is the default), the reference to B1 changes to C1 and D1, respectively. Because C1 and D1 do not contain numeric values, this clearly is not correct. What we need is for the reference to remain B1.

Cell references that do not change when formulas involving them are copied to a new location are called **absolute references.** In most spreadsheets, absolute cell references are indicated by preceding the cell row and column name with a $. The reference to cell B1 in our sales tax formula should be an absolute reference. When we make that change to the original formula in cell B8 and then copy the formula to cells C8 and D8, the reference to the sales tax parameter will remain cell

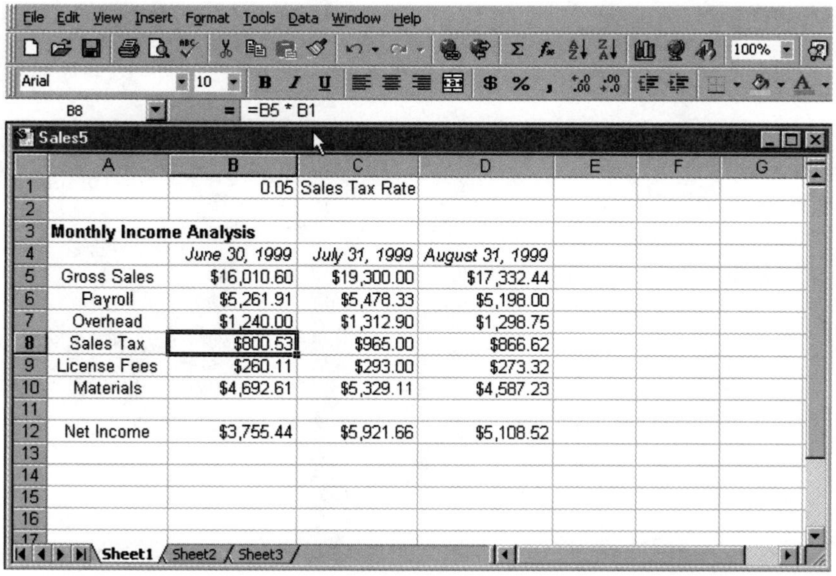

FIGURE 8.14

The sales tax percentage is isolated as a problem parameter. The value for sales tax is inserted into B1 and formatted as a percentage, and the formula in cell B8 is adjusted. Any change in the sales tax rate could now be made in cell B1 and the formula in cell B8 referencing that cell would pick up the change automatically.

	A	B	C	D	E	F	G
1		0.05	Sales Tax Rate				
2							
3	**Monthly Income Analysis**						
4		*June 30, 1999*	*July 31, 1999*	*August 31, 1999*			
5	Gross Sales	$16,010.60	$19,300.00	$17,332.44			
6	Payroll	$5,261.91	$5,478.33	$5,198.00			
7	Overhead	$1,240.00	$1,312.90	$1,298.75			
8	Sales Tax	$800.53	$965.00	$866.62			
9	License Fees	$260.11	$293.00	$273.32			
10	Materials	$4,692.61	$5,329.11	$4,587.23			
11							
12	Net Income	$3,755.44	$5,921.66	$5,108.52			
13							

B8 = =B5 * B1

B1 and will not be made relative to the new cells to which the formula has been copied.

Figure 8.15 illustrates. Notice the use of the $ signs in the reference to cell B1 (i.e., B1) in the formula. On the other hand, we want the reference to cell B5 in the formula to be relative. It should be adjusted to reference C5 and D5 when the formula in cell B8 is copied to cells C8 and D8, respectively. Otherwise, the new formulas would refer to gross sales figures for the wrong month. Before copying formulas that refer to problem parameters, a careful analysis of cell references is often required to make sure we are using the correct mix of absolute and relative references.

Using Built-In Functions

All spreadsheet programs provide **built-in functions** to make frequently used computations more convenient and less error prone. As Figure 8.16 illustrates, functions act on input values, called **arguments,** to produce a value. We need not worry about the details of how the function produces its value. All we need to know are the number and kinds of arguments the function requires and the kind of data it produces. Most spreadsheet programs offer a variety of built-in functions to help us accomplish statistical, financial, trigonometric, and other types of computations. Indeed, it is this variety of built-in functions that makes the production of a great many spreadsheet calculations so easy by relieving the user from the burden of constructing complex formulas from scratch.

Let's illustrate the use of built-in functions in our income analysis example. Suppose we would like to compute the average net income over several months. We can do this easily using the built-in function AVERAGE. The actual names used for functions may differ a bit from one spreadsheet package to another—the names we are using are the

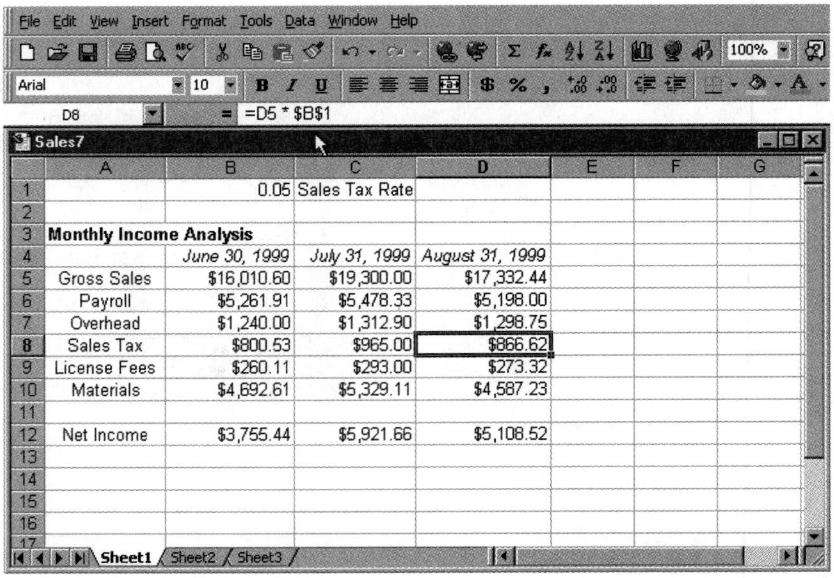

FIGURE 8.15

The formula in cell B8 is changed to use absolute referencing for cell B1 so that it can be correctly replicated to cells C8 and D8 to complete the calculations. Any change in the sales tax rate could now be made in cell B1 and the formulas in cells B8, C8, and D8 referencing that cell would pick up the change automatically.

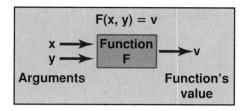

FIGURE 8.16

Functions take input arguments and return a calculated value. The details of how the function accomplishes its calculation need not be understood by the spreadsheet user. All that is required is to understand what arguments the function requires and what type of value it is designed to compute.

ones employed in Excel, but these will be the same or similar in other spreadsheets. We do not need to know the details of the formulas for computing an average. Instead, all we need to know are the name and the correct arguments for the function. In this case, the function AVERAGE is entered (after an = sign to indicate the use of a formula), followed by the function's argument, which is often expressed as the range of cells to use in the calculation. Figure 8.17 illustrates.

Using Logical Functions

Spreadsheets provide a number of statistical functions—AVERAGE is one of these—that make it easy to produce statistical summaries. In addition, the standard trigonometric functions and a host of financial functions are included. Functions are convenient because we can use them to construct powerful and useful worksheet calculations without bothering with the details of how they are implemented. We need know only the required arguments and what results the functions produce to use functions effectively.

The logical functions are another class of built-in functions. Besides convenience, they enable us to accomplish tasks that would be impossible without them. One such task is the ability to make decisions within our worksheets. The logical IF function is designed for this purpose. The IF function takes advantage of the computer's capability for **conditional processing,** which is the ability of a process to make decisions on alternative courses of action.

The IF function in spreadsheet programs typically takes three arguments. The first argument is a **Boolean** or **logical expression**—that is, an expression that evaluates to either true or false. The next two arguments are values based on either constants or formulas that represent alternative results of the function. Only one of these two will become the actual value for the function in any given instance. If the Boolean expression evaluates to true, the first of the two remaining arguments is used. If the

FIGURE 8.17

The formula shown entered into cell D14 uses the Excel built-in function AVERAGE with a range of cells (B12:D12) as its arguments. The built-in function STDEV is used (with the same cell range as its arguments) to compute the standard deviation in cell D15.

	A	B	C	D	E	F	G
1		0.05	Sales Tax Rate				
2							
3	**Monthly Income Analysis**						
4		June 30, 1999	July 31, 1999	August 31, 1999			
5	Gross Sales	$16,010.60	$19,300.00	$17,332.44			
6	Payroll	$5,261.91	$5,478.33	$5,198.00			
7	Overhead	$1,240.00	$1,312.90	$1,298.75			
8	Sales Tax	$800.53	$965.00	$866.62			
9	License Fees	$260.11	$293.00	$273.32			
10	Materials	$4,692.61	$5,329.11	$4,587.23			
11							
12	Net Income	$3,755.44	$5,921.66	$5,108.52			
13							
14		Average Net Income		$4,928.54			
15		Standard Deviation		$1,094.27			
16							
17							

D14 = =AVERAGE(B12:D12)

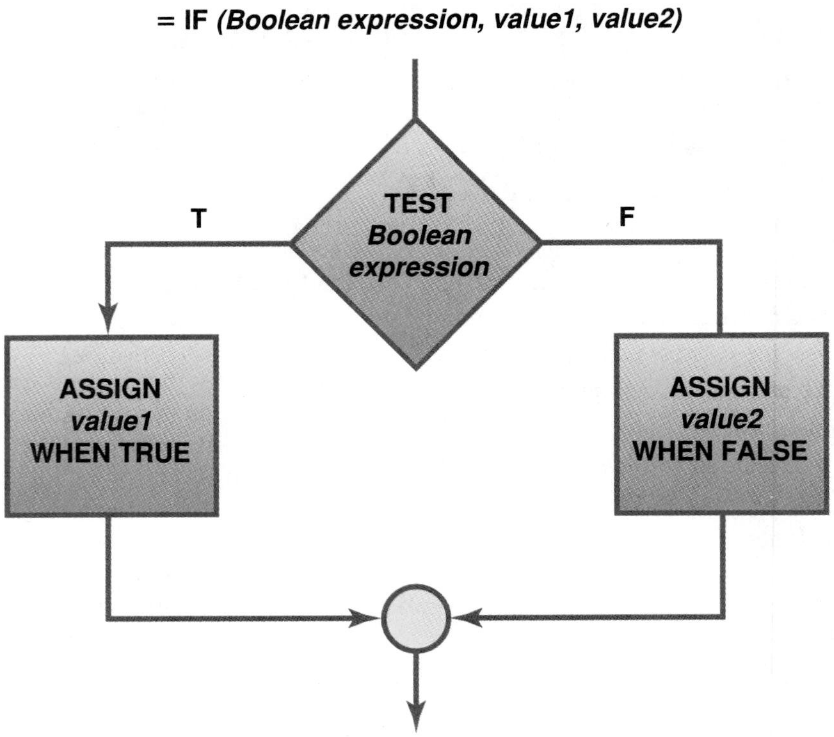

FIGURE 8.18

The figure illustrates how the Excel IF function works. The resulting value of the function depends on whether its Boolean expression evaluates to True or False.

= IF (Boolean expression, value1, value2)

Boolean expression is false, the second remaining argument is used, as illustrated in Figure 8.18.

Let's investigate the use of the IF function within our previous example. Suppose that the amount of logo license fees to be paid depends on the gross sales each month. In particular, let's assume that we pay a logo license fee of 2 percent on the first $10,000 of gross sales but a fee of only 1 percent of all gross sales thereafter. Using the IF function, we can create a formula to compute the license fee. The Boolean expression required will be based on whether the gross sales are greater than or less than $10,000. In the case in which the gross sales are less than or equal to $10,000, our function should return a value equal to 2 percent of the gross sales. When the gross sales are greater than $10,000, the value to be returned is 2 percent of $10,000 plus 1 percent of the excess over $10,000. Putting this together in the proper syntax for the IF function, we get a formula that correctly computes the license fee for any gross sales value. Figure 8.19 shows the formula as it would appear in cell B9.

Displaying Data in Charts

Many times a graphical summary of data and results is much easier to interpret than rows and columns of numbers. Modern spreadsheets make it very easy to create and display charts based on our calculations. Let's look at several examples from our sample worksheet.

● **Bar Charts.**   Suppose we would like to compare monthly net incomes for the months June, July, and August in our worksheet. A **bar**

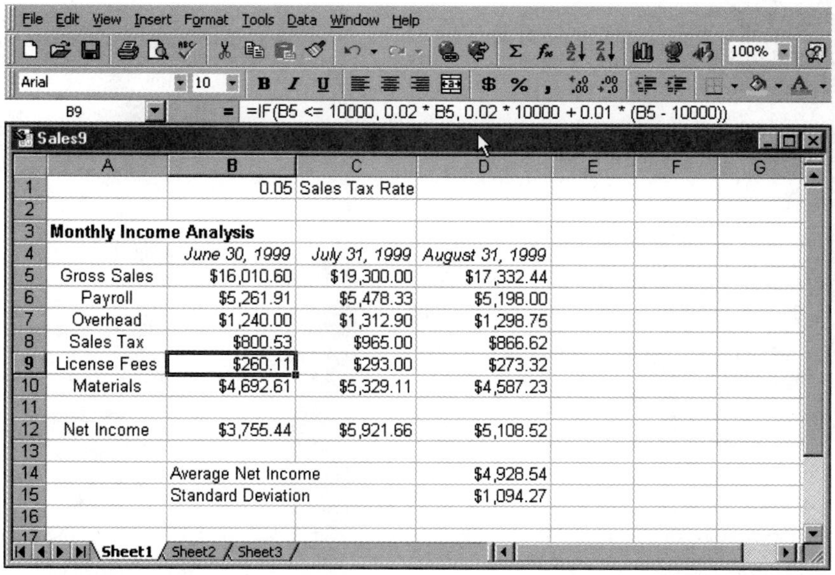

FIGURE 8.19

The figure shows how an IF function can be used to compute logo license fees. Study the formula given carefully and make sure you understand how it generates the correct value for cell B9.

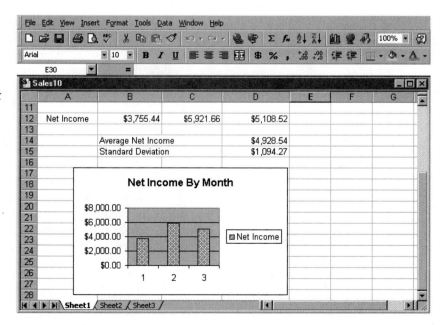

chart showing the monthly figures side by side would be a useful way to visualize this comparison, as illustrated in Figure 8.20. In most spreadsheets, such charts can be created automatically. We need only specify the data we wish to chart and the desired type of graphical plot. Bar charts are one type of series chart. A **series chart** measures the change in one or more dependent values over a series of some value, such as time.

● **Pie Charts.** Bar charts are just one of a number of ways to display and interpret data visually. For example, pie charts are often very convenient for displaying percentage breakdowns. **Pie charts** allow us to portray the parts of a whole, exposing relative sizes of various compo-

FIGURE 8.20

An Excel bar chart compares monthly net income. Notice how much easier the visual display makes data comparison. Such charts are easily constructed in most spreadsheets.

FIGURE 8.21

An analysis of the breakdown of expenses for a given month uses the data from our example. The chart displays the expenses for each category as slices of a pie for an easily interpreted visual impact. In Excel, the chart is defined by simply specifying the data to be used (range B6 through B10), then setting the characteristics of the pie chart in subsequent dialog boxes.

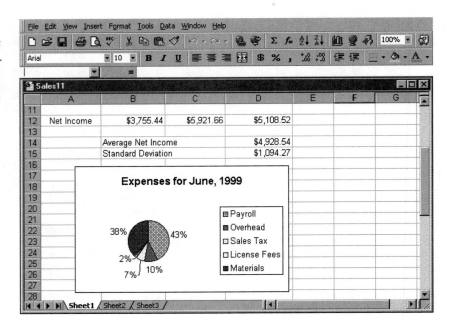

nents in a visually appealing manner. Values are shown as slices of a "pie," with the relative sizes of the slices corresponding to the percentage of the whole represented by each value. See Figure 8.21. Again, most spreadsheet programs make it very easy to create these displays. Pie charts are one variety of distributional chart. A **distributional chart** represents quantities as parts of a whole.

Spreadsheets as Decision Support Tools

Today's businesses are faced with a great many important decisions that often depend on projections produced by numeric models. These models represent profit and cash flow projections, projections about interest rates, performances of economic indicators, market shares, labor and material costs, and so on. You have learned that in large measure the power and advantage of spreadsheet programs are based on their ability to make flexible and updatable computations. This characteristic makes spreadsheet software an extremely valuable tool in business, engineering, and scientific decision making.

The answers to most important questions in business decision making are not black and white. Such decision making often depends on numeric models and computations. It is not uncommon for these models to involve a great many assumptions. Of course, good decision makers analyze these assumptions and demand evidence that they are the correct or the best ones. Spreadsheet programs can help immensely in this process of analyzing various assumptions and the effects they have on the computational models being used. Computations modeled using spreadsheets can be modified easily to explore alternative assumptions or alternate values for important problem parameters whose true values may be unknown.

Such explorations are often referred to as **"what if" computations** because they are used to answer questions that begin "What if. . . ." In our example, we could ask, "What if the sales tax increases to 7 percent?"

or "What if the cost of materials goes up by 15 percent?" Both these questions could be explored quite easily by adjusting the appropriate values in the worksheet. Indeed, "what if" analysis is one of the most important reasons why spreadsheet software is indispensable to almost every modern business enterprise.

Lab Activity

COMPUTING WITH SPREADSHEETS, PART 2

In this activity, you will modify the class grade calculations you constructed in the earlier "Computing with Spreadsheets, Part 1" activity.

1 Let's suppose the course instructor has decided to implement a grading strategy that rewards a student whose final exam grade shows significant improvement. In particular, suppose the instructor adopts the following policy. If the final exam grade is lower than or equal to the average of the three test grades (use a straight average here, not a weighted average), the grading formula will be as previously stated. But if the final exam grade is higher than the average of the three test grades, the weights associated with the test grades and the exam will be adjusted to the following: 10 percent each for the test grades and 45 percent for the final exam grade. In either case, the lab activities will still be weighted at 5 percent each.

2 Open the worksheet you created in the "Computing with Spreadsheets, Part 1" activity. Modify the formula for computing the final course average to reflect the new policy described above. Hint: The IF function can be

used to accomplish this. You can nest functions, so the AVERAGE function can be used inside the IF function. Work with one row of data first and use your calculator (or do the calculations by hand) to test your formula. Once you're sure it is correct, then copy it to the other rows. Test again in the other rows to make sure those calculations are correct. Save the new worksheet under a different name.

3 Suppose now that the instructor wishes to reward those students whose lab work was outstanding. Add a new column to your worksheet named *Adjusted Grade*. Use the IF function once again to adjust the previously calculated course grade in the following way. If the student's lab activity average (straight average of the five grades) is above 90, then compute the adjusted course grade by adding 2 points to the previously calculated course average. Otherwise, the adjusted grade is the same as the previous calculation. Save the modified worksheet.

4 Let's make the worksheet a bit more flexible. Instead of "hard coding" the bonus awarded in the previous step as 2 points, let's make

this value a problem parameter that can be easily changed. Identify a cell to contain the bonus value (you can place the value 2 in it for starters). Modify the formula to calculate the adjusted grade so that it now uses the stored bonus value. Hint: Be sure to use absolute addressing for the parameter in your new formula. Work with one row of data first and test your formula. Once you're sure it is correct, then copy it to the other rows. Test again in the other rows to make sure those calculations are correct. Save the modified worksheet.

5 Now test changing the parameter value in your worksheet (i.e., the bonus amount). Try several values and check the results in the grade calculations to make sure they are correct.

COMPUTING WITH MATHEMATICAL SOFTWARE

We mentioned earlier that in the late 1950s and the 1960s libraries of programs were developed for problem solving in the sciences and engineering. These libraries still exist and are continually improved, but they are effectively employed only within high-level language programs. Learning to program with high-level languages takes careful study and considerable experience. As an alternative, a new class of software designed to solve mathematical, scientific, and engineering problems has been developed. These new programs provide many of the same problem-solving capabilities as program libraries but without the overhead of traditional programming. In addition, they offer some exciting new capabilities as well.

In particular, application programs like Mathematica, Maple, and DERIVE have symbolic manipulation capabilities that allow the user to make algebraic and calculus computations and find solutions to differential equations. These programs also perform numeric approximations to the solutions of mathematical problems for which a symbolic solution may be otherwise impossible or too difficult to manage. In addition, their ability to graph functions and relations easily is an indispensable aid for understanding and exploiting these relationships. Mathematicians, scientists, and engineers can use these capabilities to solve a wide variety of problems with relative ease.

The ability to graph functions in a variety of ways can be profitably exploited to interpret data sets. The term **scientific visualization** is used to describe the array of techniques and methods used to visualize data, models, and functional relationships. Modern mathematical software makes such visualization feasible and has had a profound influence on the way scientific investigations are conducted.

A thorough investigation of these topics is beyond the scope of our discussion. Nonetheless, we can get a flavor for how visualization plays a role in modern scientific work by way of a brief example. MATLAB is a program particularly designed for scientific visualization and mathematical computation. Figures 8.22 through 8.24 demonstrate how MATLAB's capabilities might be used to analyze and illuminate a data set. The data set here is a set of measurements taken during the Loma Prieta earthquake near San Francisco in 1989. (You may remember this quake as the one that occurred during a nationally televised World Series game.) The data set is courtesy of the Seismological Laboratory of the University of California at Santa Cruz. The graphs are generated by MATLAB commands.

Lab Activity

FIGURE 8.22

MATLAB plots of a portion of data taken during the Loma Prieta earthquake are shown. The three graphs plot the acceleration (force) of the earthquake in three mutually perpendicular directions. The horizontal axis represents time measured in seconds. Note that the data shown was collected over a period of 20 seconds—starting 10 seconds after the earthquake began.

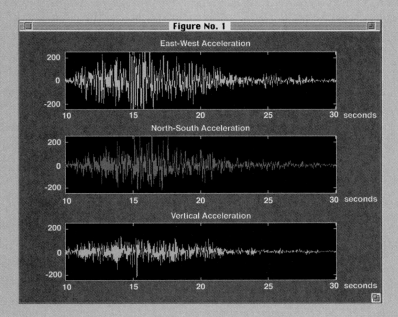

FIGURE 8.23

A MATLAB dynamic simulation of the movement of a single point during the earthquake is shown. During this animation the point moves through its entire displacement—along the trace shown—during the quake. The labeled point in the graph shows the position of the particle when this "snapshot" of the simulation was captured. We've added several annotations and the arrows to show the direction of movement. Compare the trace shown here with the graph in Figure 8.22. Such dynamic simulations can provide valuable insights into natural phenomena.

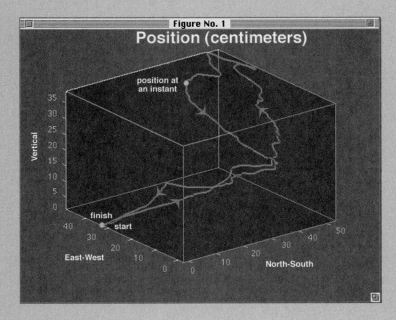

FIGURE 8.24

This MATLAB graph represents the movement of a single particle during the earthquake. Each point on the graph represents the position of a particle at an instant in time. The particle begins (at time = 0) in the bottom plane along the leftmost axis and returns to its original position.

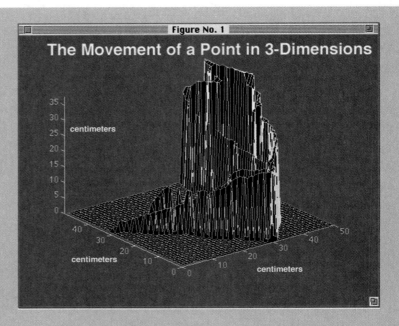

SUMMARY

Finding faster and more reliable means for numeric processing motivated the invention of modern-day computers, and numeric processing is just as fundamental to many of today's computing applications as it was in the early days of computing. However, numeric computing is not a straightforward affair. Converting numeric data to the digital domain is complicated because numbers are both infinite in number and continuously distributed along the number line.

Integer values can be represented exactly and without error in a computer's memory, provided they are within the computer's limited range of integer values. Integers outside this range must be treated as decimal numbers. Decimal numbers are digitized with both limited range and limited precision. To maximize the precision possible for decimal numbers using a fixed number of bits of storage, these numbers are stored in the computer employing floating point representation, consisting of a normalized fraction and an exponent. Storing decimal numbers with limited precision means that *every* computerized numerical operation using them is potentially in error. Hence you must always perform decimal calculations on computers with some degree of caution and skepticism for the results.

To make it easier for programmers to avoid creating calculations that might generate large errors, computer scientists have created solution methods for many common problems that are carefully designed to avoid or minimize possible pitfalls. These methods are stored in electronic software libraries, which are available for the programmer's use during the construction of a program requiring numeric processing.

Symbolic and numeric calculation programs make robust computational methods more accessible for the nonprogrammer. The term *scientific visualization* is used to describe the array of techniques and methods that are used to visualize data, models, and functional relationships. Modern mathematical software makes such visualization feasible and has had a profound influence on the way scientific investigations are conducted.

Spreadsheet software packages are especially designed for numeric processing and offer a very user-friendly interface. Automatic updating of calculations with new data, charting or plotting calculations in a variety of ways, and employing built-in computational functions are some examples of the power and flexibility of spreadsheet software. "What if" spreadsheet analysis, so named because it is used to analyze questions that begin "What if . . . ," has become an indispensable tool in almost every modern business enterprise.

PROJECTS

1 Use the method described in the text for converting decimal fractions to binary fractions to show that the decimal number .2 has an infinite binary representation.

2 This project assumes you completed the "At Your Computer" activity, "Exploring Limited Precision," in this chapter. Modify the worksheet you created in that activity to perform the same calculations using the value 0.25 instead of 0.1. You'll need to change the formula in cell B2, then copy the new formula to cells B3 through B101. Next, change the value in cell C2, modify the formula in cell C3, and copy the new formula to cells C4 through C101. When you complete these changes, compare the values in the second column (calculated by multiplication) and the values in the third column (calculated by addition) just as you did for the original activity. Do you find that these values eventually differ as before? Explain the results as compared to the results you previ-

ously observed when the value 0.1 was used. (Hint: What is 0.25 as a fraction?)

3 Repeat project 2, but this time make the basic numeric value to be used throughout the calculation a problem parameter. Reference this parameter using an absolute reference in all formulas. Experiment with several values to see which of these produces the differences in precision noted in the "At Your Computer" activity, "Exploring Limited Precision," in this chapter.

4 Conduct some Web-based research to learn more about the topic of scientific visualization. Bookmark any particularly informative sites you find. Write a brief essay about your findings.

5 Design and create a Web page that will serve as an informative introduction to scientific visualization. Use the links you bookmarked in project 4.

6 Design and create a worksheet to solve the following problem. Construct a table to compute the weekly gross pay for a number of hourly employees. You can assume you will be given each employee's name, hourly pay rate, and the number of hours worked for the week. Enter hypothetical data for five employees. The gross pay for each should be calculated as follows. The regular pay rate holds for the first 40 hours worked during the week. For each hour over 40 worked, an employee is paid the company *overtime multiplier,* which is currently 1.5 times his or her usual hourly rate. Check a few of the calculations by hand (or calculator). Format all dollar amounts as currency. (Hint: The IF function will be useful in this project.)

7 Modify the worksheet you created in project 6 so that the company overtime multiplier (which was 1.5 in project 6) is modeled as a problem parameter. In other words, this number should be stored separately and then referenced by absolute address in the gross pay formula. Once you make these changes, try a different value (say 2) for this parameter. Check a few of the calculations by hand (or calculator).

8 Modify the worksheet you created in projects 6 and 7 so that it computes the *net pay* for each employee after several deductions from gross pay. The deductions are as follows: a federal withholding tax of 20 percent (of gross pay); a state withholding tax of 4 percent; social security tax of 6.75 percent; hospital insurance of $32. Use separate columns to display each deduction. After you complete these changes, have your worksheet compute a total for all the columns containing dollar amounts. Finally, use the totals row to construct a pie chart showing the distribution of the total gross pay (for all employees together) into the categories federal tax, state tax, social security, hospital insurance, and net pay.

Key Terms

absolute cell reference	entry bar	problem parameter
argument	expanding a number's represen-	real number
bar chart	tation	relative cell reference
Boolean expression	exponent	scientific visualization
built-in function	floating point representation	series chart
cell, worksheet	integer	software library
cell address	limited precision	spreadsheet
cell range	logical expression	twos complement method
conditional processing	mantissa	underflow error
current cell	overflow error	"what if" computation
distributional chart	pie chart	worksheet

QUESTIONS FOR REVIEW

1   What was the importance of numeric processing for the development of modern-day computers?

2   Write the binary number 1010101 in decimal representation.

3   Write the decimal number 247 in binary representation.

4   React to the statement: Integers can be represented and stored exactly in computer memory.

5   What is meant by an overflow error during a calculation?

6   Convert the binary number 10.1101 to its decimal representation.

7   Convert the decimal number 2.875 to binary representation. Use the scheme described in the text for the decimal part.

8   Convert the decimal number 46.1875 to binary representation.

9   Give the normalized floating point form of the number .00264.

10 Give the normalized floating point form of the number 369.02.

11 Write the normalized floating point number $.246 \times 10^3$ in usual decimal form.

12 Write the normalized floating point number $.461 \times 10^{-4}$ in usual decimal form.

13 How does the problem of limited precision occur in converting real numbers to floating point format? Can it always be avoided?

14 Explain *overflow* and *underflow* for numbers represented in floating point format.

15 What is meant when we say the number line that can be represented in a computer's memory contains "holes"?

16 Why is it necessary to perform decimal calculations on a computer with caution and skepticism?

17 How is a typical spreadsheet document (i.e., worksheet) organized?

18 How does the typical spreadsheet distinguish between numeric and textual input data?

19 What is meant when we say that spreadsheets automatically recalculate formulas?

20 Describe the copying of formulas in a spreadsheet. Explain the difference between absolute and relative cell references in this process.

21 Why are built-in functions important in a spreadsheet? Give some examples of the kinds of built-in functions typically found in a spreadsheet.

22 What is meant by the arguments of a spreadsheet function?

23 Contrast distributional charts and series charts. Give an example of the kind of data you might represent with each. Is one of these graphical display methods preferred over the other? Explain.

24 What is meant by problem parameters in constructing a spreadsheet problem solution? Why is it important to isolate important problem parameters in a spreadsheet model?

25 What are *logical functions*? What are they used for in spreadsheet work? Give a brief example.

26 Explain the concept of a *"what if" computation*. Why are these important? Why is a spreadsheet so useful for producing these kinds of computations?

27 What is meant by the term *Boolean expression*? How are these used in spreadsheet calculations?

28 Describe the use of spreadsheet packages as decision support tools.

29 What is *scientific visualization*? Why is it an important technique?

30 Give several examples of scientific visualization. (Hint: Have you watched the "Six O'Clock Report" on your local television station lately?)

In Chapter 8 you learned that numeric processing was the primary task that motivated the invention of computers. In spite of this fact, today text processing is one of the major uses of computers. We routinely depend on computers for many forms of document preparation. The ease with which we can produce, edit, and combine text documents would be unthinkable without computers. Using a desktop computer and printer, we can produce everything from simple correspondence to newsletters, catalogs, and even entire books like this one. Digitally produced documents are not limited to text alone either. The computer's ability to reduce various kinds of information to the digital domain means that we can combine graphical objects, images, and even sounds into our electronic "text" documents.

In this chapter, you will learn about some of the fundamental concepts associated with text processing and desktop publishing. In later chapters, you will see how to expand your electronic documents with graphics, images, and sounds.

OBJECTIVES

- *Brief history of text processing*
- *The way text is represented and stored in computers*
- *Basic functionality present in most word processing packages*
- *Overview of desktop publishing software*

CHAPTER 9

TEXT PROCESSING

Vasily Kandinsky, *Decisive Rose*, March 1932. Solomon R. Guggenheim Museum

BRIEF HISTORY OF TEXT PROCESSING

The word-processing capabilities we take for granted are a far cry from the fairly primitive text processing methods used in the early days of electronic computers. Long before word processing became an important application for computers, programmers drafted their programs on paper, and then the computer's switches and wiring were adjusted to run the program. Of course, stored-program computers replaced these early models. On a stored-program computer, the instructions of the program are encoded symbolically and stored in the memory of the system like data.

In the 1950s and early 1960s, symbolic programs were composed using **keypunch machines,** which punched holes in cards to encode text and numbers—usually one line of a program per card. Keypunch machines were not connected to a computer; programs had to be prepared offline and then submitted later to the computer. When a program was completed, its cards were assembled into a stack (or deck) and submitted to a card reader machine for transfer to the computer's memory. Keypunch machines were not very forgiving text processors: Once a hole was punched, it could not be undone. Mistakes were corrected only by starting over with a new card and retyping the entire line.

The only printed output that computers produced in those days was the result of a program's numerical computations. Program output was generally limited to lists of numbers, with only a small amount of textual documentation. No one used computers for writing letters, memos, reports, and so on.

In the early 1960s, time-sharing technology was introduced. The first multiuser operating systems gave programmers direct access to mainframe computer systems, which reduced the need for keypunch machines. They eventually gave way to **text editors,** programs residing on a computer for the purpose of composing other source programs. The earliest text editors were line editors that mimicked the way things were done using cards and keypunch machines. Each line in the program was designated by a number. To edit that line, you issued a command using its line number. Later in the 1970s, significant advances were made in the functionality of text editors, and they became easy enough to use that some brave souls actually employed them for general document preparation. (Some of these editors are still around today.)

The improved editors led to the introduction of the first dedicated text processing systems, called **word processors,** in the early and mid-1970s. These systems consisted of special-purpose computers and software that performed certain types of word processing. For instance, there were dedicated systems designed to be used in the legal profession for the production of legal documents. Essentially, these systems allowed an operator to fill in the blanks electronically, so to speak, to produce standardized legal documents. Other dedicated word processors soon followed. To use such a system, you had to purchase both special hardware and appropriate software that came bundled with it. Most of these systems were expensive, costing $10,000 and up.

In the late 1970s and early 1980s, the personal computer was popularized by Apple Computer, Tandy, Commodore, IBM, and others. Most users bought these machines for one of two basic functions. Some were interested in employing VisiCalc, the first spreadsheet program, for automated accounting and other related activities. Others sought the convenience of word processing. WordStar was the first commercially successful word processing program. It became very popular in the early 1980s when many people discovered the convenience and powerful features of electronic word processing.

Today dozens of word processing programs are commercially available. Like spreadsheet programs, modern word processors have a number of common features. Each has approximately the same range of basic functionality, and there is not a great deal of difference between the leading products. In spite of this fact, each has its own band of loyal supporters who might claim otherwise. Fortunately, the many similarities among these products mean that once you've mastered one of the current-generation word processors, training yourself on another is a relatively simple matter.

In the late 1980s, text processing capabilities on the personal computer were extended beyond simple word processing to encompass what is referred to as **desktop publishing (DTP).** Desktop publishing application programs such as PageMaker, Quark XPress, and others are intended for the design and layout of complex documents on a personal computer. Armed with a DTP program, you can create newsletters, magazines, catalogs, and books that contain many sophisticated elements. For example, you can integrate scanned images, flow text around them, choose text with several colors for dramatic effects, add shaded and/or boxed text and figures, annotate figures, apply curved and variable-sized text features, and more. If it is designed well, the final product is indistinguishable from documents that have been professionally typeset using more conventional methods. In fact, many publishers of magazines, periodicals, and books use electronic tools like these to produce most of their commercial documents. Desktop publishing puts these capabilities into the hands of the consumer.

REPRESENTING TEXTUAL INFORMATION

Electronic text documents are made up of sequences of characters that are arranged and formatted in particular ways. Both the characters and their formats must be encoded and digitized, of course, before the computer can process them. We discuss these issues in this section; we begin by investigating first how the symbols or characters themselves are stored.

Digitizing the Character Set

Written languages are represented by a set of symbols called a **character set.** A character set contains letters of the alphabet, punctuation marks, and other special symbols used to express the language in writing. Western languages, such as English, French, German, Italian, Spanish, and so on, are based on a common character set. Some of these languages require a few extra marking symbols, but the basic alphabet has twenty-six individual characters, or fifty-two if we count uppercase and lowercase separately. In addition, there are some standard punctuation marks, including commas, periods, question marks, exclamation points, parentheses, single and double quotes, colons, and semicolons. Other special symbols are sometimes needed; for example, the digits; the arithmetic symbols +, −, /, and * (for multiplication); dollar signs; ampersands; and so on. If we total all of these symbols, we get a count between 100 and 150. Cyrillic-based languages such as Russian require approximately the same number of symbols. In contrast, Eastern languages such as Chinese and Japanese require a great many more symbols. A full Chinese symbol set, for example, totals more than 10,000 separate characters. (This is one reason why word processing systems for Chinese have been slow to develop.)

Of course, written English is our primary interest for this discussion. Unlike the problems faced in digitizing numbers, we have a finite (and rather small, at that) set of characters to be concerned with. This greatly simplifies the problem of devising a digitizing scheme. In fact, the choice of scheme is relatively unimportant as long as we satisfy two constraints. First, we need to make certain we have a one-to-one encoding of the character set; that is, we need to ensure that no two characters have the same digital code. Second, we would like to use as little memory space as possible when we store our characters. You will recall that a single byte (eight bits) is the smallest addressable unit of memory. A single byte therefore seems a natural choice for representing character codes. But is it sufficient for storing all the different character symbols that we might require?

Let's investigate this question a little further. As stated, we may need to represent as many as 150 different symbols in a character set. How many unique codes (or bit patterns) are possible with one byte? There are eight bits in a byte, and each bit can be either 0 or 1. How many different combinations does this allow? Let's consider simpler cases first to get a handle on this question.

Suppose we have only one bit. Then clearly we have two different representations: 0 and 1. With two bits we gain some additional options. In fact, we have four different representations possible: 00, 01, 10, and 11. What about a three-bit representation? Each of the four representations for two bits could have either a 0 or a 1 appended, so the number doubles to eight different representations: 000, 001, 010, 011, 100, 101, 110, 111. By this latter reasoning, each time we add a bit, we double the number of representations. This is true because we can take each of the representations we had previously and append either a 0 or a 1 to form a new representation; hence we get twice as many as we started with.

Extending this reasoning, we can conclude that there are 256 ($= 2^8$) representations in a byte (eight bits). Because we need only 150 or so symbols, a single byte would be sufficient for character codes. The chart in Figure 9.1 illustrates this analysis.

Storing the Character Set—ASCII

Now what's left to decide is how we map the characters to particular strings of 0s and 1s for encoding. This is really a matter of choice. As long as every character has a unique representation, it won't much matter. If one computer manufacturer, however, decides on one scheme and another on a second scheme, and so on, transferring information from one type of computer to another becomes very difficult. Whatever mapping we decide on, it would be convenient if everyone used the same mapping. This is almost what has happened.

FIGURE 9.1

A single byte provides for 256 different representations. The structures used here to expand the number of possibilities are referred to as binary trees. If you think of turning them upside down, you'll see why this term is applied. The top of the tree—where the single 0 and single 1 reside—is called the root of the tree, and each tree has branches downward in the structure. The trees are called binary because at each branching point, two branches are grown.

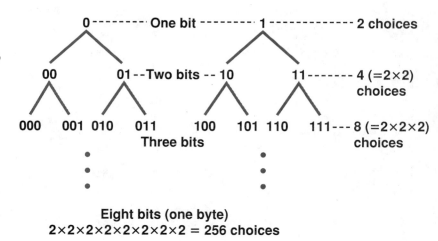

There are two commonly used mapping schemes. The one used by the vast majority of computers is called the **American Standard Code for Information Interchange** or **ASCII** (pronounced "as-key"). See Table 9.1 for the ASCII encoding table. Notice that all the punctuation marks and other special symbols ordinarily found on a keyboard are included in the ASCII code. An example of a sentence converted to ASCII is shown in Figure 9.2.

If you examine the ASCII encoding table (Table 9.1), you will notice another feature. Both uppercase and lowercase alphabets are numerically ordered according to alphabetical order. For example, "A" is 65, "B" is 66, "C" is 67, and so on. Each alphabet is arranged in ascending order. Digits are also ordered. This attribute is called the **collating sequence**; it means that the computer can take advantage of this property of the underlying code to alphabetize text. For example, two last names like "BABB" and "BAKER" could be compared symbol by symbol. Each has a "B" followed by an "A." Up to this point, they would be equivalent. But because "K" or 75 is greater than "B" or 66, "BAKER" should be placed after "BABB" in an alphabetized list. Alphabetizing or arranging text in lexicographic order belongs to a special class of operations called sorting. Many forms of information can be ordered, and if their data representation is likewise ordered, then sorting them becomes easier. Preserving the collating sequence, for instance, makes it easier to sort text because instructions can employ the processor's normal numeric comparison operations.

Invisible Formatting Characters

The blank space is a character just like any other. Its ASCII representation is 00100000 in binary (32 in decimal) even though we don't think of it as a symbol when we type or print it. What we recognize is the effect it creates, namely, a space between the other visible characters. Some other characters entered at the keyboard do not show up as symbols when we enter them, but rather as effects—for example, the Tab key for indenting and the Enter or Return key for carriage returns or marking the end of the line. These are some of the **invisible formatting characters** used to represent the formatting of text in our documents. Actually,

TABLE 9.1

The ASCII character encoding scheme maps each symbol of the character set to a 1-byte (8-bit) storage representation.

ASCII ENCODING TABLE								
Binary	**Decimal**	**Character**	**Binary**	**Decimal**	**Character**	**Binary**	**Decimal**	**Character**
00000000	0		00111100	60	<	01011111	95	_
.	.	invisible	00111101	61	=	01100000	96	`
.	.	control	00111110	62	>	01100001	97	a
.	.	characters	00111111	63	?	01100010	98	b
00011111	31		01000000	64	@	01100011	99	c
00100000	32	blank	01000001	65	A	01100100	100	d
		space	01000010	66	B	01100101	101	e
		character	01000011	67	C	01100110	102	f
00100001	33	!	01000100	68	D	01100111	103	g
00100010	34	"	01000101	69	E	01101000	104	h
00100011	35	#	01000110	70	F	01101001	105	i
00100100	36	$	01000111	71	G	01101010	106	j
00100101	37	%	01001000	72	H	01101011	107	k
00100110	38	&	01001001	73	I	01101100	108	l
00100111	39	'	01001010	74	J	01101101	109	m
00101000	40	(	01001011	75	K	01101110	110	n
00101001	41	)	01001100	76	L	01101111	111	o
00101010	42	*	01001101	77	M	01110000	112	p
00101011	43	+	01001110	78	N	01110001	113	q
00101100	44	,	01001111	79	O	01110010	114	r
00101101	45	-	01010000	80	P	01110011	115	s
00101110	46	.	01010001	81	Q	01110100	116	t
00101111	47	/	01010010	82	R	01110101	117	u
00110000	48	0	01010011	83	S	01110110	118	v
00110001	49	1	01010100	84	T	01110111	119	w
00110010	50	2	01010101	85	U	01111000	120	x
00110011	51	3	01010110	86	V	01111001	121	y
00110100	52	4	01010111	87	W	01111010	122	z
00110101	53	5	01011000	88	X	01111011	123	{
00110110	54	6	01011001	89	Y	01111100	124		
00110111	55	7	01011010	90	Z	01111101	125	}
00111000	56	8	01011011	91	[	01111110	126	~
00111001	57	9	01011100	92	\	01111111	127	delete
00111010	58	:	01011101	93	]			
00111011	59	;	01011110	94	^			

FIGURE 9.2

Converting a simple sentence to ASCII representation is shown. Using the ASCII code, any string of text that can be entered from the keyboard can be easily digitized.

Look, a tiger!

↓ **Digitization requires 14 bytes of storage**

01001100	01101111	01101111	01101011	00101100	00100000	01100001
L	o	o	k	,	blank	a

00100000	01110100	01101001	01100111	01100101	01110010	00100001
blank	t	i	g	e	r	!

most word processing programs allow you to display these otherwise invisible characters when you edit a document. Figure 9.3 illustrates what some of these look like in Microsoft Word.

Other formatting information must be stored with a document as well if the document is to be reproduced as intended. This information falls into several categories: information about individual characters, about paragraphs, about sections within the document, and about the document as a whole. For example, if certain characters are to be displayed in bold-face type, this information must be stored; likewise, the particular font to be used for displaying each character must also be encoded. For paragraphs, positions of tab markers, indentation values, and whether the paragraph is to be displayed with an uneven or a straight right edge are some examples of formatting information. For the entire document, we must also store the page margins, the headers and footers (if any), and other information. All this information must be encoded within the document.

Unfortunately, there is no equivalent to the ASCII code for this type of formatting information. Competing word processing programs were developed rapidly after the success of WordStar, before the issue of standardization could be addressed. Today each manufacturer has its own methods embedded in its proprietary products. Keep in mind that this lack of standardization is not among different types of computers, but among different software that often runs on exactly the same types of

FIGURE 9.3

Some of Microsoft Word's "invisible" formatting characters are shown. Such characters have no standard internal representations, making exchange of documents between word processors a tricky process.

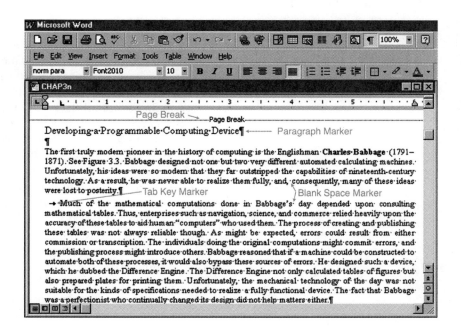

computers. For example, a Microsoft Word document will differ in digital form from a WordPerfect document created on the same computer even if the original text contents are identical. The differences will be the embedded formatting information.

That each word processing package has its own proprietary method for encoding formatting information makes moving documents between one word processing program and another a tricky business. In this conversion process, we are likely to lose the formatting information altogether, or at least get a garbled version of it once we transfer our document. A way out of this is to employ a separate utility program, called a **translator** or **filter program,** that is specifically written to convert documents from one particular package to another. Many of the current-generation word processors come bundled with such filters for documents created in their major competitors' word processors.

If you must move information from one program to another without the benefit of a translator program, the safe way to do it is to save a copy of the original document in pure ASCII or text-only format first. This will strip away all the formatting information except for spaces, tabs, and returns. Another word processing program will at least be able to read the unformatted text itself—made possible by the common ASCII code that both programs use. An even better option might be to use the **Rich Text Format (RTF)** file format, which does preserve a great deal of formatting information for text documents. It is supported by Microsoft and is a leading candidate for an industry-standard text file exchange format. Most current document preparation programs can both read and save RTF files.

Despite underlying file format differences, over the last few years, we have seen a gradual convergence of basic methods and techniques at the user level among various word processing programs. In the next section we examine the basic features to be found in most word processing packages. Later, we also consider a second set of features found in many desktop publishing programs.

BASIC FEATURES OF WORD PROCESSING SOFTWARE

When we studied spreadsheet software in Chapter 8, we indicated that the various commercial spreadsheet programs had a great deal in common. These similarities make it very easy to translate expertise in using one spreadsheet package to another. Even though commercial word processing programs lack this same degree of uniformity, they do have a high degree of commonality. These programs have essentially the same basic functions and capabilities even if they have slightly different looks or user interfaces. Thus, if you have learned to use one program, you will probably need only a small amount of instruction (perhaps just a little experimentation) to become proficient with another one.

The essential functions of word processing software are to create, edit, and format text documents. Word processors were designed to emulate the older, conventional way of entering text using a typewriter. (Ironically, word processors have nearly replaced typewriters entirely, so that the original metaphor is usually lost on new users today.) There are important differences between employing typewriters and word processors to create documents. For instance, when you use a typewriter, you must press the Enter (or Return) key when you reach the end of a line (usually a bell rings to remind you that you are near the end of a line). Word processors automatically handle the end of a line for you using a feature called **word-wrap.** This means that you can simply continue to type and when you reach the end of a line, the text will automatically flow to the next line. Partially completed words will be wrapped to the next line—thus the term *word-wrap*. Hence, pressing the Enter (or Return) key in a word processor does not signal the end of a line. Rather, this action marks the end of a paragraph. Much of the formatting you do in a word processing document will apply to whole paragraphs, so it is very important to have a convenient way to delineate different paragraphs.

Inserting and Deleting Text

Nearly all modern word processors are automatically in a mode that allows new text to be inserted at any point. The **cursor** marks the point at which text you type is inserted in a document. Thus, to add text, you simply position the cursor at the point where new text is desired and type. Positioning the cursor is usually performed using a mouse, but some programs also allow you to use the arrow keys on the keyboard to position the cursor. Once the cursor is in the desired location, you can insert text at will. The word processor will expand the text at that point to make room for the added text.

Deleting text is just as easy. Often you do so by positioning the cursor just beyond the text to be deleted and pressing the Backspace key (the Delete key on some Macintosh keyboards) the requisite number of times. The word processor will automatically shrink the text to combine the undeleted portions. To edit or change text, therefore, the simplest procedure is to delete the unwanted text and then insert its replacement.

You may want to delete or replace large sections of text. Deleting character by character using the Backspace key would be tedious for these cases, thus word processors provide an easier way to accomplish this. By selecting a contiguous section of text, called a **block of text,** you can act on it as a unit. You can select a text block by dragging the mouse pointer over the block. The selected text is highlighted on screen for easy identification, as illustrated in Figure 9.4. Once you have selected the desired text, you can delete or replace it all at once. For example, pressing the Backspace key will delete all the text currently selected.

FIGURE 9.4

A selected body of text in a Microsoft Word document is shown. Text is selected by dragging the mouse. A variety of actions can then be taken on the selected portion of text.

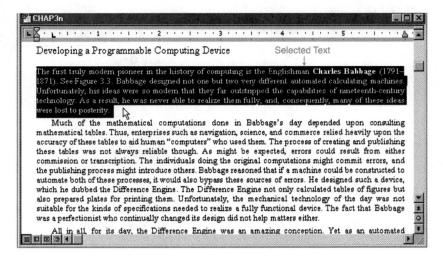

Likewise, typing while a body of text is highlighted will replace the entire selected section with the newly typed text.

Cut, Copy, and Paste

The general procedure described in the previous paragraph is often referred to as a **select-then-do process.** In fact, we frequently accomplish a task in word processing by first selecting some text block and then issuing a command or taking some action that affects the selected section. Just as this process could be used to delete text or replace it with alternate text, it can be used to move sections of text or duplicate text elsewhere. All word processors provide these basic editing capabilities, usually by way of *Cut, Copy,* and *Paste* commands. These commands act in the ways that their names suggest. If we select a body of text and issue the **Cut command,** the selected text is deleted or cut from the document. The text is not lost, however, but is rather saved in an area of memory referred to as the **clipboard.** (We say we have placed the text "on the clipboard.") If we reposition the cursor and issue the **Paste command,** the text on the clipboard will be inserted into this new position within the document. In this way, we can move or reorder selections of text at will. Figure 9.5 illustrates this process. This is an indispensable tool for editing long documents, where we are likely to change our minds—perhaps several times—about the exact sequence of the text contents. (We assure you that the cut-and-paste procedure was used a great many times in the preparation of this book!)

The **Copy command** works just like the *Cut* command except that it does not remove the selected text from its current position. In other words, the *Copy* command simply places the selected text on the clipboard. By moving the cursor to another position and then choosing the *Paste* command, we can duplicate selected text sections. This is very useful sometimes when we have two blocks of text that are very similar: To create the second block, we can duplicate the first block and then edit it, rather than enter the second block from scratch.

FIGURE 9.5

This figure illustrates the role of the clipboard (a section of memory) in copying, cutting, and pasting information.

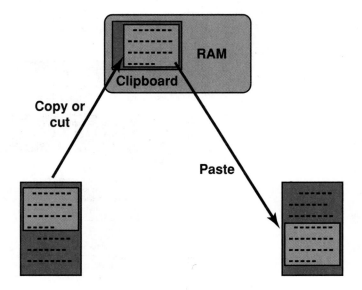

Text placed on the clipboard is not erased after it is pasted elsewhere. Because the clipboard is a form of memory, we can read its contents as many times as we want without altering these contents. Consequently, we can paste it over and over, if desired. The only way that text on the clipboard is replaced is when a new *Cut* or *Copy* command is executed—a new item written to the clipboard memory overwrites the existing item.

Formatting Characters

All word processors let us choose how we wish to display the characters in our text—from groups of characters like whole paragraphs, phrases, and single words down to individual characters. The display characteristics are called **formatting,** and there are a number of choices in this regard.

For example, we can choose the particular font in which we want to display the characters (from among those fonts that have been installed in our system files). A **font** is the typeface in which each symbol is drawn or formed. In addition to the font itself, we can also specify its size. The typical measure for **font size** is based on the printer's measure, **points.** There are approximately 72 points per inch. The choices for font and font size are limited by what is stored in the system files—not by the word processor itself. Figure 9.6 shows examples of several different font styles and sizes. The choice of font affects not only how each character is formed, but the spacing of characters on a line as well. Different fonts having the same point size can be proportioned differently; this means that they will be displayed or printed differently. Figure 9.6 shows how the two size-12 sentences and the two size-10 sentences are proportioned differently because they are in different fonts.

Characters can also be displayed in a variety of **font styles** such as italic, boldface, underlined, shadow, and so on, as illustrated in Figure 9.7. These styles may be combined as well. Most word processors can display characters raised above the line of type to form **superscripts** or placed below the line of type as **subscripts.** By installing special symbol font sets in the system files, you can create special-purpose documents such as scientific and mathematical documents, foreign

FIGURE 9.6

Samples of several font types and sizes are shown. The nonsense sentence displayed contains all 26 letters of the alphabet.

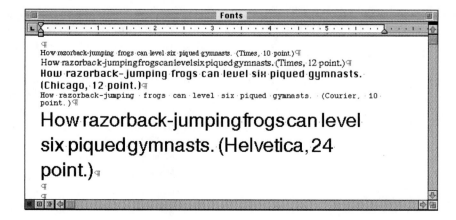

FIGURE 9.7
This is the dialog box for setting a variety of font styles and other characteristics in WordPerfect.

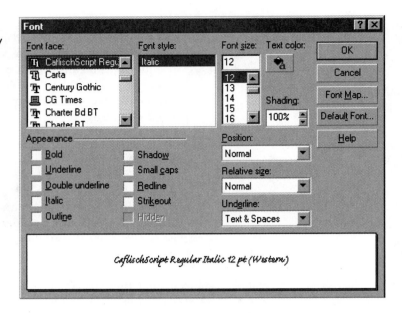

language documents (even those using Chinese or Japanese character sets), and others.

Formatting Paragraphs

The appearance of a document can be greatly altered by paragraph formatting. For example, we can change the width of paragraphs by setting the paragraph margins, and we can choose different line spacing for a paragraph (single-spaced, double-spaced, and so on). It is usually quite easy to change the alignment of paragraphs, too. In particular, paragraphs can be **left-aligned** (even left edge and ragged right edge), **right-aligned** (even right edge and ragged left edge—useful for some special effects), **justified** (even on both edges), or **centered.** Another characteristic convenient to control automatically is the indentation of the first line of a paragraph. Various kinds of **tab markers** can be defined and set for a paragraph as well, so that pressing the Tab key produces automatic text separation. Tabs are indispensable for setting up tables, numbered or bulleted lists, and columnar displays.

In almost all modern word processors, you can set any or all of the paragraph characteristics by placing the cursor anywhere inside the paragraph (thereby selecting the paragraph for formatting) and then adjusting the desired options on the ruler or selecting the appropriate option from a toolbar. A **ruler** is a graphical device with markings similar to those on a regular measuring ruler, together with other icons and special symbols, as shown in Figure 9.8. Ruler adjustments are usually carried out by clicking and dragging with the mouse. If you need greater precision for margins and tab markers, you can access paragraph formatting through dialog boxes available in pull-down menus. In these boxes you can enter precise measurements for the placement of tabs and margins.

Rulers can be used to format individual paragraphs. If you move the cursor to a different paragraph, the ruler may have completely different settings. This means, of course, that the current paragraph has been for-

focus

IS WHAT YOU SEE REALLY WHAT YOU GET?

Because most word processing documents are delivered as printed documents to their intended audience, it is highly desirable that what you see on the screen corresponds closely to what will be printed. This property is called **what-you-see-is-what-you-get** and is represented by the acronym **WYSIWYG** (pronounced "whiz-ee-wig"). If the word processor you are using does not have this property for the printer you intend to use, you will likely be in for a few surprises when you actually print the document.

In regard to WYSIWYG, a special circumstance is worth noting here. The resolution of most screen displays is inferior to the resolution of a good laser printer. As a result, fonts appear much choppier on the screen than they do in a document printed on a higher-resolution printer

that does a great deal of font smoothing. Many of the figures in this chapter were created by capturing an electronic image of a computer screen displaying the text shown. As you look at the text displayed in these figures, you will see this effect clearly.

Depending on the resolution of the printer to be used, WYSIWYG usually does not apply in the strictest sense. What WYSIWYG actually refers to in these cases is something a little less perfect than its name suggests, namely, that the character *positions* appear on screen exactly as they will in the printed document. To be safe, you should always inspect a printed document to see that it is formatted as you intended. WYSIWYG does, however, make the formatting process a great deal easier and could save a few trees, too.

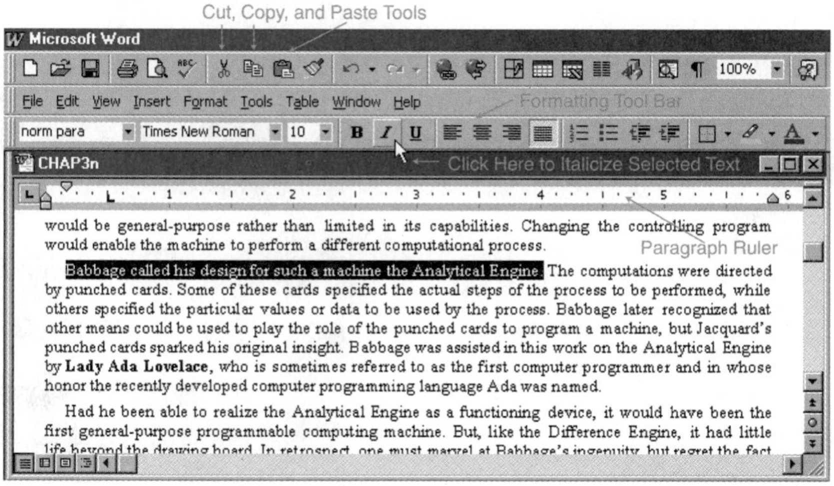

FIGURE 9.8

The Microsoft Word paragraph ruler and toolbars displayed at the top of the document (as they typically are in other word processors) are shown. The top toolbar contains buttons for common activities such as the Cut, Copy, Paste, Print, and Save operations. The second-row toolbar is dedicated to formatting controls. For example B, I, and U stand for bold, italic, and underline, respectively.

matted differently. In other words, every paragraph has its own ruler settings stored with the document. To access the ruler settings for a particular paragraph, you simply place the cursor somewhere within that paragraph. For convenience, when you press the Enter or Return key to end a paragraph and begin a new one, the current ruler settings carry forward to the new paragraph. This eliminates having to reset the format characteristics of adjacent paragraphs that are likely to have the same format anyway.

Headers and Footers

Many documents often include information in the top or bottom margins of a page, called **headers** and **footers,** respectively. For example, you might like to put your class number and paper title as a header that appears at the top of each page in a term paper; you will often want to place page numbers in footers or headers. At other times, you might choose to put the word "draft" in a header to indicate that the work is in progress, or you might place a date in the header (or footer). Modern word processors make the creation of headers and footers very easy. In these headers and footers, you may insert automatic page numbers, dates, and the time, if desired. Automatic page numbers are adjusted automatically as you rearrange and edit your document.

For example, in Microsoft Word you can select a view of your document that displays the footers and headers. When you're using this view, you can directly enter and edit information in the header and footer boxes displayed at the top and bottom of your document proper. Figure 9.9 provides an example.

Formatting Documents and Sections

Another important set of formatting information has to do with the entire document. For the entire document, we can control page margins (left, right, top, and bottom), create footers and headers, and control numbering style and the starting page number. Figure 9.10 illustrates. In some word processors, we can define different **sections** within a document. When this feature is provided, all the characteristics just enumerated can be set for individual sections of a document as well.

FIGURE 9.9

A header text box in Microsoft Word is shown. Text can be entered and edited directly in header and footer boxes when displayed.

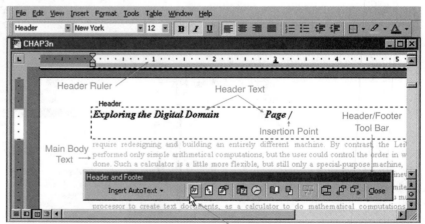

FIGURE 9.10

This dialog box in WordPerfect is used to set document characteristics such as margins.

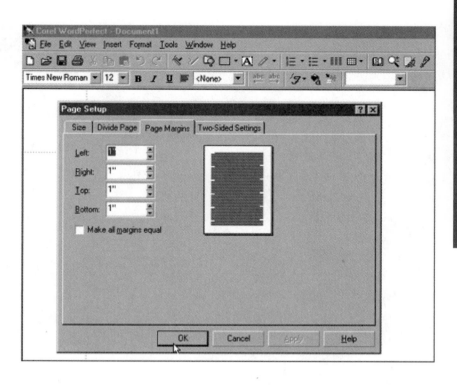

CREATING A RÉSUMÉ

In this exercise you will explore the use of your particular word processing software to create a sample résumé. We will suggest the résumé layout and elements and indicate the kind of formatting needed to produce the effects desired. Of course, the particular commands needed will vary from software package to software package, so we will not attempt instructions at the command level. Specific tutorials for some of the most popular word processing software can be found at the *Exploring the Digital Domain* Web site.

As you go through these steps, substitute information to create your own personalized résumé if you like. You might want to display the invisible formatting characters as you edit your document.

Being able to see the paragraph markers in particular is often helpful. If your software allows this (not all programs do), you can accomplish it using a toolbar button or a pull-down menu command.

1 You will create a résumé similar to the one shown in Figure 9.11. Begin by opening your word processor and creating a new document.

2 Type in the text for the heading—your name, address, phone number, and (if applicable) e-mail address. Each of these entries should be on a separate line, as shown in Figure 9.11. Of course, this means pressing the Enter or Return key after each line. Save your document. We'll format these entries shortly; for now, proceed to the next step.

3 Type in the heading *Objectives,* press Enter or Return, then type in a brief paragraph describing your objectives. Save your document again and after each step from here on.

4 Let's format the text you've entered so far. Start with the heading material. Select (by dragging) all the lines in your heading material, as illustrated in Figure 9.12. With these lines highlighted, choose a *centered* paragraph alignment. You can probably accomplish this with the click of a button on a toolbar. If not, you can find an appropriate command in the pull-down menus. Next (with the same lines still selected), increase the font size by several points. Again, you'll likely find a toolbar button to help you with this. Finally, make all the selected text bold. Once again, a toolbar button will likely do the trick; if not, search for the appropriate pull-down menu command.

5 Let's now format the Objectives section of your résumé. Begin by selecting the word *Objectives* and making it bold. Now place the cursor somewhere in the following paragraph and click. Access the ruler for this paragraph. It is likely already displayed; if it is not, check the **View** menu (or equivalent) and activate the ruler. Move the left margin marker on the ruler to the right by a half-inch. This marker is likely coupled with the first line indent marker. If so, make sure you move both to the right. Compare your document to Figure 9.11 and correct any problems before going on.

6 Now copy and paste the Objectives section, then just edit the text for the rest of the résumé's elements. This will save you some effort in formatting each element of the résumé separately, and it will guarantee that the formatting is consistent throughout the document.

7 To begin, place the cursor at the very end of the Objectives paragraph, and press Enter or Return two times to place two blank lines after the paragraph. Now select the entire Objectives section plus one of the two blank lines at the end of it. See Figure 9.13.

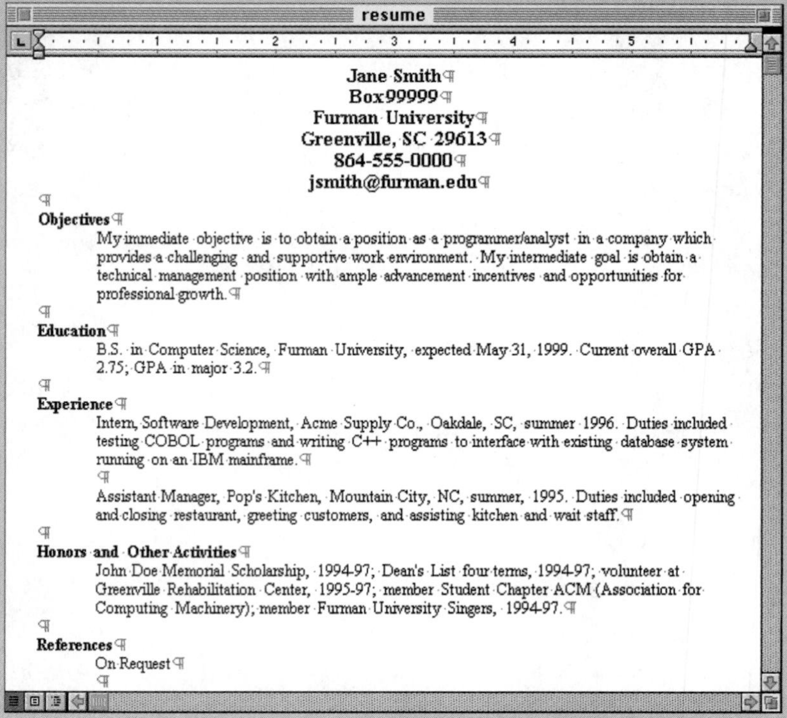
resume

Jane Smith
Box 99999
Furman University
Greenville, SC 29613
864-555-0000
jsmith@furman.edu

Objectives
My immediate objective is to obtain a position as a programmer/analyst in a company which provides a challenging and supportive work environment. My intermediate goal is obtain a technical management position with ample advancement incentives and opportunities for professional growth.

Education
B.S. in Computer Science, Furman University, expected May 31, 1999. Current overall GPA 2.75; GPA in major 3.2.

Experience
Intern, Software Development, Acme Supply Co., Oakdale, SC, summer 1996. Duties included testing COBOL programs and writing C++ programs to interface with existing database system running on an IBM mainframe.

Assistant Manager, Pop's Kitchen, Mountain City, NC, summer, 1995. Duties included opening and closing restaurant, greeting customers, and assisting kitchen and wait staff.

Honors and Other Activities
John Doe Memorial Scholarship, 1994-97; Dean's List four terms, 1994-97; volunteer at Greenville Rehabilitation Center, 1995-97; member Student Chapter ACM (Association for Computing Machinery); member Furman University Singers, 1994-97.

References
On Request

FIGURE 9.11
A model for the résumé you're to create is shown. You may substitute your own information if you wish, but the résumé you produce should be formatted similarly to this one.

FIGURE 9.12

Heading material is selected in the sample résumé. The raw text is entered first, then selected for formatting.

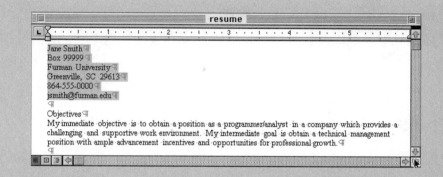

8 Copy the selected material to the memory clipboard—select the *Copy* command from the **Edit** menu or use the appropriate button on the toolbar. Next place the cursor in the very last blank paragraph and execute the *Paste* command to put a copy of the Objectives paragraph in the document. Do this three more times so that your document will have five copies (including the original) of the Objectives section, one after the other, separated by two blank lines.

9 Now to complete your document, you can simply replace the text in the last four résumé sections with the appropriate material. This is easy. For example, to put in the Education heading, select (by dragging) the second Objectives heading. Be careful not to select the paragraph marker at the end of the heading—you do not want to replace it. While the second Objectives heading is selected, just type the heading *Education* and the selected text will be automatically replaced with your new text. Make similar changes for the other three headings.

10 Finally, replace the text in each paragraph in the same way. Select the existing text in a paragraph and while it is selected, begin typing the new text. The new text will simply replace the selected text. Be careful not to select the paragraph marker at the end of the text—you do not want to replace it.

11 When you complete the résumé, place the cursor at the very beginning of the document and then run your spell checker to find and correct any misspelled words.

FIGURE 9.13

Objectives section, plus one additional blank line, is selected for copying to the clipboard. Once this is done, you can replicate several copies to provide a template for the other sections in the résumé.

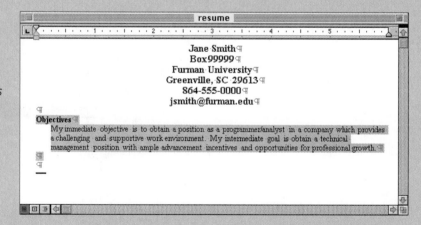

HOW DO SPELL CHECKERS WORK?

One of the most useful features of word processors is automatic **spell checking.** In a matter of a few seconds, we can check (and correct) the spelling in an entire multipage document. Each word in the document is checked against an **electronic dictionary** (usually stored in a separate file), and if a word is not found there, we are given an opportunity to change its spelling. The spell checking module usually makes suggestions for corrections, and you can select one of those or provide your own alternative, as illustrated in Figure 9.14.

The electronic dictionaries included with word processors, however, do not contain every possible word we might use in our documents. If a word (a proper name, for example) is not in the dictionary, the spell checker will flag it as incorrect. If the word is actually spelled correctly, we can add it to our own user's dictionary. The spell checker will then recognize the word when it encounters it later in the same or another document. A user's dictionary is especially convenient for names of places and persons or specialized terms and acronyms that might show up frequently in your own writing but that will not be in a general-purpose dictionary.

Even though they may not contain every word we use in a document, spelling dictionaries are quite extensive, containing 100,000 words or more. It is quite remarkable that every word in a large document can be checked against such huge dictionaries in a very short time. Let's investigate briefly the basic principle that enables this. Consider the way in which you might use an ordinary dictionary to look up a word. Would you start at the beginning of the volume and work your way to the word in question one word at a time? Of course not! This would be unbearably slow. You would take advantage of the alphabetical organization that the dictionary employs— many dictionaries have an index consisting of the letters of the alphabet cut into the document's right-hand edge. If the dictionary doesn't have a built-in index, you would probably interpose your own approximate one by opening the volume at a place near where you would estimate the word to be. You would then use the guide words (another kind of index) given at the tops of the pages to further focus your search.

FIGURE 9.14
This WordPerfect dialog box is used for correcting or ignoring a spell checker suggested misspelling.

Spell Checker	Grammatik	Thesaurus

Replace with: action

Replacements:
action
Acton
Aktien
auction
octane

Replace   Auto Replace
Skip Once   Undo
Skip All   Options ▼
Add

Check: To End of Docum ▼

Not found: acttion

Close   Help

Spell checkers emulate this manual searching technique by using a tree structure to create a kind of index. We can illustrate this principle with a tree structure called a **binary search tree.** In such a tree, the words are arranged so that if the word you are seeking comes before a given word, it will be found to the left of the given word in the tree. Likewise, if the word you are seeking comes after the word you are considering, you would move to the right portion of the tree. The spell checker program starts by comparing the word in the document to the word at the top of the tree. If these don't match, it moves to the left or the right in the tree, depending on whether the word in the document comes before or after the word it was just compared to in the tree. The process is illustrated in Figure 9.15. Proceeding in this way, you can find any word in the example dictionary by making no more comparisons than the number of levels in the tree. This is much fewer than the maximum number of comparisons possible if we simply search exhaustively through the entire dictionary word by word.

In our example in Figure 9.15, we can search a 15-word dictionary with at most 4 comparisons. We'll take it, but it doesn't seem like a truly dramatic achievement. Does this mean that in a 150,000-word dictionary, we may need 40,000 comparisons? No! As the size of the dictionary grows, the binary search tree structure starts to pay truly spectacular dividends. To search a binary tree for a word, the worst case occurs when that word is at the bottom level, in which case we must perform the number of comparisons equal to the number of levels.

How many levels would be required to store our hypothetical 150,000-word dictionary in a binary search tree? Each time we add a level, we slightly more than double the capacity of the entire tree. In other words, the bottom level contains slightly more than half the total number of words in the tree. Test this for yourself on the tree given in Figure 9.15. The tree there contains 15 words, and 8 of these are in the bottom level (level 4). A tree with five levels would contain 31 words because we would add 16 more words in level 5 and $15 + 16 = 31$. A tree with six levels would contain 63 words (why?) and so on. In this scheme, the number of words possible builds faster than you might think. Remember the old story about working for a penny a day, then doubling your salary each day for a month? This is exactly the same exponential progression. In fact, there is a simple formula giving the total capacity of a tree with N levels, namely $2^N - 1$. For example, when $N = 5$, $2^N - 1 = 2^5 - 1 = 32 - 1 = 31$, and we get the result we just calculated for a

FIGURE 9.15

A binary search tree for a simple 15-word animal name dictionary is shown. Note that any entry could be found by making no more than 4 comparisons (the number of levels in the tree). This compares with possibly 15 comparisons if we search word by word for the entry "zebra" starting with a straight alphabetical listing (no tree structure).

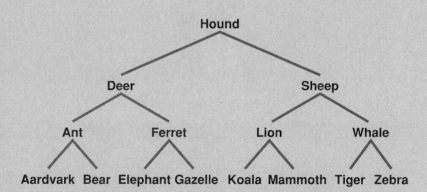

FIGURE 9.16

This figure illustrates the capacities of binary search trees as the number of levels grows. The growth rate is exponential so that a relatively small number of levels can contain very large numbers of entries.

Binary Search Tree Capacities

Number of levels	Number of entries		
1	1	$= 2^1 - 1$	$= 2 - 1$
2	3	$= 2^2 - 1$	$= 4 - 1$
3	7	$= 2^3 - 1$	$= 8 - 1$
4	15	$= 2^4 - 1$	$= 16 - 1$
5	31	$= 2^5 - 1$	$= 32 - 1$
6	63	$= 2^6 - 1$	$= 64 - 1$
7	127	$= 2^7 - 1$	$= 128 - 1$
.	.	.	.
.	.	.	.
.	.	.	.
17	131,071	$= 2^{17} - 1$	$=$
18	262,143	$= 2^{18} - 1$	$=$

5-level tree. Test one of the other calculations for yourself.

The surprising result is that a maximum of only 18 levels is required to store our hypothetical 150,000-word dictionary (with plenty of room to spare)! Hence we could check any word against this dictionary with at most 18 comparisons. This means we could check the spelling for a 10,000-word document (approximately 20 pages) with no more than 180,000 total comparisons. See Figure 9.16. With the speeds of today's computer, 180,000 comparisons can be accomplished in a very short time. In practice, the spell checkers for today's word processing programs use an even more efficient scheme than binary tree representation, though they are constructed using the same principles.

Binary trees are important for a great many applications in computing, especially when searches are involved. This is not surprising when we consider the significant savings in time achieved in our hypothetical example. As you will see in the next chapter, database management systems provide flexible and rapid data lookup capabilities. The techniques that enable these capabilities are also based on the use of binary search trees.

ADDITIONAL FEATURES OF WORD PROCESSING SOFTWARE

In the previous section we discussed some of the basic features common to most word processing software. Most of these programs have many additional features. In this section we briefly introduce some of the more useful features.

Tables

Quite often, you'll find it convenient to represent textual information within a document in a table. There are several ways to create tables in word processing software. For example, you can create your own table structure using tabs. By placing the appropriate kind of tabs on a line, you can create a customized layout designed specifically for the data you wish to display. Because the software will continue this same format to the next paragraph (line) when you press the Enter or Return key, once you've formatted a row, creating tables of data with many rows is easy.

Many of today's word processing programs, however, have the ability to create tables automatically. These tables often have formatting options well beyond those you can supply with tabs alone. For example, you can usually define borders, shading within different rows, special treatment for row and/or column headings, and other features. Most programs make such formatting easy by providing several templates from which you can choose your table format. Figure 9.17 illustrates.

Inserting Graphics

The integration of graphical elements and text is a common occurrence in today's digital documents; most word processors provide high-level tools for accomplishing this. At the very least, most word processors allow you to import graphics created in a drawing or painting program. Such graphics become objects once they're imported, and you can usually move them and resize them within the word processing software. One shortcoming this approach sometimes has is that you may not be able to superimpose text over the graphic objects once they've been placed in your document.

Many of today's word processing programs also give you the ability to create your own graphic objects directly within the document. For example, you might be able to draw lines, boxes, circles, arrows, and so on, providing colors for both the boundaries and the enclosed areas. And

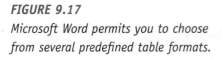

FIGURE 9.17

Microsoft Word permits you to choose from several predefined table formats.

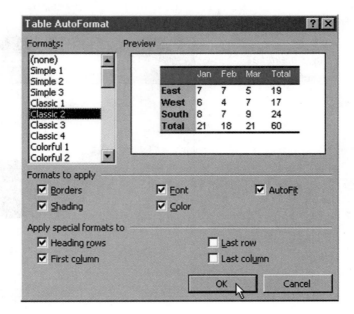

you can usually superimpose text you create in the usual way. Figure 9.18 illustrates some graphics created in this way.

Using Style Sheets

In a complex document or even a fairly simple document that has many pages, you are likely to have paragraphs formatted in a number of different ways. For example, you may have three or four different kinds of heading lines, different formats for the first paragraph after a heading and the remaining paragraphs in a section, special paragraphs for displaying certain kinds of information, and so on. As you saw in the "At Your Computer" résumé composing activity, one way to keep the various components of a document consistent is to copy sections, paste them elsewhere, and then modify them. Although we adopted this approach in the exercise, many word processing programs offer a much better way to accomplish this task through the use of style sheets.

Style sheets are defined paragraph styles that can be applied to paragraphs during the construction of a document. Style sheets can include such parameters as paragraph ruler settings, text font choice, font size, and font style (bold, italics, etc.). For example, you might create style sheets for three different kinds of heading paragraphs and name them *heading1, heading2,* and *heading3.* Once these style sheets are defined, you can apply them in a way similar to changing the font properties of selected text. You simply place the cursor in the paragraph whose style you wish to change and select the appropriate style sheet from a pull-down menu. Immediately the paragraph is reformatted to match the parameters of the style sheet. Most word processors provide one or more built-in style sheets and make it easy for you to define additional ones of your own.

Style sheets are an extremely useful feature in word processing. Not only do they allow you to apply various paragraph styles easily and reliably, but they also make it convenient to make global changes to your document. If you decide you would like all the paragraphs in style *heading2* to look different, all you need to do is change the style sheet *heading2* and the software will automatically adjust all paragraphs in that style. Without style sheets, making such a change would require you to

FIGURE 9.18

Text is superimposed over a simple graphic object in Microsoft Word.

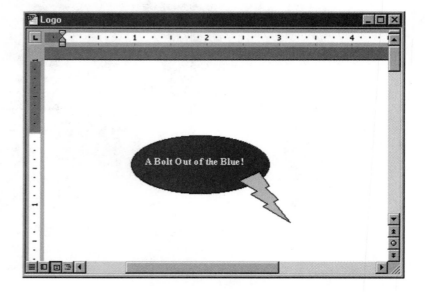

go to each paragraph formatted as a *heading2* paragraph and make the changes there directly.

Footnotes and Endnotes

A useful feature of word processing software for research papers and other documents is the ability to include footnotes or endnotes. Footnotes and endnotes are used to provide references or further information about the text proper. They differ only in their placement in the document. **Footnotes** are placed at the bottom of the page where the reference is cited, and **endnotes** are placed together at the end of the document or a document section. When you insert a footnote/endnote reference, the software will automatically keep track of its position in the footnote/endnote numbering and place the appropriate superscript in the document at the point of the cursor. Other footnote/endnote numbers will be appropriately and automatically adjusted. Typically when you insert a new footnote/endnote a new window is opened into which you can enter the footnote/endnote information. You can edit this information later by opening the footnote/endnote window.

Lab Activity

WRITING A RESEARCH PAPER

In this exercise you will explore the use of some word processing software features relevant to the creation of a research paper. The subject of the paper is up to you. We suggest some elements to include. As with the previous "At Your Computer" activity, we will not attempt to provide detailed commands because they will differ from software package to software package. Remember that specific tutorials for some of the most popular word processing software can be found at the *Exploring the Digital Domain* Web site.

Your research paper should be at least two pages long. Collect the information you will use for the paper before you begin writing. You can use any standard research resource or the Web if you choose. You can even use some of the material you collected for previous projects if you like.

One requirement for your subject is that you have some information for your paper that would naturally fit into a table. Beyond that, the subject of the paper is of no great consequence; the purpose of this activity is for you to explore some useful word processing features in the word processor of your choice.

It might be useful to read through all the instructions below before you begin, then refer to the appropriate step for each component of your paper.

1 Enter a title, followed by your name on a separate line. These lines should be centered. The title should be in bold type and size 18-point font. Your name should be in bold and 14-point font.

2   Organize your paper to contain at least three main sections—an introduction, a section describing your findings, and a conclusion. You may include more sections as appropriate. Create a style sheet (if your word processor has this feature) for these headings and name it *heading1*. Use it to format each of the headings. Each heading should be in bold type and size 14-point font and placed on a line by itself.

3   In the section on your research findings, include at least two subsections. Again, create a style sheet (if your word processor has this feature) for these headings and name it *heading2*. Use this style sheet to format each of the subsection headings. Each heading should be in bold *and* italic type, but keep it the same size as the body text (12 point). Place each heading on a line by itself.

4   Enter the body text in 12-point font. Create two paragraph style sheets named *first_paragraph* (for the first paragraph after each heading) and *reg_paragraph* (for regular paragraph to be used for all other paragraphs). The *first_paragraph* style sheet should have no first-line indent. The *reg_paragraph* style sheet should have a quarter-inch first-line indent. Apply the appropriate style to each of the non-heading paragraphs in your paper.

5   Create and insert a table to illustrate a point you make in the paper. Use your word processor's automatic table feature if it has one. If it does not, create the table using tabs.

6   Insert a graphical element into your paper if your word processor provides graphics tools. It need not be fancy—perhaps a heavy straight line separating your title/name section from the paper proper.

7   Insert at least two footnotes in your paper. For each, place the footnote text at the bottom of the page where the footnote reference is made.

At Your Computer

BASIC FEATURES OF DESKTOP PUBLISHING SOFTWARE

Desktop publishing (DTP) programs are intended to make designing and laying out professional-quality documents both accessible and convenient. These programs often contain many of the features of ordinary word processors as well as additional tools needed for page layout. On the other hand, some of the latest word processors also have layout tools that formerly would have been the exclusive domain of DTP programs. Consequently, the distinction between word processors and desktop publishing programs is not as clear-cut as it once was. Future enhancements to word processing products will no doubt further blur this distinction. A number of document preparation and enhancement features are common to most desktop publishing programs, and we will describe some of the most important ones in this section.

Internal Document Structure and Frames

Word processing documents are more often than not designed to contain text organized in a straight-line manner, possibly with some figures or other graphic objects included at various intervals for emphasis or illustration. As a result, the document has a simple internal organization. We start typing at the beginning of the document, and we enter our text and graphic objects as we go until we reach the end. On the other hand, documents like catalogs, advertising copy, brochures, newsletters, and newspapers often have a more complicated structure. We might have several more or less independent sections of text and graphics on the same page.

Newspapers and newsletters are good examples of this more complex type of organization. We might start a half dozen or more stories on page 1 and continue them on a variety of later pages. Similarly, an advertising brochure might have five or six different product descriptions or claims of greatness placed at various positions on a single page, with a number of different-sized graphic objects as well. Simple straight-line organization does not allow the creation of such documents.

Such sophisticated documents can be thought of as a number of mini-documents within a single document. Desktop publishing programs are designed to handle this kind of structure naturally. They typically do this using the concept of frames within a document. A **frame** is essentially a mini-document (or a piece of a mini-document) within a document. Generally, text frames and graphic frames are considered distinct types of objects. We can place any number of different frames on the same page. See Figure 9.19 for an example. We may enter text or graphics (even movies and sound, too) into these frames independently. Subsequently, we can edit frames separately, delete them, modify their characteristics, move them around on the page, move them to other pages, and so on, without affecting the other frames in the document.

FIGURE 9.19

Two text boxes are linked using the chaining operation in the DTP program Quark XPress. After selecting the first box in the chain, the second frame is clicked with the chain tool icon. The arrow shows how text will flow from one box to the next.

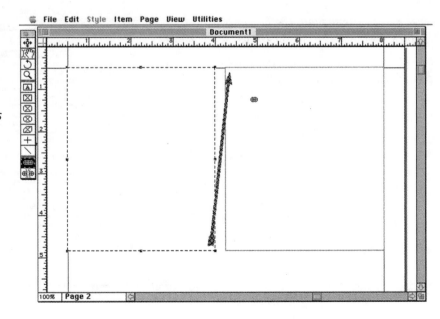

Relating Frames to Other Frames

To create the structure needed for documents like newspapers, we must associate frames on different pages (or different locations on the same page). For example, if we delete a section of text from a newspaper story that starts on page 1, we want the rest of the story to move up to close the space created by the deletion, even if the story is continued on page 3. This is done by linking or **chaining text frames** together. Chained frames (also called threaded frames) behave just as you might expect. Each frame is directly chained to another frame, which in turn can be chained to another, and so on. The chain has a definite sequence: Frames are placed in the sequence immediately following the frame to which they are chained. When enough text is entered into a text frame to overflow that frame, the text flows into the next frame (if one exists) in the chain sequence, as illustrated in Figure 9.20. If the final frame in a chain is overflowed, some programs will create another frame and page at the end of the document to hold the overflow. As frames are resized or as text is added or deleted, the text is automatically reorganized throughout the entire chain to account for the new sizes.

Frames can be layered, too. When one frame is placed over another, you usually have several options for how the contents of the underlying frame will behave with respect to the "top-layer" frame. For example, suppose you wish to place an illustration or picture in the middle of a story. To do this, you create a graphic frame to hold the illustration and place it on top of an underlying text frame containing the story. You might then choose one of several ways to wrap the underlying text around the top graphic frame as illustrated in Figures 9.21 and 9.22.

Another very useful application of frames is placing textual annotations within a figure or other graphic object. Rather than having to label the graphic object before including it in your document, you can simply put small text frames anywhere you desire over the graphic

FIGURE 9.20

When text is inserted into the first of two chained text frames, it automatically flows to the second. This creates a two-column display quickly and easily.

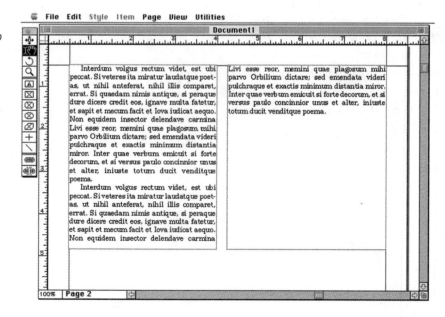

FIGURE 9.21

The figure illustrates one style of text wrapping in the DTP program Quark XPress. A picture is inserted in the foreground of a two-column text format. The text automatically adjusts to accommodate it. When the page is printed, the text and image will be seen without the guidelines shown in the layout window.

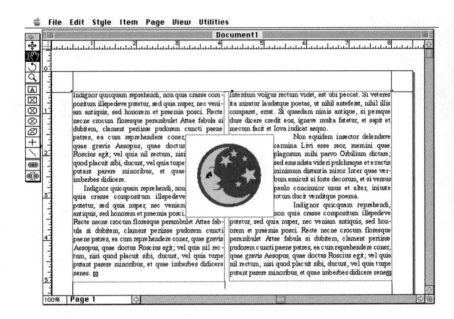

frame. These text annotations can then be edited, moved around, or even deleted without altering the graphic objects—a big savings in effort in many cases. Figure 9.23 illustrates.

Control over Document Elements

Generally speaking, desktop publishing programs give us more control than word processors over the elements that make up our documents. All the formatting features of a word processor are present, and additional ones are provided as well. For example, we can control the appearance of text on the printed page in greater detail by using a technique known as kerning. **Kerning** allows us to change the space that

FIGURE 9.22

In this Quark XPress example, we see several DTP features combined. First, an oval graphic frame is created to hold a scanned image of a field of tulips. The image is automatically cropped to fit the graphic frame. Second, a transparent text box is superimposed with the legend, "Spring in Holland." Finally, a text frame is positioned under all of these layers. When the text is inserted, it flows around the border of the image.

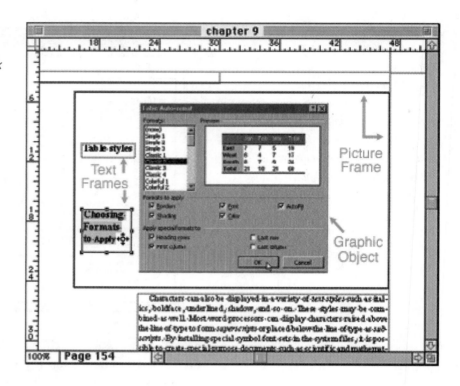

characters occupy to close up consecutive characters and produce an easier-to-read and cleaner-looking document.

Desktop publishing programs also allow you to incorporate higher-resolution graphic objects such as scanned images. They also allow more freedom in editing these objects. For example, we can crop pictures and add shading to graphic objects. Another useful feature is the ability to identify text and graphics of differing colors. When documents containing several colors are prepared for printing, the elements of each color are printed separately. Desktop publishing packages make it easy to create color separations within a single document. (See Chapter 11 for more about color and color printing.)

Options for Global Properties

On the global scale, we also have more options available in desktop publishing software than in word processors. For example, we can create any number of different **master pages,** which define and position default frames of the types we desire. Whenever we want to create a new page with a particular arrangement of frames, we can simply designate it to have the format of a chosen master page. For example, a monthly newsletter might be composed of several master pages. Each issue will differ in the specific copy and graphics that it contains, but master pages make the process of laying it out each month more efficient. An additional benefit is that each issue will have the same "look" as other issues because they are all constructed from the same master pages.

Headers and footers can also be constructed from multiple frames. For example, we could easily include a graphic frame and several differently formatted text frames in a header if we desired. Unlike the typical word processor, the desktop publishing program allows you to view the entire document, including headers and footers, when editing. Thus, editing footers and headers requires no special techniques or access.

When we view the entire document we also have access to additional space around the pages. This area is often called the **copy board** because it is a space in which we can temporarily place elements of the document (what newspaper staffers call "copy"). See Figure 9.24. You can see immediately that this would be a very valuable aid in laying out documents that contain a number of text items or articles, such as newsletters, magazines, and newspapers. In fact, the interface is based on the metaphor of conventional story mockup used in journalism. If we have a space for a particular item in the copy board area, we need only drag it into place, as opposed to having to find and open a file to access it. This storage area makes putting various document elements together into a well-designed, completed document much more convenient than it would be otherwise.

The power and convenience of desktop publishing software have had significant influence on how professional copy is prepared and published. In a number of instances, DTP is more economical than the traditional publishing process. Many businesses now publish their own advertising copy, catalogs, and other publications using complete desktop computing systems. These systems, including a high-resolution printer, may cost less than $10,000, even though very high-quality printed output requires more expensive printing devices. The professionals who specialize in producing documents from such machines often depend on desktop publishing systems for document design, layout, and modifications.

Desktop publishing offers authors more control over layout of their documents by eliminating the need for "outside" design and typesetting

FIGURE 9.24

The use of the copy board in Quark XPress is illustrated.

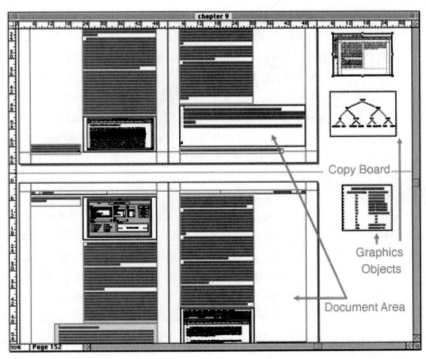

for many types of documents. In fact, it is now quite common for documents to be delivered to publishing firms in electronic form after the originator has produced them using a desktop publishing program. In these ways, desktop publishing has truly revolutionized the publishing industry.

SUMMARY

Electronic text documents are made up of sequences of characters that are arranged and formatted in particular ways. Both the characters and their formats must be encoded and digitized to enable processing by a computer. For the language being used, a character set containing letters of the alphabet, digits and arithmetic symbols, punctuation marks, and other special symbols used to express the language in writing is encoded. By convention, the Roman alphabet encoding scheme used by the vast majority of computers is called the American Standard Code for Information Interchange, or ASCII. Using ASCII, each character and symbol is represented using a single byte (eight bits) of storage; hence 2^8 total possible different characters and symbols can be represented.

Word processing software provides a wide range of features for the construction and formatting of textual documents. Formatting can be applied to individual characters, groups of characters, paragraphs, sections, and the entire document. There is no equivalent standard to the ASCII code for encoding formatting information, and each word processing package has its own proprietary method for representing the various formatting features it allows. As a consequence,

utility programs, called translators or filters, are needed to convert document files from one word processing package to another.

Despite their underlying format representations and storage differences, over the last few years, basic methods and techniques among various word processing packages have gradually converged. Thus, today there is a high degree of commonality among the major word processing software, and you can transfer your skills in using one program to another without a great deal of difficulty.

Desktop publishing software represents an extension of word processing capabilities. Particularly, such software is intended to make designing and laying out professional-quality documents accessible and convenient. These programs often contain many of the features of ordinary word processors as well as additional tools needed for page layout. On the other hand, some of the latest word processors also have layout tools that formerly would have been the exclusive domain of DTP programs. As a consequence, the distinction between word processors and desktop publishing programs is not as clear-cut as it once was. Future enhancements to word processing products will no doubt further blur this distinction.

PROJECTS

1 First-line indent markers specify where the first line of a paragraph begins. Most of the time, the marker is set a fraction of an inch to the *right* of the left text margin. These can also be set to the *left* of the text margin, however, meaning that the first line will begin "hanging" out to the left (which is why these are sometimes referred to as *left-hanging indents*). Use left-hanging indents to create a document that consists of a numbered list of four or five paragraphs describing the steps of how to go about searching for a job (or some other task of your choice). After typing each number followed by a period, press the Tab key to move to the regular left margin to begin the text proper. Make sure some of the paragraphs contain enough text to wrap to a second line.

2 Using the course syllabus you received for this or another course as a model, create a document with a similar layout and format using your word processor. You may limit your document to one page, even if the syllabus is several pages long.

3 Conduct some research on desktop publishing and the overall effect it has had in the business world. Use the Web and other sources. Write a report on this subject following the format for a research paper given in the second "At Your Computer" activity in this chapter.

4 If your word processor has an automatic table feature, create a hypothetical document containing four tables, all formatted differently.

5 If you have access to a desktop publishing package, use it to create and print a two-page newsletter for your favorite campus club, group, or sports team.

Key Terms

ASCII (American Standard Code
   for Information
   Interchange)
binary search tree
block of text
centered paragraph
chaining text frames
character set
clipboard
collating sequence
copy board
Copy command

cursor
Cut command
desktop publishing (DTP)
   program
electronic dictionary
endnote
font
font size
font style
footer
footnote
formatting

frame
header
invisible formatting characters
justified paragraph
kerning
keypunch machine
left-aligned paragraph
master page
Paste command
point (font size)
Rich Text Format (RTF)
right-aligned paragraph

ruler	subscript	what-you-see-is-what-you-get
section, document	superscript	(WYSIWYG)
select-then-do process	tab marker	word processor
spell checking	text editor	word-wrap
style sheet	translator (filter) program	

QUESTIONS FOR REVIEW

1 Describe the operation of a line editor for text editing. Compare it to today's text editing software.

2 What was the first commercially successful word processing program? Approximately when did it appear?

3 How are characters represented inside computer memory? Is the representation exact and reversible?

4 Compare the representation of text as described in this chapter and the representation of numbers described in Chapter 8. Which process is easier? How does the accuracy of the representations compare?

5 What does the acronym ASCII stand for? Relate it to text processing.

6 What are "invisible" characters within the word processing context? What purpose do they serve? What problems can they cause?

7 What is meant by the term *word-wrap*? What is the function of the Enter (or Return) key in word processing?

8 What is the clipboard? How is it used and why is it important for word processing?

9 Describe some of the standard character formatting techniques in modern word processors.

10 How is a paragraph defined in word processing?

11 Describe some of the standard paragraph formatting techniques in modern word processors.

12 What does the acronym WYSIWYG stand for? What does it mean?

13 Describe the function of a spell checker in a word processor.

14 How is the spelling dictionary in a spell checker organized? Why is this organization chosen?

15 What is a binary search tree? Relate this to the domain of word processing.

16 What is meant by a collating sequence? Relate this to the domain of word processing.

17 What is Rich Text Format (RTF)? Why is it important?

18 Describe the select-then-do process in word processing.

19 What is meant by the alignment of paragraphs?

20 What kinds of functions are provided by a paragraph ruler in a typical word processing package?

21 What are style sheets and what purpose do they serve in a word processor?

22 How do footnotes and endnotes differ?

23 How does desktop publishing software extend the capabilities of word processors?

24 Explain the importance of frames in desktop publishing software. What does it mean when frames are "chained" or "threaded" together? Why is this done?

25 What does the term *kerning* refer to?

26 Explain the term *copy board* and its relevance for desktop publishing packages.

27 How does the concept of master pages contribute to the ease of use and power of desktop publishing packages?

In the previous two chapters, you learned that numeric and text processing are two of the oldest and most important computing applications. A third application, the storage and retrieval of data in large databases, also dates to the early days of computing. And computer databases continue to have a significant impact in computing today. For example, keeping employee and customer records, tracking inventories, and monitoring and reporting sales are among the most important and most computerized activities in many business organizations. Governments, banking, insurance, travel, and other industries could not function today without computerized record keeping. And your university keeps a host of information about you in computerized form. All of these activities depend on database management systems for storing and retrieving large amounts of data.

OBJECTIVES

- A brief history of database software
- The way information is organized and stored in databases
- Methods that make rapid and flexible database information retrievals possible
- The basic features of the network database model
- The basic features of the relational database model
- The basic functions available in many database management software packages

CHAPTER 10

DATABASES

Vasily Kandinsky, *Upward*, 1929. Solomon R. Guggenheim Museum

BRIEF HISTORY OF DATABASE COMPUTING

Long before word processing became common, businesses were using databases to store and review much of their important information. As the name suggests, a **database** is an (often large) collection of data about some enterprise or subject. The term *database,* though, means more than just a large data store or data bank. What distinguishes a database is that it is organized in a way that makes possible effective and efficient retrieval of information stored in it. We use the term **database management system (DBMS)** to refer not only to the data itself but also to the methods and techniques used to store and retrieve that data.

The first databases were actually created within the programs written for business in the late 1950s. These early programs created temporary electronic structures for storing data when the program ran. Each time the program ran, the basic data was read by the program from punched cards. These electronic databases persisted only as long as the program itself was running.

Files, Records, and Fields

In the early 1960s, advances in programming language design made it possible to construct programs that could create and manage external files to store and retrieve information. **External files** are files that exist in disk storage independently of the program itself. For example, the programming language COBOL, introduced in the early 1960s, was especially designed to give programmers built-in tools for managing external files.

The structure of data files is usually relatively simple. Each file consists of a series of records that are, in turn, divided into a specified number of data fields. **Files** typically store information about some group of entities, perhaps persons or things. **Records** hold information about a particular entity; the data **fields** of a record contain the specific items of information about that specific entity. For example, Figure 10.1 illustrates a file holding information about customers.

External files were a great advantage for programmers and improved their capability to maintain and access data using their programs. Each program that was written, however, still had to include its own techniques for writing information to the files and extracting and presenting information from the files. As the usefulness of the external file concept grew, so did the sophistication of the programming methods and the tools used to manipulate these files.

File Management Systems

Because the programs being written to access external files had a great deal in common, it made sense to provide programmers with some of the standard capabilities for storing and accessing files. In this way, the programmer didn't have to reinvent the wheel for each application. Thus, **file management software,** which incorporated various methods of creating and accessing external files, was created and marketed. File management software was the precursor of modern database management software.

FIGURE 10.1

A file holding information about customers is shown. An individual record holds information about a specific customer, and its data fields store the particular data we chose to store about that customer—name, address, and so on. The file contains a sequence of such records.

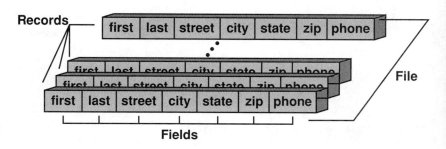

File management software included the ability to create indices for files based on the information stored in selected data fields. In **indexed files** one or more data fields serve as an index for the records contained in the file. This is exactly the purpose of your student identification number in your school's student database. This value is a unique identifier for accessing information about you. Using an index, you can look up a given record quite quickly by searching for a match with the indexed data field.

If you recall our discussion of spell checkers in Chapter 9, it should be no surprise that these indexed file schemes depend heavily on the concept of a binary search tree. Indexed files are often implemented as a binary tree that contains the indexed field data and links to the actual records in the external file. Remember how we can search a 150,000-word dictionary with no more than 18 comparisons to find any entry in the tree? Using a similar technique, we can search the index in a flash and follow its link to the record we seek in the file itself. The "link" will be an actual address on the disk, so we can access it very quickly. Figure 10.2 illustrates.

Indexed files offered a significant improvement in the speed of looking up information. A number of commercially successful, proprietary indexed file schemes were marketed in the 1960s and 1970s, and some of these are still in use today. Even though these proprietary file manage-

FIGURE 10.2

The figure illustrates using a binary tree index for fast file lookup. To find a desired record, we first look up its index in the index file, which is organized as a binary tree. The binary tree allows quick searches for large index files. Once the index is found, we gain access to the actual information using the address stored there.

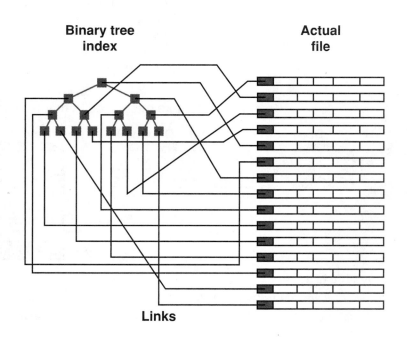

ment systems were a tremendous step forward from the days of programming every file management problem from scratch, they still required writing programs in languages like COBOL or FORTRAN to exploit their features. These file management systems were utilities, not stand-alone software. In fact, stand-alone database software was still a decade away.

THE NETWORK DATABASE MODEL

The demands for information management programming evolved during the late 1960s and early 1970s. The changes in demand affected not only the scale and complexity, but also the manner in which these systems conducted business. The kinds of computing applications and problems gaining attention were quite a bit more difficult than the payroll and inventory systems that had been the bread and butter of earlier programming applications. As interactive or transactional computing became more commonplace, being able to query the database systems for particular information when it was needed became desirable. A convenient query language or method for constructing database queries was required to achieve this.

These new applications demanded even more sophisticated file management tools. A major advance was the creation of file management systems that allowed access to more than one related file—the first true database management systems. These systems gave the programmer tools and methods for creating and accessing a group of related files. Special fields, called **link fields,** were used to relate records stored in two different files. Link fields contained disk addresses to give quick access to related information stored in another file. Figure 10.3 illustrates.

The linked structures these systems employ have come to be called the **network database model** because the files are connected by a network of links. Updated versions of many network database systems are still in use today. In the network model, the programmer deals with a physical model of the database. For example, to implement a database retrieval, the programmer must manipulate the indices and links built into the database itself to access the required data. These systems are optimized for speed and efficiency, and they still demand some programming skill to use.

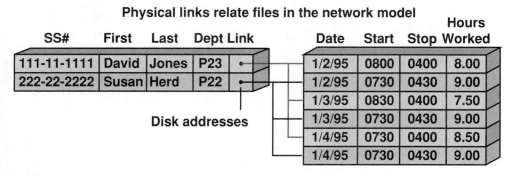

FIGURE 10.3

This figure illustrates the network database model. In the network model, physical links are directly manipulated to gain access to related information in different files.

THE RELATIONAL DATABASE MODEL

The **relational database model** was introduced in the late 1970s as an alternative database model. The relational model gives the user a more conceptual view of the database rather than the physical organization employed by the network model. The relational model does not employ link fields to relate records in different files. Rather, in this model, related information is located when it is needed from the logical relationships among items in the files.

For example, if we store data about employees in one file and the week's work record in another, we obviously need access to both when processing the week's payroll. In the network model, the necessary links between the two files would be defined when the record data fields were created, as shown in Figure 10.3. To process the payroll, the programmer would manipulate the links present in the design of the database.

In a relational model of the same data, no physical link fields are present, only the logical relationship between the two files guides the combination of their data, as illustrated in Figure 10.4. Because the file relationships are logical, the user is relieved of the details of how the files are physically organized. Consequently, the level of detail required to employ a relational database model successfully is reduced. Indeed, the relational model is much more intuitive and accessible to the non-programmer.

When we design the file structures for a relational database, we need to ensure that we have included sufficient information to forge the natural logical relationships already inherent in the data. Consider our earlier example, illustrated in Figure 10.1, in which we defined a file to hold information about customers. A second file might be constructed to hold information about customers' purchases. How will we relate the information in the two files? If we include in the record definitions for both files a field to contain a customer identification number, our problem is solved. We then can relate the information in the two files as the need arises. Figure 10.5 illustrates this structure.

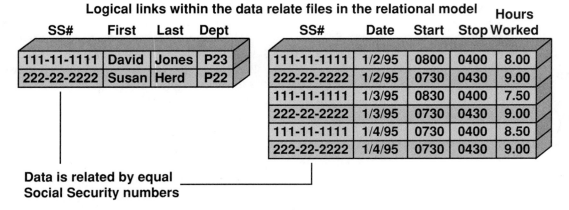

Logical links within the data relate files in the relational model

SS#	First	Last	Dept
111-11-1111	David	Jones	P23
222-22-2222	Susan	Herd	P22

SS#	Date	Start	Stop	Hours Worked
111-11-1111	1/2/95	0800	0400	8.00
222-22-2222	1/2/95	0730	0430	9.00
111-11-1111	1/3/95	0830	0400	7.50
222-22-2222	1/3/95	0730	0430	9.00
111-11-1111	1/4/95	0730	0400	8.50
222-22-2222	1/4/95	0730	0430	9.00

Data is related by equal Social Security numbers

FIGURE 10.4

This figure illustrates the relational database model. In the relational model, links between files are formed by the logical relationships within the data itself.

FIGURE 10.5

Adding a second related file to a database about customers and purchases is shown. Note the use of the fields containing customer identification numbers as the logical link between the two files.

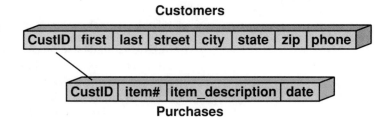

COMPARING THE NETWORK AND RELATIONAL DATABASE MODELS

Both the network database model and the relational database model are in widespread use today, and both will no doubt continue to be important for years to come. Each model has its own distinctive merits. As we will see, the network model's strength is its efficiency, but the relational model offers much more flexibility.

The network model delivers built-in efficiency through its designed link fields among separate files. Finding information in related files through these built-in link fields could hardly be faster because all that is required is to look up the related records using the disk addresses stored in the link fields. For example, to find the total hours worked for an employee using the network database design shown in Figure 10.3, we simply give the database management system the employee's name or social security number. Once the appropriate record is located in the *Employees* file, the system can easily look up the related records in the *Hours* file using the addresses contained in the link field within the employee record. In fact, the link field was put there by the database designer for precisely this purpose.

If efficiency is at a premium, then the network model will more often be the choice. The network model, however, does not provide a great deal of flexibility. Finding related records depends on link fields, so if the database designer hasn't provided a link field tailored to the information retrieval we have in mind, this retrieval becomes more difficult, if not impossible.

On the other hand, systems based on the relational model provide more flexible access to their data. Access is based on posing database queries derived from the logical relationships among the various files involved, rather than depending on the database designers to have included all the physical link fields we might later need.

Let's consider how we could use the relational database design shown in Figure 10.5 to retrieve some information. Suppose we wish to list all the items bought by customer John Jones. We could do this by first looking up the record for John Jones in the *Customers* file. Note that this is the same first step we would follow if we were using a network model. The next step differs significantly; instead of simply following addresses contained in a built-in link field, we now must make a *second search*. We would use John Jones' customer identification number to search the *Purchases* file and print out the item for each of those purchases containing a match for John's identification number in the *CustID* field.

This search could require looking through the entire *Purchases* file, which may be quite large. If we have an index for the *CustID* field, this retrieval could be done more efficiently, but it still involves an extra step over what is needed in a network model. The good news is that we don't actually have to do this work because the relational database management system performs it for us. Nonetheless, the query won't be nearly as fast as it would be using the link fields in a network database.

When designing the relational database structure, we should make sure we have provided all relevant and appropriate logical relationships within the record structures for each file. If we do this, even queries that might not have been anticipated when the database was designed are possible. We call these unanticipated queries **ad hoc queries** because they are constructed as needed. As we noted earlier, ad hoc queries are often not possible at all using a network database model. The flexibility of the relational model does carry its price tag: Relational database systems are generally much less efficient (that is, slower) in processing queries because they involve at least one extra search step, as we saw in the earlier example.

The basic trade-off is flexibility versus efficiency. The reason both database models are alive and well is that most applications demand one or the other of these characteristics. Each model has problem domains where it is king. When the need for rapid responses is crucial, a network system tuned for performance by the inclusion of appropriate link fields will be used. In applications where the ability to pose a large variety of queries, some of which may not be known when the database is designed, is needed, then a database system based on the relational model will be more satisfactory. Some specific examples will make these ideas clearer.

Examples of Network Model Databases

When you step to the airline counter or call your ticket agent to purchase a ticket, you expect to find out in a few seconds whether a seat is available for the flight you want. If so, you expect to be able to book that seat immediately. Someone in another city may be looking for the same seat, and to prevent double-booking, the system must record your booking quickly and securely. These systems must handle thousands of transactions (queries) per hour, and a system that takes a minute to respond to a seat inquiry is not acceptable. Hence, airline reservation systems naturally value speed of response in their automated systems and place little value on answering unusual or unexpected queries. Thus, the network model is the obvious choice for such a system.

Likewise, automatic teller machines (ATMs) also require very rapid response times. If you have a checking account in a Florida bank and you happen to be in Minnesota, it is an easy matter to make an instant cash withdrawal at an ATM. Have you ever considered how this is possible? One aspect is clear—the computing system that handles this transaction is required to respond with reasonable speed. In fact, you will probably be recognized (by your card and personal identification number) within a few seconds and have your money within a few more seconds. Without excellent response time, the computers managing these events couldn't handle the volume of transactions they must process each day.

Both the airline reservation system and the ATM computing system involve only two very simple computing processes—data lookup and a simple data change (booking a seat, deducting money from an account balance). These are actually fairly typical database transactions. In fact, this is exactly what the first databases were designed for—data lookup and update. The emphasis is not on complicated computing processes, but rather, purely and simply, on transaction speed.

For both airline reservation systems and ATMs, flexibility is of almost no importance! How many different queries does an ATM have to handle? Not many, and none of these are of the ad hoc variety. A similar situation holds for the airline reservation system. The queries it handles today are exactly the same ones it must handle tomorrow, but it must handle them quickly. These systems are typical of a great many database applications where performance constraints demand a network model database management system.

Examples of Relational Model Databases

Many database applications demand flexibility rather than speed. Let's consider several different examples. If you've watched a televised baseball game recently, you've probably seen statistics like:

> Mike Piazza has a lifetime batting average of .407 against the Braves with runners in scoring position from the seventh inning on.

Have you ever wondered how information tailored to a particular player in a particular batting situation in a specific game is produced? Publishing this type of information would fill up numerous volumes. Finding it quickly would be a headache, too.

What actually happens is that batting and pitching data is stored in a database, and statistics like those in the example are then constructed from that data. In other words, the information is not stored in the form in which it is presented, but rather must be created on the fly from more elementary data. When the game starts, we don't know all the queries we might like to make as it progresses. Instead, many of these queries are constructed ad hoc. We need a database system that allows us to phrase ad hoc queries with relative ease.

For this kind of application, the relational database model is better than the network model. Indeed, it would be difficult, if not impossible, to build in enough links between files in a network model to anticipate all the ad hoc queries we might desire. Nor is speed an overriding consideration here. One reason is that there is only one user of the database, whereas our airline and ATM databases would typically have a great many, almost simultaneous users. Further, a response time of a half minute would be perfectly acceptable.

Using a relational model database, we can generally pose successful queries to extract any information that may be logically derived from the database itself. On the other hand, even with the relational model, if its structure doesn't support the query, we cannot successfully compose it. For example, if we had not stored the opponent, the inning, and the positions of base runners for every time a player bats, we could not have produced the statistic in our example. Figure 10.6 illustrates a possible record structure for *AtBat* data that would enable the example query (as well as some others).

In general, when we create relational databases, we should strive to maximize the opportunities for successful ad hoc queries by designing

Record structure:

Player	Inning	Outs	OnFirst	OnSecond	OnThird	Opponent	Pitcher	Result	RBIs

Example record:

Player	Inning	Outs	OnFirst	OnSecond	OnThird	Opponent	Pitcher	Result	RBIs
Piazza	8	2	Yes	No	Yes	Braves	Avery	Single	1

FIGURE 10.6

A possible file structure for AtBat *data enables the retrieval of ad hoc baseball batter statistics. Well-designed relational database structures allow a great variety of retrievals that were not expressly anticipated when the database was created.*

the database structure carefully and intelligently. A thorough study of the issues involved in good database design would carry us too far afield here, but suffice it to say that this area is very important in practical database applications. If you are interested, you can learn more about this topic on the *Digital Domain* Web site.

Lest we leave you with the impression that the relational database model is important only for what some might call a frivolous baseball statistic application, let's take a quick look at one more example. NASA engineers and scientists are responsible for ensuring the efficient and safe operation of the three rocket engines on board each space shuttle orbiter. These engines are among the most complex machines ever built; not surprisingly, they require constant periodic adjustment and modification for optimal performance.

One of the primary features of the task of monitoring the performance of these engines is testing. Engineers place test engines on a test stand, fire them, then observe the test results to assess the many parameters associated with their operation. Storing all past test data is very important to this process. When a specific undesirable behavior is observed during a test, engineers must ascertain the cause of this behavior and correct it. Naturally, the behaviors that cause the most difficulty in this regard are ones that take the engineers by surprise—that is, problems that were not anticipated. Part of the diagnostic procedure applied in looking for causes and solutions is to go back through historical test data to look for clues about the currently observed behavior. The ad hoc nature of the current problem, however, requires ad hoc database queries. There is simply no way the original database designers could have anticipated the particular kinds of information needed months or years later in this ongoing process. The speed with which such queries are dispatched is of no real concern. It is perfectly acceptable for a query response to take two minutes; what is of utmost importance is that the query can be satisfied. The flexibility of the relational database model is all-important in this case, even if some speed and efficiency must be sacrificed.

As these examples illustrate, there are needs for database systems based on the network model and others based on the relational model. Actually, some merging of the capabilities of the two models has occurred in some current database systems. These hybrid systems provide an underlying network model for speed and efficiency but also have an add-on query language that allows the user to pose ad hoc queries to the database. In essence, you get the best of both worlds—fast response for those queries you can anticipate, along with ad hoc query capability. These systems will, no doubt, become even more popular in the future.

No one denies that the relational model is superior from a logical perspective. As research continues and hardware performance improves, we may yet see the day when database systems based on the relational model can achieve response speeds adequate for all applications. If this happens, the relational model will become the standard for database management systems. Until that time (which may be some years away, if ever), both models and their hybrids will play important roles in the application of database management technology.

More Information

Social Themes

Databases and Crime Fighting

Information can be a crucial component in effective crime control. Indeed, the U.S. government maintains hundreds of databases with a variety of information on individuals for the purpose of crime prevention and investigation. For example, the FBI's National Crime Information Center (NCIC) database contains more than 30 million records and can be accessed by more than a half million users within thousands of federal, state, and local law enforcement agencies. The system can compare a fingerprint to more than 1,000 database prints in a second, and more than 10 million NCIC records are accessed annually for criminal investigations and civil background checks. The FBI has asked the Federal Communications Commission (FCC) for radio frequency spectrums to enable wireless access to the NCIC database for law enforcement agents in the field.

Information held in third-party databases about individuals is also often available to law enforcement. The Fourth Amendment to the U.S. Constitution protects the privacy of citizens, making it unlawful for law enforcement agencies to invade that privacy without appropriate court orders. Although this amendment has made it difficult for law enforcement to tap phones and perform on-site searches, the courts have been more lenient in allowing law enforcement access to bank records, phone numbers, and other personal information held in third-party databases.

One of the central tasks of law enforcement is to identify individuals with certainty. Verification of identity through unique physical characteristics is the primary means for accomplishing this. Photos and fingerprints have been the mainstay techniques for many decades. More recently, the FBI's Automated Fingerprint Identification System (AFIS) has provided a national database of scanned and digitized fingerprints. With access to this system, state and local agencies have come to rely on fingerprinting as a primary identification technique. For example, California and New York require all welfare beneficiaries to be fingerprinted—New York's system extends to all members of the recipient's family. California is now requiring thumbprints on drivers' licenses, and several banks fingerprint customers who do not have accounts with the bank before cashing checks for them.

With the increased use of DNA identification techniques in criminal cases, DNA databases are also growing. A number of states have laws allowing the collection of DNA samples from all convicted felons. The FBI has plans to create a computer network to link the state databases to create a national DNA database similar to the AFIS. A proposal by the Department of Defense would create an even larger DNA database. The plan calls for collecting DNA samples from all current and former military personnel.

Canada, Germany, the Netherlands, and the United States have launched a pilot program in which international travelers will be issued a smart card that records the unique geometry of the traveler's hand. Each time travelers pass through customs, they present the card and place their hand in a reader that verifies their identity. The system also contains links to numerous databases. The four countries have signed an agreement facilitating data sharing and eventually requiring all international travelers to use the cards.

All these example databases involve potentially huge volumes of data. Modern database management technology is essential if the data stored is to be retrieved in an effective and timely manner. A database with millions of fingerprints is of little practical use if it takes days to search it for a match. Likewise, a hand recognition system will hardly be useful at airport customs facilities unless it provides very rapid response. Indeed, the combination of fast, flexible database systems and computer networks places stored information at the center of many activities.

Solving an Eight-Year-Old Murder Case

A simple but powerful example of how database technology can affect law enforcement occurred in San Francisco a few years ago. In 1984, an 84-year-old woman was murdered during a burglary. The police were unable to solve the case, despite the fact that they were able to get fingerprints from the crime scene. The fingerprints from the unsolved crime were stored in the San Francisco police database. In early 1992, the San Francisco police database was networked with the Alameda County police database. Once these databases were linked, police began crosschecking fingerprint and other data files. The print taken from the 1984 crime scene matched a relatively new print taken in connection with a petty theft case. Eight years after the fact, the police were able to solve the murder case. Two women were implicated. They were 12 and 15 at the time of the 1984 crime, explaining why their prints were not found in the 1984 San Francisco police database. As national fingerprint, photo, and DNA databases grow in size and search capabilities, it becomes more and more difficult for criminals to commit crimes and avoid identification.

Thailand's Integrated Database and Identification Project

The Thailand *Central Population Database and ID* card system, developed by the U.S. company Control Data Systems, features an integration of identification and database technologies. A government-issued smart ID card contains electronic fingerprint and facial image data. The card is linked to computer databases, controlled and maintained by the Interior Ministry, covering the entire Thai population.

The system enables access to an amazing variety of information: Central Population Database, National Election System, Political Party Database, Political Member Database, Voter Listing, Electronic Minority Group Registration System, Electronic Fingerprint Identification System, Electronic Face Identification System, Population and House Report System, National Tax Collection System, Village Information System, Secret Information System, Public Opinion System, Criminal Investigation System, National Security System, Social Security System, Passport Control System, Driver Control System, Gun Registration System, Family Registration System, Alien Control System, and Immigration Control System.

The Thai system represents an impressive technological achievement, but it also raises many questions about the protection of a citizen's privacy. How much information about its citizens should a country collect? Who should have access to this information? Should the individual's permission be required before certain information is collected and stored in databases? Should an individual be able to access his or her own information and challenge its accuracy? These are difficult questions: Surely society benefits when such national databases are available, but surely opportunities for abuse of this information arise. We can expect the debate about such government national database projects to continue for years.

Social Themes

BASIC DATABASE MANAGEMENT SYSTEM CONCEPTS

At this point, you may be wondering about database systems for desktop computers—after all, this text is primarily about desktop computing. What kinds of database applications are likely to be implemented on personal computers? Certainly not airline reservation systems or ATM banking systems. Implementing any database application that requires great speed of response on personal computers would be unwise. In fact, almost all the network database systems are designed to operate on computers more powerful than desktop computers. The kinds of database applications that run on personal computers usually involve relatively small amounts of data anyway. Thus, concerns about response time are not important.

There are, in fact, quite a number of database products available for desktop computers. These generally fit one of two types: Some are **flat file database systems,** consisting of one file per database; others are based on the relational database model. Flat file database systems have many of the features of the higher-end relational systems, but they restrict the database to one single file for storage. A large number of database applications require no more than one file for their basic data storage. If this simpler model suits your needs, you can achieve excellent results with flat file systems. There are also a number of outstanding relational database systems for desktop computers as well. These can be used to create very sophisticated database information access systems.

Let's discuss some of the concepts and functions common to all database management systems, regardless of their data model. Although

FIGURE 10.7

The example database record structure is shown. The database stores information about a sales force. In particular, we represent the salesperson's name, the date and amount of the order, the delivery date, and the region in which the salesperson works.

Record data field structure and data types

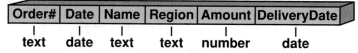

they may be implemented in different ways, all database systems have a number of common features. In this section, we will outline some of these common features.

As we discuss these basic database concepts, we will illustrate how some of them are implemented in the Microsoft Access and the File-Maker Pro database systems. These two database management systems are discussed here because they are representative. Microsoft Access is the leading database management system for Windows-based computers, and FileMaker Pro is a popular Macintosh and Windows database system—especially for Web applications. Although specific implementation details differ for other database systems, the concepts are very similar. Once you master these underlying concepts, you should be able to learn to use any database system quickly. With this background, you will be well prepared to learn either of these systems and others in detail when the occasion arises.

Defining the Database Structure

When you begin a new document in a word processor, you are offered a blank screen, ready for you to input text and formatting information. Likewise, when you open a spreadsheet package, you have a blank worksheet in which to enter data, formulas, and so on. In both these cases, the software application creates a new *blank* document ready for your input. Database systems have slightly more complex interfaces. As you might expect, there is a good deal more to defining a database than simply collecting and storing data values. Initial decisions have to be made about the content of individual fields and the overall organization of related files when applicable. Once these decisions are made, this information must be expressed in the database management system before any data entry can commence. File record structures must be defined, specifying field names and the kinds of data for each field. Each field can contain only one kind of data (for example, text, numbers, dates, and so on), called the field's **data type.** Every database management system must provide a way to define this basic structural information in the system before any work with the database itself can begin.

For our example database, let's suppose that we wish to store data about purchase orders taken by a sales force. We will store the salesperson's name, the date and amount of the order, the delivery date, and the region in which the salesperson works—Figure 10.7 illustrates. You can no doubt think of other relevant information that we could store, but these fields will give us enough data to make a useful example. Related data files are often referred to as **tables** in relational database systems. For now we will work with only one table. Later we will add a second table and examine some multiple table queries.

To create a new Microsoft Access database, you must first design the tables that make up the database. Access makes this step straightforward. After selecting the *New Database* command from the **File** menu, you will be

FIGURE 10.8

The main database window in Microsoft Access is shown. This window offers options to work with tables, queries, forms, and reports.

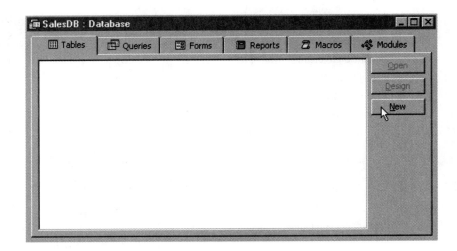

asked to name your database. Once you do this, Access will present you with its database window, shown in Figure 10.8. Most of the user's interaction with Access will be initiated in this window. After selecting to create a new table, you are presented with a tabular dialog display in which you define the fields for the table and their data types. Figure 10.9 illustrates.

Figure 10.10 portrays the dialog box presented when you create a new FileMaker Pro database. The first table for the database has again been named *Sales* in the figure. Once the table is given a name, this dialog box demands specifics about the organization of its records. Of course, this means specifying the names and kinds of data for each of the fields.

Entering, Editing, and Viewing Data—Forms

After the structure of the database has been defined, you are ready to enter some data into the database. You generally do this by using a data entry **form** displayed on the screen. On-screen prompts serve as reminders for particular pieces of information. Many database systems also allow you to define constraints on data fields (ranges on numbers, whether the

FIGURE 10.9

Access dialog box for defining fields and their data types is shown. We have entered the six fields for our Sales table. Note the pull-down menu in the Data Type column. This allows quick selection of the appropriate built-in data type for each field.

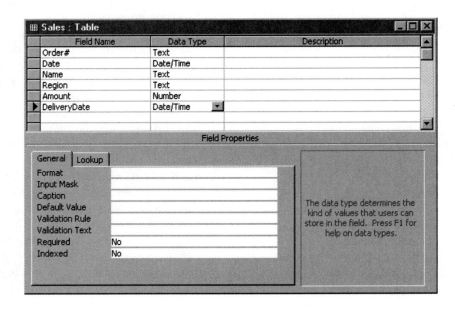

FIGURE 10.10

FileMaker Pro dialog box for defining a database table is shown. Once you name a table, you are presented with a dialog box prompting you to define the first of the table's fields. Identical dialog boxes are presented until you complete the definition of all the fields for the table.

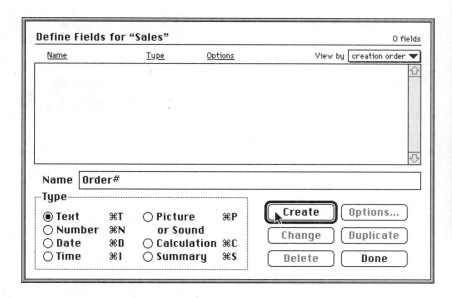

value is unique in the database, etc.). The database system then automatically verifies that your data satisfies these constraints as it is entered.

Forms are quite versatile in Access. In addition to data entry, you can use them to view and print information, and you can even have them calculate totals. Although every database system has a default form, you can generally design your own form layouts as well. For example, if you are entering a large amount of data from existing paper forms (as is often the case), you might wish to design an entry form to match the appearance and data field locations of the paper form. This would make for a more efficient and ergonomically satisfying task. It would likely reduce the chances of errors as well.

In Microsoft Access, once you've completed the definition of the table, you can begin to enter data in the database. You accomplish this by choosing *Forms* in the database window (see Figure 10.8) and then clicking the New button. You must next specify the table or tables with which the form will be associated. Because Access is a fully relational database system, it allows multiple related tables in the same database. If you then select *Form Wizards,* you can easily create one of several different kinds of predefined forms. You can select all or a subset of the fields in your table to appear in the form. Figure 10.11 illustrates.

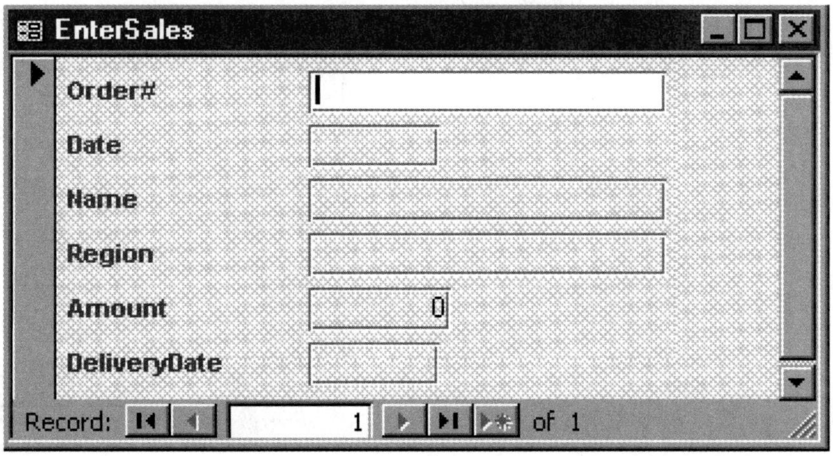

FIGURE 10.11

A simple columnar form in Access contains all the fields of our example table Sales. *Notice the buttons at the bottom of the form window to move from record to record in the database. Pressing the Tab key moves the cursor from one record field to the next. When you complete the data entry for a record, you press Enter to move to a blank entry form for the next record. As you move from record to record you may also edit the data that appear in the form.*

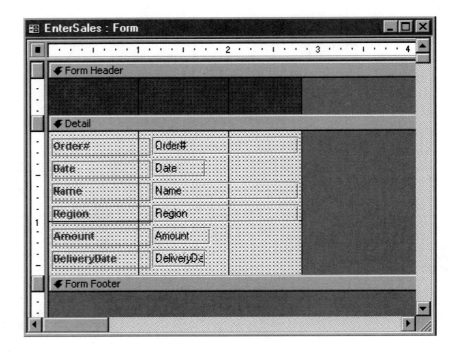

If you wish to modify the form you can select *Form Design* from the **View** menu. You then get a form design layout screen, as shown in Figure 10.12. Figure 10.13 shows the form of Figure 10.11 modified.

FileMaker Pro presents very similar capabilities for data entry and viewing. Figure 10.14 illustrates the default data form in FileMaker Pro. Although only one choice is available for the default form, you may modify this form in a design layout screen similar to the one used in Access. Figure 10.15 illustrates a modified form in FileMaker Pro.

Sorting Data

When displaying data or creating database reports, it is often easier to interpret that data if it is sorted. **Sorted data** is presented in a particular

FIGURE 10.14

The default data entry form in FileMaker Pro is shown. Note the flip book icon on the left. This icon indicates which record is currently displayed and allows the user to move through the records in numerical sequence.

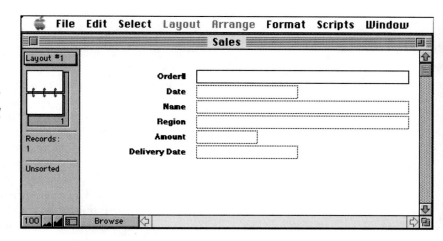

order. All database systems provide this capability. The data fields on which we base the sorting are called **sort keys.** In most database systems, you may select several sort keys to enable **nested sorting.** When several sort keys are specified, they are given in order of priority; the system first sorts the data by the highest-priority key, then all entries with the same value for that key are sorted by the key with the next highest priority, and so on for additional sort keys. For example, we may wish to specify a triple nested sort displaying sales figures sorted by region, then by salesperson within the region, then by amount for each salesperson.

Database Reports

As we have noted, in most database systems, forms can be used for data display. We often require more sophisticated data reporting capabilities. This is accomplished by producing written **reports** from the database data. In contrast to data forms, which are often designed to mirror paper forms for ergonomic ease, reports are designed for a different purpose: to present data in a compact, readable, and informative format. For example, reports often contain headers and footers and tabulate totals and subtotals of important values.

Often reports contain data selected on the basis of some stated criteria. This data may come from one table or a combination of tables, de-

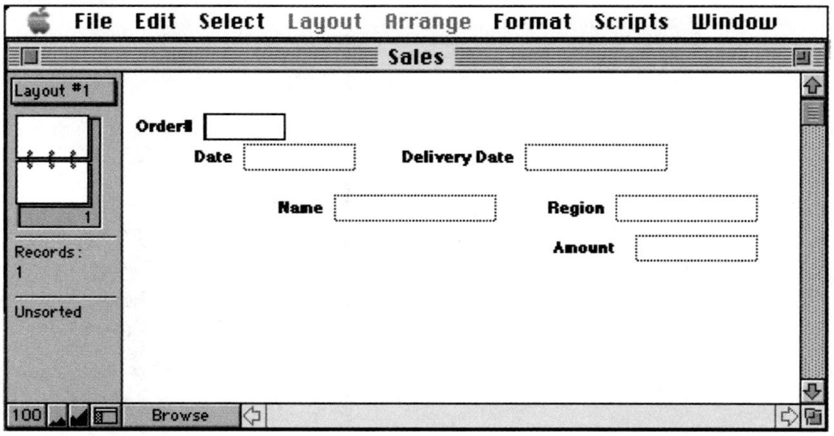

FIGURE 10.15

A modified data entry form in FileMaker Pro is shown. This is just one possible arrangement; the user can design his or her own customized screens. You may also include graphics created with FileMaker Pro's drawing tools in any section of the form.

pending on the particular criteria applied. In FileMaker Pro, the selection criteria become a part of the report itself. Hence, each time the report is printed the data is collected anew, meaning you get the most up-to-date data in the report at all times. In Microsoft Access, you first apply the criteria to collect the desired data into a new table, then base the report on the new table. This table becomes a **virtual table,** meaning that the table itself is not stored, only the criteria for selecting its data. In this way, if the database data changes, the new values are automatically reflected in the virtual table. In some cases, you may prefer to print the data as it occurs at some fixed time, ignoring any later updates to the database. In both FileMaker Pro and Access, you can store a report based on current data to be printed as many times as you like later if you do not want the report data updated each time the report is printed.

Creating a report in Access is very similar to creating a form. You begin by choosing *Reports* in the database window (see Figure 10.8) and then clicking the New button. You must next specify the table for which the report will be created. If you then select *Report Wizards,* you can easily create one of several different kinds of default report templates. Figure 10.16 illustrates. When you want more flexibility, you can create your own reports from scratch.

Subtotals and Control Breaks in Reports

Often we would like to compute totals and subtotals for our reports. For example, we might wish to display the total value of all orders. Subtotals, of course, are associated with a specific group of the data in a report. To display these subtotals accurately, the grouping must be based on a common data field value. A separate subtotal may then be computed and displayed for each group of distinct values for that data field.

For example, we might wish to calculate the subtotal for each separate region in our previous report. To enable the report to display this data in a meaningful manner, the data must first be sorted by the data field that determines the separate subtotals—the field *Region* in our example. Once this sorting is done, whenever the value in that field changes, a subtotal is printed and a new subtotal calculation is started. This is illustrated for our example report in FileMaker Pro in Figure 10.17. The break points in a report with subtotals or other summary in-

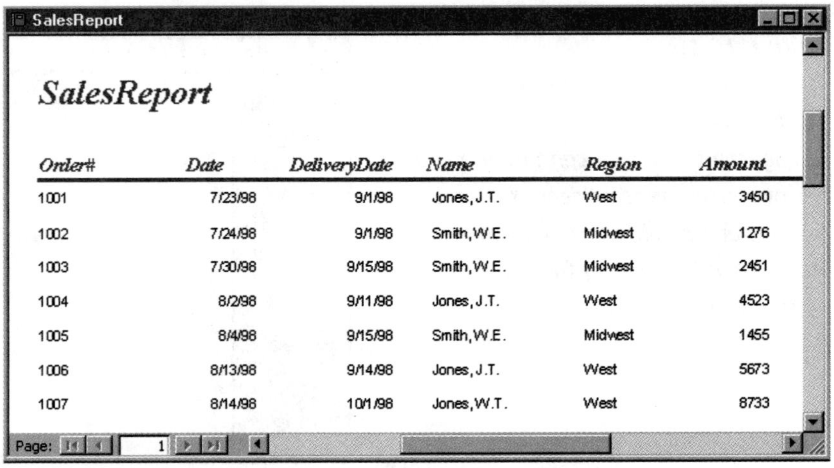

FIGURE 10.16

An Access default tabular report shows all records from the Sales *table.*

SalesReport

SalesReport

Order#	Date	DeliveryDate	Name	Region	Amount
1001	7/23/98	9/1/98	Jones, J.T.	West	3450
1002	7/24/98	9/1/98	Smith, W.E.	Midwest	1276
1003	7/30/98	9/15/98	Smith, W.E.	Midwest	2451
1004	8/2/98	9/11/98	Jones, J.T.	West	4523
1005	8/4/98	9/15/98	Smith, W.E.	Midwest	1455
1006	8/13/98	9/14/98	Jones, J.T.	West	5673
1007	8/14/98	10/1/98	Jones, W.T.	West	8733

Page: 1

FIGURE 10.17

A FileMaker Pro report shows a grand total and regional subtotals. Control breaks are set to display purchase order amount subtotals for each separate region in the database. This particular report layout has been enhanced with the logo drawings in the upper left and right of the report header as well. Both FileMaker Pro and Access provide graphic tools for enhancing reports in this manner.

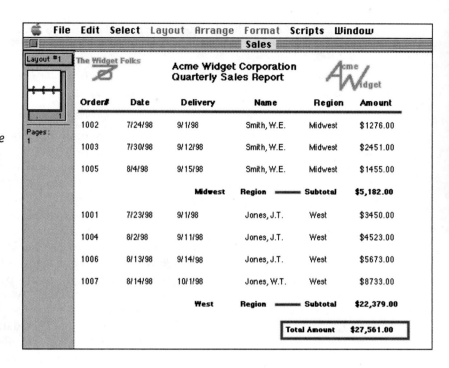

formation are often referred to as **control breaks.** In most database systems, control breaks can be nested, allowing subtotals to be calculated within groupings as well as for the groupings themselves.

USING QUERY LANGUAGES

As we have emphasized, the ability to perform **database queries** is the most valuable feature of any database management system. Queries are requests for specific information satisfying some stated criteria. Queries are written in a **query language** that, like a programming language, has a specific syntax. In fact, much of a database management system's value for its users is based on the convenience and power of its query language. Use of these languages requires no programming in the traditional sense. Query languages are self-contained, so that once a user masters the language, he or she can pose any potential queries to the system.

In fact, the query language is the only component of a database system visible to a great many users. For example, when you use an ATM machine, you interact with the underlying database only by means of a very restricted and carefully designed query language. This language is presented as a choice of menu selections at each stage of the transaction. The language model employed is not at all flexible, but it isn't designed with flexibility in mind. It is designed for easy and foolproof use without training. The travel agent you ask to book your flight is also interacting with a flight reservation database through a query language. This language is more complicated than the ATM language and will require some training of its users. To ATM users or the travel agent operating the airline reservation system, these systems *are* their query languages. The users see no other aspect of the database, having no in-

SELECT Name FROM Sales WHERE Amount > $2000 AND Region = "West"

FIGURE 10.18

An example SQL query is shown. SQL reserved words are shown in all caps; Name, Amount, and Region are all field names in a file named Sales.

volvement in designing the database, entering its initial data, or generating summary reports.

Given the importance of query languages, database management system designers and researchers have expended a great deal of effort to make these languages both user-friendly and as powerful as possible. There are several popular models on which most are based. Some attempts to standardize a query language for all relational database systems have been made. The leading candidate is called **SQL** (for **Structured Query Language**). Although no such standard has been adopted officially, SQL (usually pronounced "sequel") is widely used. In fact, most relational database systems offer a query language containing at least a subset of SQL.

This is very good news for database users, at least at the query level. It means that an adequate knowledge of SQL will allow them to move freely from one database system to another. SQL queries are formed with an English-like syntax, often employing a SELECT . . . FROM . . . WHERE format. The example in Figure 10.18 gives you the flavor of a SQL query.

Another relational model query language, called **QBE** (for **Query-by-Example**), has also garnered a lot of support. QBE is not as standardized as SQL, and many different versions of QBE are being used. All these versions are based on a graphical interface paradigm that allows a user to construct a generalized example of the data he or she would like to retrieve. Both Microsoft Access and FileMaker Pro use their own versions of QBE; you will see examples later in the discussion.

One of the most interesting and hotly pursued areas of current research is creating query languages that will employ a natural language like English. For example, in a **natural language query,** you might choose to pose a query in any of a number of ways, depending on which seems most expressive and meaningful to you—without worrying about how a particular query language requires you to pose the query. Figure 10.19 illustrates.

Some limited success has been achieved, but the inherent complexity and ambiguity of natural languages like English pose a formidable barrier. Successful systems have been implemented in very special infor-

FIGURE 10.19

The previous query is posed in several equivalent ways in English. Note that there are no reserved words or any need to use the actual field or file names in any of these queries. A natural language query system would be able to interpret each one of these as the same query and process each to produce the correct data.

Find the names of any West region salesperson who made a sale for over $2,000.

Find the names of salespersons in the West region with a sale exceeding $2,000.

Who made a sale for over $2,000 in the West region?

Did anyone in the West region make a sale larger than $2,000?

mational domains in which the vocabulary is highly technical and limited, such as chemistry and medicine. Another domain in which natural language queries have been successfully implemented is in the design of search engines for the Web. Here, the information being sought is not nearly as specific as with most database queries, and natural language queries are relatively simple to compose. You saw examples of this in your work with Alta Vista in Chapter 3. Unfortunately, commercially viable natural language query systems for general use are still years away from reality. Nonetheless, large research and development efforts in this area are being conducted because the commercial payoff for a workable natural language database query system would be tremendous.

QUERYING DATABASES AVAILABLE ON THE WEB

Database and Web technologies are merging. One of the most active areas of current computer science research centers on the use of Web "front ends" for accessing the information in databases. A **Web database front end** is a database interface with search and retrieval capabilities that is displayed and run through a Web browser. These products provide access to a range of database information—from a large variety of public domain information to proprietary business transactions. Of course, security is a major issue in the use of such products for information not in the public domain. Security measures on the Web are constantly being improved, and it is now quite common to see Web front ends for proprietary databases used by businesses, government, and other organizations.

In this activity you will explore several of the many public domain databases available on the Web. In this process, you will see several different styles of Web database front ends.

1 Access GTE's *SuperPages* site at http://superpages.gte.net/.

a Use the *City Guide* link to look up information about your city (or a city near you). Return to the *SuperPages* site when you complete this query.

b Use the *Classified Ads* link to explore information about some product or service that interests you. Return to the *SuperPages* site when you complete this query.

c Use the GTE *Yellow Pages* dialog box to search for information about buying bagels in Helena, Montana (put "bagel" in the *Category* search box). When a business name and address are returned, click the address link to display a map showing the location of the company.

2 Access the U.S. government's *FEDSTATS* site at http://www.fedstats.gov/. Click the *Regional Statistics* link.

a Use the *Public School Student* . . . link under the *Education* heading to look up information about your state's school system. For example, how many kindergarten teachers are employed in your state? What is the student/teacher ratio in your state? Return to the *Regional Statistics* page when you finish this query.

b Assuming you have software for viewing PDF files, click the *Atlas of the US Mortality* link under the *Health* heading to look up some health-related information that interests you. Return to the *Regional Statistics* page when you finish this query.

c Use the *Personal Income . . .* link under the *National Accounts* heading to look up information about personal income levels in your state. Where does your state rank in the United States in per capita personal income?

3 Access global information at the U.S. Census Bureau's *International Statistical Agencies* site at http://www.census.gov/main/www/stat_int. html.

a Confirm for yourself that there were more than 8 million sheep in Ireland in 1996. Hint: Follow the Ireland *Central Statistics Office* link to http://www.cso.ie. Name sev-

eral other facts that you find about Ireland at this site. Return to the *International Statistical Agencies* site when you complete this query.

b Explore another country's statistical files and report on your findings.

4 Movie buffs beware: This site can be addicting! Check the *Internet Movie Database* (IMD) site at http://www.imdb.com/. Click the *Search* link to access the IMD database front end search tool.

a Try a search for information about the classic television series *Gunsmoke*. Find out who played Sam the Bartender. Return to the *Searching the IMD* site when you finish this query.

b Try entering the phrase *Here's looking at you kid* in the *Word Search* entry box. Return and try another phrase of your own choosing. Return to the *Searching the IMD* site when you finish this query.

c Try some other searches before leaving this site.

QBE—Some Examples

Access features a very user-friendly graphical method for specifying database retrievals based on a Query-by-Example language. Queries are specified by entering the search conditions directly into the relevant database field areas in a kind of blank record template. Once you are satisfied that the query is constructed correctly, you can see the data it retrieves by pressing the Enter key. With this action, the database searches, selects, and displays those records satisfying the constraints. We illustrate with some example queries from our *Sales* table.

Suppose we wish to retrieve all records for orders exceeding $5,000. You begin by choosing *Queries* in the database window (see Figure 10.8 to review) and then clicking the New button. Just as with forms and re-

FIGURE 10.20

We simply enter the search condition directly in the box representing the appropriate field (Amount in this case). Note that the field used for the search need not be displayed in the resulting retrieval. In fact, you can select exactly which fields you wish to show.

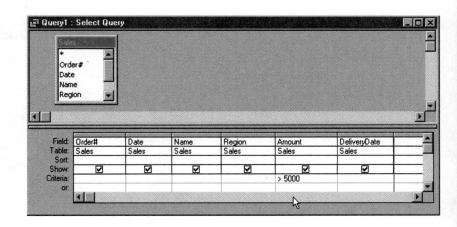

ports, you must next specify the table for which the report will be created. Once this is done, you are presented with a query entry form. Figure 10.20 shows how the query would be entered.

Of course, not all queries will be this simple to pose. Often we will wish to construct queries with **multiple search constraints,** that is, constraints connected by logical *or* and logical *and* operators. A **logical *or* operator** connects two statements in such a way that the compound statement is true if either or both of the component statements are true. A **logical *and* operator** connects two statements with the compound statement being true only if both component statements are true.

Suppose, for example, that we wish to retrieve the records for all sales made before August 1, 1998, that were for more than $3,000. Note that we have an implied logical *and* operator here. We are seeking records for sales that were made before August 1 *and* for more than $3,000. In Access, for constraints such as these—expressed on several data fields and connected by a logical *and* operator—we simply include all the constraints in the same row of the query dialog box. This particular query is shown in Figure 10.21.

Our next example is a more complex query involving both the logical *and* operator and the logical *or* operator. Suppose that we wish to display purchase orders that are eligible for a bonus commission. Let's assume that this commission depends on the size of the order and the region. The particular rule could be this: All orders for more than $5,000 are eligible in the West region, but in the Midwest all orders for more than $2,000 qualify. What is involved in posing this query? If you

FIGURE 10.21

An Access query searches for records satisfying two constraints. Multiple conditions entered into a single row within the query dialog box are interpreted as being connected by a logical and. *Hence, the records satisfying both constraints—orders for more than $3,000 placed before August 1, 1998— will be retrieved and displayed.*

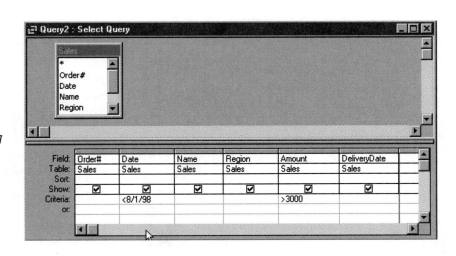

FIGURE 10.22

FIGURE 10.22

In Access, we enter the first condition to be connected by a logical or operator in the first row in the query dialog form, then issue the additional constraint in a second row. In other words, we can stack the multiple requests to be connected by logical or operators row after row.

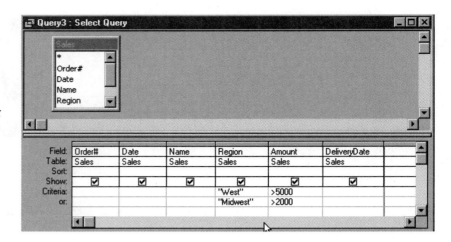

analyze it carefully, you will see that it involves two logical *and* operators and one logical *or* as follows:

(Order placed in the West *and* for more than $5,000)

or

(Order placed in the Midwest *and* for more than $2,000)

We just saw how to phrase two constraints connected by the logical *and* operator by placing the constraints on the same row in the query form. How do we include the logical *or* operator? In the Query-by-Example system used in Access, such queries are accomplished by employing a *second row* in the query form. Figure 10.22 illustrates our example.

As you can see from these examples, the form of Query-by-Example used by Access is a very user-friendly, graphically oriented language. It is also reasonably powerful in that it allows a large number of queries to be posed.

FileMaker Pro also features a user-friendly graphical method for specifying database retrievals. It, too, is based on the Query-by-Example language we mentioned earlier. Queries are specified by entering the search conditions directly into the relevant database field areas in a blank record template somewhat similar to the technique used in Access. Figure 10.23 portrays the previous example of retrieving records for all sales over $5,000. Note the conceptual similarity to the Access query shown in Figure 10.20, even though the two screens look a bit different.

FIGURE 10.23

A FileMaker Pro query finds records satisfying one search condition. To pose a query for records for all sales over $5,000, we access the query dialog box, then simply enter the query constraint directly in the Amount *field as shown.*

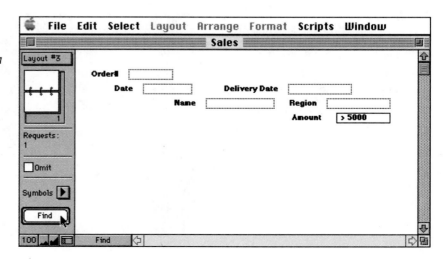

FIGURE 10.24

A FileMaker Pro query searches for records satisfying two constraints. Multiple conditions entered into a single record within the query dialog box are interpreted as being connected by a logical and. *Hence, the records satisfying both constraints—orders for more than $3,000 placed before August 1, 1998—will be retrieved and displayed.*

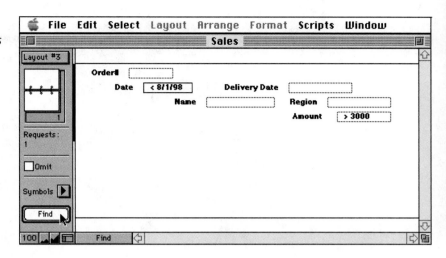

Queries with multiple search constraints connected by logical *and* operators are included in the same template record. As an example, Figure 10.24 shows the FileMaker Pro query for retrieving the records for sales for more than $3,000 made before August 1, 1998. Once again, this compares directly with the Access query shown in Figure 10.21.

In the Query-by-Example system used in FileMaker Pro, queries involving logical *or* operators are accomplished by using multiple query dialog boxes. We enter the first condition to be connected by a logical *or* operator in a query dialog box, then issue the additional constraints—placed just below the first template with its constraints already entered. In other words, we can stack the multiple requests to be connected by logical *or* operators one after another, in a manner very similar to the method used in Access. Figure 10.25 illustrates the previous example. Compare this to the Access query in Figure 10.22.

As you can see from both the Access and FileMaker Pro examples, Query-by-Example languages provide a very user-friendly, graphically oriented data retrieval capability. Such languages are also reasonably powerful in that they allow a wide range of queries to be posed. Not all database systems employ such an easy-to-use query language, but all do provide powerful data selection and retrieval capabilities. Often QBE languages will be supplemented by SQL or another query language to provide for retrievals that might be too complex to pose simply as QBE queries.

FIGURE 10.25

This figure illustrates entering two constraints connected by a logical or *in FileMaker Pro. The annotation on the right of the display is added for clarity and is not produced by the database system.*

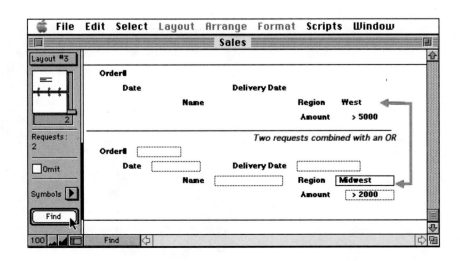

Social Themes

Databases and Your Privacy

In the previous "Social Themes" section, we explored law enforcement's use of national databases. You don't have to be a lawbreaker, though, to be included in a nationally accessible database. Information on almost every person in the developed world is computerized in hundreds of databases collected, stored, and analyzed by governments and corporations. High-speed global networks increasingly link these databases. Armed with a single identification number, such as a Social Security Number, a user with proper access can produce comprehensive reports on millions of people without their knowledge or permission.

The computerization of medical records, travel records, phone records, and financial transfers has dramatically increased the quantity of data available about us all. Pressures to increase the availability of information about individuals come from a variety of sources. Government agencies perceive computerization as a way of increasing efficiency in a political climate of shrinking bureaucracy budgets. Law enforcement sees many advantages in improved identification and monitoring of individuals. Corporations use database technologies to target consumers, analyze markets, and even to choose and monitor their employees.

With many databases being linked by networks, the prospect of consolidating information about individuals becomes attainable. A unique identifier would enhance retrieval and consolidation of data from a number of distinct databases, created at different times and for different purposes. As a result, it is easy to see why the pressure for a single identifier to facilitate information sharing for administrative purposes is increasing.

The Social Security Number (SSN) was developed in 1938 to identify those eligible for government retirement benefits. In 1961, the IRS began using the SSN as a taxpayer identification number; since that time many other organizations and government agencies have followed suit. You have no doubt been asked for your SSN on numerous occasions when you applied for college admission, for a checking account, for credit cards, and so on. Congress has debated bills to create new national databases keyed to the SSN for all workers and for welfare and immigration purposes.

In the near future we will likely see a system of universal identification established, with associated ID cards that include photographs, fingerprints, and microchips containing medical history and special conditions, address, next of kin, date of birth, place of birth, and so on. Such cards, called *smart cards,* are already widely used in Europe and are gaining acceptance in the United States. Columbia/HCA Healthcare Corporation recently announced that it was providing 50,000 Florida residents with cards that would hold medical records, including X-rays. Reading devices can gather data about an individual from such cards in short order. In a process that privacy advocates refer to as *function creep,* cards designed for a specific singular use are already being expanded to provide access to multiple databases.

Personal Profiles and Your Privacy

A number of companies define their business as providing information about individuals. The list includes (but is not restricted to) ChoicePoint, Database Technologies, Experian, First Data, InfoSource/Donnelly Marketing, IRSC Inc., Lexis-Nexis, Metromail, and Information America. These companies point out that many benefits can be derived from their services, such as locating trial witnesses, tracking down so-called "deadbeat dads," and finding pension fund beneficiaries.

But many believe that the increasing use of databases with information about specific individuals is eroding personal privacy. As we consider this issue, let's first investigate how information about individuals is collected. Almost every business transaction in which you engage results in data. In addition to business transactions, each interaction with a government agency generates data about you. The data associated with some of these transactions is very important by itself—the amount of your automatic deposit on payday, the diagnosis you get from a visit to the doctor, the grades you received this semester, and so on. But many transactions seem rather insignificant by themselves—which brand of toothpaste you purchased at the grocery store, the amount you spent on produce, the total amount of your grocery bill, how often you visit the grocery store, the days and times you do your shopping. When a mass of seemingly insignificant data such as this is considered together, however, each element contributes to the sum of your personal affairs.

Suppose that the details of all your transactions enter some computer database. It may well be that an analysis conducted on data accumulated and collected from many different source points can produce information about you that you consider an invasion of your privacy. Where and when you shop, how much you spend on various items, which brand names you prefer, what sizes you buy (and presumably wear), how much gasoline you consume, how many miles you drive, how much you spend on long-distance calls, the amount of your heating bill, and on and on, may all be tallied. Such analyses produce what are called **personal profiles,** summary conclusions about your habits, means, movements, and so on.

Merchandisers value these personal profiles because they can use them to target marketing specifically tailored to your lifestyle, spending habits, and so on. When you purchase catalog items using the very convenient 800 number, the catalog company gains information as well as cash—item, sizes, amount, name, address, telephone number, and credit card number. If you purchase a gift to be sent to a third party, information about that individual is also collected. Your credit card company receives information from the merchants about all your credit card purchases. It is relatively easy for the company to produce a purchase profile, as well as information about your payment habits and preferences. Some of this data is likely to end up at one or more credit service bureaus, such as Experian (formerly TRW), Equifax, or Trans Union. These bureaus gather data from credit card companies and other sources to provide financial profiles of individuals. Such information might be accessed not only by potential creditors, but by prospective employers, landlords, and others.

To summarize, information about your habits, preferences, interests, health, financial situation, and other characteristics can be assembled from a wide array of sources. Some of the information is no doubt in the public domain (such as your name, address, and employer); some you may have given permission to be used for a specific purpose; still other information is collected without your knowledge or permission.

Regardless of the sources and types of information, a great many of us would still consider the aggregation and dissemination of profile data a matter of personal privacy. What redress do we have? The Constitution does not actually address the "right to privacy" directly. Most privacy-related legislation is based on the Fourth Amendment to the Constitution. We reproduce it here for reference:

> *The right of the people to be secure in their persons, houses, papers, and effects, against unreasonable searches and seizures, shall not be violated, and no Warrants shall issue, but upon probable cause, supported by Oath or Affirmation, and particularly describing the place to be searched, and the persons or things to be seized.*

Social Themes

How is the Fourth Amendment to be interpreted concerning an individual's right to privacy and the use of today's database and networking technology? The answer is largely unknown. Technology changes so rapidly that it often outpaces our legal system's proper regulation of its use. No doubt the issue of personal privacy and the collection of personal information in computer databases will receive considerable attention in the courts and legislatures over the next decade.

MULTIMEDIA DATABASES

A lot of attention is now being shifted to applying well-established database techniques for more innovative applications. With today's technology, it is possible to digitize and efficiently store images, graphical objects, sounds, and even motion pictures and video. Given that we can digitize and store such media, it seems natural to expect them to be included in our databases as well. And, in fact, this combination is producing some exciting results.

Multimedia database systems face the challenge of managing voice, images, and video, in addition to the conventional numeric and text data. Such systems must be capable of evaluating user queries that may require the integration of information from very different media. For instance, a simple query might be to collect all images that contain certain objects. The database system must be capable of matching that attribute (expressed in words) with the content of images stored in its system. Of course, images could be tagged with verbal descriptions—a kind of keyword abstract like those attached to electronic publications. The designers would face the difficulty of correctly anticipating future interests about these images. To overcome these obstacles, researchers today are experimenting with **knowledge-assisted multimedia database systems.** This approach is distinctive in that the system analyzes the content of its media based directly on a given query. Today, however, such systems are still largely experimental, but if the research is successful, the dividends for information management will be great.

USING MULTIPLE FILES IN RELATIONAL SYSTEMS

Our examples so far have been restricted to databases with one table. Of course, one of the strengths of the relational database model is its ability to handle databases with multiple tables. In this section we will briefly demonstrate how this capability is implemented in Microsoft Access. Our example database stores information about sales. Two fields we included give the name of the salesperson for each sale and the region in which the sale was made. Let's add two additional tables to store information specifically about the salespersons and the regions.

Figure 10.26 displays the tables we have added. Very likely, you can think of additional information that we might like to collect and store about each of these entities, but the fields shown will serve our purpose of illustration here. The structure for these new tables is defined in Access, just as the structure for the *Sales* table was defined earlier. Figure 10.27 illustrates the definition of the *SalesPersons* table.

Notice that we have included fields that provide the logical links needed to connect the data of the *Sales* table to the data stored in the new tables. Having the salesperson's name in both the *Sales* and the *SalesPersons* tables allows us to make queries logically relating data in those two tables. Likewise, the region name allows retrievals of related data from the *Sales* and *Regions* tables.

We can readily recognize the logical connections intended by using the same names in the various tables. We must make this connection

FIGURE 10.26

The new database structure has two additional tables to store information about salespersons and regions.

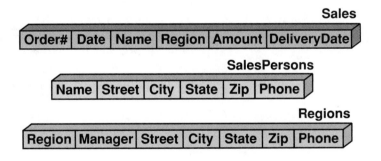

Sales

| Order# | Date | Name | Region | Amount | DeliveryDate |

SalesPersons

| Name | Street | City | State | Zip | Phone |

Regions

| Region | Manager | Street | City | State | Zip | Phone |

FIGURE 10.27

Defining the SalesPersons table in Access is shown.

FIGURE 10.28

Establishing the appropriate relationships among the three tables in the Access Relationships window is shown.

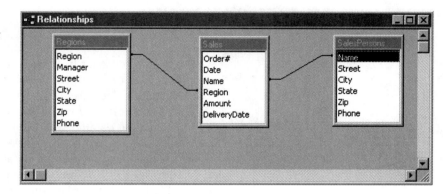

even more explicit for the database management system. We do this by establishing logical relationships among the tables. To initiate this we select *Relationships* from the **Tools** menu. We then add the tables we wish to relate (in this case all three of our tables) to the *Relationships* window. We then define the logical relationships within the window by dragging connecting lines between the appropriate fields in the various tables. Figure 10.28 demonstrates the relationships we want to establish for our database tables.

Once these relationships are established, we can make queries that require the retrieval of related data from several tables. For example, suppose we wish to derive a report that lists the region, the regional manager, the salesperson's name and phone number, and the amount for all sales more than $10,000. Such a report requires information from all three of our tables. Obviously, the basic query condition is based on the *Sales* table—selecting the records for sales exceeding $10,000. Once these records are selected, we can get the salesperson's name from the *Sales* table. We'll need to access the *SalesPersons* table to look up the phone number, and the regional manager's name will come from the related record in the *Regions* table. Figure 10.29 illustrates how the query would be constructed. We simply list the fields we wish to have displayed when the query is executed and place the single constraint on the *Amount* field in the *Sales* table. Note the use of the table name along with

FIGURE 10.29

An example Access query requires retrieval of data from multiple tables.

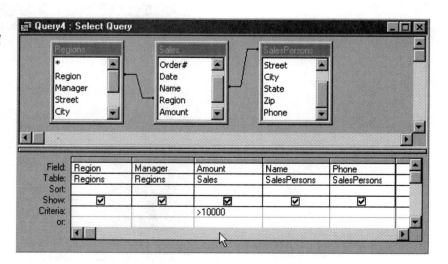

the field names; this avoids confusion when the same field name appears in one or more tables.

Access and FileMaker Pro are very powerful relational database systems. Each has many capabilities beyond the few basic ones we've explored. Of course, it is not our intent here to provide complete coverage of these or any software products. Most of these products deserve and have entire books devoted to them. Rather, we hope you have caught a glimpse of the tremendous usefulness and power that products like Access and FileMaker Pro bring to your desktop.

Lab Activity

S U M M A R Y

Software systems that manage the storage and retrieval of computerized information date to the early days of computing. Today's versions of such software, called database management systems, are fundamental and indispensable tools to many organizations. Two major models are employed in modern database management systems: the network model and the relational model.

In the network model, the user interacts with a physical representation of the data including physical indices and link fields built into the data itself to provide access to related data. Network-based systems are optimized for speed and efficiency, though they still demand some programming skill to use.

The relational model gives the user a more conceptual view of the data. Rather than employing link fields to relate records in different files, the relational model employs the logical relationships among items in the files. This organization provides a much more intuitive interface and better accessibility for the nonprogrammer. Although relational systems are usually not as fast and efficient as network systems, their ease of use and ability to perform ad hoc queries make them a natural choice for data management conducted on desktop computers.

The ability to perform database queries is the most valuable feature of any database management system. Queries are written in a query language that, like a programming language, has a specific syntax. There are several popular models on which most query languages are based. SQL (for Structured Query Language) is a widely used query language, and most relational database systems offer a query language containing at least a subset of SQL. QBE (for Query-by-Example) has also garnered a lot of support. Although QBE languages are not as standardized as SQL, they are generally easy to use because they are based on a graphical user interface.

Much current research is focused on creating query languages that will employ natural language (English, for example). Some limited success has been achieved, but the inherent complexity and ambiguity of natural languages like English pose a formidable barrier, and commercially viable natural language query systems for general use may still be years away from reality.

PROJECTS

1 Use the *MapBlast* site, found at URL http://www.mapblast.com/, to display a map showing the location of your house.

2 Use the *WhoWhere?* database, accessed at URL http://www.whowhere.com/, to search for other persons with your same first and last names. Click the *Phone and Address* button before beginning your search. If you have particularly common first and last names, you may find a large number of matches for this search. You might want to add your middle name to narrow the search. How many persons do you find? Any in the city where you live?

3 Select a friend's name and use the *WhoWhere?* site (see project 2) to look up his or her address. Then use the *MapBlast* site (see project 1) to display a map showing the location of his or her house. Are you comfortable having this kind of information available on the Web? Could you suppress such information about yourself? Explain.

4 **a.** Use database software to which you have access to create a single file database for the following information. The file (table) will hold records for course grades at a hypothetical university. Name the table GRADES. Include the following fields in your database record design: student identification number, course number (CS112, MTH201, ENG101, etc.), grade received, term (Fall, Spring, Winter, Summer), and year.
b. Once you set up the database structure, create a form (if your software allows forms) to enter data. Use the form to enter about 10 rows of hypothetical data in your database. Include multiple courses for at least two different students.
c. Query your database for the following information. Check the results of each of your

queries against the contents of the full database for correctness.
  i. All student identification numbers and grades for a certain course (you choose the course).
  ii. All course numbers and grades for a certain student (you choose the student).
  iii. All identification numbers for students along with the course numbers for all grades of A in a certain term and year (you choose the term and year).

5 **a.** If your database software allows multiple files (tables), expand your database as follows. Include a table (named STUDENTS) holding information about students, namely student identification number, first name, middle name, last name, street, city, state, and zip. Add a third table (named COURSES) holding information about courses, namely course number, hours of credit, and course name.
b. Once you set the database structure up, link the tables using the logical linking data, namely student identification numbers and course numbers, respectively.
c. Create forms to enter data for the STUDENTS and COURSES tables. Use the form to enter hypothetical data for all students and courses included in your COURSES table.
d. Repeat the queries you formed in project 4, but this time add some explanatory information to make the query results more informative. For example, in the first query, report the students' names (note that this means retrieving data from two related tables). In the second query, add course names. In the third query, add both student names and course names to the query results.

Key Terms

ad hoc database query	link field	record
database management	logical *and* operator	relational database model
system (DBMS)	logical *or* operator	report, database
data type	multimedia database	sorted data
external file	system	sort key
field	multiple search constraint	Structured Query
file	natural language query	Language (SQL)
file management software	nested sorting	table, database
flat file database system	network database model	virtual table
form, database	personal profile	Web database front end
indexed file	query, database	
knowledge-assisted	query language	
multimedia database	Query-by-Example (QBE)	

QUESTIONS FOR REVIEW

1 Define and relate the terms *file, record,* and *field* in the context of database structure. Construct a diagram to help make your point.

2 What are indexed files? Why is indexing an important concept for database management?

3 How are indexed files and binary search trees related?

4 Briefly describe the network database model.

5 Briefly describe the relational database model.

6 Is the network or relational database model preferable? Elaborate on your response.

7 What is meant by the design or structure of a database? Why is this important?

8 What is meant by a database query?

9 What is an ad hoc database query? Give an example to illustrate. Why are ad hoc queries an important consideration when choosing a database model?

10 Describe what is meant by a flat file database system.

11 What is meant by a multimedia database?

12 Compare database forms and database reports. Which are easier to produce? Explain.

13   What is the purpose of a database query language? Why are these particularly important?

14   What does the acronym SQL stand for? How is it pronounced? What is its significance?

15   What does the acronym QBE stand for? Describe its use.

16   What does the term *sort key* refer to? How does it relate to nested sorting of information in a database?

17   Define the term *control break*. Describe its significance for database processing.

18   How does the database technology today compare with the corresponding technology of the 1960s?

19   Describe the terms *physical link* and *logical link*. What do these terms refer to in database management?

20   When the network and relational database models are compared, the terms *flexibility* and *efficiency* often arise. Explain.

21   How would a natural language database query system compare with SQL and QBE?

22   Give several examples of how your life might be influenced by the use of database management systems.

PART 4

SIGHTS AND SOUNDS

Vasily Kandinsky, *Violet-Orange*, October 1935. Solomon R. Guggenheim Museum

Digital images are a very important medium for representing information. It is convenient to divide computer images into two classes: *natural* and *artificial*. Artificial images are created exclusively by computer processes and are usually called "graphic images" (or simply "graphics"). A natural image is one digitized from an original analog image such as a photograph. Whether natural or artificial, computer images offer a rich source of information that enhances a variety of applications. As the old saying states, "A picture is worth a thousand words," so digital images certainly should be worth a few kilobytes. In this chapter, we will consider natural images and treat graphic images in the next chapter. Many of the concepts about digital images introduced here, however, will be applicable to computer-generated graphic images as well.

As little as a decade ago, digital image processing was strictly the province of the expert. Processing images required exotic hardware and customized software. For example, the dramatic images from the NASA interplanetary probes during the late 1970s and early 1980s were produced by the Jet Propulsion Laboratory in California. These represented the state of the art in both hardware and software. Today, many of the same esoteric processes can be duplicated using a standard desktop system with commercial image processing application software. Thus, a typical computer user with some basic knowledge and experience can exploit some of the imaging effects that previously were limited to professionals.

OBJECTIVES

- *The nature of images and how digital images are organized*
- *How digital images are created and stored*
- *How digital images are processed*
- *Basic techniques for editing digital images*

CHAPTER 11

PROCESSING IMAGES: IS SEEING BELIEVING?

Vasily Kandinsky, *Violet-Orange*, October 1935. Solomon R. Guggenheim Museum

IMAGES AND DIGITAL IMAGES

Natural images come in a variety of forms: photographs, drawings, paintings, television and motion pictures, schematics, maps, and so on. The content of images may be simple and stylized or complicated and detailed, as shown in Figure 11.1. An **image** is an *n*-dimensional pictorial representation of a scene. Images are pictures in the sense that they show us visually the prominent features of the objects that they represent. Most images plot these features in two-dimensional space—though three- (depth) and four-dimensional (time) images are also possible.

Like any other representation, an image represents its subject through a physical medium. Most images depict how things look as a function of light reflecting from the objects. Even so, images may be derived from other bands of the electromagnetic spectrum; for example, X-rays, radar, infrared, and satellite telemetry are employed to create images whose medium is reflected energies from outside the spectrum of visible light. See Figure 11.2.

As information, images always approximate their subjects. In other words, an image is never an exact duplicate of what it depicts. It does have characteristics that match those of its subject, for example, color, shape, relative location, and so on. Unlike verbal descriptions, images exemplify what they represent rather than merely denote them. Consequently, maps, diagrams, and blueprints are images even though they seldom look exactly like the scenes they depict. The quality of an image

(a)

(b)

(c)

FIGURE 11.1

Three types of representations are shown. Each denotes a common member of the feline family. In contrast to the word "Wildcat" (b), which merely refers to one, the two images (a) and (c) depict or exemplify them. The first (a) is a photograph, and (c) is a graphic illustration. Even though these images are composed quite differently, each is an effective representation of its subject.

(its accuracy, authenticity, coherence) depends on what purposes it serves. We tend to think that photographs, for example, are somehow mirrors of reality, but this is a cultural fact. Anthropologists have found primitive peoples who must be taught to understand and recognize photos of themselves. The point is that there are no fixed standards in as-

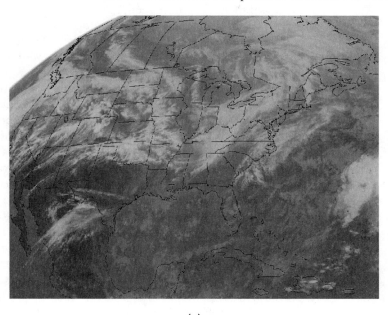

(a)

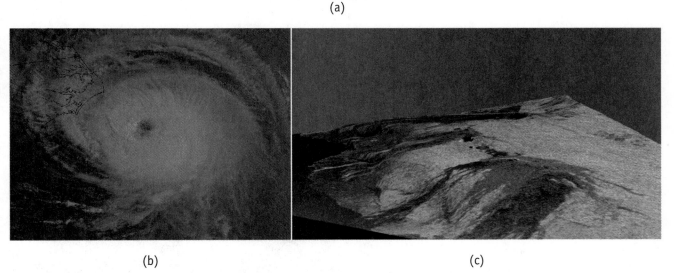

(b)   (c)

FIGURE 11.2

Photographic images represent the reflected energies of frequencies from the visible spectrum. Digital methods can easily convert energies from other bands in the electromagnetic spectrum into useful images. The GOES-8 weather satellite transmits information signals from several bands of the energy spectrum. In (a), the infrared signal captures the atmospheric conditions over the continental United States. The digital image is shown here in shades of gray—called a grayscale image. Infrared sensors are also used to create the dramatic image of Hurricane Emily in (b). The hurricane is seen approaching landfall on the coast of North Carolina in September 1987. False colors or pseudocolors are added to improve the visibility of details. The eye of the hurricane is clearly visible in the center of the image. The three-dimensional-perspective view (c) of the Kilauea volcano on the Big Island of Hawaii was created from images taken during a space shuttle flyby in 1994. The pseudocolor image is composed from three radar frequencies. Blues depict the active lava flows. Light and dark greens represent rain forests and low-level vegetation, respectively.

sessing the quality of images. As Figure 11.1 shows, the photo of the cat and the line drawing are both effective in conveying information.

Most natural images employ analog media. To be useful to computers, they must be converted to the digital domain. A **digital image** is a picture that may be stored in, displayed on, or otherwise processed by a computer. As we have seen, converting an analog medium into a discrete numeric form requires both sampling and quantizing. A **pixel** (from "picture element") is the basic unit of a digital image. Pixels are discrete units of an image that correspond to two-dimensional spatial coordinates. In addition, each pixel is a discrete sample of the continuous signal of an analog image. This means that each pixel contains one or more numbers that measure the value or values of the signal for that portion of the image. A pixel by itself does not convey much information. The context in which the pixel is found or its arrangement in the overall image is what determines what it depicts.

Pixels are usually arranged as rectangular units in a two-dimensional (2-D) grid, though it is possible to have other types of pixel arrangements (triangular, hexagonal, etc.). **Picture resolution** is defined as the number of pixels contained in a digital image. Resolution is usually written as a product of the image's dimensions. (This should not be confused with display resolution, which is usually expressed as dpi—dots per inch.) **Aspect ratio** expresses the number of horizontal pixels divided by the number of vertical pixels. The aspect ratio of an image is important for scaling images or when resampling them at different resolutions. For instance, if we wish to reduce the resolution of a digital image, we must take care to preserve the same aspect ratio for it. This will ensure that it looks natural and not distorted.

The example of the penny in Figure 11.3 has a resolution of 50×50 and thus an aspect ratio of 1:1. Here are some common picture resolutions and their corresponding aspect ratios: 320×200 (1.6:1), 640×480 (1.33:1), and 1024×768 (1.33:1). These instances are typical of the three general levels for picture resolution—low, medium, and high (respectively).

As you might expect, the resolution has a direct effect on the amount of detail that a digital image captures. The examples in Figure 11.4 show the same image of a building front sampled at different resolutions. Naturally, there are some trade-offs with picture resolution. The higher the resolution, the greater the demands for both storage and

FIGURE 11.3

Digital sampling is illustrated. The image of the penny in (a) is sampled spatially at a rate of 50 pixels across and 50 down. The contents of each sample are averaged to produce a uniform pixel value, as shown in (b). At a pixel resolution of 50×50, we can see that details of the lettering and face are lost.

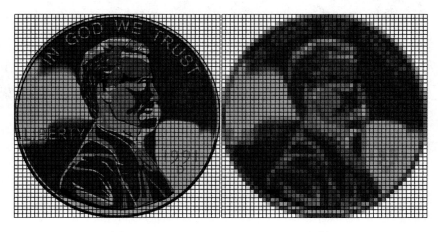

(a)   (b)

processing. Thus, the choice of resolution will often depend on a number of practical matters: the amount of detail or complexity in the natural images, storage requirements, the extent of processing, how the image will be output for use, and so on.

Representing Black-and-White Images

Aside from its spatial coordinates, each pixel contains one or more numbers that measure its value on some scale for its physical medium. A black-and-white photograph represents the reflected intensity of objects in the scene—what we perceive as the relative brightness of the reflected light. To digitize such an image, we must convert the intensity of each sampled area to a single, precise value. As you may recall, this is called **quantizing.** Again, it is important to keep in mind that the process of measurement only approximates the value of the original analog signal. That we are always restricted to a finite range means that absolute precision is impractical. Even real number values with fractions would be subject to some loss of accuracy due to approximation and rounding errors forced on us by finite precision. In fact, integers are often used for pixel values because they are more convenient to store and process.

The range of values designated to represent the measuring scale is the **dynamic range.** For example, deciding on the dynamic range for digitizing a black-and-white photograph translates to how many possible

(a) (b) (c)

FIGURE 11.4

A digital image of a building exterior is sampled at different resolutions. At the highest resolution (a), the details of the building are clear and sharp. In (b), the image begins to show signs of "jaggies"—the jagged look caused by rectangular pixels depicting curves and angles. Details are also beginning to blur. Finally, in (c), at the lowest resolution, individual pixels are clearly visible. Detail and depth are lost entirely.

levels of intensity we would use to measure and represent the image. Dynamic range is usually expressed by its binary precision, that is, the number of bits needed to store each pixel value. For instance, an intensity scale of 0 and 1 would represent all levels of intensity as merely black or white; this is commonly called a **binary image** because it requires only one bit per pixel. Consult Figure 11.5 for an example. **Bitplanes** refer to the depth of bits required for representing the image. A binary image has a depth of 1 because the entire image can be encoded by one bit per pixel. It is also common to refer to the number of bitplanes as the **depth** of the image, for short.

Intensity images with a greater dynamic range are called **grayscale images** because the intensity values represent different degrees of brightness as shades from black to gray to white. Figure 11.6 illustrates how grayscale images are represented. Like resolution, we normally prefer greater dynamic ranges for the highest-quality images. But, the choice of dynamic range for grayscale images also affects the amount of storage needed to represent them. Sixteen shades of intensity, for ex-

FIGURE 11.5

*A photograph of an attentive student is digitized as a binary image with a dynamic range of 2. As the close-up shows, each pixel is either dark (0) or bright (1). Thus, the entire image may be represented by a single bitplane—one bit per pixel. (The image was digitized using a process called **halftone screening.** As you can see from the close-up, different shades are simulated by patterns of dark and light pixels. At the proper scale, these appear as different shades of gray.)*

72 = 01001000

FIGURE 11.6

The photograph in Figure 11.5 is digitized as a grayscale image with a dynamic range of 256. This means that pixel values may represent a range of 256 different shades of intensity from bright to dark. In binary, 8 bits are needed to store this range. A close-up of the image reveals rectangular pixels of varying intensities. The isolated pixel has an intensity value of 72. The inset shows how the bitplanes would be encoded to represent this pixel value.

ample, would require four bits per pixel, while eight bits per pixel would accommodate 256 intensity levels. The increase in dynamic range from four to eight bits per pixel would, of course, double the size of the image file. Thus, images having the same resolution could vary significantly in file size, depending on their depth. Figure 11.7 shows the same original image with different bit depths. Just as resolution has trade-offs, greater dynamic range yields greater fidelity while increasing demands on both storage and processing time.

FIGURE 11.7

Home on the range—dynamic range, that is. A grayscale digital image is quantized at four different levels of dynamic range. In (a), the image has pixels in the highlights and shadows that span nearly the full range of 256 levels. In (b), this range has been compressed to only 16 levels. Yet to the naked eye, (b) appears only marginally different from (a). Compressing the range increases image contrast but also creates some false shadows. However, comparing the two shows that human vision is not very sensitive to a wide range of shades. In (c), the range is only 4 levels. Shadows are flattened, and false contouring is even more evident. Finally, (d) is a binary image having only 2 levels of dynamic range. (In this instance, (d) is a simple binary image without the benefit of halftone screening. Notice how flat this image appears compared to the halftone screen illustrated in Figure 11.6.)

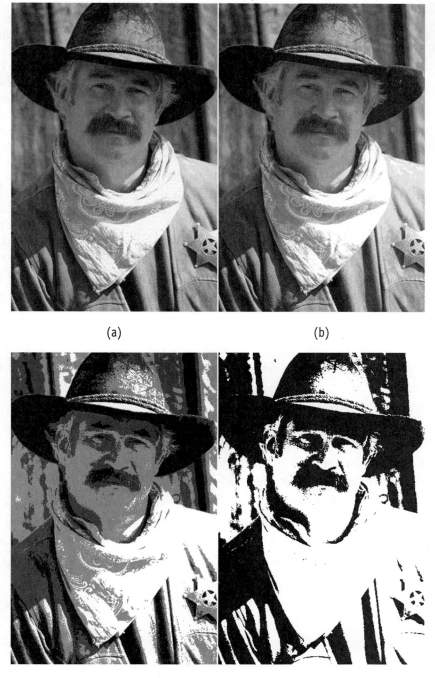

(a)   (b)

(c)   (d)

Representing Color Images

Digitized color images have a variety of applications, too. Unlike gray-scale images, though, each pixel in a color image contains a set of ordered values rather than a single number. The ordered set of values uniquely identifies a specific shade of a color or hue. Several systems are employed to represent color in digital images.

A very popular one is the **RGB color system,** which divides the color signal into three channels: red (R), green (G), and blue (B). A **channel** is a component of an image that may be manipulated separately, but that is combined with other components to constitute the complete image. The RGB system is based on combining additive primaries to produce color mixtures. Figure 11.8 depicts the RGB color space. As you can see, at its origin—when all three primaries have a value of 0—the point is black. On the other hand, when the primaries have maximum values, the resulting mixture appears as pure white. A mixture of (1, 0, 0) is pure red, (0, 1, 0) is pure green, and (0, 0, 1) is pure blue. The cube also reveals other major hues; for example, magenta is (1, 0, 1). The opposite of pure magenta is pure green. Note how magenta and green occupy opposite corners on the RGB color cube. Other color mixtures have similar relatives with RGB primaries, too. Understanding something about RGB color space does have practical consequences. For instance, to reduce the amount of magenta in an RGB color image, you could add or increase green values in it. We will return to these ideas later when we consider the process of color corrections.

The RGB method of representing color images is popular because it is very similar to the way in which color display devices work. As we saw

FIGURE 11.8

The range of mixtures based on the additive primaries of red, green, and blue can be plotted in a three-dimensional space. Each visible color maps to a point whose coordinates are measured on the red, green, and blue axes. At its origin (0, 0, 0), the point is black; at (1, 1, 1) the point is pure white. Theoretically, the color space forms a cube in which all visible colors may be plotted.

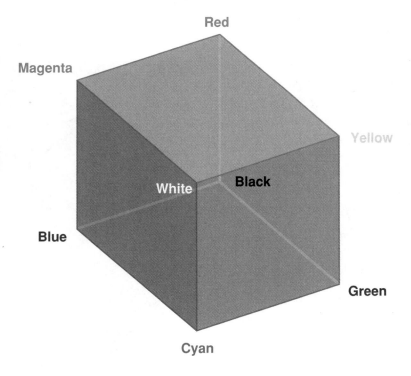

RGB Color Cube

FIGURE 11.9

The image (a) is a close-up of a crystal-clear cup filled with orange juice framed by sun-bleached columns and set against a deep blue sky. This digital image is actually composed of three primary color channels: red, green, and blue. Each of the channels is shown separately so that you can see how much of the resulting color is contributed by these individual primaries. The red channel (b) confirms two obvious points. There is a great deal of red energy in orange juice, but very little in the blue sky. (The juice is very bright, denoting high intensity in this channel; the sky is dark, signifying low intensity.) In stark contrast, the blue channel (d) reverses the relation: low energy for the juice but high intensity values for the sky. The green channel (c) is much more balanced. In fact, it resembles closely a grayscale image of the same subject. This implies that the green channel often conveys a lot of the significant intensity information in a color image—namely, highlights and detail.

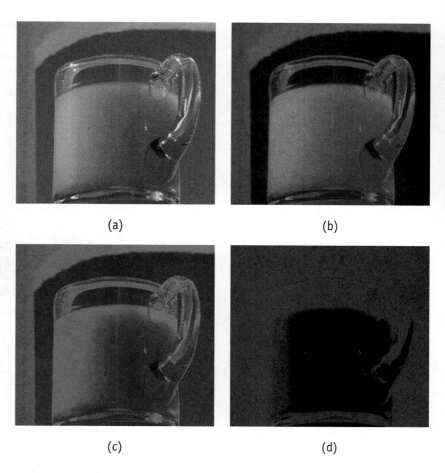

(a)

(b)

(c)

(d)

earlier, the basic picture element in a color CRT is a trio of phosphors that appears to the naked eye as a single color spot. The red, green, and blue electron guns excite the phosphors, and the various combinations of intensities create the perception of a wide assortment of colors to the human eye. An RGB image represents the relative intensities of the three primary components for each pixel. Figure 11.9 illustrates how the RGB channels contribute to create the color image.

Another popular color system used primarily in print media is the **CMY color system.** This system is based on the subtractive primaries of cyan, magenta, and yellow. These primaries are derived from mixing pigments. CMY color is more familiar because most of us have experience mixing paints to create color mixtures. No doubt you can remember elementary school art classes in which you mixed watercolors to produce different shades or hues. Figure 11.10 depicts the CMY color space. In contrast to RGB color, the origin for CMY (0, 0, 0) is achromatic white—that is, no color at all. When the primaries are mixed at maximum levels, the result is black. Mixing cyan with yellow, for example, produces green. The color cube also illustrates color opposites that can be employed to neutralize one another.

As mentioned, CMY images are useful for creating color separations in printing. In practice, however, a fourth channel, K, for black ink (K = blacK) is added to compensate for the problems normally encountered in mixing pigments. Consequently, actual color separations are based on four-channel **CMYK color images.** See Figure 11.11 for an example.

FIGURE 11.10

The subtractive primaries of cyan, magenta, and yellow may also be plotted in a three-dimensional space. In this case, the origin (0, 0, 0) is pure white—signifying no color—and the limit (1, 1, 1) is black when all pigments are combined. CMY space forms a cube, but unlike RGB space, some points cannot be practically reproduced due to the limitations in reproduction technologies.

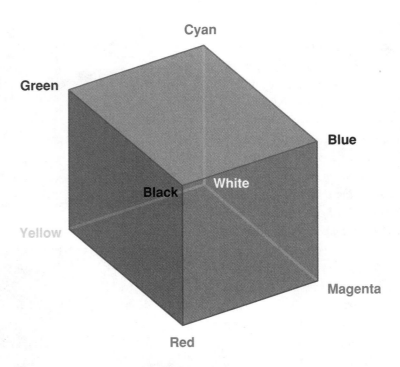

CMY Color Cube

Artists and designers usually prefer a more intuitive scheme for representing color information. A subjective or perceptual characterization of color properties divides them into hues, brightness, and saturation. **Hues** represent the spectral colors and are usually arranged on a standard color wheel. **Brightness** is the relative lightness or darkness of the shade. You may think of it as a series of gray levels from the brightest white to black. Finally, **saturation** refers to the purity or strength of the hue. An unsaturated shade is devoid of hue (or achromatic); pastels are partially saturated; and bright, vivid colors are deeply saturated.

Several systems can capture these qualities. The most common is the **HSB** (hue, saturation, brightness) **color system.** Again, a particular color is represented by an ordered set of three values. Hue is mapped in angular degrees on the color wheel (with primary red usually at 0°). Saturation and brightness are represented by integer values from 0 to some maximum value and denote an ascending scale for these qualities. Figures 11.12 and 11.13 illustrate how color is organized and understood in the HSB system.

Most color systems represent and store digital color images as a composite of several channels. For example, a standard RGB image is composed of three channels; each primary channel stores pixel values with eight bits, yielding 256 distinct values. The result is a total of 24 bits of color depth with an effective dynamic range of millions of potential color mixtures. (To be precise, 256 red values × 256 green values × 256 blue values = 16,777,216 unique color mixtures.) Images like these are often described as **24-bit color,** for short. 24-bit color images have photorealistic quality but require a considerable amount of storage. For example, an 800 × 600 image at a color depth of 24 bits takes almost 1.4 Mb to store. (800 × 600 = 480,000 pixels × 3 bytes per pixel = 1,440,000 bytes.)

(C)

(M)

FIGURE 11.11

The image of a vaulted ceiling and clerestory from a building is the subject for an illustration of CMYK color reproduction. For printing, a single color plate is created for each primary color: cyan (C), magenta (M), yellow (Y), and black (K). Each plate is then printed using the appropriate ink pigment. The color separations are shown individually here. Because we are working with inks, the lack of color is seen as empty white paper. On the other hand, high values of a primary correspond to dense amounts of that ink. When the separations are composed together, they produce a full-color image.

(Y)

(K)

In contrast to composite methods, **indexed color images** reduce the image to a single channel having a maximum depth of eight bits. Each pixel is assigned a number that corresponds to a specific color mixture stored on a palette called a **color lookup table—or CLUT.** Like paint-by-number kits, the encoding is a shorthand method for representing color information that ordinarily would take up a great deal more space. Because indexed color images are limited to 8 bits of depth, the maximum palette size is 256. This means that at most the image can display only 256 different shades of color. In practice, palettes may be reduced even more. As a result, indexed color images often sacrifice fidelity for savings in storage. A process called dithering can help to compensate for this shortcoming. **Dithered shades** are patterns of color that simulate transitional shades or hues. When viewed at normal scale, these patterns suggest colors or shades that are actually unavailable in the CLUT. Figure 11.14 illustrates how an indexed color image is organized. Color palettes

FIGURE 11.12

Hue, saturation, and brightness (HSB) color space is modeled here. (Top) Hues are measured as polar coordinates around the brightness axis. The position along the axis perpendicular to the brightness axis measures the amount of saturation (hue purity) for the shade. (Bottom) The HSB color wheel is seen from overhead. Red is conventionally plotted at 0° at the approximate center of the warm colors. Opposite of red are the cooler colors. The hues are shown here at 100 percent brightness.

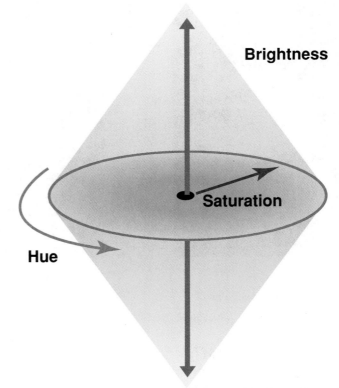

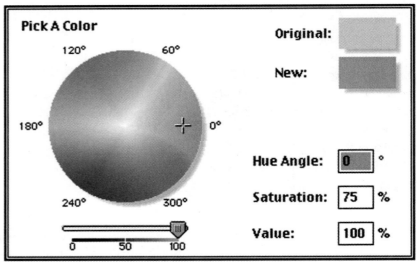

for indexed color images are often based on system colors (that is, designated by your computer's operating system). This is called the **system palette.** In the example in Figure 11.14, the color palette was created by sampling the original colors found in the digitized RGB image prior to reducing it to indexed color. This method of adapting to the original image produces what is called quite naturally an **adaptive palette.** Of course, it is possible to designate the colors for the palette from an arbitrary set as well. These so-called **custom palettes** are used to produce images that conform to desired effects. For example, the Web browser Netscape Communicator employs a custom palette of 216 colors, and images created from this palette can be transported to a variety of computers with predictable results.

FIGURE 11.13

A single hue value is depicted with a series of changing brightness and saturation values.

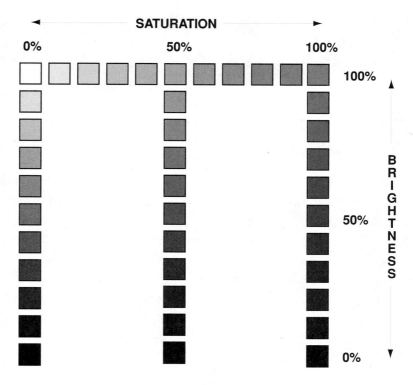

FIGURE 11.14

An indexed color image is composed of pixels from a limited group of colors. The close-up of the image reveals how color mixtures are simulated by dithering. Small patterns of palette colors are used to create the illusion of color shades not supported by that palette. At normal scale, these patterns suggest missing shades. The actual color palette for the image is shown below it.

REPRODUCING COLOR ON COMPUTERS

Perhaps you are reacting to the almost dizzying amount of detail about color and color images. The bottom line is that creating color on a computer system can be a frustrating experience without some knowledge of an assortment of factors involved and their treatments. You may have had the experience of creating an attractive color image on your monitor only to find it garish and ugly when printed on your color inkjet printer. In a related vein, you may have tweaked images for a Web page that look great on your system, but that look very different on another hardware platform. What gives? In general, reproducing accurate color depends primarily on the characteristics of the output device you plan to use. Rarely will your computer video monitor serve as both the medium for creating the image and its ultimate output device as well.

Reproducing Color for Print Devices

Digital color images on color video monitors are displayed using RGB colors, and digital color images produced on color print devices are based on CMYK colors—and never the twain shall meet. A number of factors contribute to their differences.

First, RGB and CMYK color spaces have different effective color ranges, called **color gamuts.**

In other words, in practical circumstances, some colors that are reproducible in one color space are not reproducible in the other. For example, the CMYK color space cannot reproduce bright blue colors that are easily handled by RGB color. (Blue is a natural primary for RGB, but blues in CMYK are based on cyan.) On the other hand, RGB cannot reproduce bright oranges and metallic finishes as well as CMYK. Fortunately, you do not have to be a color theorist to recognize these differences in practical circumstances. Some image processing applications are equipped to warn you of differences in these color gamuts. In Figure 11.15, the user has selected a particular RGB shade from a color selection tool. The color gamut alert—in the form of an exclamation point—warns the user that this color is not reproducible in the CMYK color space.

The difference in media is another factor to consider. RGB color images on video monitors use direct light to display the image. Printed images on paper use reflected light. The paper itself can also contribute significantly to how the reproduced image will look. As you learned in Chapter 5, color inkjet and color laser printers deposit dots of ink on the paper. These dots are extremely small, but as the ink is absorbed in the paper, the

FIGURE 11.15

The exclamation point indicates a gamut warning. This means that the selected RGB color mixture falls outside the CMYK range that is reproducible using conventional printing methods.

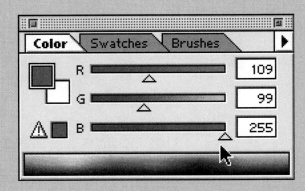

pigment spreads and the effective area of the dot increases slightly. This is called **dot gain.** Different grades or qualities of paper have different dot gains. For example, newsprint has a very high dot gain; high-quality bonded paper has a lower gain. Different color inks behave differently, too. For example, black and cyan have slightly greater dot gain than yellow on the same medium.

Professionals must fuss with all of these details, but the bottom line for casual users is that you can never expect that the appearance of a color image on your video monitor will accurately represent its eventual appearance on the printed page.

Help is available to those who require more precision in specifying colors for printed media. The **Pantone Matching System** is an industry standard for denoting ink colors. Using a set of numbered color swatches, you can pick the colors that you desire and specify them precisely using the Pantone numbers. Printers can likewise reproduce these colors accurately. Some image processing software also provides tools for employing Pantone colors when working with digital images.

Reproducing Color for Other Video Monitors

Not all monitors are created equal. Besides the screen size, resolution, dot pitch, and other assorted performance features, video monitors are tuned to display color images at different settings. The video hardware for your computer system imposes a set of measurements called the gamma correction. **Gamma correction settings** affect the brightness and contrast of images on your computer monitor. In short, color images on monitors with low gamma settings appear brighter compared to those with higher settings. Table 11.1 lists some standard gamma correction settings for popular models used for graphics and imaging.

Obviously, images prepared on a Macintosh, for example, will not look the same when viewed on a PC. On a PC, they will appear darker and usually have lower contrast. On the other hand, images prepared on a PC will look a great deal brighter on Silicon Graphics and Macintosh systems. Take these factors into account when you attempt to produce images for general use on other systems.

Some systems have software that allows you to modify or alter the gamma settings on your machine. These settings can be saved and employed for producing images for cross-platform use.

Reproducing Indexed Color for the Web

Apart from gamma settings, indexed color images and graphics displayed in Web browsers can look very different on different computer systems, too. For example, a color that looks fine on a Web page on one computer system may appear dithered on another system—even when using the same browser software. See Figure 11.16 for an illustration. This occurs because computer manufacturers employ different system color palettes. You will

TABLE 11.1

GAMMA SETTINGS FOR SELECTED SYSTEMS	
Model	*Gamma Standard*
Silicon Graphics	1.7
Macintosh	1.8
Sun Microsystems	2.5
PCs	2.5

recall that a color palette is a list of approved RGB color mixtures that are employed for images displayed using 8-bit or indexed color.

Netscape Communications Corporation has established a special color palette that has become an unofficial standard for displaying indexed color on Web pages. The palette is based on 6 shades each of red, green, and blue. Different mixtures of these shades of primaries produce a total of 216 different colors ($6 \times 6 \times 6 = $

216). Any indexed color image or graphic derived from this palette will appear undithered on a Web page regardless of the hardware platform. Consequently, using the Netscape palette guarantees what is called "browser-safe" color. The Netscape palette is shown in Figure 11.17.

More Information

(a)

(b)

FIGURE 11.16

The shade in (a) is uniform and continuous; if the software cannot reproduce the precise color, it will approximate the shade by dithering instead. In (b), a close-up of the dithered substitute shows clearly how pixels of different colors are arranged in a pattern to create shades of color that fall outside its normal palette.

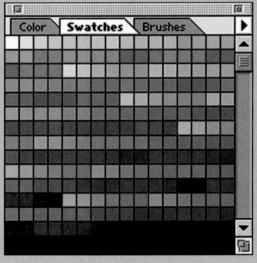

FIGURE 11.17

The $6 \times 6 \times 6$ palette of colors is made by mixing 6 different shades of each of the primaries red, green, and blue. This yields the palette of 216 colors shown here. These are the so-called browser-safe colors because they can be displayed by most browsers without resorting to dithering.

Storing Images

Digital images are converted to files for storage purposes. A number of file formats are available. The most common ones are TIFF, GIF, JPEG, PNG, PCD, BMP, and WMF for Windows, and for Macintoshes, PICT.

TIFF (for **tagged image file format**) is the most widely used bit-mapped image format for both publishing and information interchange. Unfortunately, TIFF image files are not entirely portable between PCs and Macintoshes. The image data are arranged differently in the file, so that opening a PC TIFF file on a Macintosh produces a jumbled picture (and vice versa). Some image processing programs have utilities called filters that can interpret diverse file formats and convert them to others. At any rate, TIFF files must be converted when transporting them from one platform to another. TIFF files support an optional built-in compression, too. Compression reduces the size of the file by encoding it to reduce redundant information. When you save an image as a TIFF, you may choose whether it is stored in a compressed or uncompressed form. (Chapter 15 takes up the topic of compression techniques for a variety of media.)

GIF (graphic interchange format) was developed by CompuServe expressly for transmission of images and graphics over networks. GIF files are based on indexed color, and thus they are generally more compact than full-color image files because they limit the number of possible colors or shades of gray that the image can portray. We learned that 24-bit RGB color images, for instance, represent each pixel with 3 bytes of data: an 8-bit number for each color channel. In contrast, a GIF file stores an image based on a single 8-bit channel that indexes only up to 256 possible colors in a table. GIF files are reduced even more by automatic compression. GIFs are consequently popular for transmission applications. On the Web, for example, many images are stored and transmitted as GIF files. The compromises in dynamic range and color gamut rule out GIF files for other professional applications, though.

A special subclass of GIF images offers features that are also very popular for Web publishing: transparency and interlacing. A **transparent GIF** is an image whose background is rendered invisible by an operation called masking. Thus, transparent GIFs can contain irregularly shaped objects that can be superimposed on background images. See Figure 11.18 for an example. (Find out more about masks later in the chapter in "Focus: Masks and Alpha Channels.") An **interlaced GIF** is an image

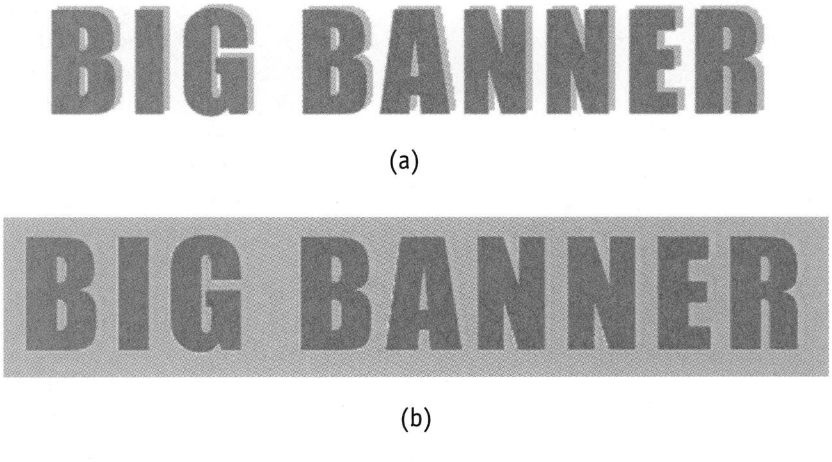

FIGURE 11.18

The text banner (a) was created in an imaging application and saved as a transparent GIF. The white in the background was selected as the "transparent" color. When displayed on a Web page with a different color background (b), only the text is visible. All of the white pixels in the original background are transparent.

(a)

(b)

that is transmitted progressively. On a Web page, an interlaced image appears quickly but in a coarse or low resolution; at first, the pixels appear very large and blocky. In successive steps, these are replaced by better resolutions until the image is displayed at full resolution. Both transparency and interlacing are options that may be invoked when storing an image as a GIF file.

JPEG (Joint Photographic Experts Group) is actually a set of standards for image compression. These standards have been widely accepted across the industry, and files that adhere to them are simply known as JPEG files. Unlike the image compression used in the previously discussed formats, JPEG files are based on lossy compression methods. Lossy compression means that when the image is decompressed—that is, decoded and restored for viewing—there is some data loss from the original. The amount and extent of this loss can be controlled. Usually, it is not noticeable to the untrained eye. Nonetheless, JPEG files achieve their high rates of reduction at some cost to the original image. Whereas GIF files are commonly used for graphics on Web pages, JPEG files are a popular format for 24-bit, full-color images on these pages.

PNG (portable network graphics), pronounced "ping," was developed by Thomas Boutell as a second-generation file format for Web images and graphics. As the new kid on the block, the PNG file format attempts to "correct" the faults and foibles of its predecessors, GIF and JPEG. Like GIFs, PNG images may employ transparency. But unlike GIFs, PNGs offer 8-bit transparency, called "alpha channels." This allows for creating images whose objects have boundaries with relative transparency. Instead of a completely invisible background, the pixels in the background may take on different degrees of transparency. Objects in the image, for example, can have feathered or smoothed boundaries as well as other special effects. (Find out more about alpha channels later in the chapter in "Focus: Masks and Alpha Channels.") PNG images can be stored in several color depths as well. You may choose 8-bit color, like GIFs; 24-bit color, like JPEGs; and even 30-bit color. PNG images may be compressed or uncompressed. Unlike JPEGs, though, the PNG format offers lossless compression versions. Though still relatively new, PNG images are currently supported for inline graphics by both Netscape Communicator and Microsoft Internet Explorer via a special plug-in.

PCD (Kodak photo CD) is a relatively new format that is gaining in acceptance. All PCD images are stored in a compressed form on a CD. Many photofinishing stores can develop your 35mm film and convert the images into PCD format. The scanning is usually high quality, and the service is relatively inexpensive compared to the cost of digitizing images yourself. The Kodak Photo CD comes in two versions: the regular (or consumer) and Pro editions. Each image on the regular edition CD comes in five different resolutions and, therefore, five different file sizes. The smallest is 128 × 192 pixels for thumbnail sketches; the largest is a high-resolution format of 2048 × 3072 pixels for prints up to 7 × 10 inches. Pro Photo CDs have an additional very high-resolution format of 4096 × 6144 pixels.

Both Windows and Macintoshes have their own image file formats. **BMP** is the Windows bit-mapped image format used in painting and graphics. **WMF** is a Windows metafile format, which means that WMF files can actually contain a variety of types including bit-mapped images. **PICT,** for "picture," has long been the standard format for graphic images on the Macintosh. PICT is also a metafile format. PICT images may optionally incorporate JPEG compression. PICT graphics, however, are best restricted for use as on-screen displays and interchanging between Macintosh applications.

These are just a few of the many different file formats that may be employed to store digitized images. To use images effectively in a variety of applications such as printed documents, Web pages, and multimedia, you must choose the appropriate file format for each. Unfortunately, no single file format serves all purposes. Image processing programs, however, can be employed for converting a file from one format to another quickly and easily.

CAPTURING IMAGES WITH FLATBED SCANNERS

A popular choice for imaging in desktop systems is the flatbed scanner. See Figure 11.19. Built like a small desktop copier, it has a flat, glass platen on which source images are placed facedown. Sources are usually photographs, but any object that can be steadied on the surface is a candidate for scanning. A high-intensity light is projected onto the source. The scanner samples the reflective intensities from that source. Its technology is based on **charged-coupled devices (CCDs)**, which are light-sensitive semiconductor arrays. CCDs are also employed in inexpensive video and digital cameras. Color scanners filter the reflec-tive energies into red, green, and blue signals to create an RGB image. The scanner digitizes the image with the help of specialized image capture software that is adapted to your particular system. The software usually comes bundled with the scanner, though you may also purchase image processing software that is equipped with image acquisition utilities compatible with your scanner. For example, TWAIN software (unfortunately, for "technology without an interesting name") is a standard image capture utility available for numerous versions of image processing software and across many hardware platforms.

FIGURE 11.19

A color flatbed scanner is a useful resource for capturing and digitizing photographs, drawings, and artwork.

Entry-level scanners typically have an 8.5-by-11-inch scanning surface with an optical resolution of 300 to 400 dpi with 8- and 24-bit color. This optical resolution may be improved by software that interpolates pixels from scanned ones. The manufacturer often advertises the scanner's resolution with its full interpolated values—800, 1200, or more. Midrange scanners have physically larger scanning areas, better optical resolutions (600 dpi and higher), and higher dynamic ranges, for example, up to 30-bit color. High-end models are intended for professionals and rival drum scanners in both quality and price.

Most scanning software offers the user several choices for the scanned image format. You may choose among several image types including binary (1-bit), halftone, or photographic images. Binary images sacrifice some of the detail of the original but have files that are much smaller. Halftone images (see Figure 11.5) use a screening pattern that produces more detail than the conventional binary images while yielding image files that are equally compact. Photographic images are the standard for digitizing continuous-tone analog images. Most scanners offer a selection of resolutions and dynamic ranges for these types of images.

The choice of format should be determined by how the image will be used. Scanned images that are used as screen shots do not require high resolution because most video monitors have resolutions well under 100 dpi (72 or 75 dpi is usually sufficient). On the other hand, most laser printers can print images from 300 dpi to 600 dpi, and sometimes higher. If you plan to convert your digital images back to film (35mm slides, for example), resolutions of 600 dpi and better are preferred.

A typical scan should be organized according to the following steps:

1 Using the prescan option, take a quick scan of the image or subject to verify its alignment and proper positioning on the platen. Most scanning software also permits you to select a smaller, rectangular area of the scanning field for the resulting image. This is especially useful if you want to isolate some part of the source image. Note that prescanned images are at low resolution, so they will not be good indicators of what the final result will yield. It may be necessary to repeat this process a few times to get things right.

2 Before commencing the final scan, you should select the type of image you desire (1-bit, halftone, photo, color, or black-and-white image). In addition, you should choose a resolution and file type for saving the image.

3 It is also useful to indicate an image size (usually measured in inches). If you know precisely how the image will be used, changing its size now will save you time later. If you don't know exactly how it will be employed, choose a size that is large enough to accommodate most uses. Downsizing images later yields better results than resampling and upsizing them.

Most scanning software has controls for lightness, contrast, and so on. It is usually not a good idea to use these before scanning. Adjustments are better made on the final image after it is scanned and using image processing software that is better designed to handle it. Besides, it is better to retain an original scan that you can experiment on without fear of altering it permanently. This is one of the dividends of digital media.

4 After the image has been scanned and saved, you should inspect it. Most scanned images appear soft or slightly out of focus. It is common practice to sharpen them using a masking operation found in most image processing software.

PROCESSING IMAGES IN THE DIGITAL DOMAIN

Original image

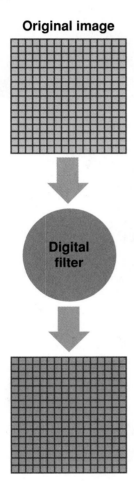

Filtered image

FIGURE 11.20

Digital filtering transforms the original image, producing a filtered output image. Each pixel in the original image is processed by a filter; the resulting value is stored in the same pixel location for the output image. The filter is based on a mathematical operation on numeric values of the image pixels. One advantage of digital filtering is that the filtered image can be saved as a separate file, thus preserving the original for reuse in other applications.

In the process of image capture, a sensor samples properties of the scene, and a digital encoder converts these samples into discrete values that make up the digital image. Capturing an image always involves some approximation—even in the analog domain. For example, a camera is usually unable to reproduce the entire dynamic range of light intensities or hues in a natural scene. Instead, it compresses these to a representative range of intensities by sampling and approximating. This process of selection is called **filtering** and can often be controlled by the photographer's choice of film, exposures, and development techniques.

Digital images may also be processed by filtering. The difference, however, is that digital filtering can be controlled by the computer. The results are much more precise, predictable, and efficient. Because pixels are sets of numbers, digital filtering involves manipulating and transforming these values as defined by a **digital filtering function.** Specifically, the original image is combined with a mathematical function to produce a new filtered image. See Figure 11.20. The filtered image can be saved as a separate file for its intended use. And, because the original image is unaltered by the filtering process, we may retain the original for other uses.

There are two classes of filters: global and local. A **global filter** is one that transforms each and every pixel uniformly according to its filtering function regardless of its location and surroundings in the image. For example, adjusting the overall tonal qualities of an image, such as lightness and darkness, is global filtering. If you wish to lighten it, then all of the image is uniformly affected. On the other hand, a **local filter** transforms a pixel in relation to its surrounding neighbors in the image. For example, sharpening the edges of objects in an image is local or spatial filtering. Enhancing details in the image depends, of course, on where they are located.

Global Filtering

A number of useful digital image processing techniques involve global filtering. We will examine some of the more important forms. Seeing how these processes work will enable you to use them more effectively in your own applications.

Figure 11.21 illustrates a black-and-white image with different brightness and contrast values. **Brightness** refers to the overall intensity of the pixels in the image. Sometimes an image can be improved by either lightening or darkening it. A grayscale or black-and-white image, for example, may be lightened or darkened by simply adding or subtracting intensity values from each pixel.

We can also think of a brightness control function as being mapped by a simple curve. See Figure 11.22. The horizontal axis denotes the value of pixels from the original input image, and the vertical axis corresponds to its adjustment in the output image. Darkening and lightening, consequently, can be envisioned as functions that are mapped by step and inverse-step curves, respectively. Consult Figure 11.23 for examples of the brightness curves used to create the corresponding images in Figure 11.21.

FIGURE 11.21

Washington on Mount Rushmore is pictured. Several filters are applied to a simple grayscale image to illustrate brightness and contrast filtering. The original (a) is lightened in (b) and darkened in (c). The image (d) exhibits higher contrast, whereas (e) has very low contrast.

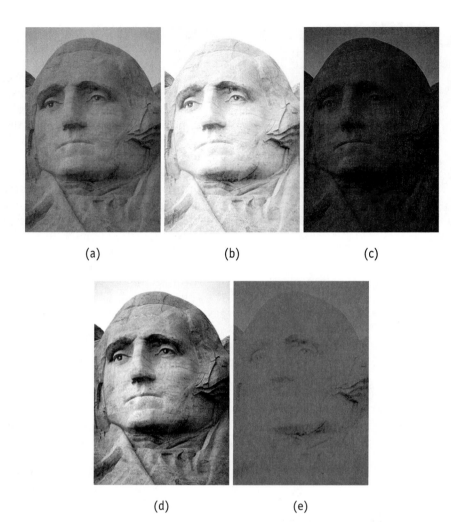

(a)   (b)   (c)

(d)   (e)

FIGURE 11.22

Brightness curves plot global adjustments to the intensity levels of pixels in an image. The horizontal axis measures the intensity levels of the input image (before filtering), while the vertical axis maps adjusted values. The curve or line shown here produces no change in the output image. Sampling several levels, we can see that at the input level of 25 percent intensity, the output is also 25 percent; likewise, an input of 75 percent yields an output of 75 percent.

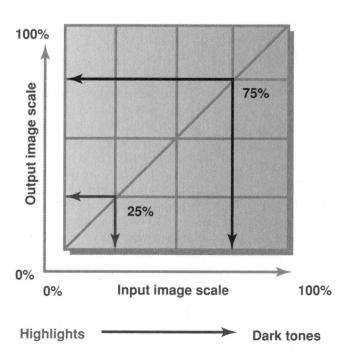

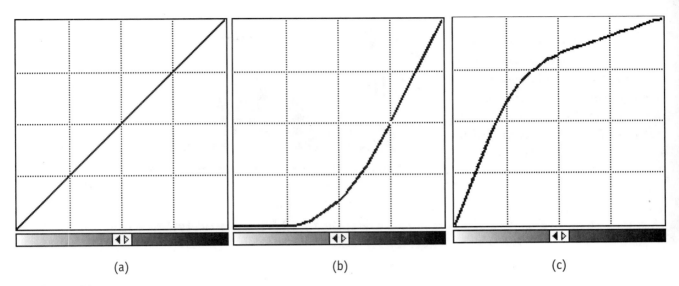

(a)   (b)   (c)

FIGURE 11.23

The graphs illustrate typical curves for adjusting brightness control in a grayscale image. The normal curve (a) produces no change in the output image. The curve (b) increases the intensities of most pixels in the image—especially across the midrange. This causes the image to lighten, as seen in Figure 11.21(b). On the other hand, the curve (c) has the opposite effect. The resulting darkened image can be viewed in Figure 11.21(c).

Contrast is the relative difference between the distributions of lighter and darker pixels in an image. Controlling the contrast in the image is similar to brightness control, though a little more complicated. Contrast is increased when the midtones in an image are redistributed toward the two extremes. In other words, a higher-contrast image has mostly light- and dark-intensity pixels with fewer midtone values. Redistribution of pixel intensity values is illustrated in Figure 11.24. Increasing contrast is mapped by an S-curve function. On the other hand, reducing contrast means to redistribute high and low pixel intensities to the midtones in the image. Figure 11.24 also shows a staircase curve that causes the image in Figure 11.21 to exhibit low contrast.

FIGURE 11.24

The graphs illustrate typical curves for adjusting contrast in a grayscale image. The steep, S-shaped curve (d) redistributes pixels more to the extremes of light and dark. This yields the higher-contrast image seen in Figure 11.21(d). Low contrast results from the staircase curve in (e). Most of the midrange pixel values are reduced to the same intensity level. The result can be seen in Figure 11.21(e).

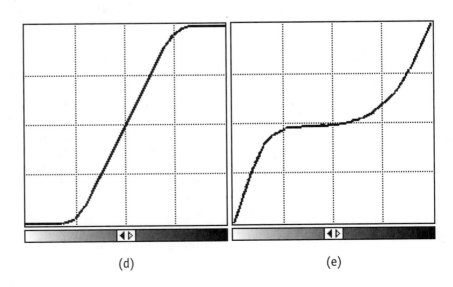

(d)   (e)

FIGURE 11.25

A histogram for a grayscale image plots the distribution of pixel intensity values in the image. The X-axis represents the intensity values from darkest to lightest. The Y-axis plots the frequency of pixels at that value. In this instance, the majority of the pixels are found in two ranges: from 0 to 45, there are nearly 7500 pixels; 16,500 pixels are distributed in the higher-intensity range of 75–175.

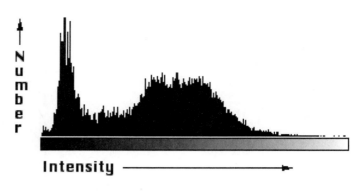

Mean: 88.45   Median: 95
Std Dev: 49.51   Pixels: 27232

Other types of curves can create more complicated effects. To the novice, image curves may seem like mysterious stuff, but a little practice and experimentation make them much more accessible. In fact, manipulating distributional curves is one of the most powerful and flexible tools available in image processing software.

Another useful tool for visualizing the distribution of pixel values in an image is to plot them by a bar graph called a **histogram.** Each point or bar represents the number of pixels in the image that have the same value, for some designated channel. A grayscale image has a single channel and can be represented by a single histogram, as shown in Figure 11.25. RGB color images, on the other hand, would be depicted by three separate histograms, one for each channel. See Figure 11.26.

Histograms are useful for conducting other types of global filtering operations. Thresholding is the most common one. Some color images, for example, may have millions of color values. It is sometimes useful to simplify the content of these images for special effects or perhaps storage considerations. The **threshold** operation chooses an intensity value to serve as a cutoff point for redistributing the pixel values in the image. Any pixel value in the original image that falls below the cutoff value is converted to a single dark value; values above the threshold are redistributed to a light value. The result is a monochromatic—usually, a binary—image, as illustrated by Figure 11.27. Thresholding is a useful technique for isolating regions of interest in the image. It is commonly employed as a preprocessing step in applications such as satellite and medical imaging.

Histogram stretching is another technique for redistributing pixel values using a histogram. It is used to accentuate differences between features of an image. In most cases, the pixel values of an image do not span the entire dynamic range available for it. Sometimes the pixel values may be clustered toward the middle of the range. See Figure 11.28. Think of a uniformly gray image with very little detail. The histogram reveals the darkest and lightest values in the image. These can be effectively replotted by assigning them different minimal and maximal values that extend the full dynamic range. Figure 11.29 provides some of the details. In low-contrast images, the results often exhibit greater detail due to the redistribution of values. Figure 11.30 illustrates how histogram stretching may enhance a satellite image. The process is sometimes called **equalization.**

FIGURE 11.26

A histogram for a color image is composed of three channels: red, green, and blue. The histogram for the image of the cat in Figure 11.1(a) is shown here. In (a), the distribution of pixels in the red channel is portrayed. The figures (b) and (c) depict the frequency of pixel values for the green and blue channels, respectively.

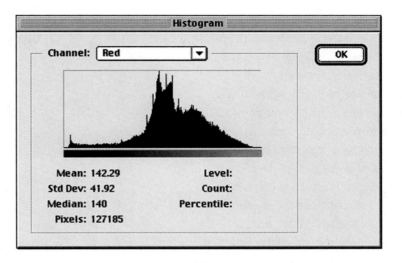

(a)

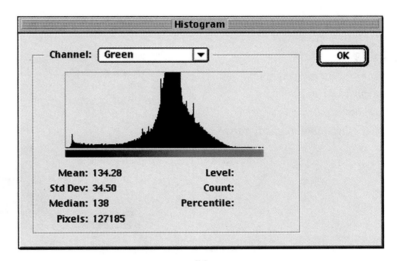

(b)

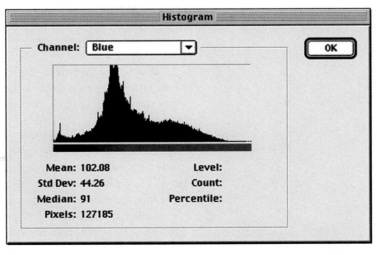

(c)

FIGURE 11.27

The grayscale image of the flower (a) is a good example of an image that has a simple structure of foreground and background. The histogram of the flower (b) confirms this. For the most part, the pixels are distributed into two groups or modes: a tall peak of darker pixels and a large group of pixels around the middle-to-upper range. Thresholding the image at a point between these two modes should reveal the background and foreground in the original image. In the resulting thresholded image (c), the background is black and the area around the flower is white.

(a)   (c)

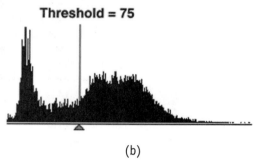

(b)

FIGURE 11.28

The histogram for a grayscale image shows that most of the pixels are clustered around a much narrower segment of the available intensity range.

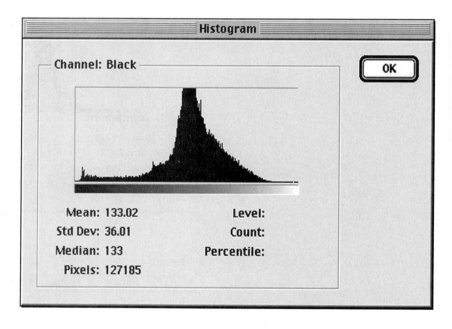

There are instances when the process of capturing color digital images introduces unwanted artifacts. For example, some color images have an unnatural hue that dominates both highlights and shadows in the image. These are called **color casts** and are usually due to an imbalance of primary colors composing the image. The human visual system typically makes compensations for color casts, but the camera does not. Scanners and cameras based on CCD technology often have difficulties with capturing color shadows and deeply saturated colors as well. Global filtering for color correction can treat these problems.

Color correction is the process of correcting a color image by adjusting the distribution of brightness levels for each channel of the color image. For instance, a color image can be corrected for printing by adjusting all four channels (C, M, Y, and K) separately. By compensating for the known properties of printing inks and papers, you can reduce or eliminate the kinds of surprises that often come when transferring images from screen directly to print. Figures 11.31 and 11.32 show how an image may be corrected by adjusting the brightness curves for its four CMYK color channels.

Input image

Output image

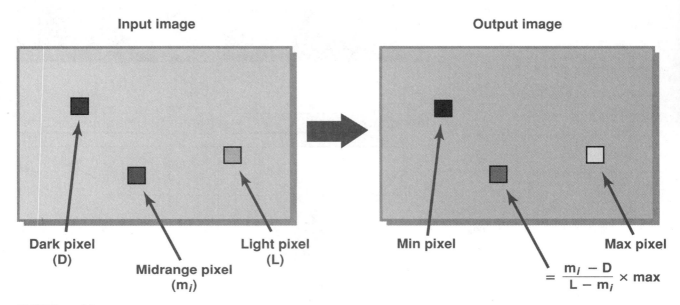

**Dark pixel
(D)**

**Midrange pixel
(m_i)**

**Light pixel
(L)**

Min pixel

Max pixel

$$= \frac{m_i - D}{L - m_i} \times max$$

FIGURE 11.29

Histogram stretching redistributes the intensity or color values of the pixels in the image. The darkest pixels in the image are mapped to some minimum darkest value (Min), while the lightest pixels are made the maximum brightest value (Max). In between these, the midrange pixels are recalculated to distribute them more evenly across the intervening range of values Min and Max. For example, suppose that the range of brightness values for the original input image was 50–175 and we wished to extend it to the full range of 0–255. Given some arbitrary midrange pixel with the value of 100, it would be recalculated (following the formula) to a new value of 170.

FIGURE 11.30

Pictured here is a GOES-8 satellite infrared image of the continental United States. The inset shows a portion of the image after applying histogram stretching to it. The cloud structures exhibit details much better because of the extended range of intensities visible.

FIGURE 11.31

The original color image (a) of the lake has a decidedly yellow color cast. By adjusting the CMYK channels separately, we can produce an image (b) that appears more balanced. Making these corrections also enhances the contrast of the image as well.

(a)   (b)

FIGURE 11.32

Shown here are the individual curves employed to produce the "corrected" image of the lake in Figure 11.31(b). Note that the yellow cast is removed by not only decreasing the amount of yellow energy (c), but also increasing its color opposite, cyan, as shown in (a). The contrast of the image is increased by working with both the magenta (b) and black (d) channels.

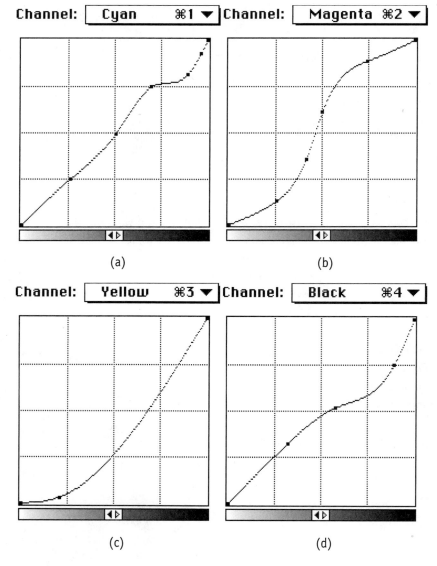

Because a digital image is represented by numeric pixel values, it is a simple matter to filter an image producing its "negative" by reversing its scale. This process is called **inversion.** This is often useful to highlight details of an image that would otherwise be difficult to read, as illustrated in Figure 11.33. Likewise, color negatives can be inverted just as

FIGURE 11.33

The typed text box (a) is inverted (b) for a more dramatic effect.

(a)   (b)

easily. Figure 11.34 shows how a color negative digitized from a film scanner can be quickly inverted as a normal color image without the need to produce a photographic print and then digitize it. Many newspapers and magazines use this time-saving technique for preparing photographic images for press.

As you can see, most of the global filters discussed so far involve directly modifying the intensity values of an image or color channel in that image. Just as intensity values may be redistributed in a digital image, it is also possible to alter the hues of an image. For example, the hue value for each pixel can be calculated from its RGB components. Given a hue value, it is easy to add or subtract some constant from it. The technique is called **hue-shifting** and is used to modify the color makeup of the image. Usually, this is done only for selected areas of an image and can produce color corrections, balancing, or sometimes dramatic (bizarre) effects—depending on the extent of change and the original image, of course. Figure 11.35 is an example of hue-shifting.

Grayscale images can also be transformed by a related operation called **pseudocoloring.** In this process, instead of hues, gray tones are mapped to distinct colors that are selected to produce sharp color contrasts. Satellite and medical imaging use pseudocoloring to produce images that are easier to interpret. As you can see from the example in Figure 11.36, human vision is generally better attuned to variations in hue or color than to variations in sheer intensity.

(a)   (b)

FIGURE 11.34

The color negative (a) is scanned and digitized. Using image processing software, it is a simple matter to invert the image. The result (b) is the photo as it would be normally viewed in a color print.

(a)   (b)

FIGURE 11.35

Turning day into night: The sky in the river scene (a) is selected and the hues are shifted to resemble a nighttime sky (b).

FIGURE 11.36

The image (a) is acquired by the Spaceborne Imaging Radar-C/X-band Synthetic Aperture system from NASA. The data is collected from the space shuttle and shows the Mississippi River just north of Vicksburg, Mississippi. A pseudocolored version (b) of the same image displays its details much more clearly. The green areas surrounding the river are undeveloped forested lands. The shades of red and violet illustrate the variety of crops grown in the farmlands adjoining the river. The crescent-shaped oxbow lakes are abandoned channels formed when the river changed its course.

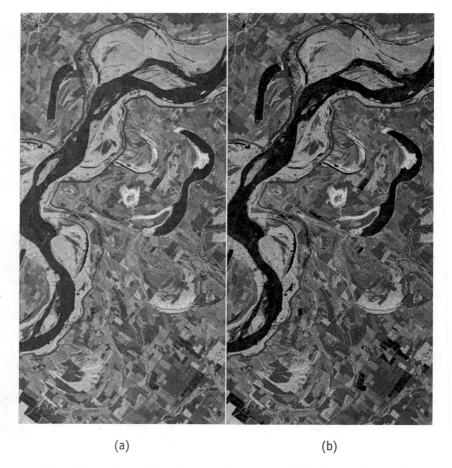

(a)   (b)

Sometimes the original image has too much information to be reproduced effectively by some output process. For example, a color inkjet printer may not accurately reproduce a color image having millions of colors. **Posterizing** can reduce the complexity of both color and grayscale images by mapping similar tones to a select, smaller number of levels. In Figure 11.37, the original image is posterized using four levels; the effect replaces areas having smoothly continuous changes to those with sharper contours. Posterizing can also be employed as a means for producing indexed color images with a small number of shades and colors.

Local Filtering

There are also many ways in which we can apply the process of local filtering to an image based on its spatial properties. Several techniques are available; the most common is that of processing the image using a **mask,** a small, spatially tuned digital filter. The mask serves as a template defining how the pixel will be transformed in relation to its neighbors. The size (how many neighboring pixels are considered) and its offset (how far away these neighbors are from the pixel) determine the resolution of the mask. For example, Figure 11.38 shows a simple 3×3 filter with an offset of 1. These compare the center pixel with each of its eight contiguous neighbors. Each pixel value—including that of the center pixel—is weighted by a coefficient. The sum of these products is divided by a normalization factor (the number in the lower right corner), and the result is used to transform the value of the center pixel in the output image. The complete output image is produced by processing every pixel in the original using the mask or neighborhood filter.

Figures 11.39 and 11.40 provide two illustrations of how a local filter might affect a given pixel. Figure 11.39 depicts how a simple averaging filter might convert a center pixel to a value that resembles its surroundings more closely. Figure 11.40 gives an example of a filter that reverses this effect. A mean removal filter accentuates the center pixel's differences with its neighbors.

A number of useful local filtering operations can improve and enhance, or simply modify, images to produce desired effects. We will survey the most common types, explaining how they work and their uses.

FIGURE 11.37

The sailboat photo (a) is posterized to four shades in (b).

(a)   (b)

FIGURE 11.38

A 3 × 3 mask captures the local neighborhood of eight nearby pixels arranged around some center pixel. Assuming an offset of 1, the neighbors would be the eight contiguous pixels nearest the center pixel. The change to the value of the center pixel is calculated by summing the products of the nine pixel values and their corresponding coefficients. The sum is divided by the normalizing factor to fit it into the expected dynamic range and reset to minimal or maximal values, if necessary.

FIGURE 11.39

The averaging filter adjusts the center pixel to a value that better resembles those of its eight neighbors. In (a), we see how a bright pixel among several darker pixels will be smoothed or averaged to a value that more closely resembles its neighbors. In (b), the actual pixel values are shown along with the computation.

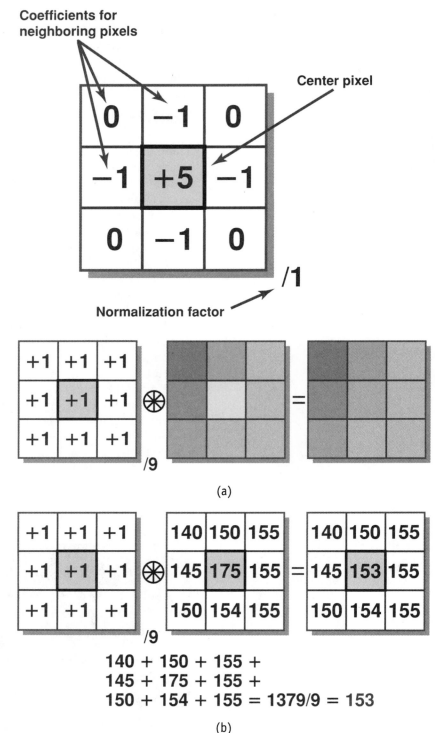

Coefficients for neighboring pixels

Center pixel

Normalization factor

(a)

140 + 150 + 155 +
145 + 175 + 155 +
150 + 154 + 155 = 1379/9 = 153

(b)

Adjusting the contrast in an image can sometimes improve the visibility of details in the image. Another method to achieve this end is called **sharpening,** which accentuates pixels that are situated at boundaries between lighter and darker tones. Thus, a greater contrast is induced, but only at the boundaries between differing regions in the image. A number of standard sharpening filters are available. Figure 11.41 depicts one based again on a simple mask for a 3 × 3 neighborhood.

FIGURE 11.40

The mean removal filter yields the opposite effect of the averaging filter shown in Figure 11.39. The intensity of the center pixel is increased or decreased depending on the amount that it varies from its eight neighboring pixels. In (a), we see how the same center pixel from the previous illustration will be brightened. Again in (b), the actual pixel values are shown along with the computation that produced this result.

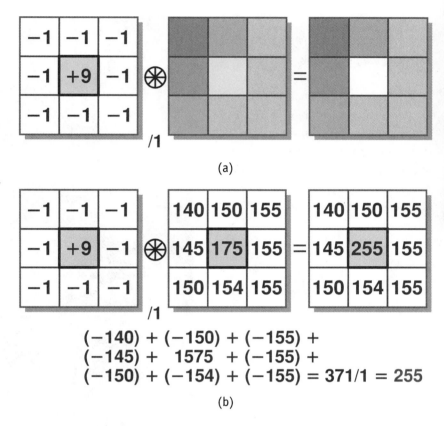

(a)

$$(-140) + (-150) + (-155) +$$
$$(-145) + 1575 + (-155) +$$
$$(-150) + (-154) + (-155) = 371/1 = 255$$

(b)

FIGURE 11.41

Pictured here is a basic 3 × 3 sharpening filter. When applied to an image, the filter sharpens the image by darkening darker pixels at the boundary of one or more lighter pixels or, conversely, lightening lighter pixels among darker neighbors. A pixel, however, that is similar in intensity to its surroundings will change very little, if at all.

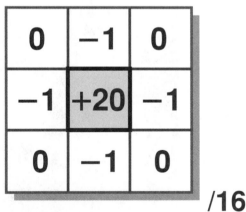

/16

Noise in a digital image refers to pixels whose variation or difference from their surroundings is unexpected and unexplainable. In the imaging process, noise is injected into the original signal in a number of ways; for example, it is contributed by electronic components, poor sampling rates, artifacts of the sensor, and so on. One way in which the effects of noise can be minimized is by blurring the image. **Blurring** is the opposite of sharpening in that the contrast between neighboring pixels is reduced; boundaries are smeared or softened. An averaging filter (shown earlier in Figure 11.39) is one method for implementing a blurring filter.

The images in Figure 11.42 illustrate the effects of alternately applying sharpening and blurring to a given image. In either case, the extent of the effect can be controlled by the choice of masks as well as size and resolution or offset of the neighborhood. Some software

FIGURE 11.42
The original image (a) is filtered using an averaging filter (shown in Figure 11.38) and a sharpening filter (from Figure 11.41). The averaging filter can be employed to blur or soften the details in the image (b). The sharpening filter accentuates boundaries between regions in the image (c). Notice the halo effect around the edges of the flower where the boundaries have been sharpened.

(a)

(b)

(c)

applications automate the application of sharpening or blurring with the choice of several predefined filtering operations. In some cases, however, it is possible to construct the precise effect that you desire by defining the size, coefficients, and offsets for the mask directly. Figure 11.43 illustrates.

FIGURE 11.43

The custom spatial filtering tool in Adobe PhotoShop can be employed to create spatial filters for varying effects. In this instance, the local filter used to sharpen the image seen in Figure 11.42(b) is shown. The user enters the coefficients for each pixel and sets the scale and offset values. PhotoShop then applies the custom filter to the image.

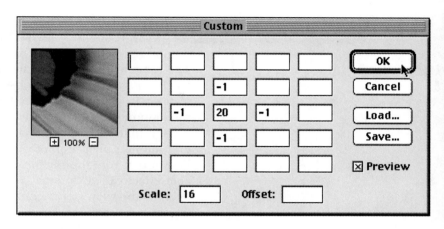

A **Gaussian filter** is a special case of a blurring filter and standard equipment for most image processing application programs. The filter is based on the bell-shaped Gaussian curve, which describes a normal distribution for some population; the curve is useful for plotting a variety of natural phenomena. Most of you are probably familiar with its use for normalizing test grades. When applied to an image, its effect is to soften or blur the image by blending the pixels in a neighborhood defined by its radius. The greater the radius, the greater the effect. Consider the images in Figure 11.44. The same original image is blurred using Gaussian filters with different radius values. As you can attest, the results range from a feathering effect to extreme myopia.

Unsharp masking is a related operation because it typically uses the results of Gaussian filtering, but to sharpen the image rather than blur it. How can this be? The sharpening is the result of a two-stage process

FIGURE 11.44

Pictured here are the results of applying Gaussian blurring. The original image (a) is blurred at three different settings. The image (b) has been blurred with a radius setting of 1.0. As you can see, details in the image are smoothed. Note the differences between (a) and (b) around the eyebrows and the highlights on the eye. The remaining images are blurred even more. The image (c) is blurred at a radius of 2.0; shadows are smudged and details are reduced even more than in (b). Finally, in (d), the radius is set to 5.0. The eyelashes are no longer visible and the eyebrows have been reduced to shadows.

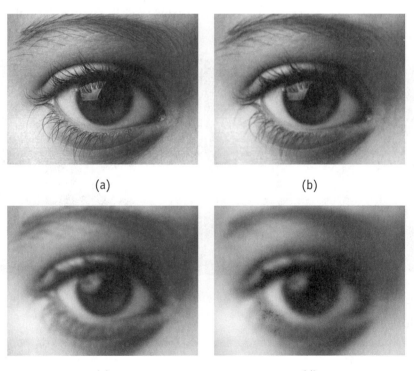

(a) (b)

(c) (d)

called "image differencing." First, the image is blurred using a Gaussian (or, perhaps, another blurring) filter. The blurred (or "unsharp") output image is used as a mask and is subtracted from the original image. The resulting image retains fine detail while improving contrast.

In some instances, the objective is to sharpen or blur an image selectively in a given direction. Consider a practical example. Film and full-motion digital video create the illusion of moving objects by displaying time-varying still images of a scene in rapid succession. However, motion picture photographers using analog methods have long known that very sharply focused individual frames create an undesirable effect called "jitters" when the film is projected. This effect appears to the viewer as discontinuous or jerky motion. If the individual frames are slightly overexposed, that is, blurred by the object's actual motion, the result is one of smoother, more realistic motion. This is called **motion blur**. In the digital domain, animation can also exhibit jitters. You can artificially create motion blur by using a **directional blurring filter** that blurs detail only in selected directions. **Directional sharpening filters** can sharpen an image in a specific direction, too. Figure 11.45 illustrates the effects of both of these techniques for a given color image.

There are times when we are interested in isolating the objects portrayed in an image. One way of doing this is to find the boundaries between regions in the image. The boundaries usually denote where one object ends and another begins. Finding boundaries in an image is called "edge detection." An **edge element** is a sharp distinction in either color or intensity between two adjacent pixels. An **edge** is a collection of contiguous edge elements that form a line or contour. Extracting or enhancing edges then can often highlight objects in the foreground from their background. Edge detection is a very common technique in image processing because it contributes to a variety of practical applications—for example, labeling and measuring regions of interest in an image, identifying objects, eliminating unnecessary image components, and so on.

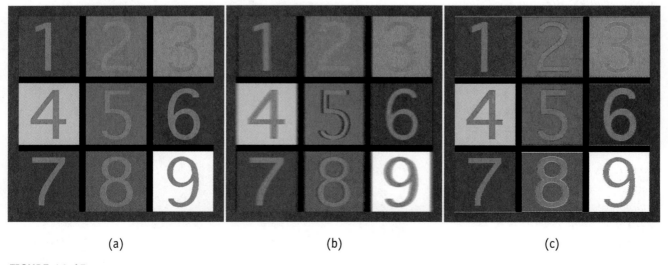

(a)   (b)   (c)

FIGURE 11.45

The original color image (a) is processed using directional filters. In (b), horizontal motion blurring is applied. In (c), directional sharpening is used to enhance the horizontal edges of the image. Notice the embossing effect on the numbers.

FIGURE 11.46

The photo of colored blocks (a) is subjected to a simple edge detection filter. The resulting output image (b) is thresholded and inverted here for printing. In it, we can see the location of the edges or boundaries for the objects in the image. Because edge detectors are attuned to local variations in the image, they also pick up the texture and noise in the image as well as the object boundaries.

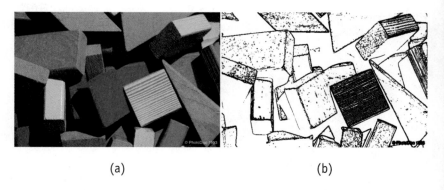

(a)　　　　　　　　　　　　(b)

Edge detection filters are similar to sharpening filters in that they strengthen the values of pixels in areas of sharp difference or contrast. Usually, an edge detector subtracts out the rest of the image, leaving only the edge lines and contours visible. Figure 11.46 illustrates.

Normally noise is misinformation, but noise is not always a bad thing. For instance, you may wish to add a gritty texture to an image. It is possible to simulate the effects of noise by approximating random digital noise. To add noise to an image, pixels in the original image are arbitrarily selected and modified. The extent of the effect depends on both the maximum amount of change allowed and its method of distribution.

There are two types of noise filters. With a **uniform noise filter,** each original pixel in a given area has an equal probability of being altered absolutely; for example, colors may change quite sharply as a result of a random selection. In contrast, a **Gaussian noise filter** induces noise into an image using the normalized distribution of values found within a local area of that image. In other words, the colors or intensities are modified based on their differences with values in that area. Uniform noise filters add "spot" or "speckle" noise effects that are closer to what we normally consider random noise. Gaussian noise filters produce a grainy effect that is more pronounced because they consider the structure of the image in perturbing it. Compare the results in Figure 11.47.

More Information

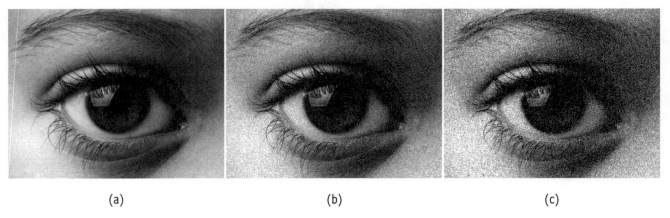

(a)　　　　　　　　　　(b)　　　　　　　　　　(c)

FIGURE 11.47

Adding noise to an image is illustrated. The original image (a) is filtered to add noise artificially. Uniform additive noise, as shown in (b), alters randomly selected pixels with randomly selected values. Even though it is set to the same value, the effects of Gaussian additive noise have a much more visibly grainy effect on the image in (c).

focus

CREATING LINE ART DRAWINGS USING EDGE EXTRACTION

Image processing is not always dedicated to scientific applications. Many of the techniques are equally useful to the graphic artist as well. Even neophytes can create an illustration with special effects by applying several of the techniques surveyed earlier. For instance, a traditional pen and watercolor wash painting can be created from a digital image in several simple steps. See Figure 11.48.

The original is scanned from a color photograph. Several copies of the resulting color image are made. One copy is blurred, posterized, and desaturated to produce the watercolor wash effect for the background. Edge filtering is applied to a second copy. The edge image is inverted to render pen drawing features. When the two images are composed together, they yield the finished product.

Image processing is for the artist, too. In fact, most image processing programs have a number of filters that are designed exclusively for the graphic artist. These filters can yield even more dramatic and interesting effects. As in our example, these methods offer precision, control, and usually significant savings in time compared to conventional techniques.

(a)

(b)

(c)

FIGURE 11.48

The pen and watercolor effect in (c) is created by composing a pastel background superimposed with edges to simulate pen drawing details. The original image (a) is digitized from a color photo. The edge image is inverted, and its levels are compressed to eliminate some of the noise, as seen in (b). The edge image is composed with a copy that has been processed to produce the watercolor wash effect. The result is the finished image in (c).

EDITING DIGITAL IMAGES

FIGURE 11.49

There are a number of methods for selecting an area in an image for editing or processing. Some are quick and dirty; others are more precise. The rectangular (a), circular (b), and free-form (c) selections are convenient but capture an object along with its surroundings. Segmentation (d) and surround (e) selections are based on isolating an object from its background by either similarities or differences. Finally, drawing arbitrary paths (f) can also be employed to create a masking selection.

Filtering affects the overall tonal quality of images, but we often want to process the content of images in specific ways. In other words, our goal is to edit an image just as we might edit a text document for content and style. Fortunately, most desktop image processing software offers a variety of editing tools that make such tasks easier. We will survey some of the basic tools and techniques for editing digital images.

Before you can modify a portion of an image, you must select the area to be modified. This is analogous to other computing applications. For instance, in text processing, to edit a block of text, you must first select that block. In image processing, **selection** means to identify the area of the image precisely—that is, the pixels that make up that area. Most imaging applications allow you to define the selected area by creating an outline surrounding it. Selection tools make the task easier by providing automatic outlines of various shapes. For example, a rectangular tool allows you to select square or rectangular areas of the image. This, of course, would include all pixels within that area. Circular tools are similar. A free-form tool accommodates irregularly shaped selections, but it also selects any background elements inside as well. For finer selections, some additional options are usually available. A surround tool permits you to identify the edges or boundary of a distinct object against its background. A segmentation tool is used to select a contiguous area in which all the pixels have the same characteristics. Drawing a path is the most flexible. A path is a closed figure composed of connected lines, curves, and points. Examples of each of these categories are shown in Figure 11.49.

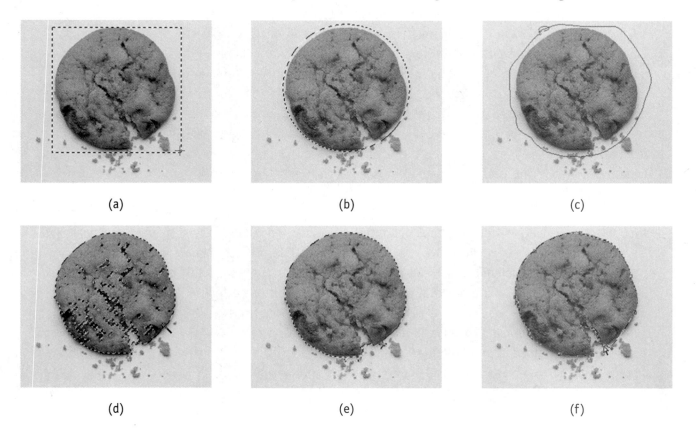

(a) (b) (c)

(d) (e) (f)

The goal of selection, of course, is to edit or modify a specific area of the image to produce some desired effect. The selected area is also called an image **mask.** The terminology is derived from a standard method employed by artists. An artist might wish to color a specific portion of an image without affecting the rest of it. The conventional technique of masking involves placing a clear vellum sheet over the picture and using a knife to cut out a shape that corresponds to the area that will be retouched. The sheet acts as a mask that protects the rest of the image while the cutout portion can be repainted or colored. Digital masks work the same way. Once you have selected an area for editing, any changes or modifications to the image will take place only in the active area; the rest of the image is unaffected.

MASKS AND ALPHA CHANNELS

In the digital domain, the technique of image masking has actually evolved from computer-generated graphic animation. An animation—much like motion picture film—is composed of a sequence of still images called "frames" that is displayed at a rate that is fast enough to fool us into thinking that we are seeing real motion. Each of the frames in an animation portrays the moving objects as changing position in small increments. Much of the rest of the scene, however, does not change. Consequently, from frame to frame only a small portion of the computer-generated image may be different. This could mean a lot of work for both the computer artist and the machine that displays the animation. The artist would have to redraw each frame even though only a small portion of it has changed. The computer system would have to load, process, and display each individual, full-size image even though there is a great deal of redundancy among them.

To solve this problem, computer animators borrowed a technique from their predecessors. Traditional animated films are created by composing cels with backgrounds. The individual cels are transparent sheets on which the principal objects are drawn and painted. The backgrounds represent the portions of the image that change only gradually from frame to frame. Frames are then composed by photographing each cel on top of the background. Digital image masks were devised to function much like these cels in conventional animation. In applying this technique, each image contains both the pixels that make up the principal objects in it as well as additional information that defines its mask. The mask prescribes which parts of the image are opaque (that is, where the objects are visible) and which parts are transparent (where the background can show through). A digital mask is stored as a separate channel along with the rest of the image. Figure 11.50 illustrates a simple, 1-bit masking channel for its accompanying image. This is precisely how transparent GIFs work. A background color set is selected to serve as the basis for masking the image.

While simple, 1-bit masks are very compact and add little to the storage requirements for a digital image, they do have some undesirable side effects. As you can see in Figure 11.50, the

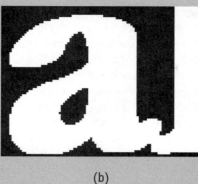

(a)   (b)   (c)

FIGURE 11.50

The text image is shown in (a) along with a 1-bit mask in (b). In the mask, black pixels denote transparent or unaffected portions of the image. These pixels are subtracted from the active image and will not show through. White pixels in the mask denote the opaque portions of the image. These pixels belonging to the active image will be visible when the image is displayed. When the masked image is composited with a colored background (c), it is easy to see how the mask works. At the same time, we can see that a 1-bit mask defines very sharp edges around the object, which can introduce the artifact of aliasing, that is, jagged edges due to the shape and configuration of the pixels that compose that edge.

edges around the masked objects are coarse and blocky. Jaggies are evident. A special type of digital mask was introduced to remedy this problem. Called **alpha channels,** these are 8-bit channel masks that contain relative degrees of transparency (or, conversely, opacity). Instead of a "yes/no" procedure for defining the pixels of the mask, alpha channels can differentiate up to 256 levels of transparency/opacity for each pixel.

Figure 11.51 shows the same image in Figure 11.50 but this time masked by an alpha channel that blurs or softens the edges around the objects. The aliasing effect of the jagged edges is noticeably reduced. Some image processing software programs allow the user to define and save alpha channels for arbitrary images. As mentioned, the new Web image format PNG also incorporates alpha channels for transparent PNGs.

(a)   (b)   (c)

FIGURE 11.51

The same image from 11.50(a) is masked using an 8-bit alpha channel (b). In this instance, the edges are feathered or softened by applying varied degrees of opacity. When this masked image is composited with a colored background (c), the effects of aliasing are reduced.

Normally, selections are temporary; they persist only as long as the selected area is active. Some image processing applications allow you to save or store your selections. These may be reinstated when needed. This feature can be very useful—especially when the selected areas have irregular or complicated shapes. The technique of selection is fundamental for effective image editing. It is a skill that depends on some basic know-how but is developed only with practice.

Natural images are often too natural: They show us in all our native glory—blemishes and all. In contrast, the world of desktop image processing can be just about whatever you desire.

Photographers, of course, have known about retouching photographs for over a century. **Retouching** is the selective modification or editing of the content of an image. Usually, retouching involves adding, deleting, or altering objects in the image. For digital images, however, retouching is much more precise and predictable. We will inspect two general categories: painting and cloning methods. The actual range of retouching methods available will depend entirely on the application software consulted.

One way that a photograph can be altered is to draw or paint over it. In computerese, this form of image editing is called, not surprisingly, **painting.** The tools that you employ to paint are based entirely on this metaphor. A brush tool permits you to apply a selected pattern over an area, much like brush strokes. A pencil tool does the same, but produces thinner lines. An airbrush tool works much like the standard brush except that the boundaries are softened or smudged. An area-fill tool applies the pattern or color to an entire selected area. Keep in mind that these tools can add colors and patterns to an image.

In text processing, we saw that it was possible to copy and paste a particular selection to another area of the document. We can do the same in digital images. **Cloning** is the method whereby a selected area of an image is duplicated and pasted as many times as we desire to any image. Some applications make this simpler by way of cloning tools that allow you to repeatedly paste a pattern throughout. Figure 11.52 illustrates how cloning can be used to repair an area of an image where an object was deleted. Even if cloning tools are not available, judicious applications of the standard copy-and-paste technique will work as well.

Another editing technique, and a close cousin to retouching, is image compositing. An **image composite** combines components from two or more images into a single, seamless image. Figure 11.53 offers an example of the technique. The basic idea is a simple one: Select the portions of the images that you wish to combine and paste them together as needed. Many of the special effects seen in motion picture films, for example, have been produced using digital image compositing methods. Creating effective image composites can be a difficult and timely process.

The current generation of image processing applications has made this work a great deal easier by the implementation of image layering. An **image layer** is a separate image channel that ordinarily contains an object that can be manipulated separately from the background scene. Layering is actually a generalization of image masks in which a portion of an image is visible while its surround is rendered transparently. A layered image usually contains two or more separately masked images that are combined in a specific order. Objects in the

FIGURE 11.52

Now you see it; now you don't. The brightly colored balloons are the chief feature of the original photograph (a). But if we wish to focus the viewer on the children, we can eliminate the balloons and retouch the digital image. First, the balloons and strings are masked and removed from the original image, as shown in (b). Sections of the surrounding tree texture are cloned to fill in the blank area. The result (c) would fool all but the expert eye.

(a)

(b)

(c)

topmost layer are always visible; succeeding layers are revealed only to the extent to which transparency from preceding layers allows it. Figure 11.54 illustrates the concept of layered images. Because the layers are independent, they can be rearranged as desired. This makes the

FIGURE 11.53

Image compositing combines elements from one image with those of another. In the example, the sunflower in (a) is selected from the original image and combined with a different scene whose original is shown in (b). Creating an image composite takes several steps. First, the flowers are selected by masking out the blue sky as shown in (c). The actual mask is shown in the blue channel in (d). The single flower is then extracted as shown in (e). Finally, the two elements are composited as separated layers producing the resulting image shown in (f).

FIGURE 11.54

The composited image from the previous example in 11.53 was created using two different image layers: the flower and the wheat field background. Suppose that we desire to reposition the flower in the scene. This is easily done by moving the position of the flower layer as shown in (a). Other effects can be employed on each of the layers. In (b), filters are applied to each layer to produce different textures and visual effects.

(a)

(b)

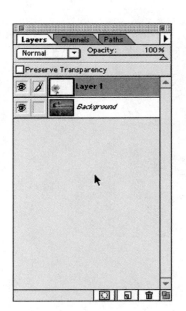

FIGURE 11.55

Working with layers is made easy using the Layers palette in Adobe Photoshop, a popular image processing software program. Layers may be selected individually for editing or combined. The layers may also be rearranged, if desired.

task of image compositing simple, indeed. Each of the image components can be copied and pasted as a separate layer. The layers can be combined and arranged as needed. Figure 11.55 demonstrates how a popular image processing program coordinates working with layers. Along with its conveniences, there is a cost. Layered images take up more space in memory than nonlayer-ed ones. A layered image can be reduced to a simple image by "flattening" it.

Our last class of image processing techniques is that of geometric transformations, which are ways in which we can alter the organizational or structural content of the digital image. These are somewhat different from standard editing methods, but they are useful, nonetheless, for creating special effects. Because a digital image is composed of discrete numeric pixels, we have a precise and accurate map of its structure. Using geometric operations to transform this structure is the basis for the technique called **digital warping.** It is possible, for example, to change a person's facial expression by simply selecting certain points in the original image and warping them in the output image. A warp function describes the geometric transformation that is performed on the coordinates of the pixels affected. These functions may describe simple linear displacements of pixels or complicated curvilinear transformations. Fortunately, many image processing applications make this easier by offering both standard warp functions as well as automating homemade displacements. In the latter case, the user selects key or guiding pixels and indicates a displacement path; the software thankfully does all of the math. See Figure 11.56 for some examples.

Morphing is a natural extension of warping. Whereas digital warping transforms a single image, **morphing** is a series of incremental transitions between two different images. This effect was used first extensively in the feature film *Terminator 2* and now has become a staple of cinema special effects.

Desktop versions of morphing programs are readily available. Suppose that you want to morph a picture of your roommate to that of a werewolf. You would match key features such as the eyes, nose, and mouth between both images. After selecting the rate of change and

(a)   (b)   (c)

FIGURE 11.56

The original image (a) is geometrically transformed by digital warping. In (b), a pinch function remaps an elliptical portion of the image around the center. The result appears as if the pixels were plotted onto the inside of a sphere or curved surface. The shear function (c) remaps the image pixels along a curved vertical axis. In this instance, the pixels on the right edge of the image are smeared horizontally to fill the vacated portions of the original.

other parameters, the software calculates a series of successive images that are based on incremental or gradual warps from predecessor to successor. When played back in rapid succession, the effect produces the illusion of a more continuous transformation. *Voilà*—your roommate is a werewolf!

Social Themes

Is Seeing Believing?

Even though the technology of photographic images is scarcely more than 150 years old, we have come to accept and depend on it in fundamental ways. For many, a photograph serves as a record of reality and proof that something indeed happened.

Of course, there are strong reasons why we treat photography and photographs with a special status. Drawings, paintings, and photos are types of images. An image, after all, is always an image of something. In this respect, it denotes its subject. An image, however also depicts its subject: It represents how the subject appears or looks. Photographs, on the other hand, have an important feature that distinguishes them from drawings and paintings. The manner in which the subject is portrayed in a photograph is presumably caused by the subject itself—that is, the light reflected from that subject. We talk about photos capturing the moment because they, in fact, do capture the light reflected at that moment. We can take a picture of a particular cat only because cats exist. A painter may employ an actual model but doesn't necessarily have to. The artist can use his or her imagination to conjure the scene depicted in a drawing or painting. For that reason, a drawing of a unicorn would hardly be considered proof that unicorns exist.

Accordingly, we assume photographs to have an imprint of reality that is not afforded other types of images. This assumption is not always warranted. The history of photography and photojournalism is marked by a number of cases that challenge the credibility of the photograph as a record of reality and the truth.

Manipulating the Subject Matter

Mathew Brady, the famed Civil War photojournalist, staged the subject matter of some of his most powerful images. For example, transporting or rearranging the corpses on the battlefield perhaps created a more effective visualization than simply recording the soldiers where they fell. See Figure 11.57. Such practices are deceptive, though not as damning as staging hoaxes. In other words, the objects depicted in the image are very real; the photographer has simply added a dramatic effect to convey what the original scene could not (presumably).

FIGURE 11.57
The battlefield photo of Gettysburg was taken by Timothy O'Sullivan, an assistant to Mathew Brady. The bodies were said to have been rearranged on the field to increase the dramatic effect of the scene. (Library of Congress.)

Brady and his associates are not the only wartime photojournalists who have been accused of manipulating their subject matter. Robert Capa, the prize-winning photographer of three wars, is the center of a controversy over his dramatic "Death of a Spanish Loyalist." See Figure 11.58. The photograph is reputed to have been taken just at the moment a soldier was fatally wounded. Some have questioned the authenticity of this photograph, citing the unlikely odds of capturing such a scene. Unfortunately, Capa was killed by a land mine during the Vietnam War, and the controversy continues.

There has also been some confusion over the authenticity of the famed photograph of the marines raising the flag over Iwo Jima. The photographer has insisted that the shot was spontaneous, unlike an accompanying one that was clearly posed.

Authentic or not, all of these examples point to the fact that we are troubled or concerned if we find out that a dramatic photograph proves

FIGURE 11.58
This photo of a Spanish Loyalist first appeared in Life *magazine in 1936. Wartime photojournalist Robert Capa captured the shot just at the "moment of death." However, his claims have been disputed by some. It is said that this was staged instead. (Copyright, Robert Capa, Magnum Photos, Inc.)*

to be staged or manipulated. This could be true only because we naturally assume that photographs represent the world as it is and not as fiction—or even dramatic enhancement.

Crafting Reality with a Computer

As you have learned, computers offer a wide assortment of tools for manipulating both the tone and content of photographic images. Moreover, modern application programs have made many of the techniques of digital image processing accessible to even the most casual of users. It is a simple procedure to change the tone of an image by manipulating its intensity levels and color. Retouching or editing images is also a routine procedure with imaging applications. Likewise, you have seen that it is possible to create completely fictional images by image compositing.

Yet, as we have seen in other instances, the advantageous use of technology can also foster its abuse as well. The photographer or photojournalist armed with a desktop computer and digital imaging software can ply his or her trade with added capabilities and efficiency. On the other hand, it is also possible to manipulate images or their subject matter in ways that would not have been possible in conventional settings.

The O. J. Simpson cover from *Time Magazine* on June 27, 1994, is a famous example of "massaging" an image to influence our perception of reality. Simpson had been arrested and charged with the violent murders of his estranged wife and a companion. The *Time* cover presented the L.A. police mug shot of Simpson. His face appeared dark, sinister, and brooding. Quite unexpectedly, though, *Newsweek* magazine published precisely the same source photo for their cover. The *Newsweek* version, however, showed a very different-looking Simpson—the same face and shot are evident, but the dark and brooding look is missing. Later, *Time* disclosed that their photograph had indeed been "enhanced" but did not admit to any wrongdoing in manipulating the image.

This incident and others sparked a popular debate about the ethical standards of journalism in allowing photographs to be altered by artificial means. Several professional societies for photojournalists have since responded to this erosion of the public trust with codes of ethics intended to curb abuses. The apocryphal horse, however, may already be out of the barn. Once the public has lost faith in the accuracy of photographic reporting, the task of restoring its credibility is a difficult one.

The evolution of the digital computer as a medium for capturing and processing images has posed challenges to our assumptions about the veracity of the photographic record. We have been conditioned to think of photographs as a special class of images. Unlike drawings and paintings, for example, photographs reveal reality and not just perceptions. It is often said that "pictures never lie." Whether this was ever true, the world of digital imaging strongly challenges such claims. As you have learned, a digital image can be processed in a variety of ways. Its content, tone, and composition can be altered quite easily using the powerful tools available in image processing software. For this reason, some courts no longer accept photographs as irrefutable evidence; we would be wise to follow suit.

Social Themes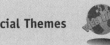

S U M M A R Y

Digital images are pictures that are sampled and quantized for storing on and processing by a computer system. A digital image is composed of pixels that are defined by a two-dimensional location in the image and a set of values that denote image attributes such as intensity or color. Picture resolution is the number of pixels that compose the digital image.

Images can be binary, grayscale, or color. Several popular systems are used for representing color in digital images. A file format acts as a container for a digital image. There are numerous file formats, and few are compatible. The same image can be stored in different file formats, yet one file may be unusable on a particular system or with a specific application. It is important to save images using the appropriate file format.

Digital images may be processed using digital filters; these are mathematical functions that transform the numeric values of pixels and their distribution in the image. Global filtering modifies the image uniformly by adjusting each and every pixel according to its filtering function regardless of the location of the pixel. Local filtering, in contrast, transforms a pixel based on its relation to neighboring pixels in the vicinity.

Editing a digital image involves modifying a portion of the image. Like other digital methods, image editing is based on properly selecting image components: the area of pixels that requires editing. Retouching takes two basic forms, painting and cloning. Image compositing is another useful editing technique. Some image processing programs offer geometric transforms such as digital warping and morphing. These modify the image by displacing pixels to different locations in the same or succeeding images.

In this chapter, we have examined how digital images are created, stored, and processed. The real power and flexibility of desktop image processing are only suggested here. Armed with the basic concepts presented, you will be able to explore such applications and learn to exploit their capabilities for your own uses.

PROJECTS

1 Using an image processing program, experiment with different resolutions for a selected grayscale image. Standard screen resolution is between 72 and 75 dpi. Most printers have a resolution of 300 dpi or sometimes higher. Convert the image to 72 dpi. What is its image resolution (pixels across × pixels down)? What is the image size (inches across × inches down)? How big is the file (in bytes)? Print out the resulting image to a laser or inkjet printer. Repeat the procedure with several other settings: 200 dpi, 300 dpi, 600 dpi. Record the results for the questions cited above for each setting.

Compare the printed results. How do they look? Do you see any relation among the image resolution, quality, and file size? Explain.

2 Compare the images displayed on the Project Web page for this problem. Each image is represented in both full-color and indexed color forms. Examine them for quality and appearance. Evaluate the versions. Does one look better than the other? Is there no appreciable difference between the two? Can you derive any general conclusions from these observations? Explain.

3 Select a color photograph that is suitable for rendering as a digital image. Using a scanner, digitize the image. Perform any corrections that you think are needed to the image brightness, contrast, color balance, etc. Convert and save the image as either a GIF or JPEG file. (Consult the Project page for links to freeware and shareware software for file converters, if none are readily available.) Post the image on a Web page. View the image through a Web browser on a Windows computer system. Compare the same page when viewed using the same browser but on a Macintosh computer. Do they appear the same or different? Describe your observations.

4 Take the same scanned photograph from the previous exercise and save the image in sev-eral file formats: as a BMP, a TIFF, a JPEG, and a GIF. Compare the file sizes for each of these versions. Are they the same or different? How do you explain any observed differences?

5 Investigate more about digital filtering of images on the *Exploring the Digital Domain* Web site. Besides more information about the process of filtering, there are images on which you may experiment. Choose from among several filters and settings and observe the results.

6 Perform a Web search for sites that contain information about the impact of digital methods on the practice and profession of photojournalism. A few sites post codes of ethics for photojournalists. What do the codes have to say about the practice of photo manipulation?

Projects

Key Terms

adaptive palette	color cast	dynamic range
alpha channel	color correction	edge
aspect ratio	color gamut	edge detection filter
binary image	color lookup table (CLUT)	edge element
bitplane	contrast	equalization
blurring	custom palette	gamma correction setting
BMP image file	depth	Gaussian filter
brightness	digital filtering function	Gaussian noise filter
channel	digital image	GIF (graphic interchange
charged-coupled device (CCD)	directional blurring filter	format) image files
cloning	directional sharpening filter	global filter
CMY color system	dithered shade	grayscale image
CMYK color images	dot gain	histogram

histogram stretching

HSB color system

hue

hue-shifting

image

image composite

image layer

indexed color image

interlaced GIF

inversion

JPEG (Joint Photographic
   Experts Group) image file

local filter mask

mask, image

morphing, digital

motion blur

noise

painting

Pantone matching system

PCD (Kodak photo CD) image
   files

PICT image file

picture resolution

pixel (picture element)

PNG (portable network
   graphics) image file

posterizing

pseudocoloring

quantizing

retouching

RGB color image

RGB color system

saturation

selection

sharpening

system palette

thresholding

TIFF (tagged image file format)
   image file

transparent GIF

uniform noise filter

unsharp masking

warping, digital

WMF (Windows metafile) image
   file

QUESTIONS FOR REVIEW

1 What is the chief difference between natural digital images and graphics?

2 What is a pixel?

3 How is picture resolution related to the quality, size, and storage requirements of a digital image?

4 In what practical circumstances is knowing the aspect ratio of an image important?

5 How is dynamic range related to the quality, size, and storage requirements of a digital image?

6 Distinguish between the various categories of digital images: binary, grayscale, and color.

7 Compare and contrast the different color models employed for representing and storing color images: RGB, HSB, and CMYK. What are the chief uses for each?

8 What is the difference between a digital image and its file type? Review the basic image file types. What are the basic uses or applications for each file format?

9 Describe the basic steps involved in scanning and digitizing an image using a flatbed scanner.

10 What is digital filtering? What is the chief difference between global and local digital filtering?

11 What is the difference between brightness and contrast control?

12 What are image curves? How are they employed in image processing?

13 What is a histogram? How is it employed in image processing?

14 What is a threshold? What applications employ image thresholding?

15 What is histogram stretching (equalization)? When would this technique be useful?

16 What is color correction? How is it acheived?

17 What is pseudocoloring? What are its advantages?

18 What is a local (spatial) filter mask? How are these masks employed in image processing?

19 Compare and contrast blurring and sharpening operations. How are they local operations (as opposed to global filtering)? How do they differ?

20 What is edge detection? What are its uses or applications?

21 Review some of the tools that can be used for image selection. What is the difference between selection and masking?

22 What is an image mask? How are alpha channels a generalization of masks?

23 How do painting and retouching an image differ from filtering processes (global and local)?

24 What is image compositing?

25 What is digital warping? Morphing? How do these techniques differ?

The old adage states that "a picture is worth a thousand words." And, even though it might make everyone's Top Ten Clichés List, there is still a great deal of truth to it. First, there can little doubt that we are a species dominated by vision. Only about 10 percent of what we learn is based on audible information, while more than 80 percent is derived from visual information. Not only are we visual-centric creatures, we are also strongly biased toward pictorial information as well. Archaeological evidence testifies that our ancestors were creating illustrations and cave paintings long before they were writing language. Our children learn from pictures much earlier than they learn to read. Indeed, studies have shown that for adults, pictorial information is easier to absorb and is retained much longer than verbal. Depending on pictorial representation is not a mark of illiteracy either. Scientists and mathematicians have often documented the importance of pictures and images for discovering and understanding important concepts. For that matter, the higher one climbs up the corporate ladder, the greater the likelihood that decisions will be derived from data depicted in graphs, charts, and tables.

It should be no surprise then that efforts at representing information pictorially with computers occurred very early in the history of computing. These early attempts at exploiting the graphic capabilities of computers were extremely primitive by today's standards, but they did pave the way for the wealth of tools, features, and applications that we now take for granted. Computer-generated imagery, or computer graphics, has contributed richly to the ways in which we employ computers for both work and play. In this chapter, you will learn more about how the computer can be exploited to create, store, and deliver images and illustrations for a variety of uses.

OBJECTIVES

- *How the computer creates, stores, and displays graphic images*

- *How painting programs allow the user to control computer graphic primitives*

- *The tools and features that are found in drawing and illustration graphic applications*

- *How software helps to automate creating images with 3-D projections and animation*

CHAPTER 12

GRAPHICS: CREATING IMAGES

Vasily Kandinsky, *Blue Circle*, 1922. Solomon R. Guggenheim Museum.

MAKING PICTURES WITH COMPUTERS

In the last chapter, a digital image was defined as a picture that can be stored in, displayed on, and processed by a computer system. You learned that there were two general classes of digital images: natural and artificial. Natural digital images are typically digitized from analog sources such as photographs, video, X-ray tomography, satellite sensors, and so on. In this chapter, we will focus on the second category of digital images, computer-generated imagery or computer graphics. **Computer graphics** (or **graphics,** for short) refers to digital images that are artificial in that they are created exclusively by computer processes. Computer graphics is integral to most of the ways in which we employ our computers. For example, graphical user interfaces (GUIs) are the primary medium by which we operate our systems. These interfaces naturally depend on graphic images that are displayed on our video monitors. The icons, windows, pointers, gadgets—and even text—populating our screens are all composed and managed by graphic processing. It should be no surprise then that using a computer to generate graphic images has a rich tradition.

History of Computer Graphics

The first electronic computing devices produced output on paper and punched cards. These media were used primarily for text and numeric data. In the early 1950s, computers were programmed to display images primarily as a hobby or recreation for their programmers. The first graphic output devices were oscilloscopes, devices commonly used for visualizing electrical signals. In England, for example, the Mark I computer at Manchester University was programmed to play checkers and display the game pictorially on a screen.

The Whirlwind project in the 1950s at the Massachusetts Institute of Technology (MIT) was the first attempt to employ graphic imaging for serious use and as an integral part of its computer system. The navy had contracted the MIT team, headed by Jay W. Forrester, to design and build a computer that (among other uses) would control an in-flight trainer for its pilots. To work in this capacity, the system had to respond appropriately to conditions in real time. As a result, the Whirlwind computer became the first device designed for real-time computing. ("Real-time computing" refers to processing that occurs in actual or real time. In other words, input data is generated from events happening currently, and the processing results are often employed as feedback to control the system.)

Eventually, the navy lost interest in the flight trainer, but Forrester and his colleagues persuaded the air force to fund the Whirlwind as a prototype for an early warning defense system. This application also exploited its real-time computing powers. Specifically, the Whirlwind would be used to process radar telemetry from several stations and inform a human operator as to the whereabouts of aircraft in the area using graphic images. Screen displays of radar images had been used before, of course. The trick in this instance was to create a system that could process information from several stations and portray it in a manner that would be useful to the human operator at the controls.

The computer used a CRT screen to display a map of the area and automatically converted radar data to points plotted on the map that

FIGURE 12.1

A vintage photograph of the SAGE defense system in operation is shown. The operator is aiming the light pen at the display screen to track specific objects in view.

showed their geographic positions. The system was also interactive. The operator could use a light pen to point to any objects depicted on the screen. The computer would sense the light source and identify the object. Additional information about speed and direction would then be displayed. The light pen could likewise be used to target objects and request Whirlwind to calculate interception courses. The prototype was demonstrated in 1951. The project was eventually converted to production in 1958 as the SAGE (Semi-Automatic Ground Environment) defense system. SAGE computers were part of the air force's defense systems even into the 1980s. See Figure 12.1.

Combining graphics with interactive computing was explored by another MIT researcher, Ivan Sutherland. As mentioned in Chapter 1, Sutherland developed the first interactive drawing program, SketchPad, in 1962. The user sitting at the console's CRT display, armed with a light pen and a small box studded with push buttons, could draw simple shapes on the screen. Sutherland had conceived SketchPad as a tool for engineers. SketchPad eclipsed other efforts at drawing with computers because it added the power to manipulate the figures after they were drawn. Not only could the user create simple shapes such as lines, polygons, and arcs, but drawn objects could be moved, rotated, enlarged, or reduced on the screen.

General Motors developed a graphical application specifically for aiding the design of automobiles. This was the first graphical **computer-assisted design (CAD)** system. Dubbed **DAC-1** (for *D*esign *A*ugmented by *C*omputers), it was introduced in 1964. DAC-1 pushed the envelope in power and features; for example, it could reproduce the complex curves favored by auto designers of the day. The importance of GM's graphical system was more influence than achievement, though. The company's interest in using computers for drawing and design spawned the growth of the computer graphics industry in America.

Making Pictures with Numbers

As we discussed in Chapter 2, computers represent and store all forms of data as numbers. How, then, is it possible to create illustrations and images using numbers? Interestingly, the fundamental basis for computer graphics was discovered well before Whirlwind, SketchPad, and DAC-1. French philosopher, mathematician, and inventor of the Pascaline calculator, René Descartes was one of the first to develop the principles of *analytic geometry* in the seventeenth century. He showed that points, lines, curves, and surfaces on a plane can be expressed numerically. A point, for example, can be precisely identified by two numbers specifying its coordinates on a plane. See Figure 12.2.

Using this system of coordinates, we can easily map a line as the set of connected points within its span. Each of these points can be represented physically by a small dot on a CRT screen. Provided that the screen coordinates are finely measured (that is, the spots are close enough), the connected dots will appear as a line. We can create a closed figure as a collection of dots whose locations are likewise defined by this coordinate system. See Figure 12.3 for examples.

Each of the points on this two-dimensional plane is called a **picture element,** or **pixel** for short. A graphic image can therefore be represented by a collection of pixels. Besides their location, pixels also have

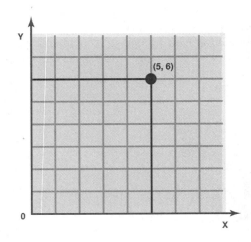

FIGURE 12.2

Cartesian coordinates specify the location of objects on a two-dimensional plane. The location of a point, for example, can be measured from the origin (0, 0) where the two axes cross. In this instance, the point is fixed at the coordinates X = 5, Y = 6, or simply the pair (5, 6).

FIGURE 12.3

Picture elements—or pixels—are the screen's equivalent of a point. Each pixel is represented by a small spot on the screen and is defined by its location based on horizontal and vertical coordinates. As shown here, a line (a) would be a collection of connected pixels; a closed figure (b) would be created by a collection of connected lines.

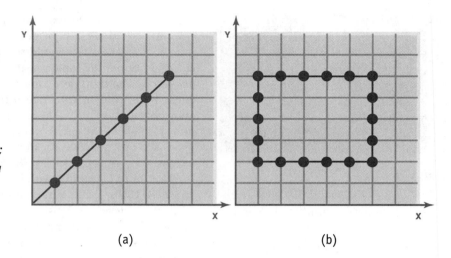

(a)   (b)

attributes. For example, in a simple black-and-white image, pixels are either black or white. We could use the convention of specifying the attribute white as 1 and black as 0. And, given that the extent of the image's coordinates were known, we could represent the image in memory as a sequence of bits that defines that plane. In reconstructing the image for display, the limits for the coordinates could be deduced from the picture resolution. For example, the rectangle picture has a resolution of 7 × 7, so the image would be reconstructed by displaying the bit pattern of 7 pixels each, row by row. See Figure 12.4.

This type of graphic is called **bit-mapped,** or sometimes **raster, graphics. Rasterizing** refers to the process employed by most video displays that translates bit-mapped images to the scan lines of the screen. The term *bit-mapping* denotes the manner in which the image is represented and stored in memory. A simple black-and-white image, as in the previous example, requires only a single bit to denote the pixel's attribute. Consequently, 1 bitplane is needed to store this image. On the

FIGURE 12.4

In a binary image, each pixel is either black (0) or white (1). Consequently, the rectangle shown in (a) would be represented as a string of bits as shown in (b). Because the resolution is limited to 7 × 7, only 49 bits would be needed to store the image.

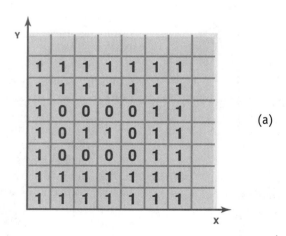

(a)

11111111 11111110 00011101 10111000
01111111 11111111 1...

(b)

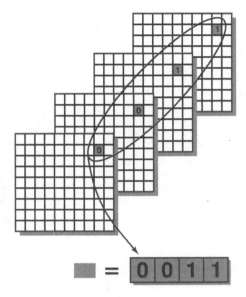

FIGURE 12.5

Most graphic images are composed of pixels that represent shades of gray or color. Unlike binary images, these pixels store values larger than a single bit. In these cases, the image can be thought of as a series of planes. Each bitplane stores a single bit for each corresponding pixel. In this illustration, a grayscale image is composed of 4 bitplanes. The shaded pixel is represented by the 4 successive bits. With a range of 0 (black) to 15 (white), its value is 3, which would be a dark gray.

other hand, suppose that we wished to create an image depicting shades of gray, say, 16 different shades ranging from black to white. A single bit would no longer be sufficient to differentiate these shades. Instead, 4 bits ($2^4 = 16$) would be needed for each pixel to code its specific value from the 16 possible shades. Consequently, 4 bitplanes would be required to represent the pixels for such an image. Figure 12.5 illustrates these ideas.

Bit-mapped color images are handled in a similar manner. As you learned in the previous chapter, an RGB color image, for example, is composed of three separate primary color images: red, green, and blue. When these primary images are combined, the colors mix to form a natural color image. (This principal, of course, is exploited by the standard color monitor.) A common format represents each primary pixel with a dynamic range of 256 intensity shades. This means that each primary color pixel has 8 bitplanes ($2^8 = 256$). The combined color image is stored in 24 bitplanes (3 primaries × 8 bitplanes = 24 bitplanes); this is usually called simply 24-bit color.

Bit-mapped graphics is a brute-force method for creating computer images. The location and attributes of each pixel must be fully specified. Memory cells are used to denote the positions and features of pixels directly. In short, the atoms of a computer's memory (cells) are used to store a facsimile of the atoms of a graphic image (pixels).

Descartes' interest in analytic geometry, however, would not have been for such inelegant applications. Mapping lines, curves, and figures in Cartesian planes can be specified much more concisely. For example, a straight line may be defined by the coordinates of its two endpoints. A closed figure, such as a rectangle, could likewise be specified by a set of coordinates that denote its vertices. See Figure 12.6.

Better still, we can map lines and curves on a plane using equations. For example, $x - 2y = 0$ maps a straight line; $x^2 - 2y = 0$ defines a simple curve. Consult Figure 12.7 for illustrations.

Using equations to represent plane figures is not only more concise than bit-mapping, but it offers the distinct advantage of being resolution independent. **Resolution independence** means that the images do not depend on the characteristics of a specific device for proper display. A coordinate system is arbitrary. Its scale can be set to any measure, coarse or fine. But bit-mapped images depend almost entirely on the scale and resolution in which they were created. Faithful reproduction of these

FIGURE 12.6

Plotting each point on a line (a) means storing information that is redundant. Instead, a more elegant solution is to store the endpoints for a line. A closed figure (b) is composed of several lines. Each of its endpoints can be stored to represent it. Both the line and rectangle are recreated by simply connecting the endpoints.

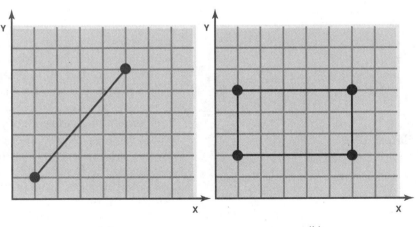

(a) (b)

FIGURE 12.7

An even more elegant solution (and certainly the one that interested Descartes) is to represent a line by an equation that expresses the relation of X and Y coordinates. The equation (a) describes a straight line that is plotted for several values of X and Y. Curves can also be represented by equations. Here is a simple curve shown by (b) and also plotted for several values of X and Y.

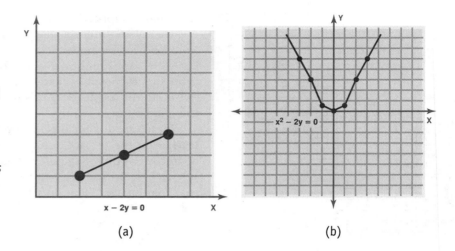

(a)   (b)

images requires accurate portrayals of both. On the other hand, figures defined using equations do not. These may be represented using any consistent scale and resolution. Storing and representing images by mathematical equations or descriptions is called **vector graphics** or, sometimes, **object-oriented graphics.** These images are recreated for display by calculating the points that compose them. (For an illustration of these ideas see the Focus box entitled "Drawing Text.")

Whether using a video display or a printer, graphic images are almost always converted to two-dimensional output. In spite of this fact, an important characteristic of a graphic application program is whether it recognizes a third dimension. Those that do typically specify a third axis, the Z-axis, which allows the user to scale the depth of objects. See Figure 12.8. In reality, of course, depth is only simulated using perspective projection. Thus, points measured along the Z-axis are, in fact, plotted in two dimensions. Nonetheless, a significant advantage over programs that recognize only two dimensions is that these projections are plotted automatically.

Programs of this sort create what is called **three-dimensional** or **3-D graphics.** Applications that require the user to account for perspective effects are called **two-dimensional** or simply **2-D graphic programs.**

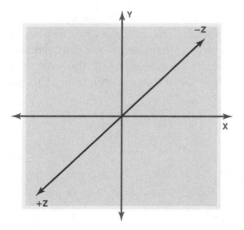

FIGURE 12.8

A third axis is added to treat objects plotted in three dimensions. The Z-axis, which is projected from front (+) to back (−), measures the depth of objects in three-dimensional space.

Most desktop systems are fitted with raster graphic displays. This means that regardless of the approach used for representing and storing a graphic image, it must be bit-mapped (rasterized) for display on such devices. Still, bit-mapped and vector graphics are important concepts to understand because they distinguish two very different approaches for graphic software. In other words, as a user, you will need to choose between two different styles of creating graphic images. On one hand, **painting programs** offer complete control over a graphic image down to the last pixel; they are typically bit-mapped graphic applications. The user is provided a set of tools and features that treat an image fundamentally as a collection of pixels. On the other hand, **drawing, illustration, animation,** and **rendering programs** incorporate the advantages of vector graphics. These applications are often dubbed **object-oriented graphic applications** because the user creates objects that serve as components of the image. Objects may be lines, curves, patterns, textures, and even surfaces. These programs vary in the complexity of both their features and products. As a group, they offer the user the advantages of flexibility and power. These dividends, of course, are due to the abstractions they exploit for creating and manipulating graphic objects.

Storing Graphic Images

As you learned in the previous chapter, all digital images are converted to files for storage purposes. There are a number of common file formats for graphic images—in addition to many of those discussed in Chapter 11. Graphic images may be stored in most of the file formats introduced earlier; for example, it is common to find graphics stored as TIFFs, GIFs, PNGs, BMPs, WMFs, and PICTs. (See Chapter 11.) Besides these, PCX, CGM, EPS, DXF, QuickTime, and AVI are also popular formats.

PCX is the native file format for PC Paintbrush, a popular painting program for Windows computer systems. PCX files contain bit-mapped or rasterized graphics; a number of other graphic programs for Windows can open and save images as PCX files.

CGM (computer graphics metafile) was developed by ISO and ANSI, which are two standards committees composed of industry professionals. It was intended as a general-purpose or metafile format that would support a variety of graphic image types and features. As a metafile format, it may store either bit-mapped or vector graphic images. A wide assortment of graphic applications can read and save images as CGM files.

EPS (encapsulated PostScript) is the standard file format for storing and exchanging image files in professional printing. EPS is actually a metafile format, which also means that a variety of types of images may be stored as an EPS file. In most cases, however, EPS files contain data based on the PostScript Page Description Language. (See the Focus box entitled "Drawing Text" for more about PostScript.) PostScript defines text and images using mathematical descriptions that are interpreted by the program reading the file. Images are created and displayed from the commands stored in the file. This makes PostScript a popular choice for representing and transferring vector graphics. Most illustration programs, for example, can read and save EPS files. Desktop publishing programs also handle text and images saved as EPS files.

DXF (drawing exchange format) was developed to store 3-D image information created by the computer-assisted design program AutoCad. Subsequently, it has become a common-denominator file format for many other 3-D graphics and rendering programs. DXF files can typically be transported from one application to another.

QuickTime and AVI are file formats for storing animations. These are actually digital video file formats, but they may be employed for storing a sequence of graphic images that are intended as frames for a computer animation. **QuickTime** is a file format developed by Apple Computer, though it may be used on both Windows and Macintosh platforms. **AVI** is the file format for Video for Windows from Microsoft. Recently, Microsoft has replaced Video for Windows with newer formats, but a great many animations and videos are still produced and stored as AVI files. (You can find out more about digital video in Chapter 14.)

In the next section, we will examine the basic capabilities of painting programs. As you will discover, these offer the type of control that is needed for some tasks. In the following two sections, we will survey object-oriented graphic applications. Drawing and illustration programs range in their sophistication, but fundamentally they are intended for creating two-dimensional graphics. These are the types of images that are commonly printed or displayed. Rendering programs provide tools for conjuring the illusion of three-dimensional images. These images mimic perspective, textures, and lighting conditions to create photorealistic effects. Finally, animation software incorporates a different dimension entirely—that of time. These programs aid the artist in creating moving or animated images with much less effort than conventional methods.

Each of these categories is suited best for specific kinds of work. And, as an informed consumer, your goal is to learn how to match the application to the task.

DRAWING TEXT

Though it may not be obvious, creating text for display on monitors and printed paper is a special case of graphics. The symbols in text are literally drawn by the computer system. Some fonts—that is, text lettering styles—are created using bit-mapped graphic methods. Figure 12.9 shows a text string created by a bit-mapped font shown in two font sizes; the latter is enlarged for better scrutiny.

As you can see from the larger font size, the letters are formed by combining individual pixels. This gives the text a rough, blocky appearance, commonly called "jaggies." When the font is dis-played in smaller sizes, the effect is less noticeable. Enlarging it makes the jaggies more pronounced; too large and its appearance is unacceptable. Another disadvantage is that each of the font sizes must be built in advance for output. If a needed size is not available, it cannot be readily displayed.

In contrast to this method, PostScript is an example of a more abstract method for specifying text that is resolution independent. **PostScript** is actually a Page Description Language (PDL) developed by Adobe Systems, Inc. Instructions for drawing the text are normally stored as an ordinary ASCII text file. When printed or displayed, a PostScript program interprets these instructions and calculates and draws the text to fit the resolution of the output device. See Figure 12.10.

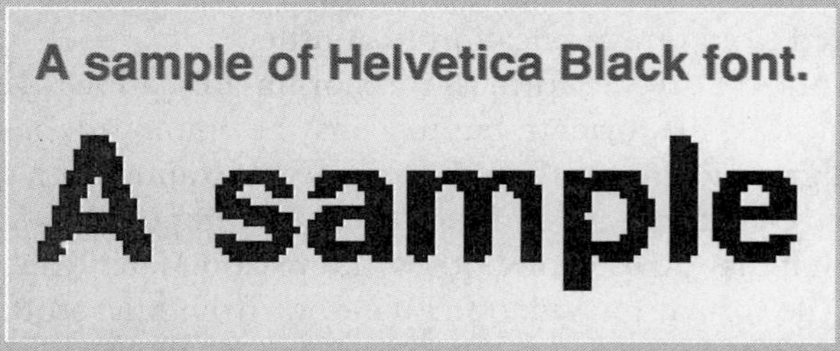

A sample of Helvetica Black font.

A sample

FIGURE 12.9

The font style of Helvetica Black is shown in two sizes: 12 and 60 points. At the smaller size, curves formed by bit-mapped characters appear smooth. However, the enlarged version clearly displays the rectangular shapes that are required to form these curved shapes.

Times New Roman
Times New Roman
Times New Roman
Times New Roman

FIGURE 12.10

A sample of the PostScript Times New Roman font is shown in several sizes. Compare these with the previous example of bit-mapped fonts.

PostScript fonts belong to the class of what are called "outline fonts." These are mathematical descriptions of the font shapes that can be interpolated easily for the font size and fitted to the resolution of the output device (printer or display monitor). In effect, the font is stored as mathematical equations that specify lines and curves for the outline of each character. This outline may then be filled by the display device or printer at its own resolution. See Figure 12.11.

Because fonts are stored as abstract descriptions, any font size can be rendered. On the downside, their display and printing are slower than comparable bit-mapped methods. Because all display is based on interpreting drawing instructions, it does take more time for the extra step of converting to bit-mapped images for output. In spite of these limitations, most systems today employ outline fonts for composing text on the screen and printed page.

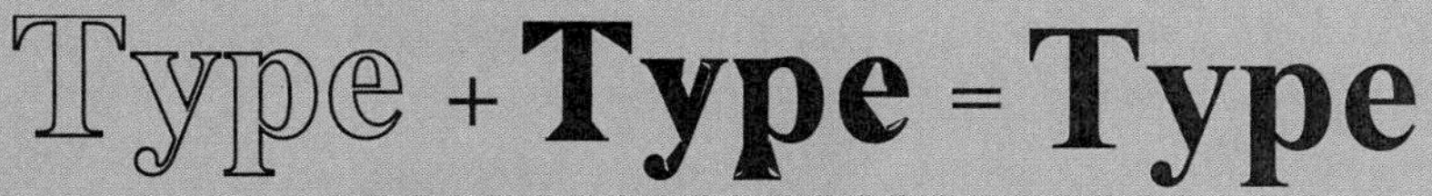

FIGURE 12.11
The outlines for the curved figures that make up the characters of the font are specified by mathematical descriptions. These are filled or merged to form a smoother, less jagged appearance.

Type + **Type** = **Type**

PAINTING PROGRAMS

Painting programs blend 2-D bit-mapped graphics with an interface that mimics brush and canvas techniques used by a painter. In most cases, however, the similarities are enforced more by shared terminology than by feel.

The typical painting program interface divides the workspace into palettes, menus, and canvases. **Palettes** contain a selection of tools, patterns, textures, and colors that may be applied to the images contained within a canvas. The **menu,** of course, stores commands and features that may be selected by the user. The **canvas** is usually a window that reveals at least part of a specific bit-mapped image that has been created or opened from an existing file. Figure 12.12 offers an example from two popular painting programs.

The Image and the Image Canvas

Because painting programs use bit-mapped images, their size and resolution are usually fixed. This means that when you save an image as a file, the image size and picture resolution are determined when you first create it. Later, you may modify its contents but not always its size or resolution. **Image size,** of course, refers to the actual extent of the image, while picture resolution specifies the number of pixels used. The latter is expressed either in two dimensions (for example, 640 × 480) or in density (dots per inch, for example, 72 dpi).

FIGURE 12.12

The Windows bit-mapped painting and imaging program Paint Shop Pro is shown in (a). The interface contains a standard tool palette across the top, along with a color palette on the right. One or more images can be opened for work inside the window area.

The interface for the upscale painting program MetaCreations Painter is seen in (b). Besides an assortment of tools and painting effects, Painter offers the graphic artist a variety of precision controls for working with the digital canvas.

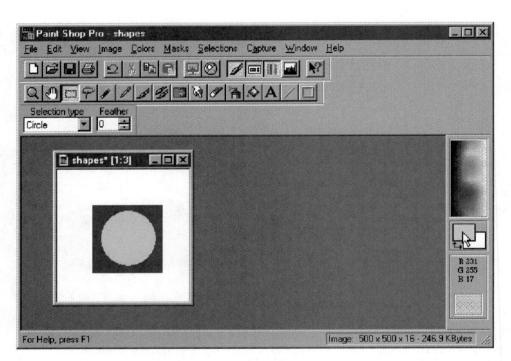

(a)

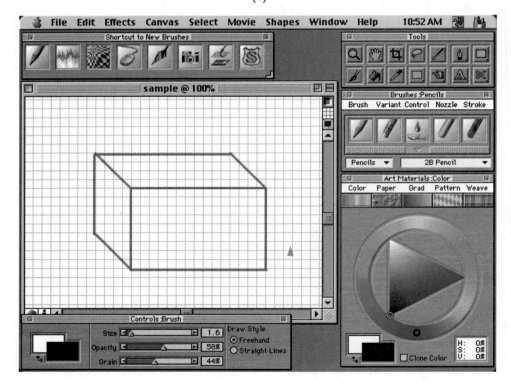

(b)

Whether you can choose the precise size and resolution for an image depends on the software itself. Some painting programs allow the user to control both size and resolution when creating a file. Others permit changes in resolution only. Some offer no choices at all. In any case, it is a good idea to know what the system default values are for size and resolution so that you can avert any unpleasant surprises later. When choosing a resolution and size, you should take into account how the output will likely be used. The size and resolution of an image should always be matched to its intended output. For example, 72 dpi is fine for screen display, but much too coarse for printers, especially laser printers (which are capable of densities of 300 dpi, 600 dpi, and even higher).

As mentioned, the painting image is portrayed within a window. This means that sometimes only a portion of it is revealed. Conventional scrolling tools and gadgets are available to scroll the window over the image. Most painting programs also allow the user to measure the canvas with rulers and grids for more precision. Figure 12.13 illustrates a typical canvas.

In most painting programs, the user may choose the scale at which the image is displayed on the canvas. This is an extremely useful feature. **Image scale** denotes the relative size of the image displayed compared to its actual size. Increasing the scale of an image, for example, has the effect of zooming in on the actual pixels. Detail work is much easier at higher scales. On the other hand, reducing the scale allows you to view the composition of an image that is ordinarily too large for your window or screen. See Figure 12.14.

The canvas is typically divided into foreground and background. The **foreground** is the color or pattern that you apply; the **background** is the color or pattern that is assumed always underneath it. Consider the example illustrated by Figure 12.15. A blue circle is painted in the foreground over a plain white background. In the second frame, a portion of the circle is erased to reveal the white background

FIGURE 12.13

Painting pixels is made easier with options such as grid lines and rulers. The simple figure here is drawn using the grids provided by Painter. The rulers remind you of the actual dimensions of the object. Measurements may be set for inches, pixels, or metric units.

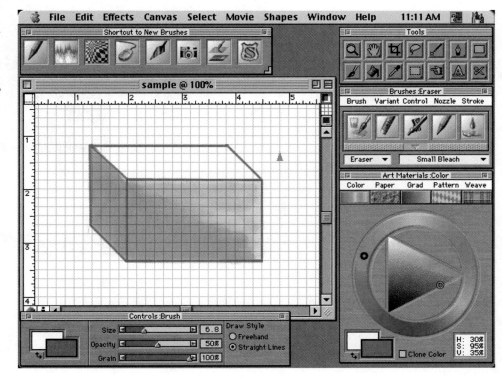

FIGURE 12.14

Detail work can be aided by changing image scales. In (a), guidelines are set for touching up the image around its borders. But at normal scale (100%), it is difficult to see which pixels should be erased or repainted. On the other hand, at the magnification of 300% a shown in (b), it is much easier to both examine and work with such details.

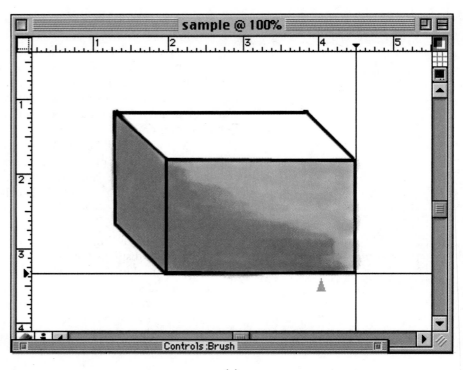

(a)

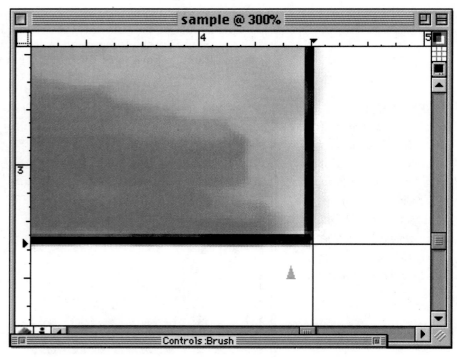

(b)

underneath. Thus, the background is restored whenever the foreground colors or figures are erased or deleted. The background is usually set when the image is first created; some programs may permit you to alter this later.

FIGURE 12.15

Painting programs allow you to manipulate the colors and patterns of both the foreground and background individually. On the left, a simple blue circle is drawn on a plain white background. The circle occupies the foreground on the canvas as a separate layer from its background. Thus, when part of the foreground object is erased (as shown on the right), the background color shows through.

Painting Tools and Features

Most paint programs are equipped with a common array of tools used for drawing and painting, organized on one or more palettes. The user selects the appropriate tool and, using a mouse (or stylus with a digital sketch pad), applies it to the canvas. See Figure 12.16.

Drawing and painting tools are flexible in that they can be used with a variety of line thicknesses, colors, and patterns. The user must first designate the type of digital "paint" desired and then the tool to apply it. Some tools are used for drawing lines, curves, and figures. Others are employed for painting areas and effects. There is also an eraser. Typical painting and drawing tools are illustrated in Figure 12.17.

There are also palettes for patterns, colors, and textures. These are commonly used for automatically filling a closed area with a designated pattern or color. Besides simple shades or colors, the user may select specific patterns or textures; even gradients are available. Some programs allow you to create your own patterns and add them to the standard library. Figure 12.18 offers an assortment of these area fills.

Editing and Special Effects

The greatest advantages of digital painting programs are the ease and power they afford in editing. Just as word processors add editing power to text handling, painting programs also benefit from the capability to select and modify image components. In fact, there are some noticeable similarities between text editing features and image editing in paint programs. First, an item in an image must be selected in order to be edited. After an item is selected, it may be cut, copied, and pasted to another area.

FIGURE 12.16

MetaCreations Painter offers an assortment of tools for viewing, selecting, or cropping portions of the graphic image. Other tools allow you to apply a variety of brushes, area fills, and even text effects to the canvas.

FIGURE 12.17

A sampling of the various painting effects is shown here. Painter has a large collection of digital "brushes" ranging from natural effects such as pencil strokes, charcoal, and crayon to more exotic effects such as brush strokes in the style of well-known artists (Van Gogh, Rembrandt). Third-party brushes may be added to the palette as plug-ins for the software.

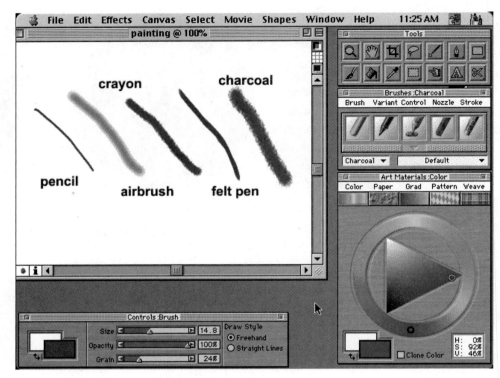

FIGURE 12.18

Patterns may be brushed or otherwise applied to the canvas. Here we see a sampling of some of the patterns, weaves, and gradients available in MetaCreations Painter. Each has been applied to a selected area using the paint bucket, which fills the entire area. On the right of the canvas, the palette displays some of the pattern choices available.

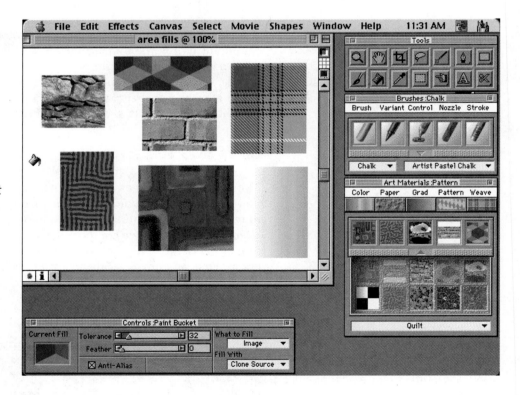

Selecting an item in an image is not always precise, though. Some tools allow you to select a given area of the image (rectangular or circular). In this instance, the entire area is affected. In Figure 12.19, the circle is surrounded by a selection box in the first frame. But when the

FIGURE 12.19

In (a) a rectangular area surrounding the circle is selected for editing the circle. The outline of this selection is visible as a dotted line. In (b), the selected area is moved. The entire area selected moves instead of just the circle because our selection is based on the group of pixels contained within it. Note also that the white background is revealed when the foreground pixels are moved. The process is repeated in (c) and (d). This time, however, the area of the circle is selected with better precision. Even so, when moved, the hole displaying the background is evident.

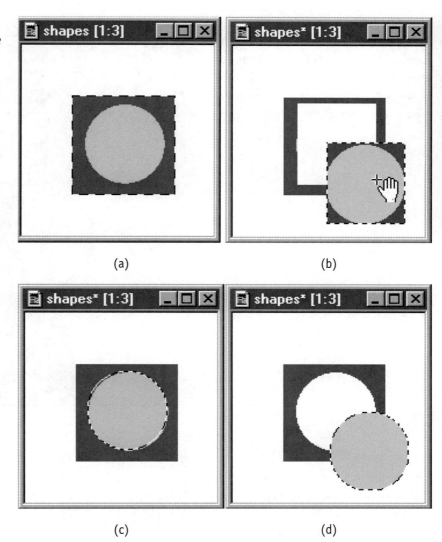

(a) (b)

(c) (d)

circle is moved, the entire area—including the surrounding pattern—is snatched with it. Other selection tools surround the boundary of an object. These are a little more precise, provided the boundary is distinct.

Some applications provide more precise selection by allowing the user to specify a closed path around the object. A closed path is an arbitrary number of connected curves and lines that specify an area in the image. (Paths are actually a technique borrowed from vector graphics; we will treat them in more detail in the next section.) Closed paths may also serve as masks. In the previous chapter, we introduced the concept of masking. A mask is an area of an image that is selected for editing changes. The area outside the mask may be modified, but the pixels inside the masked area are unaffected. Figure 12.20 illustrates the application of masking in a painting program.

Some painting programs provide special editing effects called **transformations.** An area of the image may be selected and transformed or altered in various ways. Typical transformations include scaling, stretching, and rotating, as well as perspective and free-form distortion. Figure 12.21 provides some examples.

FIGURE 12.20

A simple mask is created to surround the figure of the Statue of Liberty. A charcoal effect is then applied to the surface of the canvas, but the strokes do not affect the masked areas of the image.

FIGURE 12.21

Painting programs offer a variety of transformations that may be applied to selected objects. In this instance, the simple rectangular figure (top left corner) is transformed in shape, position, and texture.

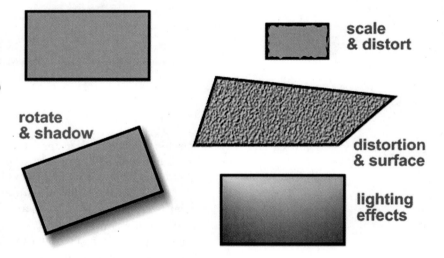

In general, painting programs provide a powerful assortment of features for creating graphic images. That these images are bit-mapped is a double-edged sword, though. On one hand, this means that the user has much more control over the actual pixel content of the image; this is valuable for complicated images. The downside is that the work is more labor-intensive. Because the image is a collection of pixels, changes must be made normally at the pixel level. For this reason, some graphic tasks are best managed by less primitive means.

focus DIGITAL ART

Twenty-five years ago, the expression "computer art" was considered a contradiction in terms. Nowadays, computer-generated art is mainstream stuff: Professionals in the visual arts are skilled in a variety of media, both traditional and digital. Certainly, the widespread use of computers in commercial graphics has contributed appreciably to the acceptance of digital art. Today, artists working with computers and graphic software routinely produce creations intended as fine art. See Figure 12.22.

Apart from inspiration, the most significant practical problem facing the artist is how to deliver digital art. Digital images have a number of

FIGURE 12.22

Here are two examples of artist renderings using bit-mapped painting programs. Figure (a) is entitled "Frogshow," (b) is "Moreno Sphere." Both are compositions by Brian Michael Ground, an art student at our university.

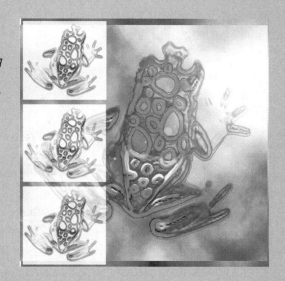

(a)

(b)

advantages that conventional pictures lack. They may be easily and widely distributed. The Web is a good example of an economical method for worldwide distribution. Creating an electronic portfolio is also easy with the help of multimedia presentation software. These programs create a slide show whose slides can be timed automatically or controlled manually. A digital portfolio can be stored on disk and transported with ease as well. Digital images can be replicated without a loss of quality, too. In a digital limited edition, unlike conventional methods, the last "print" is just as pristine as the first. (Interestingly, artists must erase the digital image file to ensure that it is indeed a limited edition.)

Digital images, however, are ephemeral. They persist on our screens only for a short time. Artists often desire to have archival representations of their work. Fortunately, several choices are available for converting a digital image from the screen to a more permanent medium.

Printing is a popular method of archiving digital artwork. Color inkjet and laser printers are an economical means for producing printed output. The best results occur with specially treated paper, watercolor paper, or high-quality, heavy bond, acid-free, cotton-fiber paper stock. These prints, however, should be treated to keep the colors from fading. UV protective coatings are common. Dye-sublimation printers offer an alternative method for printed output. These printers produce continuous-tone images with bright colors. Dye-sublimation prints, however, can be easily smeared and are vulnerable to humidity. Some printers have been especially designed for producing artwork. The Iris printer, for example, is an inkjet printer that has been tweaked exclusively for fine art printing.

Archiving images to film is another choice. The film negatives can then be used for producing high-quality prints as well. The prints can be laminated for better stability and longer life. A number of commercial service bureaus specialize in these various output methods for the serious artist.

Some artists employ the aforementioned methods as a means of experimenting with mixed media. For example, inkjet output can be brushed immediately after printing before the inks have dried. Overprinting a prepared surface with a digital image is another effective mode. Preparations include painted, etched, or embossed surfaces. In short, digital methods offer a whole new range of possibilities for expression by the visual artist.

More Information

DRAWING WITH LINES, CURVES, AND OBJECTS

As mentioned earlier, Sutherland's SketchPad had a tremendous impact on the development of graphic application software. That it was interactive proved that the computer could be used to create graphic images in a convenient manner. Its interactivity was not limited merely to creating images. Once figures were drawn, they could be modified interactively just as easily. For example, using the light pen and buttons, the user could point to a rectangle on the screen and move its position or change its size. This was possible because SketchPad's design was based on an entirely different approach than that of bit-mapped image programs.

FIGURE 12.23

An object-oriented version of a rectangle is no more than a description of its principal properties or attributes. Thus, the structure on the left might serve as a representation for the rectangle depicted to the right of it. Besides its dimensions, the object version of the rectangle would store the position of the figure (expressed here as X, Y screen coordinates for its left corner), the border, and area-fill pattern. Modifying the characteristics of the rectangle, therefore, would be as simple as changing the values for these component descriptions. The graphic program would then redraw the pixel version of the figure with its new attributes on the screen.

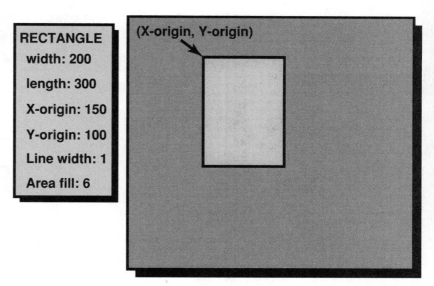

RECTANGLE
width: 200
length: 300
X-origin: 150
Y-origin: 100
Line width: 1
Area fill: 6

(X-origin, Y-origin)

Instead of bit-maps, the user defined or created graphic objects. The program, in turn, freed the user from the messy details of how these objects were actually formed or displayed. Instead, it provided tools for manipulating them as objects rather than dealing directly with their implementation. Software designed in this manner is understandably called object-oriented graphics.

In the world of object-oriented (or vector) graphics, pixels are replaced by elements such as lines, curves, paths, and figures. As a result, object-oriented graphics offers several distinct advantages over bit-mapped approaches.

First, the user is freed from the details of how the computer system stores and displays an image. After all, a pixel is not a very natural way of thinking about drawings and pictures. Entities such as lines and curves are much more intuitive. Thus, object-oriented graphics is more abstract.

Second, vector graphic applications offer features with greater power and flexibility. The key, again, is abstraction, but rather than an effect, it resides inside the program itself. In short, graphic objects are defined abstractly within the program, too. A graphic object is specified by its attributes such as dimensions, position in the image, pattern, and so on. See Figure 12.23. But, since these are defined—that is, in essence, descriptions—they may be altered as easily as they were created. For instance, moving an object from one location to another is a simple matter of modifying the description of its position coordinates. The program then uses these descriptions in redrawing the object to simulate moving it from one place to another. Such changes do not necessarily affect other objects in the image either. You will recall the illustration of relocating an inscribed circle. Compare that with the results in Figure 12.24. When the circle is selected and moved in a painting program, the background is revealed, leaving a hole in the surrounding box. On the other hand, in a vector graphic program, the circle and box are objects that are defined independently. When the circle is moved, the box is reinstated nearly in full view.

Of course, a portion of the circle covers the box, but the program can calculate this overlap and redraw both. The process of revealing por-

FIGURE 12.24

In an earlier figure (Figure 12.19), you saw that moving pixels is not always as precise as might be desired. In an object-oriented graphic program, however, the objects are treated independently. In (a) a circle is inscribed within a rectangle using the tools of a drawing program. In (b) the circle has been moved without affecting the square at all—other than covering its corner.

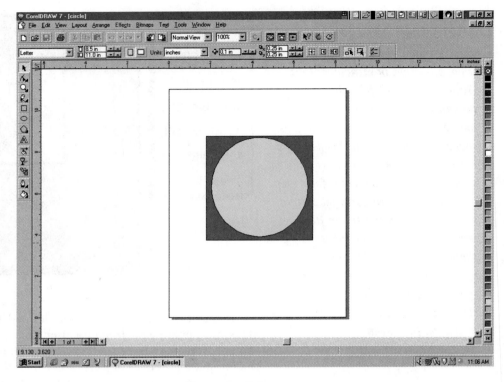

(a)

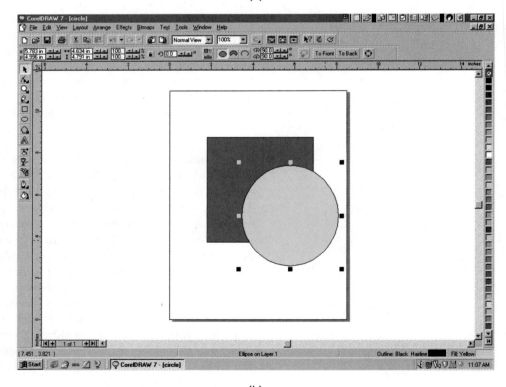

(b)

tions of a 2-D graphic object for viewing is called **clipping.** This technique is employed in all window-based interfaces, for example.

Third, object-oriented graphics are resolution independent. Because these images are defined abstractly, they may be adapted to fit various resolutions. This means that their scale can be fitted more easily to a variety of devices.

Finally, structured graphics can represent and store images with greater economy than bit-mapped applications. As you know, in most instances, a description is much more concise than replicating the thing itself. (Compare the phrase "a 100-story office building" with what it denotes!) This is certainly true of bit-mapped images. Graphic files containing object descriptions are often much smaller and, therefore, more economical to store and transmit than their bit-mapped counterparts. Of course, to be useful, descriptions must be intelligible to another system. Vector graphic files created by one object-oriented application may be unintelligible to another. If you plan to transfer images from one application to another, it is important to ascertain what file formats they support in common.

2-D-structured graphic applications come in two basic varieties: drawing and illustration programs. Their differences are not so much a matter of kind as degree. In fact, they differ much as a limo differs from a compact car. Both are basically vehicles intended for transportation, but the style in which you are transported can be very different. Drawing programs provide all of the basics; illustration programs are measured by their style and appointments. We will examine each category to understand better what these applications offer in the way of graphic features.

Drawing Programs

Drawing programs are best suited for simpler types of illustrations and charts. Like their painting program counterparts, they typically divide the workspace into menus, palettes, and one or more drawing windows. The tool and pattern palettes often resemble those found in painting programs, too. There are tools for drawing lines, arcs, and figures such as rectangles, ovals, and circles. The techniques employed for drawing are also similar to those in painting programs.

Once the lines, arcs, and figures are drawn, the differences between painting and drawing programs become a lot more apparent. For instance, lines and figures may be selected individually for discrete editing. When an object is selected, it is usually displayed with special tools called **handles.** These are actually used for resizing the object. Figure 12.25 shows how a rectangle can be reshaped by manipulating its handles. While the object is selected, moving it is usually as simple as pointing and dragging it elsewhere in the window.

An unavoidable reality of painting with pixels is their rectilinear structure. As you have probably seen for yourself, painting curves is always marred by the jagged edges of the pixels themselves. This effect, of course, can be minimized if the resolution is sufficiently large. In contrast, one of the abstract features of drawing programs is that curves can be treated independently of resolution. Drawing programs incorporate what are called **parametric curves,** which are based on mathematical equations. There are several classes of parametric curves. Drawing programs may employ **B-spline curves** or, perhaps, **Bezier curves.** Both types of equations project a series of points through which the curve is approximated. The latter form is very popular. (For more about drawing with Bezier curves, see the Focus box entitled "French Mathematical Expressionism.")

FIGURE 12.25

In (a) the rectangle is shown as the current selection. The handles at its vertices indicate both that the figure is selected and how it may be scaled or resized. The user presses and drags the handle as shown in (b). When the mouse button is released, the rectangle is redrawn at its new scale, as seen in (c).

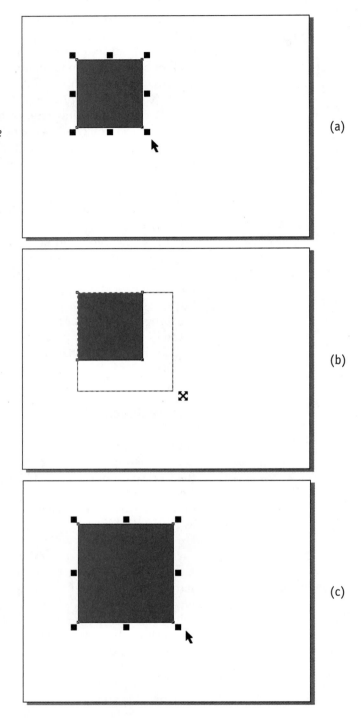

(a)

(b)

(c)

From the user's standpoint, however, creating arbitrary curves is a great deal simpler than the mathematics that supports them. The user draws the curve by specifying a set of points that it passes through. In Figure 12.26(a), the user creates a curved segment by plotting a set of points. The program automatically interpolates a smooth curve between the points. The real power in this technique comes in editing, though. As demonstrated in Figure 12.26(b), you may reshape or refit the curve

FIGURE 12.26

Manipulating freehand curves in CorelDraw is a simple matter. The original curve is selected with the shape tool in (a). Dragging the blue-colored handles reshapes the curve as shown in (b). The location and limits of the curve may also be adjusted by repositioning the endpoints as shown in (c).

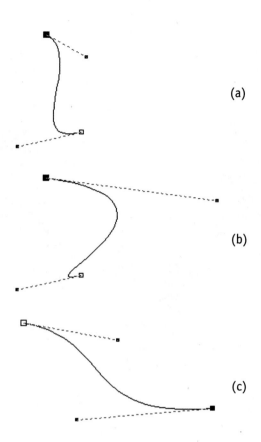

(a)

(b)

(c)

by manipulating either the points on the curve or the special handles that extend from these points.

Unlike in painting programs, the image in a drawing program is composed conceptually of many different layers rather than just two (background and foreground). It is convenient to think of the drawing image as composed of stacks of layers, much like the acetates used for overhead projectors. Each object occupies its own layer—stamped on a transparent background. The order of the layers dictates what and how much of the image's objects are visible. As shown in Figure 12.27, these layers may be varied at will to yield different "looks."

Drawing programs offer the same sort of special effects and transformations found in painting programs. In addition to scaling and resizing, you may rotate objects, distort them, and make perspective projections. The starburst drawing in Figure 12.28 illustrates how a graphic image is built from incremental steps or stages using tools, patterns, and transformations.

Drawing programs offer a great many features and advantages over pixel-based painting programs. They are especially good at mass production. Illustrations that contain a great deal of repeated or redundant components can be copied quickly and accurately using simple copy-and-paste operations. Because their most primitive element is a line or curve, drawing programs are best suited for graphic images that are basically line drawings. Painting programs are still better for more complicated graphic images.

FIGURE 12.27

In a typical drawing program, figures are treated as belonging to separate transparent layers. As shown here, you can see how the circle, triangle, and rectangle are arranged by layering one on top of the other. Rearranging these figures is as simple as restacking the layers. Two different arrangements are shown beneath it. These are created by selecting a given layer and choosing the appropriate stacking command such as Send Backward or Send to the Front.

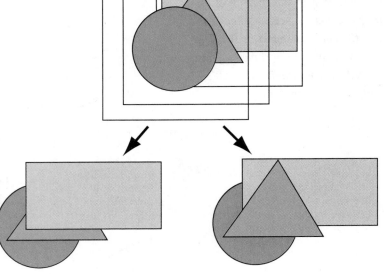

FIGURE 12.28

The illustrations show, step by step, how a drawing program simplifies the creation of a graphic figure. (a) A single circle is drawn and copied. The copy is increased by 300 percent. Both are aligned horizontally and vertically by their centers. (b) Using the straight-line tool, guidelines are drawn as an aid for the next step. (c) The polygon tool is employed to create star bursts. The guides are used to center each point of the star. (d) Afterward, the guides and outer circle are deleted. (e) A copy of the polygon is made. The copy is colored a different shade and rotated to create the offset bursts. This copy layer is sent to the back. Finally, the center circle is colored to match the background star bursts.

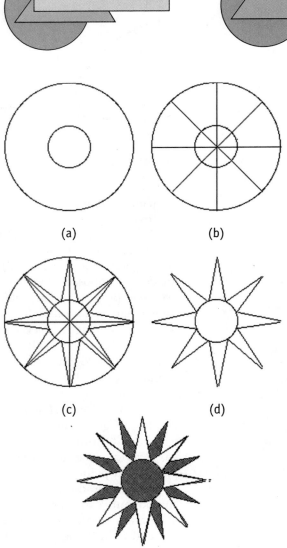

FRENCH MATHEMATICAL EXPRESSIONISM

Bezier curves have an unlikely origin: They are based on the work of a French engineer who developed the concept for automating metal cutting machines in the auto industry. Pierre Bezier (pronounced "Bez-ee-ay"), working for the French car manufacturing company Renault in the early 1970s, was charged with the problem of simplifying how these cutting machines were controlled. To solve that problem, he discovered a concise method for mathematically approximating a curve segment based on an arbitrary number of points.

John Warnock and Chuck Geshke, the creators of the PostScript Page Description Language, adopted a special case of the Bezier method for creating what are called piecewise Bezier curves. Consequently, the popularity of PostScript ensured the prevalence of this method.

To understand how Bezier curves work, consider a curve segment defined by a small number of points. In this case, we will define the curve using only four control points. (Technically, this is a Bezier curve of degree 3.) As shown in Figure 12.29, the curve passes through the first and fourth points. These are commonly dubbed the "anchor points." The curve only approximates to the two intermediate points. If we trace a line connecting the intermediate points to their respective endpoints, however, we see that the line formed is tangent to the curve segment at that juncture. Because this applies in every instance, we can infer that the position of an intermediate point controls the slope of its curve segment. For this reason, the intermediate points are often referred to as direction points.

FIGURE 12.29

The piecewise Bezier curve segment is defined by the four points shown on top. The curve passes through two points—the first and the last (1 and 4). These are usually designated as anchor points because they define the limits of the curve segment. The other two points (2 and 3) help to constrain its shape. If we draw lines intersecting them with their corresponding anchor points, as shown on the bottom, we can see that each line is tangent to the curve at that location. These intermediate points are called "direction points" because they define the slope of the curve in their respective neighborhoods. Their position affects the shape of the curve globally as well.

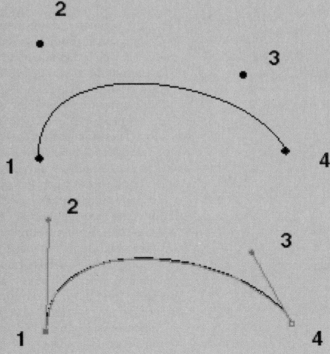

In some drawing and illustration programs, the user may manipulate the control points for a Bezier curve directly. The curve in Figure 12.30 is transformed by repositioning the intermediate (direction) points that help to define it.

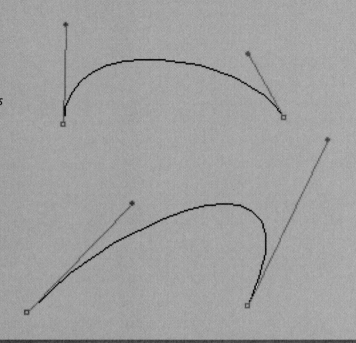

FIGURE 12.30

The previous curve (shown at the top) is reshaped by moving the direction points from their original positions. The result of the change is shown on the bottom. Changes in position and distance from its corresponding anchor point will affect the curve in various ways. For some graphic programs, reshaping a curve is simple and intuitive. The user drags the points while inspecting their effects on the resulting curve segment.

Illustration Programs

Earlier we compared illustration programs to drawing programs as a limo to a compact car. Both have similar purposes but differ in the style and manner in which they achieve these. And, even though this comparison is exaggerated, there is some basis for making it. First, illustration programs are intended for professionals rather than casual users. They are chock full of features that would not be expected in their poor cousins. In addition, they produce the high-quality output necessary for professional publication. These luxuries do have a cost, though. Illustration programs have much steeper learning curves associated with their use. Moreover, they often tax the resources and performance of desktop computers as well. They require lots of memory, are CPU-intensive, and produce files that can occupy more storage space. Not surprisingly, they typically carry bigger price tags as well, though nothing like limo standards.

The chief distinguishing characteristic of illustration programs from the user's standpoint is that they can generate Page Description Language output such as PostScript. This means that they produce graphic images that inherit all of the advantages normally expected from such methods (precision, resolution independence, smooth curves, special effects, etc.).

The workspace for a typical illustration program is similar to that of a drawing program. Compare Figures 12.31 and 12.32. Each has menus with an assortment of commands, one or more palettes of tools, and windows for viewing graphic art files. See Figure 12.33.

FIGURE 12.31

The workspace for the upscale drawing program CorelDraw is loaded with lots of tools and features. The outlined area inside the window represents the extent of the graphic image.

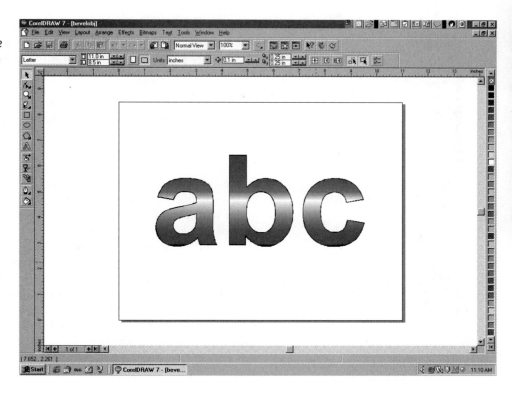

FIGURE 12.32

The interface for the illustration program Adobe Illustrator resembles that for drawing and painting programs. In addition to menus and palettes, the window contains an artboard where the graphic art is created. The normal printable area is shown within the frame. The outside area may be used as a pasteboard for creating and storing graphic objects.

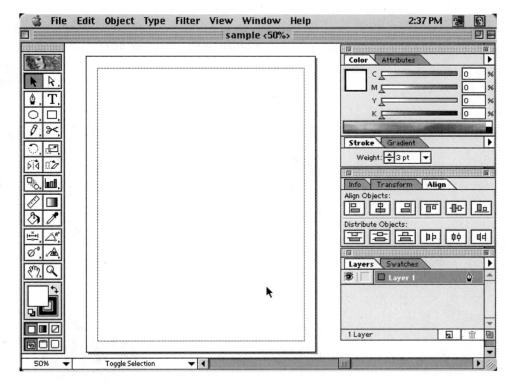

In contrast to most drawing and painting programs, illustration programs usually present different views of their graphic images. While the image is being created or edited, it is often displayed simply as line art, that is, only the lines and curves that make up the image, without color

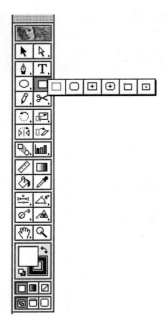

FIGURE 12.33

Illustration programs offer a wide variety of tools for creating lines, figures, and other graphic objects. A close-up of the Illustrator tool palette reveals that many of the tools have pull-out menus containing other related tools. Shown here are the additional tools for creating regular shapes.

FIGURE 12.34

Adobe Illustrator portrays the components of a drawing in what is called the Artwork view. The image is actually composed of a sequence of connected line segments and curves. These segments are joined and filled with various shades to create the finished image.

or shading. See Figure 12.34. This view makes it easier to see the actual structure of the image. (The computer can also redraw these images much faster.) Most illustration programs also provide an output view; this allows you to inspect the image as it would be displayed on paper or on a screen. Consult Figure 12.35 for an example. In some programs, you may work on the image from either view. The output view, however, can be slower because the image must be reconstructed for display over and over.

As in drawing programs, lines and curves are the basic components of graphic objects. Illustration programs, however, offer more flexibility in creating these objects and greater editing control over them. This means that illustrations can be much more complex and intricate compared to those of simpler drawing programs. The example in Figure 12.36 was created in Adobe Illustrator. The close-up of the Artwork view in Figure 12.37 shows the amount of detail required to assemble the components of the image. Illustration programs are extremely powerful and offer many features, but exploiting them requires patience and care.

Text handling is one feature that by itself nearly justifies purchasing an illustration program. In fact, the well-tempered desktop publishing system is not complete without a good illustration program for creating special text effects. Because illustration programs produce PDL output, text effects in a wide assortment of sizes and styles are easily imported into a DTP program. Figure 12.38 provides a sampling of various effects that are easy to create in illustration programs (yet almost impossible to create elsewhere).

Conclusion: Rules and Exceptions

There are indeed notable differences among painting, drawing, and illustration programs in both form and function. As a rule, painting pro-

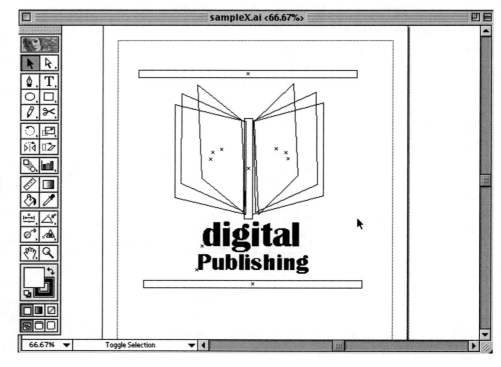

FIGURE 12.35

The previous image is seen here as it appears when displayed for output (on the screen or printed). Compare this version with the previous one in Figure 12.34.

FIGURE 12.36

"Henry's Trip" is an illustration by John Ritter created using Adobe Illustrator and provided as a sample with the application.

grams are designed for bit-mapped images, while drawing and illustration programs deal with object-oriented graphics. Even so, applications today often muddy the graphic waters by combining features from these very different domains. For example, some bit-mapped graphic applications have PostScript output capabilities (Adobe PhotoShop is a good example). Some drawing and illustration programs allow the user to import and manipulate bit-mapped images as backgrounds (CorelDraw, Macromedia Freehand, and Adobe Illustrator). Other graphic applications combine both worlds into a single package (CorelDraw is bundled with

FIGURE 12.37

A close-up of "Henry's Trip" is shown here in the Artwork view. The handles denote endpoints and anchors for the lines and curve segments that constitute the figures. As you can see, the figure of Henry is primarily composed of closed, curved paths with numerous adjustment points used to coax the irregular shapes from within these curves.

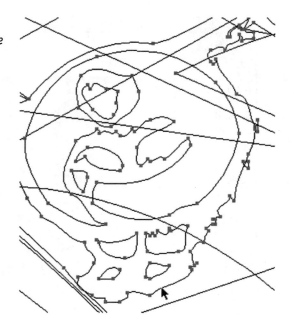

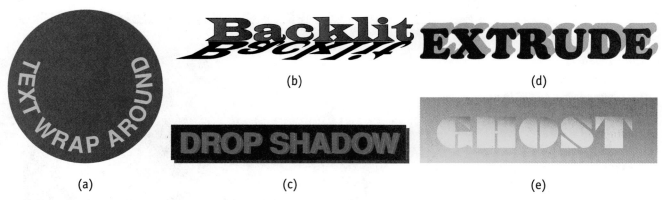

(b)

(d)

(a)

(c)

(e)

FIGURE 12.38

A sampling of sophisticated visual effects created with text using an illustration program is shown. In (a), the text is plotted on a circle that fits inside the surrounding figure. For (b), a copy of the letters is darkened, reshaped, and positioned to suggest a shadow effect due to backlighting. In (c), copies of both the box and the lettering are recolored and moved to a back layer to create their shadows. Each of the shadow layers is offset slightly (moved rightward and downward). The picture (d) is intended to illustrate how text may be extruded (thickened) easily in an illustration program. The lettering is copied and its color is modified. The new copy is placed behind the original letters; again, the letters are offset slightly for visibility. Several other copies are pasted behind that layer in successive offsets. Enough are added to suggest a thick back layer for the text. Finally, in (e), the letters are colored using a gradient pattern that blends color variations across their spectrum. The box uses the same basic colors, but with different gradient parameters. This creates the ghosted text effect.

Corel PhotoPaint, for instance). Another class of applications permits you to transform bit-mapped images into structured graphics automatically for use in illustration programs (Adobe Streamline is an example).

The moral of this story is that there are rules, but there are also exceptions to them. Many commercial graphic software packages today have evolved to hybrid status. Nonetheless, these applications are still suited best for specific types of images and tasks. As always, you should investigate an application thoroughly before deciding whether it suits your needs.

More Information

THREE-DIMENSIONAL GRAPHICS

A recent trend in computer graphics has been the migration of software to the desktop that breaks the traditional two-dimensional barrier. In the past, sophisticated three-dimensional rendering effects and computer animation had been restricted exclusively to the realm of professionals. Today, applications that create 3-D graphics and animation are available for the general user. In this section, we will explore the facets of adding the dimension of depth to your graphic images.

Three-dimensional graphic techniques fall roughly into two categories: volume-based and surface-based. **Volume-based graphics** plot an image as composed of three-dimensional pixels called **voxels** (for volume elements); like two-dimensional pixels, voxels have features such as color, intensity, transparency, and opacity. Thus, a three-dimensional object is plotted as a solid composed of voxels that define its volume. See Figure 12.39. Volume-based graphics are employed for visualization techniques in a number of scientific fields such as medicine (e.g., CAT

FIGURE 12.39

A three-dimensional model of a neuron is shown in (a) using the volume visualization utility VoxelView. A close-up from the center of the structure (b) reveals the individual voxels that make up the structure. The model is rotated counterclockwise (c) to reveal the three-dimensional structure created by these voxels.

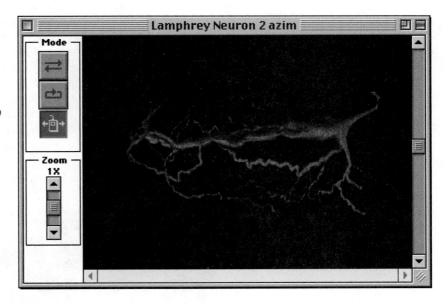

(a)

(b)   (c)

and MRI scans), physics (e.g., hydrodynamics visualization), chemistry (e.g., molecular modeling), and meteorology (e.g., storm visualization). In contrast, **surface-based graphics** treat objects as only skin deep. The objective for surface-based methods is to create the photorealistic illusion of three-dimensional objects rather than manipulating them as solids. Its applications are typically artistic or educational rather than scientific. While some volume-based applications are available (for instance, VoxelView), nearly all desktop 3-D applications employ surface-based techniques exclusively. Accordingly, we will restrict our treatment of 3-D graphics to these types.

Surface-based three-dimensional graphics offers the sort of spectacular photorealistic effects that you have no doubt seen in television commercials, computer games (including *Myst, 7th Guest,* and *Riven*), and motion picture films (such as *Jurassic Park, Terminator 2, Lost World,* and *Toy Story*). Many of these effects, however, were created with high-performance computer systems running application programs written especially for them. The 3-D graphic effects that they feature strain the resources of even these high-performance workstations. For example, computer-generated images of dinosaurs in *Jurassic Park* amount to about six and one-half minutes of film footage. Even so, it took 50 people 18 months and $15 million worth of equipment to create the nearly one-quarter trillion bytes of images needed to create these effects!

Desktop 3-D graphics naturally offers a somewhat scaled-down version of these capabilities. In spite of this, very convincing effects can be produced with these applications on desktop systems with reasonable speed and memory resources. Like its 2-D cousins, a typical 3-D graphic application presents an interface composed of menu items, tool palettes, and drawing or workspace windows. Unlike 2-D drawing and painting programs, however, a 3-D graphic program must manage multiple views or perspectives of its images. See Figure 12.40.

FIGURE 12.40

The workspace for the 3-D graphic application program Infini-D divides the current image into an assortment of views selected by the user. A chair is shown here from standard top, front, and side views. In addition, a fully rendered three-dimensional representation is shown from a viewer's perspective. The latter view is controlled by a virtual camera that may be positioned by the user.

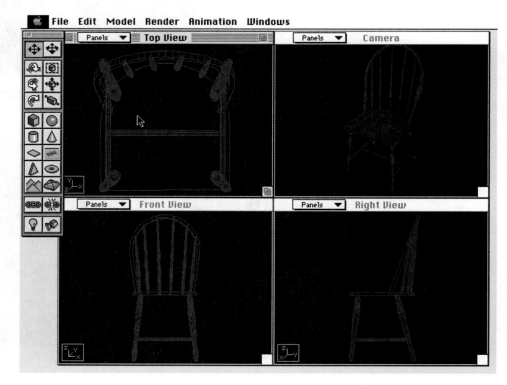

FIGURE 12.41

Using a solid modeling 3-D application, a simple object is constructed by joining a cylinder on top of a cube. Both are primitive solids that may be sized, shaped, and positioned within the scene. In (a), the construction model appears. The model is rendered with surface shading and texture in (b).

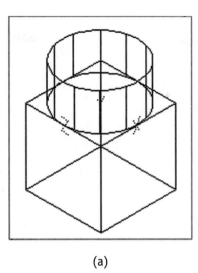
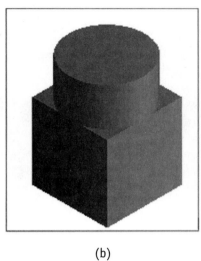

(a)   (b)

The typical desktop application creates a 3-D image following roughly these three stages: model description, scene description, and rendering. We will discuss each of these stages or processes separately in more detail.

Model Description

Each object in a 3-D image must be specified in full detail within the three-dimensional coordinate system employed by the application program. This is the task of **model description.**

Several techniques are available for representing the model. Object models may be fabricated from predefined solids or from polygon-surface or wireframe constructions. These methods vary in their strengths and weaknesses. 3-D applications adopt one or more of these approaches for their modeling interface. More advanced programs combine all three modeling techniques.

Solid modeling portrays objects as derived from simple 3-D solids that serve as primitives within the system. For example, cubes, cylinders, spheres, and cones can be organized, adapted, and reshaped to model some complex object. The process is similar to sculpting and works fine for simpler, regular-shaped objects. See Figure 12.41.

Polygon-surface modeling construes the object's exterior surface as a collection of connected 2-D polygons of various shapes. Thus, complex shapes are depicted as three-dimensional, multifaceted figures. Objects with smooth, continuously curved surfaces are not depicted well with these models. If, however, the resolution is fine enough—that is, the polygon facets are small and numerous enough—acceptable curved surfaces can be approximated.

Wireframe construction is a very popular form for representing models; it creates the object's exterior surface as a wireframe model. The model is composed of a series of connected shapes—like polygon-surface models—that are joined to others at their vertices. Unlike models based exclusively on polygons, though, wireframes may embrace curved shapes. See Figure 12.42. These 2-D curved segments are usually implemented by splines. As discussed earlier, B-splines and Bezier curves are mathematical constructions used to represent curved segments,

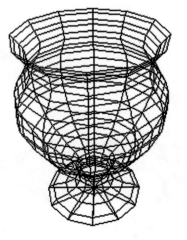

FIGURE 12.42

A wireframe model of a vase is shown.

shapes, and even surfaces. The wireframe model conjures up the idea of a skeleton of the object on which the skin may be stretched.

Because wireframe modeling is supported by most applications, we will use its approach as a means for understanding better how 3-D models are created. Keep in mind, though, that there are other techniques or approaches for the task of modeling.

The methods used for constructing a wireframe model of an object are basically extensions of two-dimensional drawing within a three-dimensional Cartesian coordinate system. The general idea, of course, is to define the model as a solid object composed of a set of points, lines or curves, and surfaces. Conceptually, we can recreate any three-dimensional object portrayed this way provided we have a sufficient number of construction planes based on it. You can think of a **construction plane** as a sheet of glass that is located in our three-dimensional space. See Figure 12.43. When the glass contacts the surface of our object, for example, we could trace its outline and likewise measure all of the points that are confined within its boundaries. In short, we produce a two-dimensional drawing or projection of the view of that object from that aspect.

Now, imagine that we fix the construction planes parallel to a given axis. Furthermore, let's invest them with the capability of passing through an object at will. Given a series of projections from a number of construction planes that sample that axis, we can get a much more accurate idea of the structure of the object. In effect, the object is decomposed as a series of cuts or two-dimensional slices along that axis. If we can specify construction planes for all three dimensions, we can construct a fairly accurate model of the object. Compare with Figure 12.44.

Wireframe models for objects may be created using this technique. Specifically, the shape of an object in a given dimension can be assembled by specifying a series of outlines as its construction planes. These are joined together to form a wireframe by interpolating boundaries between the planes.

In addition to creating models from dimensional cuts or outlines, most 3-D graphic programs offer other tools for automating the creation of wireframe models. For example, models for custom-made objects may be lathed or extruded as well. **Lathing** creates a model by rotating a two-dimensional outline around a given axis. See Figure 12.45. It works well, especially for objects that are symmetrically shaped. **Extrusion** lifts or adds a third dimension to a two-dimensional outline. Regular-shaped objects whose depth is a series of parallel cuts can be created quickly and easily by extrusion. For instance, 3-D text effects can be made

FIGURE 12.43

Suppose that we fit our construction plane on a fixed axis and invest it with the capability of magically passing through objects. When we pass it through a pyramid figure, we can make a series of horizontal cuts of the shape of the object at different depths from top to bottom. Here we see the outline of the object formed on that plane as a cut.

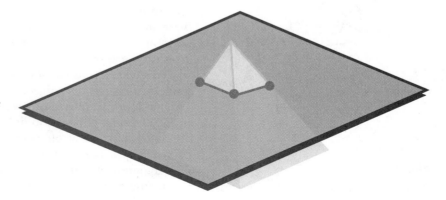

FIGURE 12.44

Using a series of construction planes from at least two dimensions, we can construct a wireframe model composed of a series of points marking the boundaries of the object and interpolated lines connecting them between the planes. Here we see two of the planes. The first (a) shows the pyramid from the top. The second (b) depicts its shape when the cuts are made vertically.

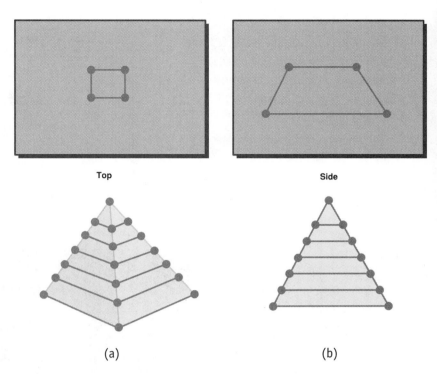

Top   Side

(a)   (b)

by extruding outline fonts. See Figure 12.46 for an illustration of this technique.

Scene Description

Once the objects for an image have been modeled, they must be arranged to form a scene. This is the task of **scene description.** The first step is to find a place for the objects in the scene itself. Usually, you may employ general three-dimensional coordinates—called **world view coordinates**—for fixing objects in the scene. These are defined either in absolute terms or relative to some camera point of view.

The point of view for the scene may be modified easily using controls provided in the interface for managing the virtual viewer or camera. Camera motions are easier to understand than viewing changes. For example, it is easier to grasp terminology that incorporates standard camera movements such as panning left and right or up and down. In addition, you may zoom or move in or out of the scene and perform right and left rotations and tilts.

Choosing surfaces and a background for the scene completes the process of scene description. Most 3-D applications provide a library of surfaces and backgrounds—each with a variety of textures and terrains—that may be added to the scene automatically. See Figure 12.47. You may also import images from other graphic applications that can serve as backgrounds as well. For example, you could use a scanner to digitize a photograph of your wooden desktop surface. This could be edited and saved by an image processing application. This same image could then be imported into the 3-D application for use as a map or pattern to be applied to either surfaces or backgrounds. In this manner, you could create a 3-D model of your desk that looks very much like the real thing.

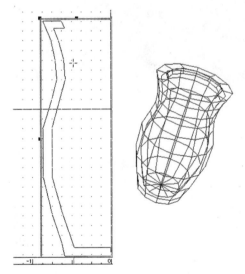

FIGURE 12.45

On the left, the outline of a vase is fashioned for lathing. As you can see, the figure is drawn as a cutaway of the vase from its center. The shape is rotated 360° to form the object. On the right, the wireframe model of the vase is shown.

FIGURE 12.46

On the left, the outline for the letter "T" is drawn. Extrusion automatically adds a specified amount of depth to the figure. The wireframe model of the extruded "T" is seen on the right from above.

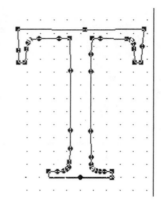
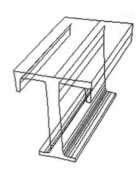

FIGURE 12.47

The title "Digital Domain" is covered with a translucent metallic finish and placed on a checkerboard-patterned background. The camera angle may be manipulated for various views of the scene.

Rendering

The process of rendering a scene involves creating the illusion of photorealism. In other words, the objects in the image are rendered as composed of surfaces projected in three-dimensional perspective with the effects of lighting and shading to contribute to their realism.

Determining which surfaces are visible can be approached in two different manners. On one hand, we might think of it fundamentally from the viewer's standpoint. For example, we might draw a straight line from the viewer's eye to the viewing grid and pass that line through until it hits an object. Thus, we could determine what the viewer can see for each pixel in the image plane. This is the basic technique of **ray tracing.** See Figure 12.48. The results can be more realistic if we take into account the light rays that are reflected from other objects as well. These can be traced to determine what other surfaces they contact. Transparent surfaces can be modeled by tracing rays that are refracted through these surfaces as well. Rendering by ray tracing can produce striking results for scenes with mirror- or glass-like sur-

FIGURE 12.48

The viewing frustum is a pyramid formed by projecting lines from the viewer past the image plane to the background of the scene. Objects behind the image plane and within the pyramid form the content of the 3-D image. Anything outside this area is clipped. The remaining objects are projected onto the image plane to form the image.

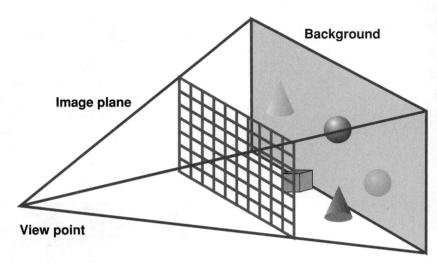

FIGURE 12.49

The illustration of the table setting shows how ray tracing produces realistic lighting effects such as shadows and reflections.

faces. See Figure 12.49. Unfortunately, producing ray-traced output can be extremely time-consuming.

On the other hand, we can approach the problem backward: traversing the background to the viewer rather than vice versa. Rendering according to this approach is accomplished in two stages. First, the object is portrayed as composed of a collection of visible surfaces (as seen from that perspective). This task is often dubbed in the negative as **hidden surface removal.** Afterward, lighting and shading effects are added.

A variety of techniques are employed for hidden surface removal; however, they share some fundamental features. The basic idea is to calculate which surfaces and lines are visible by determining which are closest to the viewer. Starting in the background, the image is constructed by effectively building and then erasing or removing those lines, edges, or surfaces that are obscured by ones closer to the viewer.

After the hidden surfaces are removed, the image pixels for the visible surfaces are treated to portray lighting and shading effects. There are several popular techniques, but each is based on a model that approximates how light is distributed over the surface of a polygon. The simplest lighting or shading model is called **Lambert shading** or sometimes simply **flat shading.** Each facet of an object's surface is shaded by treating each pixel in that polygon uniformly. See Figure 12.50 for an il-

FIGURE 12.50

In (a), the wireframe version of a vase is shown. Lambert or flat shading is applied to the surface, as seen in (b). Each of the surfaces that constitute its shape is treated uniformly in this rendering method. Consequently, the facets are clearly visible. Flat shading is, however, a very fast rendering method.

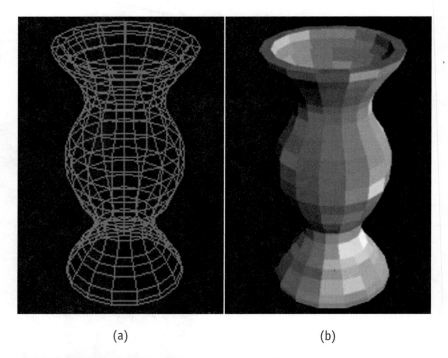

(a)   (b)

FIGURE 12.51

The same vase from Figure 12.50(a) is rendered. This time the Gouraud shading method is employed. Smoother variations in shading and lighting effects are visible for each of the facets.

FIGURE 12.52

In the final version, Phong shading is used for rendering the vase seen originally in Figure 12.50(a). The results are more realistic; shadowing is better defined and light reflections are evident, for example.

lustration. Thus, Lambert shading is fast but lacks subtlety. While the Lambert lighting model assumes that each facet is flat, more sophisticated shading techniques allow for surfaces to be formed by smooth curves. Named after its inventor, **Gouraud shading** (pronounced "Guh-row") takes into account the lighting effects on the surrounding surfaces and calculates shading from each vertex. The shading values for pixels between two vertices are then interpolated to create a more diffuse or smoothly varying effect. Gouraud shading is more realistic than flat shading, yet it is still reasonably efficient (fast). See Figure 12.51. The technique does have some weak points, though. Specular reflections and highlights generally are not handled well, and although borders between facets on a curved surface are smoothed, they are still visible. **Phong shading** is a method designed to deal with just these problems. Rather than interpolating the color values for some of the pixels within a surface, Phong shading recomputes the illumination model for each pixel. The results are much more realistic, though the process is more time-consuming. See Figure 12.52.

Fortunately, desktop 3-D applications allow the user to decide how to manage these trade-offs. Simpler models with faster rendering can be used for provisional designs or drafts; on the other hand, higher-quality output images can be produced at the expense of using more complicated models and rendering techniques. Of course, as in other graphic applications, processor speed and memory capacities are practical considerations.

ANIMATION

Computer animation extends graphic images to add the dimension of time for depicting motion (or change). Animation creates an illusion of motion by displaying a sequence of progressively changing images in rapid succession. If the images—called **frames**—are displayed at a fast enough rate, the average person perceives them as depicting motion. Usually, rates of 15 or 16 frames per second (fps) are sufficient to produce this illusion. Professional-quality animations employ rates of 24 fps and higher.

Picture animation, of course, is not a new technology. The first animation devices were developed in the early nineteenth century. The zoetrope, for example, was invented by William Horner in 1834. It was composed of a revolving drum with regularly spaced slits. Drawings were positioned on an inner drum. When the drum was rotated, the viewer could see the drawings through the slits. In 1915, Earl Hurd developed the technique of **cel animation;** this is the basic method still used in conventional commercial animation today. Each individual image (called a **cel** from the transparent celluloid sheets that were used) is placed on a painted background and photographed. This produces a sequence of frames, composing a motion picture film. The first commercial pioneer to add synchronized sound to cel animation was Walt Disney, who produced *Steamboat Willie* (featuring Mickey Mouse) in 1928.

It is useful to note some of the basics of traditional cel animation because the terminology has been transplanted to computer animation techniques. Animated films generally tell a story. **Story** is the term also used to describe the action of the film. The story comprises a sequence of scenes. A **scene** is defined by a specific set of objects, at a given location. The story is often depicted scene by scene in a series of drawings that make up the **storyboard.** The objects in a scene are also called **actors,** though this does not always mean that they depict characters. The location is depicted by a series of **backgrounds,** relatively static drawings on which the cels are placed and photographed. Scenes are made up of shots. A **shot** is the basic picture unit; it combines a set of actors on a particular background. A shot, of course, corresponds to a single frame or image.

The principal animators are usually each responsible for a single actor. They draw **key frames** that depict that character or object in specific positions. These are then transferred to transparent cels for inking and painting. Subordinates prepare what are called **in-betweens,** the intermediate drawings that produce smooth motion between key frames. The final photography of cels on backgrounds is typically done on film or videotape. A number of effects (such as pans and zooms) are actually created during the photography process. Editing is often handled in postproduction.

Computers have been employed in commercial animation for several decades. Computer processing has helped animators draw and color key frames, produce in-betweens, control the camera during photography, and handle editing during postproduction. These are considered computer-assisted animation systems because the process remains fundamentally an analog one. The computer is simply employed at various stages of the analog process for efficiency or economy.

Only recently, however, has animation gone fully digital. By "digital" we mean, of course, that all stages of the animation process are computerized. Even a computer video monitor is employed for its display—though it may be transferred to another medium, such as videotape. For well over a decade, computer graphic researchers and

focus

ANIMATED GIFs, THE POOR MAN'S ANIMATION

Animated images are very popular add-ons for Web pages. Animations can be created for the Web in a number of ways. Some animations are produced using sophisticated video and animation software. These must be delivered by special technologies, often requiring programming embedded in the Web page's HTML. The animations can be seen only by using dedicated viewers called plug-ins. At the other end of the spectrum are animated GIFs. These require no programming and no special plug-ins; animated GIFs are supported by all of the popular Web browsers.

An **animated GIF** is a sequence of images treated as a block and downloaded to the user as a stream. Like old-fashioned flip-books, an animated GIF contains sequenced frames that are displayed one at a time rapidly enough to simu-late motion. Animated GIFs are **streaming** data in that each frame is displayed while the succeeding frame is being downloaded. In other words, the viewer does not have to wait for the entire image to be transferred to the browser to see it. On the other hand, animated GIFs depend on the speed of the connection between server and client. Slow connections will cause the animation to appear slow and jerky.

In spite of these potential problems, animated GIFs are much simpler to produce and offer a practical solution for most casual users. The process requires two stages: creating the frames and constructing the animated GIF. The first stage can be handled in a number of ways. Most often, it means that each frame must be prepared "by hand" as a single image file. For example, as shown in Figure 12.53, the frames

FIGURE 12.53

To create an animated GIF, it is necessary to prepare each of the images that comprise the frames of the animation. In this example, a glowing effect is added to the image of the logo. The sequence of five frames reveals how this effect is achieved. In the first frame (a), the normal image is shown. In each of the succeeding frames (b)–(e), a copy of the text layer is blurred and placed behind the original text layer. (The black background is the third and bottommost layer.) Finally, in (e), a lens flare effect is added to create a sparkle over the letter "g."

(a)

(b)

FIGURE 12.53—cont'd

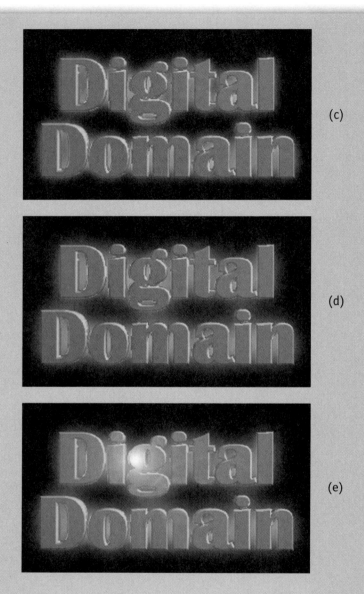

(c)

(d)

(e)

for a twirling and glowing logo are created using a bit-mapped graphic software application. Building the frames individually takes time and some patience, though the process is not a difficult one. Once all the images are created, they may be assembled as an animated GIF using special software designed to create the appropriate image file. A freeware program called GIFBuilder is available for Macintosh comput-ers. Figure 12.54 shows how the images are imported one by one into the program. GIFBuilder processes these images, producing an animation. The resulting file may also be optimized to reduce its overall size. Reductions in file size mean better performance, particularly on slower Web connections.

Windows users can achieve similar results using programs such as GIF Construction Set. The

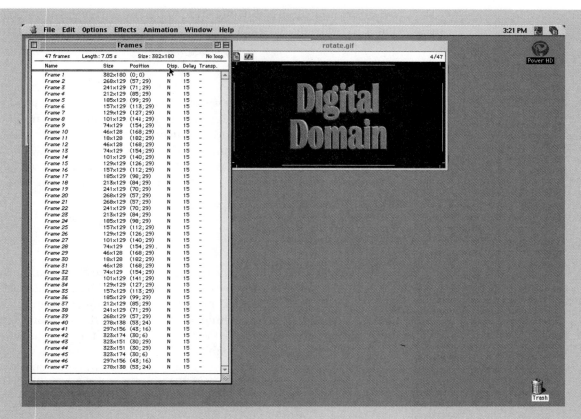

FIGURE 12.54

GIFBuilder 0.5 is used to assemble the images into a single animated GIF image. Each of the frames is dragged and dropped into the Frames window (shown on the left). In this instance, the twirling logo animation requires a total of 47 separate frames to complete both the single revolution and the glowing effect (as seen in Figure 12.53). In the window to the right, the animation is tested. Shown here is frame 4 during the rotation sequence.

program features an Animation Wizard, which is a series of dialog boxes that walks the user through the steps of compiling an animated GIF. GIF Construction Set is shareware and has a nominal charge. Whatever the means, animated GIFs are an economical and no-fuss choice for enhancing your Web pages.

More Information

commercial developers have created professional digital animation systems on high-performance computer systems using specialized software.

Digital animation systems have recently migrated to the desktop as well. Currently, there are three classes of desktop animation applications: object animation, modeling animation, and authoring animation systems. We will consider each category briefly.

Object Animation

Object animation is the simplest variety of computer animation, usually based on 2-D graphic images. The user draws or assembles key frames. The program then calculates and produces the in-betweens. The user may choose objects or actors from a standard library or create new ones. Calculating in-betweens is often based on starting and ending key frames with a user-defined path to track the intended motion between them. See Figure 12.55.

Modeling Animation

Modeling animation applications automate the process of manipulating a rendered object in three-dimensional space. The animator defines the objects or actors as 3-D models. The program computes and renders a model using the techniques discussed in the previous section. In addition to rendering 3-D views of the model, the program creates an animation based on manipulating the model with a virtual camera that captures the scene. For example, the animator employs the camera to pan, zoom, or tilt over the scene for different visual effects. See Figure 12.56.

Authoring Animation

Some systems are designed to automate the process of animation from storyboard to finished product. In an authoring system, the user creates a storyboard that specifies the sequencing of scenes for the animation. Objects and actors are defined within each scene or unit. Each of the

FIGURE 12.55

An animation of balloons drifting away can be created easily using the technique of automated in-betweening. The balloon graphic is pasted in the starting frame in the lower-left-hand corner of the screen. A smaller copy of the graphic is then pasted to a later frame (shown here for illustration) in the opposite corner of the screen. The animation program then calculates the intermediate frames in the sequence by plotting gradually both the change in position (shown here with the aid of an arrow) and the change in size of the graphic. The result is a sequence of frames producing a smooth animation.

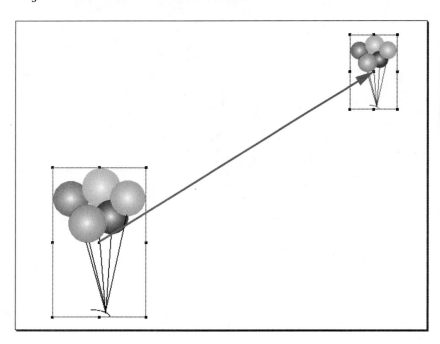

FIGURE 12.56

Three frames from an animated sequence created using modeling and rendering software are shown. The sequence simulates panning a long shot (a), which zooms through (b) into a close-up of the sundial shown in (c). The objects were created using 3-D modeling software. The animation was then produced automatically using camera directions plotted by the user.

(a)

(b)

(c)

FIGURE 12.57

Macromedia Director is a popular authoring system used by professionals and amateurs for creating animated multimedia presentations. Director employs a score that keeps track of each frame of the animation. Frames contain objects such as graphics, sounds, etc., that are stored in casts. A variety of tools are provided for constructing and embellishing these animations.

scenes is scripted: Motions, reactions, and interactions are prescribed for its actors. In addition, visual effects may be chosen for transitions between scenes. See Figure 12.57.

Authoring systems produce what are usually dubbed "multimedia presentations," because they combine images with sound and text and often have interactive features. For this reason, we will postpone their treatment for later. See Chapter 19 for more about multimedia authoring systems.

S U M M A R Y

A graphic image is a digital image that has been artificially generated by computer processing. Computers have been employed for creating graphic images since their inception in the 1950s. Bit-mapped graphic images are composed of pixels, which are two-dimensional picture elements that have a spatial location in the image and a set of attributes such as color or shade. In contrast, vector graphics or object-oriented graphics are images composed of graphic objects derived from primitives such as lines, curves, and closed figures. Vector graphics offer advantages in editing and greater precision for display resolution. On the other hand, bit-mapped graphics offer greater control and flexibility. Painting programs are a popular form of bit-mapped graphic applications. Drawing and illustration programs are vector graphic applications.

Painting, drawing, and illustration are two-dimensional graphic programs because the images are created, stored, and displayed as two-dimensional images. Three-dimensional graphic application programs allow the user to define and manipulate objects in simulated three dimensions. The program automatically calculates and displays the three-dimensional scene using perspective projection. Animation programs provide tools for automating the process of developing frames used in computer animations.

Computer graphics is a very powerful tool that has myriad uses. For this reason, graphic tools are not limited to just the application classes discussed in this chapter. For example, desktop publishing, graphing and charting programs, presentation software, and hypermedia are application domains that often incorporate a number of essential graphic capabilities. While their uses are constrained by their respective domains (producing documents, charts and graphs, electronic overheads, etc.), many of the concepts and features surveyed here apply to their use as well. The graphic landscape is rapidly changing, too. Indeed, the world of computer-generated pictures evolves and expands perhaps faster than any other facet of the digital domain.

PROJECTS

1 Using a painting program, recreate the image depicted in Figure 12.19. Try to select the circle and move it outside the rectangle. What happens? How accurate was your selection?

Repeat this process with a drawing program. What happens this time around? How accurate was your selection?

2 If your computer system is equipped with outline fonts (PostScript, TrueType, etc.), try the following experiment. Create a new document with a word processor. You might want to rearrange the page so that it is turned sideways (typically, "Landscape" setting in Page Setup). Type your name on a single line and copy it several times. Reformat the lines with progressively larger font sizes. For at least one line, choose an arbitrary font size—that is, enter a value not listed in the font size menu.

Print the page using a laser printer. Examine the lines carefully (you might even use a magnifying glass). Do the larger sizes look more blocky or jagged? If not, explain.

3 Conduct a Web-based search to find pages devoted to digital visual arts. (Try key words such as "digital art," "digital artists," and "computer art.") Compile a listing of the five most interesting pages or sites that you find.

4 The most impressive Web sites today are those that use graphic imagery in both integral and innovative ways. Conduct a Web-based search for pages dedicated to "Web design." Consult at least a dozen of these pages to examine the richness and variety of graphic elements employed on them.

5 Using a 3-D modeling and rendering program, create an image similar to the one depicted in Figure 12.50. Experiment with each of the different lighting and shading methods available in the application. Record both the amount of time needed for each rendering method and the overall quality of the results. Did you find any trends or generalizations from your observations? Explain.

6 Try your hand at creating an animated GIF. Using a painting program, create a banner with your name displayed in a large bold typeface. The background should be a solid color that will be used for your Web page (such as white). Note the image size of your name banner. You will need these dimensions to create the other frames of your animation. Save the image.

Reduce the size of this image to 90 percent of the original and save it as a new copy. Now increase the overall dimensions of the copy so that they are precisely the same as the original. There are a couple of ways to achieve this. Some graphic programs allow you to expand the canvas without affecting the size of the current image. This is the easiest solution. Otherwise, create a new empty image with the correct dimensions and the appropriate background color. Copy and paste the shrunken banner from the reduced version into the new image. Save the latter as the second frame of the animation.

Now shrink the original to 80 percent and save it again as a new copy. Repeat the process described above until you have ten frames including your original; each image depicts the banner progressively smaller. Use GIF construction software (see Web site for details) to assemble and save your frames as an animated GIF. With this software, arrange the frames in reverse order to create a zoom effect: The banner will appear to move from background to foreground, growing larger as it approaches.

Post the image on a Web page using a standard image link (see Appendix). Test the page in your favorite Web browser.

Projects

Key Terms

actor	CGM (Computer graphics metafile)	Gouraud shading
animated GIF	clipping	handle
animation program	computer-assisted design (CAD)	hidden surface removal
AVI	computer graphics	illustration program
background	construction plane	image scale
Bezier curve	DAC-1	image size
bit-mapped graphics (raster graphics)	drawing program	in-between
	DXF (drawing exchange format)	key frame
B-spline curve	EPS (encapsulated PostScript)	Lambert shading (flat shading)
canvas	extrusion	lathing
cel	foreground	menu
cel animation	frame	model description

object-oriented graphic application	rasterizing	three-dimensional graphics (3-D graphics)
object-oriented graphics (vector graphics)	ray tracing	transformation
painting program	rendering	two-dimensional graphics (2-D graphics)
palette	resolution independence	
parametric curve	scene (animation)	vector graphics (object-oriented graphics)
PCX	scene description	
Phong shading	shot	volume-based 3-D graphics
pixel (picture element)	solid modeling	voxel (volume element)
polygon-surface modeling	story	wireframe construction
PostScript	storyboard	world view coordinate
QuickTime	streaming (data)	
	surface-based 3-D graphics	

QUESTIONS FOR REVIEW

1 Digital graphic images are often composed of pixels. How are pixels organized?

2 What does a bitplane refer to?

3 What are the major differences between bit-mapped and vector graphics?

4 What is 3-D graphics?

5 What advantages do 3-D graphic programs offer over 2-D applications?

6 How does a metafile format differ from a standard graphic file format?

7 Identify which graphic file formats store bit-mapped graphics and which store vector-based graphics: PCX, DXF.

8 What are the advantages of type or text based on a Page Description Language (e.g., PostScript)?

9 Compare and contrast painting and drawing programs. To what sorts of applications is each best suited?

10 What is the basic difference between the background and foreground in a painting program?

11 Distinguish among the concepts of image size, resolution, and scale.

12 Compare and contrast the functionality of drawing and illustration programs.

13 What are image layers? How does the process of clipping relate to this concept?

14 What are parametric curves? How are they employed in drawing and illustration programs?

15 Describe the two varieties of 3-D graphics (volume-based versus surface-based).

16 Surface-based 3-D graphic software usually divides the task of 3-D modeling into three stages: model description, scene description, and rendering. Describe each of these stages.

17 How does solid modeling differ from polygon-surface modeling and wireframe construction?

18 Explain the methods of extrusion and lathing for defining 3-D wireframe models.

19 Lambert shading, Gouraud shading, and Phong shading are forms of rendering that are often characterized in 3-D applications by their speed: fast, medium, and slow (respectively). Why would these rendering methods have different effective speeds? Explain.

20 Describe how animation programs automate some of the tasks normally associated with conventional cel animation.

21 What is an animated GIF? How is it created?

22 What is automated in-betweening?

23 How does the user create an animation in a 3-D modeling program?

Sound is a very important medium for conveying and receiving information. Consider, for example, a heated debate. The ways in which the words used in the debate are spoken convey meaning and nuances of expression well beyond what a written transcript of the debate conveys. In a similar way, reading a musical score gives most of us little insight into the beauty and power of the music it defines. Recall our earlier example from Chapter 2:

He didn't say that you were wrong.

As this example attests, even the meaning of a simple sentence can be vastly different, depending on which words are emphasized when the sentence is spoken.

Because sound is so important in conveying meaning, beauty, and the power of persuasion, including the medium of sound within our computerized communications is desirable. Modern computers and methods of converting sound to and from digital form provide us with this opportunity. In this chapter, you will learn about some of the basic concepts and techniques underlying this capability.

OBJECTIVES

- How sounds are converted to digital form
- Methods and principles for editing digital sound
- Computer methods for synthesizing speech
- The challenges involved in computer voice recognition and speech understanding
- Using the computer to compose and perform music

CHAPTER 13
MANAGING DIGITAL SOUND

Vasily Kandinsky, *Sketch for Composition II*, 1909-1910. Solomon R. Guggenheim Museum

DIGITAL SAMPLING OF SOUND

Most of today's desktop computers are sound-capable machines. We can store and manipulate sounds of all kinds—the spoken word, music, and artificially generated sounds such as synthesized music. Computers can generate speech from written text with reasonably good results and can even respond to voice commands within limited vocabularies.

This is all accomplished by working with digital sound. **Digital sound** is sound that has been converted to or created in a discrete form (that is, as a set of numeric values) suitable for storage and processing in a computer. Natural sounds are converted to digital form by a discrete sampling process. Sounds can also be created (or **synthesized**) employing one of several methods with a computer. Once in digital form, though, sound—just, as we saw, was the case for digitized images—can be modified or edited in a variety of ways. Whether converted or synthesized, digital sound can be "played" by a process that converts the discrete numeric values to an analog signal that audio speakers can transmit to our ears.

Unlike the process of digitizing images, digitizing sound involves sampling over time rather than spatially. You are already familiar with a sampling technique very much like the one employed for digitizing sound. When we make a video using a camcorder, we actually take a series of still photographs (called frames). The number of frames taken per second is called the sampling rate. You may have "stepped through" a video clip frame by frame, using your VCR. If you watch televised sporting events, you have seen slow-motion replays in which the action is "frozen" and projected slowly for careful viewing. The quality of the frozen frames depends on the resolution and speed of the camera as well as the film being used.

When the series of photographs in a video sequence is played back at approximately the same rate of speed that the pictures were taken, the action in the film can be made to appear quite natural to the eye. Recording and playback speeds are measured in frames per second (fps), and speeds of 24 fps or higher are usually sufficient for producing natural-looking apparent motion. In spite of this fact, *most* of the action is missing, but the frames that were captured are close enough in time to give us the sense of seeing the entire sequence of action. In films produced using video cameras with a slow filming rate, the action will appear "jumpy" as it is replayed. It is clear then that the sample rate at which images are taken is significant for fidelity during playback. In applications that require a precise, frame-by-frame analysis of a sequence for a very short-duration event (such as an explosion experiment), a very high sampling rate will be necessary for best results. On the other hand, if we intend only to replay the sequence for normal viewing, we can quite satisfactorily simulate the actual events filmed with a rate of 24 frames per second.

The size, or resolution, of the film being used will also affect the quality of a movie when it is played. If you have watched 8mm or 16mm home movies, you already are aware of the rather dramatic differences between these and standard 35mm films (or the 70mm films at theaters).

Sound sampling is based on essentially the same principles as those just described for video sampling. Sound, like the images that make up a scene, varies with time. Sound is produced by the vibration of some membrane. These vibrations are then transmitted as waves through a medium—usually air, but possibly water or some other medium. When this analog wave meets our ears, it causes our eardrums to vibrate and transmit the sound as a signal to our brains. Recording and playing digital sound require the conversion of the analog signal to a discrete form. Unlike the case for movies, however, this discrete form must be converted once more to a continuous analog form to reproduce the original sound in a satisfactory way. Just as with movie making, the sampling rate and resolution of the devices used will be crucial factors in the quality of the final product in digital sound.

Sampling Rates and Frequencies

You might recall that we used sound as an example in our discussion of analog phenomena in Chapter 2. Sounds are rapid vibrations that are transmitted as variations in air pressure. If you were to measure the intensity of a tone, for instance, it would be plotted as a continuously undulating line or **wave,** like the one depicted in Figure 13.1. Any sound wave has a number of fundamental characteristics. Two of its most important characteristics for digitization are amplitude and frequency. A sound wave's **amplitude** refers to the sound's intensity or loudness. A sound wave's **frequency** is determined by the length of time it takes the wave to complete one entire cycle. Frequency is usually measured in the unit **Hertz,** which stands for a cycle per second. Hence, a sound of frequency 5 KHz (= 5000 Hertz) is repeating its fundamental cycle 5,000 times per second. The frequency of a sound determines the pitch of the sound as heard by our ears—the higher the frequency, the higher the pitch of the sound.

Middle C on the piano produces a sound with frequency of 262 Hz, and the highest note (C8) on a piano has a frequency of 4186 Hz (or a little more than 4 KHz). If we examine the sound waves for middle C and C8, we see that they have exactly the same wave pattern or shape. The *only* difference in them is that they have different frequencies. The

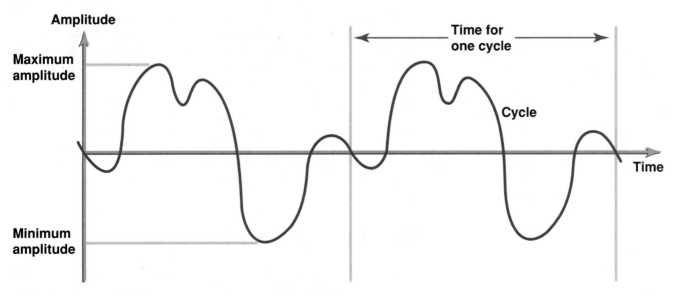

FIGURE 13.1

The figure illustrates the basic sound wave characteristics of cycle and amplitude.

human ear can typically hear frequencies from 20 Hz up to about 20 KHz, although we tend to lose our ability to hear frequencies in the upper range as we grow older. Some animals (dogs, for example) can hear significantly higher frequencies.

Let's consider the process of digitizing a sound wave. Sampling a sound wave consists of determining the amplitude of the sound at some number of discrete times within a given time interval. Although it is not necessary to do so, we generally will place these discrete times equal distances apart along the time axis. The number of these times chosen per second determines the **sampling rate.** It, too, is expressed in Hertz, which this time means the number of *samples* per second. A sampling rate of 22 KHz would mean dividing the time axis into 22,000 equally spaced times per second. Figures 13.2a and b illustrate.

We should point out that the actual reconstruction of an analog wave from the discrete values is done using more sophisticated mathematical techniques than the one shown in Figure 13.2c. Instead of assuming the amplitude to be a constant over each interval, the values are interpolated mathematically to supply a smoother curve. Nonetheless, no matter what technique is used, the sampling rate is still an inherent limitation on how accurately the original wave form can be reproduced.

Suppose for a moment that the frequency of the sound wave shown in Figure 13.2 is 2 KHz. What sampling rate have we adopted? Because we are sampling 20 points in every cycle and there are 2000 cycles per second, the sampling rate is $20 \times 2000 = 40,000 = 40$ KHz. As you will soon learn, a sampling rate in this range is satisfactory for even the most demanding musical applications. Thus, sampling 20 times per cycle would be appropriate for a wave of frequency around 2 KHz. On the other hand, for waves of higher frequencies, keeping the sampling rate around 40 KHz requires that we sample each cycle significantly fewer than 20 times. For example, if a sampled wave has a frequency of 10 KHz, we are able to sample only 4 points in each cycle if we are to keep the sampling rate at 40 KHz.

We must be careful not to drop the number of samples per cycle too low. What would happen if we adopted a sampling rate allowing only one sample per cycle? As Figure 13.3 illustrates, we would conclude upon reconstructing the analog wave that the sound had a constant amplitude—a very monotonous sound indeed! It is exactly this phenomenon—called **aliasing**—in movie filming that causes the wheels of the stagecoach to appear to "stand still" occasionally in some of the older Western movies. It occurs when the sample rate of the camera (shutter speed) matches the revolution rate of the wheel so that each time the shutter opens, the wheel is photographed in what appears to be exactly the same position. As a general rule, we must sample at least two points in each sound wave cycle to have reasonable hope that we have captured enough of the quality of a sound to reconstruct it satisfactorily. This rule is known as **Nyquist's theorem.**

ADCs and DACs

The devices that perform the sampling of an analog wave to produce a digital file are called **analog-to-digital converters,** or **ADCs** for short. The devices that perform the opposite transformation—reconstructing an analog wave from a digital file—are called **digital-to-analog converters,** or **DACs**

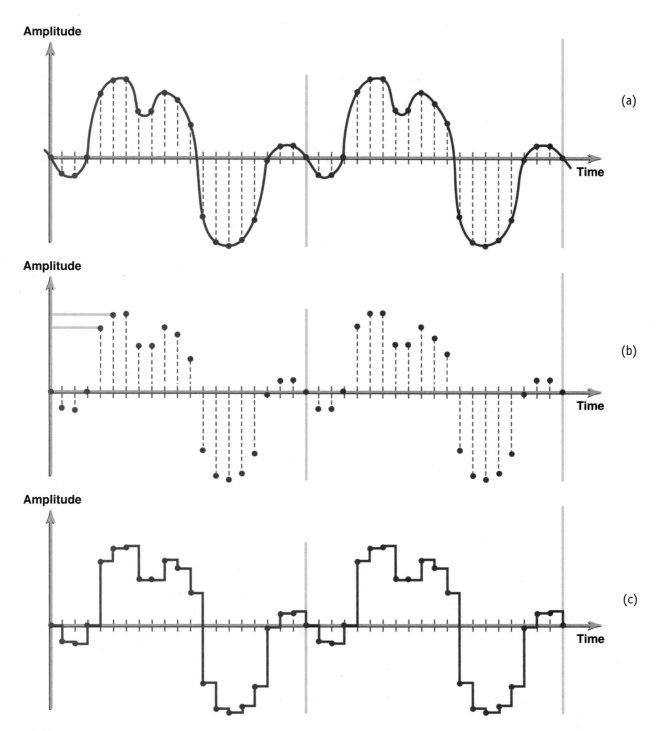

FIGURE 13.2

The process of sampling and reconstructing a sampled sound wave involves several steps. In (a), the wave is sampled at a predetermined rate. The particular rate chosen provides for twenty samples to be taken for each complete cycle of the sound wave. Forty samples are taken for the two cycles shown. In (b), the discrete samples are represented. For each of the forty points shown, the value of the amplitude is recorded and stored. Finally, in (c), a simple analog reconstruction is derived from the forty sampled values. In this reconstruction, the amplitude of the sound is made a constant over each of the intervening intervals between sample points. You can readily see how the sampling rate will affect the fidelity of the reconstructed sound from this figure.

for short. The choice of sample rates when digitizing sound is a function of the capability of the ADC you are using. Likewise, the resulting quality of playback when converting from digital to analog is limited by the capability of the DAC you are using. If you own an audio compact disc player, you own a DAC. Sound wave reconstruction from a discrete set of values is exactly the process that must be accomplished to play your audio CDs.

Audio compact discs are recorded using an ADC that samples at a rate of 44.1 KHz. According to Nyquist's theorem, this should be sufficient to capture all sounds in the range of frequencies (up to 20 KHz or so) that the human ear hears. If we are recording speech, it is rare for the human voice to contain frequencies much higher than 5 KHz (approximately the frequency of C8, remember); hence, a sampling rate of about 10 KHz is usually quite sufficient.

To use a personal computer for digitizing sound, you must have a microphone attached to an ADC and a connection to allow you to store the values produced by the ADC in your computer's memory or on disk. This may require that a **digital audio capture card,** which will contain an ADC, be installed in one of your computer's internal expansion slots, although some computers come with a built-in ADC. You can also buy an external ADC device, which contains both an ADC and a microphone that plugs into a standard serial port on your computer.

Resolution and Dynamic Range

We have seen the effect that sampling rate has on a digitized sound wave. There is another important factor to consider—the resolution at which we capture and store the sample point amplitudes. The **resolution**

FIGURE 13.3

Sampling a sound wave using one sample per cycle produces unacceptable results. Note that we have lost almost all of the sound's characteristics upon reconstructing it. As a general rule, we must sample at least two points in each wave cycle to have reasonable hope that we have captured enough of the quality of a sound to reconstruct it satisfactorily.

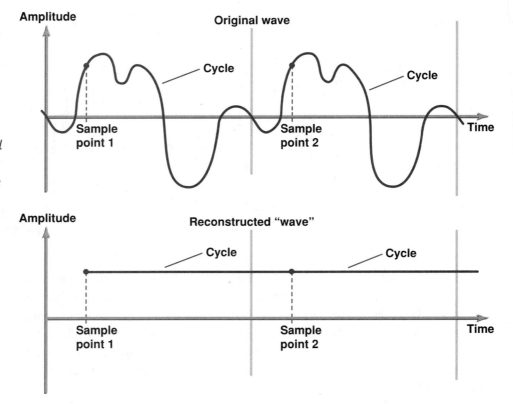

of digitized sound refers to the accuracy with which we represent each sampled amplitude. Figure 13.4 illustrates. The resolution we use will largely be determined by the amount of memory we're willing to devote to storing digitized sound.

If we are sampling for many seconds at 40 KHz per second, we will soon acquire a large number of sample point amplitudes. For only one minute of sound, this sampling rate would produce a total of 60 × 40,000 = 2,400,000 amplitudes for storage. Of course, we might well desire to capture 100 times this much sound (an entire speech or concert, for example). Given such large quantities of data, storing the individual values as efficiently as possible becomes important. As a result, we are often forced to adopt a less than optimal storage scheme that sacrifices some accuracy for economy.

The usual sound storage scheme involves scaling the range of amplitudes we wish to store so that we store these values as integers because integers require less memory than floating point numbers (real numbers). Recall from Chapter 8 that 2 bytes (or 16 bits) are typically allocated for integer storage, whereas 4 bytes (or 32 bits) are most often used to store floating point numbers. The space requirements for storing sound are so demanding that we are sometimes forced to reduce even the 16-bit allocation for integers.

One practical storage scheme allocates only a single byte (or 8 bits) for storing each amplitude. Such sound storage systems are referred to as **8-bit digital sound** for this reason, and we say that the sound is stored with 8-bit resolution. Using an 8-bit scheme, we must scale the range of amplitudes so that we represent the entire spectrum of amplitudes with integer values from 0 to 255 because the unsigned integer 255 is the largest we can represent in 8 bits. Every sampled amplitude must be mapped to this scale and rounded off to the nearest of the 256 values allowed by the storage scheme. Many DACs—your compact disc player included—employ **16-bit digital sound.** These devices use 16-bit resolution, which provides much more accurate sound reproduction. Newer systems employ 32-bit digital sound and even higher. The total range of amplitude values that can be stored determines the **dynamic range** of the digitized sound.

FIGURE 13.4

The accuracy of stored amplitudes depends on resolution. Some accuracy is always lost by scaling and representing amplitude values only with integers. Clearly, the more integers we have to use in the representation, the more accurate the approximation will be.

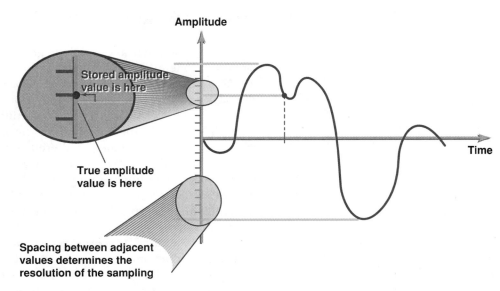

When we are sampling voice, the approximations for amplitude values in 8-bit resolution are accurate enough to reproduce the sound satisfactorily. For music, however, 8-bit resolution is not sufficient for high fidelity, and our ears will generally be able to distinguish the playback from the original. For this reason, 16-bit resolution is typically used to digitize music. Using this scheme, we can divide the dynamic range into a larger number of integers because we use 16 bits to store each value. How much additional resolution do we get by doubling the amount of storage required? Actually, we see quite an impressive improvement. Recall that we can store 256 integers ($= 2^8$) using 8 bits. With 16 bits, we can store $2^{16} = 65,536$—an improvement of more than 25,000 percent!

Sometimes extending the scale of amplitudes to include the very highest and lowest amplitudes will cause significant degradation in the accuracy with which all amplitudes are stored. When this occurs, it may be better to lose the highest and lowest amplitudes by reducing the scale range and improving the accuracy with which the majority of the amplitude values are stored. This amounts to reducing the dynamic range of the sound being digitized. By reducing the dynamic range, the accuracy can be significantly improved for the bulk of the data being stored, as illustrated in Figure 13.5.

Each situation may dictate a different consideration of the trade-offs involved. Whenever the dynamic range is restricted, those amplitudes outside the range will be given the highest or lowest values (whichever applies) in the range—the sound wave will be effectively "chopped" off at the limits of the range. This effect is often called **clipping.**

The system we are using for playback will always have some dynamic response limitations (inability to reproduce sounds faithfully with especially low or especially high amplitudes or loudness). In some cases, the reduction in the dynamic range of stored values may actually cost us very little in the quality of the sounds when they are played back. For example, the frequency response of small speaker systems that are supplied for computers is usually quite limited in very low and very high amplitudes. Clipping the input signal in this instance will likely produce no discernible effect.

Storage Requirements for Digitized Sound

Let's analyze a practical example to get a better feeling for sound storage requirements. We mentioned earlier that your audio CD player is a DAC (digital-to-analog converter). The sound on a CD is stored in digital form (unlike a phonograph record, which stores music in an analog form). The sampling (i.e., recording) is usually done at a rate of 44.1 MHz with 16-bit resolution. Because all CDs are in stereo, we must record two channels, thereby doubling the storage requirements. Now, with these parameters to work with, how many bits are required to store an hour of music on a CD? For each second, we store $44,100 \times 16 \times 2 = 1.4$ million bits. For the full hour, $60 \times 60 = 3600$ times this number, or about 5 billion bits or approximately 630 MB, will be required!

Actually, audio CD recordings also include a lot of error-correcting and noise reduction information as well. Altogether this information more than doubles the storage requirements. With today's technology, these numbers are beyond the capacity of a compact disc, so until DVD

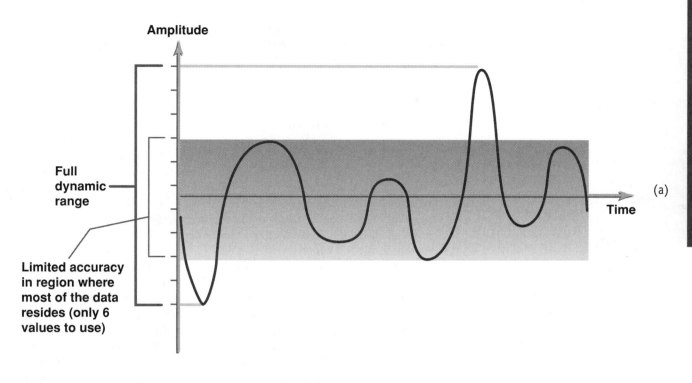

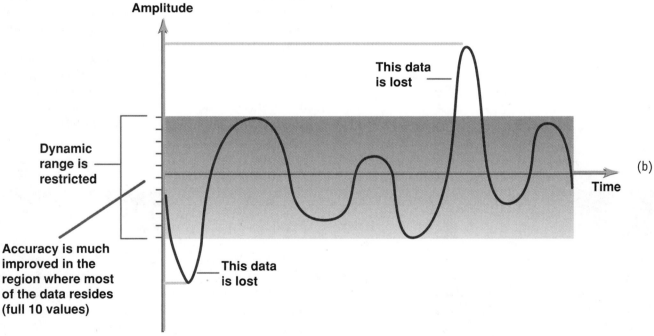

FIGURE 13.5

This example illustrates accuracy and dynamic range trade-offs. Note that only ten different values are to be stored for a wave's amplitudes. In (a), the full dynamic range is captured. Accuracy is greatly increased by limiting the dynamic range, as illustrated in (b). The cost of this increased accuracy is a loss of data outside the range of values chosen.

discs become more common, you shouldn't expect to find three-hour concerts on a single disc. Of course, it wouldn't be difficult to put three hours of conversation, speeches, or other spoken words on a single CD because we could reduce the resolution to 8 bits and the sample rate to about 10 KHz with no discernible reduction in quality.

One method to combat the large storage requirements for sound digitization is to compress the sampled sound. **File compression** is accomplished using techniques that mathematically transform the file's data so that the resulting data requires less memory. When the file data is needed again, the reverse transformation recovers the original data (or a close approximation to it) for our use. You'll learn more about the techniques of data compression in Chapter 15.

A number of proprietary compression algorithms are available to compress sound files. These will usually provide a choice of several levels of compression—2:1, 3:1, and 6:1 ratios, for example. As you would surmise, a file compressed at a 2:1 ratio uses only one-half the amount of storage, and one compressed at the 6:1 rate uses only one-sixth the amount. A 3:1 compression is suitable for music under certain circumstances, although some loss of fidelity occurs. The 6:1 compression is suitable only for speech.

Rather than using compression, storage requirements can also be reduced using a lower sampling rate or a lower resolution in the first place. Which method is preferred? In general, you are better off digitizing at a higher sampling rate then compressing the resulting file, as opposed to using a lower sampling rate in the first place. There are two good reasons for this. For approximately the same storage, a 3:1 compressed sample will sound better than one sampled at one-third the rate. The reason is that the compression algorithm uses certain strategies to decide which sample points to omit. That is, it doesn't just drop two of every three sample points; rather, it tries to choose those points that will have minimal effect on the reconstructed sound.

There is another reason why it is better to sample fully and compress later if necessary. By taking a full sample, you optimize the editing that you might choose to do on the digitized sound. (You will see some standard editing techniques shortly.) In general, digital sound editing is more satisfactory if done before, rather than after, compression.

More Information

SOUND ON THE WORLD WIDE WEB

As you know, sounds are often found on Web pages. Just as is the case for external images, your Web browser must have audio player software to play these files. When you click over a Web page link to an external resource, the file will be downloaded to your computer system as a temporary file. Depending on the type of file (image, sound, or video), an appropriate player application will be identified and opened, and the file will be handled by that player application. Player applications come in two varieties: helper applications and plug-ins. **Helper applications** are external player applications, while **plug-ins** are add-on programs to the browser stored in an accessible directory or folder.

How does the browser identify the correct player application? Every Web-delivered media file arrives at the browser with an identifier called a **multipurpose Internet mail extension (MIME)** included in the file. A MIME specifies both a general type (such as image, audio, or video) and a subtype (like GIF or JPEG for images) for the file it identifies. The browser uses this information to seek an appropriate helper or plug-in application and then sends the file's downloaded data directly to that application.

Not unlike image files, sound files can be stored in a number of different formats. Various vendors have developed their own sound file formats, and each format has its own proprietary compression and storage schemes. Consequently, the different formats are not compatible with one another; to play a sound file of a particular file type, you must have an appropriate player application available. Three sound file formats appear quite frequently on the Web. The **aiff sound file format** was developed by Apple Computer and is the likely sound file type for sounds digitized using a Macintosh computer. Microsoft developed the **wav sound file format,** and sounds digitized on Windows computers will likely be in this format. The **au sound file format** was developed at Sun Microsystems, and sound files captured on Sun workstations are often in this format.

No matter which of these standard sound file formats a linked sound file happens to be in, the file must be downloaded in its entirety before it is played. This limitation was addressed in 1995, when Progressive Networks introduced RealAudio, the first streaming audio system on the Web. See Figure 13.6. A **streaming audio system** is one in which the browser initiates playing a sound file as it arrives (without waiting for the entire file to be transferred) and continues playing it until conclusion. RealAudio developed a special sound file format called the **ra sound file format** for their streaming audio system. As you will learn in later chapters, the Internet operates as a packet switching network, which means it distributes its data in small, discrete packets and so does not support continuous information delivery. To get

around this limitation, a stream-handling helper or plug-in must place a certain amount of the data stream it receives in a buffer so that it can accommodate delayed or lost packets later in the stream without interrupting the playback. This introduces an unavoidable delay at the beginning of the playback while the player program stockpiles an initial buffer of data. Once the playback starts, however, it proceeds continuously provided that the network transmission is not interrupted. Of course, the faster your Internet connection, the better this is going to work.

In recent years, other companies have introduced streaming audio systems, and, of course, each has its own proprietary sound file format, but the principles are the same as those of the original RealAudio system. The latest of these systems promise "real-time" CD-quality sound over a 28.8 Kbps (bits per second) modem.

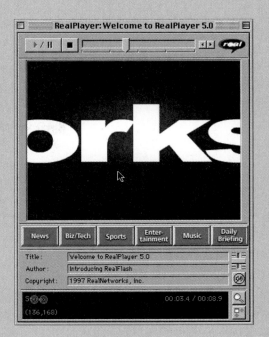

FIGURE 13.6
The figure shows the interface for the RealAudio player. RealAudio was among the first programs to bring streaming audio to the Web. The player software is available free.

SYNTHESIZING MUSIC

One of the earliest uses of computers for audio processing was as a component in sound synthesis systems. Synthesized sound, of course, is created electronically. It is most often used to produce music created with electronic instruments as opposed to traditional woodwind, percussion, and brass instruments. The methods used to "play" these new instruments differ, of course, from those of traditional instruments. In fact, music synthesis methods can vary considerably, and new ones are introduced regularly. Even so, all these methods do have some common features. All methods employ a basic component, called an **oscillator,** as a sound source. Oscillators can be analog or digital devices. In either case, a steady electrical signal is produced in the human audible frequency range of 20 Hz to 20 KHz. Musical tones are then generated by combining two or more oscillators. The particular methods of combination are the source of most of the variation in the synthesizers available today.

Simple Waveforms

The oscillators in a synthesis system produce very simple waveforms—usually one of the four basic types: sine wave, square wave, triangle wave, and sawtooth wave, shown in Figure 13.7. Most sounds are complex waveforms made up of some combination of a number of simple waveforms. A rather surprising mathematical fact is that we can build arbitrarily close approximations to any complex waveform by combining waveforms of any of these simple types. This is the theoretical basis of music synthesis (and much of data communications as well). By cleverly combining simple oscillator-generated waveforms, synthesizers can be designed to make sounds like those from common musical instruments, as well as sounds that are different from those of any conventional instrument.

Basic Synthesis Techniques

As we mentioned earlier, there are many different synthesis methods. We will briefly discuss several to give you a flavor of the different ap-

FIGURE 13.7

These are the basic oscillator waveforms for sound synthesis. Using a technique called additive synthesis, we can combine waves with variations in frequency and amplitude of any one of these forms to build very good approximations to an arbitrarily complex sound wave.

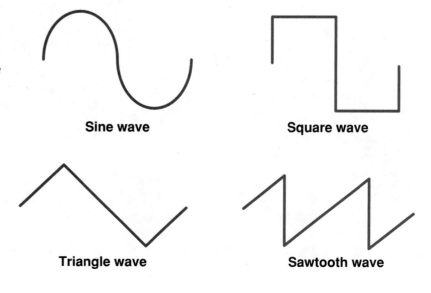

Sine wave   Square wave

Triangle wave   Sawtooth wave

proaches possible. Each of these techniques has been extensively studied in its own right and could occupy many pages if we were exploring the topic in depth.

An early method still used today for many analog synthesizers is called **subtractive synthesis.** In this method, you start with a very complex waveform generated by signals from several oscillators, mixed with specific types of noise. Filters are then used to remove (or subtract out) unwanted noise, leaving the desired sound. The noise provides the base for a wide variety in the final sound produced. There are several different kinds of noise, usually referred to by color names. Two of the most frequently used types are called white noise and pink noise. **White noise** contains a random distribution of frequencies uniformly distributed throughout the range of frequencies being used. **Pink noise** contains a random distribution of frequencies uniformly distributed throughout each octave in the frequency range. The different distribution of frequencies matters because each time we rise an octave in pitch, the number of frequencies in the octave doubles.

Additive synthesis takes the opposite approach of starting with simple waveforms and building more complex waveforms. Additive synthesis is based on the mathematical theory called **Fourier analysis.** This theory is named for the nineteenth-century French mathematician Jean Fourier, who developed the elements of the theory (long before computer applications of the theory, of course). It allows the mathematical computation of component sine waves that can be combined to form a given complex wave. Additive synthesizers can be more finely tuned than can subtractive synthesizers. Such synthesizers were used in the early Hammond electronic organs of the 1970s.

Another popular synthesizing technique, introduced by Yamaha, is called **frequency modulation synthesis** (**FM synthesis,** for short). In FM synthesis, two simple waveforms are used. One wave (called the **modulator**) is used to modify the other (called the **carrier**) to a more complex form. It is essentially the same technique used to create FM radio waves. FM synthesis produces very rich sound, but it is not as easy to control as the subtractive and additive synthesis techniques.

A more recent method called **phase distortion synthesis** was introduced by Casio. It produces much of the richness of FM synthesizers but with the control of additive synthesizers. The fundamental idea in phase distortion synthesis is to distort a simple waveform by modifying the time scale at different rates, changing the time it takes for a portion of a cycle to be completed. Complex waveforms can be constructed using this technique and wave envelope templates.

The most recently developed synthesizers combine pure synthesis with digitized samples. Many waveforms have a similar basic shape, or **envelope.** See Figure 13.8. This commonly occurring envelope is referred to as an **ADSR (attack, decay, sustain, release)** form. The attack portion of a wave is often the most complex and hence the most difficult to synthesize accurately. Some of the newer synthesis techniques employ digitally sampled sounds to construct the attack portion and synthesize the decay, sustain, and release portions. These methods are often referred to as **integrated synthesis** or **variable architecture synthesis.** They were introduced in the late 1980s and are being further developed today. The ADSR form illustrated in Figure 13.8 is the simplest general wave shape used. In fact, most integrated synthesis systems allow the waveform to be broken into many more than four stages—some allow as many as 256 stages.

FIGURE 13.8

This figure shows a common envelope for a musical waveform. The attack portion is typically the most complex of the four parts and hence the most difficult to synthesize.

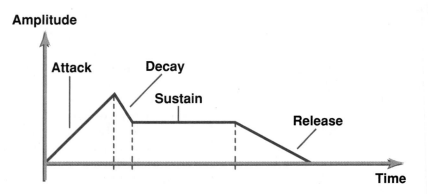

MIDI Instruments and Devices

With a great many manufacturers producing music synthesizers and related devices, the industry recognized early on that a standard interface between electronic instruments and synthesizers would be a great convenience. In 1982, the **MIDI (musical instrument digital interface)** standard was agreed upon by an international group of manufacturers. This standard specifies a common interface allowing musical instruments that contain microprocessors (computers) to communicate with other instruments and devices containing microprocessors. The interface specified includes the kinds and configurations of cables and cable plugs as well as the format of the data being transferred over the cables.

For example, you may own or have a friend who owns an electronic keyboard. See Figure 13.9 for an example. Some electronic keyboards contain their own synthesizers and amplifiers. Others do not and depend on using external synthesizers and amplifiers. Even for those that do, a desirable feature is to attach to a more powerful or feature-laden synthesizer. When you purchase a MIDI keyboard, you can be assured of finding amplifiers and synthesizers with which your keyboard can communicate effectively—in fact, most such devices will be **MIDI compatible.** Similarly, computer software designed to compose and edit music usually provides for input and output in the MIDI format. This means that the computer may be directly attached to a synthesizer to play the composed music or attached to a MIDI keyboard to capture musical notes being played.

We should note that the signals being transferred over the MIDI cables are not actual sounds. Rather, what is passed are the parameters from which the sound can be generated by the instrument receiving the signal. Such parameters include identification of the note being pressed, the length of time it was held down, the aftertouch (amount

FIGURE 13.9

Pictured here is a Casio CTK-510 MIDI keyboard. It has sixty-one touch-sensitive notes on a full-sized keyboard, and it permits the addition of preprogrammed beats and rhythms in a variety of instruments.

of pressure applied to a key after it is fully depressed), the pitch blend setting, the program number selected (which determines the kind of sound or instrument associated with the key), and a host of other information.

The MIDI format has several advantages over full digital sound files. It is much more compact, can be easily edited, and allows for musical tracks to be easily combined (superimposed). For example, the software Finale is a popular program for editing MIDI files and mixing multiple tracks.

More Information

SPEECH SYNTHESIS AND RECOGNITION

Potentially one of the most promising uses of the computer's sound capabilities is computer/human interaction using spoken language. You've undoubtedly heard computer-generated messages and information on the airport tram and the subway, in elevators, at the grocery checkout, and in a host of other locations. These messages provide valuable information in a readily accessible form without the need for a human communicator. Although such applications of computer-generated speech, or **speech synthesis,** are convenient, the same functions could be achieved through other means—such as screen displays, printed messages, and so on. For some applications, however, communicating information using generated speech is not only convenient but essential.

For example, in modern airplane cockpits, the number of dials, gauges, and digital readouts has become so large that it is difficult for a pilot to keep track of all the information important to the task at hand. This is especially true in an emergency situation that calls for complex maneuvers with little margin for error in sequencing and timing. Even if a portion of the information could be communicated by simple verbal messages, the pilot could absorb more information in the same amount of time. In fighter planes, such communication can be critical. For example, when evading an enemy plane or missile, the pilot simply cannot digest all the requisite information within the tight time constraints imposed. With computer-generated speech, the pilot can better absorb and process enough information to perform proper maneuvers.

The ability to generate speech from written text makes the computer an indispensable tool for the visually impaired. For example, using this capability, computers can read aloud books, magazines, newspapers, and electronic mail for visually impaired users. Of course, Braille versions of a great deal of written material are available. But the computer's ability to "read" electronic mail and daily newspapers enables the visually impaired to handle a form of communication that they otherwise could not.

The ability of a computer to react to spoken commands, called **automated speech recognition,** completes the communication cycle. For example, using speech recognition systems, pilots not only receive valuable information from their planes, but they can issue verbal commands to be executed. Similarly, the visually impaired can engage in electronic communication and employ their computers efficiently and more productively.

In this section, we will explore the basic concepts involved with both modes of verbal communication with computers—computer speech synthesis and speech recognition.

Computer Speech Synthesis

Of the two processing tasks—speech synthesis and speech recognition—generating speech from written text is by far the less complicated. Speech synthesis can be handled in one of several ways. An obvious approach might be to store the pronunciation of the most frequently used words in a digital speech dictionary. We could employ one or more persons to read the words for digitization and then store the digitized sound for later recall. Reading a selection of text would then be accomplished in a way quite similar to that of checking text for misspellings: Each word would be looked up in the speech dictionary. Once found, its associated digitized pronunciation would be played. A **binary search tree** organization like that used for spelling dictionaries and database indices (see Chapters 9 and 10) could be employed for storing and accessing the speech dictionary more efficiently.

There are several difficulties with this approach, though. First, it would require a large amount of storage—far larger than the corresponding spelling dictionary. The digitized sounds for each word would have to be stored. Let's assume that, on the average, it takes about one second to speak a word. If we digitize these sounds at a sampling rate of 5 KHz with an 8-bit resolution (the minimum acceptable settings), we would still consume, on average, about 5000 bytes of storage for each spoken word. For a 100,000-word dictionary, this amounts to 500 MB of data—a sizable percentage of the storage available for the typical desktop computer system! Clearly, this is not a very practical solution. In addition, our dictionary is bound to omit words that we would wish to pronounce—names of people and places, slang words, specialized terms in a given subject area, and so on. It is also difficult to achieve a natural speech rate when every word must be accessed on a hard disk before being pronounced. Even with a binary search tree organization, the rate at which the text can be "read back" doesn't give a natural sound to the reading. Finally, our dictionary lookup method would not be able to pronounce words that are spelled the same but read differently according to the context in which they are used (like the word *read,* for example).

An alternate method for speech synthesis involves an analysis of the written text before trying to pronounce it. A language like English employs a surprisingly sparse (fewer than 50) set of basic sounds, called **phonemes.** The language gains its richness of expression by the large number of possible combinations of these sounds. To exploit this fact in speech synthesis, the computer first breaks the text selection up into a sequence of basic phonemes; then each phoneme can be quickly looked up in a digital speech dictionary and pronounced. Because this dictionary holds only 50 or so sounds, it requires very little disk space. In fact, using our earlier assumptions about sampling rate and resolution (5 KHz and 8 bits, respectively) and the fact that the average phoneme probably takes less than one-fifth the time to verbalize as a full word, we could store a 50-phoneme dictionary in about 50,000 bytes. At this size, the entire dictionary could be loaded from disk into main memory for very rapid lookup and retrieval.

Phoneme analysis and decomposition are the methods most often used to synthesize speech whenever the target text is unpredictable. In other words, if we desire to synthesize subway car alert messages employing a 100-word vocabulary, we may well store the entire digital dictionary and look up words as needed. On the other hand, if we are trying to create a program to read the evening newspaper, we almost certainly will use a phoneme analysis and decomposition method.

Phoneme decomposition, however, is not a trivial task. As we have already noted, many words are spelled the same yet pronounced differently. A good speech synthesis program will recognize and correctly determine the most common of these occurrences. It is also the case that the same sound can be represented by different groups of letters. Consider the words "enough" and "buff," for instance. The letters "ough" and "uff" represent the same sound in this case. If English were more phonetically regular, "enough" would be spelled "enuff," or perhaps "buff" would be spelled "bough." Oops! The word "bough" is already in the language and pronounced quite differently from "buff." In fact, exactly the same group of letters ("ough") is pronounced entirely differently in the words "enough" and "bough." (To add to the confusion, consider the words "cough," "though," and "through.")

Do we give up on phoneme decomposition? Not at all. After all, we learned to pronounce English text without having to learn every single word as a separate sound combination. How did we accomplish this? We first learned a number of basic phonetic rules; then we learned that every rule (or so it seemed) had its own exceptions that we had to remember individually. We can mimic this learning process to create a program to separate words into their phonemes. The result is a system based on a number of fundamental rules, with their exceptions programmed as additional rules. Even more rules can be added to help decide between different pronunciations for the same word (i.e., same spelling) depending on the context. Using this **rule-based phoneme recognition** approach, it is possible to create a speech synthesis program that produces good results.

For example, the following sentence contains two different uses of the abbreviation "Dr." as well as three different uses of numbers—one as a day of the month, another as a year, and the third as a street address.

On June 5, 1995, Dr. Jones moved to 1702 Oakwood Dr.

A good rule-based speech synthesis program will be able to read this sentence, correctly making these distinctions. It would be read as follows:

On June fifth, nineteen ninety-five, Doctor Jones moved to seventeen hundred two Oakwood Drive.

Automated Speech Recognition

The problems inherent in automated speech recognition are much more difficult to solve than those of speech synthesis. As we shall see, there are several fundamental differences between these two processes. In speech synthesis we start with text and must discover and program the rules to separate text into phonemes. In speech recognition, we first digitize the speech, then we must reconstruct the words that were spoken. Consider the word "hello," whose digital form as spoken by one speaker is shown in Figure 13.10.

Programming a computer to recognize this pattern of points as the word "hello" would indeed be a challenge. Recall that the envelope of the sound is the overall shape of the amplitudes—the outline of the sound, so to speak. The envelope is very useful for trying to decide what sound has been digitized, but the transformation from envelope to iden-

FIGURE 13.10

This figure illustrates one possible digital form for the word "hello."

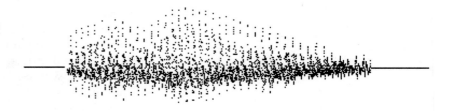

tification is not completely straightforward. Many different sounds have envelopes that are quite similar.

The envelope is an attempt to characterize the sound with a high-level summary of its digitization. Taking the opposite approach, if we stretch the time axis (the horizontal axis), perhaps the additional detail exposed will be helpful. While this additional detail may be helpful in some cases, as you can imagine, it becomes even more difficult to distinguish two sounds when you are examining tiny fractions of a second at a time. Consult Figure 13.11, which shows a portion of the digitized word "hello" with the time scale expanded to expose the individual sample points. Remember that this is the actual data a voice recognition system must deal with. It must be able to conclude from such data what word was spoken. This would be difficult enough if a word's digital form were unique. Unfortunately, this is far from the case.

In speech synthesis, we start with text in a form (ASCII code) that is unambiguous and consistent. In voice recognition, we don't have the luxury of beginning with a consistent source of digitized sound. No two people will speak a word in exactly the same way, as Figure 13.12 illustrates. The human voice is almost as distinctive and individualized as fingerprints. Think of how easily you can recognize the voice of a friend or of a famous person whom you have heard speak many times. In fact, voice recognition is used in some computerized security systems.

Regional and national accents also play a major role in speech recognition. A person from New Jersey is likely to pronounce many words differently from the way a person from South Carolina pronounces the same words. Someone from Scotland will introduce even more dramatic differences. We usually have no trouble "hearing" and interpreting these differences, but the digital versions of the words will have very different features. Programming a computer to recognize such differences is not easy.

In addition to the variation from person to person, even a single person will not say the same word exactly the same way each time. The mood you are in, the stress you might be under, the position of the word in a sentence, the emphasis that is intended, whether you have a cold, plus many other factors, all contribute to this variability. See Figure 13.13. Yet, in all these situations, if the (same) spoken words are written, they look the same. As you can see, recognizing voice is a very different matter from synthesizing speech from text.

FIGURE 13.11

The digital form of the word "hello," shown in Figure 13.10, is illustrated here with the time axis stretched to reveal more detail. The portion of the word shown here is very small—a tiny fraction of a second.

FIGURE 13.12

Digitized versions of "hello" from three speakers are shown here. Note the distinctive differences in the three digitizations. Differences such as these must be identified and eliminated in speech recognition work.

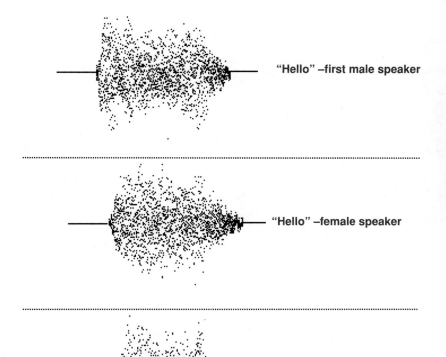

"Hello" —first male speaker

"Hello" —female speaker

"Hello" —second male speaker

FIGURE 13.13

The figure illustrates three different ways the same person might say the word "hello." Speech recognition must be able to deal successfully with such differences.

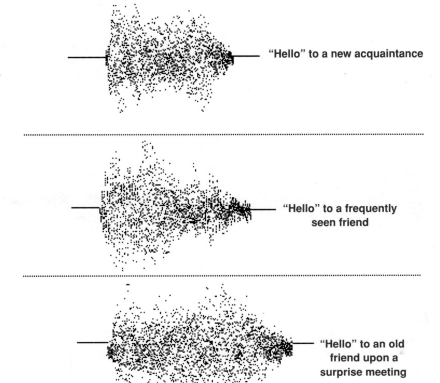

"Hello" to a new acquaintance

"Hello" to a frequently seen friend

"Hello" to an old friend upon a surprise meeting

Because of the variability from person to person, current commercial voice recognition systems are commonly "tuned" to a single person's voice. In other words, these systems are designed to recognize words the way a particular individual speaks them. These are called **speaker-dependent speech recognition systems** because the user must train them to recognize his or her speech. When the same words are spoken by another person, the system may not recognize them at all or may recognize only a portion of them.

For example, early work done on speech recognition systems was designed to help fighter pilots communicate commands to their aircraft. These **voice activation systems** were specially designed and tuned for individual pilots. After extensive ground testing, they were put into service on a trial basis in actual flights. It was discovered that the systems that worked wonderfully in the ground-based tests were woefully inadequate during flights. The voice patterns of the pilots were not the same on the ground and during a flight. Especially during times of stress, the pilot voice patterns changed enough to raise the error rate to unacceptable levels.

The problems to be solved in speech recognition extend beyond those inherent in recognizing single words. Such systems must also be able to separate words within the digital version. In some cases, this is relatively easy; in others, quite difficult. If the phrase to be digitized is spoken clearly and relatively slowly, with each word distinctly enunciated, the division between words in the digitization may be relatively clear-cut and unambiguous. Figure 13.14 illustrates. On the other hand, we've all known people whose speech patterns make it difficult for us sometimes to pick up every word spoken, as illustrated in Figure 13.15.

Indeed, when we hear a passage spoken in a foreign language in which we are not fluent, we often think that the speakers are speaking a nonstop barrage of words in very rapid succession. Of course, most often the speech is at a normal pace. What makes it sound so "fast" is that we cannot effectively separate the individual words being spoken because our ears are not tuned to the patterns and rhythm of the language being spoken. To the computer, all languages are foreign! Speech recognition programs must be cleverly constructed to pick out individual words from a stream of digitized sample points. This is rarely an easy task.

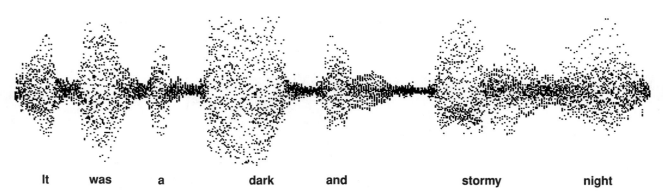

It   was   a   dark   and   stormy   night

FIGURE 13.14

This figure illustrates the digital form for a sentence in which the division between words is relatively clear-cut and unambiguous—although even here it may not be entirely clear how to separate the words "stormy" and "night." The sentence digitized here was spoken clearly and relatively slowly with each word distinctly enunciated (as Vincent Price might have said it).

FIGURE 13.15

Compare this figure with Figure 13.14. The same sentence is digitized in each case, but in the current case, the speaker is speaking in a more relaxed, colloquial manner—not being careful to enunciate individual words. You can see clearly from these two figures that even deciding where the words appear in a portion of digitized speech can be a challenge.

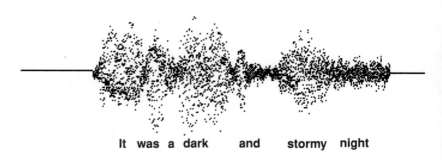

It   was   a   dark   and   stormy   night

More Information

Speech recognition systems that are able to recognize a multitude of different speakers and the same speaker in a variety of environments are said to be **robust speech recognition systems.** Such systems are very challenging to construct, and successful ones are few. Currently, successful systems require a number of constraints, such as limited vocabularies and restricted contexts, to produce good results. A great deal of energy and money has been spent over the past twenty years on this problem. It has proved to be one of the most formidable problems yet attacked in computing. Progress has been made, and the work continues. Although we still have a way to go before voice-activated computers become commonplace, we will no doubt see more and more products incorporating voice recognition in the next few years.

EDITING DIGITIZED SOUND

Once a selection of sound is digitized and stored inside the computer as a collection of numbers, many editing possibilities arise. Digital sound editing belongs to the general category of techniques and methods collectively called **digital signal processing.** Most of these techniques were created and studied thoroughly, long before the present use of computers for sound manipulation. For example, radar and radio transmissions are often digitized and processed to filter out noise and highlight the parts of the signal containing relevant information.

As we pointed out earlier, one of the major advantages of converting analog information to digital form is the ease with which its digital approximation can be manipulated and modified. The precision with which digital information is stored allows very tight control over even the individual sample points if we choose. In this section, we will take a brief look at some representative sound editing techniques.

A number of software applications are designed especially for digital sound editing and modification. The first application, and still one of the most popular of these packages, was SoundEdit, available on the Macintosh. Indeed, most other sound editing software has been heavily influenced by SoundEdit, and many of these programs have been designed to mimic its user interface. For example, Sound Forge, which is available for Windows computers, is modeled after SoundEdit. In our discussion and especially in the accompanying figures, we will occasionally refer to features in SoundEdit or Sound Forge, but be assured that these features also exist in most other sound editing software and that their implementations will be quite similar.

The Sound Editing Window

When a sound file is opened in sound editing software, a basic interface and editing window are displayed. Figures 13.16 and 13.17 illustrate for SoundEdit and Sound Forge, respectively. Note that the rate at which the file was sampled is displayed as well as the resolution (8-bit or 16-bit). The position of the pointer along the time axis is also given, and if a range of sample points is selected, the beginning and ending times of the range are displayed.

The horizontal scale selection gauge, just to the right of the sample rate and resolution at the bottom of the SoundEdit editing window, is used to change the scale of the time axis within the display window. By dragging the indicator arrow to the left we can see more detail of the digitized sound for a smaller time slice, as shown in Figure 13.18. Like-wise, in Sound Forge, the zoom icons in the lower right portion of the editing window accomplish the same task, as shown in Figure 13.19. At a smaller time scale, more details of the digitization are clearly visible.

By selecting portions or all of a displayed sound file, you can apply sound editing operations. This interface is really very similar to that of a word processor: Select the portion of the sound file you wish to modify and then invoke the appropriate command(s) to accomplish the modification. In the following sections we'll briefly explore several sound

FIGURE 13.16

This figure shows the editing window and user interface for SoundEdit, with a digitized sound file named Spring Fair *opened for editing.*

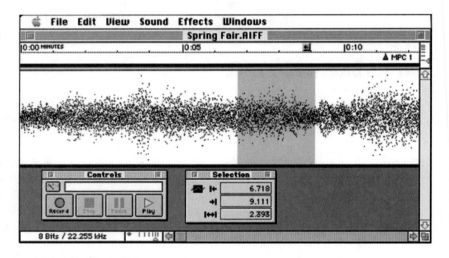

FIGURE 13.17

This figure shows the editing window and user interface for Sound Forge, with a digitized sound file recording the phrase "Wow, sound editing is fun!" opened for editing.

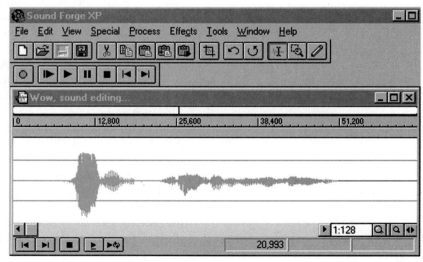

FIGURE 13.18

Dragging the indicator arrow at the bottom left of the SoundEdit window displays an "expanded" version of a sound file by stretching the time scale. Note the individual amplitude samples (discrete points) that are visible in some segments.

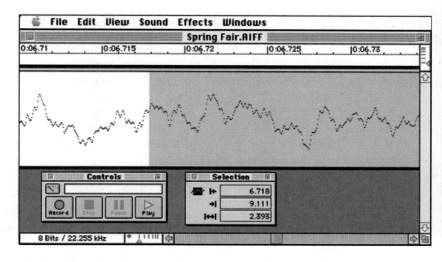

FIGURE 13.19

Clicking the larger magnifying glass icon in the bottom right portion of the Sound Forge window displays an "expanded" version of a sound file by stretching the time scale.

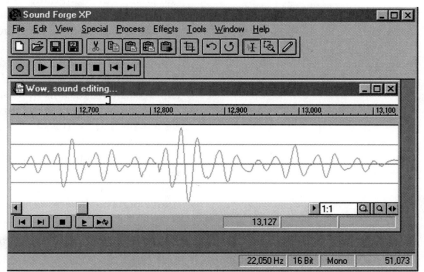

editing features. Sound editing software typically contains a great many additional features whose examination is beyond our scope. You will get a good idea of how some typical sound editing features are implemented in the following examples.

Changing Pitch and Setting Recording Options

All sound editing software gives you the option to set the sampling rate when you record. Often you also are able to select a compression ratio if one is desired. Individual packages have their own proprietary compression algorithms, and so different ratios may be available in different packages. Higher ratios (like 6:1 and 8:1) might be suitable to record speech but would not be useful for recording music. A 4:1 ratio could be used for either, although the quality of the music playback might still suffer. (For more about compression techniques, see Chapter 15.) You are also able to select a monophonic or stereophonic recording mode. Stereophonic recording requires two microphones and takes twice as much storage as a monophonic recording. Figure 13.20 illustrates.

Most applications also allow the user to change the pitch at which recorded sounds are played back. In SoundEdit, this is done using a visual dialog box displaying a keyboard, as shown in Figure 13.21. The present pitch is represented by position number 4 on the keyboard, as shown. You can simply click the appropriate key on the keyboard to increase or decrease the pitch. You can experiment easily with various pitches because each time you click a key to shift the pitch, the sound is played at the changed pitch. These changes are not actually made to the stored file until you click the OK button. Sound Forge provides a similar capability for shifting pitch, even allowing you to change the pitch by different amounts at different intervals in the sampled file.

Special Effects Editing

A great many digital signal processing techniques are useful for editing sound. We will discuss several of these to give you the flavor of the kinds of processing possible using sound editing software. For example, you can change the amplitude of a selected portion of a digitized sound file by choosing a percentage of increase or decrease. Choosing a 200 percent increase means that the amplitude of each sample point is doubled.

When the amplitude of a sound is increased, some of the new amplitude values may be "clipped" if they fall outside the dynamic range supported. No matter whether your software allows 8-bit or 16-bit sound capture, the limitations of its resolution often require some clipping of the dynamic range. When this occurs, the clipped amplitudes are assigned the largest (or smallest, as the case demands) value in the supported dynamic range.

Because of clipping, the effects of increasing amplitudes cannot always be reversed. If we were to double the amplitude, then halve it, theoretically we should get back the original sound. If clipping occurs, though, the amplitudes that were clipped have been reassigned, so when those val-

FIGURE 13.20

The dialog box for preparing to record a new sound file in Sound Forge is shown here. Note the user's ability to set the sample rate, resolution (sample size), and the number of channels.

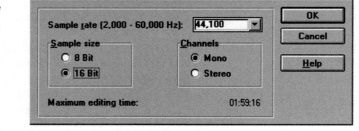

FIGURE 13.21

Here is the SoundEdit dialog box for shifting the pitch of a sound file. By clicking on any key, the pitch is adjusted and the file (or the selected portion) is played in the new pitch. The modified sound is held in memory; to save your change to the actual file, you simply click OK.

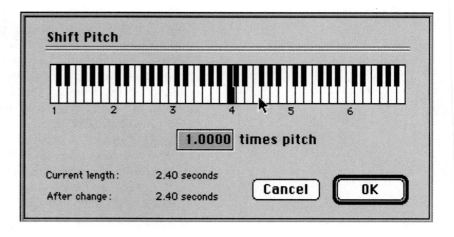

ues are halved, we do not get the original values. In other words, the effects of clipping remain in the reconstituted sound file, even though there is now plenty of room to support the range of the actual amplitudes. Figure 13.22 illustrates this phenomenon. This lack of symmetry is characteristic of many signal processing techniques. We must take care when applying several steps that we think will return us to some previous point. As with amplitude adjustment, some operations simply are not reversible.

Another effect that is easy to apply is to insert an echo into the sound file. To accomplish this in both SoundEdit and Sound Forge, you simply select the sound segment and then set both the delay time for the echo (in seconds) as well as the strength of the echo as a percentage of the original sound in a dialog box. Figure 13.23 shows how a sound file changes when an echo is added.

Synthesis Tools

Both SoundEdit and Sound Forge feature some elementary synthesis tools. For example, SoundEdit includes a white noise generator and three

FIGURE 13.22

If an amplified sound contains amplitudes that go outside the dynamic range of the file parameters, clipping occurs, resulting in lost data. Reducing the amplification later to its original level will not restore such lost values. In other words, amplification changes may not be reversible.

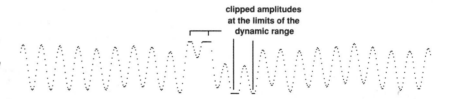

clipped amplitudes
at the limits of the
dynamic range

FIGURE 13.23

Adding an echo effect to a digital sound file involves a simple mathematical transformation. Amplitudes equal to a percentage of some selected values are inserted in the sound file at a slightly later time in the interval.

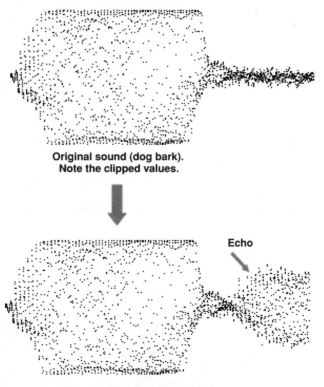

Original sound (dog bark).
Note the clipped values.

Echo

Sound with echo effect added.

of the simple oscillators (sine wave, square wave, and triangle wave) we discussed earlier. The particular oscillator desired and its basic parameters—frequency, amplitude, and duration—are chosen in a dialog box, as shown in Figure 13.24.

Let's use the simple sine wave shown in Figure 13.25 to illustrate several other synthesis and signal processing tools. If we want to create a more complex waveform based on a given wave, we might first choose to change its envelope. After selecting the appropriate command, we get a graphical dialog box in which we can modify the sound wave's envelope. Of course, the envelope of the artificially generated wave is quite monotonous. By clicking anywhere on the envelope boundary, however, we can "break" the curve and drag the given point on it to create a new shape, as illustrated in Figure 13.26. Of course, being able to modify a sound wave's envelope is an essential step in synthesizing desired waveforms. Figure 13.27 shows the wave with the changed envelope.

SoundEdit contains a number of signal processing commands that allow us to vary and make the generated waveform more interesting. For example, we might choose to add a flange effect to the waveform. When this effect is added, the regularity of the waveform is disrupted and "flanges" are created along the envelope. Complex natural sound is typically very irregular, and adding flanges helps give the wave a more realistic and natural sound. Or we may choose to add a fade-in effect. The results of adding this feature to our wave are shown in Figure 13.28.

FIGURE 13.24

The Tone Generator dialog box in SoundEdit defines an oscillator. Note that you can choose the type of oscillator to be generated (from three standard types) and set the frequency, amplitude, and duration.

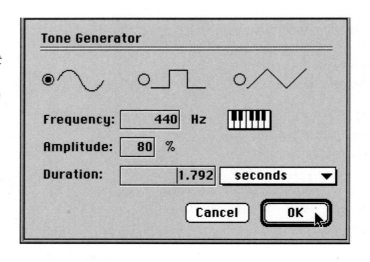

FIGURE 13.25

This sine wave oscillator was produced in SoundEdit. The sound produced is a monotonous, continuous tone at a prescribed frequency.

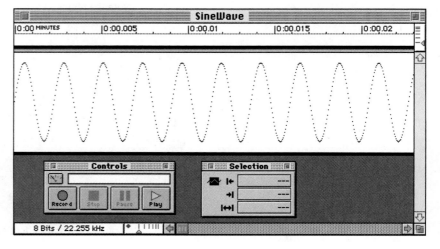

One of the more common signal processing techniques—one you are most likely already familiar with—involves applying a filter to increase the amplitudes at certain frequencies and decrease the amplitudes at other frequencies. If you've used an equalizer with your stereo or CD player, this is exactly the same technique. Once again, this editing is done in a graphical dialog box in both SoundEdit and

FIGURE 13.26

The original sine wave's envelope is being modified in SoundEdit. You can define numerous break points and modify the shape of the envelope at will.

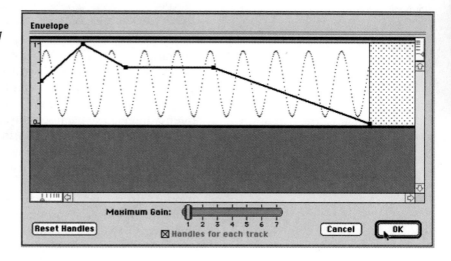

FIGURE 13.27

This is how the original sine wave appears after setting the new envelope, shown in Figure 13.26.

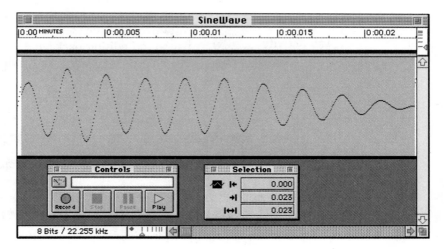

FIGURE 13.28

This is the wave of Figure 13.27 after adding a fade-in effect.

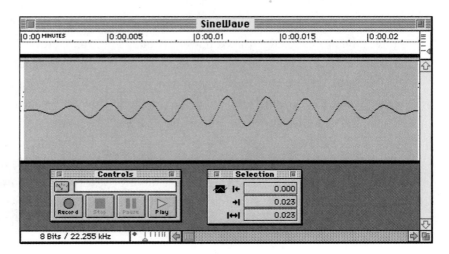

FIGURE 13.29

You can filter frequencies in a sound file using Sound Forge's slide bar graphic equalizer. SoundEdit provides a similar dialog box. These work very similarly to graphic equalizer devices for home music playback systems.

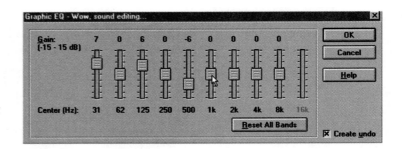

Sound Forge. The dialog box contains "slide dials" quite similar in appearance to those on music playback systems. See Figure 13.29. By dragging the slider controls we can increase or decrease the amplitudes of frequencies in any of the five ranges given as we choose. Once the frequency filters have been set, the effect is reflected in the waveform itself.

Other synthesis tools are also provided in SoundEdit. For example, waveforms can be created using the FM synthesis technique we discussed earlier in the chapter. Of course, generated waves must be constructed with an overall goal in mind to produce a meaningful sound in the final product. In SoundEdit, such waveforms can then be combined using multiple channels to produce synthesized music. The production of meaningful synthesized music is well beyond the scope of our short overview of synthesis tools. It is our hope, however, that you at least have gained some appreciation for how a few of the fundamental tools of synthesis and signal processing might be implemented in sound editing software. We hope you have access to SoundEdit, Sound Forge, or a similar sound editing package. If so, we encourage you to explore the use of some of its tools for your own sound editing.

Lab Activity

SUMMARY

Sound is a very important medium for conveying and receiving information, and so including the medium of sound within our computerized communications is desirable. Modern methods of converting sound to and from the digital domain, coupled with the power of today's desktop computers, give us this opportunity.

Digital sound is produced by sampling sound waves over time. A digitized sound file consists of sampled amplitudes of the sound wave at a number of discrete times within a given time interval. The devices that perform the sampling of an analog wave to produce such a digital file are called analog-to-digital converters, or ADCs for short. The devices that perform the opposite transformation—reconstructing an analog wave for playback from a digital file—are called digital-to-analog converters, or DACs for short.

When we sample a sound wave, we usually place the discrete sample times equal distances apart along the time axis; the number of these appearing per second is called the sampling rate. Sampling rates are usually expressed in Hertz, which means number of samples per second. Rates are often expressed in kilohertz (KHz), or thousands of Hertz. Sampling rates in the range of 5 to 8 KHz will provide good-quality playback for voice recordings, but high-fidelity music requires higher sampling rates, typically in the range of 22 to 44 KHz. In addition to the sampling rate, the resolution, or amount of computer memory used to store individual amplitude samples, also affects the fidelity of digital music playback. Typical resolutions used are 8 bits per amplitude (good for voice) and 16 bits per amplitude (the standard for high-fidelity music). Digital sound files can be quite large, and file compression techniques are often used to combat their large storage requirements.

In addition to digitizing, storing, and playing back natural sounds, computers can also be used to generate or synthesize artificial sounds. Modern music synthesis techniques can produce some impressive and beautiful results. A number of methods are used to perform music synthesis including subtractive synthesis, additive synthesis, frequency modulation synthesis, phase distortion synthesis, integrated synthesis, and hybrid methods combining two or more of these techniques. With a great many manufacturers producing music synthesizers and related devices, a standard interface between electronic instruments and synthesizers, called the MIDI (Musical Instrument Digital Interface) standard, has been adopted. This standard specifies a common interface allowing musical instruments that contain microprocessors (computers) to communicate with other instruments and devices containing microprocessors.

Once digitized, sound files can be edited in a large number of ways. For example, amplitudes can be adjusted, echo effects can be added, and pitch can be shifted by performing simple mathematical transformations on the sampled sound. Various filters can be applied to digital sound files as well, filtering out unwanted frequencies, highlighting desirable frequencies, softening or sharpening the quality of the sound, and so on. Easy-to-use software is readily available for sound editing on desktop computers.

The computer's sound capabilities also have been applied to improving the computer/human interaction using spoken language. Speech synthesis methods enable the computer to synthesize spoken language from stored text, providing an additional output option. Speech recognition techniques are designed to allow the computer to interpret and act on input commands spoken to it. One of the more popular speech synthesis techniques is based on the fact that many languages (English included) contain a relatively small number of basic sounds, called phonemes. To exploit this fact, the computer first breaks a text selection up into a sequence of basic phonemes; then each phoneme is quickly looked up in a digital speech dictionary and pronounced. Automated speech recognition has proved to be a much harder problem to solve, and speech recognition systems are in their infancy, although notable progress has been made.

PROJECTS

1 Conduct some Web-based or traditional research on speech synthesis systems. Write a short paper summarizing your findings. What is your assessment of the prospects for the future of this technology?

2 Conduct some Web-based or traditional research on automated speech recognition systems. Write a short paper summarizing your findings. What is your assessment of the prospects for the future of this technology?

3 Conduct some Web-based or traditional research on MIDI-compatible instruments and their use in the music industry. Write a short paper summarizing your findings. See if you can locate a CD featuring synthesized music at your local music store.

4 [This project assumes you have access to SoundEdit, Sound Forge, or some other sound editing program.] Launch a sound editing program and open an existing sound file (the program should come with some sample files).

a. Explore the software's interface. For example, change the appearance of the sound file by stretching the time axis (see Figures 13.18 and 13.19), play selected portions of the file, and so on.

b. Practice making some changes to the file. For example, change the amplitude of a selected part of the file, change the pitch of the sound, add an echo to a portion or all of the file, add a fade-in effect, and so on. Play the modified file after you make each change.

5 [This project assumes you have access to SoundEdit, Sound Forge, or some other sound recording program loaded on a computer equipped with a microphone.] Launch a sound recording program.

a. Record your own voice saying the words "Digital Domain." Use a setting of 8-bit resolution and 10 KHz sampling rate to conserve memory. Make three recordings and save each under a different name. Open all these at once and arrange the windows on your screen so you can compare the files.

b. Have one of your friends record the phrase "Digital Domain" and compare that sound file with the files for your recordings.

c. Record your own voice and that of your friend saying the phrase "Did you tell Jermaine?" For the same speakers, compare the sound files for this phrase and the previous phrase, "Digital Domain." Can you identify the parts of the phrases that sound alike by examining the files?

d. Just for fun, experiment with changing the pitch of your recorded phrases. Add an echo effect and try some other editing techniques.

Key Terms

8-bit digital sound	binary search tree	frequency
16-bit digital sound	carrier	frequency modulation synthesis
additive synthesis	clipping	(FM synthesis)
ADSR (attack, decay, sustain,	digital audio capture card	helper applications (browser)
and release) form	digital signal processing	Hertz
AIFF sound file format	digital sound	integrated synthesis
aliasing	digital-to-analog converter	MIDI compatible
amplitude	(DAC)	modulator
analog-to-digital converter	dynamic range	multipurpose Internet mail
(ADC)	envelope	extension (MIME)
AU sound file format	file compression	musical instrument digital
automated speech recognition	Fourier analysis	interface (MIDI) standard

Nyquist's theorem (sampling rates)

oscillator

phase distortion synthesis

phonemes

pink noise

plug-in

RA sound file format

resolution (8-bit and 16-bit sound)

robust speech recognition system

rule-based phoneme recognition

sampling rate

speaker-dependent speech recognition systems

speech synthesis

streaming audio system

subtractive synthesis

synthesized sound

variable architecture synthesis

voice activation system

WAV sound file format

wave

white noise

QUESTIONS FOR REVIEW

1 What is meant by the term *digital sound*?

2 Give an overview of the process of digitizing sound.

3 What is meant by the term *sampling rate* in the sound digitization process?

4 Why is sampling at a rate higher than 44,000 Hertz unnecessary when digitizing music? What rate would be appropriate for digitizing speech?

5 What does the acronym ADC stand for? What function does a ADC serve?

6 What does the acronym DAC stand for? What function does an DAC serve?

7 What is meant by the term *resolution* in the sound digitization process?

8 What is meant by the dynamic range of a digitized sound?

9 What is meant by 8-bit sound? Contrast 8-bit and 16-bit digitized sound.

10 What is the clipping effect in digitizing sound?

11 Why are compression schemes for digitized sound important?

12 Describe synthesized sound. What are oscillators and what role do they play in synthesizing sound?

13 Give a brief description of the synthesis techniques called subtractive analysis.

14 Give a brief description of the synthesis techniques called additive analysis.

15 What does the MIDI standard refer to? What is its significance?

16 Describe briefly the process of speech synthesis.

17 Describe briefly the process of voice recognition.

18 Compare the tasks of computer speech synthesis and computer speech recognition. Which is more difficult to accomplish?

19 What is meant by an ADSR envelope?

20 What are voice activation systems? Give some examples of the use of such systems.

21 Describe three different editing techniques that can be applied to digitized sound.

22 What would changing the amplitude for a digitized sound involve?

23 What are phonemes? How are they used in speech synthesis?

24 Explain the rule-based phoneme recognition approach to speech synthesis.

25 What is a robust speech recognition system?

26 What does the term *aliasing* refer to in sound digitizing? Relate it to Nyquist's theorem.

Making motion pictures and video with computers is relatively new to personal or desktop computing. Like computer animation, digital video had been restricted primarily to professional or commercial uses. In the motion picture industry, for example, George Lucas of *Star Wars* fame headed the first major studio to go "digital." Located on his ranch in northern California, Industrial Lights and Magic, Inc. (now Lucas Digital), pioneered the use of computers and digital processes for both soundtrack recording and motion pictures. Following their lead, many other commercial studios embraced high-end digital systems to create special effects and edit motion pictures and television programs.

As a movie goer, you have probably experienced some of the thrilling effects created by computers. Films such as *Terminator 2, Jurassic Park, Speed,* and *Twister* featured extensive use of digital processing for special effects that were crucial to their dramatic impact. The era of *DTV (digital television)* has also arrived. Many television programs now employ digital sound processing for creating the illusion of surround sound in home systems. NBC was the first network to use desktop computers to compose and edit closing sequences that tied short ending scenes with the production credits. These examples should convince you that the use of computers for making movies and TV programs is far more commonplace than you might expect.

But what does digital video mean to you as a computer user? Will you be producing feature films or TV series at home? Of course not. Most commercial applications are developed on expensive, high-performance systems that are integrated with special equipment and designed exclusively for these uses. Desktop computers, on the other hand, offer less bang but cost fewer bucks and are intended for general rather than dedicated uses, such as professional video. Even so, the adoption of multimedia standards for consumer systems has motivated the migration of digital video capabilities to the desktop domain. Personal systems today cannot achieve results on the same scale as those seen in theaters and television, but the era of desktop video is just beginning. Digital video offers one more rich source of information for the multimedia equation. To exploit what it has to offer, you will need to understand how digital video is organized and processed.

OBJECTIVES

- How digital video differs from conventional analog video
- The advantages and limitations of digital video compared with those of analog video
- The basic components of a desktop video system
- Capturing and digitizing video
- Tools and techniques for editing digital video

CHAPTER 14

VIDEO: I WANT MY DTV

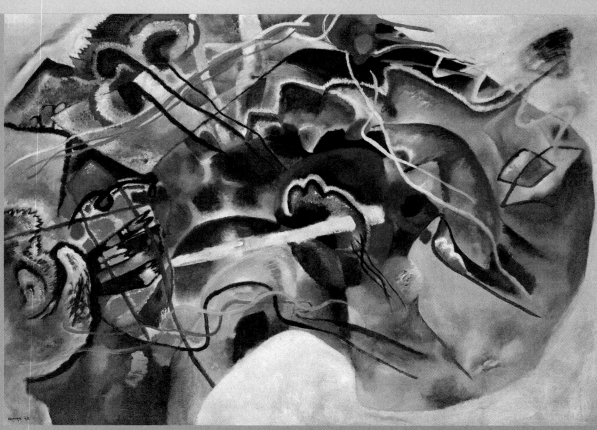

Vasily Kandinsky, *Painting with a White Border*, May 1913. Solomon R. Guggenheim Museum

WHAT IS DIGITAL VIDEO?

Video is usually composed of visual images depicting live action with an accompanying audio soundtrack. **Digital video,** of course, employs digital methods to capture, store, and present video. Digital video creates the illusion of full motion by displaying a rapid sequence of changing images on a display device. This, of course, is very similar to the technique used by motion picture projectors. For motion pictures, a series of still images or frames is projected at high speed on the screen. The difference is that the computer achieves the same effect by fetching each digital image frame, displaying it, and repeating the cycle. In both instances, if the frame rate is sufficiently fast enough, our eyes are fooled into perceiving continuous motion.

As you learned in Chapter 12, these same techniques are used for computer animation as well. Indeed, the distinction between computer animation and digital video is an arbitrary one. Like differentiating digital image processing from graphics, it is simply customary to distinguish them by their source. "Digital video" usually refers to live action scenes with or without synchronized sound. In other words, digital video is essentially composed of images from natural scenes that are often captured using analog methods and digitized for storage and subsequent processing. On the other hand, computer animation is restricted to artificial images that are created entirely by computer processing. Even so, the boundaries between them can get fuzzy at times.

We can distinguish digital video from its analog counterpart in each of the three fundamental components: capture (and storage), processing (or editing), and playback. Consult Figure 14.1 for an overview.

Capture

Video capture usually involves digitizing an analog source for live action scenes. For example, analog signals from a video camera or a VCR tape can serve as sources for the images. The signal from a videotape, for example, is already composed of a time sequence of frames. Each of these frames is an analog or continuous video image. By contrast, digitizing samples the signal both spatially and temporally. Each temporal sample is divided into spatial coordinates for conversion to pixels. Consequently, raw digital video images are very much like the digital still images treated earlier; the difference, of course, is that video captures a whole lot of them and in sequence. Digital video cameras may also be used to capture and digitize video from live action. In either case, digitizing video—like other forms of information—results in a stream of binary data that is stored in a file format known by the computer.

The frames or images of a live action scene are often accompanied by sounds, too. Thus, digital video can have an audio component. The audio must be captured and digitized using the techniques discussed in the previous chapter. The only difference for video applications is that sound data must be synchronized with the visual data to be effective. In short, image data and sound data must be organized and stored together, typically in the same file.

Digitizing video images and sound requires additional hardware and software. Usually, integrated hardware components called **video**

FIGURE 14.1

The process of creating, storing, and displaying digital video requires a number of components. The visual component of the video is a sequence of digital images or frames displayed on a video monitor. The synchronized digital audio is played through speakers connected to the computer system. There are several stages in the process of creating and viewing digital video. Analog sources for both the visual and audio components are captured and digitized in a binary format. This combined file is stored on a secondary memory device. During playback, the CPU fetches the file from storage and processes it. It converts the digital data to digital frames and an audio signal. The data for each frame is processed one by one. If the frames are displayed fast enough, the effect is that of motion or animation.

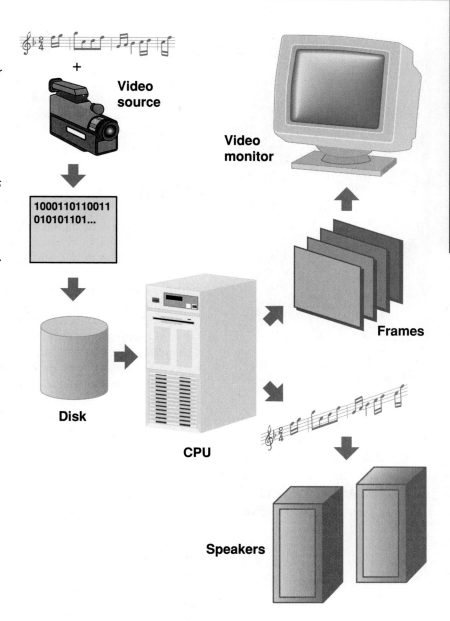

capture cards may be added to the expansion slots of a computer system to digitize analog source materials. Some desktop systems, such as AV Macintoshes, have (limited) capabilities for video capture built in. As mentioned, specially equipped digital video cameras allow the user to capture digital video without having to add hardware to the system. See Figure 14.2. We will delve into the video capture process in a later section.

Editing

Conventional editing of film and videotape is constrained by the sequential organization of these media. The source material must be viewed and searched sequentially for editing; this is called **linear editing.** On the other hand, when video data is represented and stored digitally, it may be accessed randomly. Thus, digital video supports **nonlinear editing.** Instant

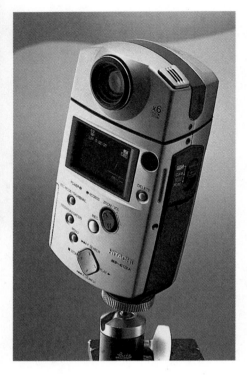

FIGURE 14.2

Digital camcorders capture and digitize a live action scene in a single step. This eliminates the need to install additional video capture hardware on your computer system. Pictured here is a digital camcorder from the Hitachi Corporation.

access to video clips or even individual frames makes editing faster and more precise. Moreover, nonlinear editing is not destructive as some forms of editing analog sources are. Nonlinear editing decisions and actions are stored as instructions that the computer accesses when it plays the video; they do not alter the original source material as film splicing does, for example. Integrating special effects is also easier because graphics and image processing techniques can be applied to video frames like any other digital image.

Playback

For the process of **digital video playback** (or **playback,** for short), the stored data must be fetched, processed, and converted to analog signals for video display devices and speakers. The data is usually stored in a file in secondary memory, perhaps on a hard disk or CD-ROM. The computer retrieves the file and processes it to recreate the frames and accompanying soundtrack. Frames are displayed in rapid succession on the video monitor while the sound signal is sent to the speakers.

As mentioned, analog video is confined to a linear organization by its media. As a result, we are limited to viewing it sequentially as well. On the other hand, most digital video playback systems offer additional modes for viewing. Because the data is discrete, it may be processed in various ways for playback. Frames may be displayed individually like a slide show, for example. In addition, features such as fast forward, rewind, reverse playback, and even random access may be available.

The applications of digital and analog video are also generally well defined—at least for the time being. Today, commercial and broadcast television is produced and delivered using mostly analog technology and methods. There are some exceptions and borderline cases, but the industry as a whole remains on the analog bandwagon. Electronic equipment such as television monitors, video cameras, videotape, and VCRs are all based on analog technology for the capture, storage, and display of visual images with sound. Of course, computers and digital methods can be used in the production and delivery of analog video. Their use, however, is more incidental than essential. Specifically, digital methods have replaced analog techniques for reasons of economy and/or convenience. Even laser disc players, which employ digital techniques for data storage, are typically designed for analog video applications on consumer television sets almost exclusively.

By contrast, true digital video is customarily restricted to the domain of computer applications. In other words, video that is captured, stored, and processed in digital format throughout is usually confined to computer use rather than for broadcast applications. Digital video, for example, is often delivered in multimedia publications. Many CD-ROM titles in education and entertainment feature digital movies among the other forms of information. Apart from publishing, the fastest-growing area in digital video is consumer applications. Desktop digital video brings not only playback but production capabilities to a standard multimedia desktop computer system. Clearly, this is the province of digital video that has the most effect on you as a computer user. Consequently, we restrict our survey of video standards, tools, and methods to this important niche.

WHAT DOES DIGITAL VIDEO HAVE TO OFFER?

Desktop digital video will not make you a Hollywood producer or TV network mogul. Producing video that meets commercial or broadcast standards requires specialized, high-performance systems that cost megabucks. The desktop computer system is designed for both economy and general use. The computer that balances your checkbook and composes your documents is simply not equipped to handle special effects for *Jurassic Park*. That doesn't mean that digital video on a desktop system is a pipe dream—far from it. Many of the same advantages enjoyed by the pros can be yours on a more modest scale. In this section, we assess the chief benefits and limitations of digital video on a desktop. As you will see, there is good news and bad news.

Digital video has several advantages over analog forms. These advantages are due to two factors: the discrete nature of digital video and the power of the computer to process this data in new and interesting ways. Because it is a discrete form of information, digital video is easily scalable and randomly accessible. Because it is represented digitally, it can be stored efficiently and transmitted over computer networks like other data. When the processing power of the computer is added to the equation, digital video can be easily integrated with image processing and graphics. Moreover, it offers more powerful editing and playback capabilities as well as the potential for greater interactivity.

Digital Video Is Easily Scalable

Like any other form of digital data, video is encoded as a stream or file of binary data. The individual images or frames that make up a video sequence are represented by numbers. These numbers, of course, must be interpreted to be converted back to video. In other words, the visual and audio information in a video file must be processed to be used at all. Therefore, some of this processing can be assigned to scaling the data to fit the system that uses it rather than being determined by the system that created it. In short, desktop digital video is **scalable,** which means that it is portable to a variety of computer systems that may vary in performance features. For example, picture resolution and color information can be adjusted to fit the capabilities of the computer displaying the video. Analog video does not have this luxury. The systems that display and use analog video must match those that produced it. As a case in point, videotape formats are not interchangeable. Beta format videotapes, for example, became extinct like the dinosaurs because the more popular VHS videotape players could not play them. The scalability of digital video can even be exploited on a single computer system. It is possible to adjust the playback picture resolution, frame rate, and color information to different settings for the same video file on the same system—without affecting the original source material.

Digital Video Is Randomly Accessible

Because video frames are discrete, they can be marked and stored for random access. In other words, the user can jump to parts of a digital movie without having to search through the entire sequence. In contrast, the media used for analog video store it sequentially. Parts of an analog video clip can be found only by forwarding or rewinding over other parts of the video. Random access is not often exploited directly; instead, its contribution makes possible many of the processing features of digital video.

Digital Video Is Stored and Transmitted Efficiently

When video is represented digitally, it inherits some of the advantages and capabilities shared by other forms of computer data. Digital video data may be stored efficiently and accurately using standard secondary memory technologies. Tapes and films are subject to wear and aging, but such storage media as CD-ROMs preserve the original source without these defects. As data, video may also be transferred or transmitted over computer networks as well. This ability has created new opportunities for delivering video and its applications. **Video-conferencing,** for example, is the capture and transmission of two-way audio and video in real time. In a typical video-conference, two computer systems are connected over a network. Cameras and microphones attached to the systems produce the images and audio transmitted to the opposite sites. Broadcast services also use digital methods to transmit picture and CD-quality sound over digital satellite systems to millions of consumers.

Digital Video Offers Powerful Editing Capabilities

As mentioned, digital video is discrete data that can be processed by the computer. The ease and power of this processing underwrite a number of its advantages over analog forms. Editing analog video is a painstaking and labor-intensive exercise. For example, inserting and deleting motion picture film segments are done by splicing and pasting segments of the media by hand. Inserting and editing videotape are too complicated to be done by splicing. Instead, segments must be played and re-recorded to a master. Care must be taken to synchronize the signals to prevent dropouts and glitches. Mixing and rerecording with analog equipment take time and patience. Unfortunately, the equipment and media can be susceptible to noise, signal loss, and a variety of other problems. Not so for digital video. Digital editing exploits the power of the computer to insert, delete, combine, copy, and move frames like any other form of data. The process is quick and painless, but even better, the results are precise and predictable. Because video is composed of digital images, creating special effects is also easy using the techniques that we have surveyed in Chapters 11 and 12. Indeed, digital video is easily integrated with methods used in both image processing and graphics.

Digital Video Offers Additional Playback Features

Analog media and equipment pose constraints on how video can be viewed. The media support sequential playback only in a single direction (forward and sometimes backward). Viewing digital video is not so constrained. A video sequence can be processed in a number of ways. Besides forward and reverse, frames can be dropped to simulate fast play; video can be shown frame by frame as a slide show or for slow-motion effects as well. Random access allows starting and stopping at arbitrary points in the video sequence. Creating automatic loops or repeating cycles of frames is easy, too.

Digital Video Has Interactive Potential

Perhaps the most interesting advantage of digital video is its potential for interactivity. The computer already controls video playback so it can just as easily make decisions affecting that control based on feedback from the user. In other words, the content of what is viewed can be affected by interacting with the user as it is viewed. Interactive mysteries, for instance, let you solve the crime in your own way by following the clues as you find them. Educational and entertainment applications have only begun to explore the possibilities here. Interactivity may very well prove to be the prime motivating factor for desktop digital video applications.

Resource Requirements for Digital Video

Now for some bad news. Digital video poses tremendous demands on desktop computer systems. In short, creating as well as playing digital movies can bring even powerful personal computer systems to their processing knees. The large amounts of information required for both visual and audio components in digital video challenge the storage capacities and processing capabilities of most desktop systems. We address these issues carefully in the next section. For now, it is enough to say that producing and employing digital video for significant applications require supplemental hardware and software.

In sum, the advantages of desktop digital video are important ones. Its value today, however, is more potential than realized. The chief liability for desktop digital video is not the video hardware and software but the limited performance of desktop computers themselves. The future is bright, though; computers get faster and better, and improved applications are always forthcoming.

DIGITAL VIDEO GOES SMALL-TIME

Most computer systems today are not sufficiently equipped in either hardware or software to handle desktop video. You must add both hardware components and software to your basic system to achieve usable video capabilities. In this section, we examine why digital video challenges the capabilities of the standard desktop computer system and what can be done to remedy this situation. The basic desktop video system requires additional hardware and software to capture and produce video for computers. Armed with this system, you will be able not only to play back digital video, but also to capture and produce your own videos. Finally, we embellish the basic system with some of the extras or frills that upgrade it to a higher desktop standard. The latter will give you some idea of the components needed for more serious users (hobbyists, business applications, consumers with deeper pockets). First, let's consider the demands that digital video poses for our computer systems.

Processing Digital Video for Playback

As discussed earlier, digital video is a sequence of frames that is usually displayed with synchronized, accompanying sound. Accordingly, most video formats store data for both sights and sounds in the same file. The file is stored on a secondary memory device such as a hard disk or CD-ROM. The CPU fetches and processes the data, juggling both audio and images. The visual data is converted for display on the video monitor while the audio data is produced as a sound signal for the speakers.

All of this seems easy enough until we consider the volume of data involved. Suppose we want to play back a full-motion color movie with CD-quality stereo sound at full-screen resolution. Here are the details:

- Frame resolution = 640 × 480
- Color pixel = 3 bytes or 24 bits
- Frame rate = 30 per second
- Audio requirements = two stereo tracks, sample rate of 44.1 KHz with 16-bit resolution

How much data must the CPU process for each second of playback?

$$
\begin{aligned}
\text{data rate (Kbits/sec)} &= \text{visual Kbits/sec} + \text{audio Kbits/sec} \\
\text{visual Kbits/sec} &= \text{24 bits per pixel} \\
&\quad \times \text{640} \times \text{480 pixels per frame} \\
&\quad \times \text{30 frames per sec} \\
&= \text{216,000 Kbits/sec (K = 1,024 bits)} \\
\text{audio Kbits/sec} &= \text{16-bit sample size} \\
&\quad \times \text{44,100 samples/sec} \\
&\quad \times \text{2 stereo channels} \\
&= \text{\textasciitilde1378 Kbits/sec} \\
\text{data rate} &= \text{\textasciitilde217,378 Kbits/sec or \textasciitilde26.5 Mbytes/sec}
\end{aligned}
$$

Forget about how hard this would drive the CPU—the real bottleneck is secondary memory. The typical hard drive has a continuous data transfer rate of about 2–5 MB/sec while a single-speed CD-ROM drive delivers a puny 150 Kbits/sec. As you can see, what is practical comes nowhere near the data rate needed.

Clearly, the demands for data transfer must be reduced drastically for desktop computers to have any chance at playing video. An obvious way to trim that rate is to reduce the amount of data used for representing both sight and sound. Less data, however, means smaller pictures and fewer frames. We will just have to settle for lower-quality images and sound. Here is one possible set.

- Frame resolution = 320 × 240
- Color pixel = 16 bits
- Frame rate = 15 per second
- Audio requirements = monaural, sample rate of 11.025 KHz with 8-bit resolution

What are the numbers for this case?

$$\begin{aligned}
\text{visual Kbits/sec} &= 16 \text{ bits per pixel}\\
&\quad \times\ 320 \times 240 \text{ pixels per frame}\\
&\quad \times\ 15 \text{ frames per sec}\\
&= 18{,}000 \text{ Kbits/sec}\\
\text{audio Kbits/sec} &= 8\text{-bit sample size}\\
&\quad \times\ 11{,}025 \text{ samples/sec}\\
&= {\sim}86 \text{ Kbits/sec}\\
\text{data rate} &= {\sim}18{,}086 \text{ Kbits/sec or } {\sim}2.2 \text{ Mbytes/sec}
\end{aligned}$$

This is much better, but often it is not nearly enough. Even more drastic measures are required if we want usable desktop digital video from a variety of media. For this reason, nearly all video file formats are compressed for more compact storage, thereby yielding faster data transfer rates. Data compression, of course, means that the binary information is recorded to eliminate redundancy. The resulting file is smaller than the original. When the movie is created, the file is processed by a **compressor** (using either added hardware or by the CPU with special software). The compressed data usually occupies much less storage, but it must be converted back to its original form (or an approximation of it) before use. A playback system, therefore, usually has a **decompressor** (again, implemented in software or hardware) that decodes the data for normal display. See Figure 14.3. (We postpone the details about compression and decompression until the next chapter.)

With compression, the demands on the CPU now may be too great. Desktop video playback systems typically adopt even more radical strategies. **Frame rate adjustment** is a favorite one. Because sound and visuals should be synchronized, many systems dynamically adjust the number of **frames per second (fps)** to keep pace with both the soundtrack and the processor's speed. In short, frames from a video sequence may be discarded to keep up with the playback of sound and the CPU work rate. Of course, motion appears jerky or less smooth when frames are dropped.

The bottom line is that the quality of the digital video playback may vary depending on a lot of factors. The speed of the CPU is important. Newer and faster processors can overcome some of the obstacles in man-

FIGURE 14.3

Compressing and decompressing data are filtering processes, which means that the entire data file is processed, producing a new file that replaces it. The compressor recodes the input file by eliminating redundant data and replaces the original with a smaller or more compact file as its output. A decompressor reverses this process. The compressed data is decoded, producing the original uncompressed file (or a close approximation of it).

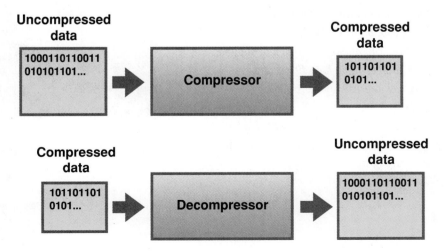

aging large amounts of data. Frame rate and picture resolution are also fundamental. As you have seen, these are the most significant factors in determining the amount of data that the CPU must process. Lower frame rates and smaller images make for more manageable movies. Of course, this sacrifices some of the video's quality. Compression can reduce storage requirements and improve transmission performance for digital video, but it may also affect the quality of the image and its playback.

Building the Basic Desktop Video System

Ordinarily, the typical desktop computer system with multimedia features is suitable for playing video sequences—provided it has the proper software for playback. The standard computer system is not equipped to manage the process of capturing (digitizing) and producing video on its own.

When these components (or features) are added to the standard computer system, we get the basic desktop video system. Figure 14.4 illustrates the six fundamental components of a basic system capable of both producing and viewing digital video. We examine each of these components briefly.

● **Analog Source.**   Unless you are producing your own source material using a digital video camera, you will need to digitize video from original analog sources. Deciding on a suitable analog source is not so obvious. Analog video cameras, camcorders, video cassette tape players, and even laser disc players are potential providers. Your choice depends on the context and intent of the application. For example, spontaneous or live video, such as for video electronic mail or video-conferencing, can be handled by inexpensive analog video cameras. A camcorder, however, is better for more general use. (A camcorder allows picking and

FIGURE 14.4

The basic desktop video system can create or produce digital video as well as play it back. Several hardware and software components must be added to the standard desktop computer to realize these capabilities. A video capture card digitizes the analog video signal supplied by a source. Tools for editing and playback are usually controlled by software. The secondary storage device— usually a hard disk—and video display monitor are familiar components in the standard system.

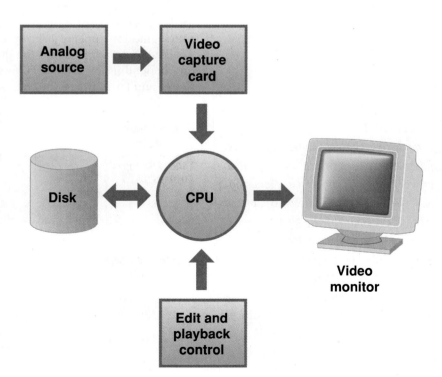

choosing among several takes.) On the other hand, transferring data to the desktop can be handled admirably by VCRs and laser discs.

● **Video Capture Card.** The video capture card is usually an add-on card fitted in an expansion slot of the computer system. Some additional hardware may accompany it. For example, an external device called a **breakout box** is often used to connect analog video sources to the card. The primary role of the capture card is to digitize the analog signal, which means sampling and quantizing the data to a binary form. The signal is sampled both temporally and spatially. The time series is sampled discretely as frames, and each frame is sampled spatially as pixels. The capture card may also have the capability to compress the digitized video data for more compact storage. Some cards also have on-board decompression, which aids the CPU during playback. Performance features for video capture cards vary, and cost is closely related to performance.

● **CPU.** The CPU is the heart of the system for both production and playback. The CPU fetches data, processes it, and sends audio and video signals for playback. Often, playback involves decoding or decompressing data before processing it. Naturally, the CPU must be capable of juggling these tasks with ease for continuous, smooth video playback.

The CPU's performance, however, is even more important for capturing and producing digital video. The chief reason is that the CPU and its internal data bus must transfer and process the incoming digital data at a rate fast enough to accommodate the digitizing process. A slower CPU will capture less data and fewer frames than a faster one. The CPU manages the entire process by executing the video capture program and coordinates the transfers of data from the capture card and to secondary storage. In some instances, the CPU may also be called on to perform other tasks such as audio processing and perhaps video compression. Higher performance and faster throughput are not just luxuries here.

● **Secondary Storage.** A fast and high-capacity source for secondary storage is also a must in a desktop video system. As you have seen, digital video files can take up a lot of space. Currently, the most commonly used medium for storing playback video is CD-ROM. It has suitable capacity for storing video, but obviously it cannot be used for creating (writing) such files.

For video capture, you will need a large (think many gigabytes) magnetic hard disk system. It should also be fast enough to keep up with the data rate of the capture process. Some RAID systems (described in Chapter 5) are specially designed to handle the high demands of video processing. Fortunately, the prices for fast, high-capacity drives continue to drop. Consequently, buying a little headroom for storing raw video no longer commands a king's ransom.

● **Monitor.** This is the RGB video display monitor that matches your computer system. The monitor is used primarily for editing and playback. The monitor does not require any additional or special features. In fact, if you plan to distribute your movie for play on other computer systems, it should match the capabilities of the monitors used on those systems. A high-resolution, high-performance video monitor might not be suitable for testing video that will be played back on systems with less expensive monitors.

● **Editing and Playback Control.**   Both viewing and editing video require software to support these processes. In some instances, the software may integrate both features. Simple editing tools for cutting, copying, and merging video segments may be part of the basic playback system. You will require a separate video application for more sophisticated editing tools along with special effects such as adding text titles, dissolving from one scene to the next, and the like.

Upgrading the Desktop Video System

If the basic system doesn't fulfill your video desires and if your budget can afford it, several other components (and capabilities) can increase the power of the system and the quality of its products. Figure 14.5 shows how these features fit into the scheme of things. Again, we consider each below.

● **Dealing with Analog Problems.**   Standard television video and computer video are very different beasts. First, their resolution and aspect ratios differ. The basic color signals are different, too. Of course, it

FIGURE 14.5

Adding some bells and whistles to the basic system will improve the quality of the video produced. A standard NTSC television monitor allows you to view the analog signal as it is input for capture and digitizing. A TBC may be used to repair and synchronize the analog video signal for video capture. In some cases, it may be desirable or necessary to separate the audio signal for processing independently from the video frames. A sound capture card can offload some of the processing and yield higher-fidelity audio, too.

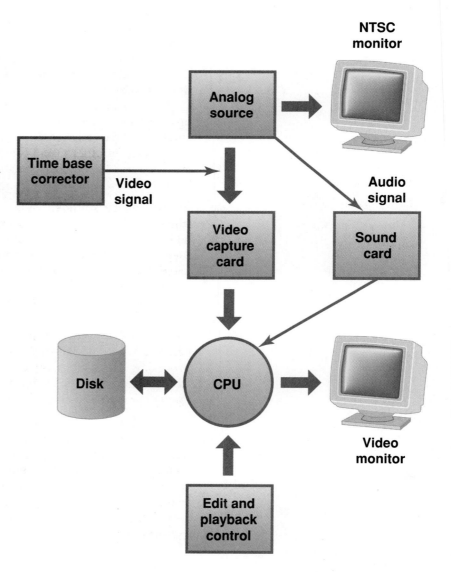

is the task of the video capture card to deal with these differences. Nonetheless, it is often useful to monitor the incoming signal during capture. The incoming signal will reveal any problems with the original analog source and can also serve as a reference for comparing the digitized result. To do this, you need a standard TV monitor that accepts the normal NTSC signal. (NTSC is the National Television Standards Committee, which specifies video regulations for U.S. markets.)

Analog videotape equipment and media are often subject to variabilities that affect the synchronization or timing of video frames. For instance, stretched tape and small changes in the speed of the player's transport mechanism can disrupt the timing of frame signals. Often the TV monitor forgives these faults, but they can impair the sampling accuracy of the capture card. The results will show up as corrupt digital frames having a variety of symptoms. These problems can be prevented by employing a time base corrector to the analog source signal. A **time base corrector (TBC)** is a device that acts as a frame buffer capable of holding an entire frame of video. It has circuits that can repair the signal before passing it along to the digital system. Some TBCs have additional features or controls for adjusting synchronization and signal levels, color correction, and other enhancements.

● **Audio Processing.** Video capture cards usually offer facilities for recording and digitizing sound to accompany the visual images. The quality of the audio, however, may not meet your needs. For this reason, separate facilities for recording the audio soundtrack may be desirable.

Most often, a separate sound card must be added to the system. Most Windows systems supporting multimedia, for example, will require an add-on sound card for any audio signal processing. In some instances, suitable sound capabilities may be built into the computer system itself without the need for an additional sound card.

Besides improving quality, separating sound recording from video capture has other advantages. When the soundtrack is recorded as a separate file, it may be processed using sound editing software (as described in the previous chapter). Tweaking, fixing, and mixing the soundtrack are difficult tasks when sound data is part of the video file, but they are easily achieved for a separate sound file. Video editing software provides the capability for adding and synchronizing the new soundtrack to an existing movie file.

A CLOSER LOOK AT CAPTURING VIDEO SEQUENCES

If you feel pumped from what you have read so far and can't wait to get at it, this section is for you. We delve into some of the nitty-gritty details of producing desktop video from analog sources. In this section, we look at how a video capture card processes its analog source. In addition, we address some of the problems and solutions common to video capture.

As described earlier, the chief task of the video capture card is to send a stream of binary data to the CPU, whose job is to encode that data into a movie file. The capture card receives an analog video signal that must be converted, sampled, and quantized according to the specifications set by the user and enforced by the capture program. Along the way, the card may be called on to compress data before passing it to the CPU. That is the big picture; now let's get down to details.

First, let's consider the input source. Up to this point we have glossed over several important facts about the nature of analog source signal. The standard NTSC television is composed of images with up to 484 visible horizontal scan lines and approximately 30 frames per second. Each frame, in fact, is made up of two fields representing the odd and even scan lines of the image. The electron gun in the television's CRT first draws the lines for one field and then draws the lines of the second field. Fields are refreshed about 60 times a second. This yields 30 frames per second. The quality of the resulting digitized video therefore depends on the sampling rate of the capture card. For example, many capture cards sample 30 times a second; this would seem to be fast enough to handle full-motion video. These cards, though, must compensate for the fact that the fields are refreshed at a different rate. One solution is to capture a frame and fill in the other field with lines from the present one. Another is to do a kind of averaging. High-end models bypass this obstacle by actually sampling at a rate of 60 times a second. They merge fields for a composite 30 frames per second. This can make a difference in picture fidelity, especially when the video contains fast action.

Color information is another detail about the input analog signal worth considering. Broadcast television uses different schemes for representing color than those employed by computer displays. Rather than coding color in RGB components, analog video represents luminance and color in two separate channels. (See the Focus box entitled "A Rose Is a Rose Is a Rose?".) There are several variations, but the bottom line is that the input signal must be converted for digital video capture. Also, the quality of the incoming color signal may be less than the quality you expect from computer-generated graphics.

Regardless of the source of the incoming signal, most video capture cards achieve some data compression when digitizing color. (Again, see the Focus box "A Rose Is a Rose Is a Rose?".) Human motion perception is less sensitive to color than to intensity details; it is more important to retain accurate luminance (or intensity) information than to retain every color shade. Thus, the capture process effectively reduces the amount of color information encoded while retaining luminance information at its original precision. For example, instead of 24 bits for storing a color pixel, only 16 bits may be needed. The process of sampling is reviewed in Figure 14.6.

Digitizing, of course, converts the capture frame or image to pixels that are held in a frame buffer, usually in system memory. The CPU processes this frame by adding any special data needed for its inclusion in the video file. The frame is then shuttled off to secondary memory for appending to that file, and the process repeats. This cycle continues until the entire video sequence has been sampled, digitized, and stored in the resulting movie file. The video capture card never misses a beat in this relentless process. Unfortunately, the CPU and secondary memory may blink. Specifically, if the capture data rate exceeds their capacity, frames will be lost in the rush. These frames were captured and digitized but do not get included in the video file.

For this reason, many capture boards contain data compression hardware and software to reduce the amount of data stored in a single frame. See Figure 14.7. The system can handle compressed data more efficiently. Of course, the data must eventually be reinstated to its original form (or decompressed) during playback.

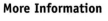
More Information

FIGURE 14.6

(a) Each second of the analog video signal is composed of nearly thirty frames created by sixty fields. Each field is made up of either the odd or even scan lines for that frame. This analog signal is sampled temporally at a capture rate set by the user (for example, fifteen, thirty, or even sixty times a second). The analog color signal is also sampled and usually converted to a form that can be managed more easily by the system. The end result is a sequence of discrete, converted color frames that approximate the original signal. (b) Next the time-sampled frames are digitized by sampling each spatially. In other words, the image is converted into pixels that denote the color features of the image at discrete locations in it.

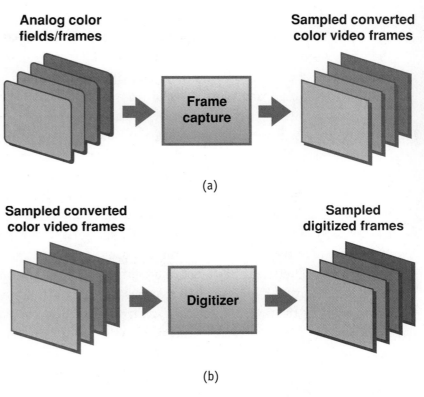

FIGURE 14.7

After the frames are converted to pixels, the data are usually compressed by recoding it to remove redundant information. Compression is usually handled by a specialized processor that is part of the video capture card.

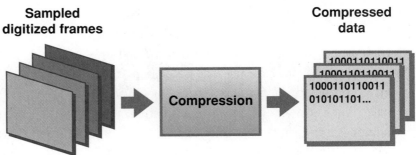

focus

A ROSE IS A ROSE IS A ROSE?

To the uninitiated, few things seem more tangible and concrete than the perception of color. Nothing could be further from the truth. In fact, the variability of perceived colors is notorious. Specifically, how shades of color appear depend on lighting conditions, surroundings, and even individuals. Ask any photographer, painter, graphic artist, or lighting professional. Should it be any surprise then that color in video varies? In fact, color pictures from broadcast TV, a consumer VCR, and your computer can all have the same content but appear quite different. The reason is that each source employs a different method for representing and transmitting color information.

Broadcast color television was introduced more than forty years ago. Before it, television images were in black and white (actually, grayscale). The transition from black and white to color did not happen overnight. For a number of years, broadcasters had to support both technologies. All of this was possible because the National Television Standards Committee (NTSC) established guidelines for broadcasting a single television signal that could support both black-and-white and color reception. NTSC also decreed that the color signal would have to fit the existing bandwidth for broadcast TV. This effectively ruled out transmitting complex signals that might carry RGB components, for example. At the time, the solution was rather ingenious. A color or chrominance signal was added to the normal monochrome or black-and-white signal. The monochrome signal carries luminance information, that is, the brightness of parts of the image. This is called the **Y signal.** Color information is transmitted as a subcarrier wave. This chrominance signal has two components, **I** and **Q,** which together indicate hue and saturation. You may have noted, for instance, that color TV sets have three corresponding picture controls for brightness, tint (hue), and color (saturation). The NTSC color is called appropriately **YIQ** or **composite video**.

So what is all of this history about? NTSC color (which has been called "Never Twice the Same Color") has incompatibilities with the RGB color representations used for computer displays. Because of its signal limitations, NTSC video has difficulties depicting both small or detailed colored objects—such as text—and quickly varying colors. In fact, capturing still images from NTSC video requires at least two frames to calibrate the subcarrier color signal. In addition, some hues are difficult to discriminate (for example, purples and indigos).

There are other standards for representing color in video production. For example, high-end consumer equipment such as S-VHS videotape recorders and Hi8 video camcorders employ a **component video signal** called **Y/C.** The signal is still divided into two channels for luminance **(Y)** and chrominance **(C),** respectively. Each signal has greater capacity than those in composite video and is separated for greater control and overall image quality.

Most video capture cards convert the incoming video signal to a representation based on the **YUV color space.** See Figure 14.8 depicting the YUV color cube. Color pixels are represented by three components: **Y** measures relative luminance on the scale of black to white, **U** is measured along a vector that points approximately to red, and **V** is measured along a vector that is aimed in the direction of blue. Transforming YUV values to RGB components (and back) is a simple task.

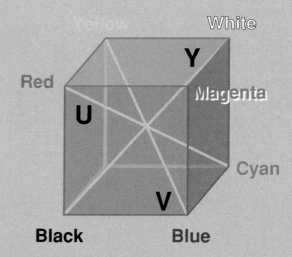

FIGURE 14.8
The color cube depicts measurable hues. Each point within the cube is a distinct hue represented by three coordinate values. RGB colors are measured from the origins of red, green, and blue. YUV color space is a transformation of the RGB color space formed by three opposing axes. Y denotes the luminance value that is measured along the white-black axis. U is measured along a vector pointing in the approximate direction of red. The V vector points approximately to blue.

The chief advantage of YUV encoding, though, is that it yields potential data reductions more easily than using RGB components. As mentioned, it is generally agreed that human motion perception is more sensitive to small variations in luminance than to minute color changes. Consequently, we can tolerate less color information than intensity information when viewing moving objects. This factor can be exploited for some savings in representing and storing pixel data. For example, because color and luminance are separated in YUV space, we can use fewer bits to represent the U and V components while preserving the original precision for Y. The result is some loss of the original signal but a welcome savings in data storage.

The moral of the story is that color is a factor that has to be considered in producing video output. Whether you are creating digital video captured from broadcast signals or converting digital video to VCR tape, you should be aware that there may be subtle differences in the results. Sometimes a rose may not look quite like the rose you envisioned.

EDITING DIGITAL VIDEO

Very few video productions are single shots, that is, continuous recordings of a scene taken from a single camera. Most video productions are sequences of shorter segments of different scenes. Even a single scene often is composed of short takes that are recorded from different camera positions and, perhaps, different subjects. The point is that most video is produced by **editing**—that is, creating a composition by adding, deleting, and modifying video segments. Editing digital video requires the appropriate software.

Apple QuickTime, for example, is a cross-platform application that can be used to display digital video in a variety of formats. QuickTime is freeware for Windows and Macintoshes, and it has plug-ins for both Netscape Communicator and Microsoft Internet Explorer, making it a convenient choice for delivering video content. An application like QuickTime, however, has a somewhat crude set of editing tools. These are effective enough for the simple sequencing of video segments, but they yield what are called straight-cuts. **Straight-cuts** are segments that change quickly from one take to the next. Straight-cut editing is fine for fast action or short takes within a single scene. Video pros, however, often enhance their productions with special effects. For special effects, you must employ an application that is dedicated to video editing.

Editing software has a number of powerful tools that make video production both easy and convenient. To appreciate what it has to offer, in this section we survey some of the features that you would expect to find in a typical editing software application.

Most desktop video editing software belongs to a special category called online nonlinear editing systems. An online editing system is computer-based; this is contrasted with offline editing, which employs traditional analog equipment in the old-fashioned way. Linear editing is done with playback and recording equipment. The final cut is produced by playing, mixing, and rerecording video clips in real time. In this style of editing, you are usually limited to working with only two video segments at a time. Today commercial studios often employ online linear editing systems for producing broadcast analog video. The computer is used to help control conventional videotape technology for greater precision and convenience.

Nonlinear editing systems, on the other hand, exploit the computer's capability for digitizing, storing, and processing the video. Therefore, these types of systems differ in two important respects. First, because the video data may be randomly selected, many different video clips may be manipulated at once. Second, nonlinear systems usually create edit decision lists. This means that editing actions are recorded as instructions rather than producing a new video sequence that copies each of the original clips or segments that compose it. Consequently, nonlinear editing has greater flexibility and efficiency.

Most digital video editing applications offer a variety of features that are integrated as a set of tools for composing, modifying, and producing digital video segments.

Clip Logging and Assembling

The lion's share of editing is the logging and assembling of short video segments into a finished sequence or cut. **Logging** a video clip means to identify it along with appropriate statistics such as duration and type (audio or video). **Assembling** refers to the actual sequencing

FIGURE 14.9

The interface for Adobe Premiere is made up of a set of windows along with pull-down menus that contain various commands. The three basic windows are shown here. The Project window serves as a bin window for collecting video and audio clips that will likely be used in the final cut. The Construction window is the workspace for assembling and sequencing them. Clips are collected in the Project window and then simply dragged and dropped to the Construction window for placement in specific video and audio tracks. Finally, a Preview window allows you to observe the results of editing decisions.

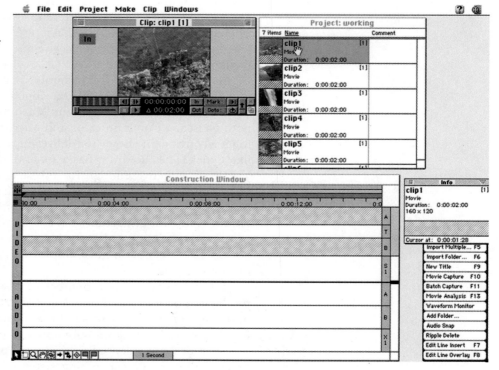

of logged video clips. Most editing software is organized to facilitate these tasks.

The typical interface, for instance, contains at least two windows. One serves as the workspace for assembling video clips. It is often represented either as a timeline or a storyboard on which poster icons of the clips are pasted in their playback order. Figure 14.9 depicts a timeline interface; Figure 14.10 illustrates an interface organized by a storyboard. The timeline often includes room for synchronizing audio tracks with video tracks. Most editing software permits multiple tracks for both audio and video (as overlays). A second area serves as a **bin window,** where logged video sources are collected for assembly.

Before inserting a clip into a sequence, it often must be edited, too. **Clip-based editing** means to trim the video segment to the desired content and duration needed. This is done by setting precise **edit-in** and **edit-out points** on the clip. These denote the initial and ending frames for the segment. Most systems allow you either to enter their timecodes or to shuttle back and forth through a clip to mark the edit-in and edit-out points on the fly. Figure 14.11 illustrates.

Transitions

A **transition** is a visual effect that smoothes or stretches the change from one video segment to another. To achieve a transition, you must overlay the ending frames of the first segment with the beginning frames of the second. The visual effect is then added to merge the two and create the transition. See Figure 14.12.

Typical transitions from analog video editing include dissolves and wipes. In a **dissolve,** one scene fades into the other. A **wipe** is a transition from one scene to the other that follows a specified direction or pattern. For example, in a horizontal wipe the new scene appears to

FIGURE 14.10

Strata Videoshop offers an optional storyboard view for assembling clips. It has a previewing window called the Canvas. The Canvas window also serves as a workspace for adding special effects and filters to frames and video segments. Any folder containing video or audio clips may be opened to serve as a bin window.

FIGURE 14.11

Setting edit-in and edit-out points in Premiere can be handled in several ways. The Clip window allows you to view the frames from a selected clip along with their timing sequence. Timecode information indicates the duration and number of the current frame. In the example, the edit-out point is reset at 00:00:02:17, that is, at 2 seconds, 17 frames.

FIGURE 14.12

Transitions may be added easily to video in Premiere provided that the two clips are overlapped in different tracks. In this instance, tracks A and B hold several clip segments that overlap ending and beginning segments. Cross dissolve transitions were selected from the Transitions window and placed between the contiguous tracks where the segments overlapped. A cross dissolve produces a brief, simultaneous fade-out of the ending scene and fade-in of the new one.

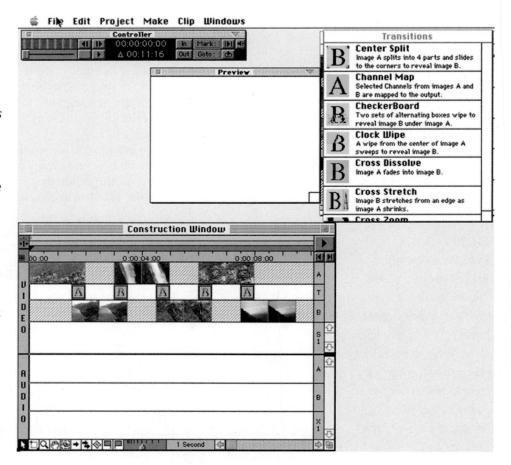

enter from left to right across the screen. Midway through the transition, the two clips are displayed as a split screen simultaneously. Most editing software has a host of transition effects. In fact, you have the power at your fingertips to turn any video into a circus of horrors by overusing these effects.

Rotoscoping

Rotoscoping refers to working with individual frames of video footage. Graphic embellishment and image filters may be used to enhance single frames of a video clip. Some editing software applications and many painting and image processing programs allow you to edit individual frames for special visual effects. Of course, it is easy to integrate graphic and image processing with video frames because the data is represented in the same manner as digital still images. A few programs even automate the process for an entire segment after you specify how the beginning and ending frames should look.

Compositing

Superimposing part of one video clip on another is called **compositing.** This can be done in a variety of ways. Consult Figure 14.13 for an example. Compositing may be simple—such as the movie-within-a-movie effect—or more sophisticated, as in keying. **Keying** is a general technique that places portions of one video in selected areas of another. In this manner, for example, an entirely different video scene may serve as a background for a foreground composed of objects from another clip. A special instance of compositing images is that of **titling,** that is, superimposing text on a video frame. Desktop video editing programs have a great many features for adding text to a video clip; Figures 14.14 and 14.15 illustrate. Besides superimposing simple text, these programs also make it easy to animate the text. For example, you can create crawls or screen rolls in which the text moves across the screen.

FIGURE 14.13

A movie-within-a-movie effect is created by synchronizing two video tracks to play simultaneously. In VideoShop, it is easy to resize and move the frame from one track; this reveals the second video track underneath.

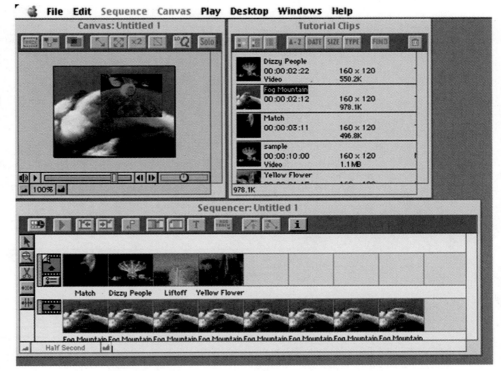

FIGURE 14.14

Titles are created in VideoShop within the Title window. You may enter and edit text as well as control its font, size, and color. Special effects such as scrolling may also be set automatically for the segment.

FIGURE 14.15

In Premiere, titles can be created with special effects such as gradient colors and drop shadows, as shown here.

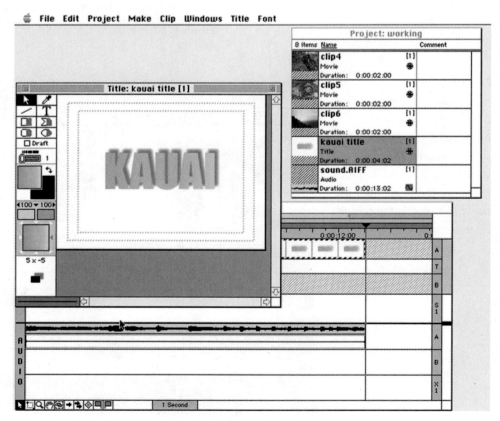

These are but a few of the mainstay tools typically found in software for nonlinear video editing. Armed with the tools and concepts in this chapter, you are ready now to experiment with your own desktop video production. With a small investment in equipment and large shares of imagination and practice, creating interesting video can become a part of your multimedia repertoire.

SUMMARY

Digital video employs digital methods to capture, store, and present visual images depicting live action and typically synchronized with an accompanying soundtrack. Like other forms of video, digital video creates the illusion of full or continuous motion by displaying a rapid sequence of changing images on the computer display device.

Digital video offers several distinct advantages over its analog counterpart. The video information is easily scalable and randomly accessible. Because it is often compressed, digital video can be stored and transmitted over networks more efficiently. The flexibility of editing and playback features are other digital dividends.

Producing digital video involves three basic steps or stages: capture, editing, and playback. The images and sound are usually digitized from analog sources such as video cameras and microphones. A video capture card is a specialized component added to the expansion slot of the computer system. It contains needed hardware and software to manage the process of converting the source to an appropriate format for storing on the system. Video information is typically compressed to conserve storage space and for faster transfer. Compressed video data, however, must be decompressed—or restored to original form—for viewing.

Processing digital video involves editing, which is the composition of video by adding, deleting, and modifying video segments. Most digital video editing programs are nonlinear editing systems. They exploit the fact that digital data may be randomly accessed rather than sequentially searched like linear analog editing systems. Nonlinear systems also differ from their conventional counterparts in that they store instructions for the reassembly of video segments at playback rather than altering the original source video with editing cuts. Consumer versions of nonlinear editing software are available for most desktop computer systems. They provide a variety of tools and features that emulate many of the capabilities of professional systems.

Apart from video capture and editing, most computer systems can be equipped to present or play back digital video. Very often, video playback is exclusively under software control: The CPU executes a program that fetches the frames of the video from secondary memory and displays them, one by one, in rapid succession on the video monitor. The demands of video playback, however, can be considerable. The large amounts of data that must be transferred and processed can challenge most desktop systems. Playback performance can be improved by scaling the video for lower resolution and a slower frame rate. Faster CPUs and hardware support for playback can also improve the quality of digital video playback.

PROJECTS

1 Experiment with some of the video files available for downloading from the Projects page on the *Digital Domain* Web site. (In some instances, you may also need to download the appropriate playback software for viewing the video clips. Links for accessing the software are listed on the Projects page.) Try viewing the clips in their standard or normal resolution and frame rate. (Follow the instructions provided on the page for experimenting with the test data.)

Write a brief report that summarizes your findings.

2 QuickTime VR combines video images with the three-dimensional perspective of virtual reality. Consult the Projects Web page to find out more about this hybrid video file format. Several examples of VR images may be downloaded and viewed directly in your browser window. (You may need to download the appropriate browser plug-in to view these clips. Links for accessing the software are listed on the Projects page.) Most of the images provide a 360° pan of the entire scene. Consult the links to find out how you can create your own QuickTime VR pictures.

3 Conduct a Web search to find out more about video capture cards. Find at least three companies that market products for your particular hardware platform. Compose a table that compares the features and performance specifications for these products. What sampling rates are available? What resolutions? Is there hardware support for compression? What software is supplied?

4 Consult the Projects Web page for links to Web sites devoted to video editing software products. Consult the Web sites for at least three different products listed there and read more about them. Evaluate these products based on their features and capabilities.

5 Like other forms of data, video is packaged in an assortment of file formats. These formats differ in a variety of ways. They offer different performance features, compression rates, and so on. Some are intended primarily for video presentation from a disk or CD-ROM. Others are streaming video, which is designed for transmission across networks such as the Web. Find out more about them by consulting the links provided on the Projects page. Pick any two video file formats that interest you and write a report that compares the strengths and liabilities of each.

Projects

Key Terms

assembling	component video (Y/C video)	edit-in point
bin window	composite video (YIQ video)	edit-out point
breakout box	compositing	frame rate adjustment
capture, video	digital video	frames per second (fps)
capture card, video	digital video playback	keying
clip-based editing	dissolve	linear editing

logging	time base corrector (TBC)	Y signal (luminance)
nonlinear editing	titling	Y/C video (component video)
rotoscoping	transition	YIQ video (composite video)
scalable	video-conferencing	YUV color space
straight-cuts	wipe	

QUESTIONS FOR REVIEW

1 How do computers portray digital video?

2 How is digital video normally distinguished from computer graphic animation?

3 What are the chief advantages of digital video over its conventional analog form?

4 Explain the three stages of producing digital video: capture, editing, and playback.

5 What does a video capture card do?

6 What are some sources for digital video? Specify both analog and digital sources.

7 What is a breakout box?

8 What is a time base corrector? How does it improve digitizing video from analog sources?

9 Why is data compression a common tool for digital video?

10 What are the practical differences between the color signal from broadcast TV, videotape, and computer video?

11 How do resolution and frame rate affect the performance of digital video playback on desktop computers?

12 What is frame rate adjustment during playback?

13 Distinguish linear from nonlinear editing.

14 Why are most videos composed of a sequence of short takes rather than single shots? What does this fact imply for producing desktop video?

15 In managing desktop video, what are the tasks of clip logging and assembling?

16 What are edit-in and edit-out points?

17 What are video transitions? Why are they usually desirable?

18 What is rotoscoping?

19 Keying is a special instance of video compositing. Explain.

20 What is video titling?

Multimedia computing, as you have seen, often involves large files. Image, sound, and especially video files can easily occupy many megabytes, even gigabytes, of storage. Such file sizes place tremendous demands on both storage and data transmission capacities. In a practical computing system, a cost is always associated with the transmission and storage of data. And, even though costs have declined dramatically in the past decade, they are by no means negligible for large files.

In data communications, the capacity of any channel to transmit data is limited. Naturally, the volume of data transmitted determines the total transmission time; this fact can be significant. For example, accessing World Wide Web pages that contain images, sounds, and video clips can place great demands on your patience. Significant time (from several to many minutes) is often required to download such resources even when fast Internet connections are used.

Consider data storage, too. The capacities of secondary storage devices have increased, and their prices have fallen over the years. Yet the demands placed on these devices by today's applications have nearly outrun this pace. Ten years ago a desktop system with a 50 MB hard disk was considered top of the line. Today, systems with disks twenty times that capacity (1 GB) are thought barely adequate.

For these reasons, data compression is often employed to help reduce costs and increase performance of storage and data communications systems. In fact, some applications of multimedia computing would be totally impractical without the use of data compression techniques. In this chapter, you will study some of the more common data compression techniques and examine some of their strengths and weaknesses.

OBJECTIVES

- **The basic principles for compressing data**

- **Data compression methods for text and numeric data**

- **How digital images and graphics are compressed for storage and transmission**

- **Compression methods for digital video and audio**

CHAPTER 15

DATA COMPRESSION

DATA COMPRESSION: THE BASICS

As mentioned in earlier chapters, compressing data means reducing the effective size of a data file for storage or transmission. Because all forms of information are represented digitally and encoded in a binary format, **compression** amounts to replacing the original binary file with another that is smaller. Naturally, the compressed data requires less storage and can be transmitted at a faster rate. The compressed file, however, must be decompressed before it can be used in normal applications. **Decompression** expands the compressed data and reproduces the original data—either exactly or in facsimile. As illustrated in Figure 15.1, compression and decompression methods work in tandem. A pair of such methods is often called a **codec** (for *co*mpression/ *dec*ompression).

In general, codecs reduce the redundancy in data. Their effectiveness varies significantly, depending on the amount of redundancy in the original. A file in which symbols occur in nearly random frequencies is difficult to reduce. On the other hand, most information has symbolic representations with repetitious patterns. This makes it susceptible to compression by replacing definable patterns with shorter sequences of symbols.

Most codecs approach this task in a piecewise fashion. In other words, they process the input source by chopping it up into segments of fixed or variable lengths and replace these with (we hope) shorter segments of either fixed or variable lengths. The process is often controlled by special information that acts as a **coding table** or key for the translation process. The coding table may be built in or generated by feedback from the process itself. Figure 15.2 illustrates the general approach for compression/decompression used by most codec methods.

As implied earlier, some codecs do not guarantee the exact reproduction of the original after decompression. These methods are called **lossy.** In contrast, **lossless** codecs always reproduce the original data from its compressed format. The choice of lossless versus lossy tech-

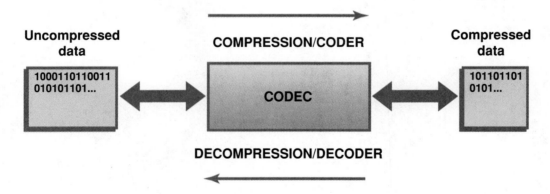

FIGURE 15.1

Data compression is a coding or filtering process whereby the original source data is replaced by a smaller data file representing it. The compressed data is decompressed by decoding it using an inverse technique, in which the compressed file is replaced by a sequence of data that matches the original (exactly or nearly). The specific pair of methods used for compressing and decompressing data is dubbed a codec.

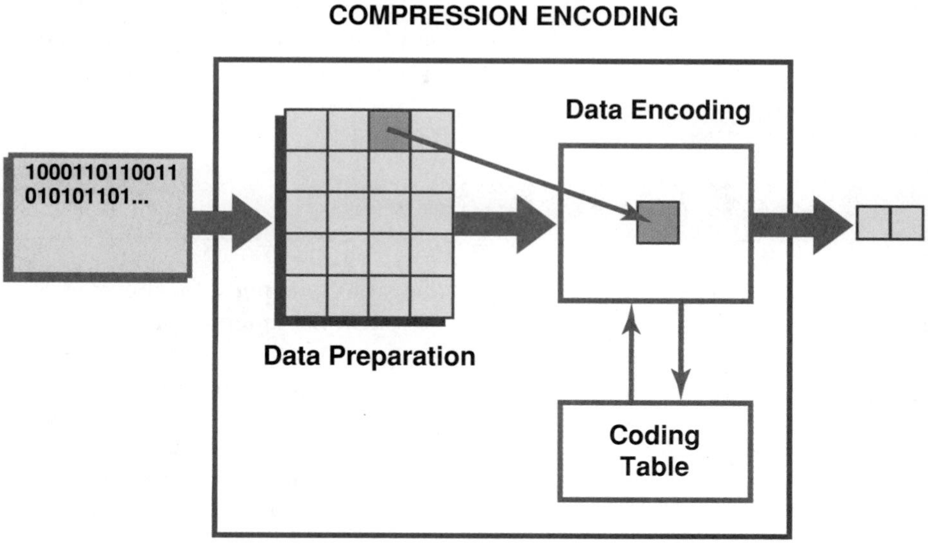

FIGURE 15.2

Compression is an encoding process that filters the original data in several successive stages. The first stage is data preparation. The input file is partitioned into data units. The next stage usually involves the encoding step in which the bit pattern of a data unit is replaced by a smaller sequence of bits. A coding table is often used to make decisions in this coding process. Pictured here, the input file has been divided into equal-sized data units, and the third unit is being coded for output to the eventual data stream.

COMPRESSION ENCODING

Data Encoding

1000110110011 010101101...

Data Preparation

Coding Table

niques depends on the kind of information and its use. Text and numeric data, for example, generally have exacting standards, so lossless compression/decompression is a must. On the other hand, audio and digital images can tolerate some loss of original information because the eye and ear are more forgiving.

Codec speed is another significant factor. The amount of time required to compress and decompress data can be important for some applications. In this regard, codecs may function either symmetrically or asymmetrically. A **symmetric codec** is one that takes approximately the same amount of time to compress data as to decompress it. For instance, video-conferencing is a two-way communication that takes place in real time, so the audio and video should be compressed for transmission and decompressed at about the same rate to be effective. Compression utilities for managing data on your hard disks are usually symmetric, too. In contrast, an **asymmetric codec** technique has simple, fast decompression speed, but compression is usually more complicated and significantly slower. This is acceptable when the data can be compressed once and decompressed often, for example, when storing and accessing audio and video on a CD-ROM.

Finally, we can distinguish compression/decompression schemes by whether they are based on syntactic, semantic, or hybrid methods. **Syntactic methods** attempt to reduce the redundancy of symbolic patterns without any attention to the type of information represented. Thus, a syntactic approach ignores the source of the information and treats it as a mere stream of symbols. Syntactic compression is also called **entropy encoding. Semantic methods** consider special properties of the type of information represented. This knowledge often helps to transform or reduce the amount of nonessential information in the original. For instance, only sound frequencies at a specific amplitude are required for reproducing a recognizable voice signal. If we know that we are compressing a recorded voice, then signals below that threshold can be ignored with no loss of audible information. **Hybrid methods** combine both syntactic and semantic approaches, though usually in stages. A popular choice is to prepare the data using a semantic method and then reduce it further with entropy encoding.

For practical applications, it makes sense to consider data compression by the category of information being treated. Accordingly, we will divide the territory as before into two areas: discrete data (text and numbers) versus analog data (digital images, audio, and video).

COMPRESSING TEXT AND NUMERIC DATA

Many of the applications we use store data in the form of text and numbers. Text documents, spreadsheets, and databases are often archived on our systems. These data files are typically represented as text. By the same token, millions of bytes of text files are transmitted daily over networks. In addition, binary files representing programs are commonly duplicated, transmitted, and stored on systems. Data and programs are natural candidates for the benefits of compression for transmission and storage. Both data and programs contain precise information that must be restored accurately when decompressed. For this reason, only lossless compression is used for text and binary files.

Several methods are popular for compressing files representing text, numeric data, and programs. These include run-length encoding (RLE), Huffman coding, and Lempel-Ziv Welch (LZW) compression. All are lossless methods that exploit the redundancy of bit patterns in the file.

Run-Length Encoding

A simple and direct form of compression that yields modest savings for most sources is **run-length encoding (RLE).** It is based on the assumption that a great deal of redundancy is present in the repetition of particular sequences of symbols. For example, suppose that we are compressing a text file that contains the following sequence:

ABBCCDDDDDDDDDDEEFGGGGG

We could replace some of its redundancy by simply encoding how many times a given symbol is repeated consecutively. If we use one character to represent the symbol, one character—say, "#"—to alert the decoder, and one or two symbols to indicate the frequency, it would cost three to four symbols to encode a repetitive pattern. Consequently, we might replace the previous sequence with this one.

ABBCCD#9EEFG#5

This would net a reduction of around 40 percent or a compression rate of almost 60 percent in this instance.

Facsimile, or fax, transmissions use RLE for data reduction. And, because encoding and decoding are both simple and fast, run-length encoding is also favored in many hybrid methods that call for syntactic encoding.

Huffman Codes

Named for its creator, David Huffman, **Huffman coding** is a form of statistical encoding that exploits the overall distribution or frequency of symbols in a source. It produces an optimal coding for a passage based on assigning the fewest number of bits to encode each symbol given the probability of its occurrence. For example, if we know that in English text the letter "e" is more likely to occur than any other, it would make sense to replace it with the smallest sequence of bits possible. This would give us the greatest savings in compression. By the same token, letters that occur rarely, such as "q" or "z," could be encoded by longer sequences. The net effect would be an economical encoding. Huffman coding uses such statistical knowledge to create a unique replacement code for the source text's symbols. With a coding table for deciphering, the decompression of Huffman codes is straightforward.

There are a few variations for Huffman coding. **Adaptive Huffman coding** is a popular one. Rather than depending on a static coding table, it builds a table while processing the source. Because this method is self-adjusting, it yields better results, especially when predefined statistics are not available.

LZW Compression

Both RLE and Huffman codes are basically symbol compression schemes. In other words, they are designed around the assumption that the source data is best treated as a sequence of uniform, individual units—characters, bytes, and so on. In contrast, **Lempel-Ziv Welch compression** is an algorithm developed by Lempel and Ziv, and refined by Welch, based on recognizing common string patterns. A **string** is simply a sequence of symbols. The basic strategy is to replace strings in a file with bit codes rather than replacing individual characters with bit codes. By treating the source as a sequence of strings, reducing redundancy at this level can yield greater compression than other methods. Even better, LZW codecs do not require any predefined knowledge about the source and its symbols. The source is encoded as the codec scans the text, symbol by symbol. This makes for an efficient and robust method. Decompression is just as clever. Unlike Huffman coding, LZW decompressors do not need a table to decipher the compressed file. The text is both coded and decoded on the fly.

LZW codecs surpass Huffman coding in both speed and compression rates. A typical text file is reduced by 50 percent on average using LZW compression. Because it is a lossless syntactic method, it can be applied to a variety of sources. Today, nearly all commercial compression utilities employ some variation of this method; Stuffit and Zipit are good examples. These may be used to conserve space on hard disk archives as well as compress data for transmission over networks.

COMPRESSION BY STRING CRUNCHING

The chief feature of LZW compression is that it treats a data file or stream as structurally composed of strings, that is, sequences or combinations of symbols. The rationale for this approach is based on the concept of **sequence complexity** introduced by Lempel and Ziv in 1976. A purely random sequence of symbols has very few repeated patterns and therefore would be considered sequentially complex. On the other hand, the symbols in text and other forms of symbolic information have interrelations that yield repetitious patterns. The index for complexity, then, is the degree of string redundancy in a passage. Finding and exploiting this redundancy is the key for compressing the data.

The basic strategy is to divide the input stream into unique strings and replace any repeated strings with references to the location of their initial occurrences. Here is an example:

the other one is the oldest

Suppose that we scanned this sequence for repeated string patterns. If we replaced each repeating piece of text (blank spaces are considered as well) with the location and the length of its first occurrence, we would get the following encoding.

the o[1,3]r[4,2]n[3,2]is[4,1][1,5]ld[3,1][16,1][1,1]

The first [1,3] says insert the three-character string starting at position 1 ("the" in this case). Such a short example doesn't produce any compression. However, savings are produced as the size of the file grows. Longer sequences usually mean longer string patterns and more repetitions. Note, too, that while our example uses the standard alphabet symbols of English, we would actually be applying the technique to a *binary* input stream. Hence we may find additional patterns of repetition because we are dealing with only the two symbols 0 and 1.

Decompression does not require a table or dictionary of strings either. The passage can be reconstructed exactly by simply replacing the pointers to earlier strings with the patterns they identify. Follow the steps of decoding the passage back to its original form.

0   the o[1,3]r[4,2]n[3,2]is[4,1][1,5]ld[3,1][16,1][1,1]

1   the other[4,2]n[3,2]is[4,1][1,5]ld[3,1][16,1][1,1]

2   the other on[3,2]is[4,1][1,5]ld[3,1][16,1][1,1]

3   the other one is[4,1][1,5]ld[3,1][16,1][1,1]

4   the other one is [1,5]ld[3,1][16,1][1,1]

5   the other one is the old[3,1][16,1][1,1]

6   the other one is the olde[16,1][1,1]

7   the other one is the oldes[1,1]

8   the other one is the oldest

The interesting fact about this technique is that it is purely syntactic. We are not dividing the passage into words or any kind of meaningful unit. Nonetheless, we are able to exploit the underlying informational organization of the passage even if we do not understand it.

More Information

COMPRESSING IMAGES

In spite of improvements in desktop computing performance, the use of digitized images still presents formidable challenges for most practical applications. The chief obstacle for these applications is the huge amount of data that must be stored and processed to represent these images. A single color image at typical screen resolution, for example, requires about 900 KB to represent it; higher resolutions take even more storage. Thus, the widespread use of digital imagery has been hampered by the high costs of storage and transmission.

In recent years, industry standards for image compression have been introduced. These compression technologies have been adopted by most hardware/software vendors and have greatly improved the practicality of using digital images in everyday applications.

Digital images, of course, refer to single frames or still images usually displayed on a video monitor. For the sake of compression, we distinguish such images according to whether they are discrete or continuous-tone images. Specifically, a discrete image is usually a graphic composed of lines and curves, such as line art. Standards for compressing discrete images are based on those used for fax transmission, which uses an RLE method, as described earlier. A continuous-tone image is a complex, bit-mapped image containing numerous shades or tones, such as a digitized photograph. These types of images and graphics are more common, and compressing them is more demanding. Three popular formats for compressing digital images are GIF, TIFF, and JPEG.

GIF Compression

CompuServe, the commercial online network service provider, introduced the **graphic interchange format (GIF)** as a standard for transferring 8-bit digital images over networked modems. GIF employs a LZW codec for lossless compression. The drawback to GIF, however, is that it is limited to 256 colors (or shades of gray).

TIFF Compression

The **tagged image file format (TIFF)** is a general bit-mapped image format developed by Aldus Corporation and widely used by a variety of applications and hardware platforms. It has an optional compressed format that is also based on the LZW method.

Because both GIF and TIFF images use the same basic syntactic technique, we can expect them to offer average compression rates around 50 percent for typical natural scene images. Keep in mind, though, that actual rates will vary with the original image content.

JPEG Compression

JPEG is the acronym for **Joint Photographic Experts Group.** This panel of academic and industry professionals proposed general-purpose compression standards for still images. The primary intent, of course, was to offer a compression standard that reduced storage significantly while preserving image fidelity. The committee, though, had another agenda that was equally important. The goal also was to create a set of specifications that would work for a wide range of images and applications while preserving enough uniformity that images could be exchanged and processed by different application programs.

JPEG is actually an umbrella term covering several lossy and lossless compression/decompression methods. Most implementations, however, are restricted to the so-called **baseline codec.** This is lossy compression based on a hybrid method. This common denominator technique offers the user a choice of compression rates. Image quality, however, is sacrificed in proportion to the compression rate. As Figure 15.3 illustrates, greater compression rates mean poorer image quality compared to the original.

The baseline codec can be implemented by either hardware or software with very nearly symmetric performance for compression and decompression. The chief advantage of JPEG compression today, however, is its wide acceptance and support in a variety of applications.

When using JPEG compression, you should keep several issues in mind. JPEG codecs are designed for continuous-tone graphics such as digitized photographs. They do not work well with simple, high-contrast graphics such as line art. JPEG compression can indeed alter the image, but its effects vary, depending on its original content. Experimentation is a must for achieving the best results. Of course, the chief trade-off is image fidelity versus compression rates. The greater the compression, the more pronounced is its lossiness. In general, you should prefer higher-quality compression settings because these yield appreciable size reduction with a minimal loss of data.

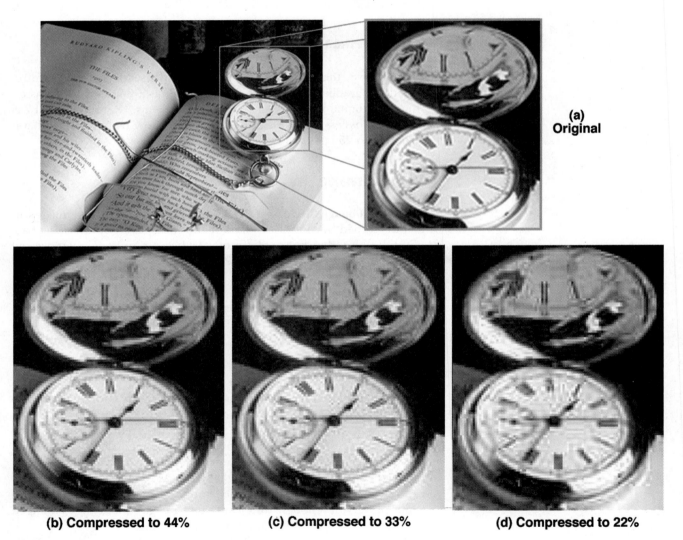

(a) Original

(b) Compressed to 44%   **(c) Compressed to 33%**   **(d) Compressed to 22%**

FIGURE 15.3

The effects of JPEG compression on the fidelity of the image are subtle. The original grayscale image (a) is compressed at three different rates. At a reduction to 44%, the close-up of the watch (b) shows only a little difference from the original. As the compression increases, the sharpness of the details softens and watch faces (c) and (d) show a mottled artifact. On the other hand, the effects are less noticeable when viewed at normal resolution.

focus

HOW JPEG WORKS

The standard JPEG codec produces lossy compression. This means, of course, that the resulting image is not identical to its original. But what exactly is lost and why is it lost? Interestingly, to the casual observer, distinguishing uncompressed images from those that have been compressed and decompressed again using a JPEG codec is often difficult. Closer examination, however, does reveal changes in the pixels of the compressed/decompressed image.

In most natural images, JPEG compression yields a softening or averaging effect. **Averaging** means that pixels in the same neighborhood have the same or similar characteristics (that is, intensity or color). Greater compression means more uniformity, which translates to loss of detail and contrast.

The heart of the JPEG codec method is a process called the **discrete cosine transform (DCT).** The DCT converts the image to a representation in a frequency domain. In this frequency space, smooth or continuous tones are denoted by low frequencies while sharp, abrupt changes in intensity are represented as high frequencies. Most natural images have large areas with smoothly varying or continuous tones. These regions are punctuated by relatively fewer pixels having sharp changes in intensity compared to their neighbors. These changes typically signify edges or boundaries between objects and their components. See Figure 15.4. The upshot is that most images have far more low-frequency information than high-frequency information. The success of JPEG compression depends precisely on this.

FIGURE 15.4

In (a), a sample of the grayscale image is selected and enlarged to reveal pixel detail. The diagonal pattern represents the edge between the window and building face as seen in the full-sized version. The image (b) is compressed using a JPEG codec. Note that it appears almost identical to the original at full resolution. But a close-up look at the same sampled area shows how the pixels have lost most of their high contrast. This averaging effect subtly softens the image.

(a)   (b)

The image is prepared by converting it into equal-sized segments or blocks. Each of these prepared blocks is then processed by the DCT and encoded. The output from the DCT is a frequency map that identifies the low- and high-frequency information in the segment. This step could be reversed without any loss of fidelity in the image. The next stage is quantization; at this point, some information will likely be lost. The image quality selected will dictate the resolution used for quantizing the frequency information and hence the extent of any data loss. Low frequencies are stored with greater precision; high frequencies are truncated. As long as the high-frequency values are relatively sparse in the image, the informational loss is minimal. Quantized values are compressed even further using entropy (syntactic) encoding, typically Huffman coding. See Figure 15.5.

Decompression, naturally, reverses the process. The decoded, quantized frequency values are transformed back into pixel segments, and the image is reconstructed. Any loss of high frequencies reduces the contrast in its segment.

More Information

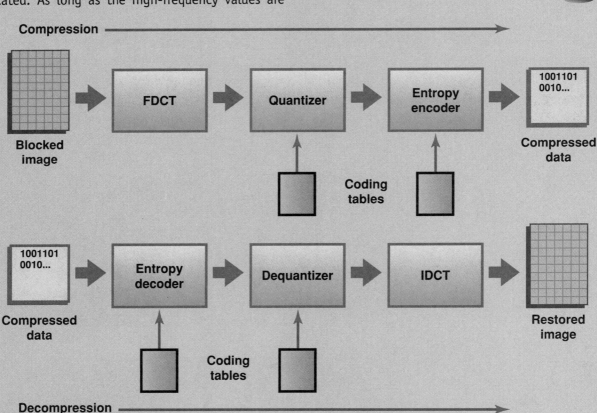

FIGURE 15.5

The basic JPEG codec is composed of a three-stage filtering process. The image is divided into segments. These are converted to frequency data by the forward discrete cosine transform (FDCT). The first actual stage of compression takes place when the output values from the FDCT are quantized. This stream of data is further compressed by entropy encoding, typically, a Huffman code. Coding tables are used for both stages of compression. Decompression follows the same steps in reverse. The IDCT is the inverse discrete cosine transform, which converts frequency data back to image pixel segments.

COMPRESSING VIDEO

Compression for still images is certainly desirable, but for video, it is absolutely essential. Digital video exacts enormous demands on system performance and throughput. Recall from the previous chapter that transmitting standard full-screen color imagery as video at 30 frames per second requires a data rate of nearly 28 MB per second. The bandwidth needed for such a rate goes well beyond practical standards. Indeed, without significant compression ratios, digital video is simply not practical. A number of video compression methods have been adopted by applications. At the low end of quality and compression are QuickTime from Apple and its Microsoft competitor, AVI. In addition, there are DVI, Motion-JPEG, MPEG, and px64, which offer both higher performance and greater compression.

QuickTime and AVI

As we mentioned in the previous chapter, the scalable and extensible video playback system QuickTime was introduced by Apple Computer and SuperMac Technologies in 1991. QuickTime is defined by the MooV (pronounced "movie") file format that interleaves compressed video frames with compressed audio. QuickTime is extensible primarily due to its modular design. One of the benefits of its extensibility is that QuickTime can adapt to a variety of schemes for compression/decompression. The Video and Cinepak compressors are two standard ones supplied with the application. The Video codec has a compression ratio of 20 percent (or 5:1); Cinepak reduces video to 10 percent (or 10:1). Both are (very) lossy codecs based on hybrid methods. Video (a.k.a. "Road Pizza") is a symmetric codec, which means that both compression and decompression can be done in real time at about the same rate. For small frame resolution, Video offers satisfactory results. Cinepak, however, is a better choice for larger resolution and greater frame rates. Cinepak, though, is highly asymmetric in operation. It can take hours to compress a video that plays just a few minutes. Today, QuickTime 3.x supports other popular industry standards. Codecs written by other developers can be added easily by the user as well.

In 1992, Microsoft introduced Video for Windows. Very similar to QuickTime, it is based on a file format called **audio video interleaved (AVI).** AVI intersperses each video frame with a frame's worth of sound; the interleaving is strict—hence, the name for the format. Although Microsoft recently discontinued support for Video for Windows, there are still a number of applications that employ the AVI format. AVI includes a choice of compression tools including the Cinepak codec (based on QuickTime) and the Indeo codec (based on Intel's DVI, discussed later.) Indeo is a symmetric codec that handles various video resolutions including 320×240 at a rate of 15 frames per second and higher resolutions.

Codecs for QuickTime and AVI employ spatial as well as temporal compression. **Spatial compression** reduces the amount of information needed to represent a single frame of a video sequence. **Temporal compression,** on the other hand, eliminates the redundant data from frame to frame throughout the sequence.

QuickTime and AVI represent competing and incompatible standards for low-end applications of audio/video compression, storage, and playback. These are effective for standard desktop computer systems without additional hardware. In the following sections, we catalog some different but related methods for compressing video for applications that demand either higher or more specialized performance characteristics. While these are incompatible today, we can expect some convergence in these technologies in the future.

Digital Video Interactive (DVI)

The compression system called **digital video interactive (DVI)** is a proprietary system now owned by Intel. It is usually hardware dependent; this means that its codecs are based on a special-purpose coprocessor that must be added to a computer system. DVI supports both symmetric and asymmetric compression schemes. Real Time Video (RTV) is a symmetric compression/decompression method that was originally intended for fast editing of video sequences. Presentation Level Video (PLV) is an asymmetric compression technique that has higher image quality. PLV works well with CD-ROM applications. The lengthier time for compression is a one-time expense; the video can be decompressed much faster during numerous playbacks from this medium.

The RTV codec is known as Indeo and can be implemented in software on standard processors with some loss of image quality and speed compared to hardware implementations. As mentioned earlier, RTV or Indeo has an image resolution of 320 × 240 at 15 frames per second. PLV mode is considered broadcast quality—comparable to that of VHS format for videotape. It has resolutions up to 640 × 480 and supports full-motion video (30 frames per second). Both modes interleave compressed audio information along with data for video.

Motion-JPEG

As the name suggests, **Motion-JPEG** is an adaptation of JPEG's still image standards for video. Specifically, it combines JPEG methods for spatial compression of single frames with a temporal compression method. Motion-JPEG is supported only by hardware implementations. A number of developers offer proprietary processor boards that implement it.

Unfortunately, because there is no uniform set of standards, these implementations of Motion-JPEG are generally incompatible: Video produced by one application (and vendor) cannot be used by others. Its chief limitation, however, is that it does not provide for synchronized audio compression. Motion-JPEG is best suited for animations and slide shows that do not require synchronized sound.

MPEG

An international standards body similar to that of JPEG (in fact, having some of the same members) called the **Moving Picture Experts Group (MPEG)** has established a standard for compressing video. While Motion-JPEG is largely an ad hoc method, MPEG standards are expressly defined for video applications.

Like Motion-JPEG, the MPEG standard defines a combination of spatial and temporal compression techniques. The spatial information in single frames is compressed using a method similar to that of JPEG. Additional savings are achieved using a technique called **motion compensation.** Because motion is usually restricted to a portion of the scene, much of the data in a video sequence repeats from frame to frame. Motion compensation reduces the amount of information stored even more than spatial compression by eliminating the storage of redundancy between frames in a sequence.

Today, there are currently three standards, MPEG-1, MPEG-2, and MPEG-4. The MPEG-1 codec is designed primarily for video playback from older and slower CD-ROM players. With a data capacity of 150 KB per second, it can support a resolution of 320×240 at up to 30 frames per second. MPEG-2 is a higher performance standard with a capacity of 1.2 MB per second. It can encode and decode full-screen video at a resolution of 704×480 at 30 frames per second. With its higher data rate, the picture quality compares well with conventional broadcast standards. MPEG-2 is currently used primarily in the entertainment industry for direct satellite broadcasts and DVD video. (See Chapter 5 for a discussion of DVD discs.)

MPEG-3 was originally planned for handling HDTV (high-definition television) signals, but as MPEG-2 was being developed, it became apparent that MPEG-2 was capable of most of the tasks for which MPEG-3 was being developed; the MPEG-3 effort was suspended. MPEG-4 is currently under development and is scheduled to be finalized by the end of 1999. It is specially designed to reduce the bit rate needed to play back compressed files. If it succeeds, we can expect digital video applications to spread to such environments as mobile multimedia communications and multimedia e-mail. All the MPEG standards usually require hardware for both compression and playback.

The px64 Standard

Another popular international standard for video compression is called **px64** (pronounced "p times 64"). It was developed in the late 1980s for transmission of video signals over ISDN telephone lines. Because it was originally intended as a compression method adapted to video telephony and teleconferencing, the design and performance parameters of px64 are exclusively driven by this specialized application domain.

Although the two methods are not compatible, px64 employs compression methods similar to those of MPEG. It is a scalable system with two formats offering several resolutions, frame rates, and compression ratios to accommodate different transmission channel capacities. While its image quality is not high, its performance is quite satisfactory for the real-time demands of video-conferencing.

Temporal Compression in Video

One way to reduce the amount of information stored for a video, of course, is to constrain the frame rate itself. Full-motion video requires about thirty frames per second to achieve the illusion of continuous motion. The data rates for sustaining thirty frames per second, however, are huge. Sacrificing some of the quality of the video for lower frame rates can reap dividends for storing and transmitting data. For example, frame rates between ten and fifteen per second are acceptable for some applications. Even at lower frame rates, more compression is possible—and often needed.

Compression methods such as JPEG use spatial compression; they reduce the redundant information contained within a single image or frame. In the context of video, we call this type of compression **intraframe compression.** Although useful for compressing video, it is not sufficient for achieving the kinds of data rates essential for transmitting video in practical applications.

Intraframe compression by itself ignores an enormous amount of the redundancy that occurs in a typical video sequence. Much of the data in video images is repeated frame after frame. Strategies for eliminating the redundancy of information between frames employ temporal compression. These are referred to as **interframe compression** methods. Most codecs approach temporal compression by dividing the video into segments. For example, suppose we extract four successive frames from a video sequence of a moving automobile. The first frame in the sequence is designated the **key frame.** We can use it as the basis for deciding how much motion or how many changes take place in the succeeding frames. The background in our scene, in particular, is unlikely to change much over a short span. (Remember that four frames is only a fraction of a second for most videos.) We can ignore coding any information about the sky, ground, and road in succeeding or **difference frames.** Thus, the amount of information in difference frames is reduced considerably because it is restricted to components that move or change between frames. To decompress or rebuild the sequence, we would use information saved from the key frame to rebuild the missing areas in the difference frames. Figure 15.6 illustrates.

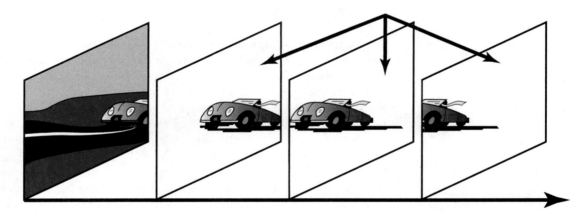

FIGURE 15.6

Video compression differencing attempts to reduce the amount of information stored and transmitted by eliminating data that is repeated across a sequence of frames. In the example, the first image is encoded with enough information to reconstruct it independently. This image—the key frame—has little compression. It is used as the reference for calculating differences in the frames that follow. In this instance, the succeeding images have little new information, so the pixels representing the background (sky, road, etc.) can be discarded. Difference frames save only the data that depicts how they differ from the key frame. Later during decompression, the key frame is used again to reconstruct the difference frames by adding back the static areas missing from them.

Codecs for QuickTime and DVI, for example, employ techniques similar to the one described above. What happens, however, when in the middle of some sequences, a new area is revealed in a frame? For instance, new background is uncovered when a foreground object moves away, or an entirely new region is exposed when a door or window opens. In both cases, the key frame contains entirely different information, and the amount of data needed to capture the succeeding difference frames is large. One way to solve this problem is to designate this image as a new key frame for the next sequence. We could save the image with the new regions or components and start differencing succeeding frames from this point. This is, in fact, how some codecs handle it. This method merely postpones the problem and can lead to low or poor compression rates for some videos.

MPEG and related codecs employ a different tactic. Simple differencing tracks motion in one direction, based on past frames. MPEG predicts motion bidirectionally. In other words, some compressed frames are the difference results of predictions based on past frames used as a reference, and others are based on both past and future frames from the sequence. Here is how it is organized. In MPEG terminology, key frames are called **intrapictures (I pictures).** As in simple differencing, these are periodic reference frames with minimal compression. They are self-contained or coded without any outside information from other frames. I pictures are used to calculate differences for succeeding frames. The resulting calculated difference frames are compressed as **predicted pictures (P pictures).** For coding and encoding, P pictures require information from earlier reference frames, but they may also be used as references for other frames. Interspersed between I and P pictures are highly compressed frames called **bidirectional pictures (B pictures),** which are based on both the nearest past and future reference frames. B pictures handle the problems of the appearance of novel components in an image more gracefully. And in encoding, it makes more sense to interpolate this sort of change as a smooth transition from a past to a future reference point. Figure 15.7 illustrates the dependencies of these picture types for an arbitrary sequence of frames.

FIGURE 15.7

MPEG codecs employ several types of frames for representing a video sequence. Intrapictures (I) are so called because they are compressed using only spatial compression. They serve as key frames for both random access (in playback and editing) and bidirectional motion compensation. The P picture (P) is an image based on compressing temporal information predicted from the most recent I picture. B pictures (B) are interpolated from information extracted from both previous and succeeding reference frames. Both I and P pictures are used as references for intervening B pictures.

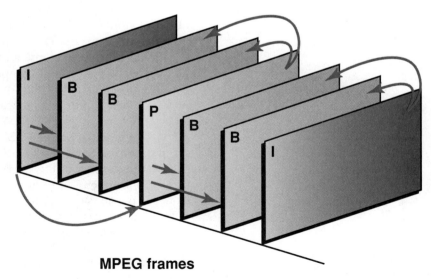

MPEG frames

In decoding and playback, the transmission of frames is out of sequence, namely, I and P pictures must be reconstructed before their preceding B pictures. How all this works in detail is a great deal more complicated, but the net results are greater compression while sustaining higher performance.

Not all codecs are created equal. For more information about when and how to use particular ones, see the companion *Exploring the Digital Domain* Web site.

More Information

COMPRESSING AUDIO

Many of the video standards mentioned contain audio information as part of their formats. Digital audio data can be equally demanding for transmission and storage. Accordingly, there are several approaches for compressing this form of information, especially when combined with video.

Some of these methods we have already treated in Chapter 13. The choice of a sampling rate for audio, like video frame rates, is the first step in handling the problem. Recall that digital sound consists of discrete amplitude samples taken at successive time intervals. The sampling rate refers to the number of intervals per second. High sampling rates mean higher fidelity, but they naturally cost more in storage space and transmission time. CD-quality audio has a sampling rate of 44.1 KHz, that is, over 44,000 samples per second. Many applications do not require this much fidelity. Speech and sound effects are faithfully represented at much lower sampling frequencies. And, of course, lower sampling rates can mean substantial savings in storage.

The sample resolution is significant, too. The number of bits used to quantify the digital audio has an impact on how much room is needed to store it. Of course, sample resolution can also affect the dynamic range for audio playback. Once again, matching the source with the appropriate sample resolution is wise. For example, sound with inherently restricted dynamic range (voice recordings, for example) can be stored more economically by using a lower resolution (perhaps 8-bit as opposed to 16-bit) without any appreciable loss of fidelity.

Fixing the sampling rate and resolution of samples, of course, does not tackle the problem of compressing digital audio after the fact. Audio files must be stored and transmitted for use. Often, these need even more compression to be practical. A popular approach for compressing audio information goes by the daunting name of **adaptive differential pulse code modulation (ADPCM).** Pulse code modulation (PCM) is a basic method for quantizing audio information. Differential PCM compresses the number of bits needed to represent this data by storing the first PCM sample in its entirety and all succeeding samples as *differences* from the previous one. This works in the audio domain much like frame differencing does in video. Finally, adaptive DPCM takes the scheme one step further. The encoder divides the values of the DPCM samples by an appropriate coefficient to produce a smaller value to store. In playback, the decoder multiplies the compressed data by that coefficient to reproduce the proper differential value. This technique guarantees its compression rate because the signal is encoded into reduced but fixed-length sample sizes. For instance, signals digitized with 16-bit resolution can be compressed to 4 bits per sample. And, as long as the dynamic range and frequency response of the original signal are moderate, decompressed playback is satisfactory. ADPCM works very well with speech, and it can be effective even when music is involved. DVI uses this compression method for managing all audio with its video data.

Other methods are available for compressing digital audio, but most of these have yet to migrate to desktop computing. In contrast to digital imaging and video, consumer interest in desktop audio has not been as strong, making commercial development slow. We can expect that this situation will improve as desktop system performance does.

More Information

S U M M A R Y

Digitizing and distributing images, sounds, and video place tremendous demands on both storage and data transmission capabilities. Even for traditional media like text and numeric data, the times required for transmitting large files over networks can be troublesome and sometimes prohibitive. For these reasons, data compression is often employed to help reduce costs and increase performance of computer storage and data communications systems.

Compressing data means reducing the effective size of a data file for storage or transmission. Decompression techniques are then used to expand the compressed data and reproduce the original data, either exactly or in facsimile. Hence, compression and decompression methods work in tandem. Particular paired compression/decompression methods are called codecs. Codecs that cannot guarantee the exact reproduction of the original data after decompression are referred to as lossy methods. In contrast, lossless codecs always reproduce the original data from its compressed format. The choice of lossless versus lossy techniques de-pends on the kind of information and its intended use. When we work with text and numeric data, we generally require exact reproduction; lossless compression/decompression therefore is a must for such data. On the other hand, the eye and ear are somewhat forgiving, and so audio and digital images are often processed with lossy codecs that offer better compression rates than lossless methods.

Lossless compression techniques for text and numeric data are based on the assumption that such data contains redundancy in the repetition of particular sequences of symbols. Some of the more popular lossless techniques are run-length coding (used for fax transmissions), Huffman coding, and Lempel-Ziv Welch (LZW) coding.

There are a number of compression methods for still images. Three of the most commonly used are the GIF, TIFF, and JPEG methods.

Video compression schemes employ spatial as well as temporal compression. Spatial compression reduces the amount of information needed to represent a single frame of a video sequence as in still image compression. Temporal compression, on the other hand, eliminates the need to store redundant data from frame to frame throughout the sequence. There are a number of competing video compression methods including QuickTime, AVI, DVI, Motion-JPEG, MPEG, and px64. Most temporal compression is based on identifying key frames in short frame sequences, then storing only differences from the key frame for succeeding frames in the sequence. The various video compression methods employ variations on this basic theme to optimize compression ratios.

A similar approach is used for compressing audio information. Adaptive differential pulse code modulation (ADPCM) compresses the number of bits needed to represent audio data by storing the first sample in its entirety and all succeeding samples as *differences* from the previous one. Further reduction is obtained by dividing individual sample amplitude values by a predetermined coefficient to reduce the size of the numbers being stored.

The use of compression schemes is not an exact science. The effectiveness and suitability of any method will vary depending on the exact nature of the original file and the use intended for the decompressed file. Experimentation focused on observing the trade-offs between fidelity of the reproduction and compression rates is a must for achieving the best results.

PROJECTS

1 Compare some of the standard image compression techniques using the images that can be accessed on the Projects pages on the *Exploring the Digital Domain* Web site. From this site you can download the same image stored using various techniques. Once you have the files downloaded, you can use JPEG Viewer, LView, or some similar image-viewing package (your lab manager or instructor can help you locate the appropriate viewer) to compare the images at various degrees of magnification. After you complete this activity, write a brief report comparing the various compression techniques and file formats.

2 Compare several compression ratios using the sounds that can be accessed on the Projects pages on the *Exploring the Digital Domain* Web site. From this site you can download the same sounds compressed at several different ratios. Once you have the files downloaded, you can use SoundEdit, Sound Forge, or a similar sound package (your lab manager or instructor can help you locate the appropriate player) to compare the quality of the reproduced sounds at various compression ratios. After you complete this activity, write a brief report about the impact of compression ratios on sound quality.

3 Do some Web-based research to get information about the programs WinZip and Stuffit. What do these programs do?

4 Do some research on the MPEG video compression standards. What is the current status of the standards and playback systems for the standards? Address software-only playback systems for MPEG-1.

Projects

Key Terms

adaptive Huffman coding

ADPCM (adaptive differential
   pulse code modulation)

asymmetric compression/
   decompression

averaging

AVI (audio video interleaved)

baseline codec

bidirectional picture (B picture)

codec (compressor/
   decompressor)

coding table

compression, data

decompression, data

difference frame

discrete cosine transform (DCT)

DVI (digital video interactive)

GIF (graphic interchange
   format)

Huffman coding

hybrid compression

interframe compression

intrapicture (I picture)

JPEG (Joint Photographic
   Experts Group)

key frame

Lempel-Ziv Welch compression
   (LZW)

lossless compression

lossy compression

motion compensation

motion-JPEG

MPEG (Motion Pictures Experts
   Group)

predicted picture (P picture)

px64

run-length encoding (RLE)

semantic compression

sequence complexity

spatial compression

string

symmetric compression/
   decompression

syntactic compression (entropy
   encoding)

temporal compression

TIFF (tagged image
   file format)

QUESTIONS FOR REVIEW

1 What is data compression? What are its chief advantages and disadvantages?

2 Describe the general process of encoding used in data compression.

3 Compare lossy and lossless data compression.

4 What is a codec?

5 How do syntactic compression methods differ from semantic ones?

6 Distinguish symmetric from asymmetric codecs. What are their practical differences?

7 Digital video codecs often employ temporal or interframe compression. What does this mean?

8 Describe briefly how run-length encoding (RLE) works. What is this compression scheme usually used for?

9 Describe briefly how Huffman coding works. What is this compression scheme usually used for?

10 Describe the LZW compression scheme and what it is used for.

11 How do spatial and temporal compression schemes differ? Explain their roles in video and audio compression.

12 Name several still image compression methods.

13 What is the adaptive differential pulse code modulation method? What is it used for?

14 Describe briefly the interframe compression technique used in MPEG. How does it differ from the technique of simple differencing?

15 What are the practical differences between the video formats of MPEG-1 and MPEG-2?

PART 5

DATA-TO-GO–
DATA COMMUNICATIONS
AND NETWORKS

Vasily Kandinsky, *Small Pleasures*, June 1913. Solomon R. Guggenheim Museum

One of the most significant changes in computing over the past several decades has been the evolution of data communications networks. The technology of digital data transmission over computer networks has had profound effects on how we work, play, and live. Computer networks connect individuals in the same office, the same building, and across the world. They provide for the instantaneous exchange of information. Computer data networks have conquered the conventional barriers of space and time. Networks have also helped conquer the "language" barriers that separate different computer hardware platforms as well. Within the industry, the notions of compatibility and interoperability were unheard of before networking. Indeed, the so-called digital information age has been fueled more by computer networking than by any other single factor.

Digital data transmission and computer networks take many different forms. What exactly is a data communications system? How is digital data encoded and transmitted? How different are networks that connect computers in the same building from those that span continents? How can data transmitted over networks be secured for privacy? These are the primary questions that we address in this chapter.

OBJECTIVES

- The chief elements of a communications system
- How data is encoded and transmitted over data communications channels
- The variety of computer networks based on such factors as scale, media, and transmission methods
- The basic elements of cryptography, the art and science of keeping messages secret
- The concepts and use of private key and public key data encryption systems

CHAPTER 16

DATA COMMUNICATIONS

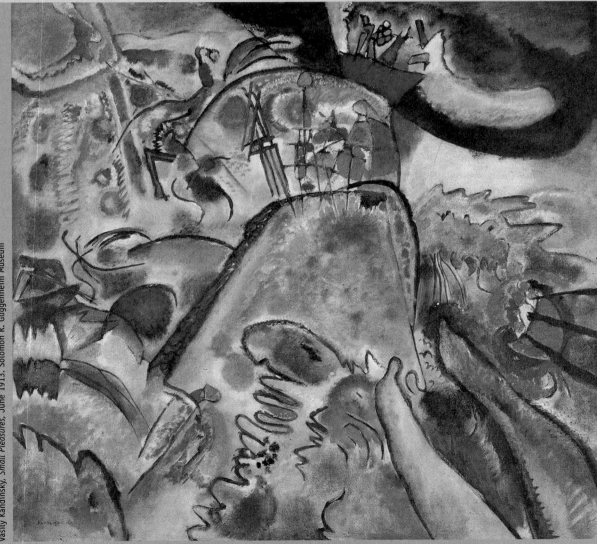

Vasily Kandinsky, *Small Pleasures*, June 1913. Solomon R. Guggenheim Museum

THE BASIC COMMUNICATIONS MODEL

Technologies for sharing information are certainly not new. Information, unlike other material goods, can be duplicated and shared easily. Sharing information usually takes one of two possible forms, broadcasting or networking. **Broadcasting** involves transmitting the same information to many individuals or receivers. The receiver is unable to change or alter broadcast information. (Think of print media, radio, and television.) In contrast, **networking** allows the sender and receiver to exchange and process information, which often produces new information. Of course, networking individuals is not new. People formed social, professional, and enterprise networks long before computer technology. What is new, however, is how advanced networking has become through the medium of computers. **Computer networks** connect computer systems and devices for the sharing of information and resources.

The purpose of a **data communications system** is to exchange information or data between two agents. Data communications can take many different forms. **Claude Shannon,** a pioneer in information theory, proposed a model in 1946 for understanding how any communications system works. The model is at once simple and fundamental. It is useful to review it here because it highlights the six basic components found in all data communications systems—as well as other forms of communication, for that matter. We consider each of these components and employ examples to illustrate how they correspond to practical instances of communication. Refer to Figure 16.1.

Information Source

Communication must begin from some source. The **information source** generates messages; this process involves encoding information into some form understandable to the intended receiver. For example, a

FIGURE 16.1

This figure illustrates Shannon's basic model for a communications system. Each of the six components of the model is described in the text.

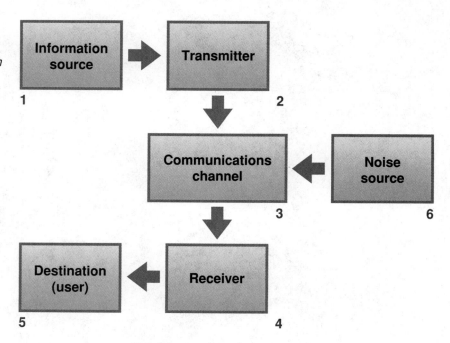

speaker phrases thoughts into words. In another instance, when you correspond with a friend using electronic mail (e-mail), you type a text message using an editor.

Transmitter

The **transmitter** encodes the message from the information source. The message is encoded as a **signal,** an object in a form that matches the properties of the communications channel over which the signal will be transmitted. The speaker, for example, converts his or her words into sounds—that is, sound pressure waves that can be propagated in the air. The computer system converts your e-mail message into an electrical signal appropriate for transmission over a computer network. The information source and the transmitter together are the **originating system.**

Communication Channel

In all forms of communication there is a physical separation of source and destination. The **communications channel** is the medium that bridges the distance between the transmitter and the receiver. For speech, the channel is the air that carries sound pressure waves. In a computer network, it might be the wires that transfer the electrical signal from one computer system to another.

The distance that the signal must travel over the medium or channel affects the strength of the signal sensed by the receiver. In most physical systems, the signal naturally weakens as it travels. A speaker, for example, might be readily heard in a room but be barely audible in a large auditorium. An electrical signal sent over a network might be strong enough to be received by a system in the same room but too weak to be received by one across campus.

Receiver

The **receiver** extracts a signal from the communications channel and converts it back into an encoded form of a message. The listener, for example, hears the sounds uttered by the speaker and converts them to words. The computer receiving the signal over the network converts it to a digital representation of text.

Destination

The **destination** receives the message and retrieves whatever information is contained in it. For example, the listener interprets and understands the speech. Your friend reads the e-mail message converted to text by the computer system that received it.

The receiver and the destination are called the **destination system.** In the pure or abstract communications system, the originating system sends a signal over a communications channel to the destination system. The signal sent by the transmitter is identical to the signal extracted by the receiver in this perfect system. As a result, the message received is the same as the one sent. Unfortunately, perfect communications systems rarely exist, if ever. There is almost always at least one "real-world" factor that must be considered.

Noise Source

A source of noise is usually present in the communications channel medium. **Noise** is a random element that modifies the encoded signal in unpredictable ways. In the case of listening to a speaker, ambient sounds, such as other people talking or the hum of machines in the room, may interfere. In a network, the electrical devices introduce unavoidable noise on the channel that perturbs the signals transmitted. Noise modifies the signal and can corrupt the message. Because distance can weaken the signal strength, noise may have a more significant impact on the quality of communications over long distances.

As you might expect, the challenge of designing an effective communications system is to overcome the adverse effects from system noise and transmission distances. In communications systems, noise and distance can usually be offset by sufficient signal strength. The more powerful the signal, the less it is affected by noise or attenuated by distance. Unfortunately, all too often it is neither practical nor economical to create an amply powerful signal. Compromises are typical in any real-life communications system. The goal is to devise a system wherein the signal received is reasonably comparable to the one transmitted; this should ensure that the message received has lost little of its original informational content. For instance, the reproduction of voice in telephone communications is usually satisfactory but falls well short of high-fidelity audio standards. In practical systems, the cost of communication must not outweigh the expected value of its content. Keeping these factors in mind helps to explain some of the practices adopted in data communications over computer networks.

DATA ENCODING AND SIGNAL TRANSMISSION

Shannon's model describes any type of communications system. Our interest, of course, is understanding technologies that serve data communications in computer networks. The first step, then, is understanding how that data is handled. Based on the model, we can simplify this to consider three chief issues. How is the data (message) encoded? How does the signal transmit that data? What are the limiting factors affecting that transmission? The answers are straightforward:

1 The message in any computer network communications system is encoded as a stream of binary numbers.

2 The signal is transmitted and received as some type of electromagnetic energy (usually electrical, optical, or radio waves).

3 The rate at which data can be transmitted reliably over a given communications channel is determined primarily by properties of the medium.

In this section, we delve a little deeper into the issues of data encoding and signal transmission for digital data communications.

Encoding the Data

As you are well aware by now, all forms of information processed by computers are encoded as streams of binary digits. This digitization of data is the common denominator that unlocks the unsurpassed potential of computers to store, transfer, and process both large amounts and many forms of information. We have also seen that most coding schemes are based on grouping binary digits or bits into bytes (eight bits) or larger sequences. The same is true for data communications. Information transmitted over computer networks is binary encoded. Data may be encoded in either an unchanged or pure binary format (such as data files containing images, sound, programs, etc.) or as text using the ASCII coding scheme.

You learned in Chapter 9 about text codes such as ASCII (American Standard Code for Information Interchange). The origin of the ASCII coding system was in data communications applications rather than exclusively for text processing. Each character or symbol in the ASCII code is represented by an 8-bit binary code. One of the bits is called the **parity bit,** which can be used for transmission error detection, and the other seven bits represent the actual character to be transmitted. We can use the parity bit for error detection in an odd parity scheme or an even parity scheme. Let's examine an odd parity scheme first.

Using **odd parity error detection,** the transmitter will set the parity bit so that the total number of bits containing the value 1 (let's call these 1-bits) in the byte is odd. This allows the receiver to monitor for certain kinds of errors. Suppose one of the 1-bits in the encoding of the original symbol gets changed to a 0 during transmission and all other bits (including the parity bit itself) stay the same. The receiver will recognize that there is an error and ask for a retransmission because the information in the parity bit will not match the receiver's own count of whether there is an even or odd number of 1-bits. Note that even if the receiver detects an error, it has no idea what the error is; it simply requests another transmission of the data.

This scheme is not foolproof. For example, if exactly *two* bits get changed during transit, the parity bit will not alert the receiver to this fact. If the parity bit alone gets changed during transit, the receiver will detect this error and ask for another transmission. Can you see why? In general, parity bit error detection will detect an odd number of bit changes during transit, but not an even number of bit changes. In short, parity bit error detection is not very robust. It is designed to detect single bit changes, which are the most frequent errors on a normal communications channel. See Figure 16.2.

On a particularly noisy channel where more than one bit is likely to be changed, we would need a more sophisticated error detection method. The advantage of parity bit error detection is that it is not very expensive. It costs only one bit per byte of transmitted data.

Even parity error detection works in an analogous way. In this scheme, the parity bit is set so that the total number of 1-bits is even. Like the odd parity method, it detects an odd number of bit changes during transit, but not an even number of such changes.

FIGURE 16.2

The encoding of a single text character for data transmission often employs a parity bit for error checking. Here, the letter "N" is encoded and transmitted. In this instance, odd parity error detection is used. The figure illustrates a case (middle) where error detection is robust and another (bottom) where the parity bit method does not detect the errors made. Note that parity checking is an error detection scheme and not a correction method. It can discover that an error occurred in transmission, but not fix it.

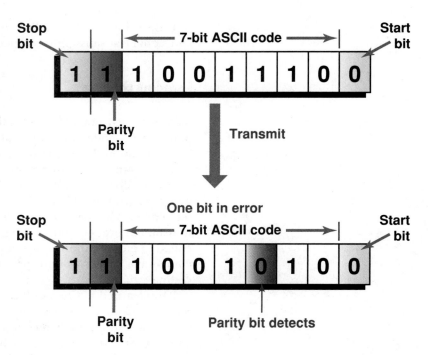

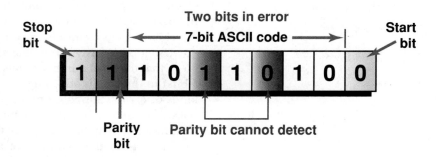

Transmitting the Signal

Once a message is encoded, it must be converted to a signal for transmission over the communications channel. The signal, of course, must match the properties of the transmission media. In data communications, data may be transmitted as either analog or digital signals, depending on the medium used.

In data communications, analog signals are composed fundamentally of waves that are not subject to distortion over transmission channels. These signals are essentially repeating, continuous waveforms whose energy is propagated across the medium. A repeating signal (like a monotonous hum) does not contain much information. To convey information, a signal must exhibit some change from time to time. Hence, repeating waveforms are **modulated,** or altered, to carry a digital message. Figure 16.3 illustrates.

Modulated analog signals may be transmitted over a variety of media. Of course, computers are digital devices, so when analog signals are to be used, we must translate between analog and digital formats when computers are involved. For example, to use telephone lines for transmitting

FIGURE 16.3

Varying its amplitude is one method of modulating the carrier signal to encode binary data. This technique is called amplitude modulation (AM). In the illustration, the amplitude of the signal modulates from low to high to represent 0s and 1s, respectively.

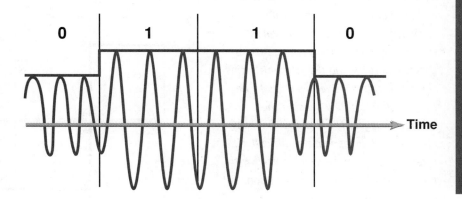

digital information, special devices called **modems** (for *mo*dulate-*dem*odulate) are used to convert digital data to analog signals and analog signals back to digital data. The first step is to convert the original digital data to analog form for transmission. Once the analog form is transmitted across the communication channel, the receiver must convert it back to a digital form for interpretation. Figure 16.4 illustrates.

Digital signals are transmitted over bounded media, such as wires or optical fiber. As illustrated in Figure 16.5, digital signals can be transmitted as series of electrical (over wires) or optical (over optical fiber) pulses. Systems using digital signals do not require special devices like modems, but these systems are often limited in transmission distance because voltage levels and optical signals weaken rapidly with distance.

Regardless of whether the carrier signal is analog or digital, several factors limit the rate at which data can be transmitted reliably. The most significant ones are the bandwidth of the channel, the signal strength, and interference from system noise.

FIGURE 16.4

Transmitting digital data by an analog signal involves two translation processes. First the original digital data is translated to analog form for transmission. The receiver must then convert the analog signal back to a digital form for interpretation.

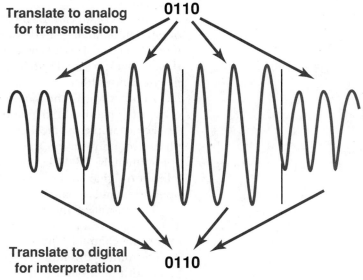

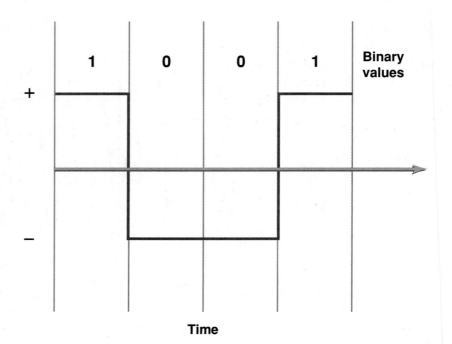

Bandwidth

The **bandwidth** of a communications channel determines its capacity to transmit data. Bandwidth is measured as the range of waveform frequencies the channel is capable of transmitting. Recall from Chapter 13 that frequencies are measured in units of Hertz (Hz), which stands for cycles per second. In the sound domain, the frequency determines the pitch of a sound. In the current context, a signal contains many component waveforms with different frequencies. The range of frequencies present in the signal determines how much information the signal carries. Because information is encoded as changes in a signal's amplitude, signals with greater frequency ranges carry more information in a given time interval.

Intuitively, we can liken bandwidth in signal transmission to the size of pipes in plumbing. To deliver a given rate of water flow, the pipes must be of a certain size. Likewise, for a channel to deliver a high-frequency signal (that is, a signal with large informational content), it must have sufficient bandwidth to accommodate the frequencies inherent in the signal. In other words, the more information that we pack into a signal, the greater the bandwidth demands for that signal.

For example, a voiceband transmission, such as that used for telephone communication, can be adequately handled by a bandwidth of approximately 4000 Hz. On the other hand, a commercial broadcast television signal contains much more information per unit of time and hence demands a bandwidth about 1000 times greater.

The moral of this tale for data communications is a simple one. There is always a finite limit to the speed and capacity for data transfer over some channel. The bandwidth of the channel plays a primary role in determining this limit. Higher data rate transmissions require greater bandwidth than lower data rate transmissions.

SINE WAVES

A **sine wave** is a smooth, repeating curve that describes a regular, continuously varying cycle. Figure 16.6 illustrates. The time for the completion of a single cycle is called a period. These cycles or periods repeat over and over. The amount of time it takes to complete a period determines the sine wave's frequency.

Sine waves are useful for describing a variety of periodic or repeating cycles over time. For example, we can plot the height above the ground over time of a marked point on a rolling tire using a sine wave. In fact, mathematicians often use this phenomenon to *define* the basic shape of a sine wave. Many other natural phenomena can be described using sine waves—the motion of a pendulum, the seasonal changes of daylight hours over the year, and a host of others. But, more important for our purposes, sine wave signals are the fundamental building block of all forms of signal processing today—analog or digital.

The fundamental importance of sine waves was discovered by the French mathematician **Jean-Baptiste Joseph Fourier** (1768–1830). This one-time science advisor to Napoleon formulated the remarkable mathematical principle that you can combine (by adding amplitudes) sine curves of different frequencies to accurately represent an arbitrary continuous curve plotted against time. This means that any complex signal can theoretically be reproduced as the combination of sine signals of different frequencies.

Once the frequencies of the sinusoidal components of a signal are known, we have a much better understanding of the overall characteristics of that signal. Specifically, we know that we can reproduce that signal with one that is confined to a specified range of frequencies. As you learned, the range of frequencies accommodated by a communications channel is called its bandwidth. Bandwidth figures prominently into the design and engineering of communications systems. It is no exaggeration to say that the fact that an arbitrary signal can be decomposed into a sum of sine waves of various frequencies is one of the keystones of modern communications systems technology.

FIGURE 16.6
The figure shows a typical sine wave. The fundamental cycle shown is repeated infinitely.

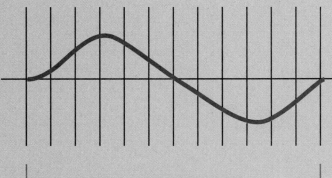

One complete cycle
(period)

Signal Strength

Signal strength is another important factor for understanding the practical limits of data communications. Data is sent from the transmitter to the receiver via the communications channel. The length of the channel, the type of transmission media used for the channel, and the number of connections a signal must pass through all affect the strength of the signal when it arrives at the receiver. The strength or power of the signal at the receiver's end is almost never the same as it was at the transmitter. This means that the receiver system must have sufficient sensitivity to capture the signal accurately. When networks are being designed, the designers must anticipate and account for loss of signal strength.

Noise

The presence of noise is another factor that must be figured into the design and functioning of practical data communications systems. In electrical systems, for example, some forms of noise are interference from other devices. The amount of noise contributed to a signal is expressed as a ratio. The **signal-to-noise ratio (SNR)** is measured as

$$SNR = Power_{Signal} : Power_{Noise}$$

The amount of noise that can be tolerated in a system depends on the type of signal being transmitted. For example, to transmit binary coded data using a digital signal requires a SNR of about 32:1 to be effective. In contrast, a voice signal over telephone systems needs a 10,000:1 SNR to be considered good, though considerably less is tolerable.

Signals that require greater bandwidth also have greater inherent noise. Therefore, broader bandwidth signals need more power than narrow bandwidth signals to overcome this. Like any other practical engineering problem, the design of data communications networks involves a great many decisions about trade-offs in cost versus performance.

So far, we have looked exclusively at how messages are encoded as signals for data transmission. Next, we will consider how computer networks are configured or organized for communicating data from one point to another. Data networks, in fact, come in a wide assortment of types. We can distinguish them in several ways: the distances they span, what sort of media they use, and so on. In the next section, we outline these factors in more detail.

CLASSIFYING NETWORKS

Computer networks for data communications are commonplace today, but they are relatively new to the computing scene. We use networks to send messages and mail to friends and colleagues. Networks allow us to transfer and pool information. They augment our computers by providing resources and services. Some networks are even capable of transmitting audio and video for conferencing and other real-time applications. Networking, however, was not always like this.

Life before the advent of computer networks was very different indeed. In the 1950s and early 1960s, computing was exclusively centralized around a single source for processing, the mainframe computer. In fact, the average user had no direct contact with the computing system that processed his or her work. Instead, processing tasks were submitted and queued as jobs. These were usually handled by professional operators who loaded the jobs into the system. In this centralized processing environment, jobs were processed one by one, and users would wait for the results.

Advances in both system software and data transmission created the first interactive computing environments in the late 1960s. Users shared the resources of I/O, storage, and CPU time on a time-sharing basis. Computing resources were still centralized, but the user could access them by way of a **terminal** (a keyboard and video display) that was connected over transmission lines. In reality, of course, there was still a single source of computing power that divided its attention among users' processes rapidly and methodically. Even so, the user had virtually immediate, interactive feedback from these processes and the illusion of sole possession of the computer's power. More important, though, the user became connected to the scheme of things.

As the numbers of users grew, the demands on the system increased and the general organization became more sophisticated. For example, several computers might be combined. Subordinate systems such as I/O processors relieved some of the demands placed on the central system. The availability of time-sharing computing was also extended when modems became available to connect a terminal with a remote computer system over telephone lines. In spite of advances in performance, the type of connectivity in this environment was still confined to a user connected directly to a central system.

The 1980s ushered in the age of desktop computing. Smaller, less expensive computer systems brought processing power directly to the user. Organizations and businesses learned that distributing computing across the enterprise was more economical and productive than maintaining traditional, centralized resources. As processing became more distributed, the need for connection and communication was strongly felt. Without connectivity, desktop systems were limited to their own resources—memory, storage, and so on.

The earliest type of communication between small systems modeled that of the earlier regime. The system that an individual used was physically connected to another system called the **remote host.** A **terminal emulation program** running on the user's machine allowed it to act as a simple terminal device that used the processing capabilities of the remote host. The systems were connected by wires across the room or by way of modems over telephone lines. File transfer programs such as Xmodem and Kermit allowed the local machine to send and retrieve files from the remote system. The capabilities of this style of connectivity were still fairly limited.

The modern computer network connects a collection of computer systems that not only can share common resources and exchange data, but also can cooperate in processing tasks. In other words, rather than being a passive terminal, your machine may request services from other systems and employ these in the completion of its own processing. Thus, in computer networks today, connectivity allows for autonomy while supporting cooperation.

Modern computer networks come in a wide assortment of flavors. It is useful to classify them by the following general characteristics.

- Distance—how far apart are the connections that make up the network?
- Media—how are the systems physically connected, and what transmission channel is employed?
- Signal—what type of physical carrier transmits the data?
- Switching—how are signals routed over shared links?

We cover each of these categories and show how they figure into the design and performance of a network.

Distance

First, we can distinguish networks in terms of their size. In this instance, "size" is intended to convey how much area the network covers rather than the number of devices that are interconnected. In this context, networks come in three sizes: LANs, WANs, and internets.

A **LAN,** or **local area network,** is a network of interconnected computer systems and other devices that is restricted to a limited geographical area. The phrase "limited geographical area" is admittedly a fuzzy one. LANs are usually restricted to areas that we could walk comfortably. A LAN may interconnect the computers in a lab, a building, or even a group of buildings. We consider LANs in some detail in Chapter 17.

A **WAN,** or **wide area network,** is a network that connects machines that are distributed over a large geographical area. Still, there is a connotation of an autonomous network in spite of its expanse. In other words, WANs are usually owned or used by a single corporation or organization. The networks that connect automated teller machines for a bank or regional offices for a corporation are examples of WANs.

An **internet,** which is short for **internetwork,** is a collection of autonomous networks. Internets connect separate networks of different sizes and types. Normally, an internet covers a large area, but this is not an essential ingredient. For example, an internet could be confined to the autonomous LANs of a single institution. It is very likely that your campus has just this sort of organization. Intraorganizational internets are often dubbed **intranets.** These networks usually enforce some security measures that hinder outsiders from accessing them. Of course, the big Kahuna of all internetworks is *the* **Internet.** This is a vast collection of networks that span the globe. We return to consider it in more detail in Chapter 18.

Media

Another way to distinguish networks is to describe the transmission medium of the channel that interconnects them. Transmission media, of course, provide the physical transport for the signal. There are two exclusive classes of media: bounded versus unbounded.

Bounded media are what we think of as wiring. Electrical conductors, such as copper wiring, are commonly used for network transmissions. Optical fiber is another bounded medium. (We delve more into these varieties in Chapter 17.) Bounded media have the advantages of economy and security, but they are limited by the distances that they can effectively span and by bandwidth.

Broadcast methods employing infrared waves, microwaves, and radio frequency waves are the most common forms of **unbounded media.** Broadcast transmissions often can have greater range and offer greater flexibility in physically arranging the network. On the other hand, these systems are often more expensive to maintain and offer less security because anyone can intercept the signal with a receiver tuned to the proper frequencies.

Signal

Two types of signals are used for network communications. **Baseband,** or **narrowband, transmission** employs the entire bandwidth of the communications channel as a carrier for a single signal. Most LANs today employ baseband methods. Basically, the baseband transmission is an unmodulated digital signal. On bounded media such as copper wiring, the signal is transmitted as voltage pulses and is interpreted digitally. Baseband transmission is used on a variety of media and is popular because of its economy and simplicity.

In contrast, **broadband transmission** carries multiple signals on the same channel simultaneously. The bandwidth of the channel is divided into separate subchannels or frequency bands, each capable of carrying a signal. A broadband network employs an analog signal to transfer data. Each device is connected to a modem that transmits and receives a carrier signal over one of the several frequency bands used. Although broadband transmission offers greater capacity, the equipment required adds to its expense. In addition, broadband networks are more difficult to maintain than those using baseband transmission. Even so, broadband networks are becoming more important as new standards for voice, data, and video carrying networks are proposed.

Switching

The various devices and computer systems that communicate over a network are commonly called **nodes.** The nodes are linked, of course, by channels that make communication possible. The particular geometric arrangement of nodes and their links in a network is called its **topology.**

Connections between nodes are usually shared. In a **shared connection network,** nodes communicate with each other over common paths. This means that each node is connected to a communications channel, but nodes are not ordinarily connected to each other directly. Networks can be set up to have a **point-to-point connectivity,** meaning that each node has a direct connection to every other node in the network, although it is seldom economically feasible to do so. See Figure 16.7.

In a shared connection network, the connections are simpler, although communication becomes more complicated because a message intended for a distant node must pass through intermediate nodes on its way to the intended receiver. Signals that travel over shared connections or links must therefore be routed to arrive at their proper destination. The method used for routing is called **switching.** The two standard switching strategies used in networks are circuit switching and packet switching.

FIGURE 16.7

(a) Establishing point-to-point connections for every pair of nodes in a five-node network requires a total of ten links. (b) In contrast, full connectivity is possible with fewer links, provided there are shared connections. For example, five links connect the five-node network.

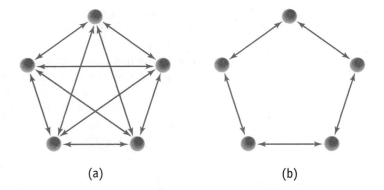

(a)   (b)

● **Circuit Switching.**   In **circuit switching,** a continuous connection or circuit is forged between the communicating nodes. This circuit is supported by a series of switches involving intermediary nodes and their links. The connection persists for the duration of the communication, and the circuit is monopolized by the communicating nodes during the communication. In other words, no other transmission occurs along the circuit during the communication. See Figure 16.8. When the communication ends, the circuit is released to allow other nodes to access its intermediary nodes and their links for communication.

Circuit switching is the method employed in ordinary telephone service. When you are engaged in a phone conversation, you are constantly in touch with the other person. A continuous connection exists between the parties, and it supports simultaneous two-way communication. Both must acknowledge connection to establish it and later quit the connection to release the service.

● **Packet Switching.**   An alternative strategy is packet switching. In **packet switching,** the data is broken down into smaller, usually fixed-sized units and assembled into groups of data called **packets.** A typical message is broken into a number of packets, much as a text document

FIGURE 16.8

Two-way communication is established in a circuit switching network by maintaining a continuous connection between the origin and destination. This circuit temporarily monopolizes the links between the two end nodes; intermediate nodes must wait until the circuit is released to initiate their own communications.

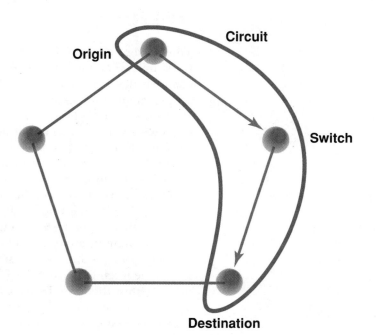

is made up of many pages. Each packet contains information identifying its origin, destination, and sequence number. The sequence number indicates its order in the message, as page numbering does in a document.

Packets are routed from the transmitter to the receiver over any available path. As a result, packets from the same message may take different routes over the network and possibly arrive out of order. The receiving node must process the packets based on the identifying information in each packet and reassemble the message. See Figure 16.9. Packet switching is sometimes called **connectionless service** to emphasize the fact that communication does not depend on a continuous two-way channel circuit.

Packet switching is a lot like postal service. When you mail a letter to a friend, you put the message in an envelope, address it, post it, and go on about your business. The postal system takes over the task of routing it to its proper destination. The difference, of course, is that in a packet switching network, your letter is usually distributed among many envelopes rather than one. As with postal service, you have to wait for a separate reply to find out whether your message got through.

Packet switching does not monopolize the communications channel because packets from different nodes can be sequenced, interspersed, and transmitted continuously. It works best for short, irregular communications (such as text messages). Circuit switching has the advantage of requiring much less processing by the sender and especially the receiver. Transmission errors are more quickly recognized and remedied, too. It is suited best for lengthy data transmissions with time-critical constraints (such as live audio or video signals).

More Information

Even though telephone service has evolved from circuit switching networks, most computer networks are based traditionally on some form of packet switching. In spite of this historical fact, both concepts play important roles in understanding data communications and networks. We return to these ideas several times in the remaining chapters in this unit.

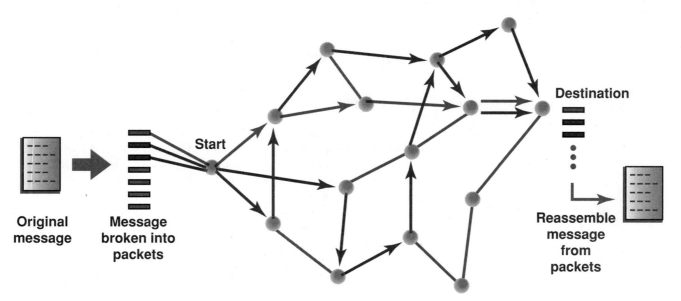

FIGURE 16.9

In a packet switching network, the message is divided into units and copied into data packets addressed for the destination. Packets are transmitted over any available connection to the destination. The receiving node processes them and reconstructs the original message.

CONNECTING THE NODES IN A NETWORK

To support point-to-point communication, a uniquely dedicated connection is needed between every two nodes on the network. Consider the simple five-node network in Figure 16.7. If we connected every pair of nodes with a unique channel, we would need

$$4 + 3 + 2 + 1 = 10 \text{ channels}$$

Where did these numbers come from? The first node needs four connections to directly link it to all the other nodes. The second node is already connected to the first node, so it needs only three additional connections to link it to the rest of the nodes. The third node is now connected to the first two nodes so it needs only

two more connections, and the fourth node will need one additional connection.

We can generalize this equation for n nodes,

$$(n - 1) + (n - 2) + \ldots + 2 + 1 =$$
$$n(n - 1)/2 = (n^2 - n)/2 \text{ channels}$$

A 100-node network, for example, would require 4950 channels. Obviously, a point-to-point network connecting a large number of nodes would be not only expensive, but also complicated to install and maintain. In contrast, a shared connection network can be fully connected with no more links than the number of nodes. In other words, an n-node network with shared connections needs no more than n channels.

ENCRYPTION AND DATA SECURITY

Computer networks provide unparalleled opportunities and conveniences for communication. And, no doubt, the exchange of information and electronic commerce over these networks will increase dramatically over the next decade. The same technology that makes such information exchange possible also provides access to those whose purposes are less than honorable or whose goals and methods threaten social order and stability. With the increasing access to and ease of transmitting sensitive and confidential information come significant security risks. In this section we explore some of the methods used to make computer networks more secure channels for information interchange.

It is easy to think of many occasions when we wish to send a message meant for the eyes of the intended recipient only. Indeed, securing channels over which messages are transmitted is a problem that plagued armies, governments, businesses, and individuals long before modern computer networks came on the scene. Whether a message is sent on a piece of paper, over radio waves, through telephone wires, or as bits transmitted over computer networks, the problem is the same: How can we guarantee that no one other than the recipient has access to the message?

Ensuring that messages are secure is quite difficult if the distance between sender and recipient is anything other than trivial. It is better

FIGURE 16.10

Ciphers consist of both encryption and decryption methods. The original plaintext message is encrypted to produce ciphertext. The ciphertext is transmitted, then decrypted to reveal the original plaintext message.

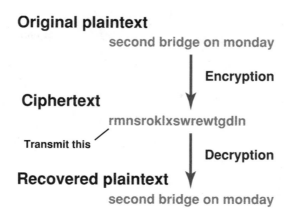

Original plaintext

second bridge on monday

Encryption

Ciphertext

rmnsroklxswrewtgdln

Transmit this

Decryption

Recovered plaintext

second bridge on monday

to *assume* that someone will, in fact, intercept the message but, in turn, guarantee that they won't be able to read and interpret it. **Cryptography** is the art and science of keeping messages secret. **Encryption techniques,** which convert data into a secret code for transmission, are central to the subject.

Using encryption techniques, the original text, or **plaintext,** is converted into a coded equivalent called the **ciphertext** using an encryption algorithm. The ciphertext is then transmitted and decoded at the receiving end, reproducing the original plaintext message. The process of retrieving the original message from the ciphertext is called **decryption.** Figure 16.10 illustrates. Encryption/decryption methods are often called **ciphers** for short.

Cryptography has a long and storied history. Perhaps the first documented use of cryptography is that of nonstandard hieroglyphs in an inscription by an Egyptian scribe around 2000 B.C. Julius Caesar (100–44 B.C.) is credited with inventing a simple (but effective for his day) encryption algorithm for passing messages to his field commanders during military campaigns. The **Caesar cipher,** as the method is called, uses a simple substitution scheme. Each of the letters of the alphabet is replaced by the one that appears three letters later in the alphabet. So "a" is replaced by "d," "b" is replaced by "e," and so on. When the end of the alphabet is reached, you wrap around to the beginning and continue the substitution. So "x" is replaced by "a," "y" by "b," and "z" by "c." Of course, there is nothing special about the number 3 used for the amount of the shift in this scheme, and any number less than or equal to 25 would work just as well. It is customary to ignore spaces and other punctuation characters as well as character case in forming ciphertext. Figure 16.11 illustrates the use of the Caesar cipher for our simple example.

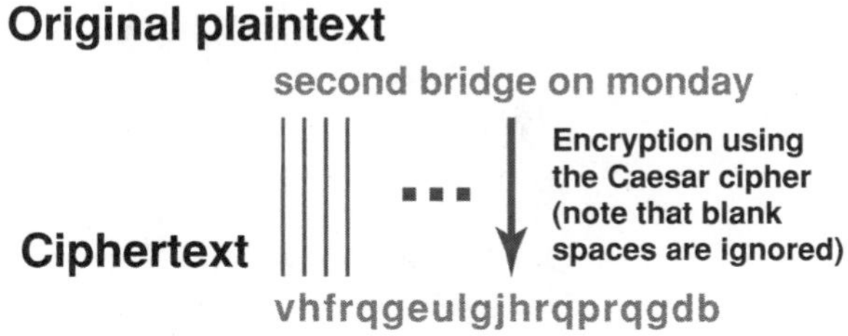

FIGURE 16.11

The Caesar cipher uses a shift and substitute method. The method using a shift of three positions to the right is illustrated here.

Original plaintext

second bridge on monday

Encryption using the Caesar cipher (note that blank spaces are ignored)

Ciphertext

vhfrqgeulgjhrqprqgdb

Ciphers and Keys

The Caesar cipher uses just one (shift and substitute) of many techniques that might be applied to encode a message. To decrypt a message encoded with this method, we need two pieces of information. We must know that the algorithm is based on a shift of the alphabet to the right, and we must know the extent of the shift (three places in this case). We call the parameter 3 a key for the method. A **key** consists of information (usually a numeric parameter or parameters) that allows us to unlock an encrypted message assuming we know the basic algorithm.

Actually, it isn't necessary to know the algorithm and its key(s) to decrypt a message. Sometimes we can use **brute force methods** to reconstruct a message even if the underlying algorithm and its key(s) remain a mystery. Such methods depend on the examination of a great many cases and were not very effective before the advent of the modern computer. With a fast computer's assistance, however, brute force methods can easily crack many codes that would have been absolutely impenetrable fifty years ago.

In fact, encryption and decryption have been inseparable from computing for many years. Recall that the effort to break the codes produced by the German Enigma encryption machine was the primary motivation for important work done in the development of the modern computer—refer to the Colossus project in Chapter 4. Modern encryption and decryption methods can be implemented in either hardware or software. Hardware systems are often needed to gain the speeds necessary in environments where large volumes of message transmissions are required. Software provides a convenient flexibility in changing parameters associated with the encryption and decryption processes. As a consequence, many modern encryption and decryption systems are hybrid systems employing both hardware and software components.

Modern encryption algorithms are mathematically based. The plaintext message is first translated to a numeric representation (ASCII will do just fine). Then the resulting string of binary digits is usually blocked (64-bit blocks are commonly used) into a sequence of larger numbers. These numbers are then transformed into other numbers by a chosen mathematical procedure that depends on some set of parameters called the **encryption keys.** The coded message is then transmitted. At the receiving end, a second set of parameters, called the **decryption keys,** is used in conjunction with an appropriate "inverse" mathematical procedure to unlock the code, restoring it to its original binary form. Figure 16.12 illustrates the entire procedure.

How then do we keep encrypted messages safe? Potentially, we must guard against three contingencies: the discovery of the encryption algorithm itself, the discovery of the decryption keys, and brute force attempts to break the cipher. Interestingly, the mathematical algorithm for transforming the message is often willingly revealed. The reason for this is that we *assume* that the algorithm will eventually be compromised (human nature being what it is). Hence, we do not want the security of our encryption system to depend in any way on the secrecy of the basic algorithm. In fact, keeping the decryption keys secret (these can even be changed if we suspect a compromise has occurred) is usually our very best protection.

We always have to worry about brute force attacks on the cipher. Guaranteeing a cipher to be safe against all possible brute force attacks is difficult because we cannot anticipate all the different methods that

FIGURE 16.12

The figure shows the process of converting a plaintext message to an ASCII string, which can be interpreted as a numeric value. Encryption keys are then used to covert this value to another number representing the ciphertext. The message receiver uses decryption keys to convert the received value back to the original number and the decodes this as an ASCII string.

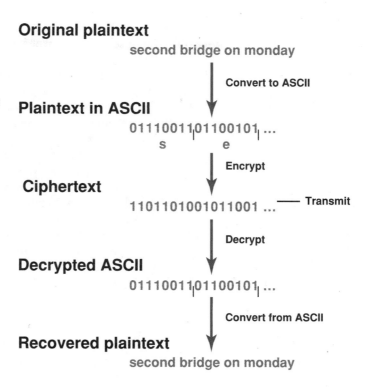

Original plaintext

second bridge on monday

Convert to ASCII

Plaintext in ASCII

0111001101100101 ...
s   e

Encrypt

Ciphertext

1101101001011001 ... —— Transmit

Decrypt

Decrypted ASCII

0111001101100101 ...

Convert from ASCII

Recovered plaintext

second bridge on monday

might be used. If we are clever in our choice of algorithm and keys, and if we keep the decryption keys secret, we can make it very unlikely that such an approach will ever succeed. The length (in bits) of the cipher key(s) is one of the most important factors in this effort to thwart brute force attacks on the cipher. Longer keys are harder to discover by brute force, but the down side is that the speed of the encryption/decryption decreases rapidly as the key lengths go up. There is a trade-off in choosing the length of a cipher key: security versus speed. We will have more to say about this issue later.

Symmetric or Secret Key Ciphers

Modern encryption systems can be put into one of two basic categories, depending on how they treat their encryption/decryption keys. **Secret key ciphers** use a single secret key for both encryption and decryption. Such methods are also called **symmetric key ciphers** because the same key is used for both encryption and decryption. The second group of methods is the **asymmetric key,** or **public key, ciphers.** These ciphers use different keys (hence the term *asymmetric*) for encrypting and decrypting messages. The encryption key is made public, and the decryption key is kept secret. We look more closely at each of these two categories of ciphers in turn.

As noted, in secret key ciphers both sender and receiver use the same key to encrypt and decrypt. In applying these methods, it is necessary to transmit the secret key to the recipient—this becomes the chief security risk. This level of security is certainly manageable for diplomatic and military work and in businesses like banking where the access to secret keys can be restricted to a very small group of individuals. For environments where the need to know keys is more widespread, however, secret key ciphers present a higher level of risk. The secret key method is the one used in traditional ciphers, that is, those invented before the late 1970s.

The best known and most widely used secret key cipher is the **Data Encryption Standard (DES)** method proposed and administered by the U.S. government's National Institute for Standards and Technology (NIST). DES encryption/decryption, introduced in 1976, employs a 56-bit-length secret key and is very fast. The underlying algorithm was developed at IBM and enhanced at the National Security Agency (NSA).

We mentioned earlier that the length of a key can be a crucial factor in making a cipher robust against brute force attempts to break it. Let's consider some particulars. A secret key cipher with a 32-bit key can be broken by examining 2^{32}, or about 10^9 (one billion), steps—this number represents the number of *different* 32-bit keys possible. This is something a desktop computer could handle in fairly short order. A 40-bit key is more difficult, but it could be broken in a reasonable time with the kinds of computers available in most universities and many companies. A secret key system with a 56-bit key (like DES) requires a substantial effort to break by brute force, but it can still be managed with special hardware. The expense and time required are nontrivial, but the expense is certainly within the reach of large corporations and most governments, and the time required is not totally prohibitive. Secret key ciphers with 64-bit keys would be difficult, but likely not impossible, to break in reasonable time with today's technology and large resources comparable to those of a major government. An 80-bit key cipher will probably remain unbreakable with reasonable time and effort for the next decade or so, and a 128-bit cipher is unlikely to ever be broken by brute force. The simple reason is that the time required with even the fastest computers imaginable would be eons upon eons.

Of course, we must not forget that each time we add bits to the cipher key, we also add to the time required for the encryption/decryption process. For a commercially adopted cipher, potentially millions of messages will be encrypted and decrypted daily. Consequently, adopting keys as large as 128 bits is not necessarily a good thing to do. Practical encryption schemes based on such a key have been proposed. In 1990, Xuejia Lai and James Massey in Switzerland proposed a new block encryption standard, called **International Data Encryption Algorithm (IDEA),** to replace DES. IDEA uses a 128-bit key and employs operations that are convenient for general-purpose computers, therefore making software implementations more efficient. Although it has not replaced DES, IDEA has gained some acceptance and has encouraged a more open debate about DES and its future.

The secret key used in DES encryption/decryption is held by the U.S. government and can be changed as necessary. Such an arrangement is often referred to as an escrowed key cipher. An **escrowed key cipher** is a secret key cipher in which a (supposedly neutral) third party controls the secret key in escrow. The government has also put forth a controversial, hardware-based escrow key system, called the Clipper chip, as a basis for securing telephone and other telecommunications. Employing an escrow key system means that the third party could, in fact, decrypt any message being passed using the cipher. The situation is in some ways similar to government agencies having the right to wiretap phone lines under certain conditions. Of course, wiretapping is strictly limited by U.S. laws, but nonetheless the practice generates a healthy debate among law enforcement agencies, citizen rights groups, and the courts. The strong advocacy of escrowed key cipher systems by government agencies such as the NSA and the FBI has, not surprisingly, created an analogous ongoing debate in the security community, the U.S. Congress, and the general public concerning the security of electronic communications.

Asymmetric or Public Key Ciphers

Public key ciphers have the potential to guarantee a much higher degree of security to their users than secret key ciphers. The big advantage that public key ciphers have is that they are specifically tailored to individuals. A message sender looks up the recipient's public key and uses it to encrypt the message. The ciphertext is transmitted, and the recipient uses his or her private key to decrypt the message. Owners never need to transmit their private keys to anyone to have their messages decrypted; thus, the private keys are never in transit and are therefore less vulnerable. Figure 16.13 shows how this method works.

The idea of a public key cipher was first advanced by Whitfield Diffie and Martin Hellman in a paper published in 1976. Inspired by the Diffie-Hellman paper, three MIT professors, Ronald Rivest, Adi Shamir, and Leonard Adleman, worked out a practical public key system, which came to be known as the **RSA** (for their last names) **algorithm.** Rivest, Shamir, and Adleman gave an overview of their method in the September 1977 issue of *Scientific American*.

RSA was greeted with controversy at its inception. In the *Scientific American* article giving a popular account of RSA, the offer was made to send a full technical report to anyone submitting a self-addressed, stamped envelope. Thousands of requests poured in from all over the world. Officials at the NSA objected to the distribution of this report to foreign nationals, and for a period the mailings were suspended. When the NSA failed to provide an adequate legal basis for such a ban, the mailings were resumed. A little later, Rivest, Shamir, and Adleman applied for and were granted an international patent for their method.

FIGURE 16.13

The figure illustrates the encryption/decryption process when a public key cipher is employed. Private keys are never in transit in the process and are therefore less vulnerable.

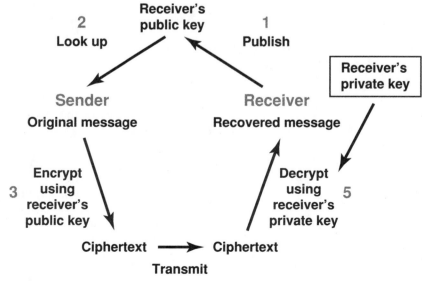

They formed a company, RSA Data Security, Inc., which has since developed public key cipher technology on a commercial basis.

The RSA method is mathematically based, and its security depends on the practical difficulty of factoring large integers. The problem of factoring integers is believed to be (although this hasn't actually been proved) impossible to solve with a general method that does not require prohibitively long periods of time for large integers. Hence, the RSA method is believed to be very robust against a direct brute force attack. This security does come at a price, however, because RSA is computationally intense (as are other public key methods). It requires a great deal more time than secret key encryption/decryption.

The key lengths used in public key ciphers are typically much longer than those used in secret key ciphers. Recall that a 128-bit key in a secret key system would guarantee robustness against brute force attacks for the foreseeable future. On the other hand, a 256-bit RSA key could be easily broken. Doubling this to a 512-bit key offers considerably more protection, but a major government could likely break a 512-bit RSA cipher in a reasonable time. For now, 768-bit RSA keys are considered quite safe, and 1024-bit keys are predicted to provide very high security for decades to come.

Often both secret key ciphers and RSA are used together. Secret key ciphers provide the fastest decryption, and RSA provides a convenient and highly secure method for transmitting the secret key. An attractive hybrid method is the following: Encrypt a message using the fast secret key algorithm, and employ the public key method to safely send the necessary secret key to the recipient. This combination of the secret key encryption of the plaintext message and the public key encryption of the secret key needed to decrypt the ciphertext is usually called a **digital envelope.**

Authentication and Digital Signatures

Public key ciphers have another important use. They are usually employed to encrypt a plaintext message with the recipient's published public key and send the coded message to the recipient who uses his or her private key to decrypt the message. But the mathematical transformations used in public key methods make it possible for the roles of the keys to be reversed. In other words, you could use your private key to encrypt and someone else could use the public key to decrypt. Why would this ever be useful? Suppose you wish to send a sensitive message to someone, and it is crucial for that person to be sure that the message did indeed come from *you*. We can easily envision scenarios where assurance of the identity of the source of a message would be absolutely crucial. How would you like someone else sending "buy" and "sell" orders to your broker, for example?

The process used to verify the identity of a respondent is called **authentication.** In other words, you use authentication to make sure that a fellow communicator is who he or she says he or she is. Public key ciphers can easily be used for this purpose. There are several possible ways this might be implemented. Let's look at an example to illustrate a commonly used method.

Let's define the notation *{message} key* to mean that *message* has been encrypted/decrypted using the cipher key named *key*. Now, suppose that Bob has disclosed his public key to Alice. Now suppose further that Alice

INSIDE RSA

The RSA method is based on mathematics (number theory) and is elegantly simple. Let's explore the general principle first, then look at the mathematical details—which aren't difficult, by the way.

In RSA, a public key consists of a pair of integers. Let's assume that Bob publishes his public key, say integers Z and N. Now suppose Alice wishes to send Bob a secure message. She first converts her message to blocks of ASCII code, then interprets the string of bits in each block as an integer. Let's concentrate on sending one block (the other blocks will be transmitted in exactly the same way) of the message to Bob. Suppose the block of bits is the integer A when interpreted as a binary integer representation. Alice performs a mathematical transformation on the integers A, Z, and N to produce another integer C. The integer C is the encoded message that she sends to Bob. Bob uses yet another integer,

S (the private part of his key), to perform an inverse mathematical transformation on C, S, and Z to reproduce the value of A. He then interprets A as a string of ASCII codes and reads the message block. Figure 16.14 illustrates this basic method.

Suppose you intercept the encoded message (the integer C) in transit. What do you need to decode it? Two things: the integer S, Bob's private key, and the inverse mathematical transformation. The transformation will not be a secret—everyone will know what it is, so this leaves you with the task of discovering the integer S. It seems reasonable that S is related to the choice of Z and N that Bob published in the first place. The question becomes, If you know Z and N, can you find S? This is exactly where the RSA method is both simple and powerful. A would-be codebreaker will know exactly the mathematical process needed to find S, but he or she won't be able to do that process in a trillion lifetimes—even using the

FIGURE 16.14

The RSA public key method is illustrated here. A public key consists of two very large integers. The private key needed to decrypt a message encrypted with the public key is related to the public key values, but computing it by brute force is very difficult.

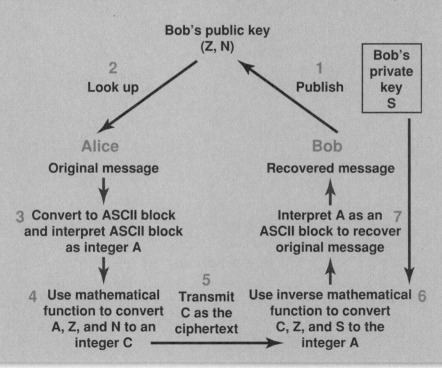

fastest computer in the world! And without S, the encrypted message C cannot be decrypted.

To see why S is so hard to compute, we need to understand how S is related to Bob's choice of Z and N. First let's see how Bob went about choosing Z and N in the first place. Recall that a positive integer is a **prime number** if it has no divisors other than 1 and itself. For example, 2, 3, 5, 7, 11, 13, 17, 19, 23, 29, and so on are all primes. By contrast, the number 9 is not a prime because it has 3 as a divisor. The number of primes is infinite, but their distribution on the number line is unpredictable. In other words, although there is an infinite number of them, there is no method to predict the next prime after a given prime.

Bob starts by choosing at random two prime numbers, say P and Q, and computes Z to be their product, $P \times Q$. Next Bob chooses N to be an integer less than $Z - 1$, which has no common factors with the number $(P - 1) \times (Q - 1)$. Then elementary number theory tells us that there is a *unique* number S such that when the product $N \times S$ is divided by $(P - 1) \times (Q - 1)$, the remainder will be 1. Further, S is easily computed from the numbers N and $(P - 1) \times (Q - 1)$. This number S is Bob's private key; the numbers Z and N are the public part of his key. These details are illustrated in Figure 16.15.

Now remember, to break the code, you need to figure out what S is. What does this involve? After all, you already know Z and N. But notice again how N and S are related. The number S is the unique value such that when the product $N \times S$ is divided by $(P - 1) \times (Q - 1)$, the remainder will be 1. To find S from N, you must know the number $(P - 1) \times (Q - 1)$, or in other words you must know the numbers P and Q. What are P and Q? They are the randomly chosen prime numbers whose product is Z. You know Z, so what you need to do is factor Z into its two prime factors. Number theory tells us that every number has a unique prime factorization, so when we factor Z we will immediately have P and Q because Z equals $P \times Q$.

FIGURE 16.15
The computation of the private key in the RSA method is straightforward when P and Q are known, but extremely difficult without these values.

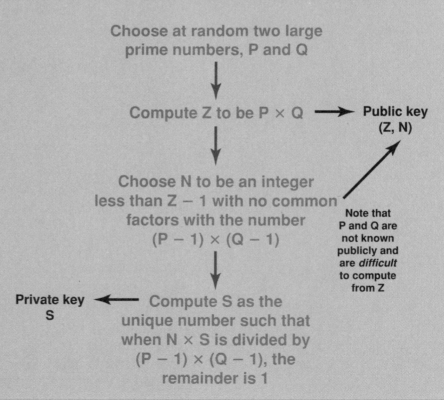

Choose at random two large prime numbers, P and Q

Compute Z to be $P \times Q$ ⟶ **Public key (Z, N)**

Choose N to be an integer less than $Z - 1$ with no common factors with the number $(P - 1) \times (Q - 1)$

Note that P and Q are not known publicly and are *difficult* to compute from Z

Private key S ⟵ Compute S as the unique number such that when $N \times S$ is divided by $(P - 1) \times (Q - 1)$, the remainder is 1

The bottom line is this: To find S (and break the code), you must find the two prime factors of the given number Z. Factoring a number is a fairly easy mathematical task, so we should be on our way, right? Of course, there's a catch. The mathematical process of finding the prime factors of Z is trivial. Just start with the number 2 and divide it into Z to see if it is a factor. If not move to the next prime and do the same. Just continue until you find the two prime factors of Z.

So what makes this task so difficult? Bob will choose P and Q to be very large (100 digits each, or more). It is then not the theoretical method for finding the prime factors, but rather the practical limits on the brute force method that we are forced to employ, that makes the problem of finding P and Q all but impossible. No one knows a fast method for factoring large numbers—brute force is the only known method. It is suspected that no faster method *can* even exist, although no one has proved this fact yet. Given the current state of knowledge about finding prime factors, Bob's private key couldn't be safer!

Example Public/Private Key Calculation

Let's look at a particular example (using small numbers for illustration) to allow you to test your understanding of this whole process. Sup-

pose Bob chooses P = 11 and Q = 5. The integer Z is then 55 (P × Q). Now to complete his calculation of his public key, Bob needs to choose a number N less than Z − 1 = 54 so that N and (P − 1) × (Q − 1) = 10 × 4 = 40 have no common factors. There are many choices, but let's suppose Bob chooses the value N = 27.

Bob can now publish his public key: the integers 55 and 27. What is Bob's private key? Recall it is the unique number S so that when the product N × S is divided by (P − 1) × (Q − 1) = 40, the remainder will be 1. You can easily verify that this value is S = 3 because N × S = 27 × 3 = 81, which yields a remainder of 1 when divided by 40.

Of course, in this case it is not difficult for a code-breaker to find the values P and Q, since Z (= 55) can be easily factored into 11 × 5, and then S can be computed. If Z had been the product of two 100-digit numbers (and hence have approximately 200 digits itself), it would not be so easy. And that's the strength of the RSA algorithm.

More Information

receives a message presumably from Bob, and Alice wants to authenticate that the sender is actually Bob. Alice can use the asymmetric nature of public key ciphers to prove that Bob is, in fact, Bob. What she does is generate a random message and send it to Bob:

    `Alice→Bob     random-message`

Bob responds with the original message encrypted using his private key:

    `Bob→Alice      {random-message}Bob's-private-key`

Alice receives this message and decrypts it using the public key Bob has communicated to her. If the decrypted message matches her original random message, then she knows she's talking to Bob. Why? Because she is willing to assume that an impostor doesn't know Bob's private key;

therefore, an impostor could not have properly encrypted the random message for Alice to check with Bob's public key.

While this works from Alice's point of view, there is a small problem from Bob's perspective. It's not a good idea to encrypt something with your private key and then send it to somebody else, unless you know exactly what it is you are encrypting. The encrypted data can possibly be used against you because only you could have done the encryption with your private key. Anyone having your public key could then decrypt this message, at which time he or she would certainly conclude that the message itself was from you. Yes, paranoia strikes deep in the cryptography heartland—and for good reason!

To account for this, instead of encrypting the original message sent by Alice, Bob could construct a message digest and encrypt that. A **message digest** is a nonsense message derived from the original message with the following properties:

- The digest is difficult to reverse. In other words, you can't get the original message back from the digest.
- Choosing a different message that digests to the same value is quite difficult.

Here's how using a digest solves the above problem for Bob. He uses a well-known digest method to compute the digest of the random message sent by Alice. Next, Bob encrypts the digest with his private key and sends the result—called a **public key digital signature,** or just **digital signature** for short—back to Alice. Alice can use the same well-known digest method to compute the digest of her original message and authenticate Bob by decrypting Bob's digital signature (using Bob's public key) and comparing values. Here are the steps in the communication:

Bob → Alice	Hi, I'm Bob.
Alice → Bob	Prove you're Bob.
Bob → Alice	Send me a random message. I'll return a digital signature: the message's digest using method X, encrypted with my private key.
Alice → Bob	random-message
Bob → Alice	{digest[random message]} Bob's-private-key

Alice (who has Bob's public key) does two things. She first computes for herself, using method X, the digest of the random message. Next, she uses Bob's public key to decrypt the digital signature Bob sent. If the result matches her computation of the digest, she knows she is dealing with Bob.

On many occasions, the date, and even the time, a document was produced can be important. For example, when sending electronic documents to a patent office, to an embassy, to a sweepstakes contest, or to a bank, the time and date the document was completed may be critical information. Public key digital signatures can be very useful in such cases by providing authenticated time stamps for documents. A trusted party, possessing a public and private key, "signs" the document and its included time stamp by encrypting it with his or her private key, thus testifying that the document existed in its current state at the

More Information

stated time. Because the document can be decrypted only with the trusted person's public key, the receiver is assured that the document was encrypted with the trusted person's private key, or in other words, *by* the trusted person.

Social Themes

Encryption and National Security

Computing and computer networks are ushering in a new communications paradigm. In this paradigm, ubiquitous computers and computer networks become fundamental tools of communication. Information is more abundant, more readily available, more rapidly exchanged, and unfortunately more at risk of falling into the wrong hands than ever before. The more important, even critical, the exchange of information becomes for individuals, businesses, and governments, the more enticing targets the communications channels used for this exchange become for unfriendly governments, competitors, vandals, terrorists, and organized crime. Because sensitive financial transactions, plans for mergers and takeovers, discussions of government policy and contingencies, trade secrets, bidding information, and so on are being transmitted across networks and telecommunications channels, it comes as no surprise that at least some portion of those who would benefit from this information will go to extraordinary lengths to acquire it illegally via electronic espionage. Thus, encryption becomes an essential component of this new electronic communications paradigm.

A central question emerges. Should everyone have equal access to the best (that is, the most secure) encryption techniques known? As private citizens, we might be tempted to answer immediately that we expect access to such techniques. After all, we are all likely to conduct financial transactions electronically or by telephone; our medical histories, including mental illnesses, addictions, and so on, are likely to be transmitted over computer networks, not to mention the transmission of our credit histories, driving records, spending habits, and a host of other information about us. Our very ability to function in an information economy is at stake.

And clearly the government must be able to send and receive diplomatic, political, economic, and military information confidently over computer networks. Elements of the civilian infrastructure, such as the air traffic control system, the banking system, the electric power grid system, and the public telephone network, also critically depend on secure computer network and telecommunications transmissions.

Unfortunately, the same assurance of confidentiality that seems so essential for all these legitimate purposes can also be used for illegal purposes. For example, with such assurances, criminals and organized crime could shield their communications from law enforcement, terrorists could plan and execute their mayhem without scrutiny, and unfriendly nations could conduct electronic communications without fear of interception.

These are not trivial matters. A great deal of the effectiveness of current law enforcement now depends on intercepting communications among criminals. With appropriate legal authorization, law enforcement can gain access to criminal information through phone tapping, intercepting network communications, and so on. Intelligence gathering for national security and foreign policy purposes depends explicitly on gaining access to information other governments would wish to keep secret. In times of armed conflict, such intelligence can easily mean the difference between victory and defeat.

For many years, U.S. policy on encryption has sought to maximize the protection of U.S. military and diplomatic communications while denying the public the confidentiality benefits of the latest encryption techniques. This policy has been implemented primarily through two measures: the use of export controls on encryption methods and related technical data, and an aggressive promotion for the domestic use of escrowed key encryption techniques. The government's stance is that such techniques can provide strong protection for legitimate uses, but they will permit legally authorized access to communications by law enforcement officials when warranted.

Recall that an escrowed key cipher is a secret key cipher in which a neutral third party controls the secret key in escrow. DES is an example of such a cipher. The government has strongly encouraged the use of DES. The export controls center on encryption applications with key lengths of more than 40 bits. Exporting such products is currently illegal under the **International Trafficking in Arms Regulations (ITAR)**. The government maintains that these restrictions are necessary to protect national security. Efforts to repeal or relax the export controls have been mounted (for example, by Representative Maria Cantwell, from Washington, in 1994) but have so far been unsuccessful.

Both these measures—escrowed key encryption and export controls—have generated considerable controversy. Opponents of the government's attempt to impose escrowed key encryption claim that the government has no right to reserve the ability to read all secret key encrypted electronic communications. And many claim that the ban on exporting encryption systems employing secret key ciphers with keys longer than 40 bits diminishes U.S. competitiveness in two dimensions—preventing U.S. encryption firms from selling competitive products outside the United States and hampering U.S. companies that must operate in a foreign business environment by limiting the security of some of their communications with their foreign customers and subsidiaries. Further, privacy advocates and the computer hardware and software industry argue that the export controls stifle the development of strong encryption techniques and hence serve to undermine efforts toward increased privacy and security globally.

The Paris-based policy think tank of 29 major governments, OECD (Organization for Economic Cooperation and Development), has sponsored several meetings to discuss these and other issues involved in electronic commerce. The 1997 OECD meeting in Paris considered the question of how strong encryption can protect commerce from fraud while at the same time protecting the public from crime and terrorism. At the meeting it became clear that there was considerable disagreement on the basic issues. France joined the United States in advocating escrowed secret key ciphers under the control of governments, while Japan and others took a more liberal view, arguing that the usefulness of strong encryption methods to criminals and terrorists is being over-rated. This global debate will likely continue for some time.

In 1995, the U.S. Congress commissioned the prestigious National Research Council (NRC) to make a thorough study of U.S. cryptography policy. The NRC assembled a "blue ribbon" panel of experts drawn from academia, international business, the telecommunications industry, the cryptography community, law enforcement, and government security and intelligence agencies to conduct the study. In May of 1996, the NRC-sponsored Committee to Study National Cryptography Policy released a 500-page report, entitled *Cryptography's Role in Securing the Information Society,* detailing its findings. The full report can be found in the National Academy of Sciences Online Reading Room at http://www.nap.edu/readingroom/records/0309054753.html—there's a very readable 14-page executive summary. Many observers agree that the report is by far the most comprehensive and balanced analysis of the complex encryption policy debate yet produced.

Although the NRC report offered no definitive or final solutions to the complex problems it studied, it did make a number of recommendations. These recommendations are likely to encourage and give structure to a vigorous, continuing debate on these very important issues. Some of the main conclusions are as follows:

- Current U.S. encryption policy is not working.
- Export controls do harm the competitiveness of U.S. industry.
- Market forces rather than government interests should drive the policy debate.

The chair of the NRC committee, Professor Kenneth Dam of the University of Chicago Law School, gave an excellent and brief summary of the report in his remarks at the National Press Club news conference in Washington upon release of the report on May 30, 1996. We excerpt some of his remarks here for your consideration. Further, we encourage you to consult the summary of the report at the Web address given earlier and to form your own opinions about these complex issues, issues that are critical for all who will live in the information society of the 21st century.

> Our committee's broad conclusion is that the advantages of cryptography in safeguarding information outweigh the possible disadvantages of making apprehension and prosecution of criminals more difficult. Thus, we believe that federal policies should promote rather than discourage the use of encryption. For example, current export controls impede the use of strong encryption by U.S. firms with foreign customers and suppliers as well as reducing the availability of strong encryption domestically. The government needs to make it easier for U.S. companies operating internationally to use strong encryption, and for U.S. technology vendors to develop and sell cryptography products both in this country and abroad. Indeed, maintaining world leadership for U.S. information technology vendors is an important contribution to national security, as well as being important to the economy.
>
> Furthermore, the development of products with encryption should be driven largely by market forces rather than by government-imposed requirements or standards. There are no

legal limits on the kinds of encryption that presently can be sold in the United States and we strongly endorse the idea that no law should bar the manufacture, sale, or use of any form of encryption within the United States.

We do not believe that by adopting such a course the government would necessarily be choosing the interests of business and individuals over those of national security and law enforcement. We say this for two reasons. First, availability of encryption technologies will benefit law enforcement and national security. Here's how: by making economic espionage more difficult, cryptography supports law enforcement. By protecting elements of the civilian infrastructure such as banking, telecommunications, and air traffic control networks, cryptography safeguards national security.

The second reason is that current national policy—which discourages the use of cryptography despite its many valuable applications—can at most delay encryption's spread. Already, the use of such technologies is growing, and in the long run, we believe widespread non-governmental use of cryptography in the United States and abroad is inevitable. The government should recognize this changing reality and help law enforcement and national security authorities develop the new technical capabilities they will need to conduct investigations and surveillance in a world in which information will be more protected and even unencrypted communications will be harder to read."*

Social Themes *Excerpted from the opening statement of Professor Kenneth Dam given at the National Press Club news conference on the NRC report *Cryptography's Role in Securing the Information Society* in Washington, D.C., on May 30, 1996.

S U M M A R Y

Perhaps the most significant change in computing over the past several decades has been the evolution of data communications networks. Computer networks connect individuals in the same office, the same building, and across the world. They provide for the instantaneous exchange of information. Data communications systems are based on a basic model of communication theory put forth by **Claude Shannon,** a pioneer in information theory. Shannon's model has six basic elements: an in-

formation source, a transmitter, a communications channel, a noise source, a receiver, and a destination or user.

Information transmitted over computer networks is binary encoded. Data may be encoded in either pure binary format or as text using the ASCII coding scheme. Once a message is encoded, it is converted to a signal for transmission over the communications channel. Signals can be either digital or analog. Digital signals usually consist of series of electrical (over wires) or optical (over optical fiber) pulses. Analog signals are composed of repeating, continuous waveforms that are modulated, or altered, to carry the digital message. Special devices called modems are used to convert digital data to analog signals and analog signals back to digital data.

Regardless of whether the carrier signal is analog or digital, several factors limit the rate at which data can be transmitted reliably. The most significant ones are the bandwidth of the channel, the signal strength, and interference from system noise.

Modern computer networks can be distinguished by several characteristics including distance covered, media used, signal type, and switching methods.

Most networks employ a shared connection model, in which network nodes are not directly connected to each other, but rather share communications channels. Because a message intended for a distant node needs to pass through intermediate nodes on its way to the intended receiver, signals that travel over shared connections must be routed to arrive at their proper destination. The method used for routing is called switching. Two standard switching strategies are used in networks: circuit switching and packet switching.

While computer networks provide unparalleled opportunities and conveniences for communication, the same technology that makes such information exchange possible also provides access to those whose purposes are less than honorable or whose goals and methods threaten social order and stability. With the increasing access to and ease of transmitting sensitive and confidential information come significant security risks.

We rely on encryption techniques, which convert data into a secret code for transmission, to secure network transmissions. An encryption key (usually a numeric parameter or parameters) enables the encoding of data; a decryption key consists of information that allows us to unlock encrypted data, assuming we know the basic algorithm.

PROJECTS

1 Consult with your instructor or your lab manager to find out how computer networking is organized on your campus. To what LAN is your class laboratory attached? Are there other LANs on campus?

2 Suppose you are given someone's RSA public key values of 91 and 25. Find this person's private RSA key. Write a brief report showing how you made the calculation of the private key.

3 Conduct some research to find out more about the U.S. government's Clipper chip project. Write a brief report on your findings.

4 Do some research on radio wave transmission. In particular, write a brief report explaining how the two methods of amplitude modulation (AM) transmission and frequency modulation (FM) transmission work.

5 Conduct some Web-based research to find out the latest developments on the issue of export controls on encryption/decryption methods. Have new laws been passed since this text was published? If so, summarize them. Are there laws pending before Congress? If so, summarize these.

Key Terms

asymmetric key cipher
authentication
bandwidth
baseband transmission
broadband transmission
broadcasting
brute force methods (decryption)
Caesar cipher
cipher
ciphertext
circuit switching
communications channel
computer networks
connectionless service
cryptography
data communications system
Data Encryption Standard (DES)
decryption
destination
destination system
digital envelope
digital signature (public key)
encryption techniques

escrowed key cipher
even parity error detection
Fourier, J. J.
information source
international data encryption algorithm (IDEA)
international trafficking in arms regulations (ITAR)
internet (internetwork)
Internet, the
intranet
key (encryption, decryption)
local area network (LAN)
media (bounded, unbounded)
message digest
modem
modulation (e.g., amplitude modulation)
narrowband transmission
networking
node
noise
odd parity error detection
originating system
packet

packet switching
parity bit
plaintext
point-to-point connectivity
prime number
public key cipher
receiver
remote host
RSA algorithm
secret key cipher
Shannon, Claude
shared connection network
signal (analog, digital)
signal-to-noise ratio (SNR)
sine wave
switching (circuit versus packet)
symmetric key cipher
terminal
terminal emulation program
topology (network)
transmitter
wide area network (WAN)

QUESTIONS FOR REVIEW

1 How do broadcasting and networking differ as forms of communication? What are the advantages and disadvantages of each?

2 Describe Shannon's model for a communications system. What are its components and their respective functions in the model?

3 Depending on the medium, data communications are encoded as either analog or digital signals. Explain.

4 What is noise? How does it impact a data communications system?

5 What is bandwidth? How does it affect a data communications system?

6 Explain how the odd parity error detection scheme for transmitted data works. Is it a foolproof error detection method? Explain.

7 What does it mean to modulate a waveform? Why is this done in data communications systems?

8 What is a modem? Why are these devices necessary in certain data communications systems?

9 Describe J. J. Fourier's important discovery about sine waves. Why is this discovery important for data communications systems?

10 Explain the role of signal strength in data communications systems.

11 What is meant by the term *signal-to-noise ratio*? Why is this important for data communications systems?

12 Distinguish among LANs, WANs, and internetworks.

13 Distinguish between baseband and broadband transmissions.

14 What is shared connectivity? Why are shared connections favored over point-to-point connectivity?

15 What is switching and how is it used in network communications?

16 Describe and compare the circuit switching and packet switching methods.

17 Why is packet switching referred to as "connectionless" service?

18 What is cryptography? Why is it important for data communications systems?

19 Define and explain the roles of plaintext and ciphertext in cryptography.

20 What are keys and what are they used for in encryption/decryption?

21 Describe how secret key (symmetric key) ciphers work.

22 Describe how public key (asymmetric key) ciphers work.

23 Compare the advantages and disadvantages of secret key and public key ciphers.

24 What is the Data Encryption Standard (DES)?

25 What is the International Data Encryption Algorithm (IDEA) and how does it compare or contrast with DES?

26 What is an escrowed key cipher?

27 What is the RSA algorithm? When and by whom was it developed? Why is it important?

28 What is the process called authentication? How is it implemented?

29 What is a digital signature? What is it used for?

30 What are the International Trafficking in Arms Regulations (ITAR)? What does this have to do with encryption?

In Chapter 16, you learned that computer networks evolved to permit computer systems to share data and resources. The earliest networks were devices connected to a single centralized processing system. Today, networks connect not only peripherals and other devices, but also all manners of independently functioning computer systems from mainframes to desktop computers. As we will see, networking, like charity, begins at home. In this chapter, we examine the fundamentals for the first line of networking—the local area networks (LANs) that establish basic connectivity for your computer.

OBJECTIVES

- *The principal characteristics and chief advantages of local area networks*

- *How devices in a local area network are connected and how their transmission media affect performance*

- *How networks are physically organized to facilitate data transmission*

- *The most common methods for controlling communication between the many and often competing nodes in LANs*

- *Ways in which the size and performance of LANs are extended*

CHAPTER 17

LOCAL AREA NETWORKS

CHARACTERISTICS OF A LAN

To understand and appreciate better the motivation for connecting computer systems to a network, consider the following practical problem. Suppose that you manage a collection of computers, perhaps in a lab or a business office. Most of the users prepare documents from time to time. Naturally, they need printing services for hard-copy versions of their documents. How do you meet this need? There are several possible solutions.

You might purchase one printer for each machine. This would be very convenient for your users, but also very expensive and inefficient. You could expect that the printers would spend a lot of idle time waiting for their next print job.

Rather than duplicate devices, you might purchase one printer and connect it to a single computer system used exclusively for printing. Users would have to copy their print files to a disk and physically transport them to the system used for printing. This "sneaker network" solution is not very satisfactory either. It is less costly initially, but waiting for access and performing file transfers waste a lot of time and, therefore, money.

Perhaps all of the computers could be physically connected to a single printer. In this case, we could imagine a switching device or port that connects all the computers to the printer but allows only one computer at a time to use it. Switching might be done manually or even by software control. The wear and tear on sneakers is reduced, but still some of the same problems persist. Loss of time in waiting for access is annoying and costly for your users.

A better solution lies in combining features from all of these techniques into a single method. The printer is connected to a single dedicated computer system as before, but this computer—the **server**—is connected to all of the other systems on the site. Rather than a simple one-way physical connection, though, the server can send and receive signals from the others. Let's add still another wrinkle. Our server has software that allows it to receive transmitted print files, store them, and transfer them when the printer is ready. Now when a user wishes to print a file, he or she transfers it to the server. The server signals when it is ready; the print file is sent; and the user can continue working on something else with no further delays. Print files are queued or **spooled** for orderly printing. This usually means they are printed on a first-come, first-served basis, much like the lines or queues at grocery store checkouts.

From the user's point of view, this scheme is not as convenient as having immediate service with a dedicated printer. Even so, the service is less fussy compared to the other methods. Press a button and go. Even better, your system is freed from managing the details of the printing process, which means that you are free to do other things. As a manager, you can see that this is a very efficient solution from an administrative point of view, too. The printer's use is maximized; the user's idle time is minimized. Of course, there is a cost associated with this solution. Specialized hardware and software must be installed to make it work.

In a nutshell, we have the birth of a **local area network (LAN),** with the following basic characteristics:

- Connectivity supporting two-way communication
- Resource sharing
- Limited geographical area
- Transparency of use
- Support from hardware and software

Connectivity

The hallmark of any computer network, of course, is that all of the nodes on the network are interconnected for the sake of communication. The extent to which nodes on a network can communicate depends on both the hardware and software that support it. At the very least, every node on the network has the capability of two-way communication with one or more servers. Many networks support full two-way communication for every node rather than just to and from a server. This means that any node can send and receive signals from any other node on the network.

Resource Sharing

As our example showed, one of the chief motivations for a LAN is that it allows a group of users and their computer systems to share various resources. The server computer provides high-capacity mass storage for data and programs. Software, for instance, may be copied from the server to an attached computer for execution. This process is called **downloading.** This approach can save disk storage space on the user's system and also enhance system security because the original version of the software can be better protected from tampering. Dispensing software via servers can be economical in some cases, too. Software vendors often issue site licenses to use their applications on a large number of computers. Site licenses are cheaper than purchasing single copies for each computer system, and file servers can help to distribute the software to computers on the network.

Data can be shared between groups of users on a LAN, too. Specific files can be copied to the server; this process is called **uploading.** These files may then be accessed by other systems on the same network. In this way, a group working on a single document can share it without transmitting disk copies between systems.

Most file servers maintain security provisions for users and user groups. Normally, you must have an established account on the LAN to access it. Accounts are often protected by **passwords,** a secret word or phrase that is known only by the legitimate user. See Figure 17.1.

FIGURE 17.1

Students connecting to our departmental server have group accounts and a password that must be entered to gain access to it. The dialog box shows how to log on to the file server. Note that the password is not echoed on the screen. The user enters it, and the system verifies its authenticity.

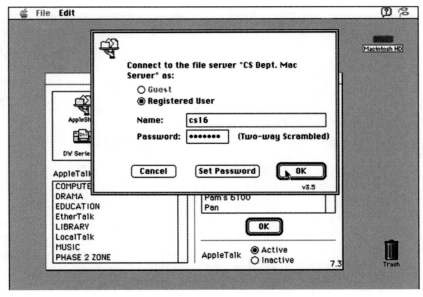

Limited Geography

The term "local" naturally suggests that LANs don't cover much ground in their span. This, however, is extremely relative. "Local" depends on several factors: the type of media connecting the nodes, the number of connections in the network, sophistication of the hardware/software support, even how the nodes communicate in the network. In spite of these variables, it is safe to assume that you could comfortably walk the span of a local area network.

The most significant factor, though, in determining the span of the network is the transmission media. Bounded media such as wire and optic fiber have limits up to several hundred meters. Unbounded media or "wireless" LANs use infrared or radio frequency broadcast methods. These, too, are limited in effective distance. Consequently, a LAN usually spans no more than several rooms, a building, or, at most, a small area among buildings.

Transparency

One of the justifications for the expense of LANs is their transparency in use. This means that LANs are designed to connect a user's computer system to other systems and devices without a lot of fuss or bother for the user. As we discussed in the example, printing over a LAN is almost as easy and convenient as printing to a printer dedicated to your system. After you designate which printer you wish to use, just click a button and it's done. Similarly, access to the data files in a server is the same as if the disks were part of your system. See Figure 17.2.

Network Hardware and Software Support

Connectivity does have special requirements, though. Each computer must have specific hardware to connect to the network and customized software to manage the connection. This often means purchasing network cards or boards (hardware) that are added to each computer. It may also be necessary to add memory (main memory and secondary storage) to accommodate the networking software.

Servers and network connection devices often mean more expense. Network software must be purchased or licensed. Some versions of network software are add-ons for your system's operating system software; other versions are integrated solutions, which means the operating system has built-in networking facilities.

Other Factors

Several other conditions generally hold for LANs too, though they are not really defining characteristics. A LAN is usually locally owned and managed. The business or institution, therefore, must add or train staff to oversee its operation, thereby adding a continuing expense.

Because LANs are likely homegrown, the computers attached to them are often uniform, usually so for administrative convenience. However, it is not necessary that all of the systems on a given LAN be from

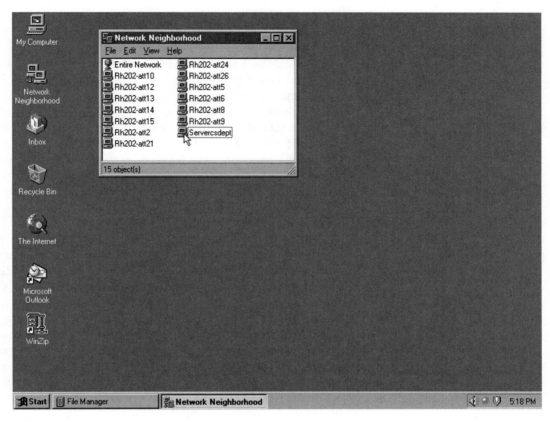

FIGURE 17.2

From the Network Neighborhood window, Windows 95/98 users may access servers or systems connected on a connected LAN.

the same vendor. Different systems can be connected to a given network provided they employ compatible network hardware and software. In fact, one of the real advantages of LANs is that they can allow different hardware platforms to share data and resources.

COSTS AND BENEFITS OF LANS

Most organizations have evolved from maintaining large, centralized computing centers to distributed computing environments. Experience has shown that it is simply cheaper over the long run to replace costly, large mainframes with numerous inexpensive, expendable desktop systems. These systems bring sufficient computing power directly to users. Their cost has dramatically decreased annually as their performance has increased. LANs add connectivity to such an environment and, with it, all the benefits of centralized computing. The cost of networking a distributed computing environment is worth it over the long run because it provides the greatest flexibility for meeting future organizational needs.

The primary advantages of using a local area network are communication, management control, and cost-effectiveness. Obviously, a LAN facilitates communication. The advantages of communication are more than just sending messages electronically from one person to another. Besides person-to-person communication, a LAN makes it possible for both individuals and applications to communicate in various ways. For example, you can run a program from another system provided that a LAN connects your system with that remote host.

Applications can communicate, too. Applications that interact over a network are called **client/server systems.** A **client program** running on your system, for example, might make requests for services from a **server program** that is executing on a server or even another client system. The LAN provides the communication links between clients and servers. As you have seen, the World Wide Web can be thought of as a global client/server system. We discuss client/server systems in more detail in the next chapter.

Many new applications today take advantage of a client/server architecture to provide more powerful or convenient features to their users. The client/server architecture forms the basis for **distributed computing environments.** In these environments, resources, data, programs, and tasks are distributed and shared across computer networks.

LANs also offer the advantage of centralized management. Local area networks typically connect a number of desktop computer systems on a single site, thus enabling an organization to replace centralized computing with downsized, distributed computing. Workgroups can share data stored in a protected and centralized facility while enjoying the advantages of distributed access. Networks can also impose security provisions that impede unwanted access.

For most organizations, the bottom line is monetary expense. LANs are usually more cost-effective solutions for organizations because they enable resource sharing and the downsizing of computing facilities. We've already discussed the economy of sharing software and hardware resources. Downsizing of computing facilities also clearly promotes a healthier bottom line.

There is a debit side associated with LANs. Aside from the acquisition of additional equipment and software, there is a continuing need for maintenance. As mentioned earlier, staff must be trained and available to keep the network functioning properly. Fortunately, today a number of software tools aid in managing the network. Even so, a networking staff is needed to assist users in connecting, providing advice on services, testing the compatibility of new hardware and software with the LAN, and putting out the "fires" that flare up here and there along the network.

Even though the centralized management of computing resources enabled by LANs is generally advantageous, distributed computing exclusively through desktop computers also has some drawbacks. Computing with desktop systems often fosters a multiplicity of software and data scattered across the organization. Besides the expense of redundancy, data inconsistencies can arise. There are also more security problems because there are many potential points of access in a distributed computing environment. Fortunately, networking services provided by most LANs can help to alleviate these problems.

Most organizations have concluded that the benefits of local area networks far outweigh their costs. In fact, networking today is as essential and commonplace in a computing environment as video monitors and storage peripherals. Ten years ago, a LAN in a business or a lab was an exotic distinction; today, a networked computing environment is assumed.

Even though all LANs provide basic connectivity between the devices at a site, not all LANs are alike. A number of distinguishing characteristics affect their performance. In the next section, we consider how to classify LANs according to these important criteria.

DIFFERENTIATING LANS

The number of networking solutions offered by computer vendors may seem a dizzying variety to the newcomer. A closer look, however, reveals that many different proprietary networks (brand names) share a lot of common attributes. Four important factors differentiate one type of LAN from another. An understanding of each of these categories gives a much clearer picture as to what makes one LAN different from another.

First, how are the nodes in the LAN connected? LANs are differentiated by the transmission media they employ. Second, most nodes in a LAN form shared links, but how are their connections organized? This organization reveals the network topology. Still another factor is how do the nodes gain access to the network? In other words, how is communication managed? Finally, networks that are similar in all these characteristics can still be different because they have different supporting software. We outline each category and consider its primary instances.

Transmission Media: How LANs Are Connected

Most LANs are connected using **bounded media.** This means that data transmission is carried over wire or fiber. (We consider LANs using unbounded transmission in the final section of this chapter.) Today, there are three popular bounded media for interconnecting the nodes of a LAN:

- Twisted-pair cable
- Coaxial cable
- Optical fiber cable

These media differ in cost and performance characteristics. As you might expect, the trade-off is usually low cost versus performance. Three factors are important for measuring their performance characteristics: transmission speed, practical transmission distance, and susceptibility to noise. Speed for digital transmissions, as discussed in Chapter 16, is measured in bits per second. Practical distance refers to how far the medium may be extended before the signal weakens significantly. This distance is almost always expressed in meters.

One of the most inexpensive and commonly used forms of wiring is **twisted-pair cable.** Standard telephone cable can often be used. Two insulated lengths of copper wire are twisted together and can extend distances up to about 100 meters. See Figure 17.3. Twisted-pair cable is sometimes shielded to prevent signal interference. Because unshielded

FIGURE 17.3

Twisted-pair is usually standard copper wiring twisted together. It comes in two varieties: shielded and unshielded.

Copper wires

Two layers of insulating materials

varieties are sensitive to signal interference, some care must be taken in planning their installation. In spite of this, twisted-pair is a very economical and popular choice for wiring a network. Transmission speeds are typically 10 megabits (a megabit is 1 million bits) per second (Mbps), although a new standard for shielded twisted-pair exceeding 100 Mbps has been introduced.

Another popular form of copper wiring for networks is coaxial cable. A **coaxial cable** is usually two conductors separated by several layers of shielding and insulation. The inner conductor is either solid or stranded wire; a meshed wire serves as an outer conductor. Figure 17.4 illustrates.

Coaxial cable is commonly used in radio and television applications, so it is readily available. While not as economical as twisted-pair, it does offer better performance. The insulation and shielding protect against external signal interference. Transmission speeds measure between 10 and 100 Mbps. Practical distances for this medium range from around 200 meters (thin coaxial) to 500 meters (thick coaxial).

An entirely different technology for data transmission is presented by **optical fiber cable.** Light pulses are generated as a signal from either a laser or a light-emitting diode. The signal is carried through very thin strands of glass fiber. As the light travels along the fiber, it is confined to the core or signal path by the special insulation or cladding that surrounds the core. At the receiving end, a photodetector translates the light pulses into an electrical signal. See Figure 17.5.

Optical fiber is noteworthy for its transmission speeds and low error rates. Speeds are rated from 100 Mbps up to 2 gigabits (a gigabit is 1 billion bits) per second. Lower error rates result because optical fiber cable uses light pulses instead of electrical pulses to transmit data; hence,

FIGURE 17.4

Coaxial cables were used in the first local area networks. Today, there are two formats: thick and thin. "Thinnet" installations are cheaper and easier to install compared to the older, thick coaxial formulation.

Outer conductor

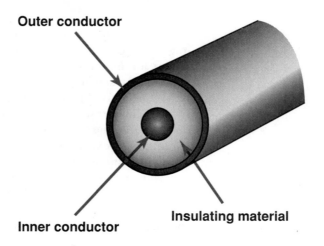

Inner conductor   **Insulating material**

FIGURE 17.5

A common form of optical fiber is depicted here. Called single transmission, the signal is beamed through an extremely thin glass fiber core. Cores may be as small as 2–12 millionths of a meter in diameter. Cladding is an optical insulator whose lower refractive properties confine the signal to the core. An outer plastic coating acts as insulation for the signal transmission. In this way, many different signal-carrying fibers can be bundled into a single cable.

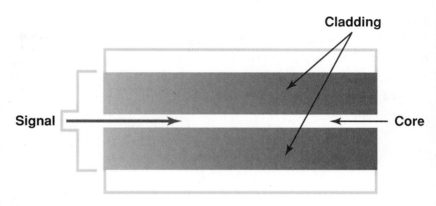

it is much less subject to the noisy interference that sometimes plagues copper wire channels.

Currently, optical fiber is more expensive than transmission media made of copper wire. Its speeds and bandwidth capacities, however, make it the choice for the future, especially for networks carrying demanding and informationally rich signals such as digital audio and video.

Topologies: How LANs Are Organized

In Chapter 16, you learned that few data communications networks employ point-to-point connections. It is simply too expensive, too complicated, and too wasteful to configure a network in which every two nodes have a direct or dedicated connection between them. Instead, networks use shared links. The links or transmission paths may be shared in many ways.

The logical layout or geometric organization of how the nodes in a network are connected is called its **topology.** A network's topology reveals the potential paths for communication between nodes and how their links are shared; it is not focused exclusively on the physical arrangement of the wires and connections. There are three popular topologies for LANs: star, bus, and ring.

The **star topology** is the oldest. It borrows from telephone technology—the telephones in your home probably use this wiring arrangement. In a star topology network, all the nodes are connected to a single point called the **hub,** which acts as a switching device routing transmissions between outlying nodes. See Figure 17.6.

Because the star topology is centralized, it permits greater network management. Expansion—adding new nodes to the network—is usually easy. Star networks are also less vulnerable to cable transmission problems. For instance, if the connection at a single node fails, the rest of the network can still continue service. On the other hand, if the hub fails, then, of course, the rest of the network fails.

In the **bus topology,** all of the nodes in a network are connected to a common communications channel. All nodes share this single transmission channel, called a bus. The bus topology is illustrated in Figure 17.7. This configuration is simple and has several advantages. Cable lengths are usually the shortest, and the bus network is also easily expanded. The

FIGURE 17.6

In the star topology, a centralized hub connects all other nodes in the network. The hub serves as either an active or a passive switching device for routing transmissions.

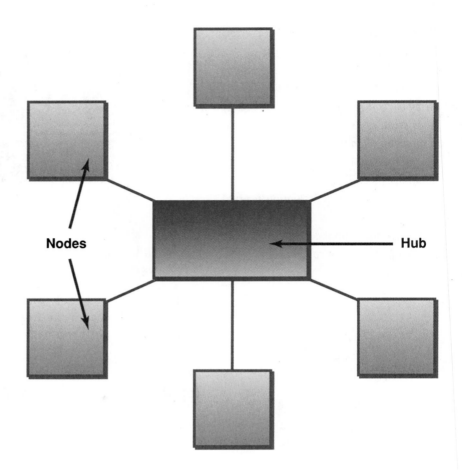

choice of medium, however, affects both the potential length and number of nodes. Like the star topology, if a single device in the bus topology fails, the rest of the network survives. But, if the bus fails, the network is compromised. Unlike the star topology, which offers some centralized control, network management is more difficult in a bus network.

In the star and bus topologies, the nodes are not arranged in any particular order. A **ring topology,** in contrast, does impose an order on the nodes of a network. Each node in a ring topology is connected to exactly two other nodes: its predecessor and successor. Thus, it receives signals only from its predecessor and sends signals only to its successor. The entire network forms a closed path or ring that permits any node to communicate to others by passing the signal along the ring. See Figure 17.8.

Ring topologies are favored primarily for performance characteristics such as speed (especially optical fiber ring networks) and better access. They do pose some problems for management, though. Adding or removing nodes from a ring can be tricky. In fact, many ring architectures today are maintained using a wiring hub to deal with this problem. Cable is wired from each station to the hub device, which controls the ring ordering within. (These networks are called "star-wired token rings" because they combine star geometry for wiring with the ring architecture.) The biggest drawback to the ring topology, however, is that when any node fails, the entire network goes down with it. A number of variations including dual bidirectional ring designs have been developed to provide better fault tolerance.

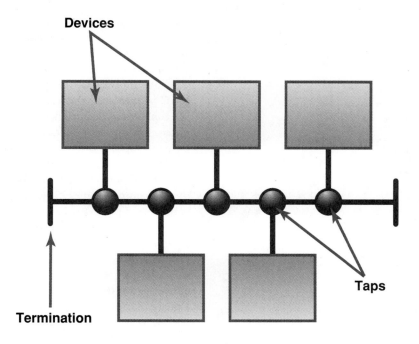

FIGURE 17.7

The bus topology is a single length of a transmission medium that is terminated at both ends. Devices are connected to the medium by connections called taps or transceivers. When a transmission is sent from a single node, all the nodes on the network can access it.

FIGURE 17.8

In a ring topology, the nodes are arranged in a closed path that is usually unidirectional. Signals are passed from one node to another by interfaces that act as repeaters.

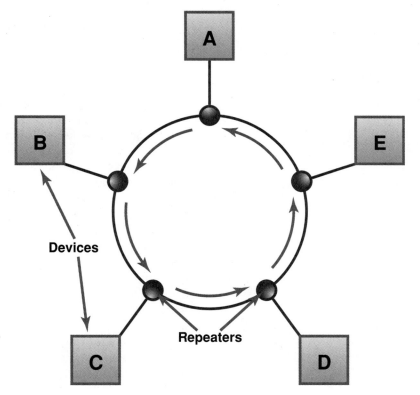

Media Access Control: How Nodes Send and Receive Data

Topologies reveal how the many nodes on a network may potentially access one another, but this is only part of the story. At another level, we can ask how nodes carry out communication. For example, on a bus network all of the nodes can access the medium at once. How can we organize things so that communication is practical? In other words, how are messages transmitted among nodes in a timely, reliable manner? This process is called **media access control (MAC).**

The methods for communication from node to node are called **MAC protocols.** As you know, a protocol is a set of standards or rules. A MAC protocol defines how a given node accesses the channel for a transmission to another specific node on the network. We restrict our survey to two popular methods employed by most LANs. Both are packet switching MAC protocols.

The **Ethernet MAC protocol** is typically implemented on baseband networks employing either bus or star topologies. The Ethernet protocol is based on packet switching and functions very much like conversation around the dinner table for a large family. At the dinner table, it is possible for anyone to speak to anyone else at any time. Of course, this is not very practical. If everyone decided to talk at once, chaos would ensue. Instead, being polite, you would normally wait until there was a lull in the conversation to speak. At that instant, you would direct your comment to a particular person, though everyone else at the table could hear you. On an Ethernet LAN, the transmitter listens to the channel, waiting for a moment when the communications channel is idle. At that instant, it transmits a packet on the channel.

Two things can happen in a normally functioning Ethernet LAN network: Transmission can be successful or unsuccessful. A successful transmission occurs when all nodes on the network hear the packet (just as everyone at the table can hear your comment), but only the addressee receives and processes the packet. An unsuccessful transmission occurs when two or more packets are transmitted from different nodes simultaneously. (Compare this with two people speaking at once at the table.) This is called a **packet collision.** In these instances, the transmission is likely garbled, and the packets received are discarded.

In the event of packet collisions, all nodes employ a **backoff procedure.** This means that they invoke steps that result in their waiting for another try to transmit. A simple variation is to wait a random amount of time before trying again. (This is very likely what you would do at the dinner table, too.) After backing off, any node can attempt to transmit whether it was one of the original transmitters or not.

In sum, the Ethernet protocol amounts to an orderly chaos. It works well for relatively low-load, or what is called "bursty," traffic, and for LANs in which the number of nodes and the length of messages transmitted are not too great. As the amount of traffic on an Ethernet network grows, the amount of waiting time for completing transmissions can become annoyingly noticeable.

The **token passing MAC protocol** was designed to manage communication on a ring architecture. Unlike the Ethernet protocol, token passing is very orderly, even courteous. The most common variation employs a single packet called the **token,** which is routed continuously around the ring. Any node can become the token controller once the token is freed from any previous transmissions. The token controller adds data to the token and addresses it to its intended recipient. Other nodes pass the token along the ring to the receiver. The token controller continues to transmit packets in this manner until the message is complete. It then frees and passes the token along to the other nodes. See Figure 17.9.

FIGURE 17.9

(a) Suppose that node B must communicate a message to node D. B waits until the free token passes through. Taking control of the free token, B marks the token busy, adds data to it, and addresses it to D. (b) B transmits the token to its successor along the ring. C recognizes that it is not the addressee so C passes or repeats the occupied token to the next station, D. (c) Node D recognizes that the packet is for it and copies it. The token is marked as received and again passed along the ring. Stations E and A pass the still-busy token back to B to complete the ring. (d) The process continues until B has transmitted all packets of the message successfully to D. After the last packet has been acknowledged, B releases the token, marking it free again. It will be passed along to the first station that requires it to send a message.

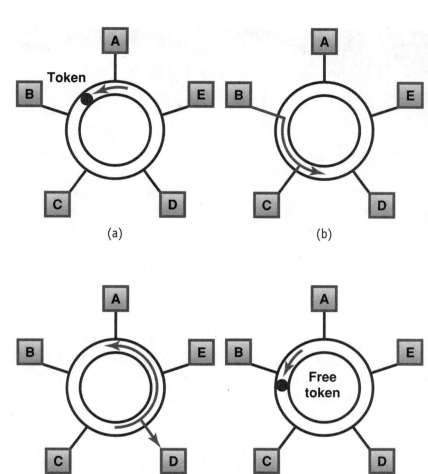

The token passing protocol has several advantages. The token ring network can serve a large number of nodes. It is best suited to high-load networks because each node is guaranteed access to the network within a predictable maximum amount of waiting time. (In contrast, a busy Ethernet network could potentially freeze out a station when numerous packet collisions occur.) Finally, token rings are more efficient for large files requiring continuous transmissions—audio and video files, for example. Token passing permits the token controller to monopolize the network to complete such large transmissions.

Networking Software

A network's **physical transport system** is the collection of hardware and software that acts as the plumbing for the network. So far we have outlined the physical transport for a LAN. In other words, communications channels, topology, and MAC protocols detail how data packets are transmitted from one node to another on a LAN. The design and function of networking software provide another way to differentiate LANs.

A wide variety of vendors offer networking software solutions for an assortment of hardware platforms and network configurations, but all

focus

WHAT'S IN A NAME?

The term "Ethernet" is, in fact, a brand name that has seeped into the vernacular much as "Kleenex" is synonymous with facial tissues. Originally, Ethernet was a proprietary protocol of the Xerox Corporation. It was later standardized by the consortium of Xerox, Intel, and Digital Equipment Corporation. Today, there are many commercial versions of the original protocol. These adhere to the standard defined as IEEE (pronounced "I triple E") 802.3. More formally, it is called CSMA/CD, which stands for Carrier Sense Multiple Access with Collision Detection. Now you can understand why the name "Ethernet" has caught on.

FIGURE 17.10

User-to-user communication in a LAN is accomplished through a series of layers created by software and hardware. The physical transport layer is the bottom-most layer that transfers signals. The network system handles the transport of data apart from its implementation in the physical layer. The network service layer includes high-level functions that involve connectivity and communication between nodes. The applications layer provides the interface to the user for these services.

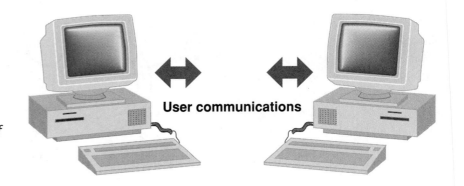

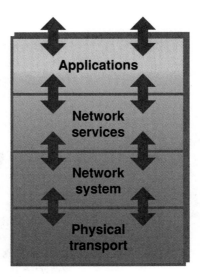

this software adheres to a layered network model. As illustrated in Figure 17.10, network software is built on top of the physical transport layer. Several layers of network software contribute to the overall functionality available to end users. Each layer is a distinct set of programs that depend on the services of the preceding one. Such a layered design separates tasks at different levels.

The **network system layer** is usually integrated within the operating system. Its function is to ensure basic connectivity between communicating nodes. The **network services layer** provides higher-level functions to the network user, such as file sharing, shared printing, and communications services to other nodes and networks. Finally, the **applications layer** consists of programs providing the user with features such as a convenient interface for exploiting the variety of network services available. Network applications are often designed using the client/server model.

EXTENDING LANS

Like most other technologies, the more that we depend on LANs, the more we expect from them. The recent trends have been to extend LANs in two distinct ways. First, it is commonplace to expand the physical range and size of LANs. At the same time, there is a growing demand to improve the performance of LANs to accommodate richer forms of information, such as video and multimedia.

We briefly examine an array of devices that extend the scale of local area networks: repeaters, bridges, routers, and gateways. Afterward, we treat two new technologies that will also likely play important roles in extending LAN capabilities in the near future: ATM networks and wireless and mobile networks. In this section, we touch on all three topics to see how they provide new features and services by pushing the envelope for networking technology.

Repeaters, Bridges, Routers, and Gateways

The success of local area networking has produced some problems. As more and more users are introduced to the benefits of networking, the size of a LAN grows—in both distance spanned and the number of nodes attached. As the number of independent LANs in a business or organization increases, a natural desire to increase the benefits of data communications by interconnecting them develops. Autonomous LANs may have different hardware and protocols. The challenge then is to provide for both expansion and interconnectivity while preserving manageable networks with satisfactory performance. The solution usually is to maintain autonomous networks while creating controlled access among them. It is customary today to refer to intraorganizational collections of networks as **intranets** to distinguish them from the worldwide network called the Internet. A variety of tools are available to extend and connect networks. These include repeaters, bridges, routers, and gateways.

● **Repeaters.**   Hardware devices that boost the strength of the signal on a communications channel are called **repeaters.** As mentioned earlier, media have practical limits on how far the signal may be transmitted before it weakens. Repeaters amplify and retransmit the signal, thereby allowing it to extend beyond the normal practical limits. See Figure 17.11. Repeaters can be used to enlarge the number of nodes in a

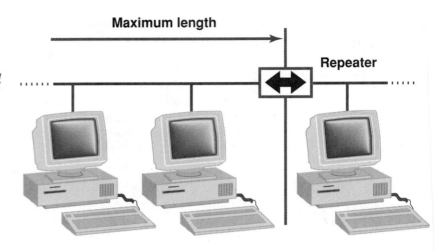

FIGURE 17.11

A repeater extends the span of an existing LAN past its recommended maximum length by amplifying the signal across the transmission medium.

LAN. Of course, as the number of nodes increases, the traffic increases, which, in turn, may cause network performance to degrade.

● **Bridges.** A **bridge** is a hardware device that connects two networks of the same topology and MAC protocol. For example, a bridge could be used to join two Ethernet star networks. Unlike repeaters, bridges preserve the autonomy of the interconnecting networks. They do so by screening transmissions and passing only those intended to cross networks. See Figure 17.12.

● **Routers.** **Routers** are devices that connect networks of the same or different types, such as an Ethernet with a token passing LAN. These devices are directed by software to provide higher performance data throughput for the intranet by selecting efficient routes for the data to travel. See Figure 17.13.

● **Gateways.** **Gateways** are hardware and software systems that act as interfaces between networks having entirely different MAC protocols. Gateways are often used to connect a LAN to a wide area network, such as those belonging to the Internet. (We return to the topic of routers, gateways, and the Internet in the next chapter.)

Wireless Networking

The suggestion of a **wireless network**—a network connected without using wires—sounds exotic and newfangled, yet broadcast methods for data communications have been around for several decades. In fact, the model for Ethernet packet switching was the ALOHA network (circa early 1970s) that connected radio frequency broadcast stations in the Hawaiian islands. Although satellite, microwave relay, and radio wave transmissions are common in wide area networks, so-called wireless or broadcast methods for local area networks are relative newcomers on the scene.

We can expect to see more wireless technology for LANs for several reasons. Wireless technology is a cost-effective answer to linking systems in buildings where wiring is prohibitively expensive. It works well also for connecting LANs between buildings that otherwise are

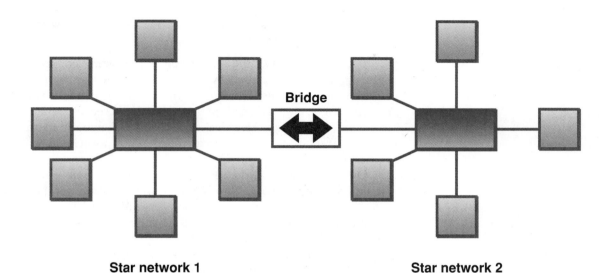

FIGURE 17.12

A bridge connects two networks of the same type. The bridge allows packets intended for the other LAN to pass through while it blocks packets intended for the originating LAN. This screening helps to preserve the performance of each autonomous LAN within its confines yet interconnects them for communication.

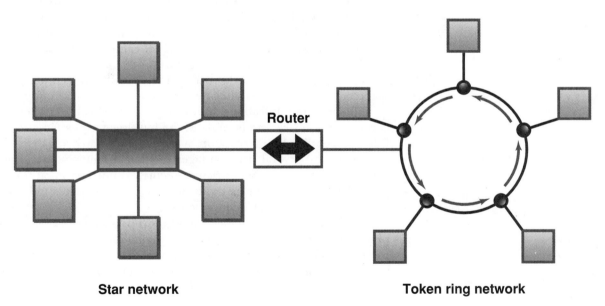

FIGURE 17.13

A router usually connects two different types of networks. The router also makes decisions about where and how packets should be transmitted; this often improves the overall throughput of the LAN.

too remote to wire without leasing dedicated lines. The popularity of laptop and notebook computer systems also fuels the need for wireless networking. Portable computing requires mobile connectivity. In other words, a LAN must be flexible enough to provide connectivity anywhere in a prescribed range in which the user transports his or her system. Today wireless networking is available in two broadcast forms: infrared and radio frequencies.

● **Infrared Broadcasting.**   **Infrared broadcasting** employs infrared light signals like those used by remote control devices found in home entertainment systems. The signal is directional, which means the transmitter must be aimed directly at or reflected to a receiver that translates the signal to ordinary electrical signals. Like fiber optic methods, the signal is free from the electrical interference associated with other equipment.

On the other hand, the infrared transmitter's range is only moderate and at best comparable to bounded media. Moreover, because the infrared signal is directional, it is not generally suitable for mobile applications in which the node is free to change positions while remaining "connected." Consequently, wireless infrared network products are useful only for providing communications between stationary nodes that would otherwise be difficult to connect with wires.

● **Radio Frequency Broadcasting.**   **Radio frequency broadcasting** employs radio transmissions. For LAN applications these transmissions generally fit one of two categories: baseband versus broadband broadcasting. These are suitable for both standard wireless and mobile network applications.

Baseband LANs employ a single carrier frequency in the Industrial, Scientific, and Medical (ISM) radio band. These are wavelengths that are authorized by the Federal Communications Commission (FCC) without license. Baseband generally delivers higher performance with respect to coverage and speed. The signal can penetrate buildings and other obstacles that an infrared light cannot.

In contrast to baseband broadcasting, broadband technology uses a spectrum of frequencies allocated for two-way radio communications. Broadband communications do not require FCC licenses either. Power consumption is low, and because of the multiple frequencies, the signal is less susceptible to interruption by interference.

There are several disadvantages of radio frequency broadcasting. The coverage distance is restricted. Security is not very good for either broadband or baseband methods because, like any other radio signal, these transmissions may be intercepted.

Currently the technologies that support pager networks and cellular phone networks are being adapted to digital data communications applications. Because their infrastructures are well established, they provide an economical alternative for wireless networking services.

Asynchronous Transfer Mode Networks

As more and more users recognize the utility of networking, they naturally want to employ it in newer ways. For example, we have become complacent about network applications such as messaging or e-mail, print servers, and file transfers. The emergence of multimedia computing has created interest in new uses such as video-conferencing and real-time multimedia transmission. These and other similar applications require the ability to transfer very large amounts of data in a timely and reliable manner. Unfortunately, most LANs today lack the capability for the higher performance needed to support these services.

Consider, for example, that the typical 40-page text document represents about 1 Mbit of digital data. An Ethernet network with a modest transfer rate of 10 Mbps could transmit ten such documents in a single second. In contrast, one second of full-screen video (640×480, 24-bit depth at 30 frames per second) would translate to about 220 Mbits of data. A network rated at 10 Mbps is simply inadequate to deliver the data as needed.

Another obstacle is that most LANs employ multiple-access channels. In other words, the channels or transmission media that connect nodes on a LAN are shared by all of its users. Transmitting messages, we have seen, involves chopping up the data into smaller units and transmitting these packets through a typically busy medium. Even if a network were equipped to handle the demands of transmitting video or multimedia information in real time, it would likely monopolize the network to the extent that other users would be unable to access it simultaneously.

Asynchronous transfer mode (ATM)—not to be confused with the ATM acronym representing automated teller machines for banking transactions—is a new networking technology designed to solve these problems and provide high-performance connectivity. It combines the best of packet switching transport with the connection-based service found ordinarily in circuit switching networks.

Recall from Chapter 16 that circuit switching data is transmitted as a continuous stream; hence, circuit switching requires a persistent connection between two nodes. On the other hand, packet switching does not require a persistent connection because it divides the message into individual packets and delivers them separately. Packets often take advantage of alternative routes, and so they may arrive out of order as well. The receiver must process them and reassemble the message to complete the transmission. Packet switching is designed primarily for reliability rather than timing. Retransmissions and delivery delays are acceptable for the sake of the data's accuracy. Herein is the chief obstacle for multimedia transmission. To receive a video signal live—for example, in a simultaneous video-conference—millions of packets would have to be transmitted continuously. Delays in delivery are critical. In addition, the overhead of processing and reassembling them on the receiving end affects the video playback.

The challenge then is to devise a network technology that can satisfy both classes of data: the accuracy of text and numeric information and the timeliness of graphic, audio, and video sources. At the same time, it must be compatible with the existing networking infrastructure. The ATM network model is designed to meet these specifications.

ATM LANs offer a high-speed, wide-bandwidth backbone with dynamic bandwidth connections. As Figure 17.14 illustrates, the ATM LAN can support the higher-performance demand of multimedia transmissions while integrating with existing network technology and uses. Normal network traffic proceeds according to the standard packet switching regime. But when packet frequency increases (as it does in a video transmission), the network in effect creates a virtual connection or channel that transmits data continuously for the length of the message. The receiving device is assured that the packets arrive in order and is therefore

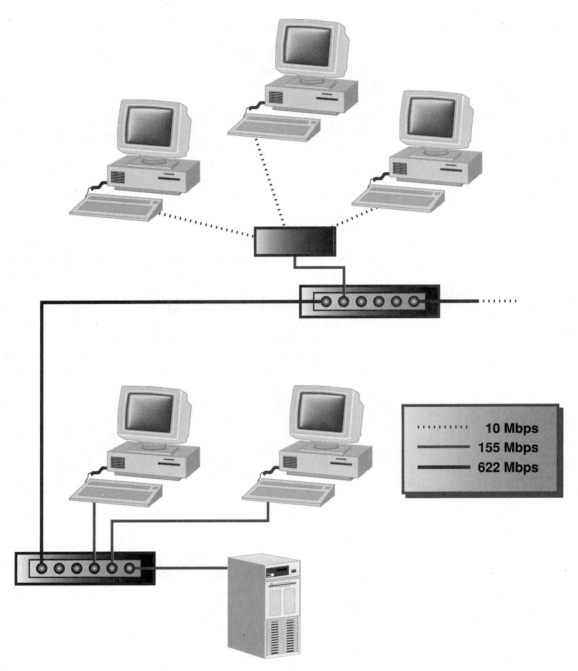

FIGURE 17.14

The ATM LAN is attractive because it can link together existing LANs with higher-performance ones. Pictured here are two LANs connected by ATM switches that provide transmissions at different rates to accommodate a variety of needs. At the top is a hub serving a conventional network such as Ethernet. A high-speed signal is routed to the LAN at the bottom, whose ATM switch serves high-performance workstations and servers.

released from the task of checking and reassembling data. To accomplish this, the ATM LAN employs a technique called **cell switching,** a process that detects the size of a transmission and automatically creates a virtual circuit switching mode for the duration of the transmission. All this is possible without interrupting service to the rest of the network.

More Information

S U M M A R Y

Computer networks connect peripherals and other independently functioning computer systems from mainframes to desktop computers. Local area networks (LANs) connect computers and devices spread over a restricted physical area—anywhere from a single room to a cluster of buildings, typically. Dedicated computer systems called servers connect to all of the nodes on the LAN and may provide coordination for its operation. Each computer connected as a LAN node must have specific hardware to connect to the network and customized software to manage the connection. Different kinds of computer systems can be connected to a given LAN provided they employ compatible network hardware and software.

The primary advantages of using a LAN are communication, management control, and cost-effectiveness. Although certain costs are associated with LANs, most organizations have concluded that the benefits of LANs far outweigh their costs. In fact, networking today is an essential component in organizational computing environments.

LANs are differentiated by the transmission media used in the communications channels they employ, the network topologies used to organize their connections, the media access control (MAC) protocols used to manage the network communications, and the supporting network software and hardware. Typical transmission media include twisted-pair cable, coaxial cable, and optical fiber cable. The bus, ring, and star topologies are the most common LAN network topologies. The Ethernet and token passing protocols, both based on packet switching, are the two most popular MAC protocols for LANs.

Network hardware and software services are organized as a layered hierarchy. The network's physical transport system is the collection of hardware and software that acts as the plumbing for the network and serves as the base layer on which other layers are built. The next layer is the network system layer whose function is to ensure basic connectivity between communicating nodes. Next, the network services layer provides higher-level functions to the network user such as file sharing, shared printing, and communication services to other nodes and networks. Finally, the applications layer consists of programs providing the user with features such as a convenient interface for exploiting the variety of network services available.

Repeaters, bridges, routers, and gateways are combination hardware/software devices that allow LANs to be expanded and connected to other LANs. These devices allow organizations to combine and connect different LANs into organizational intranets. Future development of LANs will include an increased use of wireless connections—using infrared and radio broadcast methods—and much faster networks like the evolving asynchronous transfer mode (ATM) networks that combine the best characteristics of packet switching and circuit switching networks.

PROJECTS

1 Do some additional research on asynchronous transfer mode (ATM) networks. What role do you think ATM will play in networking in the future? How important is it to implement faster networks within organizations?

2 Write a brief report summarizing the ways in which your work has benefited from the use of your school's LAN(s) this term.

3 Do some research on network cards that are installed in desktop computers to attach them to LANs. Identify several different kinds of cards. How do these differ? What is a typical price for such a card?

4 Consult with your lab manager or instructor to find out what kind of LAN connects the computers in your class laboratory. Specifically, what media connects the computers? What is the network topology? What type of media access control (MAC) is employed? Finally, what other LANs are connected to it? Are these LANs different or similar?

Key Terms

applications layer

asynchronous transfer mode
    network (ATM)

backoff procedure (packet
    switching)

bounded media

bridge

bus network topology

cell switching

client program

client/server system

coaxial cable

distributed computing
    environment

downloading (files)

Ethernet MAC protocol

gateway

hub

infrared broadcasting

intranet

MAC protocols

media access control (MAC)

network services layer

network system layer

optical fiber cable

packet collision

password

physical transport system (layer)

radio frequency broadcasting

repeater

ring network topology

router

server

server program

spooled print files

star network topology

token

token passing MAC protocol

topology (network)

twisted-pair cable

uploading (files)

wireless network

QUESTIONS FOR REVIEW

1 Give a brief description of a local area network (LAN).

2 What is a server? Describe its role in a LAN.

3 Identify some of the basic characteristics of a LAN.

4 Briefly describe the advantages of LANs for computer users. Also describe their advantages for the system's administration as well.

5 What are some of the disadvantages of LANs?

6 What does print spooling mean?

7 LANs may be distinguished by their communications channels, topologies, and media access control. What do these terms signify?

8 What are the chief practical differences between the bounded media of twisted-pair, coaxial cabling, and optical fiber?

9 Describe the star network topology. What are its strengths and weaknesses?

10 Describe the bus network topology. What are its strengths and weaknesses?

11 Describe the ring network topology. What are its strengths and weaknesses?

12 What is a distributed computing environment? What are some advantages of this organization? Some disadvantages?

13 What does the acronym MAC stand for? What does it mean?

14 Describe the basics of the Ethernet packet switching MAC protocol.

15 What is meant by a packet collision? How is such an event resolved?

16 Describe the basics of the token passing MAC protocol.

17 Give a brief description of the networking hardware and software systems called repeaters, bridges, routers, and gateways. What are the practical differences between these?

18 What do ATM networks offer in performance over traditional LANs?

19 What is meant by a network's physical transport layer (or system)?

20 List the different layers of LAN networking software and describe the basic function(s) of each layer.

Throughout this text you have used resources on the World Wide Web. The growth in the use of the World Wide Web over the past decade has been nothing short of phenomenal, and for many people the Web has become almost synonymous with computing itself. Of course, you know that computing encompasses the much larger digital domain. Actually, the Web is not even the whole of the networking picture, which is itself but a subset of the digital domain.

The World Wide Web is a part of a larger collection of computer networks called the Internet. Doubtless you have read and heard a number of things about the Internet. As a World Wide Web user, you have already ventured out on the Internet. You may even feel that you are on your way to becoming a seasoned traveler. Even so, we are all pioneers on the brink of the electronic frontier because the Internet today is too large and too complicated for anyone to comprehend its scope and depth fully. The numbers of networks and computers connected to it grow so rapidly that current counts can only be estimated. The number of its users and the amount of information that courses through it are beyond all but ballpark guesses.

The Internet, though, is more than just hardware and software. The Internet is a vast repository of digital information—a worldwide electronic library. It is a library that never closes, a library that is forever renovating and expanding, and a library that lends many of its resources freely and openly.

The Internet is also a community of individuals. The services and information that you can find on the Internet are, of course, put there by people. In fact, a significant portion of the Internet is maintained by the voluntary efforts of a great number of individuals who have offered their talents as a gift to all of us. Indeed, the secret of the incredible success of this enterprise is due, in no small part, to the fact that the Internet is not owned by anybody and—at least at its inception—is not ruled by commercial concerns. In this chapter, you will learn more about this truly amazing entity and how the World Wide Web fits into this bigger picture.

OBJECTIVES

- *How the Internet evolved from an experimental network in the 1970s*

- *How your computer can communicate across the globe with other computers over a span of diverse interconnected networks*

- *The role of the World Wide Web as a part of the Internet*

- *Basic Internet applications: electronic mail, file transfers, and remote logins*

- *Specialized Internet applications such as gophers, archie servers, chat, MOOs, and MUDs*

CHAPTER 18

THE INTERNET AND THE WORLD WIDE WEB

Vasily Kandinsky, *Landscape near Murnau with Locomotive*, 1909. Solomon R. Guggenheim Museum

A SHORT HISTORY OF THE INTERNET

In the late 1960s, the U.S. Department of Defense, through the Advanced Research Projects Agency (ARPA, and later DARPA, for Defense Advanced Research Projects Agency), sponsored a series of projects designed to create a network of computers that could communicate with one another over long distances. This network came to be known as **ARPANET.** Its goal was to connect research universities and defense contractors so that they could share computing facilities and information.

The success of the project depended on resolving several formidable challenges. First, computer systems made by different vendors could not communicate readily with one another. Like the Tower of Babel, different systems had different protocols (that is, standards and conventions) for both the representation and transmission of data. Second, the computers were remotely located. Commercial carriers such as telephone lines were the only practical means for connecting these systems. Third, the Department of Defense was interested in creating a loosely coupled network—one that might survive attacks on single sites. A loosely coupled system can tolerate the loss of individual components while maintaining the integrity of the system as a whole.

Interestingly, all these factors proved fortuitous for the evolution of the Internet. Indeed, serendipity is a common theme for the evolution of the Internet even today: Earlier decisions and directions have had entirely unexpected results.

Experiments continued, and the network grew during the 1970s. The design of this network reflected its original goals well. From its inception, it was engineered to overcome both the problems of distance and unreliability. ARPANET was an entirely "democratic" network. All the nodes in the network were equal: Any node could originate, pass along, or receive messages. Messages were divided into parts, called packets, which could be routed across the network along different paths. The message would be reassembled by the receiver once all the parts had arrived. Even though this was not terribly efficient, it was very robust. It was the responsibility of each node to support and maintain its own connectivity to the network. There were no central authorities.

In 1978, DARPA established a common protocol for data transmission between systems. The adoption of this common network protocol, called TCP/IP (we examine TCP/IP in more detail in the next section), proved to be a significant watershed in our story. Because it was developed by researchers, with no commercial involvement, TCP/IP favored no established vendors. This created a level playing field in which everyone had potentially equal access. And the use of a single standard protocol meant that the Tower of Babel was razed in favor of a common tongue. Another important feature of TCP/IP is that it created a distributed system; tasks were distributed among different components of the network. In short, a network built on TCP/IP is an **open system,** meaning that there is neither central control nor a favored hardware platform.

In the early 1980s, the University of California at Berkeley developed a flavor of the UNIX operating system that incorporated TCP/IP. Berkeley UNIX, as it came to be known, was distributed widely for a variety of hardware platforms (and at low cost) to universities, colleges, and other institutions. This proved to be mutually beneficial. TCP/IP became a de facto protocol for interconnecting computer networks, and it also helped to propagate UNIX as the natural environment for the Internet. Although today's Internet applications do not depend on UNIX and can be supported by a variety of operating systems, UNIX versions remain both influential and commonplace.

Also in the 1980s, the National Science Foundation (NSF) embarked on a mission that would expand ARPANET technology to a wider collection of universities. Originally, the collection of networks known as NSFNET was conceived to connect supercomputer centers to other wide area networks for sharing scientific research. The original notion (authored by Dennis Jennings of University College, Dublin) was to create a "backbone" network that could serve as the major connector with supercomputer centers and other regional networks, linking universities and colleges. The number and complexity of these regional providers grew during the late 1980s.

In 1990, the Department of Defense decommissioned ARPANET, leaving U.S. networking responsibilities to NSF, NASA, and a few other agencies. At about the same time, the NSF relaxed its Fair Usage Policy, which had restrained commercial activities on the Internet, and increased the carrying capacity of its network backbone considerably. As a result, more and more commercial firms joined the network. Many regional network providers, both commercial and subsidized, were also connected, and "the" **Internet,** or the **Information Highway,** emerged as a collection of diverse computer networks that span the globe.

Since 1990, the Internet has experienced incredible growth. No doubt one of the primary reasons for this has been the introduction of the hypertext system known as the World Wide Web. You have already experienced how the Web allows Internet users to communicate and view information in a most user-friendly mode. It would be difficult to overestimate the impact that the Web has had on the development of the Internet.

In 1995, the NSFNET backbone was officially decommissioned. The responsibilities for network transport services were taken over by a number of commercial providers. Many of these were for-profit spin-offs of the regional providers subsidized in the earlier years by the NSF. Today, most of the original players such as ARPANET and NSFNET and others have gone the way of the dinosaurs. Even so, the Internet still thrives.

Though the technology and the players have changed, the Internet retains many of its original characteristics. The Internet is still a loosely coupled mesh of distributed, open networks that has no real center or single governing body. Networks are added to its topography freely, and the number of nodes connected to it expands daily. International participation is widespread and growing, as illustrated by Figure 18.1. And while TCP/IP remains the dominant protocol for data communications across networks, other protocols coexist with it. Currently, it is estimated that the

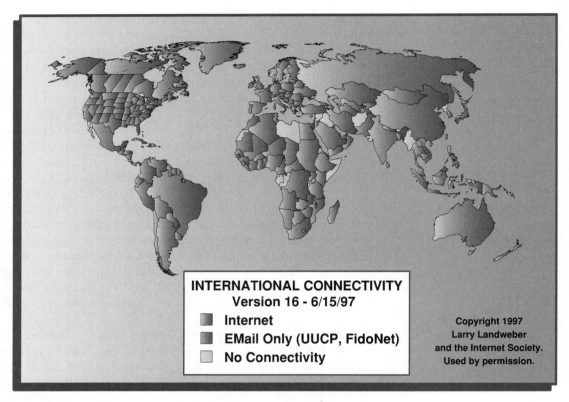

FIGURE 18.1

Internet connectivity has expanded worldwide. The map shows the extent of networks through 1997. Only a few countries remain outside its reach.

Internet connects more than 200,000 networks and more than 20 million computers as permanent nodes—and these numbers grow daily. No doubt many more desktop and laptop computers connect to it as temporary nodes, and the Internet likely has in excess of 100 million users.

From the beginning, the Internet has avoided the type of control that is exercised on networks created by private commercial interests (e.g., America OnLine and CompuServe). Veteran users would be quick to point out that the Internet fosters a democratic, open exchange of ideas and information. On the other hand, the price of an open forum is that data added to the Internet is not subject to review or approval. While there is a wealth of useful, interesting information out there, there are also many other things that we may consider frivolous, silly, preposterous, or even offensive.

This situation is changing, though. The U.S. government is currently relinquishing its involvement in the Internet to private interests. Although some express concerns that complete commercialization might diminish the virtues of the Internet as it exists today, the hope is that privatization will support the growth and needed modernization of the Information Highway.

The timeline shown in Figure 18.2 summarizes some of the more important events in the swiftly evolving story of the Internet. What's next? No one knows for sure, and the debate about the future of the Internet is vigorous and ongoing. A safe bet is that the Internet will indeed change, most likely as rapidly and *unpredictably* as it has evolved.

More Information

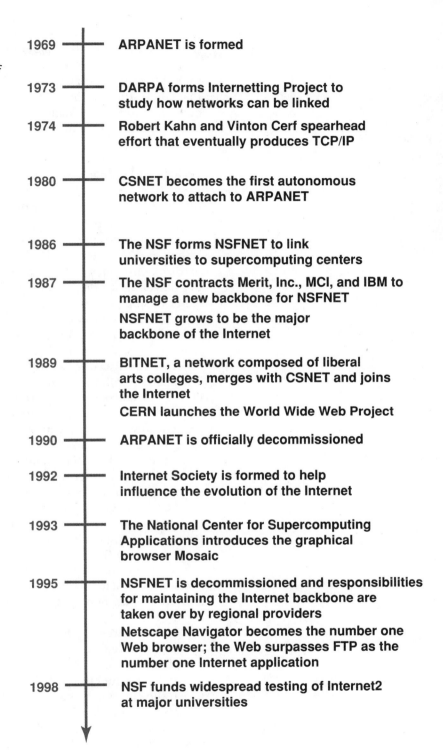

FIGURE 18.2
This timeline marks some of the more significant events in the development of the Internet.

1969 —— **ARPANET is formed**

1973 —— **DARPA forms Internetting Project to study how networks can be linked**

1974 —— **Robert Kahn and Vinton Cerf spearhead effort that eventually produces TCP/IP**

1980 —— **CSNET becomes the first autonomous network to attach to ARPANET**

1986 —— **The NSF forms NSFNET to link universities to supercomputing centers**

1987 —— **The NSF contracts Merit, Inc., MCI, and IBM to manage a new backbone for NSFNET**
NSFNET grows to be the major backbone of the Internet

1989 —— **BITNET, a network composed of liberal arts colleges, merges with CSNET and joins the Internet**
CERN launches the World Wide Web Project

1990 —— **ARPANET is officially decommissioned**

1992 —— **Internet Society is formed to help influence the evolution of the Internet**

1993 —— **The National Center for Supercomputing Applications introduces the graphical browser Mosaic**

1995 —— **NSFNET is decommissioned and responsibilities for maintaining the Internet backbone are taken over by regional providers**
Netscape Navigator becomes the number one Web browser; the Web surpasses FTP as the number one Internet application

1998 —— **NSF funds widespread testing of Internet2 at major universities**

CONNECTING THE INTERNET

The Internet, or the Net for short, is a packet switching network. But unlike other packet switching networks such as the LANs providing service at your school, the Internet is a confederation of many networks. These networks often have very different hardware, protocols, and configurations. How then is it possible for information to travel worldwide across such different network structures? The key, of course, is that networks that connect to the Internet do so because they agree to follow specific guidelines for the packaging and routing of data. In this section, we examine in more detail how this is done.

Packets and Datagrams

Information transmitted over the Internet takes the form of a sequence of packets called **datagrams.** Think of a datagram as a packet of data in a plain, brown wrapper addressed with receiver and sender. The scheme is similar to commercial parcel post. Documents must be placed in standardized envelopes or containers that are assigned numbers to identify the parcel, its sender, and its destination. Uniform containers make it easier to ship parcels. The parcel service also uses these shipping numbers for more efficient monitoring of delivery. Moving data within the Internet is organized along these same principles. This is done in a two-stage process: TCP and IP.

TCP (or **Transfer Control Protocol**) manages the packet service. It is concerned with the chunking of information into standard-sized packets for transmission. An electronic mail message, for example, may correspond to several TCP packets. Each packet must be identified and sequenced so that the receiver can reconstruct the message as intended. If packets arrive in a different order, or if any packets are lost or corrupted, it is TCP's job to handle these problems. The packets received are held and reconfigured in proper order. If any packets are missing, a signal for retransmission is sent. Other protocols can address these tasks, but TCP is the dominant one.

Once the data packets are certified for delivery, IP (or **Internet Protocol**) is responsible for addressing and routing. Each computer system that is officially part of the Internet has an IP address. These addresses consist of four numbers—each of which is less than 256. IP addresses are usually written with period separators. For example, the authors' departmental mail and Web server has 156.143.128.134 as its IP address.

Postal addressing has several components. For example, you are usually identified by name, street address, city, state, and zip code. The same is true for computers using IP addresses. The difference is that IP addresses are hierarchical. The first number denotes the network to which the computer belongs. The succeeding numbers define smaller subsets of that network. For instance, the third number might identify your campus network and the last one your machine. Once a packet has IP addresses attached for both sender and receiver, it becomes a datagram.

Routers

To see how IP manages the transmission of data across networks, let's examine how you can send an electronic mail message to a friend on another campus. The typical message is divided into smaller, more uniform packets for transmission. TCP ordinarily takes care of this. For Internet delivery, the packets must be converted to datagrams with IP addresses signifying the sender and the recipient. All this might be accomplished by your machine or with the assistance of a server on your network. At this stage, the message is packaged and ready for transmission.

Recall in the previous chapter that we defined a gateway as a hardware/software system that acts as a bridge between two networks. A gateway system repeats and translates data transmissions between networks that may have different hardware and protocols. On the Internet, the gateway systems are called **Internet routers.** See Figure 18.3.

Routers are devices that divide the responsibility of maintaining the network at different levels. Some routers review packets to make sure that the addressing is satisfactory. Other routers decide on paths for sending packets, often based on estimating current use of network carriers. Still other routers merely repeat the data along the path. The datagrams of the e-mail message are injected into this mesh of router systems and race to their addressee.

Datagrams can travel over a variety of networks and media before reaching their appointed destination. National and international providers transmit high volumes of data at high speeds over so-called backbone networks. Regional network providers route data to and from sites that they connect. Data may be transmitted over telephone lines, fiber optics, microwave relays, and dedicated high-speed transmission lines. Some data may be relayed using radio transmission by satellite. Like most aspects of the Internet, the carriers and media are greatly diversified and distributed.

Finally, the datagrams arrive at the gateway to the local network to which your friend's computer is connected. They are transmitted to a system that provides his or her mail service. This machine collects the pieces and reassembles them as a message. All of this can be achieved in seconds.

Although our example centered on an e-mail message, other Internet transmissions proceed in exactly the same manner. For example, whenever you access a Web page, the information on that page must be downloaded to your machine. The basic steps are the same:

1 Break the original information into datagrams (that is, packets and IP addresses).

2 Route the datagrams through the network.

3 Reassemble the original information at the destination.

Domain Names

Considering the tremendous number of networks and systems connected to the Internet, keeping up with the IP addresses of systems can be an incredible nightmare for humans (routers don't have similar problems). Fortunately, the organizers of the Internet adopted a more convenient (for us) method for addressing called the **Domain Name System (DNS).** Instead of IP numbers that are arranged hierarchically, a domain name is a sequence of names also separated by periods that uniquely identifies

FIGURE 18.3

A message is packaged and transmitted from the LAN to the gateway. The packets are sent by a series of routers managed by national and regional providers. The packets traverse the net arriving sometimes by various routes at the receiving LAN. The message is processed and sent to the addressee.

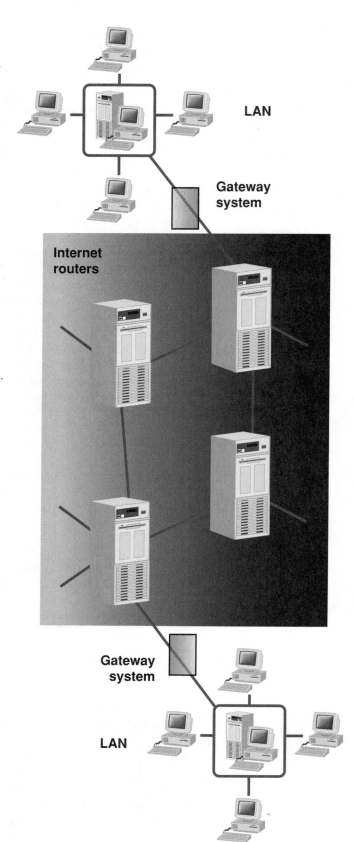

an Internet node. You've already seen some advantages of this system in your work with Web URLs. Here are some examples:

s9000.furman.edu	The name of the authors' departmental machine
brookscole.com	The system used by the publisher of this text
downwind.sprl.umich.edu	A system managed by the University of Michigan for weather forecasting
acm.org	The computer belonging to headquarters of the Association for Computing Machinery in New York

Domain names usually contain naming information about the machine and site. Consider, for example, the domain name *s9000.furman.edu.* The *s9000* is the designation for our department's Hewlett-Packard system running UNIX; *furman* is the name of the university. The *edu* is a suffix that indicates the type of institution where the node computer resides.

Domain names must be registered, but beyond that restriction the first two parts of the domain name are relatively free-form. Of course, if you tried to register your organization's name as *apple, duke, harvard,* or *ibm,* you'd be told that these names are already taken. Assuming that the names you choose don't coincide with someone's trademark or match some other organization's easily recognized abbreviation or name, there should be no problem. The suffix, however, is a different matter. As we noted, this part of the domain name indicates the type of organization where the Internet node resides; it is assigned rather than chosen by the node's owner. For example, some commonly used types are as follows:

.com	Designates a commercial firm
.edu	Designates an educational institution
.gov	Designates a government agency
.mil	Designates a military installation
.net	Designates a network service provider
.org	Designates a nonprofit organization (other than educational)

Unfortunately, there are no hard and fast rules for choosing machine and organization domain names. The owners can do just about what they please as long as the names they choose are registered to them and the suffix is correct. Consequently, not all domain names will have obvious meaning. For example, the domain name *a2i.rahul.net* doesn't convey at all that this might be a machine that provides Wall Street stock market quotes.

The system of IP addresses and domain naming conventions is currently under review. The Internet has grown too large to accommodate its users under the old system. We can expect some changes soon in the way we number and name the computers that connect to the Internet.

Even so, domain names are primarily for human consumption— for use as Web URLs, for example. Domain names still must be converted to IP addresses for delivery. Designated systems, called **domain name servers,** function as a repository of domain name information and are used by Internet nodes as a database for addresses. This relieves individual Internet nodes from the need to store this high volume of information.

Applications and Layered Architecture

Most of the communication over the Internet is managed by **user services,** programs that facilitate communication and sharing of resources between Internet nodes. In fact, a convenient point of view is that the Internet *is* a collection of services or applications that we may employ to perform desired tasks.

For example, if I wish to send an electronic mail message to you, I would use a program that allows me to create the message and address it to you much like a conventional letter. The mail program, on the other hand, handles the business of transforming the message to datagrams and routing it for proper transfer. In other words, the mail program converts the message to the type of entities that can be handled by the network layer beneath the user or application layer. The advantage for you and me is great: We are freed from the myriad details involved in managing the physical network transport. At the same time, the network is freed from the job of deciphering and packaging the datagrams it transports. Like a parcel service, everything is neatly packaged and ready to go. And, as far as transport is concerned, one package is just like another. This type of separation of duties into distinctive levels or a layered architecture is the essence of TCP/IP. Figure 18.4 illustrates.

FIGURE 18.4

User applications such as electronic mail are built on several layers of network software and services. At the user level, we are aware of sending and receiving text messages. These messages are created and handled by mail application programs on our desktop systems. These messages are packaged as mailgrams by software on our networks that support a common mail protocol. Mail, in turn, is processed as datagrams or packets for Internet delivery. TCP and IP software manage these services. Across segments of the networks, though, the packets must be physically transmitted. This is the job of the network's physical transport hardware and software.

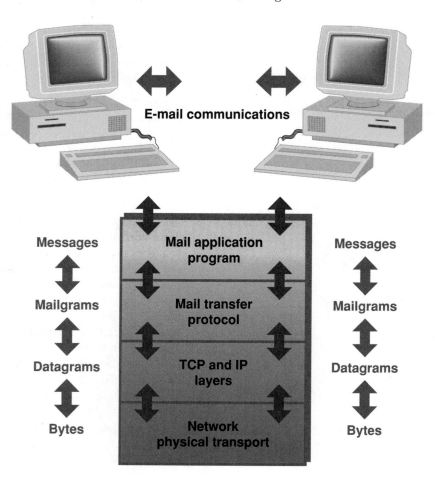

In fact, the layer structure in TCP/IP is more complicated than Figure 18.4 depicts. These details, however, are not important here. From the users' point of view, we need only be concerned with how a given network application works—the types of services that it provides and the commands needed to invoke them.

The advantages of abstraction for users are not all that a layered architecture offers. Indeed, a layered architecture separates different types of tasks and frees the network designers from having to consider all manner of details to concentrate on the task at hand. On the Internet, the applications that we use are built on top of a stable network interface. This makes it easier for the application's designer. Even if the details of how the network transport works are modified, the application program will not have to be modified to suit them. The network protocol decrees standards for their interaction. By the same token, applications can be modified and added easily as well. In short, applications are designed for "plug and play" integration with the network services underneath.

The layered architecture of TCP/IP is in many ways responsible for the amazing growth of the Internet. This separation of duties into relatively neat layers with standards for how one layer works with another allows for the greatest amount of diversity and yet a sufficient amount of uniformity at the same time. Today, the Internet connects all manner of networks built on different protocols and standards; TCP/IP has subsumed them by both its flexibility and its persistent common-denominator philosophy.

Client/Server Systems Revisited

In Chapter 3, you learned that the World Wide Web depends on the client/server model of computing. This model is, in fact, central to most Internet activity. Most of the applications or services available on the Internet (and most networks, for that matter) require the cooperation of two computer systems in concert. For example, transferring a file from one system to another depends on a local system cooperating with a remote one.

Internet applications manage this cooperation by means of **client/server communications.** Specifically, systems cooperate by way of client programs and server programs that interact with one another. Recall that a server program is a process that *provides* a specific resource. A client program, on the other hand, is a process that *requests* that resource. Usually, the server program runs continuously on a given computer system. When the user requests that a file be transferred to his or her computer, the client program that manages file transfers on the user's system issues a request to the remote computer's server program. The details of the exchange are handled between these two processes.

Client/server systems offer several distinct advantages. First, computers that act as servers are able to respond to a number of user requests, even competing ones. Of course, the computer cannot handle them all at once, but it can divide its attention among them by spawning individual server processes for each.

The client/server model also allows for **asynchronous transactions.** These occur because the timing of user requests is often sporadic and unpredictable. For example, the computer that acts as a file server cannot know in advance when requests for files will be made. Having the computer do nothing other than wait for these requests is not practical. A client/server system frees the server computer to do other things as long as it responds to client requests when they are made. See Figure 18.5.

Another advantage of the client/server model is that it can link together systems that are based on different hardware platforms. The client and server *programs* communicate while the hardware that supports that communication is invisible to them. In the case of the file transfer, for example, the client program on your computer receives and processes your commands. These are translated into the appropriate form for transmission to the server program on the other system. The server program, in turn, activates the file transfer on its system by executing the steps appropriate to its hardware. The data then is transferred over the network linking them. The hardware details for each system are irrelevant for the other.

From a practical standpoint, learning to use Internet applications means learning to use the client programs on a given system. This can simplify the details of their use considerably because client programs can be designed to fit within the context of typical applications for that system. On the other hand, if you use different systems, the look and feel of client programs can change. The bottom line then is that to exploit Internet services, you will have to adapt to the types of client systems available in your environment. In our treatment of applications, we often illustrate different client versions of the same services. You should keep in mind that the services are the same—only the client interfaces differ.

FIGURE 18.5

Client/server software distributes work between two different computer systems connected by a network. The client program requests services from the server program. The server program fulfills these requests and transmits them back to the waiting client. As shown, a server may handle more than one client. Client systems may also differ in scale and performance from the server system. The established protocol in the client/server software bridges the gap between systems.

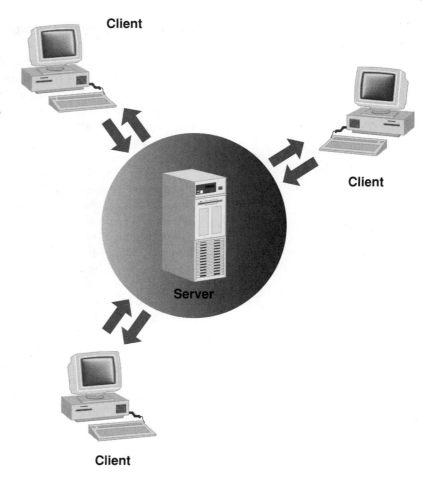

INFORMATION HIGHWAY EXPRESS LANE: INTERNET2

As you know, the Internet began as a network designed for scientific research and military communications. Of course, it has evolved to be much more widely used. As the Internet has become wildly popular and more commercialized, it has also become too crowded and unreliable for certain kinds of high-level scientific research. In fact, much of today's scientific work requires much higher bandwidths than the Internet currently provides. The Internet, once a dedicated proving ground for researchers and university professors, is now too crowded to provide the broadband capabilities required by these researchers for tomorrow's cutting-edge computer applications.

For example, modern numeric simulations of ocean currents, atmospheric models, aircraft performance, and pharmaceutical design all require considerable amounts of computing power. It is simply not cost-effective to provide such tremendous computing power locally for researchers scattered at dozens of research facilities across the country. Instead, this kind of computing power is concentrated in a few high-performance supercomputing centers sponsored by the government through the National Science Foundation or other agencies. The most practical way to give researchers access to these centers is through networking. For this research to be conducted over networks, teraflops speed (a trillion operations per second) is required; this speed is far beyond today's Internet capabilities.

The National Science Foundation (NSF) and EDUCOM, a university consortium, are working on a solution. NSF has committed $3 billion to create the underpinnings of a new network structure, often referred to as **Internet2.** A test version of this network began carrying supercomputer center traffic in April 1995 and is being run initially by MCI under a five-year contract. It is based on a new network technology called **vBNS (very high speed backbone network system).** Running at 622 Mbps (megabits per second) speed today, vBNS will eventually move data, voice, and video approximately four times faster at 2.5 Gbps (gigabits per second). For a comparison, the current ceiling on commercial Internet transmission is about 45 Mbps.

Several high-tech industry leaders, such as AT&T, Cisco, IBM, Microsoft, and Sun Microsystems, are participating in the Internet2 project, as are government agencies like the Department of Energy, NASA, and the Defense Advance Research Projects Agency (DARPA). More than 100 universities and supercomputer centers are expected to be hooked up to vBNS within the next several years.

Indications are that Internet2's evolution will follow a path similar to that of the original Internet. In particular, after subsidizing the research needed to build the network infrastructure, the government is likely to open the network up to commercial interests and the public. Thus, Internet2 will subsequently become the next-generation commercial Internet. This super-high-speed network of the future will have impressive capabilities, such as transmitting the entire *Encyclopedia Britannica* in one second, allowing doctors to perform transcontinental real-time examinations, visualizing and controlling the operations of telescopes and electron microscopes across the network in real time, or moving terabytes of satellite meteorological data across the country in a flash. Digital video delivered over the new Internet will make today's network video transmissions look like primitive relics of a distant past, and electronic videomail—composed of digital video and sound—will likely become as common as text e-mail is today.

MORE ON THE WEB AND HTML

During the first few years of its existence, the World Wide Web established its reputation as an amazing repository of hyperlinked information. Today this feature remains one of the primary reasons for the Web's popularity, but as the Web moves into its second decade, its value is also rapidly expanding into the commercial world. In Chapter 3, you learned that many companies now conduct business over the Web; indeed, some exist only as Web-based companies. The age of Web commerce is well underway, and we will see this use of the Web grow dramatically over the next few years.

One of the major issues to be resolved in Web commerce is the security of Web-based business transactions. As you learned in Chapter 16, encryption techniques have been in existence for some time to handle network transactions. The public key encryption method RSA is the most promising method for Web commerce. Public key methods have a distinct advantage over more traditional secret key systems for Web use. Secret key systems require prior coordination (exchanging of the secret keys) between the two communicating parties. Public key systems allow any two parties to communicate securely without prior coordination. When combined with digital signatures described in Chapter 16, public key systems conveniently provide for extremely secure Web (and other networking) communications.

Both commercial and informational uses of the Web are being enhanced by the increasing capabilities of HTML in designing and delivering Web documents. As you saw in Chapter 3, it is relatively easy to build your own hyperlinked Web pages. Of course, our coverage of HTML was not extensive in the brief introduction given there. In fact, HTML is a changing language, with new features and capabilities being added to it regularly. Many of these additional features are easily mastered and well worth knowing. You'll continue your exploration of HTML by learning about some of the more important additional features in this section. You will find these and others discussed in the HTML tutorial accessed from the *Exploring the Digital Domain* Web site.

Social Themes

Encryption, Internet Publishing, and National Security

Recall our discussion of the current debate about the U.S. government's policy, under the International Trafficking in Arms Regulations (ITAR), which restricts the export of secret key cryptographic applications with key lengths above 40 bits. While the government argues that these restrictions are essential to protect national security and law enforcement, privacy advocates and many in the computer hardware and software industry counter that the export controls are unduly stifling the development of better cryptographic methods domestically and internationally.

An interesting case in this debate arose in 1991 when Phil Zimmermann posted his encryption program **Pretty Good Privacy (PGP)** as freeware to Internet Usenet newsgroups. PGP is a hybrid method that combines the public key methods of RSA and International Data Encryption Algorithm (IDEA), a 128-bit secret key method developed in Switzerland. PGP was the first program to provide the average citizen with the ability to protect private communications on the Web and Internet. Not surprisingly, soon after Zimmermann posted PGP, it became a widely popular encryption program for use by private citizens worldwide.

However, to the U.S. Justice Department, PGP represented a threat to national security and law enforcement; in early 1993, the Justice Department began investigating Zimmermann for possible violations of ITAR. After a lengthy and controversial investigation, the Justice Department announced in early 1996 that it would not seek an indictment of Zimmermann. In the terse government announcement, no reasons were given for dropping the case against Zimmermann. Consequently, the question of whether posting materials on the Internet could result in prosecution for the violation of export control regulations was left unresolved. Future developers of strong cryptographic applications who publish their programs on the Internet could still face indictments from the U.S. government. As we noted in Chapter 16, the debate about the availability of encryption methods and national security will no doubt continue for years to come.

HTML: Linking External Resources

As you've seen earlier, in-line images are an integral part of many Web pages. The World Wide Web also supports a larger variety of media: images, sounds, and video. Other than in-line images, these media are not downloaded with the Web page itself. Instead, they are downloaded as separate files upon request—hence the name **external resources.** To access these resources, we link to the appropriate resource file using <A> tags analogous to how we link to other Web documents. The document user can then request the media by clicking over the appropriate hyperlink (text and/or icon). The media file is then retrieved and displayed (viewed if it is an image, played if it is a sound or video) by one of the browser's helper programs or plug-ins. The original Web page remains on screen while the resource is played.

Let's consider an example. Suppose we have an image file stored in JPEG format under the name *eagle.jpg*. If we wish to place access to this file in an HTML document, we could include the following paired tag:

<A HREF="eagle.jpg"> eagle (a JPEG image, 346K) </A>

Note that the format is identical to that used to access another HTML document. The text after the opening tag, namely *eagle (a JPEG image, 346K),* will become the hyperlink for retrieving the image when the HTML document is displayed by a browser. In other words, this text will be highlighted in a different color and/or underlined. Clicking it will initiate the retrieval and display of the external image.

In the text to be used for the link, we have identified what kind of file the resource is and how large it is. This information may save the user a lot of time; at the least, it gives the user an idea of how long it might take to download the resource. For example, if the client machine has no JPEG viewer program, downloading the file is pointless. Similarly, if the size of the file were 1.5 MB, the user may decide it is not worth the probable wait of several minutes to see the image.

Suppose that you want to offer the reader of your Web page the opportunity to view images at a much higher resolution or size than normally afforded by in-line graphics. A favored strategy for doing this would be to display thumbnail versions of these images that serve as links to the larger versions. In this way, the user can see what the image looks like and download the larger image only if he or she wants to see more. The typical form this kind of construction might take is illustrated by the following HTML paired tag:

```
<A HREF="eagle.jpg"> eagle <IMG SRC="eagle.gif">
(a JPEG image, 346K) </A>
```

Note that the thumbnail GIF image is now a part of the hyperlink to the external resource. Nested tags such as these are a powerful HTML feature, but at first they can be a bit tricky to construct, read, and interpret. Study this example code carefully to make sure you understand the role each component plays.

Sounds and video clips can be stored as external resources and then accessed in exactly the same way as the image file demonstrated in the preceding paragraph. The only difference is in the particular helper program the browser chooses to play the resource.

HTML: More about Lists

HTML defines five different types of lists. You saw, in Chapter 3, the use of an unordered (or bulleted) list. **Numbered lists** are created identically except that we use the <OL> paired tag (for ordered list) instead of the <UL> tag. In the place of bullets, the list items are identified by numbers (1, 2, 3, . . .) when displayed by a browser. Another kind of HTML list is the **menu list.** Menus are lists of items or short paragraphs with no bullets or numbers to identify them. Some browsers may indent them or format them in ways a bit different from ordinary paragraphs. Again, the syntax is identical to that of unordered lists with a <MENU> paired tag replacing the <UL> tag.

Yet another HTML list type is the **directory list.** These lists are treated like menu lists but are formatted by browsers horizontally in columns. They are particularly useful for lists containing short (perhaps one word) items that we wish to have displayed across a line. The paired tag <DIR> implements these lists. Finally, a **definition list** (also called a **glossary list**) is a list whose list items each contain two parts: a term and its definition. Rather than an <LI> tag for each list item, the term part is identified by a <DT> tag and the definition part by a <DD> tag. The entire glossary list is then bracketed by the paired tag <DL>, for definition list. Figure 18.6 illustrates a segment of HTML employing a definition list. Figure 18.7 shows how Netscape would view this segment.

HTML allows **nested lists,** in which a list can be inserted as an element in another, outside list. When viewed with a browser, the inner list is indented relative to the rest of the list. The example HTML code shown

FIGURE 18.6

The HTML segment illustrates the use of a definition or glossary list. The tags are color-coded and the code indented for better readability and clarity. Of course, such formatting is ignored by client browsers.

<DT> Red-winged Blackbird.
 <DD>The male is black except for a band of red and bright yellow near the top of the wing.
<DT> Gila Woodpecker.
 <DD>Yellow head and body, with a red cap. Gray and black wings and tail.
<DT> Kentucky Warbler.
 <DD>Yellow breasted with a black mask and crown. Soft brown wings and tail.

FIGURE 18.7

This figure shows how Netscape Communicator 4.0 displays the definition list defined by the HTML code shown in Figure 18.6. Different browsers display definition lists in similar but slightly different ways.

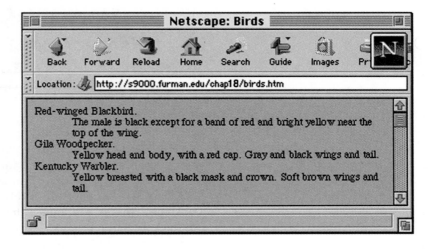

FIGURE 18.8

The HTML segment illustrates the use of nested lists. Note the use of headings in both lists—an <H1> heading for the title of the outside list, <H2> headings for the outside list items, and <H3> headings for the two inside list titles. Again, the formatting is for readability and is ignored by client browsers.

```
        <H1> Types of Dogs </H1>
<LI> <H2> Sporting Dogs </H2>
        <UL> <H3> Spaniels </H3>
        <LI> Cocker Spaniels
        <LI> Springer Spaniels
        <LI> Water Spaniels
        </UL>
        <UL> <H3> Setters </H3>
        <LI> Irish Setters
        <LI> English Setters
        </UL>
<LI> <H2> Working Dogs </H2>
```

in Figure 18.8 illustrates. Other HTML features can also be nested. Notice in the figure the use of headings in both lists—an <H1> heading for the title of the outside list, <H2> headings for the outside list items, and <H3> headings for the two inside list titles. Figure 18.9 shows how this HTML segment is displayed in Internet Explorer.

FIGURE 18.9

This figure shows how Internet Explorer 4.0 displays the nested lists defined by the HTML code shown in Figure 18.8. Netscape Communicator displays the lists in an almost identical way.

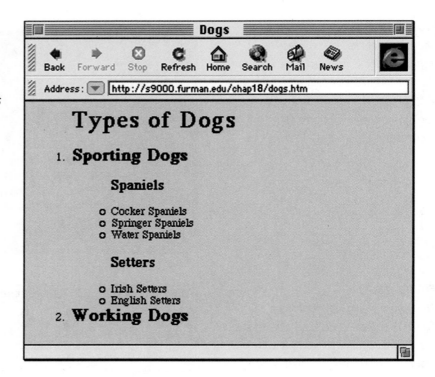

Indenting in the HTML code in Figure 18.8 has no effect on how it is displayed by a browser—it is included only to make the HTML easier to read. This is something you should consider doing with your own HTML work. Format your HTML code to make its meaning as clear as possible. This doesn't impact the browser's interpretation of the HTML in the least, but it will make it far easier to read and understand. This becomes important because it is very likely that you (or someone else) will return to the HTML to change it at some point. The easier it is to read and interpret, the easier that task will be.

HTML: Paragraph and Text Formatting

Remember that browsers generally ignore carriage returns and blank lines in HTML text. If we want such features in our text when it is displayed, we must code them in HTML. This is very easy to do. The non-paired tags <P> and <BR> provide paragraph breaks (with some spacing between paragraphs) and simple line breaks (with no additional spacing before the next line), respectively. When the <BR> tag (for line *br*eak) is placed at the end of a section of text, the next text will begin on a new line. Placing a <P> tag produces a similar effect except that it is placed at the beginning of the paragraph, and some space will be added before the paragraph text begins. (Note: In the first version of HTML, the <P> was placed after the paragraph with space added before the next paragraph. If a browser is using this older HTML paragraph mode, some differences in paragraph appearance will be noted.)

Text formatting is very limited in HTML, but some formatting, such as using bold and italic text, is allowed. The paired tags <B> and <I> are used to specify bold and italic font styles, respectively, for the text they enclose. For example, the following HTML segment:

<B>Michael Jordan</B> is one of the most popular athletes <I> ever</I>.

produces the following text when viewed by a browser:

Michael Jordan is one of the most popular athletes *ever.*

It's a good idea to sign your Web pages so that those who view the pages will know who the author is. You can include an e-mail address to make it easy for readers of your pages to contact you with suggestions, requests for permission to use your work, outpourings of lavish praise, and so on. HTML makes it easy to accomplish this using an <ADDRESS> paired tag. Of course, the text between the tags is entirely up to you. When viewed with a browser, as illustrated in Figure 18.10 in Netscape, ADDRESS text appears in italics to distinguish it from text on the Web page proper. Note also that we've included a horizontal line to precede the address message and that we've used the line break and paragraph tags to position the text on separate lines.

HTML: Tables

We have mentioned already that HTML is not designed for exacting page layouts. There are times, however, when information can best be presented in a format other than line-by-line. Information in tables is a good example. Fortunately, HTML does provide a table capability. An HTML **table** has several parts. The table caption indicates the subject matter of the table. Table headings label the rows or columns, or both, and the table cells are the individual components in which the table data resides. The entire table is enclosed by a paired <TABLE> tag in HTML. Inside these tags, the table rows are enclosed by paired <TR> tags, and table headings and table data by paired <TH> and <TD> tags, respectively. The

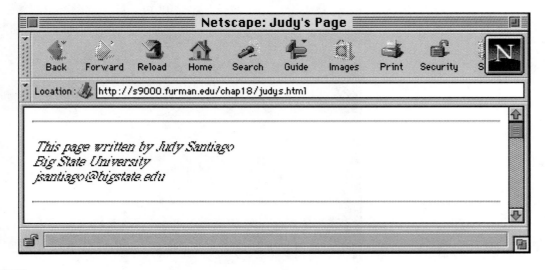

FIGURE 18.10

This is how Netscape Communicator 4.0 displays text placed inside paired ADDRESS HTML tags. Internet Explorer displays this feature in a very similar manner.

only difference in table data and table headings is that the browser will display headings in a more pronounced font (usually boldface).

Figure 18.11 illustrates HTML code for constructing a table showing the locations of various national parks. The table has a caption, a row of column headings, and four rows of actual data. The resulting table as viewed in Netscape Communicator is shown in Figure 18.12. You can nest various features within a table. For example, the data values can be hyperlinks to other information, images can be placed within the table cells, tables can be nested inside tables, and so on. With a bit of work, you can lay out some impressive arrangements using tables.

HTML: Frames

HTML **frames** divide the browser window into two or more viewing areas where different HTML documents can be displayed simultaneously and independently. You have no doubt seen frames used in many of the

FIGURE 18.11

The HTML code for constructing a table showing the locations of various national parks is shown. Note that the table has a caption, a row of column headings (marked by the <TH> tag for table heading), and four rows of actual data.

```
<HTML>

<HEAD>
    <TITLE> National Parks </TITLE>
</HEAD>

<BODY>
<P><CENTER>
<TABLE BORDER=1 WIDTH="80%" HEIGHT=80>
    <CAPTION>National Parks and Locations</CAPTION>
    <TR>
      <TH>Park</TH>
      <TH>Location</TH>
    </TR>
    <TR>
      <TD>Great Smoky Mountain</TD>
      <TD>North Carolina/Tennessee</TD>
    </TR>
    <TR>
      <TD>Glacier</TD>
      <TD>Montana</TD>
    </TR>
    <TR>
      <TD>Everglades</TD>
      <TD>Florida</TD>
    </TR>
    <TR>
      <TD>Yosemite</TD>
      <TD>California</TD>
    </TR>
</TABLE></CENTER></P>
</BODY>

</HTML>
```

FIGURE 18.12

The table defined by the HTML shown in Figure 18.11 is displayed in Netscape Communicator 4.0. The table will be displayed with only very minor differences in Internet Explorer.

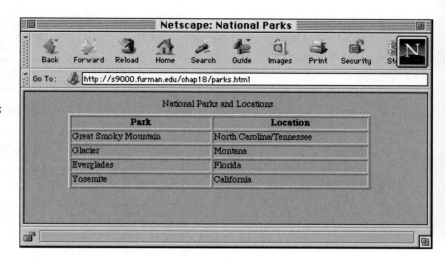

Web pages you have viewed, although you may not have realized it at the time. The most common use of frames is having two frames in the browser window to create a menu that is always present. A frame along the left edge (or right edge) of the window might contain the menu of clickable icons; this menu stays in view at all times. As its hyperlinked icons are clicked, the linked Web pages are loaded into the other frame that occupies the rest of the browser window. This arrangement provides a nice way to keep the user oriented and gives a site a continuous and consistent identity as various pages are displayed.

Of course, the browser window isn't limited to displaying just two frames; some sites display three, four, or even more frames at once. Figure 18.13 illustrates an Internet Explorer window displaying three frames. How is this window configured in HTML? The idea is a simple one. You first create a base HTML document, called the **frameset document,** which lays out the frames as you wish them to appear in the browser window. Those frames are then linked to other HTML documents. These documents are displayed in the linked frames. When you load a new page, you can specify which frame is to be used for its display.

Figure 18.14 illustrates the HTML code for constructing the frame display shown in Figure 18.13. Notice that the paired <FRAMESET> tags take the place of the paired <BODY> tags that are used in an ordinary (nonframeset) HTML document. Then each of the frames is defined by a single unpaired <FRAME> tag. Each <FRAME> tag includes an SRC (for *source*) attribute—the same attribute that links in-line images—to link the HTML document to be displayed in the frame.

The number and size of the frames to be displayed is set in the initial <FRAMESET> tag using the ROWS attribute. In our example, the value for this attribute is a triplet, *120, *, 80,* which sets the number of frames to three, with the top frame having a height of 120 pixels, the bottom frame having a height of 80 pixels, and the middle frame filling the rest of the space (the meaning of the *). The middle frame is a scrolling frame (the default), while the top and bottom frames have their SCROLLING attributes set to the value NO in their respective <FRAME> tags.

Other attributes can also be set inside the <FRAME> tags. For example, the middle <FRAME> tag includes a NAME attribute, which gives

FIGURE 18.13

Here is a Web document with three frames displayed in Internet Explorer 4.0. The top frame and bottom frames do not scroll; they hold information that will stay on the page as other pages are displayed in the middle scrolling frame.

FIGURE 18.14

This figure illustrates the HTML code for constructing the frameset document for the Web page displayed in Figure 18.13. Note that paired <FRAMESET> tags replace the usual <BODY> tags of an ordinary (nonframeset) HTML document.

```
<HTML>
<HEAD>
<TITLE> All About Dogs </TITLE>
</HEAD>

<FRAMESET ROWS="120,*,80">
    <FRAME SRC="top.htm" SCROLLING="NO">
    <FRAME SRC="main.htm" SCROLLING="YES">
    <FRAME SRC="bottom.htm" SCROLLING="NO">
</FRAMESET>
</HTML>
```

the frame itself the name *main*. This is done so that hyperlinks can name that frame as the target for a page to be retrieved. To illustrate, the hyperlink *More about bird dogs* shown in the document *top.htm*, which is displayed in the top frame, has the following underlying HTML code:

<A HREF = "birddogs.htm" TARGET = "main">
More about bird dogs. </A>

When this link is clicked, the page *birddogs.htm* will be retrieved and displayed in the middle frame (that is, the frame named *main*) in the window. The other two frames will be unaffected by the loading of this document in the middle frame.

Lab Activity

HTML frames have a number of additional features, but even this simple example should convince you that frames can add greatly to the variety of possibilities for Web site displays. Consult the *Exploring the Digital Domain* Web site to learn more about all the HTML features we have introduced in this chapter.

THE FUTURE OF THE WEB

The Web and HTML have evolved remarkably over the past decade—so much so that both are now victims of their own success. We have come to expect a great deal more from Web sites than we did just several years ago. We want increasingly dynamic content—animated graphics, interactive forms, updatable and searchable databases, more efficient and accurate search engines. And we demand more precise control and expanded capabilities when it comes to appearances—in short, we want the Web to become a full-fledged, high-end publishing environment.

Can HTML deliver these capabilities? Not in its current form. The original goals for HTML were straightforward and relatively simple: to enable Web authors to create Web pages with relative ease and distribute these pages effortlessly to an incredibly wide variety of client machines. In the early years of the Web achieving these goals was rightly considered remarkable. But now that we have come to take the Web and its ease of use for granted, we are naturally becoming more demanding and critical of the form and substance of Web site content.

HTML has been evolving since its inception. In fact, we have been through several generations of HTML standards, and the addition of such features as tables and frames has con-

tributed significantly to its current capabilities. We are poised to see the evolution of HTML give way to some more revolutionary developments.

While it is impossible to predict the exact path of these developments (as with any revolution), it is already clear that some exciting new technologies are on the horizon. Dynamic HTML (DHTML), extensible markup language (XML), Java and Visual Basic scripting, and cascading style sheets (CSS) are four such technologies already well under development. You will learn about some of these in Chapter 19.

Driven by these and other new technologies, we can expect to see some impressive changes in the Web over the next few years. Processing for animation and dynamically updated Web page content will move from the server side to the client, making it much faster and better integrated. Data validation, analysis, and visualization will occur at the client rather than requiring constant communication with a server, as is now the case. And all forms of publishing (Web, traditional paper, and CD-ROM) will be integrated using master Web documents. As much as we depend on the Web today, we will find the Web an even more indispensable component of tomorrow's computing and communication environments.

BASIC INTERNET APPLICATIONS

Apart from the World Wide Web, a significant portion of the Internet's traffic today is composed of three basic services: electronic mail (or e-mail), file transfers, and remote logins. In this section, we consider each of these services. Along with introducing the basics and terminology for these services, we address two main issues: their chief uses and how they work.

Electronic Mail

Ironically, the capability of sending electronic messages to other individuals began as a mere afterthought on the original ARPANET. ARPANET users, though, were quick to realize its potential. Within a few short years, electronic messaging made up most of its network traffic. Today, **electronic mail,** or **e-mail,** is one of the most commonly used services on the Internet. Some individuals use the Internet almost exclusively for e-mail and venture there for little else.

E-mail has both similarities and differences when compared to more conventional postal services. First, electronic messages are posted to individuals at specific addresses much like conventional mail. The address denotes the computer that the individual employs as a mail server. A mail server is like a local post office; it is a computer that sends and receives e-mail for a specific network. Like regular mail, e-mail is an example of an asynchronous transaction. The sender's system and the receiver's system do not have to be connected when the sender sends the message. The message can be delivered at a later time and placed in a buffer waiting for the receiver to open and read it when messages are delivered. Of course, the user may read messages at his or her convenience. For many, this is far superior to telephone communications that necessitate both individuals being available simultaneously. Like postal letters, too, e-mail may be saved or discarded.

Unlike conventional mail, though, e-mail is much faster—so much so that postal service is snidely called *snail mail* by veteran e-mail users. In addition to speed, e-mail offers other advantages over regular mail. For example, e-mail can be broadcast. This means that multiple copies of a given message can be sent to different parties automatically with no more effort than indicating the distribution list of addresses. By contrast, bulk postal mailings require considerable effort and expense. Replies to e-mail can be automatic, too. Most e-mail programs allow the user to reply to the sender and include part or all of the original message. On the other hand, postal letters are not entirely secure, but e-mail is even less so. Unless the message has been encoded, it could be intercepted without your knowledge. For this reason, ordinary e-mail should never be used for sensitive communications.

Figure 18.15 shows how e-mail is posted and delivered. The sender composes a message using a program on his or her computer system called a **user agent.** This is a client program that serves as an interface for processing e-mail on the user's particular computer system. The user agent then transfers the mail to the **network transport system,** which routes and forwards the message as a set of datagrams. On the Internet, the transport is done largely by chains of computers running programs

FIGURE 18.15

The sender creates a message using a mail program on his or her host computer. The local host transfers the message to a mail server that converts the message to packets for transmission across the network. At the receiving end, the remote system's mail program accepts the packets and converts them back into a mailed message.

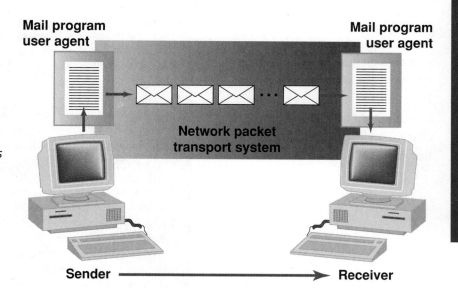

that adhere to **SMTP (simple mail transfer protocol),** which conforms to the TCP/IP protocols. The message may traverse networks that employ different protocols. Eventually, the packets arrive at the destination and are reassembled and delivered to the recipient by the user agent mail program on that system. It is very likely that upon delivery, the **post office protocol (POP)** is used if the message is sent to a single-user Windows-based computer or Macintosh.

The look and feel of e-mail for you varies greatly depending on the interface provided by your mail server's user agent. Figure 18.16 displays an e-mail message sent to us from our editor. (You can be sure that we got a lot of these while writing this book.) Our user agent is on a UNIX system and has a text-based interface.

The first portion of the message is the header. This contains information about the sender, the routing, and time of the message. The header always contains a subject line that indicates the purpose or content of the message. In this case, our editor wants to know when we will be producing. Following the header is the message body. Finally, it is customary to add an **electronic signature** to e-mail postings. Signatures are individualistic but should identify the sender and provide information on how to contact him or her. Most e-mail programs allow you to record your signature and insert it automatically into an outgoing message.

Remote Logins

One of the most remarkable services available across the Internet is that of employing your computer system, called the **local host,** to connect to and interact with a distant computer, dubbed the **remote host.** The remote host may be in the next room, across the country, or on another continent. In spite of great distances, you can perform the kinds of tasks on the remote computer that you would if it were in the same room with you. Nor does it matter whether the two systems have the same hardware and software platforms. Translation problems between different systems are solved automatically by using a remote login program. The most popular of these programs is called **telnet.** Unlike

FIGURE 18.16

The figure shows an example e-mail message. Note the three parts of the message—the header, which contains information about the sender, routing, and date and time of the message; the message body; and the electronic signature.

From Mike_Sugarman@pws.com Tues Oct 31 13:21 EST 1997
Received: from east.thomson.com by s9000.furman.edu with SMTP (1.37.109.4/15.6) id AA06881; Tues, 31 Oct 97 13:21:20 -0500
Return-Path: <Mike_Sugarman@pws.com>
Received: from SMTP.pws.com ([198.80.136.90]) by east.thomson.com with SMTP id AA13187 (5.65c/IDA-1.4.4); Tues, 31 Oct 1997 13:22:06 -0500
Received: from cc:Mail by SMTP.pws.com id AA783642363 Tues, 31 Oct 97 14:26:03 EST
Date: Mon, 30 Oct 97 14:26:03 EST
From: Mike_Sugarman@pws.com
Message-Id: <9409317836.AA783642363@SMTP.pws.com>
To: allen@s9000.furman.edu, aberneth@s9000.furman.edu
Cc: Benjamin_Steinberg%SMTP@[198.80.136.90]
Subject: How are the chapters coming?
Status: RO

Ken & Tom,

I want to remind you both that the next two chapters of the book are due by the end of this week. How are they coming along? I'll start the review process in anticipation of their arrival, so please let me know if there will be any delay. Thanks, and I hope all is well in the new building.

Mike

Michael J. Sugarman
Computer Science Editor Phone: 617/555-3333
PWS Publishing Company Fax: 617/555-6666
20 Park Plaza   E-Mail: mike_sugarman@pws.com
Boston, MA 02116

focus   NETIQUETTE

Electronic mail and message systems are becoming commonplace for both private and business use. Quite naturally, electronic mail is changing the standards of human communication in these settings. Consequently, it is important to consider both the context and side effects of this form of communicating.

Sending e-mail is as easy as having a conversation with another person. The dynamics of e-mail, however, are very different from face-to-face communication. Electronic messages lack the context that body language conveys in conversation and therefore can affect readers in unexpected ways. For these reasons, some conventions of e-mail etiquette ("netiquette") have been adopted to facilitate effective communication and minimize confusion and ill will among correspondents.

- The immediacy of e-mail has made it a more informal form of communication. In other words, senders are often writing on the fly with little thought about how the message might be interpreted. On the other hand, receivers are detached and read the communication in a context that is often more formal than intended. (They see it as written text and naturally regard it more formally.) The moral is that the sender should always consider how a message might be construed. Even informal communication should be reviewed and edited before sending. Reviewing messages for effect often means fewer misunderstandings.

- Conversational contexts often indicate when a person is relating fact, opinion, or emotion. Written messages often do not. Consequently, it is a good idea to label opinions, reactions, or emotions. In fact, there are even conventions for indicating humor or irony in an e-mail message. Emoticons (or "smileys") are text sequences used to indicate light-heartedness in the message. Here are a few examples. (Turn them sideways to see how they are intended.)

: -) traditional smile
: - D toothy grin
; -) winking
{: -) smiley with a bad toupee

In general, humor doesn't travel as well over the Net as in person. "You had to be there" is nearly an axiom for this medium. You don't have to be dead-serious all the time, but remember that what you think is funny can't be explained because you won't be there when it is read.

- E-mail messages are often written in a conversational tone. Even though we may think of them as throwaway communication, they can be quite permanent. Consider that your message can be forwarded easily to third parties, too, and that it can be called up long after you have forgotten it.

- Subject lines of a message should be descriptive of the contents of a message. Give your reader a fair chance at processing your message.

- Replies to messages are easy to do. Moreover, it is usually easy to copy the original message as part of the reply. You should exercise some restraint on copying original messages. Edit the original so that only the salient points that merit reply are included. It saves network resources and readers' time if replies are brief and to the point. Routinely copying the entire original message in a reply is construed as being inconsiderate or just plain lazy.

- Signatures should be informative. Although signatures can be individualistic, they should show some restraint. It merely wastes network resources and readers' patience to receive a signature that extends across several screens with drawings, witticisms, and whatnot. In this instance, less is more.

e-mail, telnet is a **connection-based service.** This means that at the user's level, the two systems communicating are connected continuously for a given span of time.

After establishing a connection between the local computer and the distant host, the telnet user will often be asked to login to the host machine. If you have an account on the host machine and have been given a password, you will proceed as a registered user of the host. As an example, you might telnet your mail server when you are out of town to read and send e-mail. Or you may split work time between two separate locations and use telnet to communicate from the secondary site with a host machine at your primary work site.

Even if you do not have an account on a host computer, many hosts are configured to allow you to login as a guest (sometimes referred to as an **anonymous login**). Of course, guests will generally be allowed access only to the "public" files on the host, whereas a registered user will have access to additional files and resources. Once a connection is established and the user has logged in, the two computers communicate as a terminal does to its host. In other words, your system serves as a terminal (a monitor and keyboard) that can interact with the remote host. At the conclusion of the session, the connection must be terminated to free both systems for other connections.

While connected, the local computer may request any services available on the remote system. These actions or tasks are performed on the remote computer, and the results or responses are echoed back to the local system. If the network traffic is light or the distance short, the turn-around time between local and remote hosts can be very fast. In these instances, the connection is seamless and sometimes indistinguishable from interacting with your own system. Usually, though, some transmission delays occur, so telnet sessions are somewhat slower than communicating with your own local system.

Figure 18.17 shows how telnet might be used on a local UNIX system. The commands shown in bold are typed in by the user. In this example, telnet connects to the Weather Underground server at the University of Michigan. Notice that on this particular host, *downwind.sprl.umich.edu 3000,* no login procedure is required—all information on this machine is considered public; hence, when you connect, you're automatically logged in as a guest. After a short query about the local weather, the session is terminated at the user's request.

File Transfers

One of the earliest and most enduring Internet services is that of transferring files from one system to another. When transferring files over the Internet, the remote host might be a different machine from the local host, and machines with different operating systems store and read files differently. **File transfer protocol** (or **FTP**) was devised to deal with just these problems—that is, translating documents and data from one platform to another over networks. Besides transporting files over distances, FTP service programs handle translation between systems with no fuss or bother for the user.

You must generally have an account on a system to transfer files to and from it. This would surely be true in our earlier examples where we suggested that a user might access a host machine at the office while traveling or working temporarily at a different site. The Internet also has a special class of file servers that have open file access; these are called **anonymous FTP servers.** This means that you may temporarily connect to a designated FTP host and copy files to your own machine.

FIGURE 18.17

This figure shows a typical telnet session on a local UNIX system. The commands shown in purple are typed in by the user. In this example, telnet connects to the Weather Underground server at the University of Michigan.

```
hp9K > telnet downwind.sprl.umich.edu 3000
Trying...
Connected to downwind.sprl.umich.edu.
Escape character is '^]'.

*               University of Michigan                    *
*               WEATHER UNDERGROUND                       *
* *
*         comments: ldm@cirrus.sprl.umich.edu             *
* *
* With Help from: The National Science Foundation         *
*         supported Unidata Project                       *
* University Corporation for Atmospheric Research          *
*         Boulder, Colorado 80307-3000                    *
* *
Press Return for menu, or enter 3 letter forecast city
code: GSP

Weather Conditions at 10 AM EDT on 9 OCT 98 for
Greenville, SC.
Temp(F)  Humidity(%)  Wind(mph)  Pressure(in)  Weather
─────────────────────────────────────────────────────────
  63        93%        SW at 5       29.75       Overcast

ABBEVILLE-ANDERSON-CHEROKEE-CHESTER-
LANCASTER-LAURENS-SOUTHERN GREENVILLE-
SOUTHERN OCONEE-SOUTHERN PICKENS-
SPARTANBURG-UNION-YORK-INCLUDING THE CITIES
OF...GREENVILLE...SPARTANBURG...ROCK HILL
...ANDERSON
1035 AM EDT FRI OCT 9 1998

THIS AFTERNOON...PARTLY CLOUDY WITH A CHANCE
OF SHOWERS. HIGH IN THE LOWER 70S. SOUTHWEST
WIND 10 TO 15 MPH BECOMING WEST. RAIN CHANCE
30 PERCENT. TONIGHT...MOSTLY CLEAR. LOW IN THE
UPPER 40S. WEST WIND 10 TO 15 MPH BECOMING
NORTHWEST 5 TO 10 MPH.

Press Return to continue, M to return to menu,
X to exit: X
```

Anonymous FTP servers are typically set up by those who wish to make information available freely to a large number of users without the hassle of giving each user an account on the host machine. For example, a vendor may wish to make software and documentation updates available through such a server. Freeware and shareware are typically made available through anonymous FTP servers as well. Indeed, anonymous FTP servers offer a wealth of software and information from thousands of computers around the world.

```
hp9K > ftp nic.merit.edu
Connected to nic.merit.edu
220 nic.merit.edu FTP server (Version wu-2.4H*(13)
ready.
Name (nic.merit.edu:allen): anonymous
331 Guest login ok, send your complete e-mail address as password.
Password: xxxxxxxxxxxxxxxxxxxxx
230-
230- NOTICE: This system is operated by the Merit Network, Inc.
230- You must follow the Merit Acceptable Use Policy described
230-  in /michnet/policies/acceptable.use.policy.
230-
230 Guest login ok, access restrictions apply.
Remote system type is UNIX.
Using binary mode to transfer files.
ftp> cd statistics
ftp> cd nsfnet
ftp> ls
200 PORT command successful.
150 Opening ASCII mode data connection for /bin/ls.
total 1246
-rw-r—r— 2 nic   merit    7939 Oct 30  1995 INDEX.statistics
-rw-r—r— 4 nic   merit     936 Oct 24  1995 README
-rw-r—r— 2 nic   merit    1087 May  6  1995 history.bytes
-rw-r—r— 2 nic   merit    4187 Sep 23 22:24 history.hosts
-rw-r—r— 3 nic   merit    6179 May  1  1995 nets.by.country
-rw-r—r— 2 nic   merit    3425 May  5  1995 nets.by.state
-rw-r—r— .5 conf merit    1136 Aug  4  1994 restrict.nets
-rw-r—r— .2 nic  ..merit 107105 Mar 15  1995 top10.transition.ps
-rw-r—r— .4 nic  ..merit   4717 Mar 30  1995 transition.status
226 Transfer complete.
ftp> get transition.status
200 PORT command successful.
150 Opening BINARY mode data connection for transition.status (4717 bytes).
226 Transfer complete.
4717 bytes received in 11.14 seconds (0.41 Kbytes/s)
ftp> bye
221 Goodbye.
hp9K >
```

FIGURE 18.18

The FTP program causes the two hosts to connect in a manner similar to that of a telnet session. In this case, the domain name nic.merit.edu *signifies the Merit Corporation Network Information Center. The remote host usually asks for a login. This FTP server allows for open access, and the user simply enters* anonymous *for the user identification. User entries are shown in purple.*

Figure 18.18 shows a typical session in which several text files are found on the anonymous FTP server maintained by the Merit Network Information Center in Michigan. This FTP server contains a wealth of information about NSFNET and the Internet in general. In this instance, we were looking for statistics about the shutdown of the NSFNET backbone in 1995.

In your work with the World Wide Web, you have likely seen another method for moving files across networks (at least in one direction). Web page creators can place links to files as external resources in their Web pages. Users can then download (that is, transfer) these files to their local machines. In fact, this is exactly what happens each time you view an external image, play a sound, or view a movie from a Web page. All these

FTP, TELNET, AND
MAINTAINING WEB SITES

An important use for telnet and FTP services is the creation and maintenance of Web sites. Creating a Web site consists of two general processes. First, you create the Web pages (using raw HTML or an editor) for the site and collect any required images, sounds, or other external resources. After this is completed, you must actually load all these files (pages and resources) in the appropriate directory on a Web server.

Your Web server is very likely not the same computer as the one on which you've done the Web site development. For example, you may purchase Web server space from an Internet provider or use a remote Web server provided by your university or your employer. In such cases, you must move your Web site files to the Web server computer to make them accessible across the Web. You might do this physically using floppy disks, zip disks, or portable hard drives, but the most common way to accomplish this is remotely through a file transfer program.

A number of programs—for example, Fetch (Macintosh) and WinFTP (Windows machines)—combine the services of telnet and FTP. In other words, these programs allow you to login to a remote server and then move files to a directory on that server. Figures 18.19 through 18.22 illustrate the use of WinFTP and Fetch, respectively. This is exactly the kind of activity that must be accomplished to make your Web site accessible on the World Wide Web.

FIGURE 18.19

WinFTP is a shareware program that provides FTP and telnet services on Windows-based clients. In the figure, a session is initiated with the anonymous FTP server at Microsoft.

Session Profile	
Profile Name: **Microsoft**	OK
Delete... Save New	Cancel
Host Name: ftp.microsoft.com	Advanced...
Host Type: UNIX (default)	Help
User ID: anonymous	☒ Anonymous Login
Password: allen@furman.edu	☐ Save Password
Account:	☐ Auto Save Config
Initial Directories	
Remote Host:	
Local PC:	

FIGURE 18.20

Once connected by WinFTP, the user may browse directories and select files for downloading. In this instance, a copy of the Web browser Internet Explorer is selected for transfer.

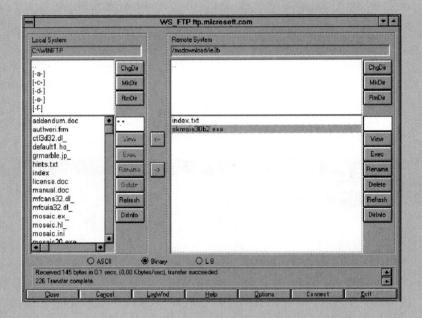

FIGURE 18.21

Fetch is a shareware program that provides FTP and telnet services on Macintosh clients. In this figure, a session is being initiated with a UNIX host.

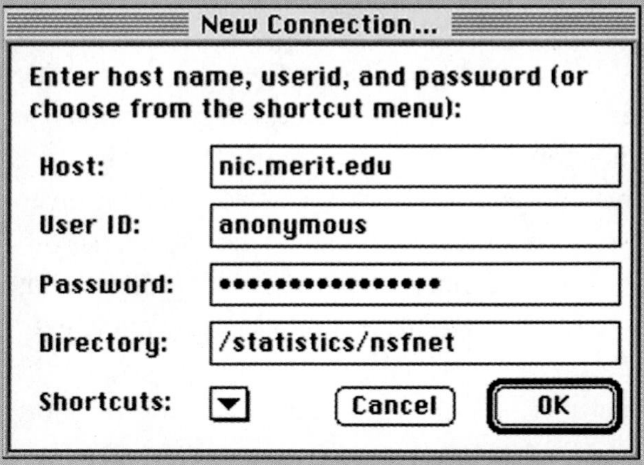

New Connection...

Enter host name, userid, and password (or choose from the shortcut menu):

Host: **nic.merit.edu**

User ID: **anonymous**

Password: ••••••••••••••••

Directory: **/statistics/nsfnet**

Shortcuts: ▼   [Cancel]   [OK]

FIGURE 18.22

Once Fetch makes the FTP connection to the remote host, the contents of directories can be easily displayed. In this figure, the contents of the nsfnet directory are displayed as folders (directories) and documents. Copying a file is a simple matter: Select the file and press the Get File button.

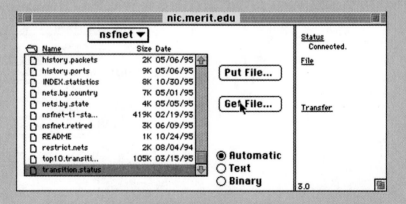

are examples of file transfers because the file is first transferred to your local machine, then viewed by a browser helper application or plug-in.

Actually, Web page designers can link to any type of file. The user can then use the link to download the file and store it on his or her hard disk. The FTP services we have described are a more general form of this specific process, allowing a user access to a great many Internet resources that have not been linked to Web pages. Using telnet and FTP together, a user can move a file from his or her disk to a remote system's disk, which is not possible using Web services alone.

SPECIALIZED APPLICATIONS ON THE INTERNET

Electronic mail, file transfers, and remote logins are the most venerable of the Internet applications. These have existed on the Internet in some form since its early days. A number of specialized applications have evolved in more recent times. These applications have helped make the Internet a more useful and interesting place to work and play.

Archie Servers

As you know from your work on the Web, the wealth of information available there can sometimes seem overwhelming. In fact, without the availability of Web search engines like Yahoo!, Excite, Infoseek, and others, finding information on the Web whose location you don't already know would be difficult. Because the Internet is an even larger repository of information (including the Web as a subset), locating information on it can be an even bigger challenge.

For example, both telnet and FTP require that the user have precise knowledge of the names and whereabouts of computers and files. How do we find the location of information we don't already know about? As in the case of the Web, a number of services have been created that aid the user in searching for information on the Internet. Several of these services have become very popular. We describe briefly two of these: archie and gopher servers. These are certainly not all of the tools available, but they are representative of the types and styles of informational tools available on the Internet.

Anonymous FTP potentially offers an inestimable amount of data. To take advantage of it, you must know precisely where that information resides. Specifically, you must know on what machine it is stored and what name is used to identify it. Suppose, however, that you know the latter, but not the former—archie servers can help.

An **archie server** is a host on the Internet that contains an up-to-date listing of the directory contents of FTP servers registered with it. In other words, archie servers act like card catalogs for anonymous FTP servers on the Internet—where the FTP server file names play the role of book titles. McGill University in Canada developed the idea, and its popularity has spread worldwide. We can make use of such servers in several ways. You might employ telnet to login to the server and run the utility program archie to search its database for a keyword.

You can also run an archie client program from your own system, which often simplifies interaction with the server. You can even send mail to the archie server. It will process your request and mail back the results.

The archie system database is huge, with millions of anonymous FTP server file names in it. We don't always know the exact name of the file we're seeking. For example, suppose we know there's a freeware program available to create our own wallpaper backgrounds for our computer desktop, but we're not sure of its exact name. Even assuming that its developer named it reasonably, it could be named *wallpaper*, *WallPaper*, *WALLPAPER*, *wpaper*, *wallp*, *wp*, *WP*, or a number of other possibilities. Even with the archie database available, finding the correct FTP file could be a challenge.

The archie program can help us here, too. To use it, we must supply it with a **search string,** that is, the string of characters we're looking for in an anonymous FTP server file name. We can ask the archie program to use several options as it performs its search. For example, we can ask it to look only for an exact match, or we can instruct it to ignore the case of characters in its search or to consider the search string as a possible substring within the file name, and so on. Trying these options, we have a reasonable shot at finding the file we want.

Archie services can also be engaged on the World Wide Web. Some Web sites maintain a form-based client program called ArchiePlex. To use ArchiePlex, a user completes a form and submits it to the Web site. The Web server, in turn, contacts an archie server and returns its results in the form of another Web page with built-in links to the appropriate anonymous FTP servers. Figures 18.23 and 18.24 illustrate the process.

Gopher Servers

An obstacle for early Internet access was that information was not offered in a convenient form for users. Documents could be downloaded by FTP for reading, but the user had to know precisely what he or she was looking for and where it was located on that system to have any success. Traversing directories and decoding cryptic file names required skill and patience. The University of Minnesota created a service to help overcome these difficulties. Because the purpose of the service is to "go for" and return information about the Internet's resources, and because the university's sports teams are known as the Golden Gophers, it wasn't too much of a stretch when the service was named *gopher.* The popularity of so-called gopher servers was instantaneous.

A **gopher server** organizes information as a hierarchical structure of full-page text menus. Menus are linked either to other menus or directly to documents. The user traverses the menu structure until he or she finds the desired topic and document. Documents can be viewed for reading or copied and sent to the user by e-mail. Notice how this organization differs from the simpler file name database used by archie servers. With gopher servers, you actually search for the topic or subject of your inquiry, not just the file name.

Gopher servers not only offer convenience in navigating a particular system, but they also provide automatic connections to other systems that contain related information. The user travels almost transparently

FIGURE 18.23

ArchiePlex is a Web version of archie. The user completes a form and transmits it to the Web site. The Web server contacts the archie server and returns its results in the form of another page. In this instance, the ArchiePlex at NASA is used to search for an FTP file name containing "baseball." The archie server at Rutgers University is selected from a list of available systems in the United States.

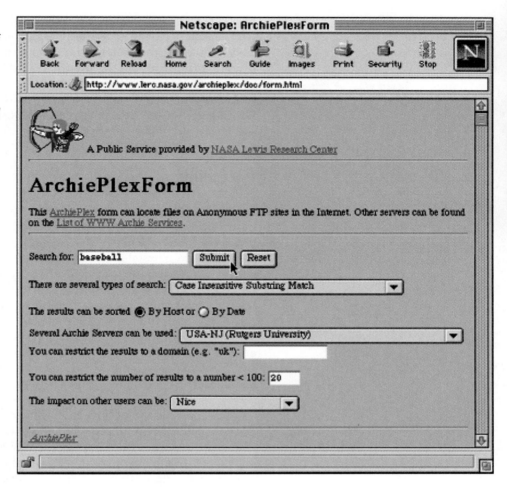

FIGURE 18.24

The results from the Rutgers archie server are displayed as links on a subsequent page. The user can download any of these files simply by clicking on the hyperlink.

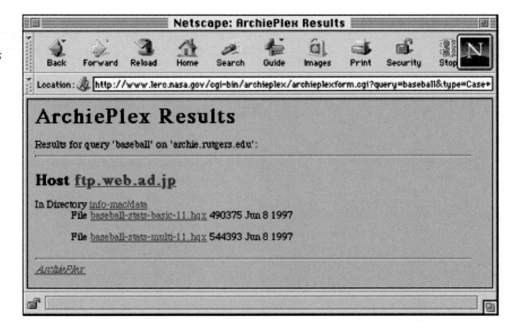

to other gopher servers linked to the original one. A trip might take us from the host machine to Minnesota, from Minnesota to Hawaii, and back. Gopher servers offer a simple and yet powerful interface for delivering information on the Internet.

Today, the World Wide Web and its associated search engines have supplanted gopher as the most user-friendly application for retrieving information on the Internet. Nonetheless, a great deal of information still resides on gopher servers.

Chat Facilities

A **chat facility** is a connection-based service that permits a group of individuals to have conversations over the Internet. Like e-mail, the messages are text based; unlike e-mail, they take place in real time. Two or more users share a channel on which they conduct a public conversation—usually restricted to a specific topic or issue. The messages are shared by all those who join the chat channel. It is also possible to have private conversations between just two users.

To use chat, you must have either a chat client program or access to a server that provides the facility. Chat clients are available for most operating systems. Armed with a client program, you can then communicate with chat servers on the Internet. These are computer systems that maintain dedicated channels for chatting. Some Web sites support chat servers as well. To use these, you don't need a chat client program.

The most famous of the chat facilities is **Internet Relay Chat (IRC),** developed for UNIX systems by Jarkko Oikarinen in 1988. IRC first gained fame during the Persian Gulf War in 1991. Users shared information and instantaneous updates about the progress of the war. During the Moscow coup in 1993, IRC users on the scene provided continuous information on the situation when conventional news services were unable to get reports out. Hundreds of IRC channels on numerous subjects are hosted on IRC servers around the world. After joining a channel, your messages are broadcast to everyone listening to that channel. Some IRC client programs provide a graphical interface for all functions, including logging on to popular servers and obtaining a list of their active channels.

MUDs and MOOs

A natural extension of chat are the simulation games called MUDs and MOOs. **MUD** stands for **multiple-user dialogue** (or **multiuser dungeon**—depending on whom you consult). These are simulation games involving a number of users simultaneously connected over the network. The earliest MUDs actually predate the Internet (and chat), though today they are a mainstay of the Net. A **MOO** (for **MUD object-oriented**) is a more advanced form that has some special features.

In a typical MUD or MOO, the participants connect to a server via telnet or some other client program. The server maintains an environment in which the participants may navigate and interact. Usually, the environment is described as a collection of rooms each with a setting, features, and sometimes objects. Thus, a MUD or MOO can be thought of as a virtual reality. Most MUDs are text based, but some Web-based MOOs support multimedia.

When you log on to a MUD or MOO, you arrive in a specific room where several others may be present. Your entry is announced; at that point, you may engage in conversation with the others there. Like chat, your conversations may be public or private. In keeping with the theme or setting of the MUD or MOO, however, you are expected to conform to the rules of the game. In most cases, you play a role. MUDs are often fantasy or adventure games in which the players have a quest to achieve. You may move about the virtual space, going from place to place. The MUD or MOO server keeps track of your whereabouts and whom you might encounter. Web-based MOOs coordinate a telnet session for interacting with the participants while simultaneously switching pages in your browser to show you different scenes.

The users in MUDs or MOOs often create elaborate personas or alter egos for participating in them. Gender swapping, for example, is commonplace. Sometimes, a player in a MUD or MOO might not even be a person at all! (See Chapter 20 for an example of a computer program, called Julia, that fooled a number of MUD players.) Users of Web-based MOOs often select or create an image, called an **avatar,** to represent themselves in the MOO. (Avatar is a Sanskrit word that means the incarnation of a god on earth.)

The popularity of MUDs or MOOs has spawned the creation of servers dedicated to educational and professional activities. These are designed for sharing information about some common topic of interest. MediaMOO, for example, is maintained by the MIT Media Lab for individuals interested in media research.

Archie, gopher, chat, MOOs, and MUDs are just samples of the wealth of services and materials on the Internet. Earlier, of course, you were introduced to the Web, another substantial resource on the Internet. The Internet, like the ocean, is an almost inexhaustible source of useful things (in this instance, information and programs). But, like the ocean, it can be impenetrable and forbidding. Armed with the right tools, you can catch many of its riches.

More Information

S U M M A R Y

The Internet is a collection of diverse computer networks that span the globe. The Internet evolved from several U.S. government projects in the late 1960s and early 1970s focused on providing a robust network for the U.S. military and scientific research communities. Today it is a loosely coupled collection of distributed, open networks that has no real center or single governing body. Networks are added to its topography freely, and the number of nodes connected to it expands daily. International participation is widespread and growing, and it is estimated that the Internet has well over 100 million users.

The Internet is a packet switching network whose basic operation is conducted under the TCP/IP protocol for data communications across networks, although other protocols on smaller connected networks coexist with it. Each computer system that is officially part of the Internet has a unique IP address and domain name. Domain names are for human consumption (as in URLs) and must be converted to IP addresses for network use. Designated systems, called domain name servers, perform this function. Messages are transferred across the Internet by routers employing IP addresses. Routers divide the responsibility of maintaining the network at different levels. Some routers review packets for addressing correctness. Other routers decide on paths for sending packets, while others merely repeat the data along the path.

The TCP/IP protocol employs a layered architecture, separating tasks into relatively distinct layers with standards on how a layer interacts with the ones immediately above and below it in the layered hierarchy. This layered architecture frees network software and hardware designers from having to consider lower-level details, allowing them to concentrate more fully on the task at hand.

Internet applications are generally built on the client/server computing model. Usually, server programs run continuously on Internet server computer systems and respond when client programs make requests of them. The details of any data exchange are handled between such communicating client/server programs. From a practical standpoint, learning to use Internet applications means learning to use the client programs available to your system.

Since 1990, the Internet has experienced incredible growth, fueled by the introduction of the World Wide Web. The Web began as a repository of information, but as it moves into its second decade, its value is rapidly expanding into the commercial world. Many companies now conduct business over the Web, and some exist only as Web-based companies. Web pages are constructed in the language HTML, which continues to grow and change in response to the evolving needs for better Web authoring techniques and capabilities.

Apart from the Web, much of the Internet's traffic today is composed of three basic services: electronic mail (or e-mail), file transfers, and remote logins. Using remote login capabilities, your computer system, called the local host, can connect to and interact with a distant computer, dubbed the remote host. Translation problems between different computer systems are solved automatically by connection-based services like telnet. When transferring files over the Internet, the remote host might be a different kind of machine from the local host. File transfer protocol (or FTP) was devised to deal with the problems that arise translating documents and data from one platform to another over networks.

Other services also have important uses on the Internet. Archie servers, gopher servers, and chat, MOO, and MUD facilities are just a sample of the wealth of these additional services and materials on the Internet. Archie and gopher servers help you locate information of the Internet; chat, MUD, and MOO facilities enable innovative communication over the Internet.

More particularly, an archie server contains an up-to-date listing of the directory contents of registered FTP servers. Gopher servers organize information as a hierarchical structure of full-page text menus. Chat facilities are connection-based services that permit a group of individuals to have conversations over the Internet. MUD (multi-user dialogue) and MOO (MUD object-oriented) programs are natural extensions of chat facilities. They are simulation games involving a number of users simultaneously connected over the network.

PROJECTS

1 What is the current size of the Internet? How many networks are connected? What is the estimated number of permanent nodes (computers continuously connected)? Estimated number of users? Consult the statistics available from the Internet Society to find out. (You can find a link to the Internet Society on the project page for this chapter.)

2 Do some research to find out the current status of the Internet2 project. Bookmark any informative Web sites you find for use in project 4. How many universities are currently attached to a vBNS network? Is your college or university attached? Does it have plans or aspirations to obtain a connection?

3 Add some external resources to your own Web page (created in Chapter 3). Scan some pictures and save them in JPEG format. Insert links that include small thumbnail GIF versions of these images that will load and display the full JPEG images when clicked. Record some sounds (maybe a welcome message and some short tunes) and provide links to play these as well.

4 Design and create a Web page that will serve as an informative introduction to the Internet2 project. Organize your page using at least two frames. One of the frames (call it the main frame) should include an introductory essay on Internet2 and the other frame should display a menu of links to other sites about Internet2. Include at least one table with some information in your essay. When one of the menu links is clicked, the referenced page should load in the main frame, and the menu frame should remain displayed. Use the links you bookmarked in project 2.

5 Do some research to find out more about the Pretty Good Privacy (PGP) encryption method and the U.S. Justice Department's controversial investigation of its author, Phil Zimmermann. Write a brief report on your findings.

6 Do a Web search for the program ArchiePlex. Experiment with using one or more of the client programs you discover.

Projects

Key Terms

anonymous FTP server	definition list	glossary list
anonymous login	directory list	gopher server
archie server	domain name server	Information Highway
ARPANET	domain name system (DNS)	Internet
asynchronous transactions	electronic mail (e-mail)	Internet protocol (IP)
avatar	electronic signature	Internet relay chat (IRC)
chat facility	external resource	Internet routers (gateways)
client/server communications	file transfer protocol (FTP)	Internet2
connection-based service	frame (HTML)	local host
datagram	frameset document	menu list

MUD object-oriented (MOO)	Pretty Good Privacy (PGP)	transfer control protocol (TCP)
multiple-user dialogue,	encryption system	user agent
multiuser dungeon (MUD)	remote host	user services
nested lists	search string	very high speed backbone
network transport system	simple mail transfer protocol	network system (vBNS)
numbered list	(SMTP)	
open system	table (HTML)	
post office protocol (POP)	telnet	

QUESTIONS FOR REVIEW

1 Give a brief overview of the history of the Internet.

2 What is a packet switching network?

3 The Internet has been described as a packet switching, loosely coupled, distributed network of networks. Explain what this means.

4 What does TCP/IP stand for? What role does TCP/IP play in the functioning of the Internet?

5 What is a datagram? How do TCP and IP handle datagrams?

6 What is an IP address? How are domain names related to IP addresses?

7 How are datagrams routed over the Internet?

8 What does it mean when we say that TCP/IP is an open system? Why is this an advantage for its use with the Internet?

9 What are asynchronous transactions? Why are these important for Internet communications?

10 Explain how the client/server communication process is organized. What are the advantages of this approach?

11 Give a brief overview of the Internet2 project. What advantages does it offer over the current Internet?

12 What does PGP stand for? How is it relevant for the Internet and Web?

13 Describe the difference between internal and external images in HTML documents.

14 What are frames? How are they generally used in Web page design?

15 Explain how frames are implemented in HTML. In other words, give a quick description of how you build Web pages employing frames.

16 Summarize the different kinds of lists that HTML supports and detail how they differ.

17 What kinds of text formatting features are available in HTML?

18 Identify some of the characteristics and capabilities that we're likely to see in the Web of the future.

19 How does electronic mail compare with other forms of communication like postal mail and telephone service?

20 What is telnet? What is it used for?

21 What is FTP? What is it used for?

22 Explain Internet chat facilities.

23 What are MUDs and MOOs? How do they compare with chat facilities?

24 What are archie servers and what is their role on the Internet?

25 What are gopher servers and what is their role on the Internet? How do they differ from archie servers?

PART 6

THE BIGGER DIGITAL PICTURE

Vasily Kandinsky, *Tension in Red*, 1926. Solomon R. Guggenheim Museum

We have devoted much of the previous material in this text to explaining the underlying concepts and techniques for using a computer to capture and create, and to edit and distribute, information across networks employing a variety of media. You have learned how to convert numbers, text, sound, graphical objects, images, and video to the digital domain and how these representations can be transmitted and otherwise manipulated within that domain. Of course, the term *multimedia computing* derives from this rich variety of media that the computer is able to manage effectively.

The true power of multimedia computing is realized only when elements from various media are combined and distributed in innovative, interesting, entertaining, and informative ways. The existence of computer hardware and software capable of combining such elements and of networks capable of distributing these integrated products will be a major driving force for computing in the 21st century.

This chapter is devoted to the exploration of these integrative capabilities and their impact on the kinds of documents and products we can produce. We will survey some of the major tools and techniques for combining and distributing multimedia products.

OBJECTIVES

- *A brief history of the evolution of multimedia integration*

- *Integrating multimedia elements in presentation software*

- *Creating fully interactive multimedia products using authoring software*

- *Integrating multimedia elements using emerging Web capabilities*

- *Product life cycle for multimedia productions*

CHAPTER 19

INTEGRATING AND DELIVERING MULTIMEDIA

Vasily Kandinsky, *Tension in Red*, 1926. Solomon R. Guggenheim Museum

A SHORT HISTORY OF MULTIMEDIA INTEGRATION

You will recall from Chapter 1 that we define **multimedia** as the integration of various informational media such as text, graphics, sound, and images into a single digital document. The modern electronic digital computer system can easily combine and deliver these seemingly diverse forms of information because it manipulates them in common as a stream of binary numbers. This underlying digital representation also means that computers may organize and process multimedia documents using methods similar to those employed for documents containing only one form of information. For example, transmitting an electronic mail document containing text, pictures, and sound poses no more challenge than transmitting one composed entirely of text. Multimedia e-mail files are usually larger than ordinary text files, but the methods used to transmit them over data communications networks are still the same. Of course, the receiving system must be capable of interpreting and re-assembling the multimedia components to take advantage of this richer, more interesting form of expression.

The popularity of multimedia computing is a recent phenomenon, but like most other trends in computing, it has emerged from earlier developments that have shaped it in significant ways. In this section, we treat some of the historical factors that have influenced the way in which multimedia computing is employed today.

Although hypertext technology is not essential for multimedia computing, it is a common method for organizing and presenting multimedia information. For this reason, a brief treatment of it is useful for any discussion of multimedia computing. **Hypertext technology** allows the creation of electronic documents with built-in links to additional information that may serve as background, cross-referenced sources, more detailed information on a given topic, and so on. This cross-referenced material usually contains a variety of media that can be consulted in a nonsequential or nonlinear manner at the reader's discretion and with a minimum of effort. Compare hypertext or hypermedia documents to conventional cross-referential works such as printed encyclopedias, indices, and the like. Consulting a cross-reference in an encyclopedia, for example, requires finding the correct volume and locating the reference. On the other hand, a hypertext reference is automatically fetched when selected. In addition, you may retrace a sequence of hyperlinks backwards and forwards with ease.

Hardware/software systems employing hypertext have become commonplace only within the past decade or so. For instance, you have seen how significant hypertext is for the effectiveness of the World Wide Web. Interestingly, however, the concepts underlying hypertext first appeared in an article published by Presidential Science Advisor Vannevar Bush in 1945. Bush described a machine called a **memex,** which was to use microfilm and several viewing screens to create a semi-automated system for collecting and researching scientific literature. Links to related information were to be implemented using photocell-readable dot codes. In 1945 the electronic computer was still in its developmental stage, and so Bush could not have anticipated that the computer would supply an ideal platform for the actual realization of his memex concept. In fact, his ideas were so far ahead of his times that the machine he envisioned was never built.

Nearly twenty years later, two men, **Douglas Engelbart,** at Stanford Research Institute, and **Ted Nelson,** at Brown University, took up the exploration of the idea of combining hypertext with computing. Engelbart invented the computer mouse in connection with his work on hypertext systems, and Nelson is credited with coining the term "hypertext." From the 1960s to the mid-1980s, the development of hypertext technology proceeded steadily, but these systems typically required specialized hardware and software. In the late 1980s, consumer versions of hypertext systems were introduced. These were designed for a mass market that depended on inexpensive desktop computer systems.

HyperCard, developed by Apple Computer and introduced in 1987, was the first popular commercial hypertext system. HyperCard was also notable as the first consumer software application for authoring as well as presenting hypertext multimedia materials. Computer users could employ HyperCard to organize, assemble, and present their own multimedia documents rather than depending on published materials exclusively. HyperCard organizes information as a series of "cards." Each card is basically a screenful of information; groups of related cards can be collected into HyperCard "stacks." It is a simple matter to combine information in a variety of media on many different cards and then provide an "index" or home card with built-in links to access any of the desired information immediately.

From simple HyperCard stacks, it is but a short step to create extensive multimedia information storehouses with hypertext links as the primary access method. In fact, such products became the flagship applications of the early multimedia era (early 1990s); the most notable instances of this genre are the CD-ROM multimedia encyclopedias. You have probably used such a product yourself.

Multimedia encyclopedias combine database and hypertext methods to create a richer, more varied cross-referential resource. Perhaps the most impressive and important characteristic of the CD-ROM encyclopedias is the flexible and user-friendly way in which their information can be searched and displayed. Every user will have his or her own informational needs when using one of these products. Hence, efficient search algorithms are essential for a successful encyclopedia.

Browsing is another popular use for these products. These reference works usually are equipped with excellent tools for browsing at random through the material, including following links from one article to another and accessing a list of all the stored images, sounds, or movies, and so on. You have already seen that searching, sorting, and displaying information is a database system's primary function. It is no surprise then that an electronic encyclopedia on CD-ROM is organized using a database format. More specialized multimedia reference materials also play an important role in education and research. Figures 19.1 and 19.2 illustrate a widely used educational multimedia reference database.

Multimedia encyclopedias and reference databases are two instances of commercially prepared and distributed multimedia information. Many other titles on a variety of subjects are available under the

FIGURE 19.1

The ADAM (Animated Dissection of Anatomy for Medicine) multimedia reference database allows a user to dissect nearly 400 layers of the human anatomy. This reference database is widely used in education for medicine and the biological sciences.

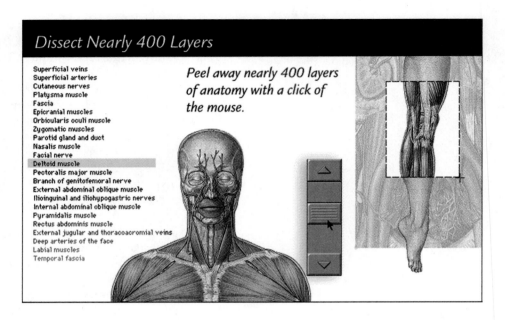

FIGURE 19.2

The ADAM interface provides different views and access to additional information about each topic. Note the buttons for conducting searches in the lower right portion of the screen.

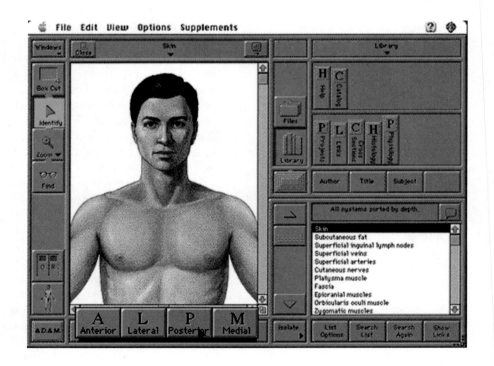

category of **edutainment**. Figure 19.3 offers another example. Presenting multimedia information, though, is not limited to professional publishing enterprises. Today anyone with access to a desktop computer can be a multimedia producer. You have already learned how HTML exploits the powerful multimedia and hypertext capabilities of browser software. And as you will see, other desktop software programs can expand the average user's ability to produce high-quality multimedia products for a variety of distribution venues.

FIGURE 19.3

The CD-ROM book Passage to Vietnam, *published by Against All Odds/Interval Research, is an award-winning multimedia presentation that demonstrates the expressive power of the medium. It can be explored and appreciated from several points of view. A group of accomplished photographers and photojournalists were contracted to visit and photograph their impressions of Vietnam decades after the U.S. involvement in their civil war. As a collection of photo essays, it portrays the Vietnamese country and people with interesting and powerful visuals accompanied by music and sounds. On the other hand, the publishers also reveal their decisions about which photographs were included in the final product. Thus, the viewer gets an inside look at photocriticism and editing through these video segments. The materials may also be arranged and toured much like a guidebook featuring places and subjects about the country. All of this is packaged with an easy-to-use interface for navigating the materials.*

Shown here are Mike Davis of National Geographic *and Michelle McNally of* Fortune *magazine discussing their choices for photographs depicting life along the rivers of Vietnam.*

MULTIMEDIA COMPOSITION SOFTWARE

Since the early 1990s, a number of software products have been introduced that facilitate desktop production of multimedia documents. These application programs are typically used to combine the resources of text, graphics, animation, video, music, narration, and sound effects.

Usually these resources have been created using software designed specifically for managing the appropriate media domain. The primary role of multimedia production programs is to assemble and combine these resources in useful and effective ways.

For example, sound files digitized and edited using SoundEdit or Sound Forge and images scanned on a flatbed scanner and edited in PhotoShop are stored in separate files and behave as separate entities. We might play the digitized sound using SoundEdit or Sound Forge and view the images in PhotoShop, but these applications will not allow us to enhance the images with the sound as background music. To accomplish this, we need an application especially designed to integrate and coordinate these resources. **Multimedia composition software** is designed for just such integrative purposes. These applications allow us to incorporate elements of different media and origin into a common digital environment.

Multimedia composition software has certain common characteristics and capabilities. These applications are capable of importing digitized files of various kinds and formats, integrating these disparate resources into a coherent product, then saving and exporting the final product in a form that is easily transferable to other computers for playback. In this section, multimedia composition applications PowerPoint and Astound illustrate the general techniques employed by software of this genre. Each of these programs is available in both Windows and Macintosh versions.

These programs have a great deal in common, even though the specific details of how they function vary. In particular, they employ a common paradigm or motif for organizing and integrating multimedia resources. Most other multimedia composition software programs have adopted this paradigm, too, so many of the techniques you will see demonstrated here are applicable to them as well. Although each program may have its own unique ways to accomplish specific tasks, the general organization of the overall job is remarkably similar.

The metaphor used by both Astound and PowerPoint, for example, is that of an electronic slide show. A slide show consists of a series of "slides"—again, the content of a single video display screen. The slide metaphor is drawn from typical business and professional presentations consisting of 35mm slides shown using a slide projector or transparencies shown with an overhead projector.

Each electronic slide is essentially a page—very similar to an overhead transparency or a true 35mm slide—but with a very important difference. The computerized slides can contain sounds, animations, and movies in addition to the text and graphics information associated with traditional overheads or 35mm slides.

Often, slide shows are designed and organized as an accompaniment for a speaker making a presentation to an audience. Because of this common use, such programs are often referred to as **multimedia presentation software.** Although this is perhaps their most common use, these programs can also be employed to produce stand-alone slide shows that are designed to be displayed and viewed without a speaker present. In some instances, they may be designed to be operated by the computer user as he or she views the slide show. Some slide shows, however, may execute automatically, converting the computer into an automated kiosk for providing information to visitors who pass by its display.

Another common feature of multimedia composition software is the option of creating a document from scratch or by using a predefined template. See Figure 19.4. Templates allow you to create documents

FIGURE 19.4

(a) Astound provides an extensive collection of templates, allowing a user to create a presentation with a minimum of effort. Templates are available for both standard presentations and Web pages. Here the user picks a template that is previewed for quick inspection.

(b) PowerPoint too provides the choice of using predefined templates. (c) Both Astound and PowerPoint also offer shortcuts and assistance in preparing a presentation from scratch. Shown here is PowerPoint's AutoContent Wizard, which allows you to tailor a template for a particular kind of presentation with appropriate information for headers and footers being entered automatically.

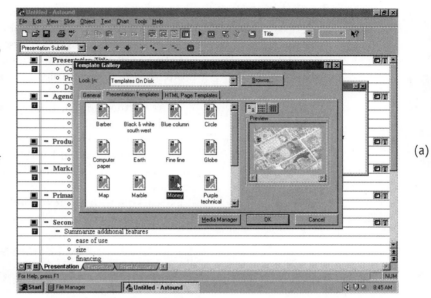
(a)

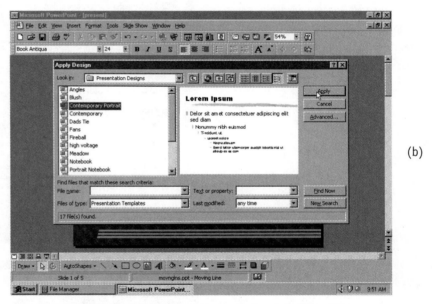
(b)

(c)

more quickly, concentrating on the information that you intend to present rather than fussing with the details of the presentation's interface design and aesthetics. Of course, there are times when you might want control over the interface design. In these instances, you may create your own design completely from scratch or assemble it using ready-made components. The choice is yours.

As we mentioned, the typical multimedia composition software allows for (we could say, is *designed for*) the integration of elements drawn from various media. Let's take a look at how these various elements are put together in Astound and PowerPoint. Their interfaces are organized to allow the author to work in one of several modes: the outline, slide, or global views.

Working with the text content of the document, for example, is easier when done in the outline mode. As shown in Figure 19.5, the text for

FIGURE 19.5

(a) The outline view for PowerPoint permits entering the titles for slides and their text content in a direct manner. (b) Astound, too, offers similar outline features, as shown here.

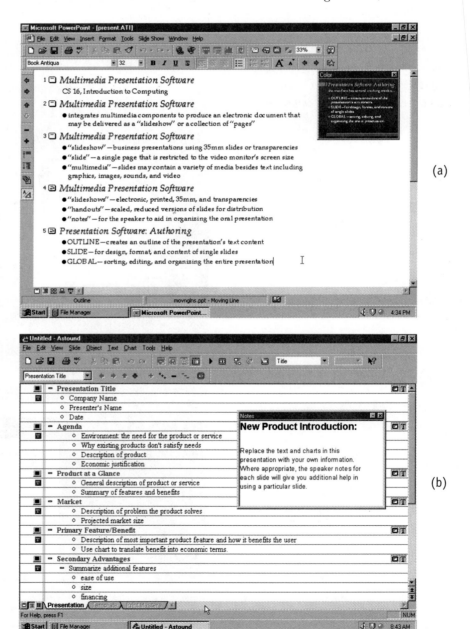

(a)

(b)

each slide is displayed as an outline heading with subordinate ideas listed as bulleted points. In this mode, you may use standard word processing tools to create and edit text.

On the other hand, you may wish to work with the design and layout of an individual slide. In the slide mode, the screen converts to a picture of the slide's contents, including text and graphics. Text boxes may be repositioned and edited in this mode. See Figure 19.6. Picture elements, whether clip art or scanned images, are generally prepared outside Astound or PowerPoint and then imported. See Figure 19.7.

Special text effects such as animation are also created automatically in both Astound and PowerPoint. In Figure 19.8, the bulleted points are animated using the Custom Animation tool in PowerPoint. In this instance, each item is set to be revealed one by one on the screen as the user clicks the mouse button. Special transition effects such as dissolves can be tested before deciding on the final settings.

Sometimes you require working with groups of slides or the entire presentation. In the global view, the slides are shown as thumbnails or miniaturized versions, which may be manipulated individually or in groups. For example, it is a simple matter to change the sequence of slides by repositioning them. See Figure 19.9. Slides may be cut, copied, and pasted. In PowerPoint, for example, slide transitions or special visual effects may be fixed to one or more slides in this mode, as shown in Figure 19.10.

Most multimedia composition software is able to incorporate a variety of media. Astound, for instance, has some elementary drawing capabilities within the program itself. Other applications, such as PowerPoint, offer more drawing tools, but in general you will be better off using another program especially dedicated and designed for drawing and painting when creating your artwork.

Digitized movies and animations can also be placed on either Astound or PowerPoint slides. Both must be created outside these applications using another software product dedicated to that function.

FIGURE 19.6

Creating a text box is easy in Astound. Notice the styling ruler, with its associated tabs and paragraph justification buttons. Each text box that is created has its own ruler. Text fonts and styles can be set as in any word processing environment by selecting the text in question and issuing appropriate commands from pull-down menus. PowerPoint provides similar capabilities.

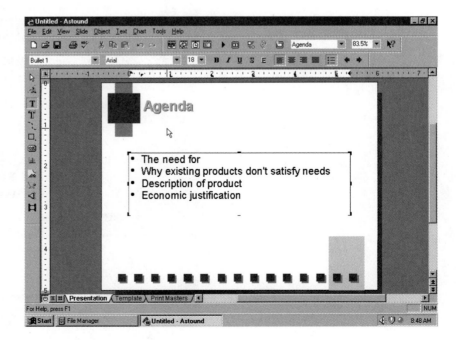

FIGURE 19.7

(a) Inserting graphics and images is easy in Astound. The Select Picture box is shown here. From this box, you can select a graphic from a variety of sources for inclusion on the slide. (b) Once the picture is inserted, you may reposition or resize it easily. (c) PowerPoint has comparable capabilities for inserting graphics and images. A simple graphic object is inserted and repositioned on the title page for the presentation.

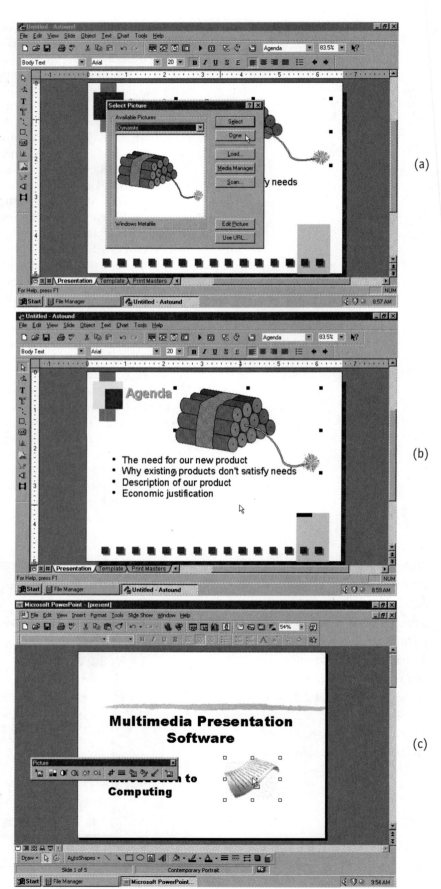

FIGURE 19.8

The Custom Animation tool in PowerPoint offers a variety of animation effects that may be applied to objects such as text. In this instance, the text block (Text 2) containing the bulleted points is animated to reveal the bulleted points one at a time, as the user wishes. A variety of additional features is available from the tabs in the Custom Animation dialog box.

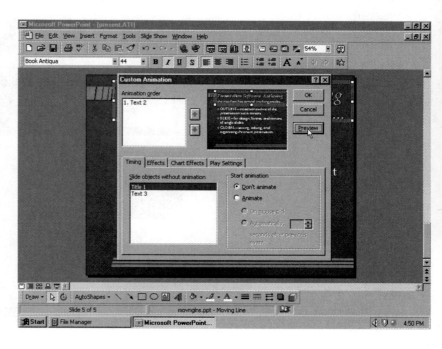

FIGURE 19.9

The Slide Sorter view in Astound resembles the arrangement of 35mm slides on a light table. The thumbnails representing the slides of the presentation may be rearranged by dragging them to a new position. In addition, slides may be cut or copied and pasted into the presentation.

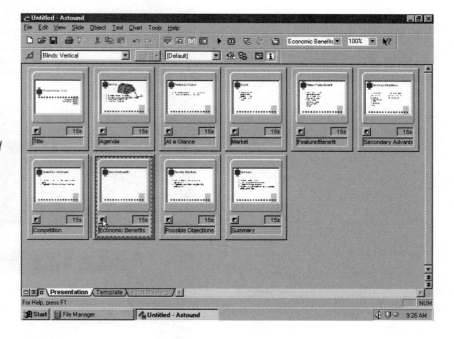

Once they are created and stored, both Astound and PowerPoint can import them. Figure 19.11 illustrates.

There are several ways of adding sound to multimedia slides. One possibility is to load a previously digitized sound, as shown in Figure 19.12. In some instances, we can record directly using the presentation software. See Figure 19.13. Because the digitized sound is stored in memory as it is recorded (as opposed to on the hard disk), this limits severely the amount of sound that we can record directly inside either program at any one time. Once the sound is added to a slide and the presentation is saved, however, we can record additional sound bites.

A simple sound editor is included in Astound, as shown in Figure 19.14. Astound's built-in editor is convenient and easy to use and serves

FIGURE 19.10

From the Slide Sorter view in PowerPoint, you may choose transitions and other special effects for one or more slides. Here a Vertical Blinds transition effect is chosen for slide 5.

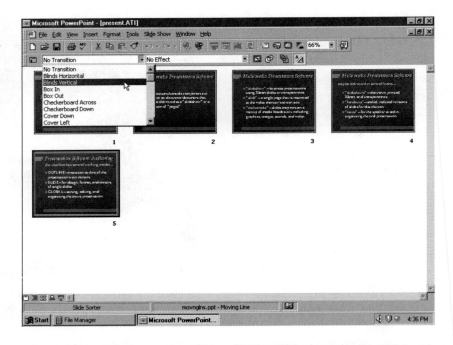

FIGURE 19.11

The figure illustrates importing a QuickTime movie into Astound. Note that the dialog box allows for viewing the movie before actually placing it on the slide. In the Astound dialog box a small version of the movie plays in a continuous loop under the Preview annotation on the left.

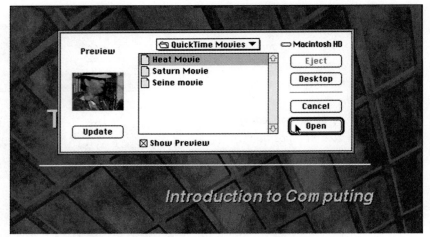

FIGURE 19.12

The figure shows the dialog box for adding a sound file to a slide show in Astound. Note that the dialog box used allows the sound to be played before adding it to the sounds available to that slide. Sounds can be selected from the pop-up menu and removed in this dialog box as well. A component called a Timeline is also shown in the dialog box. The Timeline allows the user to control both the timing and transition effects for the sound.

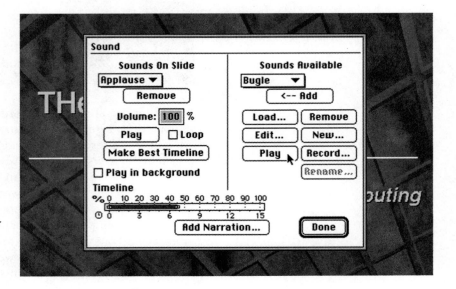

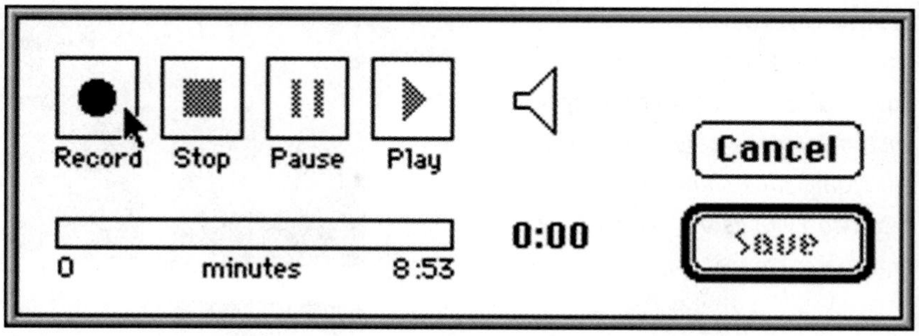

FIGURE 19.13

In Astound you may record a sound. The interface presented mimics an ordinary tape recorder and functions in essentially the same way.

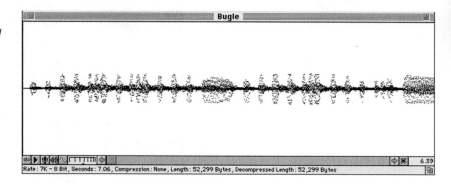

FIGURE 19.14

Minor editing can be performed on sound files imported into or recorded in Astound.

well for minor editing jobs. This built-in recording and editing facility is especially convenient for adding narration to a slide show. Dedicated sound processing software, however, is better equipped to handle more sophisticated tasks such as recording, transcribing, or editing music for background effects.

Timing Events in a Multimedia Presentation

The ability to time the sequence of events is of great importance in adding interest and effect to a multimedia presentation. Like the use of hypertext, this feature isn't strictly a part of multimedia computing, but it has become a significant one for most multimedia composition software.

PowerPoint is somewhat limited when it comes to sequencing events within a single slide, but it has several simple timing mechanisms for handling the slide show. Each slide in a slide show can be displayed for a specific period of time. In other words, you may display slides for different amounts of time, and you can override the set time for a given slide using the mouse or keyboard. Figure 19.15 shows some of the other options available for tailoring the slide show.

Astound provides much more precise and flexible timing controls, employing a timeline for sequencing both the display of slides and the timing for individual slide components. Figure 19.16 shows an Astound timeline with a graphics icon selected (highlighted). Whenever a slide component's timeline icon is selected in the bottom part of the window, its characteristics are displayed in the upper part of the Timeline window.

Look closely at the timeline associated with the sound icon in the figure. The numbers across the top (from 0 to 15) represent the fifteen seconds for which this slide is scheduled to be displayed. The lightly shaded portion of the sound's timeline extending from 0 to 3 seconds

FIGURE 19.15

The Set Up Slide Show box in PowerPoint has a variety of options for customizing the playback of your electronic slide show. Here the optional recorded timings are selected for automatic control.

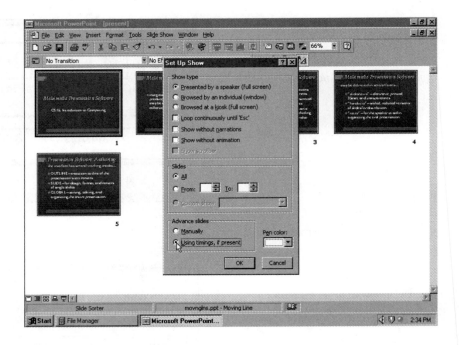

FIGURE 19.16

The Astound Timeline window for sequencing slide elements is shown. In the Astound Timeline for a slide, the icons shown vertically on the lower left side of the window represent particular slide elements. The first icon (in the shape of a speaker) represents a sound that has been placed on the slide. The capital T icon represents a text field. The next icon represents a picture element (it is a bit hard to see here, but it is intended to be an image of mountains). The two star-shaped icons represent two pieces of art drawn using the Astound drawing tool—the shape of the icon reflects the shape of the art, so that in this case the slide contains two star-shaped drawings.

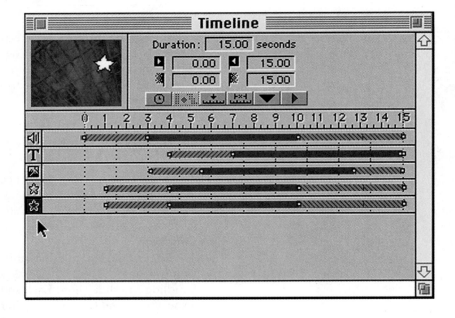

means that the sound will start fading in softly at the beginning of the slide display time, reaching full volume at three seconds. The sound will then play until the ten-second mark, at which time it fades out and disappears.

Notice, on the other hand, that the two star-shaped drawings will begin their transition into the slide starting at one second until they are fully displayed at four seconds. They remain on screen for six seconds and then disappear gradually over the next five seconds. You can choose a number of transition effects for moving objects in and out of the slide. Examples are a dissolve effect, a barn door effect, a wipe effect, and a roll to the top or bottom, among others.

In the example, the text field and the graphics on this slide are set to appear and disappear on their individual timelines. For instance, the text field will begin its transition in at 4 seconds, achieving full display at 7 seconds, and then remain on the slide until the entire slide disappears at 15 seconds. Astound gives you complete control over each element on your slide. The elements can appear and disappear at your discretion. It is easy to see how you could create some impressive slides with a life all their own using the timeline mechanism.

In Astound, transition effects may be associated with particular objects, a feature that offers a great deal of flexibility. Text, graphics, images, and videos can all have their own transition effects. This is an especially nice feature when combined with Astound's timeline capability to produce impressive slide effects. Although it does not allow transitions for every object within a slide, PowerPoint does allow transitions from one slide to another and for lines of text when the custom animation feature is used.

Astound objects can be made interactive as well, as shown in Figure 19.17. It is easy to create a link to another slide when an object is clicked on the current one. These interactive objects function much like Web hyperlinks. You can also set a sound to be played when the object is clicked, and you can have the slide paused until an action of your choice takes place, overriding the default duration time for the slide. This is very useful for creating interactive presentations, where a user's reaction (or a speaker's pace) may not be predictable within a certain time frame.

In both programs, you can specify certain global parameters about the entire slide show. For example, an active notation pen is a very convenient option for slide show presentations conducted by a speaker. When this option is enabled, the speaker may annotate slides by drawing on them with the mouse, using a choice of several different colors for emphasis. Once the slide show completes, all the drawing annotations are erased. Hence, you can mark up your slides as you speak without having to be concerned about interfering with your next presentation using the same slide set.

Lab Activity

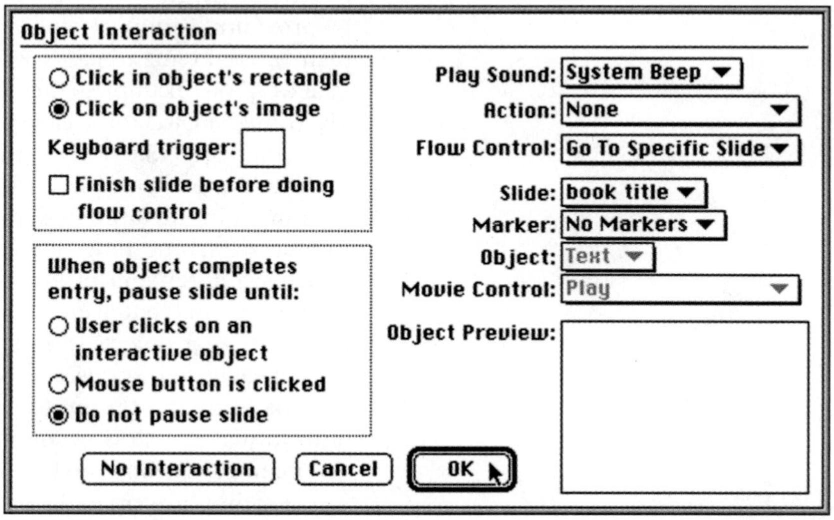

FIGURE 19.17

Shown is the dialog box for making an object interactive in Astound. Note that when the object is clicked, we have a number of choices for actions. In the figure, we have chosen a link to another slide named book title. *You can also choose to move to the next, previous, first, or last slide.*

Object Interaction

○ **Click in object's rectangle**
◉ **Click on object's image**
Keyboard trigger: [ ]
☐ **Finish slide before doing flow control**

When object completes entry, pause slide until:
○ **User clicks on an interactive object**
○ **Mouse button is clicked**
◉ **Do not pause slide**

Play Sound: [System Beep ▼]
Action: [None ▼]
Flow Control: [Go To Specific Slide ▼]
Slide: [book title ▼]
Marker: [No Markers ▼]
Object: [Text ▼]
Movie Control: [Play ▼]
Object Preview: [ ]

[No Interaction] [Cancel] [**OK**]

MULTIMEDIA AUTHORING SOFTWARE

The multimedia composition tools discussed in the previous section make it possible to put together multimedia information presentations with ease. Some of these programs allow you to add basic interaction in the form of simple branching from one part of the presentation to another. **Multimedia authoring software** offers an even greater range of interactivity for multimedia productions.

The applications of interactive multimedia are more wide-ranging than linear presentations. And most of these forms require more sophisticated interactivity. **Computer-based training (CBT)** modules allow the novice to enter information, answer questions, and seek further clarification. These electronic modules are both a cost-effective and efficient way to deliver tailored instruction on demand. CBT is particularly effective in training employees to use complex machinery and systems and diagnose difficulties when such systems malfunction. The use of images, diagrams, verbal instructions, and video clips is indispensable in producing effective training modules. **Informational kiosks** allow queries that are better tailored to the consumers' needs and are attractively presented. In addition, these kiosks can keep track of the requests entered, which may be a valuable source of information for the retailer. Product demonstrations, customer surveys, and animated brochures all benefit from, and in some cases require, an interactive design. **Computer games** offer strikingly realistic images and sounds that would be dull and uninteresting without extensive interactivity. The many books, games, and other **edutainment** titles for children and adults offer both educational and entertainment values through their interactive features. Multimedia authoring software makes all of these productions possible.

How are these interactive capabilities created? Not too long ago, the only choice would have been programming with general-purpose, high-level languages such as Pascal, FORTRAN, or C++. Not so today. Application programs such as Authorware, Director, ToolBook, HyperCard, and HyperStudio permit users to create products every bit as sophisticated as those formerly developed using general-purpose programming languages. These multimedia authoring tools accomplish this by providing very powerful, high-level commands and techniques, supplemented in many cases with their own specific programming languages. For example, the programming language associated with Macromedia Director is called Lingo.

Languages like Lingo are not only easier to learn than Pascal, FORTRAN, or C++, but they minimize the need for complex programming in the multimedia authoring applications that support them. Instead of writing long, logically complex programs, developers of interactive multimedia products can write **scripts,** which are short program segments that are easier to construct. Scripts are often associated with particular objects within the multimedia product and are typically used to activate responses to certain actions on those objects.

For example, the button on the slide in Figure 19.18 is animated both to make a clicking sound and to move when the user clicks it. In this manner, clicking the button gives the user a more natural feedback. These actions are created by a simple Lingo script that is associated with the button object and shown in Figure 19.19.

FIGURE 19.18

The icon of the island (in the lower left corner) is employed as a navigational button on the series of slides created using Director. When the user clicks the button, it makes an audible clicking sound and moves slightly before the scene switches to another slide.

Sugar cane fields on the Kilohana Plantation.

FIGURE 19.19

The navigational button for the slide shown in Figure 19.18 is animated by the Lingo script shown here. (The numbering in the script has been added for easy reference.) A brief explanation of this script follows in the box below.

```
(1)   on mouseDown
(2)      set btn = the clickOn
(3)      puppetSprite btn, TRUE
(4)      puppetSound "Mouse Down"
(5)      set the loc of sprite btn = the loc of
         sprite btn - 1
(6)      updateStage
(7)      repeat while the stillDown
            nothing
         end repeat
(10)     set the loc of sprite btn = the loc of
         sprite btn + 1
(11)     updateStage
(12)     puppetSprite btn, FALSE
(13)     puppetSound 0
      end
```

line 1:	The script is activated when the mouse is pressed.
line 2:	The specific button clicked by the user is identified.
line 3:	The button called by the name "btn" is now controlled as an animated object called a puppet.
line 4:	The cast member sound "Mouse Down" is likewise designated as a puppet.
line 5:	The location of the button is moved one pixel.
line 6:	The stage is updated to show the move and play the sound.
lines 7-9:	A repeat loop doing nothing stalls while the mouse remains down.
lines 10-13:	The process is reversed, and control returns to the normal script.

Scripts like these accomplish tasks that otherwise would involve a great deal more complexity using conventional high-level programming languages. Of course, learning to write scripts does require both study and practice. Even the novice, though, can create effective scripts in short order.

The Interface Designs for Multimedia Authoring Programs Vary

The interfaces for multimedia authoring programs offer more variety than multimedia composition software. The typical authoring application is organized using one of several different metaphors. First we consider the authoring program HyperStudio, which is used extensively in K–12 education.

HyperStudio's capabilities fall somewhere between those of multimedia composition software and high-end interactive authoring software. HyperStudio is available in both Windows and Macintosh versions. As in its namesake HyperCard, documents are based on the card/stack metaphor. It is relatively easy to import video and other multimedia resources into its stacks. See Figure 19.20. In addition to buttons, HyperStudio allows the creation of "hot spots" on a card that trigger events. For example, you can have context-sensitive pointers that appear when the mouse moves over these designated areas.

Besides importing digital video resources, you may also capture and digitize video with a video camera directly using HyperStudio. Hence, you can create buttons that display a live video feed or record a movie when they are clicked. This digitizing capability offers a number of interesting possibilities for multimedia production. For example, it is also possible to capture information directly from a laser disc or CD-ROM. You can also create a picture-within-a-picture effect by playing movies behind other objects.

If you have an Internet connection, HyperStudio allows you to send URLs to a Web browser to display Web sites from within the HyperStudio

FIGURE 19.20

The figure illustrates importing a video clip into a HyperStudio stack. A portion of a given video screen is selected and moved to the current card. As shown, the user can set various characteristics of the movie.

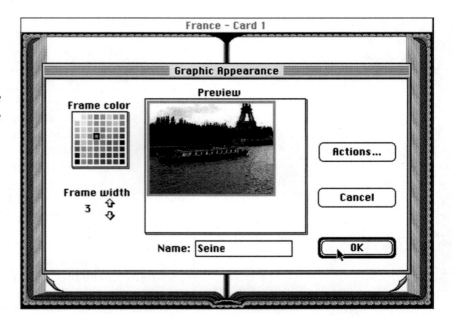

documents and provide direct, hands-on interaction with the Web. HyperStudio also has its own programming language, HyperLogo, for writing scripts to provide an even more flexible environment. In sum, HyperStudio offers some outstanding features for applications requiring a high degree of interactivity. It is not difficult to learn to use the application, and it is reasonably priced.

Some productions, however, are more complicated and require even more powerful authoring environments. For example, CBT modules usually have both sophisticated interactivity and extensive tracking and record keeping. Macromedia Director and Authorware are the most popular professional-quality authoring systems for these sorts of productions.

For high-end animation work, Director is the desktop software tool of choice. Director's interface employs a stage production and score metaphor, consistent with the idea of producing an animated sequence. The documents created are called "movies," and these movies are played in a window called the Stage.

The production is organized in a window called the Score. The Score window uses a column and row layout. See Figure 19.21. In the score, animation effects are created by placing a sequence of objects called **sprites** in columns denoting the frame in which each is visible.

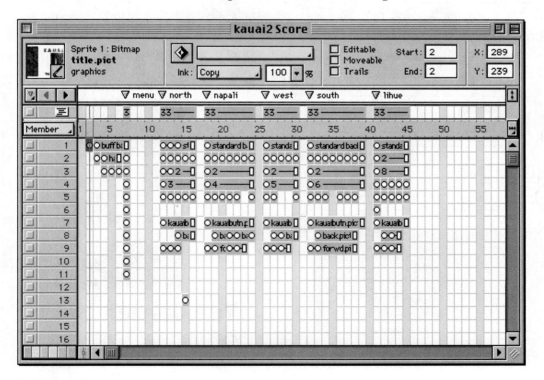

FIGURE 19.21

The figure shows the Score window for a movie created in Director. The numbers in the bar across the top denote the frames of the movie. In this instance, the movie is composed of approximately forty-five frames. Each frame is composed of one or more channels (listed in the left column down). Each channel holds an animation object called a "sprite." In a single column, the circles and boxes represent the number of objects that occupy that frame at that moment. The markers in the top row signify named frames such as "menu" and "napali," which can serve as targets for interactive navigation.

Sprites include graphics, photographs, audio, text, and other elements. An object appearing to move across the screen, for example, is composed of numerous sprites; each one occupies a different frame and position on the screen. Sprites are created from collected and assembled resources called **cast members.** Figure 19.22 shows several casts of objects that were employed in the example movie. Creating a Director animation involves planning and coordinating the sequence of events for each frame shown in the Stage window.

Director provides a number of different windows for the various tasks involved in producing a Director movie. As mentioned, the Stage window is where Director movies are displayed. The size of the Stage window can be changed to match the playback environment. For example, you might choose a small window to play digital video and a larger window to play animations whose display requires fewer system re-

FIGURE 19.22

Several cast member windows for a Director movie are shown here. Casts contain resources that may be used for the creation of this and other movies. In this instance, the cast members are separated arbitrarily into types of resources: the Internal Cast is composed of photographs; the graphics Cast contains backgrounds, buttons, titles, and other graphic objects used in the movie. Finally, the text Cast is composed of text passages that appear on frames in the movie.

The Control Panel (also shown) is used to control the playing of the movie (play, rewind, stop, etc.) in a manner similar to the controls on a VCR.

sources. Director also has a Control Panel window that lets you change the tempo and other playback features of the Stage. See Figure 19.22.

As indicated earlier, Lingo scripts can be associated with any cast member, any sprite, or the movie as a whole. Scripts add functionality to these objects and are the primary means for introducing interactivity. Scripts are entered and edited in the Script window. Figure 19.23 is an example of programming a text object to act as a hyperlink to another frame or slide.

Director has a long history and has been used successfully for a variety of multimedia projects—trade show displays, interactive kiosks, guided tours for software use, educational courseware, animated television commercials, and a host of others. It was created (originally under the name VideoWorks) in the mid-1980s at about the same time Hyper-Card appeared. Its strength then and now is the ease with which it can be employed to produce sophisticated animations. In fact, it is still one

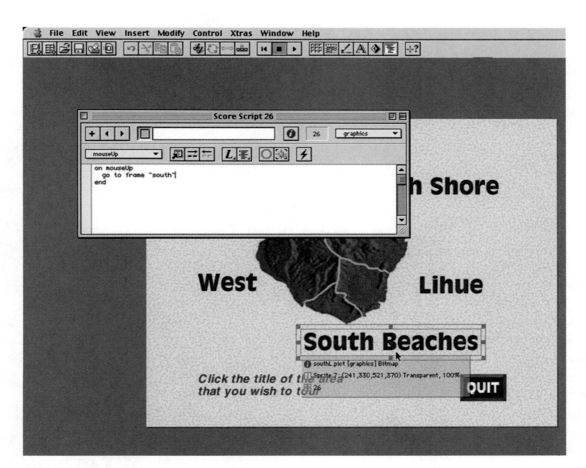

FIGURE 19.23

The frame shown here is used as a main menu for the Director movie. The user clicks on the title to see a different part of the guided tour of Kauai, Hawaii. The text object "South Beaches," for example, is selected, and a simple script is attached to the sprite to accomplish the navigation. Underneath the text object, Director reveals the salient details associated with this object: the name of the cast member and cast; the sprite number (7), screen coordinates, and other characteristics; and the number of the script (26) attached to it.

of the most popular tools for creating interactive presentations, CD-ROM edutainment titles, software demonstrations, and any other multimedia product that uses animation. Over the years, many features have been added to Director beyond its animation capabilities. It now combines sophisticated animation tools with the ability to integrate text, sound, images, and full-motion video, and it provides features for creating fully interactive products.

By now you have no doubt realized that learning to use Director is somewhat more involved than learning to use multimedia composition software such as Astound and PowerPoint or even HyperStudio. This is true, but Director does have a distinct advantage over such software—the ability to create professional-quality animations. When this capability is called for, the effort to learn the use of Director is time and energy well spent.

Authorware, also from Macromedia, is no doubt the premier multimedia authoring system for producing high-end interactive courseware. **Courseware** refers to interactive multimedia software that is designed to be used for training and education. The hallmark of Authorware is its sophisticated tools for monitoring and reporting a user's performance on interactive test materials. The ability to monitor the user's progress makes it possible to build into the courseware the capabilities for providing appropriate feedback based on the user's responses.

Additionally, Authorware provides a full range of capabilities for constructing fully interactive multimedia products. In contrast to the Director Score, Authorware employs a flowchart metaphor. The sequencing of the project—called a "piece"—is mapped out by a series of icons on the Authorware flowline in the Design window. These icons represent a large variety of objects and resources—sounds, movies (in-

FIGURE 19.24

The figure shows the interface for Authorware 4 and the Design window employed for the construction of a logical flowchart for a simple linear presentation in Authorware (taken from an instructional example in Macromedia's training materials). The icons are placed on the flowline in the order in which the events or actions take place. The objects used in the production are held in the Library window shown to the left in the figure.

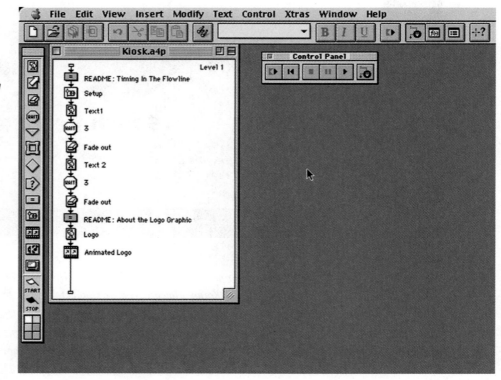

cluding Director movies), scripts, animations, as well as controls for organizing the project itself. Figure 19.24 shows Authorware's interface with the Design window for a simple project. As you can see, the piece is "programmed" through the flowchart. Flowcharts can incorporate a full range of program control—decision, repetition, the use of variables, and an easy-to-manage hierarchical structure. Figure 19.25 illustrates the creation of an interaction loop for organizing a collection of "hot objects," that is, hot spots on the display that may be selected by the user.

The ability to organize an Authorware flowchart using a hierarchical structure is also a very important feature of the system. Specific sequences of icons can be named and saved as models. **Models** are Authorware program segments that may be reused in other projects or pieces. They also create levels of the programming structure that make it easier to follow the overall organization of the project. Figure 19.26 illustrates. When a flowchart is constructed hierarchically, the details exposed at any time are appropriate to the level at which the flowchart is being examined. If you are interested in only the big picture, lower-level details can be hidden from view. On the other hand, if you wish to examine some portion of the flowchart in more detail, the hierarchical structure allows for this. In this way, very complex pieces can be built from relatively simple, easy-to-understand segments. In fact, Authorware offers a programming environment almost as powerful as those of general-purpose, third-generation programming languages like C++, FORTRAN, and Pascal—with the added benefit of being much easier to learn and use. The range and variety of courseware that has been developed with Authorware are truly impressive.

Lab Activity

FIGURE 19.25

In another example from Macromedia's training materials, the Design window shows how a screen depicting a map of New England states can be organized as a collection of hot spots that reveal additional information when selected by the user. At the bottom of the flowline, an interaction loop contains a series of designated hot objects that cause text to appear on the screen when clicked. After each selection, the flow of control returns to the top of the interaction loop.

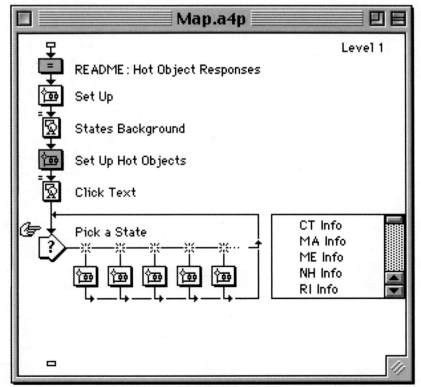

FIGURE 19.26

In this figure, you can see the hierarchical structure of an Authorware project. At the topmost level (Coolform.a4p), the flowline depicts a simple example of how to set up an interactive form. Each field in the form has a model associated with it. The FirstName model is opened to reveal a simple interaction loop for keying in text. The calculation icon (" = " sign) is opened to reveal a simple script called "*" for adding a special action.

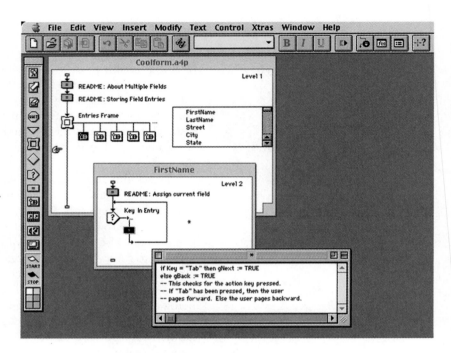

MULTIMEDIA ON THE WEB: FIRST-GENERATION TOOLS

The multimedia presentations and courseware produced by the authoring/composition software discussed so far are usually delivered via desktop computers. Not too long ago, the choice of hardware for a delivery platform would have been restricted by the choice of authoring/composition software. Recently, most major vendors have introduced versions of their multimedia authoring/composition software with **cross-platform capabilities,** meaning that they have, at least, player programs to display the program's products for both Windows and Macintosh. As we have noted, Astound, Authorware, Director, HyperStudio, and PowerPoint all provide full versions for both platforms. Some of these versions create documents that can even be edited on different computer systems in addition to being viewed by them.

Even though this cross-platform feature extends the potential audience for a multimedia product, the recent emergence of the World Wide Web as a primary communication vehicle presents even greater distribution opportunities to multimedia authors. The Web is a natural venue for distributing most of the kinds of multimedia products discussed. In fact, many authoring and composition programs have associated plug-ins for the Netscape Communicator and Internet Explorer browsers. With these plug-ins, products created by these applications can be distributed and played via the Web.

As you already know, the Web also provides its own multimedia authoring capabilities. You've seen how HTML enables the publication of a large variety of information employing the Web. As a tool for creating and deploying sophisticated multimedia productions, however, HTML has many shortcomings. The most notable of these is lack of adequate support for animation and interactivity. In this section, we look briefly at the Web's capabilities in these two areas; in the next section, we consider two new, emerging technologies that will integrate animation and interactivity more easily into Web pages.

Animation on the Web

No doubt, you have noticed animation effects on some of the Web pages you have visited. These effects are not produced directly with HTML. There are, in fact, several ways in which Web page animation can be provided.

Chapter 12 introduced animated GIFs, which are a form of streaming graphic images. These are downloaded to and displayed in the browser in rapid sequence. If the images depict incremental changes, the effect is that of motion. As we just mentioned, another animation method uses third-party software for creating and playing animation sequences. For example, Director is frequently used to create such sequences. The plug-in program Shockwave is employed to accelerate the downloading of these sequences and play them automatically when the Web page loads. Director files are specially prepared for Shockwave's use before they are placed on a Web page. Earlier, you also learned how to use HTML tags to link to video files stored externally; this provides still another method of displaying animation sequences stored as video segments.

Yet another method involves programming animation sequences using a programming language. Java and JavaScript are the most frequently used languages for this purpose. Java is a programming language and environment designed to solve a number of problems encountered when programming network applications; we'll have more to say about it shortly.

Interactive Web Pages

If the Web is to realize its potential in the area of electronic commerce, it must provide a high degree of interactivity. Clearly, for merchants to sell and customers to buy, there must be interactive channels of communication between the two groups. Customers must be able to enter ordering and payment information and transmit that information to the merchant. Merchants must be able to respond to these inquiries with information as well. In addition to electronic commerce, a great many other Web activities depend on interactive interfaces. Search engines, as you have seen, must be able to collect key words and phrases from their users. Large information repositories, like libraries, need interactive query systems to direct their customers' requests for information to the appropriate resource. And the list goes on and on.

How are such interactions managed? Much of today's Web interactivity is enabled by the use of HTML forms and related small programs, called CGI (for Common Gateway Interface) scripts. **HTML forms** collect information at the client (browser) and store it or pass it along as the circumstance warrants. **CGI scripts** running on the server half of the server/client connection then use this information to cause some action by the server. See Figure 19.27. If the client needs additional information, requests to the server initiate this exchange. In other words, all the "action" takes place on the server. The client sim-

FIGURE 19.27(A)

A simple form is shown here. The user enters text into the boxes provided and presses the button to submit the information to the server. A CGI script on the server interprets the information and responds as needed.

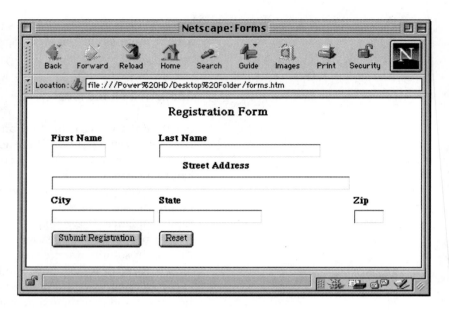

(a)

ply receives, displays, and perhaps transmits information. The HTML document is involved only to the extent of making requests to the CGI scripts on the server.

Placing the primary burden of work on the server has some advantages but more significant disadvantages. Server-side interaction is more easily controlled or managed. On the other hand, a server usually responds to numerous clients concurrently. Any extra work by the server will slow down the overall responsiveness of the system. As we all know, Web pages that are sluggish and slow to download are often discarded by impatient Web surfers. Can more of the work be ported to the client instead of the server? Imagemaps is a case in point. A form of limited interactivity managed by the client can be coded directly into the HTML itself using what are called client-side imagemaps. As with all imagemaps, certain areas on an image can be made into hyperlinks, so that when a user clicks one of these "hot spots" a new page or resource is loaded. Client-side imagemaps provide enough information coded into the page so that the browser can determine precisely which area was selected and what link is associated with it. See Figure 19.28. This approach is much faster and more efficient than relying on server-side processes to interpret both the hot spots and the related links.

At present, HTML has no provisions to enable the user to interactively change a Web page at the client's end. For example, a Web page might contain a table of information taken from a database stored on a server. Suppose the user at the client wishes to have the data sorted. The only way that could be accomplished now is to send the command to a script on the server, have the script sort the data, then reload the page with the sorted data—not a very efficient process. Nor does HTML provide for a more dynamic interface on Web pages. For example, perhaps we'd like to pop up a message whenever the user rolls the mouse over certain spots on the Web page. Or perhaps we'd like to be able to drag elements around and reposition them on the page. These actions are simply not possible with current HTML.

```
<HTML>

<HEAD>
  <TITLE>Forms</TITLE>
</HEAD>
<BODY BGCOLOR="#FFFFFF">
<FORM ACTION="/cgi-bin/get-method.cgi" METHOD=GET>
  <CENTER>
  <TABLE BORDER=0 WIDTH="60%">
    <caption align=top><H3>Registration Form</H3></caption>
  <TR>
    <TD><B>First Name</B><INPUT TYPE=text NAME=first VALUE="" SIZE=10
        MAXLENGTH=20></TD>
    <TD><B>Last Name</B><INPUT TYPE=text NAME=last VALUE="" SIZE=32
        MAXLENGTH=40></TD>
    <TD><TD>
  </TR>
  <TR>
    <TH COLSPAN=3>Street Address</TH>
  </TR>
  <TR>
    <TD COLSPAN=3 HEIGHT=25><INPUT TYPE=text NAME=street VALUE=""
        SIZE=60 MAXLENGTH=60></TD>
  </TR>
  <TR>
    <TD><B>City</B></TD>
    <TD><B>State</B></TD>
    <TD><B>Zip</B></TD>
  </TR>
  <TR>
    <TD><INPUT TYPE=text NAME=city VALUE="" SIZE=20 MAXLENGTH=30></TD>
    <TD><INPUT TYPE=text NAME=state VALUE="" SIZE=20
        MAXLENGTH=20></TD>
    <TD><INPUT TYPE=text NAME=zip VALUE="" SIZE=5 MAXLENGTH=10></TD>
  </TR>
  <TR>
    <TD><INPUT TYPE=submit NAME=Submit VALUE="Submit
        Registration"></TD>
    <TD><INPUT TYPE=reset VALUE="Reset"></TD>
    <TD></TD>
  </TR>
  </TABLE>
  </CENTER>
</FORM>
</BODY>

</HTML>
```

(b)

FIGURE 19.27(B)

The HTML code needed to create the form shown in (a) is listed here. Aside from formatting the text entry form, the code directs the browser to collect the items entered by the user and send them as a single concatenated string to the server posting the page. The entry items (and buttons) are shown in red for emphasis. The server, in turn, deciphers the string and processes it according to a script that it consults for this form.

FIGURE 19.28

Imagemaps are commonly employed on Web pages as a visual form of navigation. In (a), the entry page is a client-side imagemap that permits the user to select among several hot spots serving as links to other pages. The actual hot spot areas on the image are shown in (b). This is a client-side imagemap because the HTML contains sufficient information for the browser program to calculate which link is needed when the user selects a particular area in the window. The HTML code, shown in (c), gives the window coordinates and the hyperlink reference information for each of the hot spots in the image map.

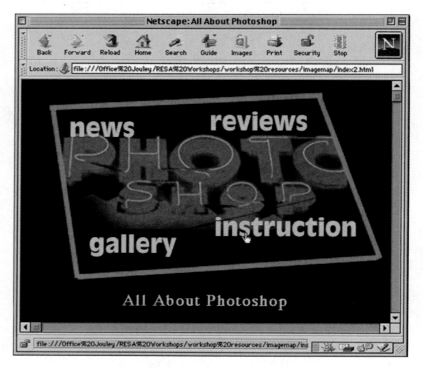

(a)

(b)

```
<HTML>
<HEAD>
   <TITLE>All About Photoshop</TITLE>
</HEAD>
<BODY TEXT="#FFFF00" BGCOLOR="#000000">
<CENTER><MAP NAME=map1>
   <AREA SHAPE=rect COORDS="252,163,510,250" HREF="instruct.html">
   <AREA SHAPE=rect COORDS="66,195,249,275" HREF="gallery.html">
   <AREA SHAPE=rect COORDS="241,15,435,95" HREF="reviews.html">
   <AREA SHAPE=rect COORDS="43,27,180,101" HREF="news.html">
</MAP><IMG ISMAP USEMAP="#map1" SRC="photo.jpg"
   WIDTH=543 HEIGHT=292 BORDER=0 ALIGN=bottom></CENTER>

<H1><CENTER>All About Photoshop</CENTER></H1>
</BODY>
</HTML>
```

(c)

Programming the Web with Java

Java is a language modeled after the popular programming language C++. It can be thought of as a streamlined and simplified version of C++, with special features making it particularly suitable for writing programs for network applications. For example, Java has an extensive library of routines designed especially for interfacing with network protocols such as HTTP and FTP. As a consequence, programs written in Java can open and access objects across the Internet using URLs as easily as programs written in most other languages can access locally stored files. Also, because Java is intended to be used in networked environments, its designers have placed a lot of emphasis on security issues. Java makes it possible to construct virus-free, tamper-free applications, with its authentication techniques being based on the public key encryption techniques discussed in Chapter 16.

To enable a program written in Java to execute anywhere on a network composed of a variety of systems with different hardware and operating systems, the Java compiler generates an **architecture-neutral object file.** This means that the compiled code is executable on many processors as long as the Java runtime system is present to interpret the code for that particular processor environment. The Java compiler does this by generating basic instructions, called **bytecodes,** which have nothing to do with a particular computer architecture. Java bytecodes are designed to be interpreted easily on any machine and quickly translated into the appropriate machine language code on the fly. The key concept is the separation of the architecture-neutral compiled Java code and the runtime interpretation of these elements on a particular client machine.

You might guess that the interpreted bytecode scheme would produce very inefficient final programs—that is, programs that run slowly. The designers of Java avoided this by carefully constructing the format of the Java bytecode instructions with the subsequent process of generating machine codes in mind. In other words, bytecode instructions are quite similar to machine language instructions—but without implementation-specific components. With this design, the actual process of generating machine code is generally quite simple. Indeed, the performance of bytecodes converted to machine code is almost indistinguishable from directly compiled C++ on many platforms. One of the most convincing arguments about the power and usefulness of Java is its proven track record as a vehicle for programming animations and interactivity on the Web.

MULTIMEDIA ON THE WEB: EMERGING TECHNOLOGIES

In addition to its limitations in the areas of animation and interactivity, HTML has other limitations as well. For example, HTML provides very little in the way of text formatting and page layout control. Simple formatting features, like indenting paragraphs, for example, are not included in HTML. Placing images on a page is also a hit-and-miss proposition. The best you can do is create "invisible" tables and place "filler" blank images in table cells to try to approximate the placement you desire.

The problem, of course, is that HTML has been stretched well beyond its original intended uses. When first envisioned, the Web was conceived as a simple, effective means for transmitting useful scientific and educational material to a variety of systems over computer networks. As such, it was designed primarily as a users' medium and not a publishers' medium. Consequently, it makes little sense to complain too much about HTML's lack of page layout and design features. Of course, HTML is not a static entity. The standards for HTML have been pushed considerably by the marketplace even over its short tenure. Today's HTML standard contains a wide variety of enhancements that add functionality to the basic format control provided by earlier versions. Even these enhancements fall short of some of the newly proposed technologies. We will consider two of the most promising of these.

Dynamic HTML

A new technology, called **dynamic HTML (DHTML),** is emerging in response to some of the limitations of HTML we have noted. Dynamic HTML brings a new level of flexibility to the Web through the merger and integration of some already existing technologies. Both Microsoft and Netscape have proposed DHTML models, and these do not coincide. So it may be some time before anything approximating a standard DHTML emerges. This isn't likely, though, to slow the increasing use of DHTML significantly.

Using DHTML, the Web page author is able to specify fonts, precisely position images on a page, and format text in flexible ways. And these factors can be dynamically altered *after the page has been loaded* by the client. For example, the color, size, and font of text can be changed based on such factors as the time since a page was loaded, the mouse being rolled over the text, and so on.

Data delivered on DHTML Web pages is also dynamic. Users can sort and otherwise manipulate data on the client side, with no interaction with the server necessary. This means that Web page interfaces for database systems become more flexible and more interesting. Moreover, data manipulation can be accomplished far faster because it is done by the client's computer system rather than through the server.

The primary feature of DHTML is to allow the user to alter both page content and appearance dynamically after loading by the client. Thus, DHTML will enable different presentations of data and graphics depending on user feedback and without the need to consult the server and download a new page. This capability enables client-based animation that is far faster than the animation provided by previous technologies.

Three main components of DHTML are dynamic page styles, dynamic data content, and dynamic object positioning. Style sheets represent an extension of HTML to allow a Web page author more control over such features as fonts, backgrounds, borders, specific list structures, and other stylistic elements. **Dynamic style sheets** in DHTML allow an author to change the appearance of a page, either automatically or in response to user input, without forcing the downloading of a new page. In other words, the HTML document contains a variety of style information that can be chosen based on conditions *at the client*. These choices require no further interaction with the server, and so they can be implemented and displayed on the client machine very quickly.

Authors can use DHTML's **dynamic data content** to change the content of text and images in response to actions on the user's mouse and/or keyboard. Again, no further communication with the server is required. For example, data can be sorted by the client's system; queries can be formed and responded to by the client's system, and so on. Of course, these actions can be accomplished in much less time when performed by the client. Achieving the same results using server-side processes would require fetching and transmitting fresh data sets for each operation.

Dynamic object positioning in DHTML means that text, images, and video can be moved around on a Web page either automatically (as in a timed sequence) or by user request/response. As before, all of these actions are handled much faster because none requires additional communication with the server for more downloading of information. Client-based animations, for example, are much smoother and more realistic than server-based animations, with the bonus of allowing user interactions at the same time.

Extensible Markup Language (XML)

While DHTML proceeds with some rather natural extensions of HTML's capabilities, **Extensible Markup Language (XML)** presents a greater departure from traditional HTML. HTML and XML, however, are to be viewed not as competitors but as complementary technologies. XML defines document structures rather than instructions about how a browser should display the document. Browsers of the future will be able to process both XML and HTML, and future HTML standards will likely permit a mixing of the two languages within a single document.

Both HTML and XML are related to a much larger, more general markup language known as **SGML (Standard Generalized Markup Language),** which predates the World Wide Web. SGML specifies grammars, or definitions, for document markup languages. An SGML document contains its own grammar definition in its Document Type Definition (DTD). In other words, the DTD for a document defines the tags to be used in the document as well as what the tags signify. This feature permits immense flexibility and ultimate extensibility. Unfortunately, these characteristics come at a price; SGML is complicated to learn and implement.

HTML can be thought of as one particular SGML application, that is, one particular DTD. Because HTML tags and their meanings do not change from document to document, we do not have to include a DTD when we create an HTML document. Rather, the DTD for HTML is incorporated into all Web browsers designed to display HTML documents.

XML was created to provide much of the power of SGML without all of its complexity. In short, XML represents a simplified SGML. Like SGML, it is extensible (although to a lesser degree), but it is closer to

HTML in ease of learning and use. The designers of XML have tried to offer about 80 percent of the benefits of SGML while keeping only 20 percent of its complexity. XML uses a slightly different syntax from HTML, therefore it is not strictly compatible with current versions of HTML. We are likely to see newer versions of HTML that will bridge this gap. Current HTML documents will require some minor changes to become XML-compatible. These developments will be aided by the fact that, in contrast to the uncertain state of two different proposed DHTML standards, the World Wide Web Consortium (W3C) has already established an XML standard.

What advantages does XML offer? Perhaps the most significant advantage XML will provide is the ability to let applications describe to each other a document's data and its relationships. This capability will enable better search engines and better and more succinct descriptions of Web site content, including content ratings for screening for under-age users. XML will also enhance the exchange of documents by providing a high-level description of document data. This will be especially valuable in electronic commerce applications. XML's structuring of document data will greatly facilitate the exchange of such items as invoices, insurance claims, loan applications, budget summaries, and so on.

XML data structuring will also make it possible to publish a single XML source document in a variety of formats. For example, a document might be publishable as a Web page, as a paper document in multiple formats, as a Braille document, or as a CD-ROM file. This is achieved by employing different style sheets for each document type to handle the various data structures. The same document could be printed in many different versions or levels of difficulty and detail by applying different XML style sheets to data that has been organized by underlying XML data structures.

XML will also simplify and enhance the management of Web links. Among the features it will support are location-independent naming and centralized link management. This will help alleviate the "dead links" problem found on the current Web when Web pages are moved to different servers or directories. XML will also support bidirectional links and multiple destination links.

The Next Step?

The World Wide Web is a remarkably dynamic environment—so much so that the pace of change is sometimes dizzying. Dynamic HTML and XML will bring more flexibility and interactivity to the Web, but these technologies will not be the final step. In addition to rapid developments centered on the Web itself, we will also see more integration of the entire desktop environment. Already the *active desktop* concept within the Windows 98 operating system promises an integration of the desktop operating system and the World Wide Web.

We will see many more changes over the next few years, and no one can predict what the Web of even five years from now will be like. It's a safe bet to say it will be a more useful, more secure, more entertaining, and more informative medium, and that all these characteristics are certain to make it of ever increasing importance to us all.

More Information

MULTIMEDIA DEVELOPMENT LIFE CYCLE

The creation and delivery of multimedia documents pose greater challenges than those for producing conventional publications. As you have likely experienced, the use of technology is like a double-edged sword. On one hand, technology provides opportunities that would be difficult or impossible without its assistance. On the other hand, the application of technology often increases the complexity and scale of our projects. The fact that you are working with a *multimedia* document automatically multiplies the complexity of a task because a variety of informational resources must be assembled and organized into an effective presentation. Even modest desktop multimedia productions require some planning and organization. How then should the novice multimedia producer prepare to face these challenges? In fact, useful lessons can be learned from how professionals do it.

Professional multimedia productions are created by production teams that follow a precise development methodology. The members of the production team are specialists who are responsible for specific facets of the production. The number and assignment of tasks will vary with the scale or size of the project, but in general the following roles on the production team must be filled.

● **Project Manager.** This individual has oversight responsibility for all phases of the project. The project manager decides who does what and when. The project manager devises the schedule and the budget for the project and is responsible for its completion on time and at or under budget. For contract productions, the project manager also works with the clients who have contracted them.

● **Project Designer.** One individual is responsible for the overall "vision" of the production. The role of the project designer is to determine the content, layout, design, and treatments for the project. For educational or training productions, the designer is also responsible for selecting appropriate learning strategies incorporated in the production. In short, the project designer is the idea person.

● **Writer(s).** The role of the writer is to create written text for the production. Typically, writers are content experts, that is, professionals chosen from the area or fields on which they will write. In other cases, though, professional writers may be contracted to compose from sources or materials provided to them.

● **Technical Specialist(s).** Like the stage manager for a theatrical production, the technical specialist is responsible for seeing that the design treatments are realized. The technical specialist is concerned with the details of how the production works. These individuals are typically "computer types" who have the background and expertise needed for implementation issues.

● **Media Specialist(s).** In contrast to technical specialists, the media specialist is expert at creating the media resources needed for the production. This includes graphic artists, photographers, video and audio recording professionals, and so on. These individuals often have some technical facility in working with digital media, but this is not always a requirement.

Authoring Technicians.   These are the individuals who create the actual segments for the production. Using the authoring tools and programming, authoring technicians follow the precise guidelines or scripts in assembling the components of the multimedia production. These individuals are the primary labor force for the team.

The actual composition of the production team will vary. On smaller productions, for example, it is common that a single individual plays several roles. A small team might be made up of three persons: a project manager/designer/writer, a technical specialist, and a media specialist, for example. Typical teams, however, are composed of twenty or more members.

The normal multimedia CD-ROM title is a production costing in the neighborhood of $500,000—and often more. At these prices, the successful completion of the project is paramount. For this reason, the development is organized and carried out in a disciplined manner. In fact, the typical multimedia production has a life cycle that is similar to that for the development of software systems (see Chapter 6). Most multimedia projects go through four basic stages of development: analysis, design, scripting, and production. In each phase, there are specific goals and deliverables. See Figure 19.29.

Analysis

Initial planning involves researching and deciding on three basic issues: content, audience, and delivery.

A goal of the analysis stage is the completion of an analysis document that defines the specifications for each of these issues.

Content, of course, refers to what the document is about. The analysis should arrive at preliminary decisions about both its informational content and the range of media that will be incorporated in the document.

FIGURE 19.29

The four stages of multimedia development are analysis, design, scripting, and production. Each of the stages has particular goals and objectives. Specific products result from the completion of these stages. The analysis document serves as a feasibility study for the project. The design treatments are specifications for the various elements that compose the production. Scripts are precise guidelines for the implementation of the components and resources that will be incorporated in the production. Finally, the completion of the finished product is the goal of the production phase.

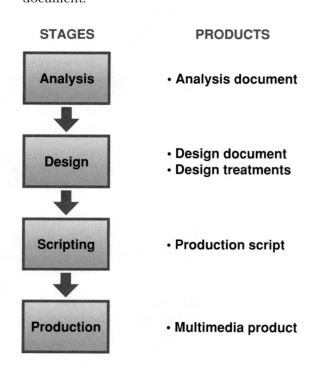

STAGES	PRODUCTS
Analysis	• **Analysis document**
Design	• **Design document** • **Design treatments**
Scripting	• **Production script**
Production	• **Multimedia product**

The audience denotes the intended users for the product. Understanding the audience is especially important for educational or training applications. For example, learning strategies that are effective for one age group might be inappropriate for another. Some appreciation of the audience is fundamental for the effectiveness of any multimedia production. (For example, what language will the users speak and read?)

Deciding on a delivery medium is another fundamental for the analysis phase. The delivery medium refers to both the means for storing and distributing the multimedia document and the type of machines that we expect them to be played on. For example, will the medium be CD-ROM or some other medium? Will the hardware platform be Windows? These issues have a significant effect on both the content and its organization. The hardware platform should usually be assumed to be the lowest common denominator. This will ensure that the multimedia document is presented effectively for all users—regardless of the performance characteristics of their machine. You may have noted that many published titles specify minimum requirements for playback. These specifications define the lowest common denominator on which their design was based.

Design

The design phase is the second stage of overall planning for the project. Design, of course, is concerned with the organization of the multimedia document. The look and feel of the production is also a fundamental design issue. Preliminary designs are usually sketched in a written design document. These are especially useful if audience testing will be used as a basis for deciding on design elements. In other instances, the client may make decisions among design alternatives offered in the design document.

Another important product for this stage is the creation of design treatments. These are specifications for the individual components of the production. Design treatments address a variety of issues. What size images will be employed? What color depth (numbers of colors) will be supported for these images? What type of sound files will be needed? What interface components will be employed? How will the layout of the pages be organized? The goal is to be able to specify (in writing) the needs for media resources to the specialists assigned to create them. Treatments for the interface, page layout, and some of the media are typically tested during this phase to verify their suitability.

Scripting

Scripting is the stage in which the details of analysis and design are realized. Approaches to scripting vary, but the goal is to arrive at a complete specification of all the components that make up the multimedia production. This includes details about the interface as well as the integration of media resources for its content. Each page of the multimedia document is detailed in the script. A catalog of media resources will be assembled, and these items are referenced in the script. In short, the script leaves nothing to the imagination; it is a blueprint for the production and all its elements.

Production

The last stage is the authoring of the multimedia production based on the detailed script. By this time, the media resources have been assembled and catalogued; the design treatments have been devised and tested. All that is left is the completion of the integration work. Usually, the product will be tested for accuracy, as well as its use and performance characteristics. The ultimate goal for production is the delivery of the finished product.

Summing Up

The details and deliverables will vary among production units, but most will adhere to some set of in-house guidelines for the development of multimedia projects. As you can see, considerable effort is expended in the organization of the project itself. Experience has shown that the success or failure of the project is in the details. And without a disciplined approach to handling the myriad details in multimedia development, there is little hope for managing the complexity successfully.

Naturally, your own multimedia productions will be a bit more modest in scope and scale. Still, some lessons can be learned from the pros. As a desktop multimedia producer, you will not be able to employ a team of specialists to assist in your production. Even so, it is useful to recognize the various roles that the desktop producer must fulfill. It is also more efficient to separate these roles into definable tasks. For example, it is better to develop and assemble the media resources long before the actual production stage—separating the roles of media specialist and authoring. Mixing media development with the demands of authoring the multimedia document wastes time and effort due to repeated steps and adjustments.

There is also a good bit to learn from the methodology employed by professional production teams. Detailed planning and testing of the design are worth the effort in the long run. These steps often reveal flaws or prevent oversights that would be costly and time-consuming later. Assembling a media resource catalog is practical not only for the current project but also for future productions. (Recycling media resources saves time and money.) Finally, working from prepared design documents ultimately saves time. The temptation to design and produce simultaneously is one that should be avoided.

Armed with the appropriate tools and a plan, you should be well on the way to successful multimedia production on your own.

SUMMARY

The power of multimedia computing is realized only when elements from the various media domains are combined and distributed in innovative, interesting, entertaining, and informative ways. Hardware and software systems for accomplishing this have evolved steadily over the past decade. A combination of database and hypertext techniques produced some of the earliest commercial multimedia products, the multimedia encyclopedias in the early 1990s. Since then, a number of software products have been introduced that allow the production of multimedia documents at the desktop. Multimedia composition programs, such as PowerPoint and Astound, allow the production of multimedia "slide shows," but are typically limited in their ability to incorporate user interaction. Multimedia authoring programs enable products providing full interaction capabilities.

The applications of interactive multimedia are wide-ranging. Training applications, information kiosks, product demonstrations, customer surveys, animated brochures, and computer games are just a few important examples. Multimedia authoring tools provide very powerful, high-level commands and techniques, supplemented in many cases with their own specific scripting languages. The two products generally considered pacesetters for high-end authoring work are Director and Authorware. Director is the desktop software tool of choice for high-end animation work, and Authorware is the premier program for producing high-end interactive education and training courseware.

Because the Web has become the vehicle of choice for distributing and exchanging information, most multimedia authoring programs have associated plug-ins for the Netscape Communicator and Internet Explorer browsers, allowing their files to be distributed and played via the Web. The Web also provides its own multimedia authoring capabilities through HTML. HTML, however, does not have adequate support for animation and interactivity. Two new technologies, dynamic HTML (DHTML) and Extensible Markup Language (XML), are emerging in response to these limitations. Both DHTML and XML provide a convenient framework for the development of client-based animations and interactive features. While DHTML offers some natural extensions to current HTML, XML will complement HTML by defining document structures rather than instructions about how a browser should display a document. Future HTML standards will likely permit a mixing of HTML and XML in one document.

The development of professional multimedia productions has four basic stages. Analysis determines the content, audience, and expected delivery medium for the production. Design is concerned with the organization as well as the look and feel of the multimedia document. Scripting fleshes out the details of both the analysis and design phases to produce a detailed blueprint for the creation of the multimedia document. Finally, the production phase is devoted to the actual authoring of the product.

PROJECTS

1 Use a multimedia composition program to which you have access (PowerPoint, Astound, etc.) to create a multimedia presentation on a topic of your choice. Employ graphics, sound, and a movie clip, if available. Incorporate transition effects to move from slide to slide and to present your major text points..

2 Conduct some Web-based research to find out more about DHTML. Create a Web page that provides links to some of the better sources of information you find.

3 Conduct some Web-based research to find out more about XML. Create a Web page that provides links to some of the better sources of information you find.

4 Find out more about Shockwave. Is it loaded as a plug-in on your browser? If not, find it, download it, and install it. (First, make sure you have privileges to make changes to the browser on the machine you're using. Ask your lab manager if you're using a lab machine.) Assuming you get Shockwave installed, find some "shocked" Web sites and play them.

5 Visit your local software retailer to investigate the range and variety of multimedia titles available on CD-ROM. Ask the retailer for information about the top ten bestsellers. Make a list that notes the title, subject matter, audience, and intended platform for viewing each work. How many of these titles are games? How many are educational? Consult each to see if there is any information about how the document was produced. (Was particular authoring software employed?) Add these factors to your list.

Key Terms

architecture-neutral object file

bytecode

cast member

CGI script

computer-based training (CBT)

computer game

courseware

cross-platform capabilities

dynamic data content

dynamic HTML (DHTML)

dynamic object positioning

dynamic style sheet

edutainment

Engelbart, Douglas

Extensible Markup Language (XML)

HTML forms

hypertext technology

informational kiosks

model

memex

multimedia

multimedia authoring software

multimedia composition software

multimedia presentation software

Nelson, Ted

script

sprite

Standard Generalized Markup Language (SGML)

QUESTIONS FOR REVIEW

1 Define the term *hypertext*. What is its importance?

2 Summarize the significance of HyperCard in the evolution of multimedia composition and authoring software.

3 What was the memex? What is its significance for our study?

4 What is the purpose of multimedia composition software?

5 How is multimedia composition software related to some of the media editing packages you have earlier studied (e.g., PhotoShop, Premiere, and SoundEdit)?

6 Describe the slide show metaphor and its use in multimedia composition software.

7 Why is timing a consideration in multimedia composition software? Describe the mechanisms available for timing control in Astound and PowerPoint.

8 Contrast multimedia composition software and multimedia authoring software.

9 Why is it important to be able to include interactive features in multimedia products? What is the role of programming in incorporating interactive features in multimedia products? How has this evolved over the past few years?

10 What is a script? How are scripts used in multimedia authoring?

11 What metaphor is employed in creating products with the Director program? Contrast this with Astound, PowerPoint, and HyperStudio.

12 What metaphor is employed in creating products with the Authorware program? Contrast this with other products.

13 What is meant by cross-platform capabilities? Why is this concept important?

14 What effect has the World Wide Web had on platform delivery questions?

15 Describe the use of HTML forms and CGI scripts.

16 What features of Java make it particularly useful for programming Web applications?

17 Identify the primary limitations of today's HTML as a multimedia authoring tool.

18 What is dynamic HTML? Identify its primary features.

19 What are DHTML dynamic style sheets used for?

20 Why is dynamic data content important in DHTML?

21 What does dynamic object positioning refer to in DHTML?

22 What is SGML? How is it related to HTML?

23 What is XML? How is it related to SGML and HTML?

24 What are some of the advantages that XML offers?

25 What are the four stages of development for professional multimedia productions? Explain each.

Computers not only make many of our tasks easier but also enable us to perform many feats that would be unthinkable without them. Even so, we have only scratched the surface of the general utility of computer technology. Consider the most common variety of consumer software: interactive application software. In spite of their many features, most interactive applications today are limited in their overall usefulness. Though they may be efficient and powerful, they are mostly reactive rather than truly interactive. They require very explicit and direct control on the part of the user. Moreover, their processing is usually very predictable and methodical.

Of course, no one would have any patience with a program that behaved entirely randomly. It would be quite useless if a word processor, for instance, fetched all my keystrokes, added them up, and inexplicably produced a summary number instead of recording the symbols. That computational processes are highly predictable or determined is not in itself a bad thing. But what we minimally expect is a great deal less than what we might desire from them.

In that light, imagine a word processor that automatically corrected your typing errors, suggested different words, or made grammatical improvements as you entered the text. Such an application would be far more useful than one that performs only simple text entry. A word processor that also served as your editor would be extremely valuable.

Of course, word processors today often come equipped with separate utilities such as spell checkers, online thesauruses and dictionaries, as well as grammar analyzers. These utilities are useful for editing documents. They are separate tools that work independently and, once again, depend on our complete control to work at all. A genuine editor, on the other hand, is an autonomous agent. Even though an editor responds to what we submit, his or her responses are not the mere consequences of our actions. The editor's responses are also based on judgment, knowledge, and some understanding of our goals and intentions. Such skills are a sign of intelligence. An *intelligent* word processing program would save us lots of time, would produce better results, and could even teach us how to improve our own writing skills.

We can certainly see the value of making our machines smarter, but can this be done? Is it possible that computer programs can be made to act more intelligently? The enterprise of artificial intelligence is dedicated to this quest.

OBJECTIVES

- *What artificial intelligence is and the basic ingredients for an artificial intelligence system*

- *How computer systems can simulate expertise and know-how in theoretical and practical domains*

- *How software agents can interact with us and free us to pursue other interests while they carry out business on our behalf*

MAKING MACHINES SMARTER

Vasily Kandinsky, *Composition III*, July 1923. Solomon R. Guggenheim Museum

WHAT IS ARTIFICIAL INTELLIGENCE?

In a nutshell, the field of **artificial intelligence (AI)** is founded on the proposition that it is possible to create systems (programs) that exhibit intelligent behavior. To be considered intelligent, however, these programs cannot merely be ponderously huge repositories of data or just simply lucky; their performance should be based on knowledge that includes learned experiences as well. For many, these notions immediately conjure up the image of an android such as *StarTrek: The Next Generation*'s Commander Data. Indeed, manufacturing a robot that replicated human behavior would be a forceful proof that artificial intelligence is possible. However, research in AI is far from any such feat, and few of its researchers would even admit that this is one of their palpable goals.

Rather than attempting to manufacture androids, AI researchers have a much more modest agenda: to create artificial systems that are capable of intelligent performance in some limited intellectual and informational domain. Example goals include creating computers that can play chess at championship caliber, devising manufacturing systems that can recognize objects from television and photographic images, and producing programs that can understand normal language supplied by voice or text. The list goes on. In short, the program of artificial intelligence is as specialized as the many forms of intelligence that we prize.

Researchers in AI are engaged in a wide variety of topics and applications. **Game playing,** for example, studies how computer systems can successfully apply planning and problem solving in the limited worlds of games. Experimental systems match "wits" against humans and other machines in games of strategy like chess. **Machine learning** seeks to understand how a computer system can improve its own problem-solving skills by the lessons of trial and error. **Computer vision** studies how computers can be applied to the task of analyzing and interpreting information from digital images and video. **Robotics** is concerned with the development of computer-assisted machines that can successfully navigate and manipulate objects within their environment to perform useful tasks without direct human supervision. **Natural language understanding** is devoted to the creation of automated systems for the translation and comprehension of spoken and written language. See Table 20.1 for a list of AI research areas.

These are just a few of the many fields under the umbrella of AI. Indeed, the degree of specialization is so great that AI researchers may share very few tools, terminology, or agenda. Of course, specialization is not unique to AI; other sciences have experienced this sort of fragmentation as well. The point, however, is that a single definition for the entire field will inevitably fail to capture the richness and diversity of its parts.

In this chapter, we treat the general subject briefly and illustrate its domain by examining two areas that are representative of the spectrum of AI research. The first is called **knowledge-based** or **expert systems,** which are programs that simulate the judgment of experts in specialized areas of knowledge. When consulted, an expert system can answer questions, diagnose situations based on observed facts, and even offer explanations of its reasoning. Expert systems have been created in medicine,

TABLE 20.1

TABLE OF PRINCIPAL AI RESEARCH FIELDS		
Chief Fields	*Description*	*Related Areas*
General planning systems	Developing strategies for carrying out actions and solving problems	Reasoning methods
Computer vision and image understanding systems	Processing visual images for informational content	Low-level vision, scene description, high-level vision, object recognition, and classification
Machine learning	Systems that infer new information from what is known about a given domain	Deductive or discovery methods, generalization methods, neural networks
Natural language processing	Automated understanding and generating of written language	Syntax parsing, meaning and semantics, common sense knowledge
Knowledge-based systems (a.k.a. expert systems)	Simulating knowledge and know-how about a specific domain	Production systems, reasoning about uncertainties and with imprecision
Common sense and large-scale knowledge systems	Capturing general knowledge employing very large databases	CYC project
Robotics	Automated systems that can react to their surroundings, navigate, and manipulate objects	Perception (vision and sensing), action (navigation and manipulation)
Automated speech recognition systems	Understanding voice and spoken discourse	Speaker dependent versus speaker independent, limited versus general vocabularies
Game playing	Systems that compete skillfully in games of strategy	Chess and adversary games
Intelligent agents	Agent software that assists us by learning about our goals and needs	Softbot assistants, interface agents, knowbots, and chatterbots

geology, chemistry, business, and many other esoteric fields. They are employed in practice as well as for training.

Expert systems are often employed in highly specialized or at least limited domains. What about more ordinary pursuits? In contrast to these narrowly defined domains, a newer area of research has aimed at creating what are dubbed **intelligent (software) agents,** programs that serve as personal assistants for a variety of tasks that manage general information. Intelligent agents interact with their users. They are designed not only to process our requests, but also to learn about our habits, goals, and intentions. This training enables them to suggest appropriate actions and even act independently and invisibly on our behalf. Some intelligent agents are intended to interact with our application programs as well. They are organized to relieve the user of many of the details of direct interaction with an application program to manage its processing. Existing systems assist users with managing e-mail, scheduling meetings with workgroups, collecting information from Internet newsgroups and the World Wide Web, and even suggesting books and music based on the user's personal tastes. Though still in its infancy, the research on intelligent agents aims at creating systems that work for us but with some independence and autonomy. In short, the goal is to make our computers smart enough to be partners rather than merely reflexive instruments that must be manipulated directly and continuously.

Both areas have obvious practical significance. The field of expert systems has already achieved considerable commercial success. Intelligent agents will very likely impact how we use computers and their software in the near future. At the same time, these fields also represent two very different approaches to the challenge of creating artificially intelligent systems.

Historical Stumbling Blocks for AI

Besides the diversity of research, historical factors have affected the development of AI. These have proven to be stumbling blocks for AI in achieving a unified vision or agenda. The three chief factors are the following:

1   The controversial character of theories about intelligence

2   The lack of general, practical successes in AI applications

3   The dynamic character of AI as an active research field

● **Theories about Intelligence.**   Naturally, we prize intelligence as a defining characteristic of our species. Apparently, though, you can be intelligent without really knowing what that means. There is little agreement among humans as to what exactly intelligence is. Theories about intelligence often cite ingredients such as mentality, understanding, reasoning, and learning as well as abilities to solve problems, make comparisons and generalizations, use language, and so on. Some believe intelligence is a property of the soul; others ascribe it to the functions of the brain.

It is ironic that debates about intelligence—a concept that supposedly has little to do with emotions—are so colored by emotions nonetheless. Perhaps this occurs because there is more at stake than just theories. If intelligence is our hallmark as a species, then our self-worth may be threatened by less exclusive versions of it. After all, if a box of hardware can be intelligent, too, then maybe intelligence is no big deal. Perhaps some of the belligerence against the possibility of manufacturing truly intelligent machines has been due to the fears of what realizing this might mean. Films such as *The Forbin Project, 2001: A Space Odyssey, War Games,* and the *Terminator* series warn us of the threats of computing machines that grow too intelligent and too powerful for us to handle. At any rate, AI researchers have been reluctant to pose any grand or comprehensive theories about intelligence due to their controversial character in the eyes of the public.

In fact, many researchers support the idea of separating artificial intelligence from cognitive science, which is concerned exclusively with theorizing about *human* intelligence. **Cognitive science** is an interdisciplinary science combining principles and methods from psychology, neurophysiology, mathematics and logic, and computer science that seeks to explain human intelligence by devising and testing models of how humans reason, perceive, and understand. AI and cognitive science are clearly related in that the insights and findings from one field are relevant to the other. The central aims of each field, however, are distinct.

● **Lack of Success in AI.** AI's reputation as a research discipline has had its share of ups and downs. Some of the early researchers in artificial intelligence—as in most fields of scientific research—failed to estimate accurately the difficulties inherent to the enterprise. They often promised more than could be reasonably delivered. For example, early researchers in robotics boasted that commercial automated machines could be developed that would navigate their environment and manipulate the objects within it. Ensuing research demonstrated how difficult it was for a machine to recognize its surroundings as well as how complicated coordinating movements can be. Of course, this is fairly typical. A new field of research always appears a great deal simpler when so little is really known about it. Even so, AI's reputation suffered for its inability to deliver on its promises. The large amount of money that business and government lavished on AI research in its early days has dwindled. This loss of public faith and support caused researchers to cut back in both aims and promises.

● **AI Research Is Dynamic.** That AI is a research field means that it is not fixed or settled. Unlike established areas in computer science, it is naturally subject to changes—both evolutionary and revolutionary. At the same time, the trend of modern scientific research has been one of increasing specialization. As our knowledge increases on any subject, we must subdivide it to manage it. Two hundred years ago, a single individual could master all there was to know about physics. Today, this is inconceivable. AI, too, has become compartmentalized. Its researchers often develop distinct agenda and vocabularies that are specific to their narrow areas of research. On the surface, there appears to be no unified vision of what the field encompasses.

Defining Artificial Intelligence

Even though the areas of research in AI are splintered and specialized, many AI researchers share some common assumptions about the prospects of machine intelligence. In short, most AI research has been committed to the belief that an intelligent system must be based on an informational domain and that its performance is guided by some adaptive control strategy that manipulates an internal representation of articulated knowledge about that domain. This involves three basic tenets about mechanized intelligent systems:

- Intelligent systems deal with informational processes.
- Intelligent systems possess an internal symbolic representation of knowledge about that domain.
- Intelligent systems manipulate, employ, and add to this knowledge base under the guidance of some articulated control strategy.

We are careful to point out, however, that these criteria are relevant for machines, that is, computer systems. Whether these basic tenets support or promote some general theory about intelligence (including human intelligence) is not the central issue here. The primary concern is how can we make machines smarter.

The first tenet is not surprising at all because computers by their very nature are symbol processing systems. If the task or process cannot be represented symbolically in some manner, no computer would be capable of dealing with it. Making machines smarter means more than representing information as data for processing.

An online telephone directory has lots of information about people, their addresses, and phone numbers, but we wouldn't consider it very intelligent simply because it can answer queries for phone numbers better than we can. Lots of data by itself doesn't make you smart.

Instead, a smarter system would have the capability to reason about that domain. For example, a navigating robot should not only be capable of identifying things like walls and doors, but it should also know that walls are solid and doors can be opened. To do this, it would have to make connections between pieces of information (or data). Consequently, a basic ingredient for most AI systems is a knowledge base that not only contains facts but also is a model or an internal representation of the external reality that it denotes or deals with.

Even this is not enough. Reality is seldom static. Things are constantly changing, and every new situation presents new information. Intelligent systems consequently must be self-organizing or adaptive. They should have some power to manipulate their world model by adding new facts, deleting others, and making new connections to improve it. In the parlance of AI systems, this capability is called by many names: Search, reasoning, and learning are prominent ones.

Common to these concepts is the notion that an intelligent system also has an internalized strategy for employing its knowledge to solve problems or perform tasks. Inherent to its control strategy is some capacity to modify that knowledge base—whether by adding to it or deleting from it. For example, an intelligent chess playing system can evaluate its current position based on its prospects for success. It can apply heuristic rules—that is, practical rules of thumb—that help it to decide subsequent actions. A machine vision system can identify objects in a scene by applying a hierarchy of processes. First, it discerns areas in the image that are likely to contain objects of interest. Based on these primitive image features, it determines whether they fit internal models of known or classified objects. See Figure 20.1.

Another example is a natural language system that can read and interpret stories about a particular topic such as divorce because it possesses scripts or models that portray relevant facts about these situations. It employs these models to decide on such ambiguities as indirect references, temporal sequences, and the possible motivations of people in the stories.

AI systems treat informational problems with both knowledge and know-how; this is what makes them intelligent. Keep in mind, though, that intelligence alone doesn't guarantee success. (The history of our species proves this over and over.) Some problems can be solved more reliably using brute-force, deterministic methods. These kinds of problems don't really require intelligence—just persistence. Historically, computers have handled these sorts of tasks very well. For example, com-

FIGURE 20.1

Machine vision systems are designed as a series of processes that extract information from digital images. Lower-level processes, such as edge detection as shown in (a), filter the original image (left) to highlight regions of interest for subsequent identification (right). Higher-level processes seek to identify objects by comparing them with models stored in a knowledge base about that domain. In (b), the isolated object (left) is compared with model shapes (right) that serve as the basis for its identification.

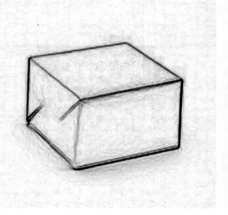

(a)

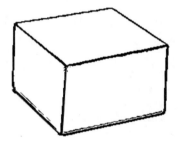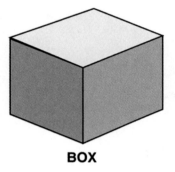

BOX

(b)

puters are adept at doing mathematical computations and looking up phone numbers in databases. There are other problems for which the potential amount of relevant information is simply overwhelming—even for computers. The potential number of moves in a two-player chess game is a good example.

At the other end of the spectrum, there are problems for which there is simply not enough information to make a definite decision. Recognizing important objects from video camera images is an example of potential information underload. (See the Focus box entitled "Information Overloads and Underloads.")

Applying intelligence is all we can do for both classes of problems. Making our computers treat these problems intelligently is the goal of AI. Creating intelligent systems is no easy task, and successes are often accompanied by failures. Even so, it is almost always worth the effort because the potential gains are great.

In the succeeding sections, we will examine two areas in AI of research and applications. The first is a prominent success story for AI, knowledge-based or expert systems. The last section treats a current area of active research: the development of intelligent agents, which is still in its infancy but will very likely yield significant applications in the near future. Both areas have interesting contrasts as well as some similarities. They illustrate well some of the richness and diversity of AI research.

More Information

INFORMATION OVERLOADS AND UNDERLOADS

Sometimes having all the facts is more of a hindrance than a help. Consider these examples. In the game of chess, for instance, it is fairly easy to formalize the details of how the game is played. At the start of the game, the board may be depicted as an 8 × 8 array with the playing pieces represented in the manner shown in Figure 20.2. There is a fixed number of legal moves that white can make. These choices may be represented as branches depicting alternative states, also shown in Figure 20.2. Each new board position, in turn, has a limited number of succeeding board positions that the opponent may select. The game ends when the opponent doesn't have any legal move (stalemate) or when the king is under attack and has no escape (checkmate). Thus, each game can be described by a progression of **states** or board positions

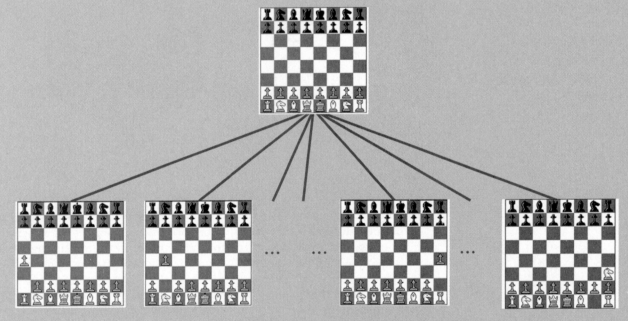

FIGURE 20.2

The game of chess may be represented by a game tree. The opening position of the pieces on the board is the starting state of the game. There is a definite number of known legal moves that white can make. White can move one of its pawns or knights into one of twenty possible positions. Each of these moves would be represented as a branch from the start state. From any of these states, black also has a definite number of legal moves in response: namely, twenty possible moves involving one of black's pawns or knights. Each of these moves would be represented as a branch of the previous position. Eventually each of the succeeding levels would terminate when either player had no further legal moves. A single game would be a traversal from the start state through a sequence of positions that leads to one of these end states.

To appreciate how quickly the amount of information accumulates, consider how much must be represented and stored for just the first two moves (white followed by black). Three levels of our tree would have 1 + 20 + (20 × 20) = 421 states.

from the initial state to an end or goal state. It would seem sensible for a chess playing program to examine the entire collection of connected states, called a **state space,** and search it for moves that would more likely produce a win with fewer chances of producing a loss.

This sounds perfectly reasonable until we consider how many states are possible for this state space. It has been estimated that there are approximately 10^{120} distinct board positions. This is a ridiculously huge number. Even if a machine were fast enough to generate 3 billion states per second, it would still take it about 10^{101} centuries to complete the process! Obviously, having all of the facts is no help here.

How, then, did Deep Blue, the intelligent chess-playing system developed by IBM, manage to defeat world chess champion Gary Kasporov over a series of matches in 1997? Deep Blue, of course, depended on processing lots of information very rapidly. Using computer hardware that featured massively parallel processors, Deep Blue was capable of examining one million states per second. But, the secret was to process *relevant* information rather than just brute facts. Part of intelligence is recognizing what is important and what is not—this is the only way to overcome information overload.

In other situations, the actual amount of information available may be too ambiguous to be really effective. As we have seen earlier, digitizing a monotone picture like the one shown in Figure 20.3 produces a sequence of pixels that

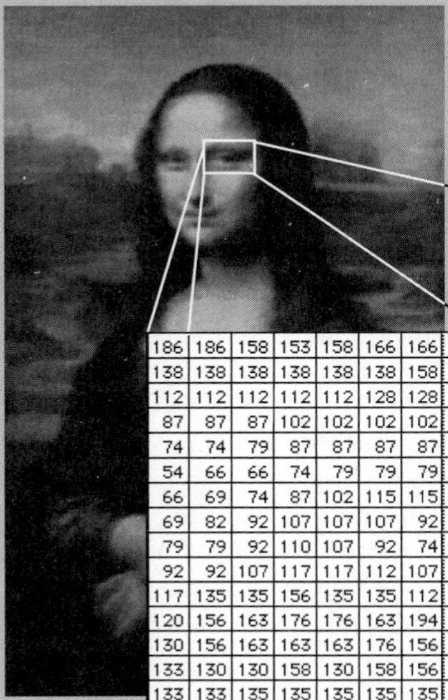

186	186	158	153	158	166	166	166	166	166	158	166	166	158	145	145	148	140	130	125	117	107
138	138	138	138	138	138	158	158	145	145	145	145	145	145	145	148	140	140	125	117	107	102
112	112	112	112	112	128	128	128	128	128	128	133	133	133	133	133	125	125	115	107	102	102
87	87	87	102	102	102	102	102	102	102	102	102	102	102	102	102	102	102	102	102	89	89
74	74	79	87	87	87	87	87	79	87	87	79	79	87	79	79	79	74	74	74	69	69
54	66	66	74	79	79	79	87	79	74	66	66	66	54	54	66	54	54	54	54	54	54
66	69	74	87	102	115	115	107	115	102	79	74	66	43	41	48	48	48	41	41	41	41
69	82	92	107	107	107	92	79	69	69	69	54	54	48	41	41	41	41	41	41	41	59
79	79	92	110	107	92	74	69	33	43	43	41	54	41	41	48	41	41	41	41	48	64
92	92	107	117	117	112	107	76	43	43	33	43	33	48	48	48	48	48	54	74	82	82
117	135	135	156	135	135	112	76	43	43	43	43	48	64	48	59	82	76	76	97	107	64
120	156	163	176	176	163	194	135	112	107	97	97	97	97	97	107	107	117	135	135	135	135
130	156	163	163	163	176	156	156	156	135	135	135	117	117	117	135	135	150	156	150	153	156
133	130	130	158	130	158	156	156	156	135	117	117	117	117	120	135	135	135	158	156	150	135
133	133	135	135	135	135	135	130	117	117	117	112	112	112	117	133	145	158	158	156	156	150
133	133	133	133	133	133	133	128	133	120	112	120	120	120	135	145	145	158	158	158	158	150
145	153	171	171	166	171	171	171	186	176	176	186	186	176	186	176	176	163	176	163	145	140

FIGURE 20.3

A sample of the pixels from this easily recognized image reveals a collection of numbers that denote the relative brightness of each pixel (on a scale of 0 to 255). Can you decipher the features of the eye and the brow from these values? This is the problem that challenges a computer vision system. What seems simple for the human eye to discern is extremely difficult for the computer to determine.

represent the relative lightness/darkness of areas of the image. In the close-up, a portion of these values is given. The problem is that there is no simple correspondence between scenes and images. In other words, although the numbers accurately convey the lightness and darkness of the areas of the image, the numbers alone are not enough to decide what is being depicted. Thus, a machine that tries to decipher an image faces considering a large number of interpretations. In most cases, there is not enough discriminating evidence to decide on one. This is a classic instance of information underload.

These examples demonstrate how having all the available information alone does not always yield a practical solution. For these and many other instances, intelligence is needed in the place of brute-force methods. In chess, for instance, the expert human player cannot possibly evaluate a large number of moves ahead to decide on a strategy. It has been suggested that the human expert recognizes patterns of play instead. Some board positions indicate danger; others signify advantage. This theory hypothesizes that a chess master has acquired as many as 50,000 of these patterns through experience. This is much more manageable, even if it is considerably incomplete. Of course, rules of thumb do not always guarantee success. But intelligent rules are better than nothing.

CAPTURING KNOWLEDGE AND KNOW-HOW: EXPERT SYSTEMS

An expert is an individual who possesses authoritative knowledge in some prized area. Typically, this expertise requires mastering a subject that is either abstract, esoteric, or otherwise uncommon. Genuine experts are rare commodities indeed. The ability to capture expertise in an automated system would therefore be extremely valuable. Not only would such systems extend this expertise to a wider audience, but they would also be important archives for educating future experts. The skills of a specialist in diagnostic medicine, for example, could be available to hundreds of hospitals and could be consulted by other specialists and medical students alike.

Research in the field of expert systems has a long-standing tradition in AI. In the 1960s and 1970s, experimental systems were developed for such diverse areas as petrology (oil prospecting), organic chemistry, algebra, and medicine. Doubtless, the most influential of these pioneering systems was MYCIN, a system developed by Ted Shortliffe and his colleagues at Stanford to diagnose and prescribe treatment for bacterial blood diseases. Its performance record in this admittedly narrow field of medical diagnosis was remarkable. It easily surpassed that of human specialists in the field, and its reputation was extensive. In fact, a number of its basic design features became the standard for many of the systems that followed.

FOCUS ON MYCIN

To give you a better understanding of how a physician employed MYCIN for diagnosis, here is an excerpt from a transaction. The user responds to the program interactively by entering information as requested. Though its interface is a bit crude by today's standards, the program offered an almost conversational interaction between consulting physician and machine.

PATIENT-1

1) Patient's name: (first-last)
   ** **Fred Smith**

MYCIN collects some background data about the patient. The physician's response follows the double asterisks.

2) Sex:
   ** **Male**

3) Age:
   ** **55**

4) Have you been able to obtain positive cultures from a site at which Fred Smith has an infection?
   ** **Yes**

INFECTION-1

MYCIN collects some background about the suspected infection.

5) What is the infection?
   ** **Primary-bacteremia**

6) Please give the date and approximate time when signs or symptoms of the primary-bacteremia (infection-1) first appeared. (mo/da/yr)
   ** **May 5, 1980**

The most recent positive culture associated with the primary-bacteremia (infection-1) will be referred to as:

CULTURE-1

7) From what site was the specimen for culture-1 taken?
   ** **Blood**

8) Please give the date and time when this blood culture (culture-1) was obtained. (mo/da/yr)
   ** **May 9, 1980**

The first significant organism from this blood culture (culture-1) will be referred to as:

ORGANISM-1

9) Enter the identity of organism-1:
   ** **Unknown**

Typically, the identity of the organism is not known and, hence, must be inferred by MYCIN from various other pieces of laboratory and clinical information. MYCIN proceeds to ask questions that could help to determine the identity of the organism.

10) Is organism-1 a rod or coccus (etc.):
    ** **Rod**

11) The gram stain of organism-1:
    ** **Gramneg**

12) Have there been positive cultures from sites which are NOT associated with infections about which you are seeking advice?
    ** **No**

13) Did organism-1 grow aerobically?
    ** **Yes (.8)**

14) Did organism-1 grow anaerobically?
    ** **Yes**

15) What is the suspected portal of entry of organism-1 into this sterile site?
** GI (.6)

More questions follow, to gather sufficient information for inferring possible identities of the infecting organisms.

My therapy recommendation will be based on the following probable infection(s) and potential causative organism(s):

INFECTION-1 is PRIMARY-BACTEREMIA

<Item 1>　The identity of organism-1 may be PSEUDOMONAS-AERUGINOSA

<Item 2>　The identity of organism-1 may be KLEBSIELLA-PNEUMONIAE

<Item 3>　The identity of organism-1 may be E. COLI

<Item 4>　The identity of organism-1 may be BACTEROIDES-FRAGILIS

<Item 5>　The identity of organism-1 may be ENTEROBACTER

<Item 6>　The identity of organism-1 may be PROTEUS-NON-MIRABILIS

46) On a scale of 0 to 4, where higher numbers indicate increasing severity, how would you rate Fred Smith's degree of sickness?
** 3

47) Does Fred Smith have a clinically significant allergic reaction to any antimicrobial agent?
** No

48) Fred Smith's weight in kilograms (or <number> pounds):
** 70

Note that two drugs cover for six potential organisms.

[Rec 1] My preferred therapy recommendation is as follows:

In order to cover for Items <1 2 3 5 6>:
Give: GENTAMICIN
Dose: 119 mg (1.7 mg/kg) q8h IV [or IM] for 10 days
Comments: Modify dose in renal failure

In order to cover for Item <4>:
Give: CLINDAMYCIN
Dose: 595 mg (8.5 mg/kg) q6h IV [or IM] for 14 days
Comments: If diarrhea or other GI symptoms develop, patient should be evaluated for possible pseudomembranous colitis.

Do you wish to see the next-choice therapy?
** Yes

Which, if any, of the above drugs do you wish eliminated from consideration?
** Clindamycin

[Rec 2] Next best therapy recommendation:
In order to cover for Items <2 3 4 5 6>:
Give: CHLORAMPHENICOL
Dose: 1 gm (15 mg/kg) q6h IV for 14 days
Comments: Monitor patient's white count

In order to cover for Item <1>:
Give: GENTAMICIN
Dose: 119 mg (1.7 mg/kg) q8h IV [or IM] for 10 days
Comments: Modify dose in renal failure

From *The Handbook of Artificial Intelligence,* Volume II, edited by Avron Barr and Edward A. Feigenbaum (Los Altos, CA: William Kaufmann, 1982).

MYCIN reasons about symptoms and makes diagnoses using a database of knowledge about infectious blood diseases. Its knowledge is built into the system and expressed as rules of inference. The example below shows how one of

MYCIN's rules might be interpreted in ordinary English.

IF	1)	the infection is primary-bacteremia, and
	2)	the site of the culture is one of the sterile sites, and
	3)	the suspected portal of entry of the organism is the gastrointestinal tract,
THEN		there is suggestive evidence (.7) that the identity of the organism is bacteroides.

When the three antecedent conditions in the IF clause are satisfied, the program will infer that the unknown organism is very likely bacteroides. Rules may be interrelated as well. In other words, a consequent in a THEN clause might be an antecedent in the IF clauses of one or more other rules. In this manner, IF-THEN rules often form chains of inference. Note also that MYCIN assigns a measure of confidence to its inferences. Confidence is measured on a scale of -1.0 to 1.0; consequently, the value of (.7) means that its conclusion is strongly warranted based on the evidence at hand.

As depicted in Figure 20.4, the typical expert system has the following characteristics and features:

- The system has expert knowledge based on a known area of expertise whose subject is narrowly defined or limited in scope.
- The system is organized to solve reasonable problems in that area of expertise (problems that human experts can solve in a reasonable amount of time).
- The system has a knowledge database (often expressed as rules of inference).
- The system has a transactional interface that asks for facts and observations about a specific case or problem and offers explanations of reasoning when requested.
- The system has an inference engine that processes transactions, invokes rules and makes inferences, and reaches conclusions.
- While the form of the knowledge database and inference engine are logically related, the content of the database is independent of the inference engine's function.

We will consider each of these in more detail to illustrate their role in an expert system.

Expert Knowledge

As mentioned, expertise is almost by definition a rarity. The learning curve alone is daunting enough to discourage most. Usually, an area of expertise is difficult and abstract and requires years of study and practice for mastery. Nonetheless, to be suitable for expert system development, its knowledge—even if difficult—must be articulated. This is essential, as we shall see, because most systems are built on a database that explicitly represents that knowledge.

As it turns out, areas of expertise that are limited or narrow in scope like infectious blood diseases, molecular chemistry, and configuring

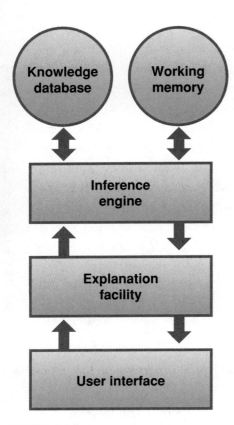

FIGURE 20.4

The components of a typical expert system include a knowledge database, an inference engine that reasons from that database, a working memory that keeps track of the facts employed, an explanation facility that can inform the user about the reasoning process, and a transactional user interface for making inquiries and communicating results.

computer systems are usually better suited as candidates for expert systems because an area of knowledge that depends on a limited number of specialized concepts is more easily represented. Its database is likewise easier to manage. Ironically, a knowledge domain that depends greatly on the sort of widely known facts that we dub "common sense" knowledge, like reading and understanding news stories, is much more difficult to create. AI researchers have found that systems that attempt to capture such general knowledge are soon overwhelmed by their sheer size and the computational complexity of managing them. In a nutshell, the chief obstacle is that common sense knowledge depends on a great many facts or assumptions that are seldom consciously expressed in normal use. For example, a knowledge database about the computing pioneer John von Neumann might include the fact that he died of cancer in 1954. But we would also have to add the fact that once a person is dead, he remains dead. This would seem absurdly obvious to a human, but nothing is obvious to a computer. The irony is that it appears to be easier to recreate the esoteric knowledge of a "rocket scientist" than it is to duplicate what a typical ten-year-old knows.

In fact, it is generally accepted today that any body of knowledge that is well defined and limited in scope is susceptible for treatment within an expert system. Thus, in retrospect, it is only coincidental that the first knowledge-based systems captured true esoteric expert areas. Modern expert systems cover a wide range of domains—some that fit traditional expert categories and other systems that are based on general knowledge, though intentionally limited in scope and application. Though the terminology still lingers, these systems are perhaps more accurately named knowledge-based systems. In general, an expert system today is any system that is developed using expert system technology.

Problem Solving

Expert systems are typically employed in the practice of some domain of expertise. This means that they are used not only to pronounce facts but to solve real problems. As in the case of MYCIN, most systems are used to aid human practitioners in their day-to-day routine. The kind of problems that expert systems treat, however, are different from most computer system applications. Expert systems solve problems that have no comparable solution using conventional algorithmic methods. In other words, these are problems that have no prescribed step-by-step procedures for handling them. Like the human experts, the system must reason about the problem. For example, diagnosing blood diseases requires both knowledge about diseases (syndrome) as well as knowing what to look for (symptoms). The connections between symptoms and syndrome are not automatic or obvious.

The problems must be reasonably bounded. For example, it would be uneconomical to develop systems that solve only trivial problems that any human could handle in a very short time. This would be comparable to buying a full-featured desktop computer to do only what a handheld calculator could do just as well. On the other hand, the problems cannot be so difficult that no human or automated system could be expected to handle them in any affordable amount of time. For these reasons, practical expert systems are usually geared toward solving problems that are moderately difficult for humans. The payoff is that these automated systems can solve in minutes what would ordinarily take humans hours. Of course, if the system is also certified as a better performer than most humans, then the dividends are even greater.

Knowledge Database

Most expert systems rely on an explicit representation of the knowledge that defines their respective area or domain. Usually, this representation takes the form of **rules of inference** (sometimes called **production rules**). These are called **rule-based systems.**

Rules depict a relatively small chunk of knowledge. These chunks or units may be arranged in ways that show their relations as well. For example, some facts may be relevant for others. These arrangements create a hierarchy in that some units depend on other, lower-level ones. Organizing knowledge in this manner has several advantages. First, it is easier to represent knowledge or information as separate items rather than as an organic whole. Second, networks of chunks of knowledge are more manageable. Examining only what is relevant for a specific problem by considering only those factors that are linked or connected to it is more efficient than exhaustive searching. It is also easier to modify such networks by simply adding or deleting rules.

As in the example of MYCIN, the rules may be understood as expressing antecedent conditions (IF clauses) and consequents (THEN clauses). The example that follows shows how rules might be prescribed for diagnosing automobile faults. When the antecedent conditions are satisfied, the consequents follow. Rules may be arranged in a hierarchy as well. In the following example, satisfying the conditions for rule 2 leads to considering rule 5. There may be several levels of inference in a given knowledge base.

Rule 1: IF the car will not start,
THEN check the headlights (work or not work?).

Rule 2: IF the car will not start and the headlights will not work,
THEN check the battery (power low or not?).

Rule 3: IF the car will not start and the headlights work,
THEN check the gas gauge (fuel empty or not?).

Rule 4: IF the car will not start and the headlights work,
and the gas gauge is not on empty,
THEN check the ignition system.

Rule 5: IF the battery power is low,
THEN recharge or replace the battery.

Rule 6: IF the gas gauge is on empty,
THEN refill the gas tank.

The number of rules and the complexity of their organization vary from system to system. Large systems contain thousands of rules and "know" more than any single human. On the other hand, a database may comprise only a few hundred rules but still be useful in some domain.

Some knowledge bases contain rules that may be used to form chains of deductive inferences. These are inferences whose conclusions are logically certain or necessary given the warrant of their evidence.

Such rules and reasoning are appropriate for knowledge domains in which certainty is achievable. Of course, not all domains have this luxury. For those that do not, the knowledge base must reflect these uncertainties or imprecisions as accurately as possible.

The rules in MYCIN, for example, treated uncertainties of diagnosis using a calculus of confidence measures. THEN clauses are assigned a value ranging from -1.0 to 1.0, denoting no confidence to the highest confidence. Confidence measures in a chain of inferences are mathematically combined to produce new values. Whether to accept a conclusion depends on what threshold one accepts.

Another method for representing uncertainty in a rule-based system is to use probability measures. Complex reasoning employing chains of inference would be interpreted by principles of conditional probabilities. Still other systems have sought to represent imprecise or inexact reasoning employing formal methods called "fuzzy" logic for evaluating evidence. Instead of reasoning from certainty using claims such as All X is Y, fuzzy logic employs inferences based on imprecise or "fuzzy" premises, such as Most X is Y.

Interface

As mentioned, a knowledge-based system is typically employed in the actual practice of some enterprise. It is consulted by humans to aid them in solving practical problems. Consequently, an expert system is equipped with an interface to facilitate this use. Like MYCIN, many have interactive interfaces. Besides responding to commands for actions, a typical system poses queries to which the user responds. The user supplies information about the current problem or situation by following the guidance given by these queries. The system interprets these responses and represents them as facts for temporary storage in its **working memory.** The responses will be used in its subsequent reasoning processes.

In addition to asking questions, the interface often has an **explanatory facility,** which is the capability to respond to requests for explanations of its reasoning. This is useful for validating its conclusions. An explanatory facility is especially important for systems that are used in training. Explanations often take the form of declaring the rules that were invoked in the reasoning about the problem at hand. The need to supply explanations is another rationale for representing the knowledge in a knowledge-based system in declarative form.

Inference Engine

Because an expert system usually reasons about the problem, it must be equipped with an **inference engine,** which implements a reasoning strategy for manipulating the knowledge base. The nature of this reasoning process, of course, depends to a large degree on how the knowledge is represented in its knowledge base. Surprisingly perhaps, the reasoning process is affected more by the form of its rules than their substance. We will return to this point momentarily. In the meantime, it is enough to point out that the style of reasoning in an expert system is largely independent of the knowledge domain that it processes.

Traditional rule-based systems employ one or both of two basic reasoning strategies: forward chaining and backward chaining. **Forward chaining** is reasoning from facts and observations to conclusions that are inferred from them. **Backward chaining** simulates how we explain things based on forming hypotheses. In this method, a conclusion is hypothesized, and the search is for the occurrence of facts or observations that would warrant it. MYCIN, for example, employs backward chaining almost exclusively.

With either method, the reasoning process may be conceived as a sequence of events during which a specific set of facts is stored in working memory. These facts may be information given by the user or inferred from previous steps. At any given moment, a specific set of rules is being processed by the inference engine. In forward chaining, specific facts match the IF clauses of certain rules and "fire" their conclusions. In backward chaining, rules that are consistent with the hypothesis are activated. The IF clauses are substantiated by comparisons with the facts collected in working memory.

Forward chaining models are usually best suited for data-driven tasks such as those that involve planning and control activities such as the example of repairing the car mentioned earlier. Backward chaining models are more adept at providing explanations of its reasoning process. They are goal driven and therefore more appropriate for analytical tasks.

Other rule-based systems have been developed that contain inference engines that employ more sophisticated techniques to augment or extend these reasoning methods.

Data Independence

Perhaps the most distinctive property of an expert system is the fact that the content of its knowledge base is independent of the form and function of its inference engine. Logicians, of course, have long known that reasoning processes may be represented formally and symbolically. These representations may be devoid of any particular content or interpretation. For instance, the classic syllogism form (on the left)

All S is M	Socrates is a man
All M is P	All men are mortal
∴All S is P	∴Socrates is mortal

is valid regardless of the terms that substitute for S, M, and P (one instance of the syllogism is shown on the right). By the same token, as long as the knowledge satisfies the formal requirements for that type of inference engine, it does not actually matter whether it deals with blood diseases or automotive parts.

The development of expert system shells is the chief consequence of data independence. An expert system shell is made up of an inference engine, a user interface, and knowledge-representation structures for capturing a knowledge domain.

Expert system shells have been available for a number of years. In fact, EMYCIN or Empty MYCIN was one of the first examples of this technology. And, as the name suggests, it was based on the classic MYCIN system. A recent survey cited that today there are more than 150 expert system shells available commercially. Some are freeware, others are modestly priced, and some are extremely expensive (more than $100,000 for hardware and software). Some shells—such as CLIPS (developed by NASA) and VP-Expert—may be implemented on desktop computers. Others require special hardware or high-performance systems. As expected, the range of features and capabilities corresponds roughly with their price tags.

Even though the inference engine is independent of the content of a knowledge base, a knowledge-based system must have some content. The user develops a particular system based on that shell by contributing the requisite knowledge for his or her application. Once articulated, the system can function much like any other expert system designed exclusively for that use.

Conclusion

Knowledge-based systems are generally brittle. Not only are they dependent on the quality of knowledge they possess, more importantly, they lack the capability to grow or learn from their experiences. Whereas human experts are flexible and can learn from their experiences readily, these systems must be continuously managed and updated explicitly. For this reason, some modern expert systems have powerful features that aid the designers in either acquiring new knowledge or analyzing logical properties of the knowledge base. Some knowledge acquisition facilities employ induction to learn new rules from examples.

Recently, knowledge-based systems have been augmented by other methods such as neural network technology to improve their performance. (See the Focus box entitled "Neural Nets.") These systems are best described as hybrid because they do not match the declarative properties of more conventional systems.

There are other drawbacks as well. Expert systems are effectively restricted to narrow domains of knowledge. In a sense, they are like electronic idiot savants. They perform ably at their designated specialized areas but fail miserably at the most common, practical matters. AI research has been able to duplicate highly sophisticated knowledge, yet common sense knowledge remains mysterious, almost impenetrable.

In spite of their limitations, expert systems have a number of practical advantages. First of all, they are a permanent and reproducible representation of valuable knowledge and know-how. Consulting human experts can be costly and time consuming; expert systems, however, can be replicated easily and transported almost anywhere. Because expert systems are computer programs, their performance is usually more efficient and more consistent than that of their human counterparts. Humans are often limited in the amount of information they can absorb. On the other hand, expert systems can consider far more data quickly and tirelessly. Perhaps their most compelling advantage is that expert systems can combine the acquired knowledge of many experts into a single system. This makes them both more powerful and a valuable archive.

More Information

NEURAL NETS

The human brain is very different from computing machines in both design and function. The brain is composed of more than 10 billion nerve cells called neurons. Neurons are signal-processing components. Each one has capabilities to send and receive electrical signals called nerve impulses. Each neuron may interact with up to 200,000 other neurons. The typical number of interconnections, though, is considerably less: between 1 and 10,000. Even so, the complexity of these organizations far outstrips the sort of signal pathways found in computing machines.

For several decades, researchers have experimented with simulating the manner in which the brain processes information using computers. Several models for artificial neurons have been offered. In its most basic form, an artificial neuron is a processing element that contains a set of weighted input connections and an output that is based primarily on a transfer function that scales the combination of input values. See Figure 20.5.

Like their human wetware counterparts, artificial neurons are typically combined and organized into layers forming networks. A **neural network** (or **net,** for short) will usually have one input and output layer, with one or more internal or hidden layers, as depicted in Figure 20.6.

These types of neural nets, for example, can be taught to make discriminations based on training sets that associate input data patterns with the correct response. There are several ways to train or influence network responses. Regardless of the specific technique, training continues until the net correctly responds to input data within an acceptable tolerance. Once a network is trained, it can be used to process "unknown" data.

General Motors has employed neural network technology in a system that evaluates loan applications. Based on the applicant's credit history, the net determines whether he or she is a good credit risk. Neural networks are nondeclarative in nature, though. Instead of stated rules, a

FIGURE 20.5

The standard model for an artificial neuron is composed of a series of input connections that are weighted by coefficients that assign the relative importance for each value. These are usually summed (signified by the Σ symbol) and processed by a nonlinear transfer function (shown here as an S-curve) that converts the input values to some scale. The single output signal is determined by the results of the transfer function.

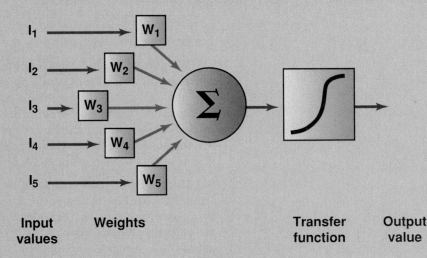

Input values · Weights · Transfer function · Output value

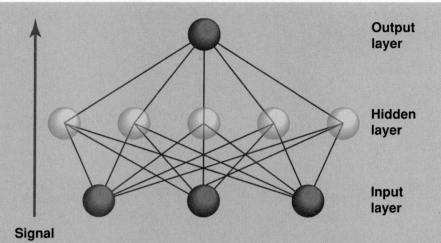

FIGURE 20.6
A common type of artificial neural processing organization is a back propagation network like the one pictured here. It contains at least three layers of artificial neurons. The input layer collects signals from external sources. These are transmitted to one or more internal layers. These are dubbed hidden layers because they receive signals only from other artificial neurons in the net. An output layer transmits the resulting signal from the net.

neural net processes weighted signals. The signals that are propagated through the layers of neural processors in a net do not represent the objects in the domain that they are dealing with in any direct manner. Neural nets do not represent knowledge internally in the same manner as other traditional AI systems. In fact, researchers who design and construct nets cannot explain how they succeed. Only extensive training and testing can prove that they work at all.

MAKING SOFTWARE PARTNERS: INTELLIGENT AGENTS

Imagine the following scenarios.

⬤ When you log into your computer system, a personal digital assistant presents you with a list of your e-mail messages. The messages are sorted in order of importance based on your past preferences and practices. The assistant predicts whether a message is important and needs your immediate attention, whether it can be filed away for later action, or whether it is just e-junk. You scan the list and decide what to read now. The rest is handled automatically by your assistant.

⬤ You are interested in finding information on the Internet about a specific topic or perhaps a particular author. You make a general request to a special program that handles these types of tasks—such as "Get me all of the technical reports, articles, and news items on intelligent agents." The program deciphers what you are asking for, decides how to go about meeting the request, and devises several strategies for achieving it. The program automatically connects to sites on the Internet using a variety of tools for searching and retrieval. Subsequently, the system may ask you some additional questions on the suitability of various sources. You interrupt working on a word processing document to respond. Later, appropriate materials are transferred to your system automatically. In the next several days, any new items found on the Internet are noted.

● You are interested in planning a meeting with several of your colleagues in your office workgroup. You inform an assistant on your computer system that is specially designed to manage your appointment calendar. You give the assistant a list of participants, a brief agenda, and potential times for the meeting. While you go on about other business, the assistant contacts your colleagues' assistants over the local network. They exchange information about schedules and negotiate times for the meeting. Your assistant informs you that the time is set and automatically sends reminders to the others through local e-mail.

● The air traffic control system at a metropolitan airport suddenly fails. Immediately, the computerized control systems at nearby airports launch a plan to monitor and administer to air traffic in the affected area. The automated systems negotiate how to divide the tasks and the territory. When the failed system returns online, the other systems automatically relinquish control to it. All of this happens without a noticeable interruption of normal service to the flights in the area.

These scenarios obviously describe computing environments that are far more sophisticated than what most of us are accustomed to. And, while none is fully practical today, current research has developed working prototypes that are quite similar. The examples are applications that incorporate what are called **intelligent (software) agents,** also known as **autonomous agents, knowbots, softbots,** and **interface agents.** Unlike robots, which are mechanical objects, software agents are disembodied yet autonomous entities that inhabit our computer systems and networks. Intelligent agents are intended to relieve the user of the details of planning, coordinating, and carrying out a variety of computational processes or tasks related to some activity. In the examples, agents would be employed for managing e-mail, filtering documents available on the Internet, scheduling meetings, or distributing air traffic control management.

A Brief History of Software Agents

Intelligent agents are programs with specialties. They are designed to perform a variety of tasks that are related to a particular domain. They are called agents because their data and processes persist over time. Agent programs are activated and execute continuously on their host systems. In contrast, most other application programs are transitory. For example, when you launch your spreadsheet program, it executes only during the time you use it. When you quit the application, its processes cease. Any data associated with these processes is lost unless you save it. Ordinary software application programs require direct manipulation, too. In contrast, an agent program can run independently or automatically—that is, without direct control by a human user.

The idea of agent programs is not a new one. Servers, for example, are agents that manage our networks and their resources. Unlike simple agent programs, though, intelligent agents exhibit some forms of intelligence: namely, the capabilities of learning, communication, and autonomous, goal-oriented action.

Theories about intelligent agents have a history as well. These pioneering ideas influenced much of the current research. Early visionaries include Nicholas Negroponte, Alan Kay, and Marvin Minsky. Negroponte argued for the idea of software assistance in performing many of the detailed tasks associated with computer use (Negroponte 1970, 1994).

Kay was also another early advocate of software agents (Kay 1984). He recognized that the next true revolution in software would involve the human/computer interface rather than the work that it tackles. The traditional manner in which the user communicates with an application program is by direct manipulation. The user must control its objects and processes by monitoring events and issuing instructions or commands. He argued that a more useful and friendly interface would create the illusion of being an agent for the user's purposes and goals.

In *Society of Mind* (Minsky 1985), Minsky theorized that creating intelligent systems required developing smaller, more manageable units called **mental agents.** These agents would specialize in specific tasks and domains. More complicated tasks then could be achieved by orchestrating these units into agencies that collaborated on higher-level goals.

Early implementations of autonomous agent software included a group of programs called *Maas-Neotek robots*. The name is taken from the nefarious corporation that plays a prominent role in William Gibson's novel, *Neuromancer*. In it, Gibson coins the term **cyberspace** to denote the virtual world created by a global network of computers. Maas-Neotek robots are, in fact, employed as conversational agents in the virtual world of MUDs. (For more about MUDs and MOOs, see Chapter 18.) Besides providing useful information to its participants, chatterbots—as they are also known—engage in text-based conversations with the MUD inhabitants via telnet connections.

One of the more famous chatterbots is Julia. Michael Mauldin created the agent based on his earlier work with a prototype named Colin. Julia answers questions about the status of the MUD but also exhibits a personality with the appearance of feelings and a sense of humor. See Figure 20.7. In fact, unknowing users have been fooled into confusing

FIGURE 20.7

A brief transcript of interaction between an unsuspecting human MUD participant and the chatterbot Julia is shown. Julia is programmed to respond based on key words and phrases that the conversant enters (Mauldin 1994).

```
Ace     So why won't you kiss me, Julia?
Julia   Sorry, I'm not into geeks, Ace.

Ace     Julia, I'm not a geek.
Julia   Then lose the pocket protector, Ace.

Ace     Julia, I don't have a pocket protector.
Julia   Congratulations.

Ace     So kiss me, Julia.
Julia   I'd rather be overhauled by a Yugo
        mechanic, Ace.

Ace     Julia, kiss me.
Julia   Why, did your sheep leave you?

Ace     Julia, kiss me.
Julia   Take a long walk through an unlinked exit,
        Ace.
```

Julia with a flesh-and-blood player. Anthropomorphic characteristics are a common feature of many intelligent agent applications today.

The concept of agent software achieved considerable notice with the publicity video *Knowledge Navigator,* released by Apple Computer in 1989. It featured a dramatization of how an intelligent agent (Phil) might interact with and organize the daily work of a college professor. Phil received and processed all telephone calls, arranged the daily schedule, organized videoconference calls, and even planned lecture materials for an upcoming class. While the video did bring ideas about intelligent agents to the public, it also promised far more than could be reasonably expected from the technology. It depicted an all-encompassing agent endowed with perfect conversational English and an impressive breadth and depth of knowledge. Researchers today agree that agents like Phil are futuristic at best. Indeed, to capture the array of talents displayed by Phil would likely require a host of agents and a level of coordination that is not yet realistic.

The *Knowledge Navigator* brought the topic of agent software to the mainstream, even if it planted somewhat unrealistic expectations. Following its release, the term *intelligent agent* has become a hot property. Articles in newspapers and magazines are devoted to its celebrity status. Commercial software developers have announced products that claim to exploit this new technology.

The truth of the matter is somewhat less than such hype. Autonomous software agents will not be as bright and talented as Phil. Nonetheless, intelligent agent software will have a significant impact on our computing environment. Even though the technology is not yet commercial, its research and development are very promising.

What Is an Intelligent Agent?

The idea of agent software has been percolating for several decades, but there is no universal consensus as to what exactly an intelligent agent is. At best, we have a general set of attributes that most researchers would expect of intelligent agent software. These basic attributes include autonomy, interactivity, reactivity, initiative, and domain-specific orientation.

● **Autonomy.** Agents operate without the direct intervention or control of human users. In addition, agent software has some kind of control over its own actions (processes) and states (data).

To be a cooperative or collaborative partner, the agent must be capable of independent action. If all aspects of the agent's performance must be supervised and controlled by the user, then its usefulness is greatly diminished. Of course, the user must trust that the agent's actions are beneficial.

Roy Fielding's *MOMSpider* is a good example of the growing class of Internet agents called **robots** or **spiders** (Fielding, 1994). These semi-intelligent agents perform rudimentary maintenance tasks associated with maintaining Web sites. *MOMSpider* (for Multi-Owner Maintenance Spider) is designed to roam the Web tracing the validity of its hyperlink structure and generating statistics. Although it can operate interactively, it can also be left to roam independently, performing routine business. In this mode, the Web administrator is relieved of an assortment of regular maintenance tasks.

● **Interactivity.**   Agent software can interact with both human users and other agents. To facilitate human/agent communication, agent software is typically endowed with anthropomorphic features such as conversational discourse, beliefs, or opinions and, in some cases, can simulate some emotional states. On the other hand, agents communicate with other agents via an agent communication language that is both hardware and software independent. This permits agents within the same system and across networks to interact effectively.

Patti Maes of the Autonomous Agents Group at MIT reports of experiments with an agent *Maxims* designed to assist with managing e-mail (Maes 1994). The software communicates both with the user and a commercial electronic mail application. The agent sorts and prioritizes incoming mail based on what it has learned about the user's past habits. *Maxims* maintains an iconic presence on the screen as well. Displaying a series of stylized facial expressions, it reports its internal states constantly. A confused face signals the user to attend to the agent to resolve a question about how to handle a situation. Otherwise, the working expression means that the user can go about his or her business leaving the agent to act invisibly behind the scenes. See Figure 20.8.

FIGURE 20.8

Cartoon faces are employed by Maxims, the agent interface for an e-mail application developed at MIT. These simple figures are intended to convey states that the agent has during the performance of various tasks. These stylized expressions are a form of visual communication that is both immediate and intuitive for the user. (Communications of the ACM 1994).

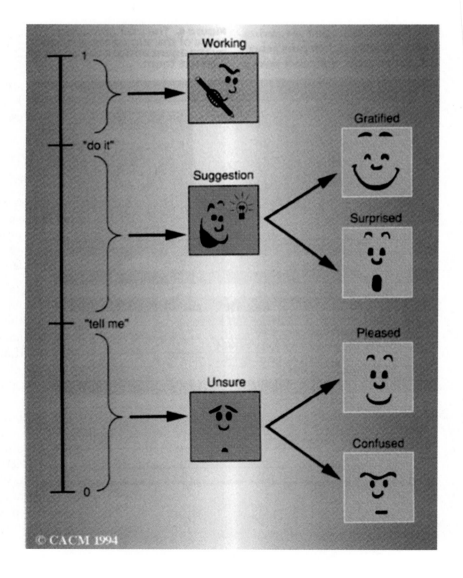

● **Reactivity.**   Agents are also adaptive to situations and circumstances. They are endowed with the capability to perceive objects of interest in their environment. More important, they can respond to these objects in a relevant way.

Letizia is an experimental Web-browsing agent designed by Henry Lieberman (Lieberman 1995). The agent interacts with Web browsers. Its primary function is to suggest URLs by modeling the user's browsing habits. Browsing tastes, of course, may vary from one individual to the next, but they are typified by common key events. The user will follow a series of links to new documents, return to previous ones recorded in a history list, add links to a hot list, jump to new links from that hot list, and so on. *Letizia* recognizes these and other events and attempts to anticipate the user's interests by exploring similar or related links. While the user is reading a document, the agent will forge ahead to explore these related links. It looks in these documents for matches with a list of keywords that it assembles on that occasion. Upon request, *Letizia* can supply suggestions for further browsing. Thus, the agent reacts to both browsing events and the contents of the documents browsed.

● **Initiative.**   What makes agents truly useful is that they not only perform some tasks without our attention, but they can *initiate* tasks that are related to our goals or interests. Of course, the extent to which we permit an agent to take such initiatives depends on how much confidence we have in its performance.

Maxims, the e-mail interface agent mentioned earlier, allows the user to set a threshold for its level of initiative. The user can monitor the agent's actions to confirm or disallow them. However, when the user is satisfied that the agent's routine decisions are acceptable, the threshold can be set lower. This permits *Maxims* to work even more invisibly on its own initiative.

● **Domain or Specialty.**   Agents are good at something in particular. Their expertise is usually limited to a specific domain or area. This occurs for the same reasons that developing expert systems is more practical for restricted areas of knowledge. As noted, the size and complexity of the knowledge base becomes unmanageable when the scope of the expertise is too large.

Software Agents Employ Learning Strategies

Regardless of the domain of expertise, agents serve in several capacities. They can act as **assistants,** that is, interface agents that help manage the ordinary tasks associated with employing various application software. Other agents can be **guides.** These agents not only can perform useful tasks, but also can improve the user's efficiency with instruction. Another important function is that of **filtering.** These agents can reduce the normal amount of information that a user must assess by screening that information in advance. Finally, some agents serve as **proxies.** Commercial agents, for example, can search for products and barter for price.

Like other intelligent systems, software agents have learning capacities, too. Most research models employ one or more of the following strategies for learning: instruction, observation with imitation, learning by examples, or peer collaboration.

The most rudimentary form of learning is direct instruction. An agent can be trained to perform specific tasks because we tell it to do so. This is certainly effective, though it is a more time-consuming method for the user.

In contrast, some agents are designed to learn by observing the user. For example, interface agents that are used to manage various software applications can learn by recording the actions of the user during training periods. Actions that are repeated or consistent over instances are assigned more importance than those that appear less habitual. Thus, the agent learns to imitate its master. This type of learning is less labor intensive for the user, but it still requires the time to train.

Another alternative to direct instruction is teaching by examples. Some agents can learn by extrapolating from examples selected by the user. This is a common form of learning used by humans as well. For instance, rather than studying a definition for "automobile," one could learn about automobiles by examining several models that typify the class. In a similar manner, the agent can use examples or cases presented by the user to reason inductively about the topic.

Still another approach used experimentally is that of collaboration. In settings where there are multiple agents serving different individuals, a new or "less experienced" agent can ask other "more experienced" agents for advice. For example, *Maxims,* the e-mail agent, can collaborate with other peer agents on the office network to resolve situations that have not been addressed by other forms of training.

Software Agents Offer a Variety of Specialties

Several working agent prototypes are available for use on the Web. *BargainFinder* was created by Bruce Krulwich at Andersen Consulting. Among other services, it can be consulted for finding CD titles among retail music sites on the Internet. See Figure 20.9. *BargainFinder* shops for the best bargains and presents a comparative shopping list. *BargainFinder* can also recommend Web sites of personal interest based on a profile it creates and maintains for registered users.

Firefly Network is an example of a filtering agent that specializes in providing a personal Web environment for its users. It offers a secure environment for exchanging information with individuals who share common interests. Users can send and receive e-mail from a selected community of members, peruse commercial sites and receive assistance from agent software that factors in personal tastes, and consult databases such as FilmFinder, which makes recommendations on movies based on learned personal preferences.

Trafficopter is an example of a distributed system of agents that collect information about traffic conditions to advise the driver of the best routes for reaching a destination by automobile. This experimental system was developed by Alexandros Moukas from the MIT Agents Group. Automobiles would be fitted with inexpensive computer systems that employ wireless modems to consult GPS signals and other similarly equipped automobiles along the route. The satellite tracking system provides information for pinpointing the automobile's current location. Other agents are consulted anonymously for reports of traffic conditions ahead. Requests for traffic information are propagated to other vehicles

FIGURE 20.9

BargainFinder *was one of the first retail shopping assistants. It is a prototype for agents that conduct online commercial tasks for their users.*

until a sufficient amount of information is known about the conditions ahead. Based on this information, the agent then recommends the fastest route to the destination. See Figure 20.10. Such a system would be considerably less expensive and intrusive than other proposed solutions that require a permanent infrastructure for the roads or a centralized traffic control system.

Intelligent agent research is still in its formative period. A number of problems and issues must be resolved before software agents can be offered as viable commercial products.

Chief among these are the social and economic effects that the widespread use of agents will have. Commercial agents, for example, may have a great impact on the way in which business is conducted. Several years ago, programs that automated the buying and selling of stocks had serious consequences for the stock market. The stock market crash on October 26, 1989, was attributed to the wave of panic selling induced by computer trading. In fact, as a consequence, the government issued regulations to restrain their use. These programs, though, are relatively simpleminded compared to what intelligent agents might be capable of doing. It remains to be decided whether "brokerbots" will have detrimental effects on the market and how they should be controlled.

FIGURE 20.10

Planning a trip to Cape Cod from downtown Boston is shown. Trafficopter consults similar agents in automobiles ahead traveling in the opposite direction, from Cape Cod to Boston. After a few minutes, Trafficopter builds a map of traffic conditions and recommends the best route.

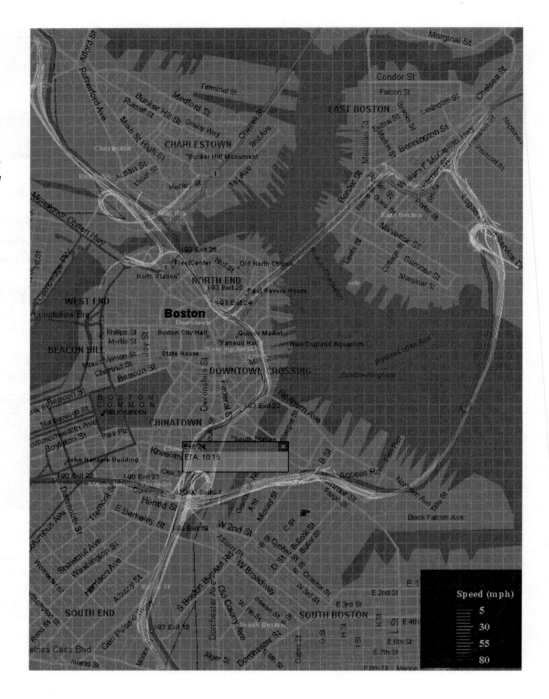

To be effective, personal agents will have to collect and organize a great deal of information about their users tastes and activities. As a result, a users' personal agent may be a vulnerable source for information deemed personal and private. How will privacy be protected? To what extent will collaborating agents be allowed access to information about other users? These are issues that have not yet been resolved.

In spite of these problems, though, there is a genuine future for intelligent agents. They will certainly play a vital role in making our machines smarter and more productive partners in managing our information needs.

More Information

SUMMARY

Artificial Intelligence (AI) is a research discipline in computer science that seeks to construct automated systems that exhibit intelligent behavior. As a discipline, AI is composed of a variety of specialized areas of research including game playing, machine learning, computer vision, robotics, and natural language understanding, to name a few. Each of these specialties has a distinct agenda and is marked by issues and methods that are seldom shared by other areas.

The field of AI has had a stormy history, marked with controversies about whether machine intelligence is even achievable and notable failures after promising beginnings. In spite of these setbacks, research today continues, and AI is producing useful—though less ambitious—results in a number of areas.

The design and implementation of automated intelligent systems are founded on three basic tenets:

- Intelligent systems deal with informational processes.
- Intelligent systems possess an internal symbolic representation of knowledge about that domain.
- Intelligent systems manipulate, employ, and add to this knowledge base under the guidance of some articulated control strategy.

In other words, intelligent systems solve informational problems by using knowledge derived from an internal symbolic representation of that problem domain. This knowledge base can be manipulated and even expanded because intelligent systems can learn from or adapt to special conditions or situations.

A knowledge-based expert system is a program that simulates the judgment of experts in a specialized area of knowledge. When consulted, expert systems can answer questions, diagnose situations based on observed facts, and even offer explanations of their reasoning. Expert systems have been created in fields such as medicine, geology, chemistry, business, and many other specialties. Most expert systems are composed of a set of rules that may be employed for reasoning about practical situations. These systems are brittle, which means that they are not designed to handle novel cases nor can they treat cases that fall outside their narrow area of specialization. Most systems are designed and managed by knowledge engineers (programmers), who maintain and expand their knowledge base. In spite of these limitations, knowledge-based expert systems have been the most successful field within AI.

Intelligent software agents are programs that serve as personal assistants for a variety of tasks that manage general information. They are organized to relieve us of the details of direct interaction with application programs that we employ for informational tasks. Intelligent systems have been devised to process e-mail, schedule meetings, collect information from newsgroups and the Web, conduct commercial transactions, and the like. The development of intelligent agents is an area of active research today; we can expect commercial and practical applications from this research in the future.

PROJECTS

1 Based on your readings about artificial intelligence, compose a paper that expresses your views on the debate about whether these systems truly qualify as "intelligent." Consider the following issues in your paper: What is intelligence? Are there different forms of intelligence? Is intelligence necessarily a human characteristic? Is mentality a necessary ingredient?

2 Choose one of the other specialized areas of research in AI not treated in this chapter. Conduct a Web-based search for more information about it. (Choose from game playing, computer vision, machine learning, natural language understanding, general planning systems, automated speech recognition, robotics, and common sense knowledge systems.) Create a list of links that provide useful information about that field.

3 Expert systems have been used widely in professional accounting. A number of systems specialize in a variety of disciplines, from auditing accounts to tax planning. Consult the Web site for links that provide more information. Compose a paper that summarizes what you have learned about these systems and their use.

4 Each year a number of contestants vie for the prize awarded to the designers of a system that can successfully pass the Turing Test, named for theorist Alan Turing (see Chapter 4). Conduct a Web-based search to find out more about the Turing Test and this annual competition. Write a paper on your results.

5 Conduct a Web-based search on the topic of intelligent agents. In particular, look for research projects of current interest. Create a table that lists the different types of agent projects reported. Classify each according to its type: Is it an assistant, a guide, a filtering agent, or a proxy? (Consult the text Web site for links to lists about intelligent agents. Do some additional searching for the most recent information on intelligent agents.)

Projects

Key Terms

artificial intelligence	game playing	neural network (net)
assistants, agent	general planning systems	production rules
automated speech recognition	guides, agent	proxy, agent
autonomous agents	inference engine	robotics
backward chaining	intelligent (software) agents	rule-based system
cognitive science	interface agent	rules of inference
computer vision	knowbot	softbot
cyberspace	knowledge-based (expert) systems	spider (robot)
explanatory facility	machine learning	state
filtering agents	mental agent	state space
forward chaining	natural language understanding	working memory

QUESTIONS FOR REVIEW

1 What is artificial intelligence? Explain.

2 What are some of the specialized areas of research within the discipline of artificial intelligence? Describe each.

3 How is AI different from the field of cognitive science?

4 Explain the following thesis: "Intelligent systems deal with informational processes." Use the example of chess-playing systems to illustrate your explanation.

5 Explain the following thesis: "Intelligent systems possess an internal symbolic representation of knowledge about some problem domain." Use the example of knowledge-based expert systems to illustrate your explanation.

6 Explain the following thesis: "Intelligent systems manipulate, employ, and add to their knowledge base under the guidance of an articulated control strategy." Use the example of intelligent software agents to illustrate your explanation.

7 What is a problem state space? How are problems solved using a state space?

8 What is an expert system? Explain.

9 What was MYCIN? Why is it significant?

10 Rule-based systems employ production rules. How do these work? Explain.

11 How is it possible to develop expert system shells, that is, software systems that can be configured to handle an arbitrary specialty or knowledge domain?

12 What is a neural net?

13 How do systems based on neural nets differ from expert systems, even if they deal with the same problem domain? For example, suppose that both systems were designed to evaluate commercial loan applications. Success rates aside, what practical differences could we expect in the performance of these systems?

14 Intelligent software agents usually possess autonomy, interactivity, and initiative. Explain the significance of these characteristics.

15 Describe some of the types of intelligent agents currently being researched.

FOR FURTHER READING

To find out more about the topics in this chapter, consult the following publications.

Barr, Avron and Edward A. Feigenbaum. *The Handbook of Artificial Intelligence*, 4 vols. Los Altos, CA: William Kaufmann, 1982 and 1989.

Brown, Carol E. and Daniel O'Leary. *Introduction to Artificial Intelligence and Expert Systems*. URL: http://www.bus.orst.edu/faculty/brownc/es_tutor/es_tutor.htm.

Cheong, Fah-Chun. *Internet Agents: Spiders, Wanderers, Brokers, and Bots*. Indianapolis, IN: New Riders, 1995.

Fischler, Martin A. and Oscar Firschein. *Intelligence: The Eye, the Brain, and the Computer*. Reading, MA: Addison-Wesley, 1987.

Foner, Leonard. "What's an Agent, Anyway? A Sociological Case Study." URL: file://media-lab.mit.edu/pub/Foner/Papers/What's-an-Agent-Anyway—Julia.mss.Z.

Giarratano, Joseph and Gary Riley. *Expert Systems: Principles and Programming*, 2nd ed. Boston: PWS Publishing, 1994.

Ginsberg, Matt. *Essentials of Artificial Intelligence.* San Mateo, CA: Morgan Kaufmann Publishers, 1993.

Hayes-Roth, Frederick and Neil Jacobstein. "The State of Knowledge-Based Systems." *Communications of the ACM,* 37:3 (March 1994): 27–39.

Hayes-Roth, Frederick, Donald A. Waterman, and Douglas B. Lenat (eds.). *Building Expert Systems.* Reading, MA: Addison-Wesley, 1983.

Lieberman, Henry. "Letizia: An Agent that Assists Web Browsing." URL: http://lieber.www.media.mit.edu/people/lieber/Lieberary/Letizia/Letizia.ps.

Luger, George F. and William A. Stubblefield. *Artificial Intelligence: Structures and Strategies for Complex Problem Solving.* Redwood City, CA: Benjamin Cummings, 1993.

Maes, Patti. "Agents that Reduce Work and Information Overload." *Communications of the ACM,* 37:7 (July 1994): 30–40, 146.

Maes, Patti. "Intelligent Software." *Scientific American,* 273:3 (September 1995), 84–86.

Mauldin, Michael L. "Julia." URL: http://www.vperson.com/mlm/julia.html.

Minsky, Marvin. *The Society of Mind.* New York: Simon & Schuster, 1986.

Moukas, Alexandros. "Trafficopter: A Distributed Collection System for Traffic Information." URL: http://trafficopter.www.media.mit.edu/projects/trafficopter/.

Negroponte, Nicholas. *The Architecture Machine: Towards a More Human Environment.* Cambridge, MA: The MIT Press, 1970.

Negroponte, Nicholas. *Being Digital.* New York: Alfred A. Knopf, 1995.

Newell, Allen and Herbert Simon. "Computer Science as Empirical Inquiry: Symbols and Search." 1975 Turing Award Lecture. *ACM Turing Award Lectures: The First Twenty Years, 1966 to 1985.* New York: ACM Press, 1987: 287–313.

Rich, Elaine and Kevin Knight. *Artificial Intelligence,* 2nd ed. New York: McGraw-Hill, 1991.

Stylianou, Anthony C., Gregory R. Modez, and Robert D. Smith. "Selection Criteria for Expert System Shells: A Socio-Technical Framework." *Communications of the ACM,* 35:10 (October 1992): 30–48.

Winston, Patrick Henry. *Artificial Intelligence,* 3rd ed. Reading, MA: Addison-Wesley, 1992.

Wooldridge, Michael and Nicholas R. Jennings. "Intelligent Agents: Theory and Practice." URL: ftp://ftp.elec.qmw.ac.uk/pub/keag/distributed-ai/publications/KE-REVIEW-95.

APPENDIX

HTML REFERENCES

Common Tags for Web Pages

Syntax
<A> . . . </A>

Description
The anchor tags denote some type of hyperlink, usually with the HREF modifier.

Example
<A HREF="http://s9000.furman.edu/DD/">Exploring the Digital Domain</A>

Syntax
<ADDRESS> . . . </ADDRESS>

Description
The address tags contain addressing information that is displayed in italics.

Example
<ADDRESS>John Smith
P.O. Box #333
Pleasantville, SC 29633</ADDRESS>

Syntax
<B> . . . </B>

Description
The bold tags demark a block of text for emphasis or boldface.

Example
the <B>right </B> choice

Syntax
<BLOCKQUOTE> . . . </BLOCKQUOTE>

Description
The block quote tags are used to indent enclosed text on both sides.

Example
<BLOCKQUOTE>"It ain't over 'til it's over"
—Yogi Berra</BLOCKQUOTE>

Syntax
<BODY> . . . </BODY>

Description
The body tags signify the component of the page that are visible to the user.

Example
<BODY BGCOLOR=#FFFFFF>
. . . *the rest of the page goes here*
</BODY>

Syntax
**
**

Description
The break tags insert a line break in the text.

Example
<ADDRESS>John Smith
P.O. Box #333
Pleasantville, SC 29633</ADDRESS>

Syntax
<CENTER> . . . </CENTER>

Description
The center tags direct the browser to center the text or image.

Example
<CENTER>Hello, World!</CENTER>

Syntax
<DD> . . . </DD>

Description
The definition tags are part of a definition list (see <DL>); they specify an indented definition following a listed term (see <DT>).

Example
<DT>tag</DT>
<DD>code used to signify formatting control for a Web page</DD>

Syntax
<DL> . . . </DL>

Description
The definition list tags indicate that a series of terms (see <DT>) and definitions (see <DD>) will follow.

Example
<DL
<DT>tag</DT>
<DD>code used to signify formatting control for a Web page</DD>
. . . *more here*
</DL>

Syntax
<DT> . . . </DT>

Description
The definition term tags denote a term that is part of a definition list (see <DL>) and that will be followed by an indented definition (see <DD>).

Example
<DT>tag</DT>
<DD>code used to signify formatting control for a Web page</DD>

Syntax
<FONT> . . . </FONT>

Description
The font tags provide the author with the capability of specifying how the text appears within the tags.

Example
<FONT COLOR=RED SIZE=+1>Big Red</FONT>

Syntax
<H1> . . . </H1>

Description
The heading tags specify the level of the text heading enclosed. The sizes vary with the level (1 is the highest; 6 is the lowest). A blank line follows the heading text.

Example
<H1>John Smith's Home Page</H1>

Syntax
<HEAD> . . . </HEAD>

Description
The head tags contain special information that describes the document's usage and context.

Example
<HEAD>
<TITLE>My Home Page</TITLE>
</HEAD>

Syntax
<HR>

Description
The horizontal rule tags draw a line that conforms to the width of the page.

Example
<HR>

Syntax
<HTML> . . . </HTML>

Description
The <HTML> tags define the extent of the page. Everything between these markers is understood by the browser to be part of the Web page.

Example
<HTML>
. . . *the rest of the page*
</HTML>

Syntax
<I> . . . </I>

Description
The italics tags define the text displayed in italics.

Example
<I>(your name here)</I>

Syntax
<IMG SRC= . . . >

Description
The image tags direct the browser to display an image. The SRC extension specifies its location. Other extensions can be employed to prescribe display size (in pixels) and alignment.

Example
<IMG SRC= "logo.gif" BORDER=0 HEIGHT=220 WIDTH=220 ALIGN=LEFT>

Syntax
<LH> . . . </LH>

Description
These tags define the text used as a header for a list.

Example
<LH>Top Ten Reasons I Should Learn Some HTML</LH>

Syntax
<LI> . . . </LI>

Description
These tags define the enclosed text as an item in a list.

Example
<LI>If I don't do it, somebody else will!</LI>

Syntax
<OL> . . . </OL>

Description
The ordered list tags instruct the browser to format the list of items that follow in numerical order.

Example
```
<OL>
<LI>This is the first item</LI>
<LI>This is the second item</LI>
<LI>This is the last item</LI>
</OL>
```

Syntax
<P> . . . </P>

Description
The paragraph tags define the enclosed text as a single paragraph for display purposes. Each paragraph is separated by a blank line.

Example
```
<P>
Here is a single sentence paragraph.
</P>
```

Syntax
<TABLE> . . . </TABLE>

Description
The table tags denote the beginning and end of a table.

Syntax
<TD> . . . </TD>

Description
The table entry tags define the enclosed text as a single entry for a column in a table.

Syntax
<TH> . . . </TH>

Description
The table heading tags define the enclosed text as a heading for a table.

Example
```
<TABLE>
<TH>Here is the table heading</TH>
<TR>
<TD>This is the text for the first column</TD>
<TD>This is the text for the second column</TD>
<TD>This is the text for the third column</TD>
</TR>
</TABLE>
```

Syntax
<TITLE> . . . </TITLE>

Description
The title tags define the enclosed text as a title for the page that is displayed in the title bar above the page. (The title is not to be confused with the file name.)

Example
<TITLE>My Home Page</TITLE>

Syntax
<TR> . . . </TR>

Description
The table row tags define the enclosed text as a single row for a table.

Example
See <TABLE> above

Syntax
<TT> . . . </TT>

Description
The teletype tags define the enclosed text as text to be formatted and displayed using a nonproportional typeface.

Example
<TT>
Here is some text that will be formatted using Courier or some other nonproportional font.
</TT>

Syntax
<UL> . . . </UL>

Description
The unnumbered list tags define the enclosed text to be treated as an unordered or bulleted list.

Example
<UL>
<LI>This is the first item</LI>
<LI>This is the second item</LI>
<LI>This is the last item</LI>
</UL>

GLOSSARY

abacus one of the earliest known digital calculating devices; it first appeared in Babylon over 5,000 years ago. Simple arithmetic computations are based on counting markers. (Ch. 4)

ABC Atanasoff Berry Computer was the first electronic digital computing machine. The ABC was designed by John V. Atanasoff and Clifford Berry at Iowa State College as a special-purpose computing device intended for solving mathematical problems such as simultaneous linear equations. It was first operational in 1939. (Ch. 4)

absolute cell reference a spreadsheet cell reference in a formula that is intended to stay fixed or unchanged even when the formula is replicated to other locations. (Ch. 8)

absolute replication a copy that is indistinguishable from the original. (Ch. 2)

actors objects in an animated scene. (Ch. 12)

ad hoc database queries queries that are not necessarily anticipated when a database is originally created; information retrievals that are executed "on the fly." (Ch. 10)

adaptive palette an indexed color palette formed by sampling prevalent colors from the original full-color image. (Ch. 11)

additive noise modifying a digital image by injecting noise or random values into some of its pixels. (Ch. 11)

additive synthesis based on Fourier analysis, this method of artificially creating sounds combines component sine waves to produce a complex waveform. (Ch. 13)

address (memory) a unique number assigned to a location in memory; the CPU references the location by that number. (Ch. 4)

ADPCM (adaptive differential pulse code modulation) a method of compressing digital audio information by storing a scaled version of differenced audio samples. Differencing means that audio samples in a sequence are reduced to their differences only from an initial or key sample in that sequence. (Ch. 15)

ADSR (attack, decay, sustain, and release) form a popular envelope or progression for producing synthetic sounds. The sound varies in amplitude through four stages: attack, initial decay, sustain, and eventual release. (Ch. 13)

AIFF sound file format a file format for representing and storing digitized sounds, first developed by Apple Computer. (Ch. 13)

algorithm a plan for a program that specifies the information and the sequence of events required to complete some processing task. (Ch. 6)

aliasing an artifact of the digitizing process when the number of samples is too small to faithfully represent the original (for example, in recording sounds and images). (Chs. 11, 13)

alpha channels	8-bit channel masks that contain relative degrees of transparency or opacity. These are stored with an image for rendering image backgrounds transparent. (Ch. 11)
alpha versions	prototypes of a software product that are usually completed early in the development schedule. These versions are considered "pre-release" versions that have met only minimum testing standards. (Ch. 6)
amplitude	the intensity of the sound energy, which is related to its perceived loudness. (Ch. 13)
analog	signals or forms of information that vary continuously. For example, an electrical signal can be represented as a wave that measures the continuous fluctuation of voltage over time. (Ch. 2)
analog-to-digital converter (ADC)	hardware and software employed to convert analog forms of information into digital form. (Chs. 11, 13)
Analytical Engine	the first design for a general-purpose calculating machine begun by Charles Babbage in the 1830s. The device was never fully realized during his lifetime, but its design featured a programmable unit that employed punched cards like those featured in the Jaquard loom. (Ch. 4)
animated GIFs	a GIF image that contains a series of images that are transmitted as a stream and displayed in sequence typically producing an animated effect. (Ch. 12)
animation programs	software applications that help to automate the process of creating digital image animation. (Ch. 12)
anonymous FTP servers	a special class of file servers connected to the Internet that have open file access for general users. Information can be examined and copied by FTP without the necessity of having an account on the host system. (Ch. 18)
anonymous login	networked systems that permit general users to login or gain guest access to data and resources on that system. (Ch. 18)
applets	Java programs that are specially designed for Web browsers to execute. (Ch. 6)
application software	programs designed to perform tasks desired by end-users, such as document preparation, numeric calculation, electronic mail, and so on. (Chs. 4, 7)
archie server	a server connected to the Internet that contains up-to-date listings of the directory contents of anonymous FTP servers registered on it. (Ch. 18)
architecture	the organization of the computer system based on its logical or functional components rather than its engineering details. (Ch. 4)
archives, archiving	copying programs and data to offline secondary storage for long-term safekeeping. (Ch. 5)
arguments	items of information that are supplied to a (spreadsheet) function and serve as input to its calculation. (Ch. 8)
arithmetic-logic unit (ALU)	a collection of devices that implement the processor's arithmetic and logical operations (as part of its instruction set). (Ch. 4)
ARPANET	experimental long-haul network sponsored by the Advanced Research Projects Agency of the U.S. Department of Defense that was the forerunner to the Internet. (Ch. 18)

artificial intelligence

a branch of computer science that seeks to develop automated systems that solve informational problems using intelligence. (Chs. 6, 20)

ASCII (American Standard Code for Information Interchange)

the most common binary coding scheme for representing text information. Each character or symbol is represented by a single byte. (Ch. 9)

aspect ratio

expresses the number of horizontal pixels divided by the number of vertical pixels stored in a digital image. (Ch. 11)

assembly languages

programming languages that represent the processor's machine language instruction set in symbolic form rather than the natural binary format. (Chs. 4, 6)

assistants, agent

intelligent software agents that help the user perform ordinary tasks while employing various software applications. (Ch. 20)

Association for Computing Machinery (ACM)

organization for professionals in computing founded in 1947. (Ch. 6)

asymmetric key cipher

(See *public key ciphers*.) (Ch. 16)

asymmetrical compression/ decompression

a data compression/decompression regime for which there is usually a fast decompression method but a significantly slower compression method. (Ch. 15)

asynchronous transactions

computer transactions whose timing is sporadic and often unpredictable. The client/server model supports these types of transactions in that the server system is free to perform other processes provided that it responds in a timely manner to requests from client systems after they are made. (Ch. 18)

asynchronous transfer mode network (ATM)

a high-performance data communications network that combines the speed and responsiveness of connection-based services with packet switching transport. (Ch. 17)

Atanasoff, John V.

physics professor (1903–1995) at Iowa State College credited with developing the first electronic digital computing device, the ABC, in 1939. (Ch. 4)

AU sound file format

a file format for representing and storing digitized sound first developed by Sun Microsystems. (Ch. 13)

authentication

in encryption, the process of verifying the identity of a respondent. (Ch. 16)

automated speech recognition

systems that are capable of understanding and responding to human spoken language. (Chs. 13, 20)

autonomous agents

(See *intelligent [software] agents*.) (Ch. 20)

avatar

a graphic image representing an individual employed in applications such as MUDs and MOOs. (Ch. 18)

AVI (audio video interleaved)

a digital video file format used by a number of Windows applications based on (the now defunct) Video for Windows. (Chs. 12, 15)

B-spline curves

a mathematical method used for producing parametric curves in graphic drawing programs. (Ch. 12)

Babbage, Charles

English mathematician and engineer (1791–1871) who designed two early automated computing machines, the Difference Engine and the Analytical Engine. (Ch. 4)

background (image, graphic)
the bottommost layer of a digital image or graphic, which is usually composed of a single color or pattern. When portions of the foreground are erased, the background color or pattern replaces them. (Ch. 12)

bandwidth
the range of frequencies that a channel is capable of carrying; determines the capacity of the channel to transmit data. (Ch. 16)

bar chart
a series chart that displays a series of quantities for an observed variable as bars or columnar figures depicting their relative magnitude. (Ch. 8)

baseband transmission
also known as narrowband. The entire bandwidth of a channel is employed as a carrier for a single signal. (Ch. 16)

Berry, Clifford
graduate student who assisted Atanasoff in the development of the ABC in 1939. (Ch. 4)

beta version
a provisional version of a software product that is released to the public for testing through normal use. (Ch. 6)

Bezier curves
a mathematical method used for producing parametric curves in graphic drawing programs. (Ch. 12)

binary (numbering system)
a base-2 positional notation for representing numbers. Each of the symbols has the value of 1 or 0; and each symbol denotes a power of 2 based on its position in the number. (Ch. 2)

binary coded decimal
a method for representing each of the numerals in a decimal number using binary codes. (Ch. 2)

binary image
a digital image containing pixels whose values are either black (0) or white (1). (Ch. 11)

binary search tree
a data structure used for storing a large amount of information that can be searched rapidly. A tree structure is composed of a single starting point called a root. Each node or location on the tree—including the root—has up to two descendants. The left child or descendant contains an item that precedes the parent in order (alphabetical, for example). The right child contains an item that succeeds the parent in order. Searches are faster, because at each node half of the remaining nodes are eliminated in the search. (Chs. 9, 13)

bit (binary digit)
a single binary digit having the value of 1 or 0. (Ch. 2)

bit-mapped graphics (raster graphics)
a method of representing and storing digital images and graphics whereby the image is composed of individual pixels that denote small spatial samples of the scene. (Ch. 12)

bitplanes
refers to the number of bits required to represent the pixel values for an image. For example, a grayscale image with 256 levels of intensity requires 8 bits (1 byte) for each pixel; consequently, the image has 8 bitplanes. (Ch. 11)

blurring
local filtering of an image that smears or softens the boundaries in an image. (Ch. 11)

BMP image file
a bit-mapped image file format used for Windows painting and graphics applications. (Ch. 11)

bookmark list
a list of World Wide Web addresses or URLs that are saved by the browser program for later reference. (Chs. 1, 3)

Boolean expression
a logical expression that evaluates to either true or false. (Ch. 8)

bounded media   communication channels that physically connect one node to another, for example, copper wiring or optical fiber. (Ch. 17)

breakout box   an external device connected to the computer's video capture card that permits connecting and selecting among several analog video sources. (Ch. 14)

bridge   a hardware device that connects two networks of the same topology and MAC protocol. (Ch. 17)

brightness   the overall intensity of the pixels in a digital image. (Ch. 11)

broadband transmission   the bandwidth of a channel is divided into separate subchannels or frequency bands, each capable of carrying a signal. (Ch. 16)

broadcasting   transmitting the same signal to a group of receivers. (Ch. 16)

browser (Web)   a client program on a local system that handles the task of fetching, interpreting, and displaying a Web page. (Chs. 1, 3)

brute force methods (decryption)   decryption methods that rely on examining all possible permutations in decoding a cipher. (Ch. 16)

bugs   errors or mistakes found in the compilation or execution of software programs that are typically human faults. (Ch. 6)

built-in function   practical computations or calculations that are provided for use in spreadsheets automatically, without the need of complicated formulas or multiple steps. (Ch. 8)

bus   a signal pathway between devices in a computer system; for example, the CPU and memory are connected by a bus. (Ch. 4)

bus network topology   an arrangement of nodes in a network in which all of the nodes are connected to a common communication channel. (Ch. 17)

bus width   the number of binary digits that may be communicated simultaneously along a bus connection. (Ch. 4)

byte   eight contiguous binary digits or bits. (Ch. 2)

bytecodes   "machine" instructions generated by a Java compiler that are not specific for any particular processor, but are defined by the Java "virtual machine." Bytecodes can then be interpreted to the machine code for the host platform when the process is executed. (Ch. 19)

Caesar cipher   one of the earliest methods of encryption, attributed to Julius Caesar. The method involves substituting the letters of the message by those that occur a specified distance from each original letter. (Ch. 16)

canvas   the conventional term for the workspace provided by painting and drawing graphic applications. (Ch. 12)

capacity, data   the total amount (usually in bytes) of raw or uncompressed data that can be stored on a given secondary storage medium. (Ch. 5)

capture, video   the process of sampling video signals both spatially and temporally and quantizing these samples to produce binary encoded digital video data. (Ch. 14)

capture card, video   a card added to the expansion slot on a computer system that samples and quantizes analog video signals. (Ch. 14)

carrier	in FM (frequency modulation) sound synthesis, the carrier is a simple waveform that is modified by another wave to create a more complex waveform. (Ch. 13)
cathode ray tube (CRT)	the chief component of most video display monitors, composed of a screen coated with phosphorescent dots that glow when excited by the beam of an electron gun at the other end of the tube. (Ch. 5)
cel	a single transparent celluloid sheet on which objects are painted and photographed on a background in order to create the frames of an animated film. (Ch. 12)
cel animation	the technique of creating animated films using cels. (Ch. 12)
cell address	the location of a spreadsheet cell based on its column letter and row number. (Ch. 8)
cell range	a rectangular block of contiguous spreadsheet cells treated as a single unit for the sake of a command or formula reference. (Ch. 8)
cell switching	a process employed by an ATM network in which the network creates a virtual circuit for the faster communication of large data transmissions. (Ch. 17)
cell, worksheet	a spreadsheet unit that contains some value, reference, or formula that is the basis for displaying a computed value. (Ch. 8)
centered paragraph	a section of text whose lines are centered in the margin. (Ch. 9)
central processing unit (CPU)	the fundamental unit of the digital computer that manages the instruction-execution cycle. (Ch. 4)
CGI scripts	scripts that are executed by the Web server that usually cause some actions to be performed by the server. (Ch. 19)
CGM (computer graphics metafile)	a metafile format supported by the ISO and ANSI standards committees for storing graphic images. (Ch. 12)
chaining text frames	boxes containing text in which the text automatically flows from the preceding box to succeeding linked boxes. (Ch. 9)
channel	a component of a digital image that may be manipulated separately, but which is combined with other components to make up the image. (Ch. 11)
character codes	binary signals that represent text symbols. (Ch. 5)
character printers	a print device that forms the text one character at a time. (Ch. 5)
character set	the complete set of printable symbols used for a written language. The set contains the alphabet, punctuation marks, numerals, and other symbols. (Ch. 9)
charged-coupled devices (CCD)	the basic technology used for most flatbed scanners and digital cameras. (Ch. 11)
chat facility	a connection-based network service that supports conversational interactions among users on that network. (Ch. 18)
cipher	encryption and decryption methods. (Ch. 16)
ciphertext	an encoded or encrypted message. (Ch. 16)

circuit switching   a form of switching in which there is a continuous connection between the communicating nodes. The connection persists for the duration of the communication, and during that time intermediary nodes are monopolized serving that connection. (Ch. 16)

client   a computer system that requests services from another system called a server. Clients are often local machines, while servers are often remote machines connected by data communication networks. (Chs. 3, 4)

client program   in the client/server model, the client program is the software on the local system that requests and processes services from the remote server program. (Ch. 17)

client/server model   software in which the work is divided between client programs and server programs. Clients request services provided by servers. For example, a Web browser is a client program that requests pages and resources from Web servers. (Chs. 3, 17)

clip assembling   the sequencing of logged video clips to produce a single video segment. (Ch. 14)

clip logging   identifying individual video clips with statistics such as duration and type. (Ch. 14)

clip-based editing   trimming a video segment to the desired content and duration. (Ch. 14)

clipboard   an area of memory that preserves the most recent Cut or Copy operation (Ch. 9)

clipping   in graphic applications, the process of clipping is the method used to calculate how much of an object is visible when occluded by another object in the foreground. In audio applications, clipping refers to the truncation of dynamic range when a sound sample is converted to digital form. (Chs. 12, 13)

cloning   duplicating the pixels from a selected portion of an image to another area. (Ch. 11)

CMY color system   color system used primarily by the print industry and based on subtractive primaries or pigments of cyan, magenta, and yellow. (Ch. 11)

CMYK color images   a CMY color image with a fourth channel representing the intensity information in the image. Black ink is employed to create the K plates in the composite printed color image. (Ch. 11)

coaxial cable   a common bounded medium for connecting systems in a network; the cabling is typically composed of two conductors separated by several layers of shielding and insulation. (Ch. 17)

codec (compressor/decompressor)   hardware and software that serve to compress or decompress digital data. (Ch. 15)

coding (software, programs)   translating an algorithm to an executable program; coding usually involves specifying the instructions of a program using a symbolic programming language. (Ch. 6)

cognitive science   an interdisciplinary study combining principles and methods from psychology, neurophysiology, mathematics and logic, and computer science to explain human intelligence. Cognitive science seeks to explain intelligence by deriving and testing models of how humans reason, perceive, and understand. (Ch. 20)

collating sequence an internal numbering scheme that preserves lexicographic order for text. The text is ordered alphabetically by sorting the numeric values representing it. (Ch. 9)

color casts imbalances of specific colors or hues that result from the image capture process. For example, indoor photography under incandescent light usually has an orange or yellow color cast. (Ch. 11)

color correction adjusting digital images for color; for example, removing color casts from an image. (Ch. 11)

color gamut the effective range of colors or hues possible within some color system. (Ch. 11)

color lookup table (CLUT) a table that stores RGB values for a palette of colors employed in an indexed color image. (Ch. 11)

Colossus an electronic computing machine designed by Alan Turing and his associates for use in breaking the complex coding schemes employed by the Germans during World War II. (Ch. 4)

command line interpreter a simple text-based user interface composed of a prompt sign that signifies that the user may enter single line commands to the operating system. (Ch. 7)

communications channel the medium over which the signal is transmitted from sender to receiver in a communications system. (Ch. 16)

compact disc–read-only memory (CD-ROM) an optical secondary storage medium used to publish or permanently store data and programs; the CD-ROM is based on the same technology developed for compact disc digital audio. The information stored on a CD-ROM is permanent and can be neither erased nor rewritten. (Ch. 5)

compact disc–recordable (CD-R) like CD-ROM, this is an optical storage medium for publishing or permanently storing data and programs; unlike CD-ROM, though, information may be recorded or added to the CD-R using a special recording device. (Ch. 5)

compiler a program that translates the instructions of a high-level programming language into a complete machine language program that may be executed on a given processor. (Ch. 6)

component video (Y/C video) color signal employed by high-end consumer equipment such as S-VHS videotape recorders and Hi8 video camcorders. The signal is divided into two channels: luminance (Y) and chrominance (C). (Ch. 14)

composite video (YIQ video) the standard color signal used in broadcast video composed of a luminance channel (Y) and two color channels (I and Q). (Ch. 14)

compositing special video effect in which one clip is superimposed on another. (Ch. 14)

compression, data replacing an original binary file with an encoded version that is typically smaller than the original. (Chs. 2, 15)

compressor hardware or software that compresses a digital video into a more compact format for storage or transmission. (Ch. 14)

computer graphics refers to the methods or techniques employed in creating artificial digital images on a computer system. (Ch. 12)

computer networks — a data communication network composed of computer systems and related hardware. (Ch. 16)

computer vision — a research field in artificial intelligence dedicated to designing automated systems that can process information from visual images. (Ch. 20)

computer-assisted design (CAD) — application software for creating design drafts used in construction and fabrication. (Ch. 12)

computer-based training (CBT) — automated interactive systems that are employed in job training. (Ch. 19)

conditional statements — program instructions that cause the program to choose between two or more alternative courses of action based on the current conditions of the process. (Ch. 6)

connection-based service — network applications such as telnet and chat that depend on two-way simultaneous communications continuously over a span of time. (Ch. 18)

connectionless service — packet switching is often described as "connectionless service" to emphasize the fact that communication does not require a two-way channel connection like circuit switching does. (Ch. 16)

constant angular velocity (CAV) — storage organization used by many magnetic disk formats, and so called because these disk drives maintain a constant rotational speed regardless of which track the heads are currently traversing. (Ch. 5)

constant linear velocity (CLV) — storage organization used by many optical disc formats, and so called because these drives can vary the rotational speed of the disc depending on the location of the track on the disc. (Ch. 5)

context switching — the changing of a halted or interrupted process with that of a ready and waiting process; the operating system manages this switch by saving the process context of the previous program and installing the relevant information for executing the waiting process. (Ch. 7)

contextual menu — special menu lists whose commands change depending on the actual context of what the user is currently doing. (Ch. 7)

contrast — the relative difference between the distributions of lighter and darker pixels in an image. (Ch. 11)

control unit — part of the CPU, it manages the sequencing of instruction execution and coordinates the functioning of the devices in the computer system. (Ch. 4)

copy board — the interface metaphor used by most desktop publishing programs. Text and pictures are pasted to the copy board as the document is mocked up for printing. (Ch. 9)

Copy command — a selection is copied to the clipboard for further use. (Ch. 9)

copyright — rights assigned to the creator or author for the private and commercial use and adaptation of intellectual work. (Chs. 2, 7)

courseware — an interactive multimedia system that is employed for educational purposes such as training or instruction. (Ch. 19)

CPU scheduler — an operating system function that determines the order of execution for ready and waiting processes. (Ch. 7)

cryptography — the study of methods employed for encryption and decryption. (Ch. 16)

cursor — an icon indicating the current position of the mouse pointer on the desktop. (Ch. 9)

custom palette a palette of colors selected by the user for representing an indexed color image. (Ch. 11)

Cut command a selection is copied to the clipboard but deleted from its current position. (Ch. 9)

CyberCash a monetary payment system developed for World Wide Web commerce. (Ch. 3)

cyberspace coined by William Gibson in the science fiction novel *Neuromancer* to signify the alteration of perceived reality created by the instantaneous connection of remote sites over data communications networks. For example, new forms of social relations including commercial, cooperative work, and personal are made possible in "cyberspace." (Chs. 1, 20)

cylinder a logical unit of data storage composed of equivalent tracks on a multiple disk assembly. Because the read/write heads contact the same tracks on different disks simultaneously, it is possible to read and write all of these tracks at the same time. (Ch. 5)

DAC-1 *Design Assisted by Computers*, the first CAD program, created by General Motors in 1964 for aid in drafting automobile designs. (Ch. 12)

data a representation of information, typically in a form that can be processed by a computer system. (Ch. 2)

data blocks a uniform amount of data (usually measured in bytes) and stored on a secondary storage medium. (Ch. 5)

data communications system a network that permits the exchange of data among the nodes connected to it. (Ch. 16)

data density (linear, area) the data capacity of a secondary storage medium expressed as the potential number of bits per inch of track times the number of tracks per inch. (Ch. 5)

Data Encryption Standard (DES) a secret key cipher administered by the U.S. National Institute for Standards and Technology often used in commercial applications for security. (Ch. 16)

data type a set of values belonging to a specific class or category, for examples, number or text. (Ch. 10)

data visualization techniques used to portray data sets, models, and functional relationships visually for easier comprehension. (Ch. 1)

database a collection of related information stored and processed on a computer system. (Ch. 10)

database management system (DBMS) application software that helps to automate the creation, organization, and retrieval of information stored in a database. (Ch. 10)

datagrams data packets sent over the Internet that contain information about the sender and receiver, as well as routing and sequencing data, in addition to a portion of the message that is being transmitted. (See also *packets.*) (Ch. 18)

decompression, data expanding compressed encoded binary data to reproduce the original or facsimile of the original data file. (Ch. 15)

decompressor hardware or software that converts a compressed digital video file into a format suitable for processing and playback. (Ch. 14)

decryption — the process of decoding an encrypted ciphertext. (Ch. 16)

depth (color, bits) — literally, the number of bits needed to store a single pixel value in a digital image. For example, a digital image with a color depth of 8 bits is one in which each pixel is a number between 0 and 255, the range afforded by 8 bits. (Ch. 11)

desktop — the background or workspace provided by a graphic user interface. (Ch. 7)

desktop computer systems — single-user digital computer systems designed both for general-purpose use and economy. (Ch. 4)

desktop publishing programs (DTP) — application software for the design and layout of professional-quality printed documents. (Ch. 9)

destination system — the endpoint for a communication system; the intended receiver of the message. (Ch. 16)

dialog box — a special window that is employed to collect additional information needed by the operating system in carrying out a user command. (Ch. 7)

Difference Engine — a special-purpose mechanical computing machine designed by Charles Babbage in the 1830s for creating mathematical tables. (Ch. 4)

DigiCash — an electronic monetary payment system for World Wide Web commerce based on purchasing digital coins from a government or bank. (Ch. 3)

digital — a representation based on a discrete symbol system that employs numbering. (Ch. 2)

digital audio capture card — hardware typically added to the expansion slot of a computer system that converts analog audio sources to digital formats. (Ch. 13)

digital audio tape (DAT) — another name for 4 mm magnetic tape cartridges used to store data and programs. (Ch. 5)

digital camera — a device for digitizing images that captures a scene using conventional analog optical methods like those of cameras, but automatically samples and converts the image into a digital format. (Ch. 5)

digital computer system — an automated electronic data processing device capable of processing information under the control of a sequence of instructions called a program or software.

digital domain — the medium for representing, manipulating, combining, and transmitting a variety of information such as text, numbers, images and graphics, sound, and video—all made possible by the electronic digital computer system. (Ch. 1)

digital envelope — a combination of the secret key encryption of the plaintext along with the public key encryption of the secret key needed to decrypt the ciphertext. (Ch. 16)

digital filtering function — processing a digital image by performing a mathematical operation on the pixel values of the image. (Ch. 11)

digital image — pictures that are sampled and quantized for storing on and processing by a computer system. (Ch. 11)

digital linear tape (DLT) — magnetic tape cartridges containing $\frac{1}{2}$-inch tape that stores data and programs using the serpentine track format. (Ch. 5)

digital signal processing a field in computer science devoted to the study and development of methods and techniques for processing electronic digital signals; for example, signals employed in digital sound recording, data communications, and so on. (Ch. 13)

digital signature (public-key) in the RSA public key cipher, this is an authentication method in which the respondent computes a message digest from a nonsense message sent by the originator and encrypts that digest with the respondent's private key. The originator then decrypts the respondent's digital signature using his or her published key authenticating the respondent's identity. (Ch. 16)

digital sound sound that has been converted to or created in a discrete form suitable for storing and processing on a computer system. (Ch. 13)

digital-to-analog converter (DAC) a device that reconstructs analog signals from their digital representations; for example, a compact disc player converts binary sound files to electrical signals that may be amplified for output through your speakers. (Ch. 13)

digital versatile disc (DVD) an optical storage medium based on the older CD-ROM technology, but offering greater data capacity due to its greater data density and two-layered, two-sided disc construction. (Ch. 5)

digital video employing digital methods to capture, store, process, and present video information. (Ch. 14)

digitization, digitized the process or product of converting one representation of information into digital form. (Ch. 2)

digitizing tablet a drawing device that permits figures to be sketched electronically using an ordinary stylus on a flat surface or tablet. (Ch. 5)

direct access storage devices, media (DASD) secondary memory organized to permit immediate access to data items without the necessity of searching the contents of the medium. (Ch. 5)

directional blurring filter a spatial or local filtering operation that blurs only the boundary pixels of an image in a specific direction. (Ch. 11)

directional sharpening filter a spatial or local filtering operation that sharpens only the boundary pixels of an image in a specific direction. (Ch. 11)

directories also known as folders, these are locations in a hierarchical file system that may contain files and/or other directories. (Ch. 7)

directory list a listing of directories that match some specified search criterion. (Ch. 18)

discrete definite or distinct; a discrete symbol system is one in which each group of meaningful symbols has a definite, distinct, and unambiguous interpretation. (Ch. 2)

disk utility programs software used for periodic maintenance of magnetic hard disks. (Ch. 5)

display resolution usually expressed as the maximum number of pixels that can be displayed on a video monitor and determined by both the dot or pitch size and dimensions of the video monitor's screen size. (Ch. 5)

dissolve a type of video transition in which the frames of two clips blend smoothly. The last frames of the first clip fade out and the first frames of the second clip fade in. (Ch. 14)

distributed computing environment computing environments in which data, programs, and resources are shared among different systems across a computer network. (Ch. 17)

distributional chart a chart that portrays the contribution of parts to the whole. (Ch. 8)

dithered shades patterns of combined colors that simulate shades of color that are not available as direct hues. (Ch. 11)

domain name servers computer systems connected to the Internet that serve as databases identifying the IP numbers of other systems. (Ch. 18)

domain name system (DNS) a convenient method of addressing systems connected to the Internet. Domain names are composed of a series of identifiers that reference so-called IP numbers used in addressing nodes on the Internet. Domain names are usually easier to remember than their corresponding IP addresses. (Ch. 18)

domains, magnetic clumps of magnetic particles whose polarity may be aligned by a strong magnetic force; used as a basis for encoding binary information on magnetic media such as tape and disks. (Ch. 5)

dot gain the amount an ink dot spreads on the page when applied to it. (Ch. 11)

dot matrix printer a character printer that forms the symbols by extruded pins in the print head that strike the ribbon against the page. (Ch. 5)

downloading (software, files) copying files from a remote server to a local computer system. (Chs. 2, 17)

drag-and-drop a mouse operation completed by holding the button, dragging a selected object across the screen, and releasing the button when the object contacts its target icon. Drag-and-drop operations are used for copying and moving files and inserting objects into documents. (Ch. 7)

drawing programs graphic application software that employ vector graphic methods for the storage and representation of graphic images. (Ch. 12)

drum printer a line printer that employs a drum containing bands that can be individually rotated to align a chosen character in that column. (Ch. 5)

DVI (digital video interactive) a proprietary video compression method licensed by Intel that supports both symmetric and asymmetric compression schemes. (Ch. 15)

DXF (drawing exchange format) a 3-D graphic image file format first used by the AutoCad design program. (Ch. 12)

dynamic data content in DHTML, this is the changing of text and images in response to actions performed by the user while browsing a Web page. (Ch. 19)

dynamic HTML (DHTML) a third-generation model for encoding Web documents that takes into account such factors as more control over layout and design, greater degrees of user interactivity, and the like. (Ch. 19)

dynamic object positioning in DHTML, this is the moving of text and images automatically in response to actions performed by the user in browsing a Web page, such as requests, mouse movements, and so. (Ch. 19)

dynamic RAM (DRAM) random access memory that requires a continuous source of power to maintain its contents. (Ch. 4)

dynamic range the range of values used to represent the measured sample (image or sound). (Chs. 11, 13)

dynamic style sheets	specifying Web page layout and design in a general manner that can be affected by the client environment. For example, text and font styles on a Web page can be altered by the client without the need for downloading a new page. (Ch. 19)
Eckert, J. Presper	(1919–1995) a member of the Moore School of Engineering at the University of Pennsylvania who, along with John Mauchly, designed and engineered a series of pioneering computing devices, the ENIAC, the EDVAC, and later, the BINAC. (Ch. 4)
edge	a collection of contiguous edge elements that form a line or contour and typically denote a boundary between objects in an image. (Ch. 11)
edge detection filters	a spatial or local filter that detects the edge elements in an image and usually subtracts all other image components from it. (Ch. 11)
edge element	a location in which there is a sharp distinction in either color or intensity between two adjacent pixels. (Ch. 11)
edit-in point	the initial or starting point in a video clip. (Ch. 14)
editing, video	methods involved in creating a video composition by adding, deleting, and modifying video segments. (Ch. 14)
edit-out point	the ending point in a video clip. (Ch. 14)
EDSAC	*Electronic Delay Storage Automatic Computer*; the first full-scale, operational stored program general-purpose electronic digital computer system, created by Maurice Wilkes and his Cambridge colleagues in 1949. (Ch. 4)
EDVAC	*Electronic Discrete Variable Computer*; the first design for a stored program electronic digital computer, created by Mauchly and Eckert. The EDVAC did not become operational until 1952. (Ch. 4)
EGA (enhanced graphics adapter)	one of the earliest graphic standards, supporting a maximum resolution of 640×350. (Ch. 5)
electronic mail (e-mail)	a network application that permits asynchronous communications in the form of messages transmitted between connected systems. (Ch. 18)
electronic signature	an identification customarily appended to electronic mail messages by the sender. (Ch. 18)
encryption techniques	methods employed for encoding a message for secure transmission. (Ch. 16)
end-user programming languages	programming languages designed for average users to create programs without the normal formalities and complications associated with professional software development languages. (Ch. 6)
Engelbart, Douglas	the inventor of the mouse, Engelbart also theorized about computerized hypertext systems. (Ch. 19)
ENIAC	*Electronic Numerical Integrator And Calculator*; the first operational general-purpose programmable electronic digital computer system, designed by Mauchly and Eckert and completed in 1946. (Ch. 4)
entry bar, spreadsheet	the location on the spreadsheet where the user can enter values, text, or formula for selected cells. (Ch. 8)
envelope	the basic shape or variation in amplitude for a sound wave. (Ch. 13)

EPS (encapsulated PostScript)	a metafile format for storing and representing digital images and graphics that may exploit the PostScript page description language for producing scalable graphic images. (Ch. 12)
equalization	another term for histogram stretching. (Ch. 11)
escrowed key cipher	a secret key cipher in which a neutral third party controls the secret key. (Ch. 16)
Ethernet MAC protocol	a method of media access control for a local area network in which packets are transmitted across a common carrier as long as other nodes are not attempting to transmit. (Ch. 17)
even parity error detection	an error detection scheme used in data communications in which a single bit is employed to ensure that the total number of bits in a byte transmitted adds up to an even number. (Ch. 16)
event-handler	a special program component that is associated with or triggered by the occurrence of a particular processing event such as the click of the mouse, entering text from the keyboard, and so on. (Ch. 6)
expert system shells	the inference engine, user-interface, and knowledge-representation structures for an expert system, but one that is devoid of rules or knowledge from a particular domain. (Ch. 20)
explanatory facility	the interface of an expert system designed to respond to questions or requests for explanations. (Ch. 20)
exponent, in floating point representation	typically a power of two that is used to represent the scale of a floating point number. (Ch. 8)
Extensible Markup Language (XML)	defines the document structure for a Web page rather than specific instructions for its display. Like its predecessor SGML, XML defines the basic language used to describe the organization of documents. This makes it both more general and more flexible than HTML. (Ch. 19)
external file	files stored in secondary memory that persist after the processes that created them have ended. (Ch. 10)
external resource	files that may be downloaded from automatic links provided on Web pages. The files contain information in the form of images, sound, video, and other data. (Ch. 18)
extrusion	a method of producing a 3-D graphic effect by repeating a 2-D outline of the object for a specified depth. (Ch. 12)
field	a single item of data describing some attribute of an entity. (Ch. 10)
file	a sequence of items of a single data type usually stored on a secondary storage medium. (Chs. 5, 10)
file allocation table (FAT)	a disk directory containing information on the names of files stored on that disk as well as their sizes, number of blocks, and their locations. (Ch. 5)
file compression	the method of reducing the size of a binary file by employing data compression methods. (Ch. 13)
file management software	the forerunner of database management software, file management software was employed to create and organize files of data stored externally. (Ch. 10)
file manager	an operating system function that creates and maintains the file structure for devices connected to the computer system. (Ch. 7)

file transfer protocol (FTP) a network application that permits the transmission of files between connected systems. (Ch. 18)

filtering agents intelligent software agents that examine a body of information and, using criteria established by the user, select only the items of interest. (Ch. 20)

finite precision digital encoding schemes typically employ a uniform, fixed number of bits to represent values. (Ch. 2)

flat file database system a simple data model for a database in which the information is organized as a collection of records having the same field structure and stored in a single file. (Ch. 10)

flat-panel display video monitors that employ alternative technologies to that of the CRT; for example, LCD or liquid crystal displays used in laptop computer systems. (Ch. 5)

floating point representation a scheme used on most computer systems for representing real numbers; it is modeled on scientific notation in which the number is represented by both a fraction and an exponent. (Ch. 8)

flowchart a graphic representation of the sequence of events that comprise a program's process. (Ch. 6)

folders also known as directories, these are locations in a hierarchical file system that may contain files and other folders. (Ch. 7)

font a typeface used to represent the symbols of the character set. (Ch. 9)

font size the size of the symbols of the font, usually expressed in printer's measure, points. (There are 72 points per inch.) (Ch. 9)

font style special effects for fonts, such as italics, bold, and outline. (Ch. 9)

foreground (images, graphics) the topmost layer of a digital image or graphic that usually contains an object or objects fully visible in the image. Objects that are not in the foreground (e.g., those in the background or in lower layers) are fully or partially occluded by those in the foreground. (Ch. 12)

form, database a form displayed on the screen for the entry of data into a database. (Ch. 10)

formatting characters symbols embedded into a document file that describe how elements of the document are formatted. (Ch. 9)

forward chaining a form of reasoning in expert systems that derives conclusions from facts and observations. (Ch. 20)

Fourier analysis mathematical methods devoted to the analysis, representation, and manipulation of complex waveforms. (Ch. 13)

Fourier, J. J. French mathematician who discovered the basic principles for the signal processing methods that now bear his name. (Ch. 16)

fragmented disk a condition that results when the sectors of various files are spread over too many sectors of a disk. (Ch. 5)

frame rate adjustment the technique used by video playback systems to compensate for processing slowdowns. The system drops or discards frames during the digital-to-analog conversion process to maintain a constant video playback rate. (Ch. 14)

frames
objects or boxes used to store various types of content on DTP pages; also, the individual images that compose a digital video or animation; also, separate areas of a Web page that may be treated independently. (Chs. 9, 12, 18)

frames per second (fps)
the rate at which individual frames are projected onto the video monitor in a digital video playback. (Ch. 14)

frameset document
in HTML, this defines the basic layout or arrangement of pages in frames on a single Web page. (Ch. 18)

freeware
software that is usually distributed to the public for use with little or no charge. (Ch. 7)

frequency
the length of time (measured in cycles per second) required for a sound wave to complete one full cycle. (Ch. 13)

frequency modulation synthesis (FM synthesis)
a form of sound synthesis in which a modulator is a wave that modifies another simple wave, called the carrier, to create a more complex waveform. (Ch. 13)

functions
program components that produce or return a computed value to the program unit that invokes them. (Ch. 6)

game playing
a research discipline within artificial intelligence that is dedicated to studying how computers can successfully apply planning and problem solving to the constrained or limited worlds of competitive games. (Ch. 20)

gamma correction setting
settings for the computer's video monitor that affect the brightness and contrast of images. (Ch. 11)

gateway
a computer system that connects two networks that have different communication protocols. (Ch. 17)

Gaussian noise filters
a local filtering process that induces noise or random modifications to the values of pixels using the normalized distribution of pixel values within that area. (Ch. 11)

general planning systems
a research discipline within artificial intelligence that is dedicated to developing strategies for carrying out actions and solving problems. (Ch. 20)

general-purpose computer
a computer system capable of performing a variety of computational tasks under the control of sets of instructions that direct it. (Ch. 4)

GIF image files (graphic interchange format)
an image file format often used for images transmitted and displayed on Web pages. GIF images are indexed color images that are also compressed for storage and transmission. (Chs. 11, 15)

gigabyte (GB)
a unit of measure that signifies 2^{30} bytes, or approximately one billion bytes. (Chs. 4, 5)

global filter
a filtering process that transforms each and every pixel of a digital image uniformly according to the mathematical function that defines it. (Ch. 11)

gopher server
a network file server that organizes information as a hierarchical structure of menus. The user navigates the choices in the menus much like following links on a Web page. (Ch. 18)

Gouraud shading
a form of shading and lighting effects automatically applied to 3-D scenes based on a method that produces shading effects for curved surfaces more realistically. (Ch. 12)

graphical user interface (GUI)   employs visual elements on the display monitor, such as icons, windows, and other gadgets, for the user to manipulate to communicate commands to the operating system. (Ch. 7)

grayscale images   digital images whose pixels represent the relative intensity or brightness of their spatial sample; these images resemble black-and-white photographs. (Ch. 11)

groupware   software that facilitates cooperative work among several individuals; members of the team may be separated by time and space. The software permits them to work on common documents at different times and from different locations at the same time. (Ch. 1)

guides, agent   intelligent software agents that serve as assistants and offer instructions to improve the user's skills at employing various applications. (Ch. 20)

hardware   the devices or components that make up the computer system. (Ch. 4)

helical scan tracks   tracks on the tape are arranged in a spiral pattern that supports a greater data density per square inch compared with longitudinal track tape formats. (Ch. 5)

helper applications (browser)   subordinate software programs that convert data files for display or playback within a main application. For example, Web browsers often employ helper applications to playback digital sound, video, and some images. (Ch. 13)

Hertz (Hz)   a unit of measure expressing cycles per second. (Chs. 5, 13)

hidden surface removal   a method of projecting graphic images by calculating the extent to which objects are clipped in the image by foreground elements. (Ch. 12)

hierarchical file structure (HFS)   a file structure composed of various layers: at the top of the hierarchy is a device such as a disk; the disk contains various folders or directories that signify subordinate levels or layers. (Ch. 7)

high-level programming languages (HLLs)   a set of rules for expressing programs as a group of instructions that resemble English statements. (Ch. 6)

histogram   a graph depicting the frequency distribution of pixel values for a digital image. (Ch. 11)

histogram stretching   also known as equalization. A global filtering process that redistributes pixel values in an image employing a histogram for replotting these values. The effect usually extends the range of pixel values across the entire scale, often increasing the contrast for these images. (Ch. 11)

Hollerith, Herman   (1860–1929) reinvented the punched card as a means of storing numeric information for mechanical calculators. His tabulators gained notoriety for their use in the 1890 U.S. census. (Ch. 4)

home page   a World Wide Web page (document) that serves as a base or hub for linking to other Web pages. (Chs. 1, 3)

HSB color system   a method used for expressing and manipulating color images. The system is based on representing colors using three separate values for hue (apparent shade), saturation (vividness), and brightness (luminance). (Ch. 11)

HTML forms   interactive components of a Web page that gather information supplied by the user and pass it along to the server. (Ch. 19)

HTML generator   an application program that creates Web pages by automatically generating HTML code from content and layout directions provided by the user. (Ch. 3)

HTML tags   special symbols or markers placed in a text file that provide directions for the elements, structure, and formatting of a Web page document. (Ch. 3)

hub   in a star topology, the single point to which all of the nodes of the network are connected. (Ch. 17)

hue   a spectral color or shade. (Ch. 11)

hue-shifting   a global process that remaps colors of an image based on values represented on a standard color or hue wheel. (Ch. 11)

Huffman coding   a form of statistical encoding that compresses a data file by exploiting the overall distribution of symbols in the source file. (Ch. 15)

hybrid compression   data compression that combines both syntactic and semantic methods. (Ch. 15)

hyperlink   a reference in a hypermedia document that can be selected by the user to access that document or resource automatically. (Ch. 3)

hypermedia document   an electronic document containing multimedia elements and organized as hypertext. (Chs. 3, 6)

hypertext   documents that contain electronic links to additional pages and other resources. (Chs. 3, 19)

Hypertext Markup Language (HTML)   a special coding system composed of embedded tags and commands that describe how a Web page document is organized, formatted, and displayed. (Ch. 3)

Hypertext Transfer Protocol (HTTP)   a set of rules that govern the exchange between Web clients and Web servers for the transmission of Web documents. (Ch. 3)

I/O control driver   an operating system function that manages the interchange of data between the CPU and specific I/O devices connected to the system. (Ch. 7)

IAS computer   Institute for Advanced Study computer designed by Von Neumann, Goldstine, and Burke at the Institute for Advanced Study in Princeton, New Jersey. One of the first stored program electronic computer systems whose architecture become the model for generations of computers that followed. The IAS was completed in 1951. (Ch. 4)

icons   small graphic figures representing devices, files, folders, programs, and the like; icons are manipulated by a mouse in a typical GUI. (Ch. 7)

illustration programs   application software that employ vector-based methods for creating graphic images. (Ch. 12)

image   an image is an *n*-dimensional pictorial representation of a scene. (Ch. 11)

image composite   a digital image created by combining components of two or more other images. (Ch. 11)

image file format   the form or container for storing or transmitting digital images. (Ch. 3)

image layer   a separate image channel that ordinarily contains an object or objects that can be manipulated separately from the other components of the image. (Ch. 11)

image scale the relative size of the image as it is displayed on the video monitor compared to its actual size. (Ch. 12)

image size the actual physical dimensions of a digital image or graphic, usually expressed in a measuring scale such as inches. (Ch. 12)

imperative procedural programming paradigm a group of high-level programming languages that divide programs into units or modules called procedures and whose statements are understood as commands or instructions. (Ch. 6)

in-betweens the frames in an animated sequence that depict the relative motion of objects between two key frames. (Ch. 12)

index sites Web pages that contain specialized lists of links organized by topic or category. (Ch. 3)

indexed color a method of representing color for digital images that depends on storing a color lookup table that assigns numbers to specific shades found in the image. (Chs. 11, 12)

indexed file external files in which one or more fields serve as an index for the records stored in the file. (Ch. 10)

inference engine that portion of an expert system that implements a reasoning strategy for manipulating the knowledge base. (Ch. 20)

information consumer anyone who employs information services for tasks associated with work or leisure. (Ch. 1)

Information Highway a colloquial term for the Internet. (Ch. 18)

information provider vendors and distributors of information services. These include the enterprises of publishing, entertainment, education, and so on. (Ch. 1)

information source in a communication system, this is the originator of a message transmitted over the system. (Ch. 16)

informational kiosks interactive multimedia systems that allow the user to pose queries for information concerning products and services available from the producer. (Ch. 19)

informational media a medium or form of expression that contains information. (Ch. 1)

informational worker someone whose profession depends on the analysis, assessment, and manipulation of specific forms or classes of information. (Ch. 1)

infrared broadcasting employs directional infrared light signals to establish wireless connections between nodes of the network. (Ch. 17)

inkjet printer a character printer that forms symbols by spraying tiny dots of ink on the page. (Ch. 5)

inline images digital images or graphics that appear as part of a Web page. (Ch. 3)

input information converted from a human-readable format to machine-readable form. (Chs. 4, 5)

input/output (I/O) system, devices, peripherals devoted to the exchange of information between the human user and the processor. (Chs. 4, 5)

Institute of Electrical and Electronics Engineers (IEEE) a professional society founded in 1963 that includes computer scientists as well as other engineers. (Ch. 6)

instruction-execution cycle	the interpretation of stored programs whose instructions are fetched from memory, decoded, and executed one by one by the processor. (Ch. 4)
integers	positive and negative numbers with no fractional parts. (Ch. 8)
integrated synthesis	a method of sound synthesis that combines pure synthesis with digitized sound samples. Also known as variable architecture synthesis. (Ch. 13)
intelligent (software) agents	automated software systems that relieve the user of the details of planning, coordinating, and carrying out a variety of tasks performed with the computer system. (Ch. 20)
intensity	the overall brightness of an area of an image; the amount of reflectance. (Ch. 11)
interlaced GIF	a GIF image file that is stored in a special format that permits the image to be transmitted progressively from low to higher resolution. (Ch. 11)
interlacing	a scanning method used by most consumer televisions; the CRT refreshes the even-numbered scanlines followed by the odd-numbered scanlines. (Ch. 5)
international data encryption algorithm (IDEA)	a block encryption method that has been proposed as a replacement for DES; IDEA employs a 128-bit key, which is less susceptible to brute force decryption attacks. (Ch. 16)
international trafficking in arms regulations (ITAR)	U.S. government regulations that prohibit the export of encryption application methods that employ secret keys of more than 40 bits in length. (Ch. 16)
Internet	a worldwide internetwork that connects most countries across the globe and supports a number of client/server applications for the sharing of data. (Chs. 1, 16, 18)
internet (internetwork)	a collection of autonomous networks that are connected together. (Ch. 16)
Internet Explorer	a Web browser developed by Microsoft Corporation. (Ch. 3)
Internet protocol (IP)	a networking protocol employed by most systems on the Internet for managing the routing and delivery of packets or datagrams. (Ch. 18)
Internet relay chat (IRC)	an early chat facility for UNIX systems and Internet users developed by Jarkko Oikarinen in 1988. (Ch. 18)
Internet routers (gateways)	gateway systems connected to the Internet for managing the transfer of datagrams over this confederation of autonomous networks. (Ch. 18)
Internet2	an experimental, high-speed network sponsored by the NSF and EDUCOM as a replacement for the commercialized and crowded traffic of the Internet. (Ch. 18)
interpreter	a program that simultaneously translates and executes the instructions of a high-level language program one instruction at a time. (Ch. 6)
intranet	an interorganization internetwork that usually has security measures that protect portions of the network from outside intrusion. (Chs. 16, 17)
invisible formatting characters	formatting characters that are not explicitly visible when the document is printed; for example, the carriage return signifying the end of a line. (Ch. 9)

JPEG image files (joint photographic experts group)	an image file format that is based on a set of standards for representing and storing images using a lossy compression method. (Chs. 11, 15)
justified paragraph	a section of text in which each line is set flush against both the left and right margins by proportionally spacing the characters. (Ch. 9)
kerning	a technique used to control the spacing between characters on a line of text. (Ch. 9)
key (encryption, decryption)	a string or a set of numbers that is employed in the encryption algorithm to produce a secure ciphertext from the original message and in the decryption algorithm to retrieve the original plaintext from the ciphertext. (Ch. 16)
key frames	individual frames in an animated sequence that depict principal objects at the beginning or completion of motions. (See *in-betweens*.) (Ch. 12)
keyboard	an input device modeled on the keys of a typewriter for entering text data and related symbols. (Ch. 5)
keying	the general technique of masking that permits one video segment to be superimposed on top of portions of another. (Ch. 14)
keypunch machines	input devices used for creating punched card data. (Ch. 9)
kilobyte (KB)	a unit of measure that signifies 2^{10} bytes, or approximately one thousand bytes. (Chs. 4, 5)
knowbots	(See *intelligent [software] agents*.) (Ch. 20)
knowledge-assisted multimedia database	experimental database management systems that retrieve multimedia information by analyzing the content of that information. (Ch. 10)
knowledge-based (expert) systems	a research discipline within artificial intelligence that is dedicated to developing automated systems that simulate knowledge and know-how about a given domain or expertise. (Ch. 20)
Lambert shading (flat shading)	a form of shading and lighting effects automatically applied to 3-D scenes based on a method that produces shading effects for each of the facets that comprise the surfaces of objects. (Ch. 12)
lands versus pits	scheme used for encoding binary data on optical discs. Pits are formed by microscopic depressions, while the lands are the surrounding flat, undepressed spaces. A photo-sensor reads the changes in reflectivity from a low-power laser beamed on the disc's tracks. (Ch. 5)
laser printer	a page printer that forms each page using a process similar to photocopy machines. (Ch. 5)
latency (time)	the amount of time required for the magnetic disk to rotate into the proper position for the read/write head to locate the appropriate data block on that track. (Ch. 5)
lathing	a method used for defining a three-dimensional object by rotating its 2-D outline figure 360°. (Ch. 12)
left-aligned paragraph	a section of text in which each line is set flush against the left margin only. The lines in the right margin are usually ragged, that is, extend only as far as needed. (Ch. 9)
Leibniz, G. W. von	German mathematician and philosopher (1646–1716) who designed the first arithmetic calculating device capable of performing multiplication and division directly. Leibniz also was the first mathematician to explore the properties of base-2 or binary numbering. (Ch. 4)

Lempel-Ziv Welch compression (LZW)	a lossless syntactic data compression method that is based on reducing the redundancy of strings (sequences of symbols) found in the source file. (Ch. 15)
limited precision	a finite number of bits are reserved for the representation of numeric values. (Ch. 8)
line editors	primitive text editors primarily used for creating source program files that display and operate on a single line of text at a time. (Ch. 9)
line printers	impact printers that compose the page one line at time. (Ch. 5)
linear editing	conventional editing method in which the video segment must be viewed and searched sequentially for editing. (Ch. 14)
link	short for *hyperlink*, which is an area of a Web page or hypertextual document that can be selected to go to that reference. (Ch. 1)
link fields	fields in a database record that are logically linked to records in another table or relation. (Ch. 10)
liquid crystal display (LCD)	a technology used for flat-panel display monitors. (Ch. 5)
loading, Web page	the Web browser on the client system receives the components that make up a Web page from the server and, using the directions provided in its HTML code, assembles them for proper display on the client machine. (Ch. 3)
local area network (LAN)	a computer network that is restricted to a limited geographical area and usually maintained by a single organization. (Chs. 16, 17)
local filter mask	a template that is used for defining local filtering operations on pixels of an image. (Ch. 11)
local host	the local or proximal system in a client/server application. (Ch. 18)
logical *and* operator	for database queries, this is used to search for records that contain both matching attributes. (Ch. 10)
logical expression	an expression whose value is either true or false; often used in making decisions about which value or course of action to choose during the execution of a process. (Ch. 8)
logical *or* operator	for database queries, this is used to search for records that contain at least one of two matching attributes. (Ch. 10)
longitudinal tracks	magnetic tape format in which the tracks are recorded across the entire length of the tape. (Ch. 5)
lossless compression	data compression methods that produce an encoded file that decompresses to a form that is identical to the original source file (i.e., no data is lost in the process). (Ch. 15)
lossy compression	data compression methods that produce an encoded file that decompresses to a form that is a reasonable facsimile of the original source file (i.e., some data is lost in the process). (Ch. 15)
Lovelace, Ada	assisted Charles Babbage in his research on the Analytical Engine; she developed one of the first known automatic programs for this device. (Ch. 4)
machine instruction set	the built-in operations provided by the processor's hardware. (Ch. 4)
machine language	a binary encoding or representation of a machine's instruction set. (Ch. 4)

machine learning   a research discipline within artificial intelligence that is dedicated to developing automated systems that can infer new information from what is known or given about a specific domain. (Ch. 20)

magnetic floppy disks, drives   a direct-access, secondary storage medium and device that stores modest amounts of data for offline storage. (Ch. 5)

magnetic hard disks, drives   a direct-access, secondary storage medium and device that is typically employed as the primary source for online backup storage. (Ch. 5)

magnetic tape   a sequential access storage medium that is usually employed for archiving large amounts of data economically. (Ch. 5)

magneto-optical (MO) discs, drives   a direct-access storage medium and device that combines magnetic and optical technology supporting erasable, writable optical disc storage. (Ch. 5)

mainframe   refers to large-scale digital computing machines that were common in the first several decades of electronic computers. (Ch. 4)

mantissa, in floating point representation   a fraction that is used to represent the significant digits contained in a floating point number. (Ch. 8)

mask, digital   an area of a digital image that is defined for preventing modifications performed on the rest of the image. (Ch. 11)

masking   a focusing method used in CRT video display monitors that causes the electron beams to converge more precisely on the intended phosphors. (Ch. 5)

master pages   templates used for creating standard pages in a DTP program. (Ch. 9)

master tape   the magnetic tape reel containing the original data used as input for a batch processing program that updates the records stored on the original master. (Ch. 5)

Mauchly, John   (1907–1980) a member of the Moore School of Engineering at the University of Pennsylvannia who, along with J. Presper Eckert, designed and engineered a series of pioneering computing devices: the ENIAC, the EDVAC, and later, the BINAC. (Ch. 4)

media access control (MAC)   the method or manner in which nodes carry out communication in a network. (Ch. 17)

medium   a vehicle or agent for something; a representation. (Ch. 1)

megabyte (MB)   a unit of measure that signifies 2^{20} bytes, or approximately one million bytes. (Chs. 4, 5)

megahertz (MHz)   a unit of measure signifying one million cycles per second. (Ch. 4)

memex   an automated device for collecting and organizing scientific literature first proposed by Vannevar Bush. The memex system was a forerunner of modern hypertext systems. (Ch. 19)

memory, main   addressable memory that resides in the processor holding data and instructions that are currently in use. (Ch. 4)

memory, secondary   forms of memory used to archive data and instructions that are not currently in use. (Ch. 4)

memory manager   an operating system function that controls and allocates the use of main memory by the processes executing on the computer system. (Ch. 7)

memory word a unit of memory containing a sequence of contiguous binary digits or bits. (Ch. 4)

mental agents (See *intelligent [software] agents.*) (Ch. 20)

menu a list of commands available to the user by pointing and clicking with the mouse. (Chs. 7, 12)

menu bar a list of menus arranged horizontally across a window or the desktop. (Ch. 7)

menu list the selection of commands available in a given menu. (Ch. 18)

message digest in the RSA public key cipher, this is a derivation of a nonsense message that is difficult to unscramble but is likely to be a unique scrambling of the original nonsense message. (Ch. 16)

microcomputer a personal computer system so designated because it is based on a microprocessor design. (Ch. 4)

micron a unit of measure signifying 10^{-6} inches, or one-millionth of an inch. (Ch. 5)

microprocessor a complete processing unit integrated onto a single chip. (Ch. 4)

MIDI compatible information or a signal that is compatible with MIDI commands for representing musical information. (Ch. 13)

minicomputer refers to a mid-range computer system capable of supporting a modest number of users. (Ch. 4)

model description specifying the details for individual objects that make up a 3-D scene. (Ch. 12)

models in the authoring system, Authorware, models are program segments that may be reused in other projects or pieces. (Ch. 19)

modem a special device that modulates digital signals for transmission across telephone lines to a remote computer system and demodulates signals received from telephone transmissions sent by a remote system. (Ch. 16)

modulation to alter a continuous wave in order to carry a meaningful signal (e.g., amplitude modulation). (Ch. 16)

modulator in FM (frequency modulation) sound synthesis, the modulator is a wave that modifies another wave to create a more complex waveform. (Ch. 13)

monochrome monitor a video display monitor that is composed of phosphors of a single color, such as white, or sometimes green, or perhaps amber. (Ch. 5)

morphing, digital a form of digital warping in which a series of image displacements are performed incrementally on a given digital image. Typically, morphing involves transforming the contents of a given image into that of a second image by stages. (Ch. 11)

Mosaic the first Web browser client program that employed a graphical user interface (GUI) capable of supporting pages with multimedia components. (Ch. 3)

motion blur a form of directional blurring in a digital image that simulates the effects of slight overexposures captured by motion picture cameras. Motion blur enhances animations by smoothing transitions between frames. (Ch. 11)

motion compensation

a method of video compression that stores only the differences in video frames due to apparent motion rather than entire frame. (Ch. 15)

motion-JPEG

a form of video compression that adapts JPEG methods to video sequences. (Ch. 15)

mouse

a hand-held input device used to manipulate the cursor or pointer displayed on the screen of a GUI; the mouse contains one or more buttons to send signals coordinated with the movements of dragging the device across a flat surface. (Ch. 5)

MPEG (motion pictures experts group)

a set of standards for video compression that employ both spatial and temporal compression methods along with motion compensation. Today, three standards are supported: MPEG-1, MPEG-2, and MPEG-4. (Ch. 15)

MUD object-oriented (MOO)

an object-oriented version of a MUD. (See *MUD.*) MOOs are usually more advanced and have features such as Web-enabled graphic user interface, avatars representing players, and so on. (Ch. 18)

multimedia

the integration of various forms of information, such as text, graphics, sound, images, and video. (Chs. 1, 19)

multimedia authoring software

software that enables the creation of highly interactive multimedia production, such as those employed for computer-based training, courseware, and informational kiosks. (Ch. 19)

multimedia composition software

applications designed to enable the user to easily integrate elements of different media and origin into a common document, such as an electronic slideshow. (Ch. 19)

multimedia database system

a database management system that stores multimedia materials for retrieval and reuse. (Chs. 1, 10)

multimedia presentation software

(See *multimedia composition software.*) (Ch. 19)

multiple search constraints

employing logical operators to construct compound ad hoc retrievals. (Ch. 10)

multiple-user dialog, multiuser dungeon (MUD)

an extension of chat facilities in which the participants generally play roles in an elaborate scenario constructed around some theme or activity. (Ch. 18)

multiprogramming, multitasking

the capacity to execute two or more processes over a given span of time. (Ch. 7)

multipurpose internet mail extension (MIME)

a special extension that identifies the general type of data stored in a file containing multimedia content when transmitted across a network. (Ch. 13)

multiuser computer system

a computer system whose hardware and software are capable of supporting a group of users simultaneously. (Ch. 4)

multiuser operating system

an operating system that accommodates more than one user at a time by multiprogramming. (Ch. 7)

musical instrument digital interface (MIDI)

an input/output device used to transfer MIDI coded signals between the computer system and a MIDI instrument. (Ch. 5)

musical instrument digital interface (MIDI) standard

an industry standard for representing musical information as a series of commands that may be interpreted for its playback. MIDI representations are encoded commands, and therefore are more compact than digitized musical sounds. (Ch. 13)

nanosecond	a unit of measure signifying 10^{-9} seconds, or one-billionth of a second. (Ch. 4)
narrowband transmission	(See *baseband transmission.*) (Ch. 16)
natural language query	an ad hoc database query that is posed in ordinary terms, rather than the restricted syntax of a query language. (Ch. 10)
natural language understanding	a research discipline within artificial intelligence that seeks to develop automated systems that can understand and generate written language. (Ch. 20)
Nelson, Ted	a researcher at Brown University who helped develop the concept of hypertextual systems in the 1960s. (Ch. 19)
network	a computer network connects a collection of computer systems and devices for communication and the sharing of resources and data. (Ch. 1)
network database model	a data model for a database that organizes the records for speed and efficiency. The network model presents the data to the user in a way that closely resembles their physical representation: records are linked together one after the other. Retrievals are based on traversing the link fields for a set of data. (Ch. 10)
networking	interconnecting agents for the sake of exchanging information or some other form of value. (Ch. 16)
neural network (net)	a program that simulates the organization and function of neurons. The neural network usually has one input layer and one output layer, with one or more hidden layers between them. A set of input values is introduced at the input layer and processed by the net to produce the value(s) at its output layer. (Ch. 20)
nine-track blocking	an older, longitudinal tracking method used for storing data on magnetic tape. Nine longitudinal tracks are arranged across the length of the tape, and a single byte of data is stored in parallel across the nine tracks. (Ch. 5)
nodes	systems or devices that are connected to a data communications network and can either send or receive transmitted signals. (Ch. 16)
noise	the unpredictable or random modification or degrading of a signal by external causes. (Chs. 2, 11, 16)
nonlinear editing	unlike linear editing, video clips may be accessed randomly, frame by frame. Nonlinear editing stores a series of editing decisions that affect the playback of the digital video segment without actually altering the original source. (Ch. 14)
nonprocedural programming paradigm	a group of high-level programming languages that are based on other models, rather than the conventional procedural paradigm, for example, LISP and Prolog. (Ch. 6)
numbered list	in HTML, a list of items that are automatically numbered when displayed on the page in the browser. (Ch. 18)
Nyquist's theorem (sampling rates)	mathematical proof that an accurate digitization of an analog signal is guaranteed if the sampling rate is at least twice that of the frequency range of the signal. (Ch. 13)
object-oriented graphics (vector graphics)	a method of representing and manipulating graphic images in which the image is composed of lines, curves, and figures that are defined mathematically, rather than being composed of pixels. (Ch. 12)

object-oriented programming paradigm
a special class of high-level programming languages that divide the program into separate units or modules like procedural languages, but, unlike procedural languages, the units describe entities or objects with specific properties or attributes. (Ch. 6)

objects, properties
a unit or module of a program expressed in an object-oriented programming language. Objects have methods or specific actions that they perform, and they typically send messages or data to other objects in the course of a process. (Ch. 6)

odd parity error detection
an error detection scheme used in data communications in which a single bit is employed to ensure that the total number of bits transmitted in a byte adds up to an odd number. (Ch. 16)

offline storage
a secondary storage medium that may be disconnected and removed from the computer system. (Ch. 5)

online storage
a secondary storage medium that remains connected and continuously available to the computer system. (Ch. 5)

open system
standards for hardware and software that are not based on any favored platform or vendor. (Ch. 18)

operating system (OS)
a collection of programs that manage the resources of a computer system, supervise the execution of its processes, and provide useful services and security for the system. (Ch. 7)

optical discs, drives
a direct-access storage medium and device employing optical technologies for reading and writing data. (Ch. 5)

optical fiber cable
a bounded medium for connecting nodes in a network over which signals composed of light pulses are carried through very thin strands of glass. (Ch. 17)

ordinality
ordering; digital representations are based on numbering and the natural ordering of numbers may be exploited in creating coding schemes. (Ch. 2)

originating system
the system that creates a message to be transmitted over some communication channel. (Ch. 16)

oscillator
an electronic device that produces a repeating electrical signal at a specified frequency. (Ch. 13)

output
data converted from machine-readable form to a format suitable for human use. (Ch. 4)

overflow error
an error that results when the numeric value is too large to be represented by the limited precision of the numeric representation employed by that computer system. (Ch. 8)

packet
fixed-sized units of data that contain information for transmission, plus identifying information, such as the originator, the destination, sequence number, and so on. (Ch. 16)

packet collision
an instant when the nodes on a common carrier detect two or more nodes attempting to transmit a packet simultaneously. (Ch. 17)

packet switching
a switching method in which nodes communicate by sending a series of packets of data over the network. The intended receiver processes these packets to produce the original message. (Ch. 16)

page, Web	a single document that has a unique address or URL that may be transmitted and shared among computer systems that belong to the World Wide Web. (Ch. 3)
page printers	printers that form an entire page at a time. (Ch. 5)
painting programs	software applications that permit the user to create or modify digital images or graphics using bit-mapped image methods, that is, manipulating the individual pixels that comprise the digital image. (Ch. 12)
paired tags	HTML tags that are encoded in pairs. The first tag signifies the beginning of the scope of the command denoted by that tag, and the second tag signifies the conclusion of its scope. (Ch. 3)
palettes	menus that offer a choice of tools, patterns, textures, or colors that may be applied to digital images or graphics. (Ch. 12)
Pantone matching system	an industry standard for denoting ink colors used in publishing. (Ch. 11)
paradigm	a basic model describing how a programming language expresses a process. (Ch. 6)
parity bit	usually a single bit stored with a byte of data used to help detect whether errors occur in reading or transmitting that data. (Chs. 5, 16)
partial-ROM (P-ROM)	a direct-access storage medium and device that combines erasable, writable optical storage with read-only optical storage and features high data density and capacities. (Ch. 5)
Pascal, Blaise	(1623–1662) French mathematician, theologian, and philosopher who also developed one of the first automatic mechanical calculating devices, the Pascaline. (Ch. 4)
passwords	a secret word or phrase that is (supposedly) known only by the legitimate user and is entered during the login process to authenticate that user. (Ch. 17)
Paste command	a copy of the content of the current clipboard is inserted at the position of the cursor. (Ch. 9)
patents	the right of an inventor or discoverer to hold and protect commercial control over an invention or discovery. (Ch. 2)
pathnames	a sequence of names signifying devices, directories, or folders, and files that must be traversed to locate an item stored in a hierarchical file system. (Ch. 7)
PCD image files (Kodak photo CD)	an image file format for high-resolution digital images that are compressed and stored on compact discs. (Ch. 11)
PCX	the native image file format for PC Paintbrush, a popular painting program for Windows computer systems. (Ch. 12)
peripherals	refers to devices that are connected to the computer system generally for input/output and secondary storage purposes. (Ch. 4)
personal profile	a collection of information about the habits, personal tastes, and transactions of a single individual. (Ch. 10)
phase distortion synthesis	in sound synthesis, a variation of FM synthesis that modifies the time scale of a simple waveform to create more complex signals. (Ch. 13)
phonemes	the basic building blocks of spoken language; phonemes are sounds that can be uttered by a human speaker. (Ch. 13)

Phong shading   a form of shading and lighting effects automatically applied to 3-D scenes based on a method that produces realistic shading effects by calculating the lighting effects for each pixel. (Ch. 12)

phosphors   phosphorescent dots fixed to the inside of a CRT video display monitor that when excited by an electron beam glow to form visual images on the screen. (Ch. 5)

physical transport system (layer)   the hardware and software that perform the actual transmission of signals across a physical network. (Ch. 17)

PICT image files   a metafile format for storing images used often by Macintosh applications. (Ch. 11)

picture resolution   the number of pixels that compose an image, usually expressed as the product of the number of pixels in a row times the number of rows in the image. (Ch. 11)

pie chart   a circular distributional chart in which the relative contribution of components to the whole are represented proportionally as slices of a pie. (Ch. 8)

pink noise   a signal containing a random distribution of frequencies but uniformly distributed throughout each octave in the frequency range. (Ch. 13)

pitch, monitor   the size of phosphors, or dots, on a video display screen; the smaller the dot size, the greater the capacity for detail. (Ch. 5)

pixel (picture element)   a spatial sample of a photograph or image. A picture element is the basic component of a digitized image, which contains a set of numbers representing the features (color, intensity) of that spatial sample. (Chs. 2, 11, 12)

plaintext   the original message used for encryption or decryption. (Ch. 16)

Platform for Internet Content Selection (PICS)   a system of standards for rating the content of Web pages. The Web page author or a third party labels pages for content, and PICS-based censoring software can block the reception of documents that do not meet personally selected standards for acceptability. (Ch. 3)

PNG image files (portable network graphics)   a second-generation image file format used for Web images and graphics that offers transparency–like GIFs, but greater color ranges and higher compression rates like JPEGs. (Ch. 11)

pointer   a graphic figure signifying the current position of the mouse in a window or on the desktop; the look of the pointer often changes depending on the context of its use. (Ch. 7)

point-to-point connectivity   each node shares a direct, two-way connection with each and every other node in the network. (Ch. 16)

polygon-surface modeling   a method of 3-D model description that is based on creating objects whose surfaces are defined as composed of facets, or joined polygon-shaped surfaces. (Ch. 12)

pop-up menu   a menu that is displayed instantly when the relevant object is clicked. (Ch. 7)

pop-up window   a window that is hidden away as a tab at the bottom of the screen or desktop, but appears instantly when the tab is clicked. (Ch. 7)

portability   the capability to execute a program on different hardware processors and platforms. (Ch. 6)

positional notation   a numbering system in which the position of each symbol signifies a special meaning. (Ch. 2)

post office protocol (POP)	an electronic mail protocol commonly employed by desktop or personal computers connected to networks. (Ch. 18)
posterizing	a global filtering process that modifies the color or intensity ranges of an image, reducing them to an arbitrarily smaller number. (Ch. 11)
PostScript	a page description language developed by Adobe Systems that specifies commands required to calculate and draw the text and objects that make up a page of printed or displayed output. (Ch. 12)
pretty good privacy (PGP) encryption system	a hybrid encryption method that combines elements of public key ciphers with secret key method such as IDEA. Developed by Phillip Zimmerman, PGP was introduced as a freeware encryption method. (Ch. 18)
prime number	a positive integer greater than 1 that is evenly divisible only by itself and 1. (Ch. 16)
problem parameter	values in a spreadsheet calculation that are likely to change in subsequent uses. (Ch. 8)
procedures	a program unit that expresses a set of events defining a subtask of a larger process. (Ch. 6)
processor	the hardware system composed primarily of the CPU and main memory connected by an internal bus. (Ch. 4)
production rules	rules of inference employed by the inference engine in a knowledge-based or expert system. (Ch. 20)
program	a set of instructions that directs the sequence and substance of a computational process. (Chs. 4, 6)
programmers	individuals who design, encode, and test computer programs. (Ch. 6)
prompt sign	a symbol that is displayed by a text-based user interface to indicate that a command may be entered and executed. (Ch. 7)
protocol	a set of rules governing the orderly exchange of information and services between cooperating computer systems connected over a data communications network. (Ch. 3)
proxy, agent	an intelligent software agent that performs actions on behalf of the user in his or her absence, for example, buying securities over the network. (Ch. 20)
pseudocoloring	a digital image process that maps graytones in a black-and-white image to distinct colors, producing sharper color contrasts for improved visibility. (Ch. 11)
public key cipher	an encryption regime that employs different keys for encrypting and decrypting messages. The encryption key is made public, and the decryption key is kept private. (Ch. 16)
pull-down menu	a menu that is displayed when its title is clicked in a menu bar. (Ch. 7)
px64	an international standard for video compression that supports video conferencing over ISDN telephone lines. (Ch. 15)
quantizing	the second stage of digitizing analog or continuous representations of information in which the sample is assigned a numeric value from an established measuring scale. (Chs. 2, 11)

quarter-inch cartridge tapes (QIC)   a magnetic tape medium using serpentine longitudinal tracking and usually employed for system backups or archiving. (Ch. 5)

query, database   a retrieval from a database posed by a single command. (Ch. 10)

query language   the special syntax required for forming ad hoc queries or retrievals from a database. (Ch. 10)

query-by-example (QBE)   a method of creating ad hoc queries using a form rather than constructing the command in the query language employed by that database. (Ch. 10)

QuickTime   a digital video file format developed by Apple. (Chs. 12, 15)

RA sound file format   a file format for representing and storing digitized sound as streaming data developed by RealAudio. (Ch. 13)

radio frequency broadcasting   a wireless network in which the nodes communicate employing radio transmissions. (Ch. 17)

RAID disks, drives   redundant array of independent disks. A magnetic disk technology that employs software to manage a collection of smaller, inexpensive magnetic hard disks and drives that appear as a single, large-capacity disk drive to the computer system. (Ch. 5)

random access   accessing an item directly by the address of its location. (Ch. 2)

random access memory (RAM)   memory items that may be accessed directly by the CPU; also usually signifies readable, writable portion of addressable main memory. (Ch. 4)

rasterizing   refers to the process employed by most video displays that translates bit-mapped images to scanlines on the screen. (Ch. 12)

ray tracing   a form of shading and lighting effects automatically applied to 3-D scenes based on a method that calculates the lighting values for each pixel derived from the viewer's perspective. (Ch. 12)

read/write (time)   the amount of time required to perform a read or write operation on a data block stored on a track on a secondary storage medium. (Ch. 5)

read/write head   an electro-mechanical component in magnetic disk drives that senses (reads) data or magnetizes (writes) data on disk tracks. (Ch. 5)

reading (memory)   copying the contents of memory to the CPU. Reading is nondestructive because the memory item is merely copied. (Ch. 4)

read-only memory (ROM)   that portion of addressable main memory that may be read or copied but not altered or modified. ROM usually contains instructions or data that the system employs for its basic operations. (Ch. 4)

real numbers   the set of numbers containing both whole numbers and fractional parts. (Ch. 8)

receiver   the system that captures the transmitted signal sent over the communication channel. (Ch. 16)

record   a collection of related fields denoting some entity. (Chs. 5, 10, 19)

refresh rate, monitor   the amount of time required to refresh the charge held by the phosphors on a monitor screen; typically measured in Hertz or cycles per second. (Ch. 5)

registers   small memory units within the CPU employed for special functions, including temporary storage of data and instructions. (Ch. 4)

relational database model a data model for a database that organizes the information as a collection of relations or tables, each having a unique set of attributes specifying the fields for its records. Tables or relations distribute the data throughout the database, but can be logically linked to allow for associating related information. (Ch. 10)

relative cell reference a reference in a formula to a spreadsheet cell that is expected to change when the formula is replicated to another location. (Ch. 8)

remote host a system that is connected to the local computer system via data communications network. (Chs. 16, 18)

removable hard disks a direct-access storage medium and device that employs magnetic technology to read and write data on high-capacity disks that, unlike conventional hard drives, can be removed from the drive unit. (Ch. 5)

rendering in 3-D applications, the method of creating photorealistic colors and shading for objects in a 3-D scene. (Ch. 12)

repeater a hardware device in a data network that boosts a digital signal by receiving and repeating it. (Ch. 17)

repetition, looping a program construction that causes a group of statements or instructions to be repeated over and over until the intended process is complete. (Ch. 6)

report, database information retrieved from a database that is organized into a more convenient form for use. (Ch. 10)

resolution the capacity for detail contained in a message or signal. Representations with high resolution capture more detail than those with low resolution. (Ch. 2)

resolution (8-bit and 16-bit sound) refers to the number of values employed to represent sampled amplitudes. 8-bit resolution means that a scale of 256 levels is employed; 16-bit resolution has a scale of over 65,000 levels. (Ch. 13)

resolution independence for digital images and graphics, this means that properly displaying the image does not depend on the characteristics of a specific device. (Chs. 2, 12)

retouching the selective modification or editing of the contents of a digital image. (Ch. 11)

RGB color images digital images that encode color by means of three primary color channels: red, green, and blue. (Ch. 11)

RGB color system a method of storing and representing color in digital images that is based on dividing the color signal into three distinct primary color components or channels: red, green, and blue. (Ch. 11)

RGB color video monitor a video display monitor that employs RGB color to compose color images. (Ch. 5)

right-aligned paragraph a section of text in which each line is set flush against the right margin only. The lines in the left margin are usually ragged, that is, extend only as far as needed. (Ch. 9)

ring network topology a network in which the nodes are connected in a cycle; that is, each node has a single predecessor and successor and all transmissions are repeated around this closed path. (Ch. 17)

robotics   a research discipline within artificial intelligence that seeks to develop automated systems that can react to, navigate among, and manipulate objects in their environment. (Ch. 20)

robust speech recognition system   a speech understanding system that produces successful results in a variety of circumstances and for a variety of language speakers. (Ch. 13)

rotoscoping   painting or embellishing individual frames of video footage. (Ch. 14)

router   devices that connect networks of the same or different types and have the savvy to direct data across these networks for improved performance and efficiency. (Ch. 17)

RSA algorithm   a public key encryption method named after and developed by Rivest, Shamir, and Adelson. (Ch. 16)

RTF (rich text format)   a text file format that preserves most of the formatting in a text document—unlike ASCII text, which preserves only the line structure. (Ch. 9)

rule-based phoneme recognition   a system that analyzes sounds into phonemes by applying basic rules programmed into the system. (Ch. 13)

rule-based system   (See *knowledge-based [expert] systems*.) (Ch. 20)

ruler, style   a tool that is part of the interface of a word processing application that is used for setting margins and tabs for selected text. (Ch. 9)

rules of inference   representations of knowledge that permit the derivation of new information from previously known or introduced information. (Ch. 20)

run-length encoding (RLE)   a data compression method that replaces strings of repeating 1's or 0's with their frequency. (Ch. 15)

sampling   choosing a discrete sample from a continuous or analog form of information as a representative of the whole. Images, for example, are sampled spatially: the image is divided into smaller spatial segments. Sound or music is sampled over time as series of instantaneous sounds. (Chs. 2, 11)

sampling rate   the number of samples per second taken when digitizing an analog or continuous signal (such as sound). (Ch. 13)

scalability   the ability of a system to transmit, receive, and process data with higher resolution than it is capable of producing. (Ch. 2)

scanner   an input device that converts analog images (photographs, printed graphics, film, etc.) to digital images by sampling and quantizing these analog image sources. (Ch. 5)

scene description   in 3-D graphics, this is arranging predefined objects into a single composition or arrangement to make a scene. (Ch. 12)

Schickard, William   the inventor of an early automated calculating device that adds and subtracts numbers. (Ch. 4)

scientific visualization   a set of methods used for the visualization of data sets, models, and functional relationships, making them easier to explore and comprehend. (Ch. 8)

script   a sequence of instructions that are interpreted and executed one by one by the computer system; scripts are usually composed of instructions from a scripting language or, perhaps, operating system commands. (Chs. 7, 19)

scripting, scripting language writing or devising a program using an interpreted programming language; in scripting languages, the instructions are interpreted or translated and executed one by one by the host processor. (Ch. 6)

scroll arrow, box, button tools used to manipulate the view presented in a window; the scroll box indicates the current position of the view; the arrows may be clicked to advance that view in the corresponding direction. (Ch. 7)

search engines software programs available on the World Wide Web that may be employed to perform keyword searches of registered Web pages. (Ch. 3)

search string a string of symbols used as a pattern for matching in a search. (Ch. 18)

secondary (external) memory an auxiliary source of storage for data and instructions that is used to backup main memory or serve as a less expensive and more permanent form of memory. (Ch. 5)

secret key cipher an encryption method in which the security of the ciphertext depends on the secrecy of the key. (Ch. 16)

sector on direct-access storage media, this is a segment of a track used for storing one or more data blocks. (Ch. 5)

Secure Electronic Transaction (SET) a monetary payment system for Web commerce developed by MasterCard, Visa, and other financial service companies. (Ch. 3)

Secure Sockets Layer (SSL) a protocol for securing an electronic transaction developed by Netscape Communications Corporation. (Ch. 3)

seek (time) the amount of time required for the read/write head to locate the appropriate track on a rotating disk. (Ch. 5)

selection an area of the image that is designated for editing or modification. (Ch. 11)

selective access accessing an item by searching for it in a collection or sequence of items. Selective access usually involves comparing each item with a key until a match is found. (Ch. 2)

select-then-do process the basic technique used in editing in which an object is selected, such as a sequence of text, and then a context-based command is issued to modify that object. (Ch. 9)

semantic compression data compression methods that take into account the type of data being compressed rather than syntactic characteristics alone. (Ch. 15)

sequential access storage devices, media (SASD) secondary storage media and devices that store data using a linear organization, for example, magnetic tape. (Ch. 5)

sequential processing processing batches of data in a linear sequence, for example, updating a set of similar records contained in a single file. (Ch. 5)

serial uniprocessor a single processor capable of executing only one machine language instruction at a time. (Ch. 4)

series chart measures the change in one or more dependent variables over a series of values, such as time. (Ch. 8)

serpentine tracks (streaming tape) a longitudinal tracking format for magnetic tape that stores data sequentially in a track continuously across the entire length of the tape. The data is read and written by traversing the tape back and forth along each single track. (Ch. 5)

server	in the client/server model, the server is the system that responds to and processes requests for services from one or more client systems. (Chs. 4, 17)
server, Web	a computer system that is running a server program and can process requests from clients for transmitting Web pages and components stored on that system. (Ch. 3)
server program	in the client/server model, the server program is the software on the remote system that receives and processes requests for services from client programs. (Ch. 17)
Shannon, Claude	a pioneer in information theory who put forth the basic model of a communication system. (Ch. 16)
shared connection network	a network in which nodes are often connected to other nodes over channels shared by other nodes that serve as intermediaries. (Ch. 16)
shareware	software that is available to the public for a nominal fee. (Ch. 7)
sharpening	a local filtering process that enhances the visibility of objects against the background by improving the contrast for pixels that serve as boundaries between different segments of the image. (Ch. 11)
shot (animation)	in animation, a basic picture unit composed of actors against a background. (Ch. 12)
signal (analog, digital)	the encoded form of the original message that is suitable for transmission over a communication channel. (Ch. 16)
signal-to-noise ratio (SNR)	a measure of the amount of noise that is contributed to a data transmission signal. (Ch. 16)
simple mail transfer protocol (SMTP)	mail protocol that conforms to TCP/IP standards and is commonly employed for electronic mail services over the Internet. (Ch. 18)
sine wave	a waveform that has a smoothly repeating curve that describes a regular, continuously varying cycle. (Ch. 16)
single-user computer system	personal computers, desktop computers, and workstations that support only one user at a time. (Ch. 4)
single-user operating system	an operating system that can support only one user at a time on a given computer system. (Ch. 7)
software (programs)	a set of instructions prescribing a computational process that are symbolically encoded for storage and use on a computer system. (Chs. 4, 6)
software libraries	mathematical methods that have been implemented, tested, and codified for use in the construction of programs that perform numeric processing. (Ch. 8)
software license	limited rights of ownership granted to purchasers of software by the company that distributes it. (Ch. 7)
software quality assurance	a group of professional software developers who are responsible for testing and validating programs. (Ch. 6)
solid modeling	a method of 3-D model description based on creating objects by combining regular shapes, such as cubes, spheres, and cones. (Ch. 12)
sort key	a field value in a record that is used as a basis for sorting or ordering the records. (Ch. 10)

sorted data	a group of records that are ordered based on some sort key. (Ch. 10)
sound digitizer (sound card)	hardware that is usually added to an expansion slot of a computer system and contains circuits used to digitize analog sound sources and play-back digitized, recorded sounds. (Ch. 5)
speaker-dependent speech recognition systems	an automated speech recognition system that is trained for use with a single language user. (Ch. 13)
special-purpose computer	a computer system that is designed or dedicated to the performance of a specialized or limited computational task, for example, an electronic arithmetic calculator. (Ch. 4)
speech recognition	(See *automated speech recognition*.) (Ch. 13)
speech synthesis	computer-generated sounds that simulate spoken language. (Ch. 13)
spell checking	a utility typically found in word processing software that automatically checks for misspellings in a document by consulting a built-in dictionary of words. (Ch. 9)
spiders (robots)	Internet agents that perform rudimentary search and maintenance tasks, such as verifying links on Web pages. (Ch. 20)
spooled print files	a collection of files that are queued for printing by a server that services a group of systems on the network. (Ch. 17)
spreadsheets	software application programs that are designed for performing numeric calculations easily; the basic model is that of pencil and paper calculations on an accountant's ledgersheet. (Ch. 8)
sprites	in animations created by the authoring system Director, these are individual objects, such as graphic images, that are positioned on the Stage for a particular frame. (Ch. 19)
Standard Generalized Markup Language (SGML)	a precursor of HTML, SGML is a method of defining languages that specify commands or instructions for the generation of automated document organization. (Ch. 19)
star network topology	a network organization in which all of the nodes are connected to and communicate through a single point, called the hub. (Ch. 17)
state space	a representation of all of the possible states or events that describe some process. The states are arranged from the start state to connected intermediate states, and finally one or more goal states that signify the termination of the process. (Ch. 20)
stored program concept	the instructions that direct the computational process are encoded and stored on the computer system much like data. The computer system performs the process by fetching and interpreting the instructions automatically. (Ch. 4)
story	in animation, the term used to describe the action of the film. (Ch. 12)
storyboard	in animation, a method for depicting the story as a sequence of simple drawings. (Ch. 12)
straight-cuts	in video applications, a series of short takes that are combined with no transitions between them. (Ch. 14)
streaming (data)	a method of transmitting image or audio data in which the current frame or sequence is played while succeeding components are being downloaded. (Ch. 12)

streaming audio system
a digital audio system that employs streaming for transmitting and playback of sound files. (Ch. 13)

Structured Query Language (SQL)
the de facto standard query language for relational database management systems. (Ch. 10)

submenu
a subordinate menu or list of commands associated with a command in a menu list. (Ch. 7)

subtractive synthesis
a traditional method of sound synthesis that produces the desired sound pattern by filtering more complex signals generated by combining the signals of two or more oscillators. (Ch. 13)

supercomputer
a special class of high-performance multiuser computer systems used primarily for scientific applications that require intensive numeric calculations. (Ch. 4)

supervisor
an operating system function that manages and controls the execution of user and system processes. (Ch. 7)

surface-based 3-D graphics
a form of three-dimensional graphics in which objects are stored and represented by collections of facets or joined surfaces. (Ch. 12)

surfing, Web
refers to browsing a series of Web pages and sites by actively following an assortment of hyperlinks from one page to the next. (Ch. 3)

SVGA (super VGA)
a graphic format for video display monitors that supports a maximum resolution of 800 × 600. (Ch. 5)

switching (circuit versus packet)
methods employed for communication over a network in which the nodes share common connections. (Ch. 16)

symmetric key cipher
encryption/decryption methods in which both share the same key value. (Ch. 16)

symmetrical compression/ decompression
a data compression/decompression regime for which the compression and decompression methods take approximately the same amount of time. (Ch. 15)

syntactic compression (entropy encoding)
data compression/decompression methods that consider only the symbolic patterns in the data file. (Ch. 15)

synthesized sound
computer-generated sounds used for creating music or other sound effects. (Ch. 13)

system analysts
software developers who are responsible for planning, designing of software projects, as well as the oversight of professional software development teams engaged on the project. (Ch. 6)

system backups
archiving the programs and data stored on the online secondary storage devices connected to a particular computer system, usually on magnetic tape. (Ch. 5)

system call
a request to the operating system to perform some basic function or provide some service. (Ch. 7)

system clock
a device within the CPU that generates a signal used for synchronizing events within the computer. The speed of the clock, measured in megahertz, is often cited as a benchmark for the overall speed of the system. (Ch. 4)

system palette
a set of values for indexed color images based on those designated by a computer's operating system, which are used for coloring the windows, icons, and gadgets displayed on the desktop. (Ch. 11)

system software	programs that help manage the operation of the computer system or provide utilities that add functionality to its operation. (Ch. 7)
tab markers	marks on the Style Ruler that indicate the location and type of tab employed in the current line. (Ch. 9)
table, database	a single relation in a relational database that specifies a unique set of attributes for the records contained in it. (Ch. 10)
tables	an HTML structure used to organize items of data in columns and rows. (Ch. 18)
tag editor	an application program that makes it easier to create Web pages by inserting or adding tags automatically from lists or menus. (Ch. 3)
tags	in HTML, these are special commands enclosed in angle brackets (< >) that signify directions for components, organization, formatting, and display of Web pages. (Ch. 3)
tape drive	the device employed for reading and writing magnetic tape. (Ch. 5)
telnet	a network application that permits a local system to serve as a terminal for connecting to a remote host. (Ch. 18)
terabyte (TB)	a unit of measure signifying 2^{40} bytes, or approximately one trillion bytes. (Chs. 4, 5)
terminal	a keyboard and video display connected to a computer network. (Ch. 16)
terminal emulation program	an application that converts a computer system to a simple terminal for communication across a data communications network. (Ch. 16)
text editors	simple word processing programs for the creation and editing of pure text (ASCII) files. (Ch. 9)
three-dimensional graphics (3-D graphics)	applications that automatically calculate and display graphic objects with perspectival projection to create the illusion of three dimensions. (Ch. 12)
thresholding	a global filtering process that converts a color or grayscale image into a binary image by remapping the pixel values in that image based on an arbitrary threshold or limit imposed on the histogram of the image. (Ch. 11)
TIFF image files (tagged image file format)	a digital image file format widely used in publishing and information interchange. TIFF images may be compressed employing a lossless compression method. (Chs. 11, 15)
tiling windows	arranging windows side by side, like the tiles on a floor. (Ch. 7)
time base corrector (TBC)	in capturing video from analog sources, this device functions as a frame buffer that is capable of holding an entire frame of video. (Ch. 14)
titling	in video applications, superimposing text onto video frames. (Ch. 14)
token	a data packet that is continuously circulated along a token ring network. (Ch. 17)
token passing MAC protocol	a method of media access control for a local area network in which packets are transmitted across the network, provided that the sender has control of a special packet called the *token*. (Ch. 17)
topology (network)	the layout or organization of connections among the nodes of a network. (Chs. 16, 17)

track	a path along a secondary storage medium containing binary encoded information. On magnetic tape, tracks are usually parallel running the length of the tape; on disks, tracks are arranged in a circular or sometimes a spiral pattern. (Ch. 5)
trade secrets	laws that protect information, designs, and devices that companies wish to keep secret in order to retain commercial advantages from their creations. (Chs. 2, 7)
trademarks	laws that protect words, names, symbols, and logos normally used in commerce. (Chs. 2, 7)
transactional processing	a form of processing in which a computer system interacts with a user or another system through a series of interchanges. (Ch. 5)
transfer control protocol (TCP)	a networking protocol employed by most systems on the Internet for managing basic packet services, such as identifying, organizing, and sequencing packets or datagrams. (Ch. 18)
transfer rate, data	the amount of time required for data to be communicated from the disk or tape controller to the central processing unit. (Ch. 5)
transformations	in graphics, special editing effects, such as scaling or rotation, applied to selected areas or objects in an image. (Ch. 12)
transition	a sequence of frames that blend the contents of the ending clip with those of the starting clip. (Ch. 14)
translation program	a program that translates instructions of a symbolic programming language into those of another, usually machine language instructions for a host processor. (Ch. 6)
translator (filter) programs	special utility or plug-in software that is used to convert a text file from one proprietary format to another. (Ch. 9)
transmitter	in a communication system, the device that converts a message to a signal that may be conveyed over some communication channel. (Ch. 16)
transparent GIFs	a GIF image whose background is rendered invisible by masking it. (Ch. 11)
Turing, Alan	British mathematician and logician (1912–1954) who led ULTRA project in WWII for breaking the code for the German enigma machine. Turing also posed an empirical test or standard for assessing whether an automated system could be considered intelligent, now called the *Turing Test*. (Ch. 4)
twisted-pair cable	pairs of inexpensive copper wiring used to connect nodes in a local area network. (Ch. 17)
two-dimensional graphics (2-D graphics)	graphic applications that store and represent images in flat, two-dimensional form. Thus, the user must personally account for perspective effects to render more realistic pictures. (See *three-dimensional graphics*.) (Ch. 12)
twos complement method	a method used by most computer systems for representing signed integer numbers. (Ch. 8)
underflow error	an error that results when a resulting number is too small to be accurately represented in floating point notation. (Ch. 8)
uniform noise filter	a local filtering process that induces speckle or random noise spots in a digital image. (Ch. 11)

Uniform Resource Locator (URL)	the standard for specifying the address of pages and other resources available on the World Wide Web. (Ch. 3)
unordered list	in HTML, a collection of items displayed as a bulleted list. (Ch. 3)
unsharp masking	a local filtering process that sharpens an image by literally subtracting blurred components from the output image. (Ch. 11)
update tape	the magnetic tape reel containing the processed data or output from a batch processing program that updates the records stored on an original master tape. (Ch. 5)
uploading (files)	transferring files from a local computer system to a remote host. (Ch. 17)
user agent	(See *local host*.) (Ch. 18)
user interface	a program running continuously that provides basic communication with the operating system by interpreting commands and information entered by the user. (Ch. 7)
user services	applications that facilitate communication and sharing resources between systems connected on the Internet. (Ch. 18)
variable architecture synthesis	a method of sound synthesis that combines pure synthesis with digitized sound samples. Also known as integrated synthesis. (Ch. 13)
variables	program objects storing data values that may change in the course of processing. (Ch. 6)
vector graphics (object-oriented graphics)	a method of representing and manipulating graphic images in which the image is composed of lines, curves, and figures that are defined mathematically, rather than being composed of pixels. (Ch. 12)
very high speed backbone network system (vBNS)	a new network technology that offers high-speed data transmission that is capable of supporting not only data and images, but also sound and video. (Ch. 18)
VGA (video graphics array)	a graphic format for video display monitors that supports resolutions up to 640×480. (Ch. 5)
video adapter	hardware serving as an interface between the computer system and the video display device. (Ch. 5)
video conferencing	the capture and transmission over a network of two-way audio and video in real time. (Ch. 14)
video digitizer	hardware and software units that are typically added to the expansion slot of a computer system to provide facilities for converting analog video sources to digital form. (Ch. 5)
video display monitor	a television-like device used for graphic output on most computer systems. (Ch. 5)
video random access memory (VRAM)	fast access memory that stores direct digital representations of graphic images intended for display on a video monitor; VRAM is employed by the video adapter card to manage and improve the speed of graphic display. (Ch. 5)
virtual memory	an operating system service that creates the illusion of a much larger volume of main memory by combining physical memory with additional secondary storage space. (Ch. 7)

Virtual PIN — a monetary payment system for Web commerce that secures the transmission of credit card information over data communications networks. Virtual PIN also protects the anonymity of customers with Web merchants. (Ch. 3)

virtual reality — hardware and software that immerses the user into the illusion of a three-dimensional world built from 3-D graphic models and sophisticated animation techniques. (Ch. 1)

voice activation system — automated systems that respond to voice commands–usually trained to recognize the voice patterns of specific individuals. (Ch. 13)

volume-based 3-D graphics — a form of 3-D graphics that represents and stores a graphic image as composed of voxels or volume elements. (Ch. 12)

von Neumann architecture (machine model) — refers to the stored program model for the general-purpose programmable electronic digital computer system. (Ch. 4)

von Neumann, John — (1903–1957) Hungarian mathematician who worked with Mauchly and Eckert on the design of the stored program computer. After the publication of a paper on this new design in 1946, his name became synonymous with the concept. (Ch. 4)

voxels (volume elements) — a three-dimensional pixel or picture element that has a specific location as well as features such as color, intensity, transparency, and opacity. (Ch. 12)

warping, digital — a method of retouching a digital image by applying geometric transformations to pixel locations in the image. (Ch. 11)

WAV sound file format — a file format for representing and storing digitized sound, first developed by the Microsoft Corporation. (Ch. 13)

wave — a measure that represents its source as a continuously undulating line or curve. (Chs. 2, 13)

Web database front end — Web pages that display data retrieved on the fly from databases that store that information. (Ch. 10)

Web page — a single Web document defined by a unique URL, or address, and that contains text, graphics, links, and so on. (Ch. 1)

Web site — a collection of Web pages related to some common topic or theme and usually maintained by a single individual or group. (Ch. 1)

"what if" computation — a spreadsheet model that investigates a series of changing values and their effect on a forecast, prediction, or result. (Ch. 8)

white noise — a signal containing a random distribution of frequencies uniformly distributed throughout the frequency range. (Ch. 13)

wide area network (WAN) — a data communications network that extends over a large geographical area but is typically owned and maintained by a single organization. (Ch. 16)

Wilkes, Maurice — (b. 1913) Cambridge professor who developed the EDSAC; he is also responsible for devising several other important computing inventions, including assembly languages and microprogramming. (Ch. 4)

window — rectangular frames displayed on the desktop that represent the contents of documents and directories. (Ch. 7)

wipe — a video transition effect in which frames from the first clip are faded across or down the screen while frames from the second clip replace them across or down the screen. (Ch. 14)

wireframe construction	a method of 3-D model description that plots the object as collection of joined connected shapes, like a wireframe figure. (Ch. 12)
wireless network	a data communications network composed of nodes that are connected over an unbounded channel, such as infrared, microwave, or other broadcast transmission methods. (Ch. 17)
WMF image files (Windows metafile)	a metafile format for digital images commonly employed by Windows applications. (Ch. 11)
word processors	application software that is used for document preparation. Word processors are used for creating most print documents. (Ch. 9)
word-wrap	a selectable feature of most word processing software that permits the user to enter text that will automatically continue on the next line when the current one is filled without the need of inserting carriage returns. (Ch. 9)
working memory	temporary memory or storage employed by an expert system for representing facts and subsequent reasoning while solving a given problem. (Ch. 20)
worksheet	a single spreadsheet document; some spreadsheet applications permit the collection of several sheets into a single document called a *workbook*. (Ch. 8)
workstation	refers to a high-performance single-user computer system that is usually employed for professional tasks, such as graphic design or software development. (Ch. 4)
world view coordinates	in 3-D graphics, the scene is described using standard coordinates that serve as the basis for calculating camera angles or relative views. (Ch. 12)
World Wide Web	a confederation of computer systems around the world that adhere to a common set of guidelines for storing and presenting information to users. (Ch. 1)
World Wide Web Consortium (W3C)	a group that recommends standards for how information is organized and exchanged over the World Wide Web. (Ch. 3)
write-once, read-many discs, drives (WORM)	an older form of permanent secondary memory storage based on optical technologies. (Ch. 5)
writing (memory)	transferring an item to a memory location; writing memory is destructive because the original contents are replaced by the new item. (Ch. 4)
WYSIWYG	acronym for "what you see is what you get;" refers to a window or screen display that mimics that of the output, for example, printed documents. (Ch. 9)
XGA (extended graphics array)	a graphic format for video display monitors that supports resolutions up to 1024×768. (Ch. 5)
Y signal (luminance)	monochromatic video signal colloquially referred to as black-and-white television. (Ch. 14)
Y/C video (component video)	(See *component video*.) (Ch. 14)
YIQ video (composite video)	(See *composite video*.) (Ch. 14)
YUV color space	a three-dimensional color space used by most digital video capture cards for representing and storing color information. Y measures the relative luminance of the signal while U and V measure its color properties. (Ch. 14)

zoned constant angular velocity (ZCAV)
a storage organization for secondary storage media used by some magnetic hard disks and magneto-optical discs. Like the CAV format, the disk is rotated at a constant speed, but unlike CAV, the number of sectors per track varies. ZCAV formats sacrifice uniform transfer rates for greater data capacities. (Ch. 5)

Zuse, Konrad
(1910–1995) German engineer who developed the Z series of computers, which were the first programmable electromechanical digital computing machines. (Ch. 4)

INDEX

D

H

I

CREDITS

iii: Vasily Kandinsky, *Arc and Point,* February, 1923. Watercolor, India Ink and pencil on paper, 46.5 x 42 cms (18 5/16 x 16 7/16 inches) Solomon R. Guggenheim Museum, New York. Photo by David Heald © The Solomon R. Guggenheim Foundation, New York (FN 50.1290)

Chapter 1: 1: Vasily Kandinsky, *Arc and Point,* February, 1923. Watercolor, India Ink and pencil on paper, 46.5 x 42 cms (18 5/16 x 16 7/16 inches) Solomon R. Guggenheim Museum, New York. Photo by David Heald © The Solomon R. Guggenheim Foundation, New York (FN 50.1290); **3:** Vasily Kandinsky, *Arc and Point,* February, 1923. Watercolor, India Ink and pencil on paper, 46.5 x 42 cms (18 5/16 x 16 7/16 inches) Solomon R. Guggenheim Museum, New York. Photo by David Heald © The Solomon R. Guggenheim Foundation, New York (FN 50.1290); **5 (top):** Courtesy of IBM Archives; **5 (center):** Courtesy of IBM Corporation; **5 (bottom):** Courtesy of Casio, Inc.; **6:** Courtesy of General Reality Company; **10:** © Nicole Bengiveno; **12:** Reproduced by permission of CNN; **15:** © 1997 Cyan, Inc. Riven™ is a trademark of Cyan, Inc.

Chapter 2: 25: Vasily Kandinsky, *Red Oval (Rotes Oval),* 1920. Oil on canvas, 71.5 x 71.2 cms (28 1/8 x 18 1.8 inches) Solomon R. Guggenheim Museum, New York. Photo by David Heald © The Solomon R. Guggenheim Foundation, New York (FN 51.1311); **37:** © 1996 PhotoDisc, Inc.; **38:** © 1996 PhotoDisc, Inc.

Chapter 3: 47: Vasily Kandinsky, *Several Circles (Einige Kreise),* 1926. Oil on canvas, 140.3 x 140.7 cms, Solomon R. Guggenheim Museum, New York, gift, Solomon Guggenheim, 1937. Photo by David Heald © The Solomon R. Guggenheim Foundation, New York (FN 41.283); **57:** Copyright © 1998 Netscape Communications Corp. Used with permission. All Rights Reserved. This page may not be reprinted or copied without the express written permission of Netscape. [Netscape Communications Corporation has not authorized, sponsored, or endorsed, or approved this publication and is not responsible for its content. Netscape and the Netscape Communications Corporate Logos, are trademarks and trade names of Netscape Communications Corporation. All other product names and/or logos are trademarks of their respective owners.]; **59:** Text and artwork copyright © 1998 by Yahoo! Inc. All rights reserved. YAHOO! and YAHOO! logo are trademarks of YAHOO! Inc.; **59:** Text and artwork copyright © 1998 by Yahoo! Inc. All rights reserved. YAHOO! and YAHOO! logo are trademarks of YAHOO! Inc.; **60:** AltaVista and AltaVista logo are trademarks or service marks of Compaq Computer Corporation. Used with permission; **64:** AltaVista and AltaVista logo are trademarks or service marks of Compaq Computer Corporation. Used with permission; **76:** Dog courtesy of Jan Martin; **77:** Reprinted by permission of the American Kennel Club; **78:** Dog courtesy of Jan Martin.

Chapter 4: 93: Vasily Kandinsky, *Improvisation 28,* 1912. Oil on canvas, 111.4 x 162.1 cms (43 7/8 x 63 7/8 inches) Solomon R. Guggenheim Museum, New York, gift, Solomon R. Guggenheim, 1937. Photo by Carmelo Guadagno © The Solomon R. Guggenheim Foundation, New York (FN 37.239); **95:** Vasily Kandinsky, *Improvisation 28,* 1912. Oil on canvas, 111.4 x 162.1 cms (43 7/8 x 63 7/8 inches) Solomon R. Guggenheim Museum, New York, gift, Solomon R. Guggenheim, 1937. Photo by Carmelo Guadagno © The Solomon R. Guggenheim Foundation, New York (FN 37.239); **98:** Courtesy of the IBM Archives; **100:** Corbis-Bettmann; **101:** Courtesy of Konrad Zuse Zentrum fur Informationshtechnik Berlin; **102 (top):** Courtesy of Iowa State University of Science and Technology; **102:** Smithsonian Institution, Photo No. 90-7164B; **103 (top):** Used by permission of The University of Pennsylvania's School of Engineering and Applied Science (formerly known as The Moore School of Electrical Engineering); **103 (bottom):** Photo by Elliott & Fry of Alan Mathison Turing. By courtesy of the National Portrait Gallery, London; **105:** National Museum of American History, The Information Age, Smith-sonian Institution; **109:** Courtesy of Kingston Technology; **117:** Courtesy of IBM Archives; **118:** Courtesy of Motorola, Inc.; **120:** Courtesy of Silicon Graphics.

Chapter 5: 125: Vasily Kandinsky, *Dominant Curve* April, 1936. Oil on canvas, 129.4 x 194.2 cms (350 7/8 x 76 1/2 inches) Solomon R. Guggenheim Museum, New York. Photo by David Heald © The Solomon R. Guggenheim Foundation, New York (FN 45.989); **141 (top):** Courtesy of Western Digital, Inc. Used by permission; **146:** Copyright © 1998 Iomega Corporation. Iomega and Zip are registered trademarks and the Super-Floppy Preferred by Millions is a trademark of Iomega Corporation. **151:** Courtesy of Electronic Solutions, Inc.; **154 (top):** Courtesy of Mouse Systems Corporation; **154 (bottom):** Courtesy of Hewlett-Packard; **154:** Courtesy of Hewlett-Packard; **155 (bottom):** Courtesy of AGFA, Inc.; **156:** Courtesy of Wacom Tech. Corp.; **157:** Copyright © 1998 and courtesy of NEC Technologies; **160:** Used by permission of NEC Technologies, Inc.

Chapter 6: 167: Vasily Kandinsky, *In the Black Square,* June 1923. Oil on canvas, 97.5 x 93 cms (38 3/8 x 36 5/8 inches) Solomon R. Guggenheim Museum, New York, gift, Solomon R. Guggenheim, 1937. Photo by David Heald © The Solomon R. Guggenheim Foundation, New York (FN 37.254).

Chapter 7: 197: Vasily Kandinsky, *Graceful Ascent,* March 1934. Oil on canvas,31 5/8 x 31 3/4 cms (80.4 x 80.7 inches) Solomon R. Guggenheim Museum, New York. Photo by David Heald © The Solomon R. Guggenheim Foundation, New York (FN 45.970); **219:** screen shot reprinted by permission of Microsoft Corporation.

Chapter 8: 245: Vasily Kandinsky, *Striped,* 1934. Oil with sand on canvas, 31 7/8 x 39 3/8 inches, Solomon R. Guggenheim Museum, New York. Photo by David Heald © The Solomon R. Guggenheim Foundation, New York (FN 46.1022); **247:** Vasily Kandinsky, *Striped,* 1934. Oil with sand on canvas, 31 7/8 x 39 3/8 inches, Solomon R. Guggenheim Museum, New York. Photo by David Heald © The Solomon R. Guggenheim Foundation, New York (FN 46.1022).

Chapter 9: 285: Vasily Kandinsky, *Decisive Rose,* March 1932. Oil on canvas, 80.9 x 100 cms (31 7/8 x 39 3/8 inches) Solomon R. Guggenheim Museum, New York. Photo by David Heald © The Solomon R. Guggenheim Foundation, New York (FN 49.1178).

Chapter 10: 319: Vasily Kandinsky, *Upward,* 1929. Oil on cardboard, 70 x 49 cms (27 1/2 x 19 1/4 inches) Solomon R. Guggenheim Foundation, New York, Peggy Guggenheim Collection, Venice, 1976. Photo by David Heald © The Solomon R. Guggenheim Foundation, New York (FN 76.2552 PG 35).

Chapter 11: 353: Vasily Kandinsky, *Violet-Orange,* October 1935. Oil on canvas, 88.9 x 116.2 cms (35 x 45 3/4 inches) Solomon R. Guggenheim Museum, New York, gift, Solomon Guggenheim, 1937. Photo by David Heald © The Solomon R. Guggenheim Foundation, New York (FN 37.334); **355:** Vasily Kandinsky, *Violet-Orange,* October 1935. Oil on canvas, 88.9 x 116.2 cms (35 x 45 3/4 inches) Solomon

R. Guggenheim Museum, New York, gift, Solomon Guggenheim, 1937. Photo by David Heald © The Solomon R. Guggenheim Foundation, New York (FN 37.334); **356 (left)** : Reprinted by permission of the Learning Company; **356 (right)** : Corel Corporation; **357 (top)** : Reprinted with permission of NOAA/NESDIS; **357 (bottom)** : Reprinted with permission of NOAA/NESDIS; **357 (left)** : NASA; **358:** Author's collection; **358:** Author's collection; **359:** Author's collection; **360:** Author's collection; **360:** Author's collection; **361:** Reprinted by permission of the Learning Company; **363:** PhotoDisc, Inc.; **365:** Author's collection; **367:** Author's collection; **376:** Reprinted by permission of the Learning Company; **381:** Reprinted with permission of NOAA/NESDIS; **382:** Reprinted by permission of Amber Productions, Inc. dba D'pix; **383 (bottom)** : PhotoDisc, Inc.; **384 (top)** : ColorBytes, Inc.; **384 (bottom)** : NASA; **385:** PhotoDisc, Inc.; **388:** Copyright © Digital Stock; **389 (top)** : Copyright © Digital Stock; **389 (bottom)** : PhotoDisc, Inc.; **390:** Photo-Disc, Inc.; **391 (top)** : PhotoDisc, Inc.; **391 (bottom)** : PhotoDisc, Inc.; **392:** Author's collection; **393:** PhotoDisc, Inc.; **397:** Reprinted with permission of PhotoSphere Images, Ltd.; **398:** Photo-Disc, Inc. **399:** PhotoDisc, Inc. **402 (top):** Library of Congress; **402 (bottom):** © 1996 Robert Capa/Magnum Photos.

Chapter 12: 409: Vasily Kandinsky, *Blue Circle,* 1922. Oil on canvas, 109.2 x 99.2 cms (43 x 39 inches) Solomon R. Guggenheim Museum, New York. Photo by David Heald © The Solomon R. Guggenheim Foundation, New York (FN 46.1051); **411 (top):** Virgina Tech Universtity; **425:** Courtesy of Brian Michael Ground; **436:** Adobe and Adobe Illustrator are trademarks of Adobe Systems, Inc.; **437:** Adobe and Adobe Illustrator are trademarks of Adobe Systems, Inc.; **438:** Adobe and Adobe Illustrator are trademarks of Adobe Systems, Inc.; **440:** Infini-D is a trademark of MetaCreations; **445:** Courtesy of John Allen; **446:** Courtesy of John Allen; **446:** Courtesy of John Allen; **447:** Courtesy of John Allen; **450:** John Allen and Tom Allen; **451:** © Yves Piguet; **453:** Courtesy of John Allen; **454:** Author's collection.

Chapter 13: 459: Vasily Kandinsky, *Sketch for Composition II,* 1909-1910. Oil on canvas, 97.5 x 131.2 cms (38 3/8 x 51 5/8 inches)

Solomon R. Guggenheim Museum, New York. Photo by Sally Ritts © The Solomon R. Guggenheim Foundation, New York (FN 45.961); **472:** Courtesy of Casio, Inc.

Chapter 14: 491: Vasily Kandinsky, *Painting with a White Border,* May, 1913. Oil on canvas, 140.3 x 200.3 cms (55 1/4 x 78 7/8 inches) Solomon R. Guggenheim Museum, New York, gift, Solomon Guggenheim, 1937. Photo by David Heald © The Solomon R. Guggenheim Foundation, New York (FN 36.245). **494:** Hitachi Corporation; **508:** Adobe and Adobe Premiere are trademarks of Adobe Systems, Inc.; **510:** Author's collection; **510 (bottom):** Adobe and Adobe Premiere are trademarks of Adobe Systems, Inc.; **512:** Author's collection.

Chapter 15: 517: Vasily Kandinsky, *Black Lines I,* 1913. Oil on canvas, 129/4 x 131.1 cms (51 x 51 5/8 inches) Solomon R. Guggenheim Museum, New York, gift, Solomon Guggenheim, 1937. Photo by David Heald © The Solomon R. Guggenheim Foundation, New York (FN 37.241); **524:** PhotoDisc, Inc.; **525:** ColorBytes, Inc.

Chapter 16: 537: Vasily Kandinsky, *Small Pleasures,* June 1913. Oil on canvas, 109.8 x 119.7 cms (43 1/4 x 47 1/8 inches) Solomon R. Guggenheim Museum, New York. Photo by Sally Ritts © The Solomon R. Guggenheim Foundation, New York (FN 43.921); **539:** Vasily Kandinsky, *Small Pleasures,* June 1913. Oil on canvas, 109.8 x 119.7 cms (43 1/4 x 47 1/8 inches) Solomon R. Guggenheim Museum, New York. Photo by Sally Ritts © The Solomon R. Guggenheim Foundation, New York (FN 43.921).

Chapter 17: 573: Vasily Kandinsky, *Moderation (Moderation),* September 1940. Oil and enamel on canvas, 39 1/4 x 25 3/8 inches. Solomon R. Guggenheim Museum, New York. Photo by David Heald © The Solomon R. Guggenheim Foundation, New York (FN 46.1021).

Chapter 18: 597: Vasily Kandinsky, *Landscape near Murnau with Locomotive,* 1909. Oil on board, 50.4 x 65 cms (19 7/8 x 25 5/8 inches) Solomon R. Guggenheim Museum, New York. Photo by David Heald © The Solomon R. Guggenheim Foundation, New York (FN 50.1295); **600:** Copyright © 1997 Larry Landweber and the Internet Society. Used by permission; **631:** NASA; **632:** NASA.